D0367875

Jordan

Bradley Mayhew

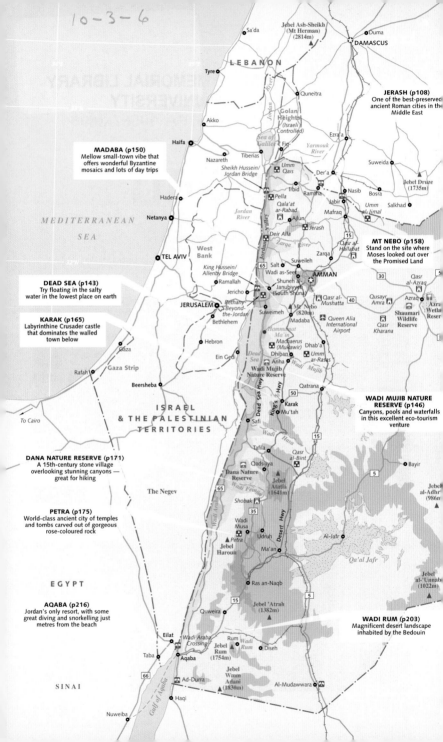

10-3-6

JERASH (p108)
One of the best-preserved ancient Roman cities in the Middle East

MADABA (p150)
Mellow small-town vibe that offers wonderful Byzantine mosaics and lots of day trips

MT NEBO (p158)
Stand on the site where Moses looked out over the Promised Land

DEAD SEA (p143)
Try floating in the salty water in the lowest place on earth

KARAK (p165)
Labyrinthine Crusader castle that dominates the walled town below

WADI MUJIB NATURE RESERVE (p146)
Canyons, pools and waterfalls in this excellent eco-tourism venture

DANA NATURE RESERVE (p171)
A 15th-century stone village overlooking stunning canyons — great for hiking

PETRA (p175)
World-class ancient city of temples and tombs carved out of gorgeous rose-coloured rock

AQABA (p216)
Jordan's only resort, with some great diving and snorkelling just metres from the beach

WADI RUM (p203)
Magnificent desert landscape inhabited by the Bedouin

Sa'da
Jebel Ash-Sheikh (Mt Herman) (2814m)
Duma
DAMASCUS
LEBANON
Tyre
Quneitra
Golan Heights (Israeli Controlled)
Akko
Ezra'a
Haifa
Sea of Galilee
Fiq
Yarmouk River
Suweida
Tiberias
Nazareth
Umm Qais
Der'a
Jebel Druze (1735m)
Sheikh Hussein/ Jordan Bridge
Irbid
Ramtha
Nasib
Bosra
Hadera
Pella
Jabir
Umm al-Jimal
Salkhad
Qala'at ar-Rabad
Netanya
Jordan River
Ajlun
Mafraq
MEDITERRANEAN SEA
Jerash
West Bank
Deir Alla
Qasr al-Hallabat
TEL AVIV
Zarqa River
Salt
Suweileh
Zarqa
Qasr al-Azraq
King Hussein/ Allenby Bridge
Wadi as-Seer
AMMAN
Ramallah
Shuneh al-Janubiyyeh (South Shuna)
Qasr al-Mushatta
Qusayr Amra
Azraq
Azri Wetla Reser
Jericho
JERUSALEM
Bethany Beyond-the-Jordan
Suweimeh
Mt Nebo (820m)
Qasr Kharana
Shaumari Wildlife Reserve
Bethlehem
Madaba
Queen Alia International Airport
Hammamat Ma'in
Hebron
Machaerus (Mukawir)
Dhab'a
Umm ar-Rasas
Ein Gedi
Dhiban
Gaza
Dead Sea
Ariha
Wadi Mujib
Rafah
Gaza Strip
Wadi Mujib Nature Reserve
Qatrana
Beersheba
King's Hwy
Karak
ISRAEL & THE PALESTINIAN TERRITORIES
Dead Sea Hwy
Mu'tah
To Cairo
Safi
Wadi Hasa
Tafila
Qasr al-Bint
The Negev
Qadisiyya
Bayir
Dana Nature Reserve
Jebel Atatla (1641m)
Wadi Feinan
Shobak
Jebel al-Adhr (986m)
Wadi Araba
Wadi Musa
Udruh
Desert Hwy
Ma'an
Al-Jafr
Petra
Jebel Haroun
Qa'al Jafr
EGYPT
Jebel al-'Unnab (1022m)
Ras an-Naqb
Eilat
Quweira
Jebel 'Atrah (1382m)
Wadi Araba Crossing
Rum
Wadi Rum
Diseh
Taba
Aqaba
Jebel Rum (1754m)
WADI RUM (p203)
Magnificent desert landscape inhabited by the Bedouin
SINAI
Ad-Durra
Jebel Wmm Adani (1830m)
Al-Mudawwara
Gulf of Aqaba
Haqi
Nuweiba

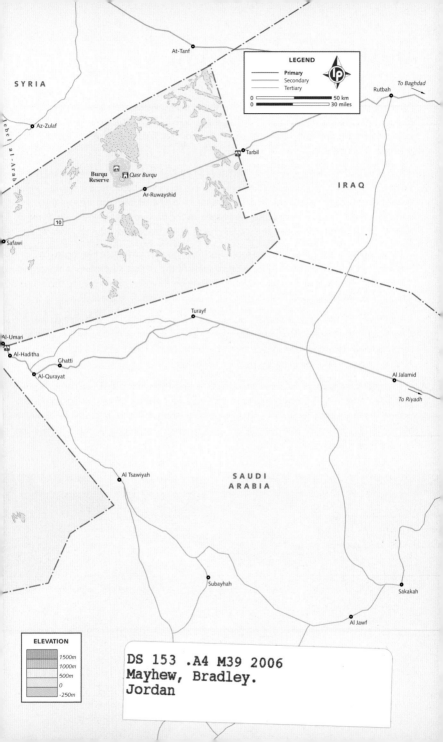

SYRIA

At-Tanf

Az-Zulaf

Jebel al-Arab

Burqu
Reserve

Qasr Burqu

Ar-Ruwayshid

10

Safawi

Turayf

Al-Umari

Al-Haditha

Ghatti

Al-Qurayat

Al Tsawiyah

Subayhah

LEGEND

Primary
Secondary
Tertiary

0   50 km
0   30 miles

Rutbah

To Baghdad

Tarbil

IRAQ

Al Jalamid

To Riyadh

SAUDI
ARABIA

Sakakah

Al Jawf

ELEVATION

1500m
1000m
500m
0
-250m

Destination Jordan

For many people Jordan begins and ends with the magical ancient Nabataean city of Petra. And it's true, Petra is without doubt one of the Middle East's most spectacular, unmissable sights, battling it out with Machu Picchu or Angkor Wat for the title of the world's most dramatic 'lost city'.

Yet there's so much more to see in Jordan – ruined Roman cities, Crusader castles, desert citadels and powerful biblical sites: the brook where Jesus was baptised, the fortress where Herod beheaded John the Baptist and the mountain top where Moses cast eyes on the Promised Land. Biblical scenes are not just consigned to the past in Jordan; you'll see plenty of men wearing full-flowing robes and leading herds of livestock across the timeless desert.

But it's not all crusty ruins. From the rock-climbing highs of Wadi Rum to floating in the Dead Sea (the lowest place on earth), Jordan offers some of the wildest adventures in the region. The incredibly varied backdrop ranges from the red desert sands of Wadi Rum to the brilliant blues of the coral-filled Gulf of Aqaba; from rich palm-filled wadis to the lifeless Dead Sea.

Ultimately it's the sensual delights of daily life in the Middle East that you'll hanker for longest after you return home; the bittersweet taste of cardamom coffee or the smell of a richly scented nargileh (water pipe); the intoxicating swirl of Arabic pop sliding out of an Amman doorway and the deafening silence of the desert.

Jordanians are a passionate and proud people and the country truly welcomes visitors with open arms. Despite being squeezed between the hotspots of Iraq, Saudi Arabia and Israel & the Palestinian Territories, Jordan is probably the safest and most stable country in the region. Regardless of your nationality, you'll be greeted with nothing but courtesy and hospitality in this gem of a country.

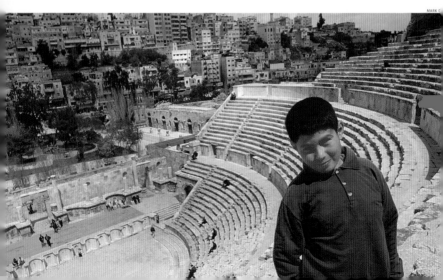

Natural Wonders

Sussing out the scene before splashing up the majestic Wadi Mujib Gorge (p147)

The Dead Sea (p143) is sure to impress

Enjoy spectacular views from the foot of Jebel Khazali out over Wadi Rum (p203)

Archaeological Treasures

PATRICK HORTON

Discover the amazing acoustics at south theatre (p111), Jerash

Take a moment in the tranquil courtyard of Beit Russan (p121), Umm Qais

MARK DAFFEY

OTHER HIGHLIGHTS

- Karak Castle (p166), arguably the most interesting of Jordan's Crusader castles, has a rich history and truly superb setting.
- Belief and archaeology meet at Bethany-Beyond-the-Jordan (p141), where John baptised Jesus.

See for yourself why Unesco has declared the desert castle Qusayr Amra (p135) a World Heritage site

DAMIEN SIM

SARA-JANE CLELAND

Reaching up to the land of the gods, the Temple of Artemis (p112) at Jerash

PATRICK BEN LUKE SYDER

The serpent and cross monument on Mt Nebo (p158) looms over the Dead Sea

It's not known as the 'Rose-red City' for nothing; the Treasury (p182), Petra

PAUL DAVID HELLANDER

Active Jordan

MARK DAFFEY

Taking the well-trodden path along the spine of the Red Sand Dunes (p208), Jebel Umm Ulaydiyya, outside Wadi Rum

JOHN ELK III

Snorkelling the reefs south of Aqaba (p227)

OTHER HIGHLIGHTS

- Join the Bedouin for 4WD jeep tours (p209) around remarkable Wadi Rum and sleep in the desert under a canopy of stars.
- For a deeper taste of the Bedouin lifestyle, try a camel trek (p210) from Wadi Rum to Wadi Musa (near Petra) or Aqaba.
- Help excavate an ancient site; join a genuine archaeological dig (p235).

Climb up to the Burdah Rock Bridge, Wadi Rum (p211)

ANDERS BLOMQVIST

Contents

Regional Map Contents

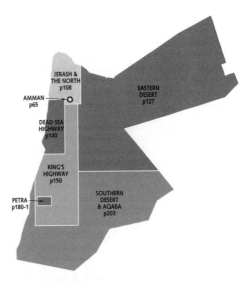

JERASH &
THE NORTH
p108

AMMAN
p65

EASTERN
DESERT
p127

DEAD SEA
HIGHWAY
p140

KING'S
HIGHWAY
p150

PETRA
p180-1

SOUTHERN
DESERT
& AQABA
p203

The Author

BRADLEY MAYHEW

Bradley has returned to the Middle East frequently since first visiting Jordan in the early 1990s as an adventure-tour organiser. Since then he's travelled the breadth of the Islamic world, from Casablanca to Kashgar, Tangiers to Tajikistan.

Bradley is the co-author of Lonely Planet guides to *Jordan, Central Asia, Tibet, Nepal* and *Shanghai* and has worked on Lonely Planet guides from *Morocco* to *Mongolia*. He has also lectured on Central Asia at the Royal Geographic Society.

My Favourite Trip

I had such a great time in Jordan that I can't recall a single place that I didn't enjoy. One of the more unexpected high-lights of this trip was reconnecting such sites as Lot's Cave and the ruins of Sodom with hazy biblical stories that were stored so far back in my childhood that I didn't even know I remembered them.

Petra (p175) was fabulous, especially hiking through deserted Wadi Muthlim and around some of the lesser known tombs. Best for me, though, was Wadi Rum (p203). Clambering up to the Burdah rock bridge with the Bedouin climber Attayak Ali; brewing up a mint tea atop Jebel Umm Adaami, the highest peak in Jordan; running with abandon down huge red sand dunes; and hiking through the labyrinthine Rakhabat Canyon all offered stunning and contrasting views of the desert, far from the 4WDs that buzzed like flies around the main sights.

Three weeks later, back home, I was still leaving little piles of powdery red sand wherever I walked; my favourite souvenir from Jordan.

Getting Started

Jordan is an easy and highly enjoyable country to visit. The logistics of travel are a breeze, from the visa you get on arrival to the ATMs parked on every street corner. The country is compact, travel times are short and transport is generally comfortable. Budget travel in Jordan is definitely doable but you'll probably get the most from the country if you can spend a bit more, every now and again splashing out for a dive or guided hike, perhaps hiring a car for a few days or dining in a upscale restaurant. The great thing about Jordan is that you can really see a lot in a short period of time, or combine the country with the other great sights of the Middle East, from Jerusalem to Damascus, both just a few hours away by road.

WHEN TO GO

For a small country, Jordan has an extraordinary range of climates. The best time to visit climate-wise is in spring (March to May) and autumn (September to November), when the daytime temperatures aren't too extreme. April is probably the best month, when temperatures are warm and wildflowers are in bloom. March can be cold and rainy in the north but is balmy by the Gulf of Aqaba and the Dead Sea.

Average daytime maximum temperatures in Amman range from 12.6°C in January to 32.5°C in August. See the Climate Charts on p240.

Winter can be surprisingly cold. Snow in Amman is not unheard of (even Petra gets the occasional fall) and the deserts can be freezing, especially at night. Make sure you have plenty of warm clothes and a windproof and waterproof jacket. Aqaba is the one exception, with average daytime maximum temperatures of around 20°C in January, and is quite a hit with deep-frozen northern Europeans during winter.

In high summer (July and August) the weather in the humid Jordan Valley is extremely oppressive – it feels like you're trapped in an airless oven – with suffocating daytime highs well in excess of 36°C. It's also fiercely hot in the desert (including Wadi Rum), though this is a dry heat

---

DON'T LEAVE HOME WITHOUT...

- Your driver's licence and/or Professional Association of Diving Instructors (PADI) diving card if you plan to hire a car or go diving
- A Syrian visa if headed north to Syria (see p251)
- A Jordanian visa if headed from Israel & the Palestinian Territories across King Hussein/ Allenby Bridge (see p257)
- A swimming costume if visiting the Red or Dead seas or canyoning in Wadi Mujib
- A sleeping sheet and/or bag if you're staying overnight in Wadi Rum or one of Jordan's nature reserves, especially outside of summer
- A torch (flashlight) for exploring archaeological sites and overnighting in Wadi Rum
- Your PIN to access cash through ATMs
- Binoculars if bird- or animal-spotting in a nature reserve
- Other handy items such as: a Swiss army knife, a few metres of nylon cord (for a clothesline), clothes pegs, a universal sink plug, an electrical adaptor, earplugs (useful if you're staying near mosques), padlocks and a towel

---

UNESCO WORLD HERITAGE SITES IN JORDAN

- Petra (1985; p175)
- Qusayr Amra (1985; p135)
- Dana Nature Reserve (Biosphere Reserve) (1998; p171)
- Umm ar-Rasas (2004; p163)

---

and thus easier to deal with. The tourist authorities usually plan festivals (such as the Jerash Festival) for the summer period. If you do visit in summer, come well prepared with a hat, sunscreen and protective clothing.

The month of Ramadan is a time when visitors should not eat, drink or smoke in public during the day so it's a tricky time to visit. Eid al-Fitr, the great celebration at the end of Ramadan, is a fun time to visit but it's best to bunker down for a few days because public transport is heavily booked and hotel rooms are sometimes hard to find, especially in Aqaba. See p244 for more on Ramadan.

Note also that most of the excellent ecotourism projects operated in Jordan's Dana, Wadi Mujib and Ajlun nature reserves only operate between April and October.

COSTS & MONEY

Jordan is not the cheapest country in the area to travel around, but it is possible to get by on a tight budget and, if you spend wisely, good value can be found all over the country.

The most basic accommodation costs from JD2 for a bed in a very basic shared room or on the roof, but most decent budget places charge about JD5/8/11 for a single/double/triple. A good midrange single/double costs from JD12/20 up to JD25/35, while top-end doubles start from JD65.

Street snacks like a felafel or shwarma sandwich (see p59) are cheap and you can get a decent budget meal for JD1 to JD3. In any midrange restaurant, expect to pay JD1 for a starter and from JD1.500 to JD2.500 for most main courses. If you're splashing out at one of Amman's better restaurants, don't expect too much change back from JD15 per person, and you'll pay more if you have a bottle of wine.

Public transport is cheap – less than 500 fils per hour of travel in a public bus or minibus, and about JD1 per hour in a more comfortable, long-distance private bus.

One of the biggest sightseeing expenses in Jordan is the entrance fee to Petra (up to JD31 for three days, depending on the season), but it's so worth it! Entry to other popular sights such as Jerash costs JD5 but most places are free or cost just a dinar or two.

If you stay in a shared room or sleep on the roof at the cheapest possible hotel, eat nothing but felafel and shwarma and use public transport and/or hitch exclusively, it's possible to get by on about JD8 per day, though JD10 is more realistic. If you add the cost of an occasional chartered taxi, decent food and the entrance fee to Petra, the cost per day for a budget-minded traveller is about JD15. For JD30, you could live comfortably.

TRAVEL LITERATURE

In the late 19th century the archaeologist Selah Merrill set off to explore what is modern Jordan, the area he called *East of the Jordan*. His book is one of the very few written in the 19th century about this area, but it can be hard to find a copy.

HOW MUCH?

souvenir keffiyeh from JD5

postcard 100 fils

cup of tea 200-400 fils

cup of western coffee JD1-1.500

two-course cheap lunch JD2

midrange dinner JD7

See also Lonely Planet Index, inside front cover.

Johann Ludwig (also known as Jean Louis) Burckhardt spent many years in the early 19th century travelling extensively through Jordan, Syria and the Holy Land, disguised as a pilgrim and compiling a unique and scholarly travelogue detailing every facet of the culture and society he encountered along the way. The result is *Travels in Syria and the Holy Land*,

TOP CHOICES

Top Five Jordanian Experiences

- Dive among the spectacular wrecks and coral of the Red Sea, south of Aqaba (p227)
- Spend a night under sparkling desert skies with the Bedouin in Wadi Rum (p212)
- Splash through the ochre-coloured canyon of a wadi (p147)
- Float on the Dead Sea for a weird been-there-done-that experience (p143)
- Organise a camel ride with a Bedouin guide up Jebel Haroun mountain in Petra (p191) or through Barrah Siq in Wadi Rum (p210)

Top Five Adventures

- The three-day camel trip from Wadi Rum to Aqaba (p210)
- Wadi Mujib – hike through gorges and slot canyons along the Maqui Trail or the Faqua-Wadi Mujib routes (p147), or explore one of Jordan's other wild wadis (p237)
- The three-day hike from Dana to Petra via Wadi Feinan, Wadi Ghuweir and Mansourah (p172)
- Climb Jebel Rum or scramble through the canyons of Jebel Umm Ishrin or Jebel Khazali (p211)
- Hire a camel or donkey or hike for two days to Jebel Haroun, Sabra and Tayyibeh (p191 and p192)

Top Five Views

- The Promised Land from atop Mt Nebo (p158)
- The Dead Sea from the Dead Sea Panorama Complex (p146)
- The Sea of Galilee and the Golan Heights from Umm Qais (p120)
- Wadi Araba from the Desert Highway headed towards Aqaba
- Wadi Rum anywhere, from towering canyon walls to red-sand dunes – even the night sky (p203)

Be Good to Yourself – Top Five Splurges

- Hammam it up with a massage, sauna and body scrub in Amman (p86) or Wadi Musa (p193)
- Pamper yourself at a Dead Sea spa (p145)
- Enjoy a cocktail as the sun sets over Petra, the Dead Sea or the Gulf of Aqaba
- Take a day off in Aqaba at a private beach (p220 or p231)
- Upgrade to a fabulous boutique hotel such as the Sofitel Taybet Zaman near Petra (p198 and p234)

Top Ten Ruins

- Petra – Nabataean capital (p175)
- Jerash – one of the best preserved Roman ruins in the Middle East (p108)
- Karak Castle – the biggest Crusader castle in Jordan (p165)
- Qusayr Amra – superb 8th-century frescoes (p135)
- Umm Qais – Roman and Byzantine city (p120)
- Madaba – Byzantine mosaics (p150)
- Shobak Castle – Crusader fortifications and tunnels (p173)
- Ajlun – Islamic castle (p114)
- Umm al-Jimal – urban architecture (p128)
- Umm ar-Rasas – churches and mosaics (p163)

Top Five Off-the-Beaten-Track Ruins

- Umm ar-Rasas (p163)
- Pella (p124)
- Khirbet Tannour (p170)
- Khirbet Feinan (p171)
- Umm al-Jimal (p128)

which mentions his 'discovery' of Petra (see p177). *Desert Traveller – The Life of Jean Louis Burckhardt* by Katherine Sim is an excellent biography of this remarkable traveller, packed with interesting insights.

The redoubtable Englishwoman Gertrude Bell wrote a few memoirs about her travels in the region in the early 20th century, including the fairly dated and light-hearted *The Desert and the Sown,* though it's mostly concerned with Syria. One of the most impressive women travellers of the last 150 years, Bell has been described as 'the architect of the modern Middle East', 'the most powerful woman of the British Empire' and 'the brains behind Lawrence's brawn'.

Annie Caulfield's *Kingdom of the Film Stars: Journey into Jordan* is an entertaining, personal account of the author's relationship with a Bedouin man in Jordan. *Walking the Bible* by Bruce Feiler is an engaging travelogue that follows Feiler's travels through Egypt, Israel & the Palestinian Territories and Jordan, searching for the physical roots of the Bible. Feiler shows considerably more empathy for people and places in Israel & the Palestinian Territories than those of the Arab world, but writes well on the archaeology of the Holy Land.

For books on Petra see p179.

FILMS

Foreign films to check out before you leave include David Lean's epic *Lawrence of Arabia* (1962), starring Peter O'Toole as Lawrence and filmed partly in Wadi Rum. The lesser-known *A Dangerous Man: Lawrence After Arabia* (1991) stars Ralph Fiennes in one of his earliest film roles.

Petra's Siq and Treasury landed a starring role as the hiding place of the Holy Grail in the closing scenes of Stephen Spielberg's *Indiana Jones and the Last Crusade* (1989), starring Harrison Ford and Sean Connery. The film plays nightly in the budget guesthouses of Wadi Musa.

The PBS docu-drama *Lawrence of Arabia – the Battle for the Arab World* (2003) is worth a look if you are interested in Jordanian history.

'One of the most impressive women travellers of the last 150 years, Bell has been described as 'the architect of the modern Middle East''

INTERNET RESOURCES

Atlas Tours (www.atlastours.net) A travel agency site but with lots of good background information on Jordan.

Bible Places (www.bibleplaces.com) Interesting rundown on biblical sights in Jordan and Israel & the Palestinian Territories.

Jordan Jubilee (www.jordanjubilee.com) Probably the single best website about Jordan, loaded with practical tips and great detail; offers a wonderful window onto Jordanian society.

Jordan Tourism Board (www.see-jordan.com or www.seejordan.org) Reasonable links to range of Jordan-related websites.

Lonely Planet (www.lonelyplanet.com). The Thorn Tree has an active range of Jordan experts who offer good advice if you post a question.

Madaba (www.madaba.freeservers.com) Excellent description of Madaba's attractions and other nearby sites.

Ministry of Tourism and Antiquities (www.tourism.jo) Online brochures, maps and more

Pilgrimage 2000 (http://holysites.com) Good rundown of Jordan's biblical sites, prepared for the millennium visit of the late Pope John Paul II.

Royal Family of Jordan (www.kingabdullah.gov.jo or www.kinghussein.gov.jo) Official websites of Jordan's Hashemite royal family, with good tourist information.

RSCN (www.rscn.org.jo) Accessible information about Jordan's environmental and ecotourism projects. Check out the 'Adventures' and 'Wild Jordan' sections.

Itineraries

CLASSIC ROUTES

AMMAN TO AQABA   One Week

One week is the minimum length of time required to truly explore Jordan on any form of transport. If you have less than a week you're better off just concentrating on Petra and Wadi Rum.

Spend your first day or half-day in **Amman** (p63) and then make a day trip to the Roman ruins at **Jerash** (p108). From Amman it's a short hop or day trip to **Madaba** (p150) to take in the Byzantine mosaics and visit nearby **Mt Nebo** (p158) where Moses is said to have died.

From Madaba head along the King's Highway to Petra, crossing Wadi Mujib gorge and the Crusader castle at **Karak** (p166). You'll have time for a flying visit to **Dana Nature Reserve** (p171), or add on a day for some hiking.

Be sure to budget two full days for **Petra** (p175). On the first day make an early start and enter the site through the Siq before the tour groups arrive. On day two enter the site through the Wadi Muthlim gorge and finish off with a visit to the Monastery.

Take the early bus to **Wadi Rum** (p203) and you'll still have time for a full-day tour by 4WD. An overnight in a Bedouin camp is a must. Next morning head to **Aqaba** (p216) for some diving or a lie on the beach; you deserve it.

A whirlwind short break that takes in a Crusader castle, views of the Promised Land, Jordan's most impressive Roman remains, desert landscapes and even some snorkelling. Use Amman or Madaba as a base for the first three days. To do all this by public transport you'd need 10 days.

AMMAN TO AQABA   Two Weeks

Two weeks is the ideal amount of time in which to see Jordan's main highlights.

After a couple of days visiting Amman and Jerash take a day tour or hire a car to visit the desert castles, in particular the caravanserai-style **Qasr Kharana** (p136) and the Unesco World Heritage site of **Qusayr Amra** (p135). If you have a car try to add on a visit to the ruined desert garrison town of **Umm al-Jimal** (p128).

Take a minibus from Amman to Madaba and use this as a base from which to visit Mt Nebo and the ruins of **Herod's Castle** (p162) at Mukawir. Hire a taxi for the day and combine a visit to Jesus' baptism site at **Bethany-Beyond-the-Jordan** (p141) with a float in the **Dead Sea** (p143) at Amman Beach, before returning via sunset views from the Dead Sea Panorama complex.

If you do have a car and are visiting between April and September you could consider making a half-day hike in **Wadi Mujib Nature Reserve** (p146). The Maqui Trail in particular is superb – reserve a place in advance.

The next day, journey down to **Karak** (p165) and spend a couple of hours exploring the crusader fort. If you spent the night at the Wadi Mujib Nature Reserve camp site or at a swanky Dead Sea resort then take the Dead Sea Highway to Karak.

Next stop is **Dana Nature Reserve** (p171), for a relaxing day of village walks or a longer hike with a guide.

On a two-week itinerary you should allocate three days for **Petra** (p175), which'll allow for some hiking and exploration of the lesser-visited sights.

Finish off with an overnight trip to **Wadi Rum** (p203) to enjoy some desert stillness, before heading down to the beach at **Aqaba** (p216).

This itinerary follows the same route as the shorter week-long version but gives you the extra time to fit in some hiking, some fine archaeological sights and explore some of Petra's lesser visited corners. Even if you use public transport most of the time, it's still worth hiring or chartering a vehicle for a few days to visit remote places.

ROADS LESS TRAVELLED

SELF-DRIVE

In two days you could make a relaxing excursion to the historic sights, limestone hills and olive orchards of northern Jordan. Drive north to Ajlun via Jerash to the Islamic castle of Qala'at ar-Rabad. From here backroads lead to the recently discovered church ruins at **Mar Elias** (p115) and on to the **Ajlun Nature Reserve** (p116), where you can do some lovely light walking. If you get good directions, you can take country roads from here to **Pella** (p124), before heading up the Jordan Valley to **Umm Qais** for more ruins (p120).

A two-day eastern loop could take in the desert castles of **Qasr Kharana** (p136) and **Qusayr Amra** (p135), plus a brief visit to **Shaumari Wildlife Reserve** (p131). Overnight in Azraq and on the second day (or a long first day) take the northern Hwy 10 to the brooding basalt ruins of **Umm al-Jimal** (p128).

From Madaba a great one-day Dead Sea loop can take in views of the Dead Sea at the **Dead Sea Panorama** (p146), a float in the sea and then a visit to the site of Christ's baptism at **Bethany-Beyond-the-Jordan** (p141), topped off by a sunset tilapia dinner at the nearby Talloubi Restaurant. If you have an extra day, tack on a splash up the Siq Trail of **Wadi Mujib Nature Reserve** (p146).

A car is also very useful for traversing the King's Highway from Madaba to Petra, via Herod's Castle at **Mukawir** (p162), the church mosaics of **Umm ar-Rasas** (p163) and the twisting tunnels of the Crusader castle at **Shobak** (p173). Two days is a good amount of time for this (overnight in Karak and Dana) or add on an extra day and go hiking in the **Dana Nature Reserve** (p171).

Hiring a car is a great idea but it's not cheap, so make the most of your time with these itineraries. Amman, Madaba, Wadi Rum, Aqaba, Petra and Jerash are all easily visited by public transport so concentrate on the other sights mentioned here by car. You can do all this in a week or take several bite-sized itineraries of a day or two.

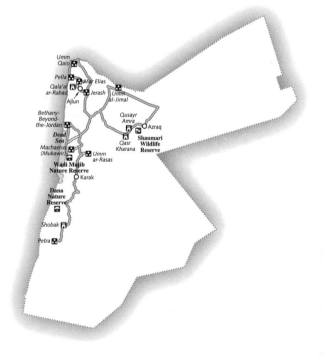

JORDAN'S NATURE RESERVES

From Amman, take the Dead Sea Highway past the resorts and shore of the Dead Sea to the **Wadi Mujib Nature Reserve** (p146). Here you can have a serious adventure on the exciting Malaqi Trail, hike the Ibex Trail for views of the Dead Sea and Nubian ibex, or just cool off by splashing up the Siq Trail.

From Wadi Mujib, travel south via Karak or Safi/Fifa to **Dana Nature Reserve** (p171), which is a great place to just relax for a half day. Join a group for a hike in the southern Al-Barra region or make a more demanding hike down Wadi Ghuweir to Feinan Lodge and then back to Dana. The easiest option is to hike down Wadi Dana (no guide required) and arrange transport back to Dana with the Royal Society for the Conservation of Nature (RSCN). One pleasant day-trip is to make the half-day hike to Rummana and arrange for the RSCN to take you back to Dana village.

After a stop in Petra, budget a couple of nights in the desert at **Wadi Rum** (p203). Most people whizz around the site in a 4WD but, for a richer, slower-paced sense of the desert, arrange in advance a couple of days of hiking and climbing in the far south. There's some great rock scrambling through Jebel Umm Ishrin and to Burdah Rock Bridge and you can reach the summit of Jebel Rum with some experience with ropes. Then there's always the three-day camel trip to Aqaba…

Finally, budget a couple of days for some great **scuba diving** (p227) among the wrecks and reefs of the Gulf of Aqaba. Remember that after diving you can't fly or drive up onto the central Jordan plateau for 24 hours.

Pack some hiking shoes and make the most out of Jordan's natural beauty through its fledgling ecotourism projects. You'll need to hire a car or taxi to get to Wadi Mujib but the others can just about be visited with public transport (Dana requires some patience). Make arrangements in advance with the RSCN (see p53).

TAILORED TRIPS

BIBLICAL JORDAN

The east bank of the Jordan has been repeatedly touched by the prophets, and modern-day pilgrims can follow in the footsteps of such illustrious company as Abraham, Jacob, Moses, Joshua, Elijah, John the Baptist and Jesus. Over 100 sites in Jordan are mentioned in the Bible alone.

Probably the single most important site is **Bethany-Beyond-the-Jordan** (p141), where Jesus is said to have been baptised and where Elijah ascended to heaven on a fiery chariot. Just north of here Joshua led the tribes of Israel across the Jordan River into the Promised Land.

From Bethany it's a short climb along the old pilgrim road to **Mt Nebo** (p158), where Moses finally cast eyes on the Promised Land before dying.

A day trip south of Madaba are the ruins of Herod's fort at **Mukawir** (p162), where John the Baptist was imprisoned and beheaded at the behest of Salome.

At the southern end of the Dead Sea is **Lot's Cave** (p148) where Lot's wife turned to salt and Lot's daughters seduced their father, after they all fled the destruction of **Sodom and Gomorrah** (p147), which is believed to lie nearby.

Back up north, Jesus performed one of his lesser-known miracles at Gadara, modern **Umm Qais** (p120), turning a band of brigands into a pack of swine.

Umm Qais

Bethany-Beyond-the-Jordan
Mt Nebo
Machaerus
Babh-Adh Dhra (Mukawir)
Lot's Cave

Snapshot

Plucky little Jordan. In the middle of a tough neighbourhood, stuck between 'I-raq' and a hard place (Israel & the Palestinian Territories, Syria and Saudi Arabia), surrounded by political extremism and the violence of the Israeli-Palestinian struggle, devoid of the region's great oil reserves and running out of water, it's been a tough few years for the tiny kingdom.

The political instability of the region, especially the Gulf, in the last 15 years has hit Jordan hard. Tourism virtually collapsed in the wake of the September 11th attacks and a recovery only started in 2005. The current American occupation of Iraq once again cut off the country's main source of cheap oil and its main market for exported goods.

Add to this high unemployment (officially 15% but actually around double that), an extraordinarily high proportion of refugees, unpredictable climatic conditions, a dangerous dependency on foreign aid and one of the highest foreign debts per capita in the world. Currently, about 30% of the government's expenditure is used to pay off its debts.

But it's not all bad. The arrival of 100,000 mostly wealthy, mostly Christian Iraqi refugees has injected life into the Jordanian economy, raising property prices in Amman by 20% in 2005 alone. Jordan hopes to benefit from the rebuilding of Iraq, especially in the service and banking industries, pitching itself as the gateway to Iraqi reconstruction. Tourism is starting to recover and money is currently pouring into several major tourism and hotel projects in Amman and Aqaba. The new joint Israeli-Jordanian 'Bridging The Rift' desert science centre straddling the border in Wadi Araba is a small but notable example of what can be achieved in the region through conciliation rather than conflict.

Politically and diplomatically King Abdullah has inherited the tricky balancing act of his father. Peace with Israel & the Palestinian Territories, support for the US and the resulting jump in fuel prices have all proved unpopular among most Jordanians. There is of course a payoff for supporting the US. Jordan currently gets US$1 billion a year in American aid and in 2000 Jordan became only the fourth country to enjoy a free-trade agreement with the USA.

King Abdullah has pushed ahead with economic reforms aimed at repositioning Jordan as a hi-tech and service centre. Political reform has been slower to arrive. Jordan now has 22 registered parties, including a communist party and the main opposition Islamic Action Front (IAF), which has connections with the fundamentalist Muslim Brotherhood. The IAF's opposition to the peace treaty with Israel & the Palestinian Territories causes disquiet but criticising the king remains unheard of (and against the law).

Change has come fast in the last 15 years but Jordan remains essentially a tribal desert monarchy, where change is coming from above not below, and an increasingly marginalised section of society has not kept up with these changes. Tensions remain between the conservative Bedouin countryside and the more Islamicised Palestinian cities, and between Western-looking modernists and conservative Islamist elements. Nor has the country remained unaffected by the rise of militant Islam. A US diplomat was murdered in Amman in 2002 and several Al-Qaeda plots in Jordan were foiled in 2004. In August 2005, militants fired rockets at a US warship docked at Aqaba. In November 2005, an Iraqi Al-Qaeda bomb attack on three Amman hotels claimed the lives of 60 people,

FAST FACTS

Local name:
Al-Mamlakah al-
Urdunniyah al-
Hashimiyah

Land Area: 96,188 sq km

Population: 5,759,000
(July 2005 est)

Human Development
Index: ranked 90th
out of 170 of world's
countries (Egypt 120th,
Syria 106th, Palestinian
Territories 102nd, Israel
22nd)

Religion: 80% Sunni Muslim, 15% Shi'a Muslim,
5% Christian

Only 4.5% of Jordan's
land is cultivated

Around 1.7 million Palestinians live in Jordan

Tourism contributes
10% of GDP and US$800
million to the economy
every year

23% of Jordanians have a
mobile phone, compared
to 7% in Egypt and 2%
in Syria

shocking the Jordanian people and provoking outraged demonstrations against the act.

The challenge facing King Abdullah is to keep Jordan on track as a modern and cosmopolitan Arab state, but one with a tradititional Bedouin heart. The success of this, unfortunately, may well depend largely on political events beyond Jordan's borders. As long as its neighbours are in turmoil, Jordan will continue to walk a tightrope in its attempts to remain the most stable country in the Middle East.

History

Jordan is a young state with a long history. Born out of the ruins of WWII, the modern state and its territory east of the Jordan River can claim to have hosted some of the oldest civilisations in the world. The region has always sat at the fringes rather than the centre of empires but its strategic position ensured that all the great early civilisations passed through. The Egyptians, Assyrians, Babylonians, Hittites, Greeks, Romans, Arabs, Turks and Crusaders all traded, built cities and fought their wars here, leaving behind rich cultural influences.

'History is but a series of accepted lies' – TE Lawrence (of Arabia).

ANCIENT HISTORY

Evidence of human habitation in the area dates back about 500,000 years, when the climate of the Middle East was considerably milder and wetter than today. Archaeological finds from Jericho (on the other side of the Jordan River, in the Palestinian Territories) and Al-Beidha (near Petra) date from around 9000 BC and can rank among the world's first cities, whose inhabitants lived in circular houses, bred domestic animals, made pottery, practised a form of ancestor worship and used sophisticated agricultural methods.

The innovation of copper smelting during the Chalcolithic (copper) Age (4500–3000 BC) was a major technological advance for the region. Remains from the world's earliest and largest copper mines can be found at Khirbet Feinan in Jordan's Dana Nature Reserve. Sheep and goat herding produced milk and wool for the first time and crops such as olives, wheat and barley were introduced, creating a split in lifestyle between the nomad and the farmer, the 'desert and the sown', that would endure for millennia.

During the Bronze Age, crafts such as pottery and jewellery-making came under the dominant cultural influence of Egypt. Permanent settlements were established in modern-day Amman and in the southern desert regions. Foreigners introduced the idea of mixing copper and tin to create bronze, a hardier material that allowed the rapid development of tools and weapons.

Neolithic skulls with holes drilled in them show that an early and crude form of brain surgery was practised (unsuccessfully!) thousands of years ago.

The Early Bronze Age (3000–2100 BC) also saw the occupation of the Jordan Valley by the Canaanites, a Semitic tribe. Along with other tribes in the area, the Canaanites raised defensive walls against invaders, creating a string of emerging city states. Trade gradually developed with neighbouring powers in Syria, Palestine and Egypt.

The later decline of Egyptian influence (though artistic influence continued) around 1500–1200 BC created opportunities for nearby tribes, such as the Hebrew-speaking people who later became known as the Israelites. The innovation of the camel saddle in the middle of the first millennium BC gave a huge technological boost to the native peoples of the Arabian peninsula.

By the Iron Age (1200–330 BC) three kingdoms had emerged in Jordan: the Edomites in the south, with a capital at Bozrah (modern Buseira/Busayra, near Dana); the Moabites near Wadi Mujib; and the

TIMELINE	**1.5 million years BC**	**8000 BC**
	Herds of wild animals graze on the shore of large lakes in the Jordan Valley	Domestication of animals and crops sees some of world's earliest settlements at Jericho, Ain Ghazal and al-Beidha

Ammonites on the edge of the Arabian Desert with a capital at Rabbath Ammon (present-day Amman). According to the Old Testament, this is the age of the Exodus, during which Moses and his brother, Aaron, led the Israelites through the wildernesses of Egypt and Jordan to the Promised Land. The Edomites barred the Israelites from southern Jordan but the Israelites managed to wind their way north, roughly along the route of the modern King's Highway, to arrive at the Jordan River. Moses died on Mt Nebo, in sight of the Promised Land, and it was left to Joshua to lead his people across the Jordan River onto the West Bank.

> The words 'Semite' and 'Semitic' derive from Shem, the eldest son of Noah.

Several hundred years later came the rule of the great Israelite kings David and Solomon. Trade reached a peak during the golden age of King Solomon, with trade routes crossing the deserts from Arabia to the Euphrates, and huge shipments of African gold and South Arabian spices passed through the ports of Aqaba/Eilat. However, in about 850 BC the now-divided Israelite empire was defeated by Mesha, king of Moab, who recorded his victories on the famous Mesha Stele in the Moabite capital of Dhiban (see p165). In 586 BC the Babylonian king Nebuchadnezzar sacked Jerusalem and deported the exiled Israelites to Babylon.

THE GREEKS, NABATAEANS, ROMANS & BYZANTINES

In 333 BC, Alexander the Great stormed his way through Jordan on his way to creating the largest empire the world had ever seen, eventually ruling everything from the Nile to the Indus. On his death in 323 BC, Alexander's empire was parcelled up among his generals: Ptolemy I gained Egypt, Jordan and parts of Syria, while Seleucus established the Seleucid dynasty in Babylonia. Many people in Jordan at this time spoke (or at least wrote in) Greek, and classically influenced cities such as Philadelphia (Amman), Pella and Gerasa (Jerash) were prospering in trade with Egypt. In 198 BC the Seleucid ruler Antiochus III defeated Ptolemy V and took control of western Jordan. By this time the Jews had gradually reestablished themselves and by 141 BC controlled much of northern Jordan.

> The amazing big-hipped, bug-eyed fertility statues created at Ain Ghazal in Jordan around 7000–6500 BC are some of the earliest sculptures in the world; check them out at the National Archaeological Museum on Amman's Citadel (see p71).

Southern Jordan at this time was controlled by a nomadic tribe known as the Nabataeans. The Nabataeans were consummate traders and middlemen (they didn't actually produce anything apart from bitumen for waterproofing boat hulls and copper) who used their almost exclusive knowledge of desert strongpoints and water supplies to amass huge wealth from the trade in incense and spices. Their empire, based in Petra, eventually spread from Arabia to Syria, peaking around the time of Christ. Speaking a form of Aramaic, the language of the Bible, the Nabataeans gradually transformed themselves from their desert trading roots into masterful architects, hydraulic engineers and craftsmen, whose influence connected Arabia to the Mediterranean.

After their conquest of Syria in 64 BC, the powerful Romans began eyeing the wealth of the Nabataeans. The Emperor Trajan finally annexed the Nabataean empire in AD 106 and absorbed it into the new Roman province of Arabia Petraea, with a capital in Petra and later Bosra (modern Syria). The Romans constructed a new road through Jordan, the Nova Via Traiana, and built a string of forts in the eastern desert at Qasr al-Hallabat, Azraq and Umm al-Jimal, to shore up the outermost

8300–4300 BC	4000 BC
Neolithic Era	Bronze Age revolution

borders of the empire. The sophisticated cities of Jerash, Umm Qais and Pella blossomed as members of the Decapolis (see p109), a league of provincial cities that accepted Roman cultural influence but retained their independence.

The decision by Byzantine emperor Constantine to convert to Christianity in AD 324 changed the face of the eastern Mediterranean, as well as its soul, and the young faith quickly became the official religion of Jordan, ushering in a period of prosperity and stability. Churches were constructed across Jordan (often from the building blocks of former Greek and Roman temples), and most were decorated with elaborate mosaics that are still visible today at Madaba, Umm ar-Rasas and Petra. Byzantine Christian pilgrims began to make the arduous trip to the Holy Land, visiting sights and building churches at the Jordanian biblical sites of Bethany, Mt Nebo and Lot's Cave. It was the archaeological rediscovery of these churches 1400 years later that confirmed the lost location of these biblical sites to a forgetful modern world.

In AD 614 the Persian Sassanians reoccupied parts of Jordan as part of their invasion from the east. Although the Byzantine emperor Heraclius forced them into a peace agreement, it was the beginning of the end for Byzantine rule and Christian rule in the region. A storm was brewing in the deserts to the south.

The legacy of Roman rule in Jordan includes the tourist attractions of Jerash and Umm Qais, as well as the Jordanian currency, the dinar, which gets its name from the Roman *denarius*.

THE ADVENT OF ISLAM

After the Prophet Mohammed's death in AD 632, his followers began to push north, exploding out of the desert. The armies of Islam lost their first battle against the Byzantines at Mu'tah (near Karak) in 629, but defeated them seven years later at the Battle of Yarmouk. Jerusalem fell in 638 and Syria was taken in 640, as the Arab forces quickly supplanted the Byzantine and Sassanian empires. Islam became the dominant religion and Arabic replaced Greek as the cultural unifier and lingua franca of the region.

When an assassin murdered the fourth caliph (and son-in-law of Mohammed), Ali (see p40), he was succeeded by the Syrian governor, Mu'awiya, who established the Umayyad dynasty (661–750), based in Damascus. The ensuing bitter dispute over Ali's succession split Islam into two branches, Sunni and Shiite, to create a powerful schism that continues unresolved to this day.

The Umayyads' rich architectural legacy included the Umayyad Mosque in Damascus and the Dome of the Rock in Jerusalem. In eastern Jordan, the Umayyads' close attachment to the desert led to the construction of a string of opulent 'desert castles' (p133), which includes the still-impressive Qusayr Amra (built in 711) and Qasr Kharana (710).

The huge earthquake of AD 747 shattered huge swathes of northern Jordan and Syria, weakening the Umayyads' hold on power to such a degree that they were soon overthrown by a rival Sunni faction, the Abbasids. The change of dynasties marked the beginning of an important political shift from Damascus to Baghdad, and from Arab ethnic superiority to Persian cultural dominance. The Abbasids followed a stricter form of Islam, and were far less tolerant of Christianity than the Umayyads.

The well-respected scholar Bernard Lewis has written several excellent books on the Middle East, including *The Middle East: A Brief History of the Last 2000 Years*. It's excellent big-picture stuff.

2900 BC	2300 BC
Emergence of city states in Middle East, including the growth of towns at Amman, Pella, Deir Alla and Tell Irbid	Sodom and Gomorrah destroyed in a cataclysmic disaster on the southeast corner of the Dead Sea

Still, the 8th, 9th and 10th centuries saw an Arab intellectual flowering that rekindled the artistic and philosophical advancements of Ancient Greece and developed standards in medicine, biology, philosophy, architecture and agriculture that were unprecedented in their day. These achievements spread into Europe through Spain and Sicily and were the major factor in sparking the European Renaissance. Far from the sophisticated mainstream of the Arab court, Jordan was virtually ignored.

In 969 the Cairo-based Fatimids (the Shiite dynasty named after Mohammed's daughter-in-law Fatima) wrested control of Palestine, Jordan and southern Syria from the Abbasids. Less than a century later the Seljuk Turks, pushed west by waves of nomadic incursions from Central Asia, conquered what remained of the Abbasid territory and took over Trans-Jordan.

THE CRUSADES & HOLY WAR

The armies of Islam and Christianity had already clashed, primarily in the 7th century, but the next struggle would be bloodier and more bitter than anything that had gone before it, and its consequences and language of religious conflict resonates to this day. Pope Urban II kicked off the 'holy war' in 1095 as revenge for the ongoing destruction of churches and to protect pilgrim routes to the Holy Land. Within five years the Crusaders had captured their goal, the holy city of Jerusalem, slaughtering countless inhabitants in the process.

By about 1116 the Crusader armies took control of most of 'Outre Jourdain' (Trans-Jordan – literally the 'Land Across the Jordan'), and built a string of fortresses to control the roads from Damascus to Cairo. Their hold was always tenuous, and only survived as long as the local Muslim states remained weak and divided.

In the 12th century, Nureddin (Nur ad-Din – literally 'Light of the Faith'), son of a Turkish tribal ruler, was able to unite the Arab world and defeat the Crusaders in Egypt. His campaign was completed by Saladin (Salah ad-Din – 'Restorer of the Faith'), a Kurdish scholar and military leader who overthrew his Fatimid employers in Egypt, declared a jihad (holy war in defence of Islam) on the invaders and occupied most of the Crusader strongholds in Jordan. The Damascus-based Ayyubids, members of Saladin's family, squabbled over his empire on his death in 1193, and the Crusaders recaptured much of their former territory along the coast.

The Mamluks, the name given to a vast group of adolescents taken from foreign lands to serve as a soldier-slave caste for the Ayyubids, had gained so much power by 1250 that they overthrew their masters. It was the Mamluks who finally turned back the rampaging Mongols, after the armies of Genghis Khan's son had taken Baghdad and killed the last caliph (the Mongol armies reached as far as Ajlun and Salt in Jordan). The Mamluks took control of Jordan and finally expelled the Crusaders. The Mamluk sultan Baybars rebuilt the castles at Karak, Shobak and Ajlun, which they used as lookouts and as a series of staging posts for message-carrying pigeons.

Just 150 years after the departure of the Mongols, the brutal Central Asian invader Tamerlane destroyed much of the Mamluk empire, the final ripple of a wave of invasions from Central Asia that by the 15th century had changed the face of the Middle East.

To see the Crusades from a Muslim perspective read Amin Maalouf's lively *The Crusades Through Arab Eyes*. The book recasts the West's memories of knights in shining armour as ruthless barbarians who pillaged the Middle East, the horrors of which still reside in the collective memory of the Middle East.

The main remnant of Ayyubid rule in Jordan is the magnificent Qala'at ar-Rabad at Ajlun – see p114.

You can visit Crusader castles at Karak (p166), Petra (p200 & p188) and on Pharaoh's Island (p231) just offshore from Aqaba.

1000–800 BC	8 BC–AD 40
Emergence of the kingdoms of Ammon, Moab and Edom, based at Rabbath Ammon, Dhiban and Bozrah (Buseira), respectively	Rule of Aretas IV, the greatest of the Nabataean kings

THE OTTOMAN STAGNATION (1516–1918)

The Ottoman Turks took Constantinople in 1453, and defeated the Mamluks in Jordan in 1516 to create one of the word's largest empires. The Ottomans concentrated on the lucrative cities of the region, such as the holy city of Jerusalem and the commercial centre of Damascus, and Jordan again became a forgotten backwater. However, four centuries later the Ottomans did build the Hejaz Railway linking Damascus with the holy city of Medina, via Amman. Jordan was briefly occupied by the Egyptians in the 1830s.

Though bombed by Lawrence and the Arab Revolt, a section of the Hejaz Railway is still in operation – see p261.

The last years of the Ottoman Empire marked the ascendency of the European powers over the Middle East, starting with European conquests of Algeria and Morocco. By the end of WWI the entire Arab world was under European domination. The debate over how Islam and the Arab world should respond to the resurgent West has dominated the last 200 years' history of the Middle East. The West may have shifted roles over the years – 'from conqueror to seducer', in the words of one historian – but the debate over the response still rages. One response – a return to the early principles of Islam, an Islamic 'fundamentalism' – continues to shape Middle Eastern politics to this day.

WWI & THE ARAB REVOLT

During WWI Jordan was the scene of fierce fighting between the Ottoman Turks, allied with the Germans, and the British, based in Suez (Egypt). By the end of 1917 British troops occupied Jerusalem and, a year later, the rest of Syria. Their successes would not have been possible without the aid of the Arab tribes, loosely formed into an army under Emir Faisal, who was the *sharif* (ruler) of Mecca and guardian of the Muslim holy places, and had taken up the reins of the Arab nationalist movement in 1914. The enigmatic British colonel TE Lawrence, known as Lawrence of Arabia (see p204), helped coordinate the Arab Revolt and secure supplies from the Allies.

In June 1916 the Arabs under Emir Faisal and his brother Abdullah joined the British drive to oust the Turks, following British assurances that they would be helped in their fight to establish an independent Arab state. This was one month after the British and French had concluded the secret Sykes-Picot Agreement, whereby 'Syria' (modern-day Syria and Lebanon) was to be placed under French control and 'Palestine' (a vaguely defined area including modern Israel, the Palestinian Territories and Jordan) would go to the British.

Look for the ghosts of Lawrence at Wadi Rum (p203), Aqaba fort (p219) and Azraq fort (p134).

This betrayal was heightened by the 1917 Balfour Declaration, the third of three utterly contradictory British declarations, which stated that:

His Majesty's Government view with favour the establishment in Palestine of a National Home for the Jewish people, and will use their best endeavours to facilitate the achievement of this object.

This contradictory acceptance of both a Jewish homeland in Palestine and the preservation of the rights of the original Palestinian community lies at the heart of the seemingly irreconcilable Arab-Israeli conflict.

111–114   **363**

| Construction of the Via Nova Traiana Roman road along the route of the King's Highway | Half of Petra destroyed by an earthquake |

AFTER WWI

As the Arab Revolt swept through Arabia and Jordan, Aqaba fell to Faisal and Lawrence and three months later the victorious Arab forces marched into Damascus. The war ended a month later, by which time Arab forces controlled most of modern Saudi Arabia, Jordan and parts of southern Syria. The principal Arab leader, Emir Faisal, set up an independent government in Damascus at the end of 1918, a move at first welcomed by the Allies. His demand at the 1919 Paris Peace Conference for independence throughout the Arab world was not so kindly greeted.

The British came to an agreement with Faisal, giving him Iraq, while his elder brother, Abdullah, was proclaimed ruler of Trans-Jordan (formerly part of the Ottoman province of Syria), the land lying between Iraq and the east bank of the Jordan River. A young Winston Churchill drew up the borders in 1921 in his role as British colonial secretary.

Abdullah made Amman his capital. Britain recognised the territory as an independent state under its protection in 1923, and a small defence force, the Arab Legion, was set up under British officers – the best known of whom was Major JB Glubb (Glubb Pasha). A series of treaties after 1928 led to full independence in 1946, when Abdullah was proclaimed king.

For something compact try *The Arabs* by Peter Mansfield, another excellent overview, with a general history followed by specific country overviews, or try the short and impartial *The Arabs: A Short History* by Philip Hitti, a Lebanese Christian Arab. For something more detailed try *History of the Arabs* also by Philip Hitti or *A History of the Middle East* by Peter Mansfield.

PALESTINE & THE BIRTH OF JORDAN

The Balfour Declaration, and subsequent attempts to make the Jewish national home a reality, was destined for trouble from the start. Arabs were outraged by the implication that they were the 'intruders' and the minority group in Palestine, where they accounted for about 90% of the population.

Persecution of Jews under the Nazis in the 1930s accelerated the rate of Jewish immigration to Palestine and violence between Jews and Arabs increased. In 1939 a white paper was drawn up calling for the creation of a bi-national state. This was rejected by both sides, however, and during WWII both sides cooperated with the British.

After the war, the conflict reached its high point. In 1947, the UN voted for the partition of Palestine and on 14 May 1948 the State of Israel was proclaimed. The British Mandate was over and, as troops withdrew from the area, Arab armies attacked the new-born state. Highly trained Israeli forces proved too strong for the ill-equipped Arab volunteers and by mid-1949 armistices had been signed.

King Abdullah harboured dreams of a 'Greater Syria' to include all the modern states of Syria, Lebanon, Jordan and what is now Israel & the Palestinian Territories in a single Arab state (later to include Iraq, as well). For this, he was suspected by his Arab neighbours of pursuing different goals from them in their fight with the state of Israel.

THE JORDANIAN FLAG

The Jordanian flag is based on the flag of the Arab Revolt and is very similar to the Palestinian version. The three bands of black, white and green represent the Abbasid, Umayyad and Fatimid caliphates, respectively; the red triangle represents the Arab Revolt of 1916; a seven-pointed white star symbolises the seven verses of the opening sura of the Quran.

632

Battle of Mu'tah between Byzantine and Muslim Arab forces, followed by Battle of Fahl in 635 and Battle of Yarmouk in 636

747

Earthquake shatters northern Jordan

At the end of hostilities, Jordanian troops were in control of East Jerusalem and the West Bank. In response to the establishment of an Egyptian-backed Arab government in Gaza in September 1948, King Abdullah proclaimed himself King of All Palestine. In April 1950 he formally annexed the territory, despite paying lip service to Arab declarations backing Palestinian independence and expressly ruling out territorial annexations. The new Hashemite Kingdom of Jordan (HKJ) won immediate recognition from the governments of Britain and the US. However, the first wave of Palestinian refugees virtually doubled Jordan's population, putting it under great strain.

The Hashemites are named after Hashem, the great-grandfather of the Prophet Mohammed, from whom King Abdullah (the founder of modern Jordan) claimed descent.

King Abdullah was assassinated outside Al-Aqsa Mosque in Jerusalem in July 1951. His son Talal ruled for a year before being declared schizophrenic, whereupon Abdullah's 17-year-old grandson (and Talal's son) Hussein was proclaimed king, finally ascending to the throne in May 1953, after completing his military education at Harrow and Sandhurst. In 1956, Hussein sacked Glubb Pasha (by then chief of staff of the Jordanian Army). After elections that year, the newly formed Jordanian government broke ties with the UK, and the last British troops left Jordan by mid-1957. Hussein then staged a coup against his government, partly because it had tried to open a dialogue with the Soviet Union.

With the (temporary) union of Egypt and Syria in 1958, King Hussein feared for his own position and tried a federation with his Hashemite cousins in Iraq. This lasted less than a year because the Iraqi Hashemite monarchy was overthrown, and British troops were sent in to Jordan to protect Hussein.

A History of Jordan, by Philip Robbins, details the modern history of Jordan from the 1920s to the present day and is one of very few specific books to focus on the Hashemite Kingdom. The main other available work is Kamal Salibi's *The Modern History of Jordan*.

In February 1960, Jordan offered a form of citizenship to all Palestinian Arab refugees and, in defiance of the wishes of the other Arab states for an independent Palestine, insisted that its annexation of Palestinian territory be recognised. Despite Jordan's opposition, the Palestine Liberation Organization (PLO) was formed in 1964, with the blessing of the Arab League, to represent the Palestinian people. The Palestine National Council (PNC) was established within the PLO as its executive body – the closest thing to a Palestinian government.

At about the same time, an organisation called the Palestine National Liberation Movement (also known as Al-Fatah) was established. One of the stated aims of both the PLO and Al-Fatah was to train guerrillas for raids on Israel. Al-Fatah emerged from a power struggle for control of the guerrilla organisations as the dominant force within the PLO, and its leader, Yasser Arafat, became chair of the executive committee of the PLO in 1969.

THE SIX DAY WAR

With aid from the USA and a boom in tourism – mainly in Jerusalem's old city – the early 1960s saw Jordan's position improve dramatically. However, all that changed within a week with the outbreak of the Six Day War.

The build-up to the war had seen increasing Palestinian guerrilla raids into Israel from Syria. The Syrians stepped up the raids once President Nasser of Egypt promised support in the event of an Israeli attack. When the Syrians announced that Israel was massing troops in preparation for an assault, Egypt responded by asking the UN to withdraw its Emergency

1187	1516–1918
Battle of Hittin – Saladin beats the Crusader armies in a decisive battle	Ottoman rule

Force from the Egypt-Israel border, which it did. Nasser then closed the Straits of Tiran (the entrance to the Red Sea), effectively sealing the port of Eilat. Five days later, Jordan and Egypt signed a mutual defence pact, dragging Jordan into any future hostilities.

On 5 June 1967, the Israelis dispatched a pre-dawn raid that wiped out the Egyptian Air Force on the ground, and in the following days decimated Egyptian troops in Sinai and Jordanian troops on the West Bank, and stormed up the Golan Heights in Syria.

The outcome for Jordan was disastrous: it lost the whole of the West Bank and its part of Jerusalem, which together has supplied Jordan with its two principal sources of income (agriculture and tourism), and resulted in yet another huge wave of Palestinian refugees.

For an overview of Arab history, the widely acclaimed work *A History of the Arab Peoples* by Albert Hourani is recommended. It's as much an attempt to convey a sense of the evolution of Muslim Arab societies as a straightforward history, with extensive treatment of various aspects of social, cultural and religious life.

BLACK SEPTEMBER

After the 1967 defeat, the frustrated Palestinians became increasingly militant and, although there was tacit agreement with the Jordanian government that they could operate freely out of their bases in the Jordan Valley, the Jordanians were not ready to give them immunity from Jordan's laws. It was not long before the inevitable showdown took place.

By 1968, Palestinian *fedayeen* (guerrilla) fighters were effectively acting as a state within a state, openly defying and humiliating Jordanian soldiers. In June 1970, things deteriorated into sporadic conflict, when Palestinian militants fired on King Hussein's motorcade and held 68 foreigners hostage in an Amman hotel.

On 6 September 1970, the rogue Popular Front for the Liberation of Palestine (an epithet that will sound familiar to fans of the film *Life of Brian*) hijacked Swissair and TWA flights to an airstrip in Jordan's remote desert. Six days later another hijacked plane arrived, then all three were spectacularly blown up in front of the world's TV cameras. On 16 September, martial law was imposed and bloody fighting between Palestinian militants and the Jordanian army broke out across Amman and Jordan. At the height of the fighting, Yasser Arafat was spirited out of Amman disguised as a Kuwaiti sheikh in order to attend an Arab League summit in Cairo. A fragile cease-fire was signed, but not before at least 3000 lives had been lost. It was not until midway through 1971 that the final resistance around Ajlun was defeated. The guerrillas were forced to recognise Hussein's authority and the Palestinians had to choose between exile and submission. Most chose exile in Lebanon.

In October 1974, King Hussein reluctantly agreed to an Arab summit declaration that recognised the Palestine Liberation Organization (PLO) as the sole representative of Palestinians with a right to set up a government in any liberated territory, nullifying Jordan's claims to the West Bank. In July 1988 the king severed all of Jordan's administrative and legal ties with the West Bank.

In the meantime, profound and long-lasting demographic changes had been reshaping the region. Economic migration, both from the countryside to the city, and also from Jordan to the increasingly wealthy Gulf States, changed social and family structures. Improvements in education, a huge rise in population and a particularly sharp rise in the percentage of young people further dramatically altered the face of the Middle East

1946, 25 May	**1950**
Independence from the British; Abdullah becomes first king of Jordan	Jordan annexes the West Bank and east Jerusalem

during the 1960s, 70s and 80s. Amman alone mushroomed from a town of 30,000 in 1948 to a city of 250,000 in 1960.

In November 1989 the first full parliamentary elections since 1967 were held in Jordan, and women were allowed to vote for the first time. Four years later most political parties were legalised and allowed to participate in parliamentary and municipal elections.

Although the Islamic Action Front occupied many of the 80 lower-house seats, royalist independents together still constituted a large majority, which continued to ensure that King Hussein remained in power.

THE GULF WAR

Jordan found itself caught in a no-win situation when Iraq (its major trading partner) invaded Kuwait in 1990. Support for Saddam was at fever pitch among Palestinians in Jordan after he promised to link the Kuwait issue to their own and force a showdown.

King Hussein's diplomatic skills were stretched to the fullest when he refused to side against Iraq, largely out of fear of unrest among Jordan's Palestinian populace. This was misunderstood in the West as support for Saddam, but King Hussein played the game with typical dexterity. Although tending to side publicly with Baghdad, he maintained efforts to find a peaceful solution and complied, officially at least, with the UN embargo on trade with Iraq. This last step won him the sympathy of Western financial bodies and, although US and Saudi aid was temporarily cut, along with Saudi oil, loans and help were forthcoming from other quarters, particularly Japan and Europe.

One UN assessment put the total cost to Jordan of the war from mid-1990 to mid-1991 at more than US$8 billion. The UN naval blockade of Aqaba, which was aimed at enforcing UN sanctions against Iraq, cost Jordan around US$300 million a year in lost revenue between 1991 and 1994.

Moreover, for the third time in 45 years, Jordan experienced a massive refugee inflow, this time of 500,000 Jordanians and Palestinians who had been working in the Gulf States. The loss of their remittances was initially seen as a blow to the economy, but the 'returnees' brought US$500 million home with them and actually helped unleash an unprecedented boom, stimulating economic growth to a huge 11% in 1992.

PEACE WITH ISRAEL

With the signing of the PLO-Israeli declaration of principles in September 1993, which set in motion the process of establishing an autonomous Palestinian authority in the Occupied Territories, the territorial question was virtually removed as an obstacle to peace between Jordan and Israel.

Compared with Syria, Jordan had long displayed greater willingness to countenance peace with Israel. On 26 October 1994 Jordan and Israel & the Palestinian Territories signed a peace treaty that provided for the dropping of all economic barriers between the two countries and for closer cooperation on security, water and other issues.

The clause in the treaty recognising the 'special role of the Hashemite Kingdom of Jordan in the Muslim holy shrines in Jerusalem' sounded

'In November 1989 the first full parliamentary elections since 1967 were held in Jordan, and women were allowed to vote for the first time'

1951	**1953**
King Abdullah assassinated at Al-Aqsa Mosque in Jerusalem	Hussein is proclaimed king of Jordan after his brother is declared mentally unstable

alarm bells in Palestinian circles. The treaty made Jordan very unpopular with the region's governments and people alike, as well as severely straining relations with other countries such as Syria and Libya.

THE KING IS DEAD, LONG LIVE THE KING

By the time of his death in February 1999, King Hussein was well on his way to becoming one of the great peacemakers of history. From his frantic efforts at diplomacy to avert the 1991 Gulf War to his peace agreement with Israel in 1994, the urbane and articulate king of a country in one of the world's toughest neighbourhoods came to be seen as a beacon of moderateness and stability in a region known for neither attribute. This reputation was secured in 1997 when a Jordanian soldier shot and killed seven Israeli schoolgirls in northern Jordan. King Hussein personally attended the funeral in a public display of grief and solidarity with the Israeli families.

And yet King Hussein also struggled to maintain his credibility among the majority Palestinian population of his kingdom. Numerous assassination attempts, fuelled by accusations that the king had been carrying out secret negotiations with the Israelis and was on the payroll of the CIA after 1957, dogged the early years of his reign. His belief that he was the true representative of the Palestinian people brought him frequently

---

KING HUSSEIN

Like all great figures of history, King Hussein has become a figure of legend. When the first king of Jordan, King Abdullah, was assassinated at Al-Aqsa Mosque in Jerusalem in July 1951, his 15-year-old grandson Hussein was by his side. By some accounts, he was hit in the chest by a bullet, miraculously deflected by a medal worn on his uniform. On succeeding to the throne on 2 May 1953 at the age of 18, the youthful, British-educated Hussein was known more for his love of pretty women and fast cars than any great political skill. Yet 45 years later he was fêted as one of the Middle East's great political survivors, still king against all the odds and the de facto creator of the modern state of Jordan.

Hussein married four times and sired 11 children. His first marriage was to the beautiful Dina bint Abedelhamid. After one year of marriage and the birth of a daughter, Princess Alia, they divorced. In 1961, Hussein married Antoinette 'Toni' Gardner, a British army officer's daughter who took the name Princess Muna upon converting to Islam. They had two sons, Prince Abdullah (the current king) and Prince Feisal, followed by two daughters, Princess Zein and Princess Aisha. In 1972 the couple divorced. That same year Hussein married Alia Toukan. They had a daughter, Princess Haya, and a son, Prince Ali, as well as an adopted daughter, Abeer Muhaisin. Tragedy struck the family in 1977, however, when Queen Alia was killed in a helicopter crash. The following year, King Hussein married his fourth and final wife, American-born Lisa Halaby, who took the name Queen Noor (see p41). They had two sons, Prince Hamzah and Prince Hashim, and two daughters, Princess Iman and Princess Raiyah.

While King Hussein was active on the world's political stage, his loyalty to his people was also well regarded. In the great tradition of *The Thousand and One Nights*, and in a role emulated by his son decades later, Hussein would disguise himself as a taxi driver and ask passengers what they really thought of the king. In November 1958, Hussein, a trained pilot, flew his air-force plane towards Europe for a vacation only to be intercepted by two Syrian fighter planes who sought to force him down. He escaped back to Jordan, adding to his already growing legend.

1967	1970
Israel wins the Six Day War, gaining Jerusalem and the West Bank	Black September – thousands injured in clashes between the Jordanian government and Palestinian guerrillas

THE ROYAL HANDSHAKE

Like any royal family worth its salt, Jordan's Hashemites have not been immune from squabbles over the royal succession. While King Hussein was in the USA for cancer treatment, the widely respected elder statesman of Jordanian diplomacy, Hassan bin Talal (Hussein's brother and Crown Prince for 34 years), took temporary charge of the kingdom. Just before his death in February 1999, Hussein returned to Jordan, stripped Hassan of power and unexpectedly announced that Hussein's son from a previous marriage, Abdullah bin Hussein, would be the new king.

While the public appearance was of a smooth transition and happy families, all was not well behind the scenes. Soon after the succession was finalised, reports began to surface from within the palace that Abdullah had agreed to become king only for a limited time, after which the more charismatic but youthful Crown Prince Hamzah, would take the throne. Neither Queen Noor nor her son, Prince Hamzah were at Abdullah's enthronement ceremony.

In 2002, unofficial reports suggested that Abdullah had changed his mind and decided to remain as king. In 2004 the crown prince was stripped of his title, leaving Abdullah's 11-year-old son Hussein next in line for the throne.

into conflict with an increasingly militant Palestinian movement. It was not until his later years, after he renounced all claims to the Palestinian leadership and to the West Bank, that the rift was officially healed. Even then, his 1994 peace treaty with Israel was branded by some Palestinians as a betrayal and this uneasy relationship remained largely unresolved at the time of his death.

After an official mourning period, Hussein's son was enthroned as King Abdullah II on 9 June 1999.

KING ABDULLAH II

Abdullah was born on 30 January 1962 to Princess Muna, King Hussein's second (British) wife. He studied in the USA and, like his father, attended Sandhurst in the UK and other military academies in the USA. He was promoted to lieutenant in the Jordanian Army at 22, and became head of Jordan's Special Forces in 1998 after he was involved in the successful (and televised) capture of two assassins.

Abdullah is a keen sportsman, pilot, scuba diver and rally driver; he enjoys Western food and speaks better English than Arabic. He is married to Queen Rania, a glamorous Palestinian dedicated to children's and women's charities, and has three young children, Crown Prince Hussein, Princess Iman and Princess Salma.

Throughout the Palestinian intifada, Abdullah has been one of the voices of moderation within the Arab world, preferring diplomacy as a means of bringing about a peace settlement. This stance has won him much respect in international circles. He has, however, come under attack from many Palestinians and other Arabs for maintaining relations with Israel and being ineffectual in his attempts to bring about a solution to the conflict. Although he has proven to be adept at following in his father's footsteps, it remains to be seen whether Abdullah's diplomatic skills are as enduring, or as ultimately effective, as Hussein's. At home, his drive to stamp out corruption has helped to maintain his popularity.

The Jordanian constitution stipulates that the parents of the king of Jordan must be Arab and Muslim by birth; King Abdullah's mother was English and a convert to Islam.

1994	1999, 7 Feb
Peace treaty signed between Israel and Jordan, ending 46 years of war	King Hussein dies; King Abdullah ascends to the throne

The Culture

THE NATIONAL PSYCHE

Ahlan wa sahlan! It's one of the most common greetings in Arabic and one that defines the way Jordanians relate to the people around them, especially guests. The root words mean 'people' or 'family' *(ahl)* and 'ease' *(sahl)*, so translated loosely the expression means 'be as one of the family and at your ease'. It's a gracious thought, and one that ends up in English simply as 'welcome', or more commonly to tourists, 'welcome to Jordan'. Among Arabs, it's used to mean anything from 'hello' to 'you're welcome' (after thanks).

Arab traditions of hospitality and kindness are deeply ingrained in the psyches of most Jordanians, especially the Bedouin. Rooted in the harsh realities of life in the desert, these traditions have been virtually codified into all social behaviour. These century-old notions of hospitality mix with an easy modernity and wonderful sense of humour that make Jordanians easy to get along with.

Writers over the centuries have commented on the dignity, pride and courtesy of the Bedouin in particular, characterising them as courageous and fierce fighters yet also intense and loyal friends.

Yet there is an increasing polarisation in Jordanian society and in many ways the modern Western-looking outlook of Amman's young middle and upper classes contrasts starkly with the conservative Bedouin morality of the countryside.

Bedouin concepts of honour *(ird)* in particular run deep, but sit uneasily with the freedoms many affluent Jordanian women have come to expect. Rapid social change connected with the rise of tourism has also led to a clash of social values in places like Petra and Wadi Musa. The effect of tourism on traditional Bedouin hospitality and lifestyle has yet to be studied.

However, Jordanians still share many values, including a deep respect for the Jordanian royal family, which itself stems in part from the ingrained tribal respect for local elders, or sheikhs. Islam dominates the Jordanian view of the world, of course, as does the Palestinian experience, which is hardly surprising when you consider that 65% of Jordanians are Palestinian.

A belief and faith in and submission (Islam literally means 'submission') to God's will sits deep in the Jordanian psyche. Ask Jordanians *kaif halak?* (how are you?) and they will reply *al-hamdu lillah* – 'Fine, thanks be to God'. Ask if peace will come soon to the Middle East, or even if the bus to Jerash will leave on time, and the reply will doubtless be *in sha' Allah* – 'God willing'. Say your goodbyes with *ma'a salama* and you will be told *Allah ysmalakh*, 'God keep you safe'.

Sharing deep ethnic and cultural ties with both Palestine and Iraq, many Jordanians are frustrated and at times even angered by American and European policies towards the Middle East, but Jordanians are always able to differentiate a government and its policies from its people. You'll never be greeted with animosity in Jordan, regardless of your nationality; only a courtesy and hospitality that is deeply impressive and often quite humbling.

The checked keffiyeh headdress is an important national symbol in Jordan – red and white for the Bedouin, or black and white for the Palestinians – held in place by the black rope-like *agal*.

DAILY LIFE

Like much of the Middle East, Jordan is a country that has deep attachments to the desert – the historical source of Arab tradition – but one that has an increasingly urban society. Over 40% of Jordan's population now lives in Amman, reflecting the deep contradiction between rural and urban lifestyles – the timeless spilt between the 'Desert and the Sown'. There is also increasing economic polarisation, especially in Amman – just compare gritty downtown with affluent Abdoun.

The middle and upper classes of Amman shop in malls, drink lattes in mixed-sex Starbucks and obsess over the latest fashions. Mobile phones dominate life in Jordan as they do abroad. Yet in other districts of the same city, urban unemployment is high and entire neighbourhoods of Amman are made up of Palestinian refugees.

At the other end of the spectrum is traditional Bedouin life, deeply rooted in the desert and semi-nomadic, centred around herding. For more on the Bedouin see p212.

Due to high unemployment, economic migration is common in Jordan and most families have at least one male who is temporarily working away from home, whether in Amman, the Gulf States or further abroad. The remittances sent home by these absent workers are increasingly important to family budgets. Each economically active person has to support, on average, four other persons too.

Family ties are all-important to both modern and traditional Jordanians and the sexes are often segregated. Most Jordanian women only socialise with other women, and often only inside the family group, while men chat with other men in male-only coffeehouses. Attitudes towards women remain quite traditional.

Marriages are often arranged and matches are commonly made between cousins. The marriage ceremony usually takes place in either the mosque or the home of the bride or groom. After the marriage the men of the family drive around the streets in a long convoy, sounding their

> Conscription for males aged 18 and over was discontinued in 1999.

SOCIAL GRACES

Etiquette is very important in Jordanian (and Arab) culture, and you'll find that Jordanians will respect you more if you follow these few simple rules:

- Stand when someone important, or another guest, enters the room
- Shake hands with everyone – but only with a Jordanian woman if she offers her hand first
- Arab men often greet good friends with a kiss on the cheek
- Do not sit so that the soles of your feet point at anyone
- Never accept any present or service of any kind without first politely refusing twice
- Proactive efforts – such as offering sweets and wishing people *eid mubarak* during the festival of Eid al-Adha – will especially endear you to your hosts
- Don't engage in any conversation about sensitive topics (eg the Jordanian royal family or Judaism) unless you are in private with a person you know well
- An unaccompanied foreign man should not sit next to an unaccompanied Jordanian woman on public transport, unless it's unavoidable
- Remove your shoes when visiting a mosque, or a private house (unless you're specifically told to keep them on)
- Never walk in front of, or interrupt in any way, someone praying towards Mecca
- Foreign couples should not hold hands, or show any signs of affection, in public
- Rather than curtly saying 'no', the way to turn down an invitation is to refuse politely with your right hand over your heart, adding something noncommittal like 'perhaps another time, *in sha' Allah*' (if God wills it)

BODY LANGUAGE

Arabs are some of the world's great gesticulators, and a whole range of ideas can be expressed without uttering a word. Jordanians often say 'no' by raising the eyebrows and lifting the head up and back. This is often accompanied by a 'tsk tsk' noise, which can be a little disconcerting if you're not used to it.

Shaking the head from side to side means 'I don't understand'. Stretching out the hand as if to open a door and giving it a quick flick of the wrist is equivalent to 'what do you want?', 'where are you going?' or 'what is your problem?'.

If an official holds out a hand and draws a line across the palm with the index finger of the other hand, they're asking to see your passport, bus ticket or other document.

A right hand over your heart means 'no, thanks'. When a Jordanian puts his thumb and fore-fingers together vertically it often means 'wait a minute'.

A foreign man asking directions should not be surprised to be taken by the hand and led along by another man; it's quite natural. Male friends often greet each other with a hug and a kiss on the cheek.

Lastly, as the left hand is associated with toilet duties it's considered unclean, so always use your right hand when giving or receiving something.

---

horns, blasting out music and making as much ballyhoo as possible. After that the partying goes on until the early hours of the morning, often until sunrise.

Many families, especially in smaller towns and rural areas, remain traditional in terms of divisions within the house. As a rule, various parts of the house are reserved for men and others for women. This becomes particularly apparent when guests are present.

Meals are generally eaten on the floor, with everyone gathered around several trays of food shared by all. More traditional families are often quite hierarchical at meal times. The grandparents and male head of the house may eat in one circle, the latter's wife and the older children and other women in the family in another, and the small children in yet another. Usually, outsiders eat with the head of the household.

Foreign women will more often than not be treated as 'honorary males'. In the case of a couple, a foreign woman may be welcome to sneak off to hang around with the Jordanian women and then come back to see how the 'men's world' is getting on. In this way, a foreign woman can find herself in the unique position of being able to get an impression of home life for both sexes.

In the evenings, most locals in the cities will probably window-shop, stroll around the streets, enjoy a leisurely meal, go to the cinema or watch TV. Men may pass the time in a local coffeehouse, playing cards, smoking a nargileh (water pipe), or perhaps watching European league football on the TV, while the kids play the real thing on the streets outside.

POPULATION

The population of Jordan stood at about 5.7 million in 2005, a substantial increase from just 586,000 in 1958. More than 1.7 million people were registered as refugees (primarily from the wars of 1948 and 1967) with the UN Relief & Works Agency (UNRWA). In an effort to reduce the expected population of eight million in 2024, the Jordanian National Population Commission is hoping to dramatically reduce the birth rate, through the promotion of family planning, to 2.1 children per family. In 1990 the fertility rate stood at 5.6 children, with the figure reduced to 3.5 by 2001.

Approximately 1.8 million people live in the capital, Amman, and a further 700,000 live in neighbouring Zarqa and suburbs. The majority of Jordanians are Arab; over 60% are Palestinian Arabs. There are also small communities of Circassians, Chechens, Armenians and Western expatriates. There are now anywhere between 200,000 and 500,000 exiled Iraqis living in Jordan.

The Bedouin are the original desert dwellers of Arabia, perceived by many as the representatives and guardians of the very essence of 'Arabness'. They form the majority of the indigenous population but today not more than 40,000 Bedouin can be considered truly nomadic. There are dozens of Bedouin tribes or sub-clans, from the influential Beni Sakr and Huweitat to the smaller but very visible B'doul and Ammareen of Petra. The traditional tribal insignias, known as *wasm*, are still used as brands for livestock.

Jordan is one of the better-educated Arab countries; about 87% of Jordanians are literate, and about 97% of children attend primary school. School is compulsory for children from the ages of five to 14.

Arabs

Over 98% of Jordanians are Arab, descended from various tribes that migrated to the area from all directions over the centuries.

PALESTINIANS

About 60% of Jordan's population is made up of Palestinians who fled, mostly from the West Bank, during the wars of 1948 and 1967 and after the Gulf War in 1990–91. The Palestinians have the country's highest birthrate so this percentage will only rise.

PALESTINIAN REFUGEES IN JORDAN

No country has absorbed more Palestinian refugees than Jordan. As at 2005, more than 1.7 million Palestinians were registered as refugees in Jordan by the UN, making up 33% of the local population. The figure is surpassed only by the Gaza Strip (74%) and the West Bank (34%).

Most of the refugees have become an integral part of Jordanian life, with many succeeding in business, politics and cultural pursuits. In the aftermath of the 1990 Iraqi invasion of Kuwait, as many as 500,000 Palestinian refugees entered Jordan. Although they placed a huge strain upon already creaking infrastructure, they also brought with them an estimated US$500 million, sparking a booming economy.

Nonetheless, around 280,000 refugees (18% of the total refugee population in Jordan) are housed in 10 camps administered by the UN Relief & Works Agency (UNRWA), which remains responsible for all health, education and relief programmes. The first four camps were set up after 1948, with the remaining six established after the 1967 war. As of December 2002, the largest camps were those at Baqa'a (with 78,163 inhabitants), 20km north of Amman, the Amman New Camp (49,034), Marqa (40,349) and Jebel al-Hussein (27,831), with large camps also at Zarqa, Jerash and Irbid. The original tent shelters have long since been replaced with more permanent structures and often more resemble suburbs than refugee camp.

The UNRWA runs one of the largest school systems in the Middle East with 184 schools in Jordan alone teaching double-shift classes (due to limited space) for 140,000 students up to Grade 10 level. The UNRWA also facilitates university scholarships.

The relief side of the UN operation is targeted primarily at special hardship cases and poverty alleviation, with special emphasis on women's programmes, rehabilitation for people with a disability and microfinance for disadvantaged individuals.

For more information on the work of UNRWA in Jordan, contact the **UNRWA Public Information Office** (☎ 06 5609100, ext 165; jorpio@unrwa.org; Mustapha bin Abdullah St, Shmeisani, Amman). For more general information about Palestinians in Jordan, contact the Jordanian **Department of Palestinian Affairs** (☎ 06 5666172; www.dpa.gov.jo; Abu Hamed al-Ghazali St, Shmeisani, Amman), which is part of the Ministry of Foreign Affairs.

All Palestinians have been granted the right to Jordanian citizenship, and many have exercised that option. Palestinians play an important part in the political, cultural and economic life of Jordan and, although many occupy high positions in government and business, they continue to dream of a return to an independent Palestine. This is partly why so many continue to live in difficult conditions in the 30 or more refugee camps that dot the landscape (see p37).

The Palestinians derive their name from the Greek name for the Philistines, one of the 'Peoples of the Sea' who invaded the Mediterranean coast around 1300 BC, settling in Gaza.

Circassians & Chechens

The Circassians (Turkic Muslims from the Caucasus) fled persecution in Russia in the late 19th century to settle in the Jordan Valley, becoming prosperous farmers. There are now about 40,000 Circassians – living mainly in Wadi as-Seer and Na'ur (both near Amman) – but intermarriage has made them virtually indistinguishable from Arabs.

Historically and ethnically related to the Circassians is the small (about 4000) Shiite community of Chechens, the only other recognised ethnic minority in Jordan.

RELIGION

Although the population is overwhelmingly Islamic, Jordan is officially secular, and freedom of religion is a statutory right of the Jordanian constitution.

Islam

Islam is the predominant religion in Jordan. Muslims are called to prayer five times a day and, no matter where you might be, there always seems to be a mosque within earshot. The midday prayers on Friday, when the sheikh of the mosque delivers his weekly sermon, or *khutba,* are considered the most important.

Muslims must cover their entire heads when they pray, which is one reason why Muslim headgear has no peak, whether it be a fez, skullcap or headdress.

While Islam shares its roots with the other great monotheistic faiths – Judaism and Christianity – that sprang from the harsh and unforgiving soil of the Middle East, it is considerably younger than both. The holy book of Islam is the Quran, meaning literally 'reading' or 'recitation'. Its pages carry many references to the earlier prophets of both the older religions: Abraham (known in the Quran as Ibrahim), Noah (Nuh), Moses (Musa) and Jesus (Isa). Mohammed is not considered divine, but rather the last in this series of prophets.

The Quran is believed to be the word of God, communicated to Mohammed directly in a series of revelations in the early 7th century. For Muslims, Islam is the apogee of the monotheistic faiths from which it derives so much. Muslims traditionally attribute a place of great respect to Christians and Jews, whom they consider *Ahl al-kitab,* the 'People of the Book'.

Among Muslims it is customary to follow a mention of the Prophet Mohammed's name with the phrase *Salla Allahu Wa Salam,* Peace Be Upon Him (PBUH).

EARLY YEARS OF ISLAM

Mohammed, born into a trading family of the Arabian city of Mecca (in present-day Saudi Arabia) in AD 570, began receiving revelations in 610, and after a time began imparting the content of Allah's message to the inhabitants of Mecca. The essence was a call to submit to God's will, but not all locals were terribly taken with the idea.

Mohammed gathered quite a following in his campaign against the idolaters of Mecca, and his movement especially appealed to the poorer levels of society. The powerful families became increasingly outraged, and by 622 had made life sufficiently unpleasant for Mohammed and his followers; they fled to Medina, an oasis town some 300km to the north and

THE FIVE PILLARS OF ISLAM

In order to live a devout life, a Muslim is expected to carry out at least the Five Pillars of Islam:

- Haj – the pinnacle of a devout Muslim's life is the pilgrimage to the holy sites in and around Mecca. The haj takes place in the last month of the year, Zuul-Hijja, and Muslims from all over the world travel to Saudi Arabia for the pilgrimage and subsequent feast of Eid al-Adha. The returned pilgrim earns the right to be addressed as Haji. Women may perform the haj with a male chaperon.

- Salat – this is the obligation of prayer, done ideally five times a day when the muezzins call upon the faithful to pray: before sunrise, noon, mid-afternoon, sunset and before midnight. Communal prayers are only obligatory on Friday, although the strong sense of community makes joining together in a masjid ('place of prostration', ie mosque) preferable to most.

- Shahada – this is the profession of the faith, the basic tenet of Islam: 'There is no God but Allah and Mohammed is his prophet' *(La il-laha illa Allah Mohammed rasul Allah)*. It's commonly heard as part of the call to prayer, and at other events such as births and deaths. People can often be heard muttering the first half of the sentence to themselves, as if seeking a little strength to get through the trials of the day.

- Sawm – Ramadan, the ninth month of the Muslim calendar, commemorates the revelation of the Quran to Mohammed. In a demonstration of the Muslims' renewal of faith, they are asked to abstain from sex, and from letting anything (including cigarettes) pass their lips from dawn to dusk every day of the month. For more on Ramadan, see p244 and p58.

- Zakat – giving alms to the poor was, from the start, an essential part of Islamic social teaching and, in some parts of the Muslim world, was later developed into various forms of tax as a way of redistributing funds to the needy. The moral obligation towards one's poorer neighbours continues to be emphasised at a personal and community level, and many Islamic groups run large charitable institutions, including Amman's Islamic Hospital.

now Islam's second most holy city. This migration – the Hejira – marks the beginning of the Islamic calendar, year 1 AH or AD 622.

In Medina, Mohammed continued to preach. Soon he and his followers clashed with the rulers of Mecca, led by the powerful Quraysh tribe. By 630, his followers returned to take Mecca. In the two years before his death, many of the surrounding tribes swore allegiance to him and the new faith.

Mecca became the symbolic centre of the Islamic religion, containing as it did the Kaaba, which houses the black stone that had long formed the object of pagan pilgrimage and later was said to have been given to Ibrahim (Abraham) by the Archangel Jibreel (Gabriel). Mohammed determined that Muslims ('those who submit') should always face Mecca when praying outside the city.

Upon Mohammed's death in 632, the Arab tribes conquered all of what makes up modern Jordan, Syria, Iraq, Lebanon, Israel & the Palestinian Territories. By 644, they had taken Egypt and spread into North Africa, and in the following decades crossed into Spain and, for a while, deep into France. The Arabic language and Islamic faith remained long after the military conquests faded into history and remain to this day a remarkable cultural unifier, from Casablanca to Kashgar, and Syria to Sudan.

The initial conquests were carried out under four successive caliphs, or Companions of Mohammed, of whom three were assassinated. In turn, the caliphs were followed by the Umayyad dynasty, based in Damascus, and the Abbasids, based in Baghdad. For more information see p25.

One of the more sensitive and accessible recent accounts of Islamic belief and practice is *Islam: A Short History* by Karen Armstrong. It's compact and also tackles the modern dilemmas facing Islam.

SUNNIS & SHIITES

In its early days, Islam suffered a major schism that divided the faith into two streams, the Sunnis and Shiites. The power struggle between Ali (the last of the four caliphs and Mohammed's son-in-law) and the Umayyad dynasty in Damascus lay at the heart of the rift that tore asunder the new faith's followers.

The succession to the caliphate had from the first been marked by intrigue. Ali, the father of Mohammed's sole male heirs, lost his struggle and was assassinated, paving the way to the caliphate for the Umayyad leader Mu'awiyah. The latter was related to Ali's predecessor, Othman, in whose murder some believed Ali was implicated.

Those who recognised Mu'awiyah as caliph (who were the majority) came to be known as the Sunnis, and would become the orthodox bedrock of Islam. The Shiites, on the other hand, recognise only the successors of Ali. Most of them are known as Twelvers, because they believe in 12 imams (religious leaders), the last of whom has been lost from sight, but will appear some day to create an empire of the true faith.

The Sunnis divided into four schools of religious thought, of which most Jordanians belong to the Hanafi school.

Northeast Jordan (including the town of Azraq) has small pockets of around 15,000 Druze, who follow a shadowy offshoot of Shiite Islam.

> The spread of Islam in the 7th century has been described by historian Bernard Lewis as 'one of the swiftest and most dramatic changes in the whole of history'.

ISLAMIC CUSTOMS

The first words a newborn baby hears are the call to prayer. A week later this is followed by a ceremony in which the baby's head is shaved and an animal is sacrificed. The major event of a boy's childhood is circumcision, which normally takes place sometime between the ages of seven and 12.

Before praying, Muslims follow certain rituals. They must wash their hands, mouth, ears, arms, feet, head and neck in running water. All mosques have a small area set aside for this purpose. If they're not in a mosque and there is no water available, scouring with sand suffices; where there is no sand, they must still go through the motions of washing.

Then they must cover their head, face Mecca (all mosques are oriented so that the mihrab, or prayer niche, faces the right way – south-southeast in Jordan) and follow a set pattern of gestures and genuflections. Muslims don't technically require a mosque to pray and you'll often see Jordanians praying by the side of the road or at the back of their shop; many keep a small prayer rug handy for such times. Mosques themselves are quite austere places, devoid of the pews, sculpture, paintings and music common in Christian churches.

In everyday life, Muslims are prohibited from drinking alcohol and eating pork (as the pig is considered unclean), and must refrain from fraud, usury, slander and gambling. Followers of Islam believe in angels, the infallibility of the Quran and parts of the Bible, a day of judgement, predestination of worldly affairs and life after death. Denial of these central tenets is considered apostasy (a renunciation of faith), which carries considerable social stigma.

> About 92% of Jordan's population belong to the Hanafi school of Sunni Islam.

> You may be surprised to hear that Islam and Christianity share many prophets, including Jesus (Isa in Arabic), John the Baptist (Yahya), Job (Ayyub), Joshua (Yosha), Lot (Lut) and Noah (Nuh).

Christianity

Statistics on the number of Christians in Jordan are wildly contradictory. Christians are believed to account for 5% to 6% of Jordan's population. Most live in Karak, Madaba, Salt, Fuheis, Ajlun and Amman – all with a bewildering array of churches representing the three major branches of

Christianity in Jordan: Orthodox, Catholic (known in Jordan as Latin) and (to a far lesser extent) Protestant.

About two-thirds of Christians in Jordan are Greek Orthodox. This church has its liturgy in Arabic, and is the mother church of the Jacobites (Syrian Orthodox), who broke away in the 6th century. Coptic Orthodox and Armenian Orthodox Christians are also represented in Jordan.

The other third are Greek Catholics, or Melchites, under the authority of the patriarch who resides in Damascus. This church observes a Byzantine tradition of married clergy being in charge of rural parishes, while diocesan clergy are celibate.

Bismillah, literally 'In the name of God, the Merciful, the Compassionate', is the opening phrase of all suras in the Quran and is used in general conversation as an expression of sincerity or to commend something to God.

WOMEN IN JORDAN

Compared to some neighbouring countries, particularly Saudi Arabia, women in Jordan enjoy more freedom and privileges: they have access to a full education (in 2002, the number of girls in primary and secondary schools was almost identical to the number of boys); they can vote (Jordanian women got the vote in 1967 but didn't have a chance to use it for the first time until 1989); many work in male-dominated industries and businesses; and they are allowed to drive cars. In 2001, the legal age of marriage was lifted from 15 years old for women and 16 for men to 18 for both, although Islamic judges are still permitted to sanction underage marriages.

THE ROYAL WOMEN OF JORDAN

Despite claming unbroken descent from the Prophet Mohammed, Jordan's Hashemite royal family is surprisingly cosmopolitan. King Hussein's second wife (and also mother of the present king, Abdullah) was English and the king himself has blue eyes.

When Hussein's fourth wife, Queen Noor (www.noor.gov.jo) met her future husband, King Hussein, she was simply known as Lisa Halaby, a Washington DC-born architect and urban planner fresh out of Princeton. Born into a distinguished Arab-American family (her father served under the administration of John F Kennedy and was head of Pan-Am for a while), she met King Hussein while working on a project for Royal Jordanian Airlines. After a much-scrutinised whirlwind romance they married in a traditional Islamic ceremony in 1978. The fairy-tale romance, however, was not without its detractors. Many Jordanians were uneasy about an American joining their revered royal family. Although five inches taller than her husband, official pictures always depicted the queen as shorter than him.

Adopting the name Queen Noor (Light of Hussein) upon her conversion to Islam, Jordan's new queen effectively signalled the beginning of a new era. Throughout her tenure she campaigned for women's rights, children's welfare and community improvement, setting up the impressive Noor Foundation. Queen Noor took an important role in explaining Jordan's stand against the 1990 Gulf War to American audiences. Since her husband's death, Queen Noor has scaled back her public presence.

Since the ascension of King Abdullah and his wife Queen Rania (www.queenrania.jo), parts of the media have been unable to resist offhand newspaper headlines such as 'Battle of the Queens'. The recent stripping of the title of Crown Prince from King Abdullah's half-brother Hamzah (www.princehamzah.jo) in late 2004 was seen as a blow to Noor's influence, since he is her eldest son.

Queen Rania has assumed a prominent position on a number of issues. Born in Kuwait to a notable Jordanian family of Palestinian origin, and educated at the American University of Cairo, she married King Abdullah bin Al-Hussein in 1993. As Jordan's new first lady she too has become a public supporter of a variety of issues and, like Queen Noor, has established her own charity based on women's handicrafts, the Jordan River Foundation. She can be seen doing everything from campaigning for the rights of women to running the Dead Sea Marathon.

In recent years Jordanian women have made great progress in male-dominated professions. Jordan gained its first female MP (Toujan Faisal) in the early 1990s (a minimum of six women MPs is guaranteed under a royal-imposed quota system), first female taxi driver in 1997, first female mayor in Ajlun in 1995, first female judge in 1996 and first ambassador to the European Union in 2001. But the rise of a few women to senior positions has yet to be matched by across-the-board equality. A majority of women work in health and education; the highest levels of inequality remain in the media and the political arena. Less than 1% of judges are women. In 1991, 14% of the labour force was made up of women; by 2001, this had risen to 20%.

Unlike some of the neighbouring Muslim countries, polygamy (by men) is rare though legal; segregation is uncommon (except in some homes and restaurants, and all mosques); there are no official restrictions about dress codes; and female infanticide and female genital mutilation are extremely rare. Very few women wear the hejab veil and almost none wear the full body chador, though many women wear a headscarf.

Amendments to the law in 2002 made it possible for women to file for divorce if they repay the dowry given by their husband, though the social stigma remains strong. The legal changes also require men who marry more than once, as Islam allows, to inform both their first and their new wives.

Arranged marriages and dowries are still common, but parents do not often enforce a wedding against their daughter's wish. A woman's 'honour' is still valued in traditional societies, and sex before marriage can still be dealt with harshly by other members of a woman's family (see below).

Over 25% of all solved murders in Jordan are described as honour killings.

Women in more traditional societies are starting to gain some financial independence, prestige and self-respect through a number of Jordanian organisations that encourage small-scale craft production (see p248 for more on this).

'HONOUR' KILLINGS

Despite a reputation as one of the most liberal societies in the region, honour killings – where a woman is killed by her brothers and fathers to protect the family honour – are a problem in Jordan. On average one women every two weeks is murdered for bringing shame onto her family, by having sex out of wedlock, refusing an arranged marriage, leaving her husband, or simply being the victim of rape or sexual assault. Women in the family are often complicit in the murder.

The actions have a cultural base rather than religious one, and the often extreme pressures felt by families are rooted in the deeply conservative tribal-based morality of the countryside, where a family feels it has a duty to protect and control a woman's purity. There is no basis for honour killings in Islamic teachings.

Part of the problem is that the killings take place in a climate of near-impunity. Articles 340 and 98 of Jordan's legal code exempt a husband or close male relative for killing a wife caught in an act of adultery and offer leniency for murders committed in a 'fit of rage'. Most murderers are sentenced to as little as six months imprisonment. King Abdullah has tried to impose tougher sentences for honour killings but in 2003 parliament again rejected a bill proposing this.

Jordanian journalist Rana Husseini has been instrumental in bringing these killings to the public attention and often writes on the subject in the *Jordan Times*.

For more information see the website www.hrw.org/reports/2004/jordan0404, or look out for the documentary *Crimes of Honour* by Shelley Saywell, which was filmed in Jordan and the West Bank.

LITERATURE ON WOMEN IN JORDAN

- One of the better books around in a genre dominated by sensationalist writing is *Nine Parts of Desire: The Hidden World of Islamic Women* by Geraldine Brooks, a former *Wall St Journal* correspondent, who includes an account of her encounter with Queen Noor

- *Price of Honour: Muslim Women Lift the Veil of Silence on the Islamic World,* by Jan Goodwin, also has a chapter on Jordan, though it dates from the mid-1990s

- Two scholarly investigations into the position of women in Islam include *The Veil and the Male Elite: A Feminist Interpretation of Women's Rights in Islam* by Fatima Mernissi, with a specific focus on Morocco, and the more historical *Women and Gender in Islam* by Leila Ahmed, from a feminist viewpoint and with particular emphasis on Egypt

- *Into the Wadi* by Michele Drouart is a readable account of an Australian woman's marriage to a Jordanian man and her attempts to gain a greater understanding of Jordanian society

---

ARTS

Despite the region's rich tradition of music, literature and arts, the comparatively modern nation of Jordan could not boast much in the way of distinctive arts and literature until the last 25 years. Jordan's emergence as a centre of contemporary arts was recognised by Unesco, which named Amman as its Arab Cultural Capital for 2002.

Handicrafts

Embroidery is an important skill among Jordanian women and most learn it at a young age. Teenagers traditionally embroider the clothes they will need as married women. Embroidery is done in social groups and provides an occasion for women to socialise, often with a pot of tea and spiced up with a pinch of local gossip. Palestinian embroidery is famed throughout the region and you'll see the characteristic red embroidery on traditional dresses, known as *roza*, in shops across Jordan.

Weaving is the craft of choice among Bedouin women and looms are set up every August/September when work in the fields winds down for the summer. Goat-hair tents, saddlebags and *mafrash* rugs (woven kilim-style rugs) are still the main products.

Jewellery is the other major handicraft. A bride traditionally receives a gift of jewellery on her wedding day as her dowry and this remains her personal property throughout (and after) the marriage. The most common designs are protective silver amulets, such as the 'hand of Fatima' (Fatima was the daughter-in-law of the Prophet Mohammed), which are used as protection from evil spirits known as *djinn* (from which we get the word 'genie'). Antique items such as silver headdresses decorated with Ottoman coins and ornately decorated Bedouin daggers (straight, rather than the famously curved Yemeni and Omani versions) are getting harder to find. Many of the most beautiful antique pieces were produced by Circassian, Armenian and Yemeni silversmiths in the early 20th century. These days gold is replacing silver as the precious metal of choice – for a glittering display of gaudy modern bracelets, chokers and necklaces check out Amman's gold souq.

For good examples of Bedouin jewellery, Jordanian crafts and traditional costumes from across Jordan check out the Folklore Museum and Museum of Popular Traditions at the Roman Theatre in Amman (p81).

Several Non-Governmental Organisations (NGOs) such as the **Noor Al-Hussein Foundation** (www.noor.gov.jo/nhf.htm) and **Jordan River Foundation** (www.jordanriver.jo) have recently spurred a revival of locally produced handicrafts,

Treasures from an Ancient Land; The Art of Jordan, by the renowned Arabist Pitr Bienkowski, gives an excellent overview of Jordanian culture, particularly pottery, sculpture and jewellery.

In addition to protective talismans, most Bedouin women safeguarded themselves from the evil eye by tattooing their foreheads or chins.

as part of a programme to raise rural living standards and the status of rural women. See p248 for some examples of what's on offer.

Music & Dance

Arab music reflects a synthesis of indigenous and Western influences. Popular music differs little from that of neighbouring Arab countries, with Egyptian and Lebanese superstars such as Amr Diab and Fairouz dominating the airwaves. Many travellers are eventually caught up in the particular magic of Arabic pop, which is probably a good thing because you'll be hearing it in one form or another wherever you go.

The Bedouin have long had their own simple but mesmerising musical traditions. The sound of men chanting at a distant wedding, drifting across the desert on a still night, is haunting. Up close, the musical aspects of the festivities are clearly rooted in ancient traditions. A row of men will, arm in arm, gently sway backwards and forwards engaged in what appears to be an almost trance-like chant. Songs deal with romantic concepts of honour and chivalry and draw their inspiration from the oral histories – part poetry, part folk song and part story – that have been handed down for generations by elders assembled around a desert camp fire.

The music in the streets of Amman today, however, has little to do with these timeless desert traditions. The most common and popular style of music focuses on a star performer backed by anything from a small quartet to a full-blown orchestra. The resulting sliding strings are more Bollywood than Beethoven, while the singers' voices slip and slide around the notes rather than lingering on them. The highly produced mix is then given a pounding percussive drive that gets the heads nodding. Western-style instruments predominate, next to local instruments such as the *oud* (lute) and *rababa* (single-stringed violin). Instrumentalists generally exist to accompany a vocalist rather than perform in their own right.

The Performing Arts Center in Amman was established in 1987 under the auspices of the Queen Noor Foundation to 'develop the value and understanding of contemporary music and dance by local Jordanians'.

Popular Jordanian singers include Qamar Badwan, the Bedouin singer Omar Abdullat and the female performer Rania Kurdi, part of a younger generation of modern Jordanian pop stars.

Literature

CLASSICAL LITERATURE & POETRY

The Quran itself is considered the finest example of classical Arabic writing and gives Arabic poetry and literature a highly regarded, even divine, calling.

Al-Muallaqat, which pre-dates the Quran and the advent of Islam, is a widely celebrated collection of early Arab poetry. Prior to Islam, a poet was regarded by Arabs as having knowledge forbidden to ordinary people, supposedly acquired from the demon. *Al-Muallaqat* means 'the suspended', and refers to traditions according to which the poems were hung for public view, possibly on the walls of the Kaaba in Mecca.

As the Middle Ages drew to a close and the Arab world came to be dominated by other forces (most notably the Ottoman Turks), Arabic literature also faded, stagnating in a classicist rut dominated by a complex and burdensome poetical inheritance until well into the 19th century.

One of the few classical Jordanian poets was Mustafa Wahbi al-Tal, also known as Irar. Born in Irbid in 1899, he was renowned for his incisive and humorous poems about Arab nationalism and anticolonialism.

Heather Colyer Ross looks into popular art forms in *The Art of Bedouin Jewellery,* a useful asset for those contemplating purchasing some pieces.

Traditional Arabic music is based on a five-tone scale rather than the Western seven-tone system, which creates its exotic, unique sound.

CONTEMPORARY LITERATURE & POETRY

Modern literary genres such as the novel have only fairly recently taken off in Jordan, largely due to increased contact with Europe as well as a reawakening of Arab 'national' consciousness in the wake of the Ottoman Empire's stagnation.

Egyptians (such as the Nobel Prize winner Naguib Mahfouz), Lebanese and, to a lesser extent, Palestinians, seem to dominate Middle Eastern literature, but there are now several renowned Jordanian writers and poets. Ramadan al-Rawashdeh has published collections of short stories, including *The Night*. His novel *Al-Hamrawi* won the Naguib Mahfouz Arabic Novel Prize, and more recently he published *The Shepherds' Songs*.

Mounis al-Razzaz, who died in 2002, was regarded by many as the driving force behind contemporary Jordanian literature. His works spoke of wider turmoil in the Arab world (most notably in his satirical final work *Sweetest Night*) as well as the transition of Amman from a small village to a modern metropolis.

Rifka Doudeen, one of an emerging number of female authors, has published a collection of short stories called *Justifiable Agony*, and a novel, *The Outcast*. Another popular Jordanian writer is Yousef Dhamra.

Other writers to watch out for are: young short-story writer Basma Nsour; Hashim Gharaybeh; novelist and playwright Mefleh al-Adwan, who won the coveted Unesco prize for creative writing in France in 2001; Raga Abu Gazaleh; Jamal Naji; Abdel Raouf Shamoun; and Abdullah Mansour.

Many Palestinian Jordanian writers graphically relate first-hand experiences of the Arab-Israeli conflict and their people's struggle for a homeland. Taher al-Edwan's *The Fact of Time*, telling the story of a Palestinian family fleeing to Amman in 1948, is regarded as an important Jordanian novel.

Jordanian-based Palestinian poet Ibrahim Naserallah has had his complex novel *Prairies of Fever* translated into English. Unfortunately few of these other titles are available in languages other than Arabic. The following titles are available abroad in English.

Diana Abu-Jaber is a celebrated Jordanian-American author who draws on her family's memories of Jordanian cultural identity and father's love of Jordanian food. Her first novel, *Arabian Jazz*, is a hit-or-miss tale of Jordanian-American family in upstate New York. Her second novel, *Crescent*, is an eloquent story of Iraqi emigrant life in Los Angeles, with a haunting and luscious tale of exile, love and food, and is recommended. For details on her latest book, *The Language of Baklava*, see p56.

East of the Jordan, by Laila Halaby, also deals with the issues of migration and the clash of modernity and tradition among four young Jordanian cousins living in Jordan and the USA.

Palestinian Yasmin Zahran's *A Beggar at Damascus Gate* is a dark novel that mixes mystery and romance, told in flashbacks from a budget hotel in Petra.

Pillars of Salt by Fadia Faqir tells the tale of two Jordanian women from different branches of life who meet in an asylum in 1920s Jordan. Her previous novel, *Nisanit*, deals with the Palestinian struggle and is harder to find.

Story of a City: A Childhood in Amman by Abd al-Rahman Munif eloquently describes life in 1940s Amman from a child's perspective. Munif's other major work, *Cities of Salt*, follows the development of a village in an unspecified country in Arabia in the 1930s, when oil is discovered. Unusually the main character is the city, and its transformation under

'Many Palestinian Jordanian writers graphically relate first-hand experiences of the Arab-Israeli conflict and their people's struggle for a homeland'

CONTEMPORARY ART

One of the first Jordanian painters to gain any international recognition was the redoubtable Fahrenasa Zeid (the great-great aunt of King Abdullah II), who exhibited works in the galleries of Europe and the USA in the 1910s and 1920s. However, it really wasn't until the creation of the Jordan Artists' Association in 1978, and the opening of the Jordan National Gallery of Fine Arts two years later, that contemporary art in Jordan was taken seriously.

Many Jordanian artists are Palestinians who fled the West Bank during the two wars with Israel: Adnan Yahya specialises in gut-wrenching paintings of Palestinian persecution; Ahmad Nawash is famous for his distinctive stick figures in pastel colours; and another famous Palestinian-Jordanian painter is Ibrahim abu-Rubb.

Other popular contemporary Jordanian painters include: Suha Shoman, Yaser Duweik, Ali Jabri, Ahmad al-Safareeni, Mohanna Durra (an internationally renowned Jordanian cubist and abstract painter), Ahmed al-Khateeb and Rafiq Lahham. Lahham is a pioneer of modern Jordanian art. His work interprets traditional Islamic architectural forms in an eclectic mix of styles, with some of his most appealing work incorporating Kufic script along with abstract elements and a striking use of colour. An emerging female artist is Samar Haddadin, whose paintings and drawings capture religious harmony. Other female artists of renown include Karima ben Othman, Basma Nimry, Clara Khreis, Rula Shukairy, Riham Ghassib, Ghada Dahdaleh and Mukaram Haghandouga. The Jordanian sculptor Larissa Najjar specialises in sandstone sculptures with different colours and unusual designs. Also renowned for their sculptures are Samaa Tabaa and Margaret Tadros.

Works by these and other Jordanian artists can be seen in the numerous art galleries and cultural centres of Amman, particularly the excellent **Darat al-Funun** (p83) and **Jordan National Gallery of Fine Arts** (p84).

the influence of the West, rather than its inhabitants. The novel was translated by Peter Theroux (brother of travel writer Paul) and banned in Saudi Arabia. In 1992 Munif was awarded the Sultan al-Uways award, the Arab equivalent of a Nobel Prize for Literature.

Honour Lost: Love and Death in Modern-Day Jordan by Norma Khouri is the now discredited story of an honour killing in Jordan. The author is accused of making up the supposedly true story.

Painting

That Islam frowns on the depiction of living beings does not mean that everyone immediately towed the line. Long-standing artistic traditions in Asia Minor, Persia and further east – including Spain and other parts of Europe – could not be completely swept away, and depictions of living creatures continued. The creation of classical-style mosaics (see p154) continued from the Byzantines into the Islamic era.

The 7th-century Umayyad rulers, who comprised the first real dynasty after the demise of the Prophet Mohammed, left behind a series of so-called 'desert castles' across the eastern desert of Jordan; traces of frescoes can be found on the walls of most of these – but none so extraordinary as those in Qusayr Amra (p136).

MEDIA

By regional standards, Jordan maintains a reasonably free media, although the government does flex its muscle about reports that displease it. The bulk of newspapers (in Arabic and English) tend to push an editorial line similar to the government's position. The Jordanian government maintains more control over local radio and TV than it does over the newspapers.

The English-language *Jordan Times* has good coverage of domestic and international events. The *Star*, subtitled 'Jordan's Political, Economic and

Cultural Weekly', is similar but published only every Tuesday. It also has a double-page supplement in French called *Le Jourdain*.

Of the many local Arabic daily and weekly newspapers printed in Amman, *Ad-Dustour, Al-Ra'i* and *Al-Aswaq* are among the more popular.

Jordan TV broadcasts on three channels. Channels 1 and 3 broadcast in Arabic, and Channel 2 airs bad Australian soap operas, worse American sitcoms, locally produced news (all in English) and documentaries in French.

Uncensored international satellite stations, such as the BBC, CNN, MTV and Al-Jazeera, are found in the homes of most wealthy Jordanians, all rooms in top-end hotels and many midrange hotels.

SPORT

Perhaps unsurprisingly, the most popular sport in the country is football (soccer). The Premier League Championship plays mostly on Friday during winter (from about September to March), and features teams from Amman and most major towns. The fans take the game so seriously that the league was cancelled in 1998 after a referee was beaten up by fans, and the game abandoned. The cancellation was not caused by the horror of the injury to the referee, but by the vehement disagreement about which team should be the 'winner' of the abandoned game.

Other sports that Jordanians enjoy watching, participating in locally and competing in at overseas events, include judo, table tennis, kite flying, volleyball and horse racing (including long-distance endurance races).

Major sporting events are often held at the massive Sports City, in northern Amman, and at Al-Hasan Sports City in Irbid. In mid-1999, Jordan hosted the 9th Pan Arab Games, with over 4000 athletes from most Arab countries. Prince Feisal (King Abdullah's younger brother) is closely involved in Jordan's sporting infrastructure and in charge of the country's Olympic committee.

The vast deserts and good roads are ideal for car rallies – such as the 700km Jordan International Rally organised by the Royal Automobile Club of Jordan – and for events such as the Amman–Dead Sea Marathon (about 50km), held every April – see p144, for details.

Environment

The true servants of the most gracious are those who tread gently
on the earth

Quran, sura 25, verse 63

THE LAND

Jordan encompasses 91,860 sq km – it's slightly smaller than Portugal
or the US state of Virginia. When King Hussein renounced claims to
the West Bank (5600 sq km) in 1988, the country reverted to the same
boundaries as the former Trans-Jordan.

Jordan can easily be divided into three major regions: the Jordan Valley,
the east bank plateau and the desert. Distances are short – it's only 430km
from Ramtha, on the Syrian border in the north, to Aqaba, in the far south.
From Aqaba to the capital, Amman, it's 335km – a four-hour drive.

The 359km Jordan River
is known to Jordanians as
Nahar al-Urdun and rises
near Jebel ash-Sheikh (Mt
Hermon) in Lebanon's
Anti-Syrian Mountains.

Jordan Valley

The dominant physical feature of western Jordan is the fertile valley of
the Jordan River, the lowest river on earth. Forming part of the Great
Rift Valley of Africa, it rises just over the Lebanese border and continues
the entire length of Jordan from the Syrian border in the north, past the
salty depression of the Dead Sea, and south down to Aqaba and the Red
Sea. The 251km-long river is fed from the Sea of Galilee (Lake Tiberias),
the Yarmouk River and the valley streams of the high plateaus to the
east and west.

The Dead Sea (see p143) is the lowest point on earth, and the highly
saline soils of this central area of the Jordan Valley support little vegetation. This half of the Jordan Valley is known to Jordanians as Ghor. Wadi
Araba in particular has a distinct Rift Valley ecosystem, with flat-topped
acacia trees that owe more to Africa than the Middle East.

The Dead Sea is the
lowest point on earth at
408m below sea level.

The Rift Valley, stretching from East Africa's great lakes to southern
Syria, was created as the Arabian plate pulled (and continues to pull)
away from the African plate (the tear also created the Red Sea). Wadi
Araba, the Dead Sea and the Jordan Valley lie right on this fault line,
which is the geological reason that tourists can soak it up in a line of hot
springs from Himmah in the north to Hammamat Ma'in and Zara in the
south. The 15-million-year-old Dead Sea basin is a direct result of this
tectonic movement. Jordan continues to move north 0.5cm a year.

East Bank Plateau

The east bank plateau is cut by a series of epic gorges carved out in slow
motion by the east–west flowing wadis Zarqa, Mujib and Hasa (a *wadi*
is a valley, often dry in the summer). Most of the plateau sits at between
600m and 900m above sea level.

This area contains the main centres of population: Amman, Irbid,
Zarqa and Karak. It also contains the historical sites of major interest to
visitors: Jerash, Karak, Madaba and Petra. The plateau ends at Ras an-
Naqb, from where the Desert Highway drops down to the desert around
the Red Sea and the port of Aqaba.

The Desert

About 80% of Jordan is desert and this is concentrated in huge swathes
of the south and east of the country. The volcanic basalt rock of the

north (the bottom end of the area known in Syria as the Hauran) gives way to the south's sandstone and granite, which produces the famously photogenic jebels of southern Jordan and Wadi Rum. The area around Wadi Rum ranks as one of the most fantastic desert landscapes in the world, and boasts Jebel Umm Adaani (1832m), the highest peak in Jordan. To the north, the stony wasteland known as the *badia* slopes down for 1000km of nothingness until it hits the Persian Gulf.

Over 80% of Jordan is desert; 95% of Jordanians cram into the remaining 20% of the land.

WILDLIFE

With a range of habitat and elevation from desert to pine forest, mountains to marshland, Jordan packs a rich biodiversity into such a small area.

Animals

Jordan is not renowned for the quantity and variety of its wildlife, and visitors will count themselves very fortunate to see anything more than a few domesticated goats and the odd camel. But this hasn't always been the case. Byzantine mosaics portray everything from bears and lions to zebras, all now extinct in the region. Palaeolithic remains prove that the region was once home to elephants, rhinos and huge herds of wild asses.

The seemingly empty eastern and southern deserts are home to desert and red foxes, sand rats, mountain and desert hares, wolves, Asiatic jackals and several species of rodent, including the jerboa (with its long legs for jumping).

In Shaumari Wildlife Reserve, you'll get a chance to see a number of rare animals such as the oryx, ostrich, gazelle and Persian onager, which are being reared for reintroduction to the wild. The ostrich is the world's largest bird and also the fastest animal on two legs.

The Gulf of Aqaba is a diver's paradise, with over 230 species of coral and over 1000 types of fish.

One of Jordan's most beautiful but hard-to-spot animals is the caracal (Persian lynx), a feline with outrageous tufts of black hair on the tips of its outsized, pointy ears. It's found in Wadi Mujib and Dana nature reserves. In Petra you'll spot lots of fabulously blue lizards.

The Jordan Valley, and the forested and sparsely inhabited hills of northern Jordan, are home to ill-tempered wild boar, marbled polecats, stone martens, jungle cats and crested porcupines, as well as species of mongoose, hyrax and hedgehog.

Wild Mammals of HK Jordan by Adnan Y Dajani, and Mammals of the Holy Land by Mazin Q Qumsiyeh, are both comprehensive and colourful.

In the rocky sandstone bluffs of Wadi Mujib Nature Reserve you can spot the majestic Nubian ibex. In the few wet and swampy areas, such as the Jordan Valley and Azraq wetlands, there are small populations of otters.

For information about underwater wonders in the Gulf of Aqaba, see p227.

Birds

Jordan's location on the edge of the Great Rift Valley means it is an important migration route for birds. Over half a million birds fly through Jordan during spring, in transit between Russia, Central Europe and Africa. About 365 species of bird have been recorded.

Commonly seen around the eastern and southern desert regions are the many species of vulture, eagle and partridge. Other desert species in the east of the country include Temminck's horned lark, the desert lark, hoopoe lark, desert wheatear and trumpeter finch. For a desert region, Dana Nature Reserve boasts an extraordinary number of bird species, including the warbler, partridge, griffon vulture and falcon. In eastern Jordan, the Azraq Wetland Reserve and the Burqu area attract a large number of migratory water bird species, such as herons, egrets and marsh harriers. You'll see a range of beautiful kingfishers in the lush wadis of central

Jordan. Around the Dead Sea, the Dead Sea sparrow, the sand partridge and the quaintly named Tristam's grackle can be spotted. In the northern hills, look for warblers and Palestine sunbirds, while in the rocky terrain off the King's Highway species include Bonelli's eagle, Hume's tawny owl, the blackstart, the house bunting and the fan-tailed raven. Aqaba has a variety of migratory birds, but little has been done to protect them, and their habitats are being eroded by development and desertification.

The Royal Society for the Conservation of Nature (RSCN) can organise bird-watching tours.

The Birds of the Hashemite Kingdom of Jordan by Ian J Andrews is the definitive work about our feathered friends.

Endangered Species

About 20 species of mammal have become extinct in Jordan in the past 100 years. Some were hunted and poached (especially after WWII, when weapons flooded the region), including species of lion, cheetah, gazelle, Syrian brown bear, onager (wild ass) and Arabian leopard. The last known leopard was killed in the area now known as Dana Nature Reserve in 1986, although there have been unsubstantiated sightings since.

The reasons for the number of extinct species – and the continuing threat to animals (24 out of Jordan's remaining 77 species of mammals are globally threatened) and birds include poor land management, such as deforestation, and the pumping of water from vital areas such as the Jordan River, Dead Sea and the Azraq Wetlands; urban sprawl; weak environmental laws; unremitting use of pesticides, especially near water sources in the Jordan Valley; hunting; air and water pollution; and overgrazing.

Jordan's national bird is the Sinai rose finch (Carpodacus synoicus), which can be found in the Dana and Wadi Mujib nature reserves.

Officially endangered are the Northern Middle East wolf and South Arabian grey wolf (both are often shot to protect livestock); lynx (always popular with hunters); striped hyena; Persian squirrel; and the Persian, dorcas, goitred and mountain gazelles. A successful breeding programme by the RSCN for the Nubian ibex (hunted to near extinction in the wild) began in the Wadi Mujib Nature Reserve in 1989 with some being reintroduced into the wild.

Endangered birds include the marbled duck; imperial and lesser spotted eagles; houbara bustard; and lesser kestrel. The killifish, unique to the Azraq Wetlands, has recently been saved from extinction but its situation remains precarious (see the boxed text 'What Happened to the Wetlands?' on p131).

Animal species such as the Arabian oryx and onager have been successfully reintroduced to Jordan after becoming extinct, though their populations are still fragile (see p132).

Plants

Jordan boasts over 2500 species of wild plants and flowers (including about 20 species of orchid) but, due to desertification, urban sprawl and pollution, at least 10 have become extinct over the past 100 years.

Anyone interested in the flora of Jordan should pick up the detailed Wildflowers of Jordan and Neighbouring Countries by Dawud MH Al-Eisawi, with beautiful illustrations and photographs (all captioned in English).

Spring is the best time to see wildflowers, particularly at Wadi as-Seer, near Amman, and Wadi Yabis in the north of Jordan. The pine forests of the north give way to the cultivated slopes of the humid Jordan Valley where cedar, olive, eucalyptus and even banana trees are dominant. In a few areas, such as the Dana Nature Reserve, acacia trees thrive. Dense ribbons of green foliage and palm trees follow the deep seasonal wadis of the central plateau. In the deserts, cacti are about the only plants that grow, unless there is heavy rain.

The national flower of Jordan is the black iris, which is actually coloured a deep purple. One of the best places to see this flower is on the eastern walls of the Jordan Valley, particularly around Pella and Wadi as-Seer.

PROTECTED AREAS

Nearly 25 years ago the Jordanian government established 12 protected areas, totalling about 1200 sq km. While environmental agencies waited for funds and battled with bureaucracy, some potential reserves were abandoned because they had suffered appalling ecological damage.

Established in 1966, the RSCN (www.rscn.org.jo) is both a Non-Governmental Organisation (NGO) and Jordan's major environmental agency. It is heavily involved in saving animal, plant and bird species from extinction, and has successfully reintroduced several species into Jordan, such as the Arabian oryx and two species of ostrich.

Other activities include conducting public awareness programmes among Jordanians, especially children; sponsoring environmental clubs throughout the country; training guides; promoting ecotourism; fighting against poaching and hunting; and lobbying against mining.

The limited resources of the RSCN are used to maintain and develop six of the reserves listed below (all except the Wadi Rum protected area). These represent about 1% of Jordan's total land area – a small percentage compared with the land allocated in Saudi Arabia (9%) and the USA (11%). Jordan also has several 'national parks' but they are more like recreational parks than protected areas.

Less than 1% of Jordanian territory is covered by forest or woodland.

For a detailed look at Jordan's nature reserves and ecotourism projects see www.rscn.org.jo.

Ajlun Nature Reserve (13 sq km, 1988) Woodlands, pistachio and oak forest, spring flowers, wild boar and martens, with a programme to reintroduce the locally extinct roe deer. It has a couple of easy trails and a fine tree-house–style campground. See p116 for details.

Azraq Wetland Reserve (12 sq km, 1977) This environmentally damaged marshland is home to hundreds of species of migratory bird, who visit in spring and autumn. A wooden boardwalk leads around the reserve, via a bird hide. It's easily accessible. See p130 for details.

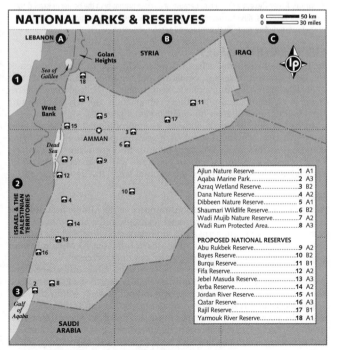

NATIONAL PARKS & RESERVES

Ajlun Nature Reserve	**1** A1
Aqaba Marine Park	**2** A3
Azraq Wetland Reserve	**3** B2
Dana Nature Reserve	**4** A2
Dibbeen Nature Reserve	**5** A1
Shaumari Wildlife Reserve	**6** B2
Wadi Mujib Nature Reserve	**7** A2
Wadi Rum Protected Area	**8** A3

PROPOSED NATIONAL RESERVES

Abu Rukbek Reserve	**9** A2
Bayes Reserve	**10** B2
Burqu Reserve	**11** B1
Fifa Reserve	**12** A2
Jebel Masuda Reserve	**13** A3
Jerba Reserve	**14** A2
Jordan River Reserve	**15** A1
Qatar Reserve	**16** A3
Rajil Reserve	**17** B1
Yarmouk River Reserve	**18** A1

Dana Nature Reserve (320 sq km, 1989) This spectacular Unesco Biosphere Reserve is home to a diverse Rift Valley ecosystem, from rugged mountains to desert, including about 600 species of plants, about 200 species of bird and over 40 species of mammal. There are walking trails, tented and hotel accommodation and several archaeological sites. See p171 for details.

Dibbeen Nature Reserve (8 sq km, 2005) One of the last Aleppo Pine forests left in Jordan, it's home to endangered species such as the Persian squirrel. See p116 for more details.

Shaumari Wildlife Reserve (22 sq km, 1975) This small reserve is more like a zoo and is specifically for reintroduced Arabian oryxes; blue-necked and red-necked ostriches; subgutu rosa and dorcas gazelles; and onagers. Nearly 250 bird species have also been identified. There is tented accommodation, or you'll find hotels in nearby Azraq. See p131 for details.

Jordan's Ministry of Environment (www .environment.gov.jo) offers environmental overviews, a list of environmental organisations and regional reports.

Wadi Mujib Nature Reserve (212 sq km, 1988) This reserve near the Dead Sea is used for the captive breeding of Nubian ibexes and has an impressive ecotourism programme, with canyon walks, waterfall rappelling and a Dead Sea camp site. See p146 for details.

Wadi Rum Protected Area (540 sq km, 1998) This stunning and popular area was managed by the RSCN but is now under the control of the Aqaba government. Camping, camel treks and the 4WD trail are popular. See p205 for details.

In addition, the RSCN and the Jordanian government hope to create five new protected areas:

Burqu Reserve (400 sq km) After the debacle in the Azraq wetlands (see the boxed text, p131), the desert lake at Burqu needs urgent protection.

Fifa Reserve (27 sq km) This area alongside the Dead Sea has rare subtropical vegetation, and is home to migratory water birds.

Jordan River Reserve (5 sq km) Based around Wadi Kharrar at the Bethany-Beyond-the-Jordan religious site (p141), this is the only section of the Jordan River that has not been ecologically damaged in some way, with environments of marsh wetland, reed beds and tamarix woodland.

Yarmouk River Reserve (30 sq km) Because of its close proximity to the border of Israel & the Palestinian Territories, this area has remained undeveloped and is home to many natural features of the forest including water birds, endangered gazelles and otters.

ENVIRONMENTAL ISSUES

In 1995, the Jordanian Parliament passed the Law of the Protection of the Environment to set up regulators and funding streams as part of a generally impressive (but recent) commitment by the Jordanian government to environmental protection. This includes the refusal of mining licences in protected areas on environmental grounds.

Jordan is not, however, without its environmental problems, most notably a lack of water, caused by a growing population, rising living standards in the cities, heavy exploitation for agriculture and wastage. Other important issues include air pollution, waste management, erosion (exacerbated by steeply graded agricultural land) and desertification.

Water

For more information on environmental issues in Jordan contact Friends of the Earth (☎ 06 5866602; foeme@go .com.jo; Amman) or check out www.foeme.org.

Water, not oil, is the most precious resource in the Middle East. It is fast becoming a major factor in regional relations, and some point to long-term strategic water concerns as an important motive behind the 1967 Six Day War and Israel's invasion of southern Lebanon. As Middle Eastern populations boom, tensions over water can only increase.

Jordan has one of the lowest water-per-capita ratios in the world and currently uses about 60% more water than is replenished from natural sources. By some estimates, Jordan will run out of water within 20 years.

One major problem is simply mismanagement: Jordan's farmers (around 5% of the population) consume as much as 75% of the water (often inefficiently). According to one report, half the water consumed in Amman is lost in leakage. Rationing has been widespread in recent years.

Jordan's only sources of water are the Jordan River and Yarmouk River and several subterranean aquifers that are already in many cases over-exploited (see p131). Since the 1960s Israel & the Palestinian Territories has drawn around one-third of its water from the Jordan River, which has now been reduced to a trickle, half of which is 50% raw sewage and effluent from fish farms.

Since the 1994 peace treaty between Jordan and Israel & the Palestinian Territories, under which Jordan was permitted to extract 50 million cu metres per year from Lake Tiberias, disputes have arisen over whether Jordan is getting its fair share.

In 2000 and 2001, the Jordanian government told farmers and irrigators in the Jordan Valley not to plant the summer crops because the necessary water would have strained resources and paid compensation for lost income.

Both Jordan and Israel & the Palestinian Territories have recently allocated millions of dollars to water projects. The joint Syrian-Jordanian Wahdah Dam on the Yarmouk River was recently completed, giving power to Syria and water to Jordan (mainly for Amman and Irbid).

Jordan is also building a 325km pipeline from Disheh to Amman at a cost of US$600 million to tap non-renewable fossil water from Diseh near Wadi Rum. Over 90% of Jordan's river water is already being diverted.

One plan on the drawing board is to construct a series of desalination plants, hydroelectric power stations and canals that would link the Red Sea with the Dead Sea (see p143), in an attempt to raise the level of the Dead Sea and create a supply of fresh water.

To make matters worse, Jordan has endured consecutive droughts in recent years: the one in 1998–99 was the worst in 50 years, and cost an estimated US$200 million in lost and damaged agriculture and livestock.

In the last 50 years, water levels in the Dead Sea have fallen by 18m and 30% of the area of the sea has vanished. For more see p143.

The 2005 Environmental Sustainability Index ranked Jordan 84th out of 146 countries; higher than any Arab country except Tunisia.

ECOTOURISM AND THE RSCN

In recent years the RSCN has initiated a major ecotourism drive in several reserves, notably Dana and Wadi Mujib, and to a lesser extent Ajlun and Shaumari. Programmes range from hiking trails to local income-generation projects, aimed at creating employment and economic opportunities for local people. The RSCN has also created some of the country's most interesting places to stay, from top-end lodges like Feinan Lodge (p173) and Dana Guest House (p173) to camp sites at Rummana (Dana; p173) and on the shores of the Dead Sea (Wadi Mujib; p147).

Dana in particular has emerged as a model for ecotourism projects in the kingdom. The production of local crafts and organic foods, the establishment of village hotels (which fund a social cooperative) and new opportunities for employment as guides or craftsmen have breathed new life into the partially abandoned village, reversing the economic emigration from the village. See p171 for more details on the project.

These days hiking in Dana and canyoning in Wadi Mujib rank among the highlights of a visit to Jordan. Prices are not cheap but at least you know that the money you spend is going to aid, not hinder, the protection of nature in the land you pass through.

Hiking groups and RSCN camp sites are strictly limited to avoid overuse (only 25 people per day are allowed on some trails) so it's well worth booking guides and accommodation in advance through the tourism department of **Wild Jordan** (☎ 06 4616523; tourism@rscn.org.jo), which acts as the business arm of the RSCN (see p70). The centre in Amman is also worth a visit for its excellent nature shop (p99).

RSCN members get a 20% discount on RSCN accommodation and 50% discount on reserve entry fees. Membership costs JD25 per person. You can also 'adopt' an animal from an endangered species, for JD40 to JD60 per year.

RESPONSIBLE TOURISM

The environmental problems of Jordan may seem insurmountable, but there is a lot we can all do to minimise our impact:

■ Leave it as you found it: for as long as outsiders have been searching for, and stumbling over, the ancient monuments of Jordan, they have also been chipping bits off, hauling stuff home or leaving their contributions engraved upon them. When visiting historical and archaeological sites, please consider how important it is to leave things alone.

■ Don't litter: plastic bags are a huge problem in Jordan, accumulating in bushes, fences and valleys all over the country. Try to keep your use of plastic bags and bottles to a minimum and dispose of litter properly.

■ Do as requested: please follow environmental regulations, eg don't touch the coral off the coast of Aqaba. Camping and camp fires are not allowed in Jordan's reserves outside designated RSCN camp sites and barbecue grills.

Effects of Tourism

Only recently have the Jordanian government and foreign NGOs fully realised the impact on the environment of mass tourism.

Tourism has also caused a rapid increase in pollution from cars and industries and demand for precious water, as well as damage to unique sites such as Jerash and Petra (see p187). Other problems are vandalism at archaeological sites, damage to artwork from flash photography, and rubbish left at hot springs and baths.

The RSCN has been at the forefront of attempts to foster ecotourism projects in recent years (see p53). Environmentally sustainable tourism is slowly taking hold as a major means of funding environmental programmes.

Desertification

Like most countries in the region, Jordan has a serious problem with desertification (the seemingly unstoppable spread of the desert to previously fertile, inhabited and environmentally sensitive areas). According to the RSCN, millions of hectares of fertile land have become infertile and uninhabitable desert. This means there are now fewer pastures for livestock and crops, and there's reduced land for native animals and plants. Jordan is home to about three million sheep and goats, but there is simply no longer enough pasture to feed them.

Desertification is usually caused by human factors such as overgrazing, deforestation and overuse of off-road vehicles, as well as wind erosion and drought.

Jordan has just 140 cu metres of renewable water per capita per year, compared to the UK's 1500, Israel's 340 and the Palestine Authority's 70. Jordan's figure is expected to fall to 90 cu metres by 2025. Anything under 500 cu metres is considered to be a scarcity of water.

Food & Drink

Eating in Jordan can be a wonderful experience, especially if you can pay a little more than rock-bottom prices. The Lebanese-influenced salads and dips, collectively known as mezze, are wonderful and the bread is as good as you'll get in the Middle East – great news for vegetarians. For carnivores, the chicken and grilled meat are similarly good. And, as you'd expect in this part of the world, coffee and tea are an important way of life that quickly open up inroads into local culture.

Jordanian food is made up of Lebanese, Syrian and Egyptian influences blended with traditional local Bedouin cuisine. Historical influences run deep, from the spices of the Arabian trade routes to the Turkish influence of Ottoman rule, while native dates and camel milk have for centuries been the staple diet of the nomadic Bedouin of Arabia. These days in Amman you can get everything from tacos to sushi.

Recipes and Remembrances from an Eastern Mediterranean Kitchen: A Culinary Journey through Syria, Lebanon, and Jordan by Sonia Uvezian is a high-quality introduction to the food of the Levant.

STAPLES & SPECIALITIES

Menus in the better restaurants are generally divided into cold mezze, hot mezze, grills and (sometimes) desserts.

Mezze

The most common way for a group to eat in any restaurant is to order mezze – a variety of small starters followed by several mains to be shared by all present.

Hummus is cooked chickpeas ground into a paste and mixed with tahini (a sesame-seed paste), garlic and lemon. Available in virtually every restaurant, it's invariably excellent and generally eaten as a starter with bread. It goes very nicely with any of the meat dishes.

Another local staple, often eaten for breakfast, is fuul, a cheap and tasty dish of squashed fava beans with chillis, onions and olive oil.

Baba ghanooj (literally 'father's favourite'), made from mashed egg-plant and tahini, is another dip eaten with bread. It often has a smoky taste. Similar but blander is *muttabal*.

Tabbouleh is a parsley, cracked (bulgar) wheat and tomato-based salad, with a sprinkling of sesame seeds, lemon and garlic. It goes perfectly with hummus in bread. Fattoosh is pretty much tabbouleh with sumach, tomatoes and little shreds of deep-fried bread in it.

The word 'mezze' is derived from the Arabic *t'mazza*, meaning 'to savour in little bites'.

Several types of cheese are available as starters, including *kashkawan* (or *kishkeh*) a soft white cheese, *haloumi* and Lebanese-style *shinklish*, a tangy seasoned cheese fried in olive oil.

Bread

Arabic unleavened bread, *khobz*, is eaten with absolutely everything and is sometimes called *a'aish* (life) – its common name in Egypt. Tastier than plain old *khobz* is *ka'ik*, round sesame rings of bread, often sold with a boiled egg from stalls throughout Jordan. A favourite breakfast staple is bread liberally sprinkled with zaatar (thyme).

The big five dishes that you'll find yourself eating on a fairly monotonous daily (or twice daily!) basis are shwarma, hummus, kebabs, felafel and roast chicken.

MAIN DISHES

Most main dishes comprise some combination of chicken, meat kebabs, or meat and vegetable stews.

Chicken *(farooj)* is often roasted on spits in large grills out the front of the restaurant. The usual serving is half a chicken *(nuss farooj)*, which

---

TRAVEL YOUR TASTEBUDS

The Bedouin *zerb* oven couldn't be simpler. Simply dig a hole in the sand and burn enough firewood to make glowing coals. Seal the oven, cover it with sand and cook for an hour or two. These can be found at all good Bedouin camps in Wadi Rum. It's best done with a whole goat or sheep, which brings us to...

We Dare You!

Traditionally the prized part of that Bedouin favourite, whole roast lamb, are the succulent eyeballs, which are presented to honoured guests – which, yes, as a foreigner probably means you!

If somehow you miss out on the dubious honour of chewing on an eyeball, you can always invite some serious bacterial infection by ordering from the *nayye* (raw) meat section of one of Amman's numerous Lebanese restaurants. Top that off with an order of steaming ram's testicles, or even fried brains, both favourite mezzes, and you have an unbeatable night (and perhaps next morning) to remember.

---

comes with bread, a side dish of raw onion, chillies and sometimes olives. Eaten with the optional extras of salad and hummus, it's a great meal.

Kebabs are another favourite, and available everywhere. These are spicy minced-lamb pieces pressed onto skewers and grilled over charcoal. *Shish tawooq* is loosely the chicken version of the same thing.

Another popular chicken dish is *musakhan*, baked chicken served with onions, olive oil and pine nuts on *khobz*. *Kofta* are delicious meatballs of minced lamb, sometimes served in a stew with tomatoes and spices.

Stews are usually meat or vegetable, or both, and make a pleasant change from chicken and kebabs. *Fasoolyeh* is bean stew; *biseela* is made of peas; *batatas* is mostly potato; and *mulukiyyeh* is a spinach stew with chicken or meat pieces. They are usually served with rice *(ruz)* or, more rarely, macaroni *(makarone)*.

A Bedouin speciality is *mensaf*. Traditionally served on special occasions, it consists of a whole lamb on a bed of rice and pine nuts, topped with the gaping head of the animal. The fat from the cooking is poured into the rice. You can buy a serving of mensaf in better restaurants in the larger cities. It's not cheap, but should be tried at least once. A tangy sauce of cooked yogurt mixed with fat is served with it.

One Bedouin dish you will see in places like Wadi Musa is *maqlub-beh*, sometimes called 'upside down', steamed rice pressed into a small bowl, turned upside down and topped with grilled slices of eggplant or meat, grilled tomato, cauliflower and pine nuts. *Fareekeh* is a similar dish with cracked wheat.

Fish *(samak)* is not widely available, and it's always relatively expensive. *Sayadieh* is an Aqaba specialty – fish with lemon juice on a bed of paella-style rice, with a tomato, onion and green pepper sauce.

Desserts

Jordanians have an incorrigibly sweet tooth, and their desserts are confected accordingly; there are dozens of pastry shops in every town, selling nothing else. Many of the pastry shops are sit-down places and are often good for solo women travellers to relax at. For some reason coffee is rarely served at an Arabic pastry shop, and neither are pastries served in traditional coffeehouses.

The basic formula for Arab sweets involves drenching some kind of filo pastry in honey, syrup and/or rose water (or, hell, all three!) and then cutting the entire mass into pieces with an implement that resembles a

Pork products are taboo in Islam but you can find pork dishes in Chinese restaurants, at a higher price than other meats.

Literary foodies will enjoy *The Language of Baklava* by Diana Abu Jabr (see p45) which combines autobiographical novel with home-style Jordanian recipe book, offering authentic recipes for *muhammara* (a walnut and pepper dip), kunafa and shish kebab, among others.

plastering trowel. Imagine Edward Scissorhands let loose on a giant-sized baklava and you get the picture. The sweetest highlight of travel in Jordan is kunafa, a highly addictive dessert of shredded dough on top of cream cheese, smothered in syrup.

Customers generally order desserts by the piece or by weight (250g is generally the smallest portion). The best thing is to simply walk into a pastry shop and try out a variety; you'll quickly find a favourite.

DRINKS
Alcoholic Drinks

Alcohol is widely available in bars and from the occasional liquor store in major towns (especially those with a large Christian minority).

For the best kunafa join the queues of sugar addicts at the takeaway branch of Habibah, hidden down an alley in downtown Amman (p95).

Amstel beer is brewed in Jordan under licence from its Dutch parent company and it's definitely the most widely available (and often the only available) beer. In Amman and Aqaba, beer imported from all over the world – everything from Guinness to Fosters – is available but at prices higher than you'd pay in Ireland or Australia. A bottle of 650ml Amstel beer costs about JD1.400 from a liquor store, at least JD1.750 in a dingy bar in Amman and up to JD3.500 in a trendy nightclub. You may also come across the local Jordanian beer Philadelphia, which is OK if you're not fussy. To get to your destination quickly there's always Petra beer with 8% alcohol content.

Arak is the local aniseed firewater, similar to Greek ouzo or Turkish raki. It's usually mixed with water and ice and should be treated with caution. Various other types of hard liquor are available in liquor stores and bars, including all sorts of 'scotch whisky' brewed locally or imported.

Some local wine is produced in Jordan, including the St George and Machereus labels. Other brands such as Latroun, St Catherine and Cremisan are imported from the West Bank. Wine costs from around JD3 per glass in a restaurant.

Non-Alcoholic Drinks

Most restaurants offer a jug of free cold (tap) water, but to be safe you are better off buying bottled mineral water; see p276). Ghadeer is one of the better brands (350 fils for a 2L bottle).

Coffee originated in Ethiopia before spreading to southern Arabia, the Middle East and, several centuries later, Europe. Its English name is thought to be derived from the Ethiopian village of Kaffa, through the Arabic name *qahwa* and then the Turkish word *kahveh*.

All over Jordan, juice stalls sell freshly squeezed fruit juices (*aseer*); these stalls are instantly recognisable by the string bags of fruit hanging out the front. Popular juices include lemon, orange, banana, pomegranate and rockmelon, and you're welcome to request any kind of combination you'd like.

Some stalls put milk in their drinks or, worse, water, which you might want to stay away from if you have a dodgy stomach.

Tea & Coffee

From the chic cafés of western Amman to the Bedouin tents of Wadi Rum, tea and coffee are the major social lubricants in Jordan. Both are served strong and sweet.

Tea (*shai*) is probably the more popular drink, taken without milk and in various degrees of sweetness: with sugar (*sukkar ziyada*), a little sugar (*sukkar qaleel*), or no sugar (*bidoon sukkar*). In some cafés the sugar will be served on the side in little egg cups. Both tea and coffee can be quite bitter without any sugar.

'Coffee should be black as hell, strong as death and sweet as love' – Turkish proverb.

In most cafés you can ask for refreshing mint tea (*shai ma n'aana*). Zaatar (thyme) and *marrameeya* (sage) herbal teas are especially delicious in Dana.

TROUBLE BREWING – COMMUNICATING WITH COFFEE

In traditional Bedouin circles the shared drinking of coffee symbolises trust and good intent between strangers. A visitor who refuses to drink is likely to have come bearing a grudge. If the host pours a cup of coffee and then deliberately spills it in front of the guest, this is an insult or indicates that the host feels wronged by that person. Likewise if a host arranges a toast and one of those assembled refuses to drink or pours away their drink before the toast, it's clear that trouble is brewing between that person and the guest being toasted.

Coffee (qahwa) is generally taken Turkish-style in strong, small, sweet shots. Remember to let the grains settle and avoid the last gritty mouthful. You can specify a small espresso-sized cup (finjan) or large cup (kassa kabira). In traditional Bedouin areas coffee is served in small porcelain bowls. You may get to see the beans roasted and then ground in a decorated pestle and mortar called a mihbash. Arabic-style coffee is generally flavoured with cardamom.

Once again you need to make clear the degree of sweetness: ask for sweet (haaloua), a little sugar (sukkar khalil), or without sugar (saada). If you just ask for coffee, or order 'American coffee', you may end up with instant coffee. Only the top-end places offer brewed or filtered coffee à la Starbucks.

Sahlab is a traditional winter drink, served hot with milk, nuts and cinnamon – delicious, if made properly. Look for it at hot drink vendors (recognisable by their silver samovars), who also offer takeaway shots of coffee or Lipton tea in white plastic cups.

> A host will always refill his guest's coffee cup. A good guest will accept a minimum of three cups but when you've had enough, gently tilt the cup from side to side (in Arabic – 'dancing' the cup). For other drinks put your hand over the cup and say *da'iman* (may it ever be thus).

CELEBRATIONS

During the month of Ramadan (see p243 for a list of upcoming dates) Muslims fast during daylight hours. The daily evening meal during Ramadan, called *iftar* (breaking the fast), is always something of a celebration. Go to the bigger restaurants and wait with fasting crowds for sundown, the moment when food is served – it's quite a lively experience.

Out of respect for those fasting during Ramadan, always eat inside or as discreetly as possible. Restaurants catering to tourists will usually still be open, though it can be hard to find a restaurant in out-of-the-way places that opens before sunset. Most Jordanians stock up on an especially large pre-dawn breakfast called *suhur*.

If you're going to be travelling around during the day, buy some food for lunch (grocery shops normally stay open during the day), and eat it somewhere discreet.

> It's generally impolite to smoke, drink or eat in public during Ramadan.

The Ramadan fast is broken by the three-day festival of Eid al-Fitr, when everyone gets dressed up in new clothes, visits friends and family, and eats a big family dinner.

WHERE TO EAT & DRINK

Some restaurants close on Friday, usually in the evening, but most places frequented by foreigners open every day. A menu in English is usually offered only by restaurants in upmarket hotels, those set up for the tourist trade and outlets of Western fast-food chains. Elsewhere, just ask what's available or point to what other patrons are enjoying. Usually someone in the restaurant will know a bit of English, and 'kebabs', 'chicken', 'salad' and 'soup' are universally understood by restaurant staff.

Before you start ordering, especially at a restaurant frequented by foreigners and where there's no menu in English, ask for the price of each dish.

Coffeehouses

Jordan's coffeehouses are great places to watch the world go by, write a letter, meet the locals and, maybe, play a hand of cards, accompanied by the incessant clattering clacking of slammed domino and backgammon pieces and the gurgling of a dozen fruity *nargileh* (water pipes). Traditional coffeehouses are generally men-only but foreign women, with a bit of courage and very modest attire, are usually welcome at most coffeehouses in Jordan (see p253).

Few traditional coffeehouses serve food. In eastern Amman, a few trendy Western-style cafés serve meals, as well as alcohol and sometimes host live music or exhibitions in the Western café tradition.

Grumpy Gourmet (www .grumpygourmet.com) is a light-hearted restaurant guide, mainly for expatriates and well-off visitors living in Amman.

Quick Eats

The two most popular local versions of 'fast food' are the *shwarma* and felafel, both well known to anyone who has travelled elsewhere in the region.

Shwarma is like Greek gyros or Turkish doner kebab ie slices of lamb or chicken from a huge revolving spit, mixed with onions and tomato in bread. The vendor will slice off the meat (usually with a great flourish and much knife sharpening and waving), dip a piece of flat bread in the fat that has dripped off the meat, hold it against the gas flame so it flares, then fill it with meat and fillings.

Felafel are deep-fried balls of chickpea paste with spices, served in a piece of rolled up *khobz* (bread) with varying combinations of pickled vegetables, tomato, salad and yogurt. Super-sized *kabir* felafel sometimes have onion inside.

Some restaurants have a 'family' section, set aside for families and unaccompanied (local and foreign) women, where female travellers can eat in relative peace. The entrance may not be entirely obvious but you'll probably be ushered in there anyway.

VEGETARIANS & VEGANS

Virtually no restaurants in Jordan specialise in vegetarian food, and there are few specific 'vegetarian' dishes. Vegetarians report varying degrees of difficulty in getting by in Jordan. Every restaurant offers a number of different mezze or salads at reasonable prices, and a couple of salads with bread often makes a decent meal. Vegetable soups are common, although they may well be infiltrated by small pieces of meat. Starters such as hummus, and traditional dishes like fuul, are meatless and will become staple foods for vegetarians.

EATING WITH KIDS

You shouldn't have any major problems finding something the kids can eat. Chicken and chips, bread, ice cream and the major soft drinks are all common, while grocery stores stock a wide range of imported Western foods.

JORDAN'S CULINARY TOP FIVE

- *Fatteh* at **Fuheis** (p106)
- Seafood and *sayadiyeh* – try **Floka Restaurant** in Aqaba (p224)
- Savour the best mezze at Amman's excellent Lebanese restaurants, such as **Fakhr el-Din** (p93, **Abu Ahmad Orient Restaurant** (p93, or **Tannoureen Restaurant** (p94)
- Desert cuisine – tear into a *mensaf* or *zerb* barbecue at a **Bedouin camp** in Wadi Rum (p212)
- For atmospheric digs – try the restored Ottoman architecture of **Kan Zeman** outside Amman (p102), or **Haret Jdoudna** in Madaba (p157)

DOS & DON'TS

If you are invited to share a meal, whether at home or in a restaurant, grab the opportunity but bear the following pointers in mind:

- If offered, always wash your hands before a meal, even if you washed them recently
- If eating from a communal plate, and there are no eating implements, always use your right hand
- Avoid licking your fingers during a meal
- Don't put food back on the plate
- Your host will often lay the best cuts in front of you, which it is polite to accept. The best food is often saved until last so remember to pace yourself
- Reaching across the food is considered impolite
- It's good manners to leave a little food on your plate at the end of the meal
- Always commend your host for a wonderful meal and express regret when you have to leave

HABITS & CUSTOMS

The most common way for a group to eat in any restaurant is to order mezze – a variety of small starters followed by several mains to be shared by all present. Otherwise, simply order one or two starters, bread (which is normally provided free anyway), main course (usually meat) and salad. Some smaller hole-in-the-wall places will specialise in one or two things only, while some just offer chicken or a couple of stews.

The New Book of Middle Eastern Food by Claudia Roden is a classic text that contains 800 mouth-watering recipes.

COOKING COURSES

You can learn how to cook a range of Jordanian mezze, main courses and desserts at a nightly cookery course held by local Bedouin women at **Petra Kitchen** (☎ /fax 2155900; www.petrakitchen.com, petrakitchen@petramoon.com) in Wadi Musa, near Petra. The price of JD30 per person isn't cheap, but it's a relaxed family atmosphere and the price includes dinner, as soon as you've finished cooking it. See p195 for details.

EAT YOUR WORDS
Useful Phrases

I'm a vegetarian.
   ana nabaatee (m)/*ana nabateeyya* (f)
What is this?
   ma hadha?/shu hadha?
breakfast
   al-futur
restaurant
   al-matam
daily special
   wajbet al-yum

Menu Decoder

Note that, because of the imprecise nature of transliterating Arabic into English, spellings will vary; for example what we give as *kibbeh* may appear variously as *kubbeh, kibba, kibby,* or even *gibeh*.

MEZZE

baba ghanouj	dip of mashed eggplant and tahini
balilah	snack of boiled salty legumes

basterma	pastrami, popular from Armenia to Lebanon
buraik	meat or cheese pie
fatayer	triangles of pastry filled with white cheese or spinach; also known as burak
fatteh	garlicky yogurt and hummus, sometimes with chicken
fattoosh	salad with sumach (a red spice mix), tomatoes and shreds of crouton-like deep-fried bread
fuul	dip of squashed fava beans with chillis, onions and olive oil
fuul masrih	fuul with tahini
fuul medames	fuul with olive oil
gallai	sautéed tomato, garlic, onion and peppers topped with cheese and pine nuts on Arabic bread
kibbeh	Lebanese-style kofta made with minced lamb, bulgar/cracked wheat and onion; served raw or deep fried
labneh	cream-cheese dip
makdous	pickled eggplant, walnut and olive-oil dip
manaqeesh	Arabic bread with herbs
manoucha/manaqish	baked breads or pies with thyme (zaatar) and cheese
mosabaha	hummus with whole chickpeas in it
mouhamara	walnut, olive-oil and cumin dip
mutaffi bethanjan	fried eggplant and sesame
muttabal	eggplant dip similar to baba ghanouj but creamier
odsieh	hummus inside fuhl
sambousek	meat and pine-nut pastry
shinklish	tangy and salty dried white cheese, sometimes grilled, sometimes in a salad
tabbouleh	salad of cracked (bulgar) wheat, parsley and tomato
treedah	egg, yogurt and meat
yalenjeh	Turkish-style stuffed vine leaves

MAIN DISHES

fareekeh	similar to maqlubbeh but with cracked wheat
fasoolyeh	bean stew
gallayah	traditional Bedouin meal of chicken with tomatoes, other vegetables, garlic and Arabic spices
kofta	meatballs, often in a stew
maqlubbeh	steamed rice topped with grilled slices of eggplant or meat, grilled tomato, cauliflower and pine nuts
musakhan	baked chicken served on bread with onions, olive oil and pine nuts
sajieh	baked dish of chicken, onion and bread
sawani	meat or vegetables cooked on trays in a wood-burning oven
shish tawouq	grilled boneless chicken served with bread and onions
shwarma	chicken or lamb sliced off a spit and stuffed in a pocket of pita-type bread with chopped tomatoes and garnish

DESSERT

ftir jibneh	large pastries
haliwat al-jibneh	a soft doughy pastry filled with cream cheese and topped with syrup and ice cream
halva	soft sesame paste, like nougat
kunafa	shredded dough on top of cream cheese smothered in syrup
ma'amoul	biscuits stuffed with dates and pistachio nuts and dipped in rose water
muhalabiyya	rice pudding, made with rose water
mushabbak	a lacework-shaped pastry drenched in syrup
m'shekel	a form of baklava
wharbat	little triangular pastries with custard inside, a bit like a Danish pastry

Food Glossary
STAPLES

beid	egg
ejja	omelette
jibna	cheese
khobz	bread
laban	yogurt
ruz	rice
shurba	soup
sukkar	sugar

MEAT & FISH

farooj	chicken
hamour	a grouper-like fish from the Red Sea
kibda	liver
samak	fish

VEGETABLES

adas	lentils
banadura	tomato
batata	potato
khadrawat	vegetables
khiyar	cucumber
khudar	vegetables

FRUIT

battikh	watermelon
burtuqal	orange
inab	grape
mish-mish	apricot
moz	banana
rumman	pomegranate
tamr	date
tin	fig
tufah	apple

OTHER DISHES & CONDIMENTS

fil fil	chillis
sumach	red-spice mix
tahini	sesame-seed paste
tum	garlic
torshi	bright pink pickled vegetables
zaatar	thyme
zayt	olive oil
zaytun	olives

DRINKS

asir	juice
maya at-ta'abiyya	mineral water
qahwa	coffee
sefeeha	a lemon and mint drink
shai	tea

Amman عمان

Amman is a modern Arab city rather than one of the great cultural centres of the Middle East; it has never rivalled Damascus or Cairo as a grand Islamic city of antiquity. For those arriving from Syria or Egypt it can, depending on your perspective, feel either refreshingly or disappointingly modern and Westernised.

Residents talk openly of two Ammans. Conservative and Islamic in its sympathies, Eastern Amman (which includes downtown) is home to the urbanised poor, with vast suburban Palestinian refugee camps on its fringe. Western Amman is a world apart, with leafy residential districts, trendy cafés and bars, and impressive art galleries. It's impossible to gain a full understanding of Amman, or even Jordan, without visiting both areas.

The city's character has been indelibly altered by the arrival of hundreds of thousands of Palestinian refugees and, more recently, 100,000 Iraqi refugees, most of whom are highly educated and have pushed the boundaries of a cultural life that had been kept under close rein by Islamic conservatives. Along with a young generation of Jordanians, these immigrants have helped to make Amman a tolerant and outward-looking city.

Don't come to the nation's captial with expectations of medieval souqs and bazaars, or wonderful mosques of Islam's grand architectural heritage. Do come to Amman to catch a glimpse of a modern Arab city, embracing an international and culturally diverse vision of the future. Whether you're in the urbane western suburbs, or the earthy, kinetic chaos of downtown, the welcome you'll receive is sure to be warm.

HIGHLIGHTS

- Take in the ruins of ancient Amman at the **Citadel** (p71), visit the impressive National Archaeological Museum there, and admire the views of the modern city

- Sit and watch Jordanians come and go from high in the **Roman Theatre** (p81), Amman's most spectacular ancient monument

- Take in an art exhibition at the tranquil **Darat al-Funun** (p83) complex, then relax in its simple café, set amidst Byzantine ruins

- Join the beautiful people for a hubbly bubbly in the cool **wine bars** and **cafés** (p95 and p96) of Shmeisani and Abdoun

- Enjoy a fine Lebanese meal at **Fakhr el-Din** (p93) or **Abu Ahmad Orient Restaurant** (p93)

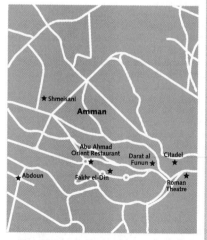

AMMAN

HISTORY

Excavations in and around Amman have turned up finds from as early as 3500 BC, when the earliest inhabitants settled on Jebel al-Qala'a (the site of the Citadel). There has been a town on this site since at least the Bronze Age; objects dated to this time show that the town was involved in trade with Greece, Syria, Cyprus and Mesopotamia.

Biblical references indicate that by 1200 BC, Rabbath Ammon (the Great City of the Ammonites mentioned in the Old Testament) was the capital of the Ammonites. King David sent the Israelite armies to besiege Rabbath, after being insulted by the Ammonite king Nahash. After taking the town, David burnt many inhabitants alive in a brick kiln. Rabbath continued to flourish and supplied David with weapons for his ongoing wars. His successor Solomon erected a shrine in Jerusalem to the Ammonite god Molech. From here on, the only biblical references to Rabbath are prophecies of its destruction at the hands of the Babylonians.

The history of Amman between then (c 585 BC) and the time of the Ptolemies of Egypt is unclear. Ptolemy Philadelphus (283–246 BC) rebuilt the city during his reign, and it was named Philadelphia after him. The Ptolemy dynasty was succeeded by the Seleucids and, briefly, by the Nabataeans, before Amman was taken by Herod around 30 BC, and fell under the sway of Rome. The city, which even before Herod's arrival had felt Rome's influence as a member of the Decapolis (see p109), was totally replanned in typically grand Roman style, with a theatre, forum and Temple to Hercules. It soon became an important centre along the trade routes between the Red Sea and Syria.

Philadelphia was the seat of Christian bishops in the early Byzantine period, but the city declined and fell to the Sassanians (from Persia) in about AD 614. At the time of the Muslim invasion in about AD 636, the town – by then named Amman – was again thriving as a staging post on the caravan trade route. From about the 10th century, however, the city declined, and was soon reduced to a place of exile.

Amman was little more than a backwater village of less than 2000 residents when a colony of Circassians resettled there in 1878. It boomed temporarily in the early 20th century when it became a stopover on the new Hejaz Railway between Damascus and Medina (Saudi Arabia). In 1921 it became the centre of Trans-Jordan when Emir Abdullah made it his headquarters. In 1948 many Palestinians settled in and around Amman and, two years later, it was officially declared the capital of the Hashemite kingdom.

ORIENTATION

Like Rome, Amman was born on seven major jebels (hills), but today it spreads across over 20. As such, it's not really a city to explore on foot, apart from the downtown area – known by locals as *il-balad*. A straight, flat road is almost unheard of in Amman.

The only way to make any sense of Amman in a short time is to pick out the major landmarks on the jebels. The main hill is Jebel Amman, home to several embassies, a few hotels and trendy restaurants. The traffic roundabouts in this central area (some now replaced with tunnels and major intersections) are numbered west of downtown from 1st Circle to 8th Circle. If you're travelling in a taxi, street names will mean little so ask for the nearest 'circle' and walk from there, or give the driver a nearby landmark (like an embassy or hotel).

Jebel al-Hussein, northwest of downtown, has the Housing Bank Centre; its mossy, terraced façade sticks out a mile. This also marks the start of the upmarket Shmeisani area, which stretches out to the north as far as the leafy Sports City. It has plenty of restaurants, shops, top-end hotels and a few nightclubs. Another trendy and affluent area is Abdoun, a few hills south of Shmeisani and home to supercool cafés and several embassies.

Closer to downtown is the grittier Abdali area, home to the Abdali bus station and topped by the distinctive blue dome of the King Abdullah Mosque.

In the far west is swanky Sweifieh, a booming shopping area. Further out, the city's outlying towns, suburbs and refugee camps have now pretty much merged into one sprawling urban area.

Maps

The maps in this guidebook should be sufficient for most visitors. If you plan to stay for some time or intend to visit places out of the centre, the 2003 *Maps of Jordan, Amman and Aqaba* published by Luma Khalaf is worth picking up. It shows just about every street in the city and pinpoints embassies and other landmarks. It doesn't, however, cover

the southern or eastern suburbs. The map is available from most bookshops.

INFORMATION
Bookshops

Amman has a good range of bookshops with titles in English but there are few bargains on books in Jordan.

Books@café (p93) has a large, eclectic selection, with a café and Internet access. The bookshop at the Jordan InterContinental Hotel (p91) has a good range of books about Jordan.

Al-Aulama Bookshop (Map p82; ☎ /fax 4636192; 44 Al-Amir Mohammed St, downtown; ⊙ 8am-8pm Sat-Thu) Good for hard-to-find locally produced (and Lonely Planet) guidebooks, maps and postcards.

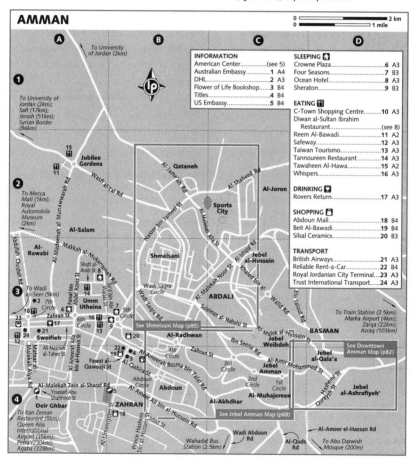

AMMAN

0 ———————— 2 km
0 ———————— 1 mile

INFORMATION
American Center..............(see 5)
Australian Embassy..............**1** A4
DHL..............................**2** A3
Flower of Life Bookshop.....**3** B4
Titles............................**4** B4
US Embassy....................**5** B4

SLEEPING 🏠
Crowne Plaza....................**6** A3
Four Seasons....................**7** B3
Ocean Hotel.....................**8** A3
Sheraton.........................**9** B3

EATING 🍴
C-Town Shopping Centre........**10** A3
Diwan al-Sultan Ibrahim
  Restaurant.................(see 8)
Reem Al-Bawadi................**11** A2
Safeway........................**12** A3
Taiwan Tourismo...............**13** A3
Tannoureen Restaurant.........**14** A3
Tawaheen Al-Hawa.............**15** A2
Whispers.......................**16** A3

DRINKING 🍷
Rovers Return..................**17** A3

SHOPPING 🛍
Abdoun Mall.....................**18** B4
Beit Al-Bawadi..................**19** B4
Silsal Ceramics.................**20** B3

TRANSPORT
British Airways..................**21** A3
Reliable Rent-a-Car.............**22** B4
Royal Jordanian City Terminal..**23** A3
Trust International Transport.....**24** A3

To University of Jordan (2km)

To University of Jordan (2km); Salt (17km); Jerash (51km); Syrian Border (96km)

Jubilee Gardens

Wasfi al-Tal Rd

Al Qataneh

Al-Shaheed Rd

Al-Joron

To Mecca Mall (1km); Royal Automobile Museum (2km)

Al-Salam

Sports City

Nasser bin Jameel St

Al-Malekah Alia St

Al-Istiqlal Rd

Abdullah Choshteh Rd

Al-Rawabi

Makkah al-Mukarramah Rd

Al-Madeenah al-Munawarrah Rd

Shatt al-Arab St

Shmeisani

Jebel al-Hussein

Khaled bin al...

To Wadi as-Seer (9km)

Faisal bin Abdel Azeez St

3rd bin Abi Talib

Umm Utheina

Wadi Saqra Circle

7th Circle

Al-Malekah Noor St

ABDALI

Wadi Saqra Rd

Suleiman al-Nabulsi St

Walid Rd

Ein Jalout Rd

To Train Station (2.5km); Marka Airport (4km); Zarqa (22km); Azraq (103km)

5th Circle

Zahran St

6th Circle

See Shmeisani Map (p85)

Al-Radhwan

Al-Malek al-Hussein St

BASMAN

See Downtown Amman Map (p82)

Sweifieh

Matbaat Alia al-Taher St

Al-Ameerah Alia bin al-Hussein St

4th Circle

Ibn Seena Rd

3rd Circle

Jebel Weibdeh

Jebel al-Qala'a

Hashemi St

Qurays St

Jebel al-Ashrafiyeh'

Fawzi al-Qawoaji St

Al-Qahira St

Ameerah Basma bin Talal Rd

Zahran St

Jebel Amman

Al-Amir Mohammed St

2nd Circle

1st Circle

Al-Malekah Zein al-Sharaf Rd

Youssef Abu Shahhout St

Deir Ghbar

Abdoun

Al-Ameer Ali bin al-Hussein Rd

Al-Muhajereen

ZAHRAN

Al-Akhdhar

See Jebel Amman Map (p68)

To Kan Zeman Restaurant (8km); Queen Alia International Airport (35km); Petra (230km); Aqaba (328km)

Prince Hashem bin al-Hussein St

Al-Irbid St

Wadi Abdoun Rd

Wahadat Bus Station (2.5km)

Al-Quds Rd

Al-Ameer el-Hassan Rd

To Abu Darwish Mosque (200m)

WHEN CIRCLES ARE SQUARES

With its endless one-way streets, stairways, narrow lanes and jebels (hills), Amman is confusing enough to get around anyway, but the ambiguous names for the streets and circles would challenge the navigational skills of even the most experienced explorer. We have used the more common names on the maps and in the text, but if street signs, directions given by locals and queries from taxi drivers are still confusing you, refer to the list below.

Don't forget that Al-Malek means King, so King Faisal St is sometimes labelled Al-Malek Faisal St. Similarly, Al-Malekah is Queen and Al-Amir (Al-Emir) is Prince. And don't be too surprised that some 'circles' are now called 'squares' *(maidan)*…

Streets

- Al-Kulliyah al-Islamiyah St – sometimes known as Zahran St
- Omar bin al-Khattab St – Mango St
- Quraysh St – Saqf Sayl St
- Abu Bakr as-Siddiq St – Rainbow St
- Suleiman al-Nabulsi St – Police St

Circles

- 1st Circle – Maidan al-Malek Abdullah
- 2nd Circle – Maidan Wasfi al-Tal
- 3rd Circle – Maidan al-Malek Talal
- 4th Circle – Maidan al-Emir Gazi bin Mohammed
- 5th Circle – Maidan al-Emir Faisal bin Hussein
- 6th Circle – Maidan al-Emir Rashid bin al-Hassan
- 7th Circle – Maidan al-Emir Talal bin Mohammed
- Ministry of the Interior Circle – Maidan Jamal Abdul Nasser
- Sports City Circle – Maidan al-Medina al-Riyadiyah

Amman Bookshop (Map p68; ☎ 4644013; Al-Amir Mohammed St, Jebel Amman; ☷ 9am-2pm & 3.30-6.30pm Sat-Thu) Just down from 3rd Circle, it has the best range of books and novels in Amman.

Bustami's Library (Map p82; ☎ 4622649; Al-Amir Mohammed St, downtown; ☷ 5am-6pm Sat-Thu) Right in the heart of downtown, this tiny bookstand is the place to go for up-to-date Western magazines and newspapers.

Flower of Life Bookshop (Map p65; ☎ 5921838; Abdoun Fawzi al-Qawaji St, Abdoun; 10am-2pm & 4-7pm Sat-Thu) Strong on archaeology, spirituality and kids' books.

Titles (Map p65; ☎ 5924130; Karadshe Complex, Abdoun Fawzi al-Qawaji St, Abdoun) Across from the Flower of Life Bookshop, with a good selection of books for sale and DVDs to rent.

Cultural Centres

All of the following foreign cultural centres regularly organise film nights and lectures (generally in their own language), plus exhibitions and concerts (in their own language or Arabic). Tourists are normally welcome at these events, but it's always a good idea to ring the centre first. You will also find details of functions at the various cultural centres listed in the two main local English-language newspapers, the *Jordan Times* and the *Star*.

American Center (Map p65; ☎ 5859102; US Embassy, 20 Al-Umawiyeen St, Abdoun; ☷ 1-4.30pm Sat-Wed, 9am-4pm Thu) Has a library with American newspapers and magazines.

British Council (Map p68; ☎ 4636147; www.british council.org.jo; Abu Bakr as-Siddiq St, Jebel Amman; ☷ 9am-6.30pm Sun-Wed, 9am-3.30pm Thu) Southeast of 1st Circle. Has a library with current English newspapers and a pleasant outdoor café. Library hours are noon-6.30pm Sunday to Wednesday, 11am to 3.30pm Thursday.

Centre Culturel Français (Map p82; ☎ 4612658; www.cccljor-jo.org; Kulliyat al-Sharee'ah St, Jebel Weibdeh; ☷ 8.30am-2pm & 4-6pm Sat-Thu) By the roundabout at the top of Jebel Weibdeh. The library is open 4pm to 6pm Saturday, Sunday and Monday, 11am-1pm and 4pm to 6pm Tuesday and Wednesday, 4pm to 8pm Thursday.

Goethe Institut (Map p68; ☎ 4641993; giammvw@ go.com.jo; 5 Abdul Mun'im al-Rifa'I St, Al-Radhwan; ☷ 9am-1pm Sun-Thu, 4.30-6.30pm Sun-Wed) Northwest of 3rd Circle.

Instituto Cervantes (Map p68; ☎ 4610858; http:// amman.cervantes.es; Mohammed Hafiz Ma'ath St, Jebel Amman; ☷ 9am-1pm & 4-7.30pm Sun-Thu) Behind Amman Surgical Hospital near 3rd Circle.

Emergency

The tourist police have an office at the Ministry of Tourism & Antiquities and there is a small tourist police booth on Hashemi St near the Roman Theatre. You can contact the tourist police through the **Halla Line** (☎ 0800 22228); free if calling from a non-mobile or public telephone.

Ambulance (☎ 193)

Fire Department (☎ 4617101, 199)

Ministry of Tourism & Antiquities (Map p68; ☎ 4642311, 4603360, ext 254; fax 4646264; Ground fl, Al-Mutanabbi St, Jebel Amman; ⏱ 8am-9pm)

Police (☎ 192, 191)

Traffic Police/Accidents (☎ 4896390, ☎ 190)

Internet Access

Amman has plenty of Internet cafés, particularly in downtown and by the University of Jordan.

Books@café (p93; per hr JD2) A highly professional set-up with fast connections.

Internet Yard (Map p82; ☎ 079 5509569; dweib@joinnet.com.jo; Al-Amir Mohammed St, downtown; per hr JD1; ⏱ 9.30am-midnight)

Meeranet (Map p85; ☎ 5695956; Ilya Abu Madhi St, Shmeisani; per hr JD2; ⏱ 24hr)

Welcome Internet (Map p82; ☎ 4620206; Al-Amir Mohammed St, downtown; per hr JD1; ⏱ 10.30am-1am) Used to dealing with travellers.

Laundry

Several tiny laundries and dry-cleaning services are hidden down side-alleys around downtown. There's one around the corner from Jabri Restaurant in downtown which charges around 500 fils per piece. Several hotels, including the Palace, offer a laundry service.

Libraries

The Darat al-Funun gallery (p83) has terrific art books. The main library at the University of Jordan is your best option for serious research. There are also small libraries at the British Council and in the American, French, Spanish and German cultural centres.

Amman Central Library (Map p82; ☎ 4627718; Hashemi St, downtown; ⏱ 9am-5pm Sat-Thu) Near the Roman Theatre. The top floor holds an eclectic range of English titles.

Media

Jordan Today (www.jordantoday.com.jo) is a free monthly booklet that includes a Yellow Pages listing of embassies, airlines, travel agencies and car-rental companies in both Amman and Aqaba, as well as restaurant listings and news of upcoming events.

The similarly monthly *Where to Go* (www.w2go.com) includes a useful collection of Amman restaurant menus. To track down a copy of either, ask at one of the tourist offices or at top-end hotels and restaurants.

The English-language *Jordan Times* and *Star* newspapers both print entertainment listings and a collection of useful phone numbers.

AMMAN IN...

One Day

Take a taxi to the **Citadel** (p71), with its ruined Roman temple and Umayyad palace, and check out the Archaeological Museum and views over downtown. Take a taxi or head east on foot and descend the series of steps to the aptly named downtown to check out the **Roman Theatre** (p81) and its museums. Follow our walking tour (p86) in reverse and shop the **souqs** around the Hussein Mosque. Enjoy a cheap local lunch of hummus and mint tea at **Hashem Restaurant** (p91) or spend a bit more on an organic salad while visiting the **Wild Jordan Centre** (p70).

In the afternoon wander the swanky districts of Shmeisani or check out the **craft shops** (p98) around 2nd Circle, before dining at **Abdoun Circle**.

Two Days

On the second day take a taxi or drive to **Wadi as-Seer** (p102) to check out the ruined Hellenistic palace and handicrafts complex of Iraq al-Amir and then continue on to **Fuheis** (p106) for a lunch or dinner of *fatteh* (fried bread with yoghurt, hummus and chicken). If you are short on time make a great day trip out to the Roman ruins of **Jerash** (p108) instead. After a hard day's sightseeing sweat it all out in the opulent **Al-Pasha Turkish Bath** (p86).

JEBEL AMMAN

Medical Services

Amman has more than 20 hospitals and some of the best medical facilities available in the Middle East. Among the better ones are those listed here. The two English-language newspapers found in Amman list the current telephone numbers of these and other hospitals, and of doctors on night duty throughout the capital. The two newspapers also publish a list of pharmacies open after hours.

Al-Khalidi Medical Centre (Map p68; ☎ 4644281; www.kmc.jo; Bin Khaldoun St, southwest of 3rd Circle)
Islamic Hospital (Map p85; ☎ 5680127; Just off Al-Malek al-Hussein St, Jebel al-Hussein)
Italian Hospital (Map p82; ☎ 4777101; Italian St, downtown)
Jacob's Pharmacy (Map p68; ☎ 4644945; 3rd Circle, Jebel Amman; ⌚ 9am-3am) One of the more convenient pharmacies.
Jordan Hospital & Medical Centre (Map p68; ☎ 5607550, 5620777; Al-Malekah Noor St, Jebel Amman)
Palestine Hospital (Map p85; ☎ 5607071; Al-Malekah Alia St, Shmeisani)
University Hospital (Map p65; ☎ 5353444; University of Jordan complex, northern Amman)

Money

Changing money is very easy and the downtown area especially is awash with banks and moneychangers. The Arab Bank, Jordan Gulf Bank and the Housing Bank for Trade & Finance are among those with widespread ATMs for Visa and MasterCard, while Jordan National Bank and HSBC ATMs allow you to extract dinars from your MasterCard and are Cirrus compatible. The Housing Bank has an ATM in the arrivals hall at Queen Alia International Airport; you get there after passing through customs so make sure you have some cash to buy your Jordanian visa if necessary.

Many moneychangers are located along Al-Malek Faisal St in downtown.
Sahloul Exchange Co (Map p82; ⌚ 9am-7pm Sat-Thu; Ground Fl, Aicco Bldg, Al-Malek Faisal St) Good for travellers cheques.

Post

There are lots of small post offices around town (ask your hotel for the nearest), including at the Jordan InterContinental Hotel between 2nd and 3rd Circles in Jebel Amman, and in the Housing Bank Centre in Shmeisani (which also houses the Royal Jordanian Airlines head office).

To send a large parcel anywhere, first go to the Parcel Post Office, in an alleyway behind the central post office in downtown (it looks more like a shop, so look out for the weighing machine on the counter), where it's weighed. Then take it unwrapped to the nearby Customs Office, diagonally opposite (look for the sign with the word 'Customs' in English on the crest), where a customs declaration must be completed. Then take the parcel back to the Parcel Post Office for packing and paying.

Central Post Office (Map p82; ☎ 4624120; Al-Amir Mohammed St, downtown; ☒ 7.30am-5pm Sat-Thu, 8am-1.30pm Fri)

Customs Office (Map p82; ☒ 8am-2pm Thu-Sat) Diagonally opposite the Parcel Post Office.

Parcel Post Office (Map p82; Omar al-Khayyam St, downtown; ☒ 8am-3pm Mon-Thu, 8am-2pm Sat, 8am-3pm Sun)

Amman's courier companies will generally pick up your package free of charge if you ring them:

DHL (Map p65; ☎ 5858487, 58005800; info@amm-co.jo .dhl.com; 7th Circle, Sweifieh) Behind C-Town Shopping Centre

FedEx (Map p85; ☎ 5511460; fedex@go.com.jo; Nasser bin Jameel St, Shmeisani)

UPS (Map p85; ☎ 5697030; ups@ups.com.jo; 21 Abdul Hameed Shoman St, Shmeisani)

Telephone

There is no central telephone office found in Amman. To make a local telephone call, use a telephone in your hotel (ask the price and minimum call length before dialling), or one of the numerous payphones (see p249 for more information). Telephone cards are available at shops close to telephone booths and grocery stores around town.

The private telephone agencies around downtown are the cheapest places for international and domestic calls.

Communication International (Map p82; Nimer Bin Adwan St, downtown) Charges 150 fils per minute to the US or UK, through a mobile phone.

Tourist Information

Jordan Tourism Board (Map p85; ☎ 5678294; Tunis St, Al-Radhwan; ☒ 8.30am-4pm Sat-Thu) Probably only worth contacting if you have a specific query or interest. It's next to the Century Park Hotel, between 4th and 5th Circles.

Ministry of Tourism & Antiquities (Map p68; ☎ 4642311, 4603360, ext 254; fax 4646264; Ground fl, Al-Mutanabbi St, Jebel Amman; ☒ 8am-9pm) The most useful place for information is this office, southwest of the 3rd Circle. The staff are friendly and speak good English. This is also the centre for the tourist police. You can also ask questions or lodge a tourism-related complaint at this office through the Halla (Welcome) Line (☎ 0800 22228; free if calling from a nonmobile or public telephone).

Wild Jordan Centre (Map p82; ☎ 4616523; www .rscn.org.jo, tourism@rscn.org.jo; Othman Bin Affan St) The place for information and bookings for activities and accommodation in any of Jordan's nature reserves, including Dana and Wadi Mujib. The centre is run by the Royal Society for the Conservation of Nature (RSCN; see p53). There's also a shop (p99) and café (p93) here.

Travel Agencies

There is a plethora of travel agencies dotted around the city: a crowd of them is strung along Al-Malek al-Hussein St, not far north of downtown near the flyover, and along the northwestern end of Abdul Hameed Sharaf St in Shmeisani. Although some claim to organise tours within Jordan, the bulk are sales agents for international airline tickets.

Atlas Travel Agency (Map p82; ☎ 4624262; www .atlastours.net; Al-Malek al-Hussein St) Reliable for airline tickets.

Universities

The **University of Jordan** (Map p65; www.ju.edu.jo) is one of the biggest universities in Jordan, and is located over 10km northwest of downtown. It boasts a Museum of Archaeology (p84) and a massive library. It also offers language courses (see p240), and is a great place to meet young locals. Numerous Internet cafés and Western fast-food outlets are dotted at various points along the main road, just opposite the university. Take any minibus or service taxi to Salt from either Raghadan or Abdali stations; the university is easy to spot from the main road.

Visa Extensions

If you're staying in Jordan for longer than 30 days (this used to be 14 days, until a change in mid-2005, so double check on arrival), you must obtain a visa extension (see p250).

The process is simple but involves a little running around. First you will need to get your hotel to write a short letter confirming where you are staying. Your hotel will also need to fill out two copies of a small card (or photocopy) that states all their details. On the back of the card is the application form for an extension, which you must fill out. It's in Arabic but your hotel should be able to help you fill it out and answers can be in English. That done, take the form, letter, photocopies of the front pages of your passport and the Jordanian visa page, and your passport to the relevant police station.

Which police station you visit depends on which area of Amman you're staying; ask your hotel for directions to the relevant office. If you're staying downtown, go to the first floor of the **Al-Madeenah Police Station** (Map p82; ☎ 4657788; 1st fl, Al-Malek Faisal St, downtown), opposite the Arab Bank.

After getting the relevant stamp, take your passport off to the **Muhajireen Police Station** (markaz amn muhajireen; Map p68; Al-Ameerah Basma bin Talal Rd), west of the downtown area. A taxi there from downtown should cost around 600 fils or take service taxi 35 along Quraysh St. A further stamp in your passport should see you with permission to remain in Jordan for an additional three months. Police stations are usually open for extensions from 10am to 3pm Saturday to Thursday, although it's best to go in the morning. Extensions are granted on the spot and you're unlikely to spend more than 10 minutes in each office.

DANGERS & ANNOYANCES

The only problem you're likely to encounter is the traffic; if driving, avoid the chaotic downtown area. The pollution can also affect those with respiratory problems, especially when dust levels are high. Nightclubs frequented by foreigners are more likely to attract pickpockets and bag snatchers, but crime in Amman is extremely rare.

The suicide bombings of November 2005 targeted tourist hotels in a worrying new development to the turmoil in neighbouring Iraq – the export of terrorism. Expect heightened security in the city's hotels and public places.

Scams

Be wary of taxi drivers who claim that your chosen hotel is closed, dirty or 'burnt down', only to recommend another hotel at which they get commission.

SIGHTS

The lion's share of the sights are downtown. Amman boasts several good museums, the best being the National Archaeological Museum in the Citadel. Amman doesn't boast any truly spectacular mosques; non-Muslims will feel most comfortable at King Abdullah Mosque.

Citadel (Jebel al-Qala'a)

The area known as the **Citadel** (Map p82; ☎ 4638795; admission JD2; ☺ 8am-4pm Sat-Thu Oct-Mar, 8am-7pm Sat-Thu Apr-Sep, 10am-4pm Fri) sits on

---

CROSSING THE STREET IN AMMAN

When you first arrive in Amman, one of your greatest challenges is likely to be making it safely to the other side of the street. This is especially true of the downtown area, although the faster-moving thoroughfares elsewhere also pose a serious hazard to your health. Contrary to what you may think, Amman's drivers have no desire to run you over; they just want to get to their destination as quickly as possible. The installation of more traffic lights has made the situation a little easier, but you'll still have a better chance of survival if you follow a few simple 'rules'. In slow-moving traffic, the name of the game is brinkmanship – whoever yields last will win. A car missing you by inches may scare the hell out of you but is actually a normal and precisely calculated course of events.

Cross wide roads a lane at a time – if you wait for a big gap you'll be there all day. Some unscrupulous travellers have even been known to hail a taxi so that it will block traffic and give them a lane's head start. Make your decision and then don't hesitate – Amman's drivers will make their decisions based on a reasonable assumption of what you'll do next. Above all, have patience; an extra minute's wait is infinitely preferable to a nasty accident. And if all else fails, put your pride behind you and ask some old lady to lead you by the hand or at least follow in their slipstream.

WORLD'S TALLEST FLAGPOLE

From most places in the city you can spot the huge Jordanian flag of the Raghadan palace compound, which at 127m high is said to be the world's largest free-standing flagpole. (A smaller but similarly impressive flag flies in Aqaba.) The award for the tallest flag pole in the world actually goes to those crazy North Koreans on the border with South Korea but that one is supported by cables, which as everyone knows is cheating.

the highest hill in Amman, Jebel al-Qala'a (about 850m above sea level) and is the site of ancient Rabbath-Ammon. Artefacts dating from the Bronze Age show that the hill was a fortress and/or agora for thousands of years. The complex is surrounded by 1700m-long **walls**, which were rebuilt many times during the Bronze and Iron Ages, as well as the Roman, Byzantine and Umayyad periods. The Citadel ticket office is on the road leading up to the Citadel's entrance.

The Citadel's most impressive series of historic buildings is the **Umayyad Palace**, which stretches out behind the National Archaeological Museum. Believed to be the work of Umayyad Arabs and dating from about AD 720, the palace was an extensive complex of royal and residential buildings and was once home to the governor of Amman. Its life span was short – it was destroyed by an earthquake in AD 749 and never fully rebuilt.

Coming from the south, the first major building belonging to the palace complex is the domed **audience hall**, designed to impress visitors to the royal palace. It is the most intact of the buildings on the site and is shaped like a cross because it was built over a Byzantine church. After much debate as to whether the central space had originally been covered or left open to the elements, consensus came down on the side of the ceiling dome, which was reconstructed by Spanish archaeologists.

A **courtyard** immediately north of the hall leads to a 10m-wide **colonnaded street**, lined with numerous arches and columns and flanked by residential and administrative buildings. Further to the north is the former **governor's residence**, which includes the **throne room**.

East of the audience hall is the **Umayyad Cistern**, an enormous circular hole with steps leading down to the bottom, which once supplied water to the palace and surrounding areas. The small disk on the floor in the centre once supported a pillar which was used for measuring water levels.

Back towards the museum to the south is the small **Byzantine Basilica**, most of which has been destroyed by earthquakes. It dates from the 6th or 7th century AD, and contains a few dusty mosaics.

About 100m south of the basilica are the remaining pillars of the Roman **Temple of Hercules** (Map p82). Once connected to the Forum (see the boxed text, p81), the temple was built during the reign of Marcus Aurelius (AD 161–80). The only obvious remains are parts of the podium and the columns, which are visible from around town. Nearby is a **lookout** with great views.

There are information boards in English and Spanish at a few places around the Umayyad Palace but, while informative, they can be a little confusing to follow. Guides will probably approach you when you arrive (or you can ask at the museum) and can really enhance your visit (up to JD5 depending on the length of time and number of people).

The **National Archaeological Museum** is just northwest of the Temple of Hercules. It has a good collection of items spanning all eras of Jordanian and regional history, ranging from 6000-year-old skulls from Jericho to Umayyad period artwork. It also boasts some examples of the Dead Sea Scrolls found at Qumran in 1952, a copy of the Mesha Stele (see p165) and assorted artefacts from Petra and Jerash. Most exhibits are well labelled in English. Pride of place are three of the Ain Ghazal statues, which date back to 6500 BC as some of the world's earliest sculpture. Finds from the Citadel itself include the head from a statue of the Greek goddess Tyche and some Egyptian-style carvings.

The only access roads to the Citadel are from Al-Malek Ali bin al-Hussein St. It's better to hire a taxi for the trip up (less than JD1 from downtown). If you decide to walk it's much easier headed downhill. Steps lead down from east of the Citadel complex, past a viewing platform to Hashemi St, opposite the Roman Theatre.

(Continued on page 81)

Royal Tombs (p184), Petra

PATRICK BEN LUKE SYDER

The Treasury (p182), Petra

ANDERS BLOMQVIST

Urn Tomb (p185), Petra

ANDERS BLOMQVIST

The Siq (p181), Petra

ANDERS BLOMQVIST

South Gate (p111), Jerash

ANDERS BLOMQVIST

ANTHONY HAM

Southern Tetrapylon (p112), Jerash

Oval Plaza (p111), Jerash

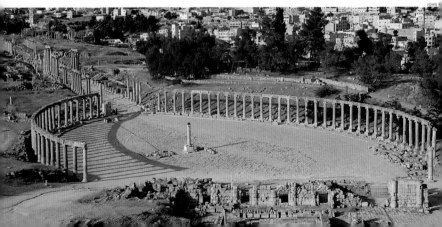

JOHN

ANDERS BLOMQVIST

View from the Burdah Rock Bridge (p208), Wadi Rum

JOHN ELK III

Wadak Rock Bridge (p208), Wadi Rum

Wadi Rum (p203)

ALISON WRIGHT

MARK DAFFEY

Qala'at ar-Rabad (p114), Ajlun

Qusayr Amra (p135)

MARK DAFFEY

Karak Castle (p166)

JOHN E

SARA-JANE CLELAND

Bedouin (p212), Wadi Rum

Female weaver, Bani Hamida Project (p163)

ALISON WRIGHT

Bedouin men (p212), Wadi Rum

JOHN ELK III

PATRICK BEN LUKE

Dead Sea beach (p143)

ALISON WRIGHT

Sunset, Dead Sea (p143)

Floating in the Dead Sea (p143)

ALISON

King Hussein Mosque (p83)

ALISON WRIGHT

King Abdullah Mosque (p83)

PATRICK BEN LUKE SYDER

Abu Darwish Mosque (p83)

DAMIEN SIMONIS

Mosaic in the Church of the Apostles (p153), Madaba

Mosaic floor, Petra Church (p187)

Mosaics of the Hippolytus Hall, Archaeological Park (p153), Madaba

(Continued from page 72)

Roman Theatre

The restored **Roman Theatre** (Map p82; admission incl Folklore Museum & Museum of Popular Traditions JD1; ☺ 8am-4pm Sat-Thu, 10am-4pm Fri Oct-Mar, 8.30am-7pm Apr-Sep) is the most obvious and impressive remnant of Roman Philadelphia and, for many, the highlight of Amman. It is cut into the northern side of a hill that once served as a necropolis, and has a seating capacity of 6000. It was built on three tiers: the rulers, of course, sat closest to the action, the military had the middle section, and the general public sat perched, squinting, way up the top.

The theatre was probably built in the 2nd century AD during the reign of Antoninus Pius (AD 138–61). Theatres often had religious significance, and the small shrine above the top row of seats once housed a statue of the goddess Athena (now in the National Archaeological Museum), who was prominent in the religious life of the city.

Full restoration began in 1957. Unfortunately, nonoriginal materials were used so the reconstruction is partly inaccurate. In recent years, the theatre has again become a place of entertainment; productions are sometimes put on here in July and August; check with the tourist office or ask at your hotel.

The best time for photographs is probably the morning, although the views from the top tiers just before sunset are superb. At night the theatre is floodlit, providing a spectacular backdrop to the very modern bustle of downtown.

TUNNEL UNDER AMMAN

In ancient Roman Philadelphia, royalty considered it beneath them to mingle with the general public unless they had to. To ease their path between the major sites, an underground tunnel was built to connect the Citadel high on the hill with the Nymphaeum and Theatre. While modern visitors to Amman might welcome having such access without having to negotiate the streets of downtown, the tunnel's precise location and state of repair is a closely guarded secret. All the locals know about it, but very few know where it is and some even doubt that it exists. Those that do know aren't telling.

The row of columns immediately in front (north) of the Roman Theatre is all that's left of the **Forum**, once one of the largest public squares (about 100m by 50m) in Imperial Rome. Built in AD 190, the square was flanked on three sides by columns, and on the fourth side by the Seil Amman stream; almost everything (including the stream, which still runs) lies underneath the modern streets.

On the eastern side of what was the Forum stands the 500-seat **Odeon** (admission free). Built in the 2nd century AD, it served mainly as a venue for musical performances. The small amphitheatre was probably enclosed with a wooden or temporary tent roof to shield the performers and audience from the elements.

FOLKLORE MUSEUM

This **museum** (Map p82; ☎ 4651742; Roman Theatre complex; ☺ 9am-7pm Sat-Thu, 10am-4pm Fri May-Sep, 9am-5pm Sat-Thu, 10am-4pm Fri Oct-Apr) is immediately to the right as you enter the Roman Theatre. It houses a modest collection of items illustrating traditional Jordanian life. They include a Bedouin goat-hair tent complete with tools; musical instruments such as the single-string *rababa* (a one-stringed Bedouin instrument); looms; *mihbash* (coffee grinders); some weapons; and various costumes, including Circassian. Don't miss the B&W photos of old Amman by the entrance. Captions are in English.

MUSEUM OF POPULAR TRADITIONS

This **museum** (Map p82; ☎ 4651670; Roman Theatre complex; ☺ 9am-7pm Sat-Thu, 10am-4pm Fri May-Sep, 9am-5pm Sat-Thu, 10am-4pm Fri Oct-Apr), to the left after you enter the Roman Theatre, has well-presented displays of traditional costumes, jewellery, face masks and mosaics from Jerash.

Nymphaeum

Built in AD 191, the **Nymphaeum** (Map p82; Quraysh St; admission free; ☺ daylight Sat-Thu) was once a large, two-storey complex with fountains, mosaics, stone carvings and possibly a 600-sq-metre swimming pool – all dedicated to the nymphs (mythical young girls who lived in and around the rivers). Up until 1947 the ancient stream and Roman bridge still stood where the road now runs. Excavations started in earnest in 1993, and restoration

DOWNTOWN AMMAN

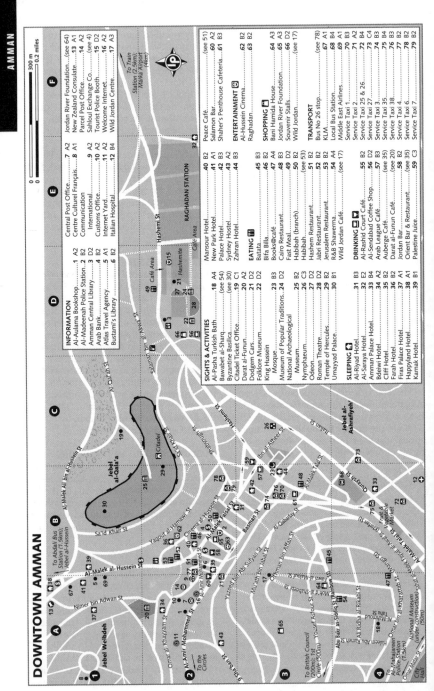

INFORMATION

Al-Aulama Bookshop	1 A2
Al-Madeenah Police Station	2 B2
Amman Central Library	3 D2
Arab Bank	4 A2
Atlas Travel Agency	5 A1
Bustani's Library	6 B2
Central Post Office	7 A2
Centre Culturel Français	8 A1
Communication International	9 A2
Customs Office	10 A2
Internet Yard	11 A2
Italian Hospital	12 B4
Jordan River Foundation	(see 64)
New Zealand Consulate	13 A1
Parcel Post Office	14 A2
Sahloul Exchange Co	(see 4)
Tourist Police Booth	15 D2
Welcome Internet	16 A1
Wild Jordan Centre	17 A3

SIGHTS & ACTIVITIES

Al-Pasha Turkish Bath	18 A4
Bawabet al-Sharq	(see 54)
Byzantine Basilica	19 C1
Citadel Ticket Office	(see 30)
Darat al-Funun	20 A2
Dodgem Cars	21 D2
Folklore Museum	22 D2
King Hussein Mosque	23 B3
Museum of Popular Traditions	24 D2
National Archaeological Museum	25 B2
Nymphaeum	26 C3
Odeon	27 D2
Roman Theatre	28 D2
Temple of Hercules	29 B2
Umayyad Palace	30 B1

SLEEPING

Al-Riyad Hotel	31 B3
Al-Saraya Hotel	32 E2
Amman Palace Hotel	33 B4
Bdeiwi Hotel	34 A2
Cliff Hotel	35 B2
Farah Hotel	36 B2
Firas Palace Hotel	37 A1
Happyland Hotel	38 A1
Karnak Hotel	39 B1

Mansour Hotel	40 B2
New Park Hotel	41 A1
Palace Hotel	42 B3
Sydney Hostel	43 A2
Zahran Hotel	44 B3

EATING

Batata	45 B3
Bifa Billa	46 B2
Books@Café	47 A4
Cairo Restaurant	48 B3
Fast Meal	49 D2
Habibah (branch)	50 B2
Habibah	(see 53)
Hashem Restaurant	51 B2
Jabri Restaurant	52 B2
Jerusalem Restaurant	53 B2
R&B Shawerma	54 A4
Wild Jordan Café	(see 17)

DRINKING

Al-Rashid Court Café	55 B2
Al-Sendabad Coffee Shop	56 D2
Arab League Café	57 B3
Auberge Café	(see 35)
Darat al-Funun Café	(see 20)
Jordan Bar	58 B2
Orient Bar & Restaurant	(see 35)
Palestine Juice	59 C3

Peace Café	(see 51)
Salamon Bar	60 A1
Shaher's Penthouse Cafeteria	61 B3

ENTERTAINMENT

Al-Hussein Cinema	62 B2
Raghadan	63 B2

SHOPPING

Bani Hamida House	64 A3
Jordan River Foundation	65 A3
Souvenir Stalls	66 D2
Wild Jordan	(see 17)

TRANSPORT

Bus No 26 stop	(see 78)
KLM	67 A1
Local Bus Station	68 B4
Middle East Airlines	69 A1
Service Taxi 1	70 B3
Service Taxi 2	71 A2
Service Taxis 25 & 26	72 B4
Service Taxi 27	73 C4
Service Taxi 3	74 B3
Service Taxi 35	75 B4
Service Taxi 38	76 B3
Service Taxi 4	77 B2
Service Taxi 6	78 B2
Service Taxi 7	79 B2

GIVING AMMAN A FACELIFT

Amman is definitely a city on the rise, with investment rates and rents skyrocketing. Several huge construction projects in particular look set to change the face of the city over the next few years.

Amman's congested downtown area is midway through a major makeover, which will include a new international-standard National Museum next to City Hall (due for completion in 2007), gardens, panoramic vantage points and pedestrian trails linking the Citadel and Roman Theatre. As part of the Japanese-funded redevelopment, many of the grimy buildings in the area have already been cleaned and the Raghadan bus station has been rebuilt, with corner towers, a tourist police booth, restaurants and shops.

Further west, the Abdali Urban Regeneration Project will house a large shopping and office complex, as well as a library and a new American University of Jordan. The project is part of a drive to relocate the Jordanian military out of some of Amman's prime real estate.

Jordan Gate/Royal Metropolis is another high-profile US$1 billion business and retail complex planned for 6th Circle. The twin 35-storey high-rise towers will house a five-star hotel and shopping complex and looks set to dominate the Amman skyline.

---

will continue for many years. Except for a few columns, an elegant archway and a few alcoves there is still little to see.

The site is easy to find, not far from the King Hussein Mosque. It's open for as long as the workers are toiling away.

King Hussein Mosque

Built by King Abdullah I in 1924, and restored in 1987, the **King Hussein Mosque** (Map p82; Hashemi St; admission free) is in the heart of downtown on the site of a mosque built in AD 640 by 'Umar, the second caliph of Islam. The mosque is more interesting as a hive of activity than for any architectural splendour; the precinct is a local meeting place and exudes an altogether Arab flavour. Non-Muslims, while generally welcome any time (except during prayer time), may feel intrusive.

Abu Darwish Mosque

On top of Jebel al-Ashrafiyeh' is the striking **Abu Darwish Mosque** (map p65), built in 1961 with unmistakable alternating layers of black and white stone. Non-Muslims are generally not permitted inside, but the views on the way up are good. Take service taxi 25 or 26 from Italian St in downtown to the mosque, or charter a taxi. It's a very long and steep climb southeast of downtown if you decide to walk.

Darat al-Funun

On the hillside to the north of the downtown area, **Darat al-Funun** (House of Arts; Map p82; ☎ 4643251; www.daratalfunun.org; Nimer bin Adwan St; admission free; ⊙ 10am-7pm Sat-Wed, to 8pm Thu) is a superb complex dedicated to placing contemporary art at the heart of Jordan's cultural life. The main building features a small **art gallery** with works by Jordanian and other Arab artists, an art library, and workshops for Jordanian and visiting sculptors and painters. A schedule of upcoming exhibitions, lectures, films and public discussion forums is available on the website and the *Jordan Times* newspaper.

Almost as significant as the centre's artistic endeavours are the architectural features of the site. At the base of the complex, near the entrance, are the excavated ruins of a 6th-century **Byzantine church**. Buildings further up the hill are mostly restored residences from the 1920s; it was in one of these that TE Lawrence wrote part of *Seven Pillars of Wisdom*. There is also a peaceful café (see p97) and gardens with superb views over Amman.

Access is easiest on foot. From near the southern end of Al-Malek al-Hussein St, head up the stairs under the 'Riviera Hotel' sign. At the top of the stairs, turn immediately right onto Nimer bin Adwan St and walk uphill for 50m where you need to take the left fork. The entrance gate (no English sign) is on the right after a few metres.

King Abdullah Mosque

Completed in 1989 as a memorial by the late King Hussein to his grandfather, the unmistakable blue-domed **mosque** (Map p68;

Suleiman al-Nabulsi St; Jebel Weibdeh; admission JD2; 8-11am & 12.30-2pm Sat-Thu, 8-10am Fri) can house up to 7000 worshippers inside, and another 3000 in the courtyard area. This is the only mosque in Amman that openly welcomes non-Muslim visitors.

The cavernous, octagonal prayer hall is notable for not having any pillars; the dome is 35m in diameter. The inscriptions quote verses from the Quran. The blue colour of the underside of the dome is said to represent the sky, and the golden lines running down to the base of the dome depict rays of light illuminating the 99 names of Allah. The huge three-ringed chandelier contains more Quranic inscriptions. There is also a small women's section for 500 worshippers, and a much smaller royal enclosure.

Inside the mosque is a small **Islamic Museum** (5672155), which has some pottery pieces, as well as photographs and personal effects of King Abdullah I. There are also a number of pieces of Muslim art, coins and stone engravings. The admission fee to the mosque includes access to the museum.

Women are required to wear something (which can be borrowed at the mosque) to cover the hair; and everyone must remove their shoes before entering the prayer hall.

Jordan National Gallery of Fine Arts

This small **gallery** (Map p68; 4630128; www.na tionalgallery.org; Hosni Fareez St, Jebel Weibdeh; admission JD1; 9am-5pm Sun-Thu) is an excellent place to gain an appreciation of contemporary Jordanian painting, sculpture and pottery and is worth an hour or more. There's an excellent small gift shop and a café. The gallery was renovated in 2005.

The gallery is signposted from Suleiman al-Nabulsi St, opposite the King Abdullah Mosque.

Museum of Archaeology

If you have an interest in archaeology, or happen to be at the University of Jordan, this small **museum** (map p65; 5355000, ext 3412; 8am-5pm Sun-Thu) is well worth a visit. Highlights include models of the Temple of Artemis and Nymphaeum at Jerash, a copy of the Mesha Stele (see p165) and finds from Bronze Age Jericho and the 6th-century BC Ammonite fort at Tell al-Mazar. Don't miss the unmarked gems laying around outside the building, including several dolmens (ancient graves). The next door Museum of National Heritage isn't up to much.

To get here, take any minibus or service taxi heading towards Salt from Abdali or Raghadan stations, then get off at the main (west) entrance to the university and head for the clocktower; the museum is just behind it.

Other Sights

The simple and solemn Martyr's Memorial houses the small but interesting **Military Museum** (Map p85; 5664240; admission free; 9am-4pm Sat-Thu), which chronicles Jordan's recent military history, from the Arab Revolt in 1916 (in which 10,000 Arab fighters were killed) through to the Arab-Israeli Wars. It does, however, airbrush over many of the controversial aspects of these conflicts – the 1948 and 1967 wars are hardly mentioned and the 1973 war only in passing.

The memorial is on the road to Zarqa, 1km east of the Sports City junction, in the grounds of the Sports City. Take any minibus or service taxi towards Zarqa, but check whether it goes past the Sports City (al-Medina al-Riyadiyah). A private taxi from downtown should cost around JD1.500.

The **Museum of the Political History of HM Late King Abdullah bin al-Hussein** (Map p68; 4621151; Al-Kulliyah al-Islamiyah St, Jebel Amman; 9am-2pm Sun-Thu) is worth checking out for its coverage of Jordan's political life in the early 20th century. It's next to the Iraqi Embassy, west of 1st Circle.

Car enthusiasts will like the display of over 70 classic cars and motorbikes from the personal collection of King Hussein at the **Royal Automobile Museum** (Map p65; 5411392; www.royalautomuseum.jo; King Hussein Park; adult JD3; 10am-7pm Wed-Mon). It's in the northwestern suburbs, north of 8th Circle.

ACTIVITIES
Swimming

The top-end hotels allow nonguests to use their swimming pools for a fee; the InterContinental charges JD15; Le Royal currently JD10. Among the cheapest is the Manar Hotel (p90), which charges JD5.

Sports City (Map p85; 5667181) in northern Amman has an Olympic-sized pool. Nonmembers are charged around JD6, which includes the use of a locker. Women may feel uncomfortable swimming here.

SHMEISANI

0 — 500 m
0 — 0.3 miles

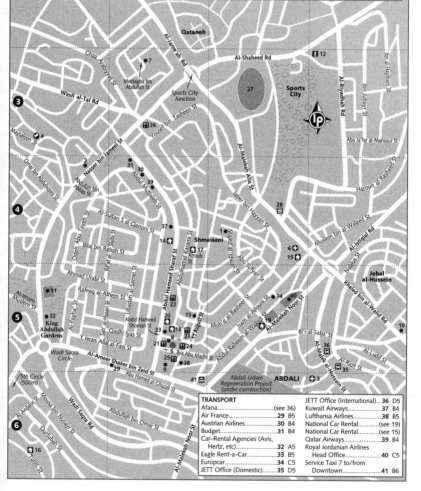

Hammams

Al-Pasha Turkish Bath (Map p82; ☎/fax 4633002; www.pashaturkishbath.com; Al-Mahmoud Taha St, Jebel Amman; ☺ 9am-2am, last booking midnight) is the perfect pampering antidote to the hills and bustle of Amman. The full service (JD15) includes steam bath, sauna, Jacuzzi, scrubbing, a 40-minute massage and two soft drinks, all done in a superb building architecturally faithful to the tradition of a Turkish *hammam*. There are male and female attendants. Couples are welcome during the day; evenings are generally for men only. It's a good idea to book ahead and bring a pair of swimming trunks. It's easiest to find if you're coming along Abu Bakr as-Siddiq St (Rainbow St) from the 1st Circle; it's the fifth street on the right. Taxis know it as near Ahliya School for Girls.

Other Activities

The Sports City complex has **tennis courts** (Map p85; ☎ 5682796) for JD1 per hour. This rises to JD2 if you play at night under lights. You will, however, need to provide your own racquet and balls.

The **Bisharat Golf Course** (Map p103; ☎ 079 5520334) comprises of a nine-hole course, putting greens and even a golf pro. Nine holes cost JD12, plus JD12 for club hire. The club is 14km south of downtown, and signposted from the Desert Highway on the way to Queen Alia airport.

To try something completely different here, gliding is sometimes possible at the **Gliding Club** (☎ 4874587) at the Marka Airport east of Amman. The **Royal Racing Club** (Map p103; ☎ 5850630) holds races (for horses and camels) in spring and summer, and offers horse-riding classes. Details are available from the club, located off the Desert Highway and on the way to Queen Alia airport.

For tenpin bowling try **Strikers** (Map p85; Kempinski Amman, Abdul Hamid Shouman St, Shmeisani) or the **Jordan Bowling Centre** (map p65; ☎ 5512987) at Mecca Mall in the northwestern suburbs. A game costs JD3.

Power Hut (Map p85; ☎ 5686349; powerhut@nets .com.jo; 11 August St, Shmeisani; ☺ 5.30am-11pm Sun-Thu & Sat, 10am-6.30pm Fri) is one of the best gyms in town. A day/week pass costs JD6/17.500 and gives access to a wide range of machines, free weights, spin and taebo classes, and a sauna and steam room. The gym is women-only from 9.30am to noon.

Club Olympus (Map p68; Grand Hyatt Amman, Al-Hussein bin Ali St, 3rd Circle; ☺ 6am-10pm Sat-Thu, 7am-10pm Fri) charges JD15 for a day's use of its gym, indoor and outdoor pools, Jacuzzi and sauna; 10 visits cost JD75.

WALKING TOUR

This walk takes you through the busiest part and most interesting sections of downtown's bustling souqs. It can be done in an hour (2km) but it's worth stopping, detouring and making a shopping trip out of it.

Start off the walk by sitting down with a fortifying hummus and mint tea at **Hashem Restaurant** (**1**; p91), before heading down Al-Malek (King) Faisal St. Just past the ornate Arab Bank, on the left, you'll see an alleyway perennially overflowing with men lining up like impatient addicts waiting for a plate of *kanafa* (shredded wheat and syrup dessert) from the takeaway branch of **Habibah** (**2**; p95); 300 fils will buy your very own sugar rush. After another 80m, turn left into the dazzling **gold souq** (**3**). After a quick window shop, cross the road and head up the alley directly opposite, by the Palace Hotel (the alley entrance is marked by a perfume stall). The eye-opening side alley is lined with risqué Islamic lingerie shops – sure to blow away any preconceived myths you have about prudish Arab women! Head up the flight of steps at the end of the alley and turn left onto Basman St, past several dress shops that stock some nice examples of Palestinian-style embroidery to views of **King Hussein mosque** (**4**; p83). The area is particularly busy on Friday lunchtimes, when hundreds of men stream out of the mosque after the weekly sermon.

Right on the junction is the **Al-Afghani souvenir store** (**5**), a tiny Aladdin's cave overflowing with tourist kitsch. The souq behind conceals a maze of other souvenir stores. Across the street, four shops from the mosque, is a tiny but excellent **keffiyeh shop** (**6**) – actually a converted stairwell!

Take your life into your hands, cross the street and head down Betra St. On the left is a traditional **Arabic medicine stall** (**7**), recognisable by its dried alligators, starfish and drawers of herbs. At the junction take in the lovely aroma of the coffee roasters and spice grinders. Take a left past these and then another left, past a small bakery on the right, whose staff are continually pulling huge pitta breads out of the ovens. Take a right into the **vegetable market (8)**, past piles of Saudi dates, Iranian pistachios and Syrian olives. A left and quick right takes you through the fruit souq. As you hit the main road a left turn takes you to couple of shops selling olives and cheeses; a right leads to the **Nymphaeum (9**; p81).

From the Nymphaeum follow Quraysh St then take a right along the busy road to plaza in front of the **Roman Theatre (10**; p81). Beyond the Theatre is **Hashemite Sq (11)**, a place for locals to stroll, sip tea, smoke the nargileh (water pipe) and watch the world go by. There are cafés, shwarma stalls, souvenir shops and even dodgem cars (like any downtown Amman street really!).

If you are feeling fit, as an add on to the walking tour you can climb the steps across the road from the Roman Theatre up to a viewpoint and then up to the **Citadel**.

AMMAN FOR CHILDREN

Dodgem cars (Map p82; Hashemite Sq, downtown; admission 500 fils; 9am-10pm) Children and the young at heart can enjoy these.

Haya Cultural Centre (Map p85; ☎ 5665195; Ilya Abu Madhi St, Shmeisani; admission free; 9am-6pm Sat-Thu) Is designed especially for children and has a library, playground, an interactive ecomuseum and an inflatable castle. It also organises regular activities and performances for kids.

Luna Park (Map p85; Khaled bin al-Walid Rd; admission JD1; 10am-10pm) Has rides and amusements for the kids. It has a branch at King Abdullah Gardens (Map p85).

The Friday brunch at Wild Jordan Café (p93) offers entertainment and environmental education for kids aged eight to 11, between 9am and 11am.

Amman Waves, 15km south of town on the highway to the airport, is a new water park but wasn't open at the time of research.

TOURS

At least three budget hotels – the Cliff, Farah and Palace – offer day trips from Amman. The most popular tours are to the desert castles (JD10 per person), or to Jerash, Ajlun and Umm Qais (JD13 per person). A day trip to Madaba, Mt Nebo and the Dead Sea is possible if you can find enough people to make up a carload. Don't expect anything more than transport on these tours.

One option, which has been recommended by readers, is the transport offered by some hotels (eg Farah) which leaves Amman at 8.30am and travels to Petra (around 6pm) via Madaba, Mt Nebo, Wadi Mujib Gorge, Karak, Shobak and Dana Nature Reserve with a brief amount of time spent at each of the various sites (JD15 to JD25 per person). A taxi for the same route costs around JD60.

The Palace Hotel plans to run a day trip from Amman to Damascus, via Jerash and Bosra, for JD20 per person.

FESTIVALS & EVENTS

Concerts, plays and performances are occasionally held at the Odeon and Roman Theatre in July and August. The Ministry of Tourism office, near 3rd Circle, is the best source of detailed information, but also check out the English-language newspapers. See p113 for information about the Jerash Festival (generally visited as a day trip from Amman), Jordan's best-known cultural event.

SLEEPING

Most cheap hotels are in downtown; there are also a few around Abdali bus station. Many midrange places are around Abdali and between 1st and 5th Circles; most top-end places are further out in Shmeisani.

Budget

The cheapest places are around the King Hussein Mosque, but these are only for deep sleepers and those for whom price is everything. Many have shops on the ground floor, a tea shop on the 2nd and rooms on the 3rd and 4th floors, so getting to your room involves a lot of climbing. All budget places mentioned here come with shared bathroom facilities unless stated otherwise; all promise hot water and some even deliver.

DOWNTOWN

Cliff Hotel (Map p82; ☎ 4624273; fax 4638078; Al-Amir Mohammed St; 3-bed dm/s/d JD3/5/6) A long-standing shoestring favourite with friendly staff, in the heart of downtown and one of the few places in Amman where you can hook up with other backpackers. The rooms are simple but bright, though you should check out a few rooms as some beds are better than others. The doubles are much better than the pokey singles. Showers cost 500 fils. In summer you can sleep on the roof for JD2.

Farah Hotel (Map p82; ☎ 4651443; farahhotel@ hotmail.com; Cinema al-Hussein St; mattress on roof/dm/ s/d 2.500/4/7/9; ☐) A backpacker-savvy place that gets good reports from travellers. The rooms are a bit dingy and the shared bathrooms consist of a shower head installed directly above a squat toilet, but the staff are friendly and eager to help. Solo travellers get a double room for a single rate.

Mansour Hotel (Map p82; ☎ 4621575; Al-Malek Faisal St; s/d JD5.500/8.800, d with private bathroom JD10) An old-school place that's central and quieter than most because it's a little back from the busy main road. The rooms are simple but well looked after and the welcome is understated but friendly. Toilets are Arab-style; showers cost 500 fils.

Al-Riyad Hotel (Map p82; ☎ 4624260; fax 4625457; Al-Malek Faisal St; s/d/tr with sink & fan JD5/5/7) The dyslexic al-Riyad/Reyad/Riyadh is a basic place with an almost exclusively male Jordanian clientele. There's little English spoken but plenty of goodwill.

Zahran Hotel (Map p82; ☎ 4625473; Hashemi St; q JD1.500 per bed, s/d JD3/4) Probably the pick of the very basic cheapies around the King Hussein Mosque, but you'll feel as if the muezzin (mosque official) is broadcasting from your closet daily at 4am. Lone women will definitely feel uncomfortable here. A hot shower costs 500 fils.

Bdeiwi Hotel (Map p82; ☎ 4643394; fax 4643393; Omar al-Khayyam St; s/d/tr JD5/7/9) Slightly away from the bustle of downtown, the Bdeiwi gets decidedly mixed reviews from travellers but it seems to depend on who's on duty at reception (ask for Feraz). The rooms are simple but generally clean, with a shared Western-style bathroom. Room 6 is the best by far and a good deal if you can get it.

Karnak Hotel (Map p82; ☎ /fax 4638125; Al-Malek al-Hussein St; s/d/tr with fan & private bathroom JD8/10/12) This is a good-value, well-run, friendly but slightly unexciting option. The rooms are freshened up a little by the pine furniture and a few have balconies overlooking the noisy street. There's a sitting area with cold drinks for sale.

THE AUTHOR'S CHOICE

Palace Hotel (Map p82; ☎ 4624326; www.pal acehotel.com.jo; Al-Malek Faisal St; s/d/tr JD6/8/12, with private bathroom JD11/14/21; ☐) The Palace is definitely the best budget and lower midrange option in downtown and is worth a little splurge if you are on a tight budget. The rooms are clean and large, all renovated in 2005, and some have balconies with good views over the street. There's a wide range of rooms, from midrange triples with satellite TV and fridge to singles with shared bathroom (four bathrooms on every floor). The hot water is reliable and it's surprisingly quiet considering the downtown location. It also runs the best value tours around the country (see p87) and has a laundry service, free local calls, Internet access, a café and free baggage storage. Breakfast is an extra JD1 per person.

New Park Hotel (Map p82; ☎ 4648145; Al-Malek al-Hussein St; s/d with fan, private bathroom JD10/13 with breakfast) Also has a nice feel about it with helpful staff and clean, fresh rooms that come with satellite TV. Hot water is available 5am to 9am and 5pm to 9pm. The rooms over the street have a balcony but the rooms at the back are quieter. Doubles are much better value than singles.

Happyland Hotel (Map p82; ☎ 4639832; fax 4628550; Al-Malek al-Hussein St; s/d with private bathroom summer JD5/8, winter JD4/6) Like most budget places in Amman, Happyland Hotel is better than its exterior suggests and is actually pretty good value because you get a private bathroom. The rooms are simple and hot water is only available between 7am and noon – at least they're honest about it.

Sydney Hostel (Map p82; ☎ 4641122; sydney _hostel@yahoo.com; 9 Sha'ban St; with private bathroom dm/s/d/tr JD4/10/15/20) The short walk from Al-Malek Faisal St means this is a little quieter than other budget places. Rooms are clean, comfortable and fresh with hot-water bathrooms, towels, a small balcony and satellite TV. Singles are good value but there's only one dorm room. A coffee shop is planned, as is free Internet access. This new place has already undergone one change of management so things may change again. They claim they'll pick you up from the airport for free if you book in advance.

JEBEL AMMAN

The following places are within a short walk of the Abdali bus station and can, therefore, be especially useful for late-night or early-morning departures or arrivals.

Merryland Hotel (Map p68; ☎ /fax 4654238; www .merryland-hotel.com; Al-Malek al-Hussein St; s/d with private bathroom from JD13/16 with breakfast & tax) Not the most stylish option, with an odd castle-like interior, but good value with clean, tiled rooms and hot water in the bathrooms.

Select Hotel (Map p68; ☎ 4637101; www.select -amman.com; 52 Al-Ba'ouniyah St, Jebel Weibdeh; s/d JD12/18; ☒ 💻) Excellent upper-budget value, quiet and well-run with a family feel. Its rooms are clean and spacious and come with TV, air-conditioning and spotless private bathrooms, though the doubles are much more spacious than the singles. Ask for one of the four rooms with a balcony. There's a bar and outside terrace. Prices include breakfast.

Midrange

Most places listed have air-conditioning, satellite TV and a fridge in the rooms and all have private bathrooms with hot water. All prices listed here include tax and breakfast unless stated otherwise. A few midrange places are in downtown, but most are around Abdali and between 1st and 5th Circles.

DOWNTOWN

Al-Saraya Hotel (Map p82; ☎ 4656791; www.saraya hotel.com; Al-Jaza'er St, s/d/tr JD14/18/22; 💻) One of a few midrange options in downtown, the Saraya, near the eastern end of Raghadan bus station, has clean, comfortable and spacious rooms, with superclean bathrooms and towels. Among the highlights are Fayez, the friendly owner. The call to prayer from the neighbouring mosque can be quite a shock early in the morning. The reception changes money.

Amman Palace Hotel (Map p82; ☎ 4646172; aplchotl@hotmail.com; Quraysh St; s/d JD15/20; ☒) A friendly midrange option if you want the convenience of being close to the interesting downtown souqs. The large rooms are a tad jaded and the hot water can be slow to arrive but it's comfortable nonetheless. Ask for a room with a window. Solo travellers should push for a double room, as they are much bigger.

Firas Palace Hotel (Map p82; ☎ 4650404; www .firaspalace.com; Nimer bin Adwan St; s/d JD23/28) Not a bad midrange choice close to downtown's colour. Rooms are spacious and comfortable, set around a large central skylight, though the carpet's seen better days.

JEBEL AMMAN

Toledo Hotel (Map p68; ☎ 4657777; www.toledohotel .jo; Umayyah bin Abd Shams St; s/d JD25/35; ☒ 💻) If you are concerned about either a late arrival or early departure by bus (though there are taxis available at any time), this Andalusian Moorish–style midrange place is conveniently located right by the Abdali bus station. Rooms here are comfortable and surprisingly quiet, and have satellite TV, 24-hour room service and even pizza delivery to the room (JD2). The lobby is on the 7th floor. The hotel can arrange airport transfers.

Canary Hotel (Map p68; ☎ 4638353; canary_h@ hotmail.com; 17 Al-Karmali St; s/d/ste JD18/24/28; 💻) In the leafy Jebel Weibdeh area, the cosy

B&B-style Canary is pleasantly aloof from the chaos of the nearby Abdali bus station but within walking distance of it. The rooms are more comfortable than luxurious, although the (smallish) bathrooms sparkle. Doubles are generally better value than the singles; the best deal is the four-bed family suite. Visa cards are accepted.

Caravan Hotel (Map p68; ☎ 5661195; caravan@go.com.jo; Al-Ma'moun St; s/d JD16/22) Almost opposite the King Abdullah Mosque, in a similarly quiet neighbourhood, is another good-value and reliable place, with a family feel and pleasant rooms, some bigger than others.

Carlton Hotel (Map p68; ☎ 4654200; jcarlton@joinnet.com.jo; Al-Kulliyah al-Islamiyah St; s/d JD35/45) After a recent renovation the rooms here vary (some are quite luxurious) so check out a few before committing. The staff are friendly and there's a Chinese restaurant, café and basement pub, and it's got a useful location between 2nd and 3rd Circles.

Hisham Hotel (Map p68; ☎ 4644028; www.1stjordan.net/hishamhotel; Mithqal al-Fayez St; s/d high season JD30/40, low season JD25/35; P ⚤ ⬜) You can't go wrong in this excellent choice, in a leafy embassy district a couple of blocks south of the French Embassy. The rooms are comfortable and spacious and there are lots of personal touches; one reason why the place is popular with journalists and diplomats. Prices are often negotiable but you should book in advance. The restaurant (mains from JD5) has nice garden seating in summer.

Shepherd Hotel (Map p68; ☎ /fax 4639197; www.1stjordan.net/shepherd; Zayd bin Harethah St; s/d JD30/40; P ⬜) The Shepherd comes warmly recommended by readers and it's not hard to see why. The rooms are good value and very comfortable, with satellite TV and a fridge, and discounts are often possible. The hotel restaurant is especially good and there's also a bar, café and terrace.

Bellevue Hotel (Map p68; ☎ 4616144; www.bellevue.com.jo; 2nd Circle; s/d JD45/55) A cosy, stylish and comfortable vibe and big bathrooms push this to the upper end of the midrange scale. The four-star facilities include a small health club (sauna and steam room), restaurant and Mövenpick ice-cream café, but the Saudi owners don't allow alcohol in the hotel.

SHMEISANI

Century Park Hotel (Map p85; ☎ 5680090; Tunis St; m.twal@jhtcc.edu.jo; s/d from JD70/85; ⬜ ⚤) Sleek lines and cool cream and brown décor lend this comfortable new four-star business hotel a surprisingly stylish twist. There's a pool, tennis court, bar and terrace, all in a quiet embassy district.

Manar Hotel (Map p85; ☎ 5662186; manarhotel-amman@wanadoo.jo; Abdul Hameed Sharaf St; s/d/tr JD20/26/30; ⚤) Decent value, especially in summer when it's one of the cheapest places in Amman with a swimming pool. Rooms are small and a bit old-fashioned but cosy.

Ambassador Hotel (Map p85; ☎ 5605161; ambashtl@go.com.jo; Abdul Hameed Sharaf St; s/d JD30/40) There's no doubt this is a big tour-group joint, but it's still a good, professionally run and friendly place. The rooms are stuck in bit of a 70s timewarp, with faded pink and brown décor and some kinky mirrors but it's not a bad choice.

Howard Johnson Alqasr Plaza Hotel (Map p85; ☎ 5689671; www.alqasr-hojo.com; 3 Arroub St; s/d JD60/70; ⚤ ⬜) Not your average Howard Johnson, this is probably the closest thing to a boutique hotel in Amman, with an excellent range of restaurants and bars (including Vinaigrette, p93, and Nai, p97) and free access to the Power Hut gym (see p86), a 10-minute walk away. The good service and facilities warrant its four stars. Ask for a free upgrade to an executive room.

WESTERN AMMAN

Ocean Hotel (Map p65; ☎ 5517280; www.oceanhotel.com.jo; Shatt al-Arab St, Umm Utheima; s/d JD37/45) Clean, spacious rooms in a quiet neighbourhood make this a quiet option, with nice terrace seating and a great Lebanese restaurant in-house (see Diwan al-Sultan Ibrahim Restaurant, p94).

Crowne Plaza (Map p65; ☎ 5510001; www.crowneplaza.com; Faisal Bin Abdel Azeez St, 6th Circle; r JD60/70; ⚤) Good value and has excellent facilities, as you'd expect. Restaurants include Mediterranean, a top-floor Arab/Moroccan terrace, the Café Vienna for salads and snacks and a brasserie. Facilities include wi-fi high speed Internet, a good fitness centre, a nightclub, indoor and outdoor pools, a Turkish bath and a tennis court.

Top End

Amman has its share of four- and five-star hotels. Many offer frequently changing rates depending on demand and you'll often get the best deal by booking from abroad or through an online agency. Prices below are walk-in rates at time of research. Prices include breakfast and tax unless otherwise stated.

JEBEL AMMAN

Jordan InterContinental Hotel (Map p68; ☎ 464 1361, 0800 22666; www.amman.intercontinental.com; Al-Kulliyah al-Islamiyah St; d JD77; 🖳) Midway between 2nd and 3rd Circles, the InterCon is suitably luxurious and well-equipped, with a shopping arcade, Royal Jordanian office, a good bookshop, a post office and a deli. There's a cool Mexican bar/restaurant at Cinco de Mayo, plus Indian and Lebanese restaurants, a 24-hour gym, indoor and outdoor pools and wi-fi Internet. All the rooms were refurbished in 2004.

Grand Hyatt Amman (Map p68; ☎ 4651234; www.amman.hyatt.com; Al-Hussein bin Ali St, 3rd Circle; s/d JD106/116; 🗶 🕃 🖳 🖳) Quite a complex, with seven restaurants, a deli, bookshop, JJ's nightclub, indoor and outdoor pools and high-speed Internet. There's a cinema and shopping complex next door.

Hotel Le Royal (Map p68; ☎ 4603000; www.leroyalhotel-amman.com; Zahran St, 3rd Circle; s/d JD95/105 discounted from JD160/170; 🖳) Amman doesn't get more ostentatious than this huge ziggurat-shaped palace, bustling with Gulf sheikhs and oil ministers. Facilities include three pools, a good gym, the biggest spa in Amman, a cinema, 13 restaurants (Japanese, French, Italian, Lebanese, café, pastry shop), a German beer hall, the funky Buddah Bar and an executive floor. Don't expect a lot of cosy intimacy here.

Radisson SAS Hotel (Map p68; ☎ 5607100; fax 5665160; Al-Hussein bin Ali St; d from JD80; 🗶 🕃 🖳 🖳) With a popular rooftop garden and poolside terrace.

SHMEISANI

Kempinski Amman (Map p85; ☎ 5200200; www.kempinski.com; Abdul Hamid Shouman St; rooms from JD120, discounted to JD77) Opened in late 2005, this is the newest place in town, with a good location in the café and restaurant quarter of Shmeisani. Facilities include Cuban and Italian restaurants, high-speed wi-fi Internet, a bowling alley, video games for the kids and cinemas to come.

Amman Marriott (Map p85; ☎ 5607607; www.marriott-middleeast.com; Isam al-Ajlouni St; s/d JD81/95; 🗶 🕃 🖳 🖳) Bright, breezy and informal

is the feel here, with Mediterranean and Italian restaurants and a popular sports bar. The two pools and 24-hour gym will please jet-lagged health nuts. There are six buses (JD6) a day which shuttle guests to its sister property on the Dead Sea.

Le Meridien (Map p85; ☎ 5696511; www.lemeridien.com; Al-Malekah Noor St; s/d old wing JD70/80, new wing JD80/90 without breakfast or tax; 🖳 🗶 🕃 🖳) Grand and stylish. For those vital business first impressions, Le Meridien is grand and stylish but couples may find it too impersonal for that romantic getaway. Still the facilities are good with a gym, pools and a spa, and a great range of restaurants and bars. New wing rooms are worth the extra JD10.

WESTERN AMMAN

Four Seasons (Map p65; ☎ 5505555; www.fourseasons.com/amman; Al-Kindi St, 5th Circle, Jebel Amman; s/d from JD120/130; 🗶 🕃 🖳 🖳) A stylish and designery option with some lovely Art Deco touches. Facilities include large rooms, wi-fi Internet, Italian and Thai restaurants, a spa, squash court (chilled towels!), two pools, free DVD rental and wheelchair accessible rooms.

Sheraton (Map p65; ☎ 5934111; www.sheraton.com; 5th Circle; r JD80 without tax) The Sheraton is another classy option, with all the facilities you'd expect.

EATING

Amman has a wide range of eating options, with budget places concentrated in downtown and, to a lesser extent, Jebel Amman, while the more upmarket restaurants serving Arab and international cuisine are concentrated in Shmeisani and Abdoun.

Budget

If money's an issue, your mainstay in Amman will be felafel, shwarma and roast chicken; these are easy to find in downtown, though bear in mind that not much is open after 9pm. The following are in downtown unless specified.

Hashem Restaurant (Map p82; Al-Amir Mohammed St; hummus 400 fils; ⏰ 24hr) A legendary place which overflows into the alley. It's popular with locals for felafel, hummus and fuul (fava bean paste). A filling meal with bread and mint tea costs less than JD1. As one reader extolled: 'nothing but bread, hummus, fuul and felafel, but everything is fresh and dirt cheap. I love this place!'

THE AUTHOR'S CHOICE

Blue Fig Café (Map p68; ☎ 5928800; Prince Hashem bin al-Hussein St; starters from JD1.650, mains JD4-8; ☺ 8.30am-1am) Travellers always seem to appreciate the global coffeehouse vibe in this supercool place near Abdoun Circle. It's great for almost any occasion, from breakfast to late-night drinks.

The menu is an extensive and imaginative mix of world fusion dishes, strong on pizza-like dishes, and with a wide range of snacks from sushi rolls to baked potatoes (JD2). Try the Bedouin-influenced *gallai* (sautéed tomato, garlic, onion and peppers topped with cheese and pine nuts on Arabic bread; JD3.500). There's also a kids' menu, sinful smoothies (JD1.800) and a full bar. Throw in some seductive world music and the occasional poetry reading and you've got a winner. And, honestly, where else could you get a 'Kyoto green tea and mint flavoured crème brulée'?

Jabri Restaurant (Map p82; ☎ 4624108; Al-Malek al-Hussein St; starters from 500 fils, mains from JD1.800; ☺ 8am-8pm Sat-Thu) Jabri is famed as a pastry place, with branches across town, but the restaurant is also pretty good, with attentive service and decent food. Highlights include *mensaf* (Bedouin dish of lamb on a bed of rice topped with a lamb's head; JD2.400), shish kebabs (JD2.250), fried half chicken (JD1.800) and a bite-sized cheese or meat pie for 200 fils. A plate of fuul for breakfast costs 500 fils. Jabri also has an outlet in Shmeisani.

Jerusalem Restaurant (Al-Quds; Map p82; ☎ 463 0168; Al-Malek al-Hussein St; mains from JD2; ☺ 7am-10pm) Another famed place specialising in sweets and pastries, but with a large restaurant at the back. The menu is in Arabic and sadly most waiters can only be bothered to translate a couple of items before getting huffy. The *mensaf* (JD2.500) is recommended. Lunchtime is busier and better.

Cairo Restaurant (Map p82; ☎ 4624527; Al-Malek Talal St; mains from JD1; ☺ 6am-10pm) This is one place we kept coming back to night after night for the best budget food in downtown. Most of the locals opt for the mutton stews and boiled goat's heads but take it from us you're better off with the excellent *shish tawooq* (JD1.750), which is enough

grilled chicken for two. Alternatively combine a tomatoey *kofta* (mincemeat and spices grilled on a skewer) and a yoghurt for another great meal. There's also *mensaf* and the ever popular chicken *maqlubbeh* (rice with vegetables). It's a clean and pleasant place, just off Sahat al-Malek Faysal al-Awal St, with a family section on the top floor.

Bifa Billa (Map p82; Cinema al-Hussein St; mains from 500 fils; ☺ noon-midnight) One of the better places in downtown for hamburgers and shwarmas.

Fast Meal (Map p82; ☎ 4650037; Hashemi St; meals from JD1.250; ☺ 8am-2am) Superclean and close to the Roman Theatre, you can get a burger/shwarma, fries and juice combo here for JD1.300, though the burgers are pretty anaemic. If nothing else, pop in for one of the superb juice smoothies (600 fils).

Batata (Map p82; ☎ 4656768; Abu Bakr as-Siddiq St; small/large/family fries JD0.600/0.750/1.500; ☺ noon-10pm Sat-Thu, 6pm-late Fri) 'Do one thing and do it good' could well be the motto here; the one thing being French fries, which come with a choice of eight sauces (100 fils each). There are also hot drinks, including cappuccino (750 fils) and hot chocolate (500 fils).

R&B Shawerma (Map p82; ☎ 4645347; Abu Bakr as-Siddiq St; shwarmas JD0.700-1.500; ☺ noon-midnight) Not your average sliced-meat stand, the shwarmas here come in three sizes – 6, 10 and 12 inches – and come in Chinese, chicken and cheese varieties. The fries are good too.

Reem Cafeteria (Map p68; ☎ 4645725; 2nd Circle, Jebel Amman; shwarma JD0.500) There are hundreds of shoebox-sized shwarma dives in Amman but few that have the punters queuing down the street at 3am. Even the royal family are rumoured to have dropped in here for a late-night kebab. And if it's good enough for them…

Lebnani Snack (Map p68; ☎ 5930018; Abdoun Circle) A reliable place for good-value Arabic fast food, such as a cheese and olive sandwich (600 fils). There is an English menu and good juices too. There are four branches around town, including at Abdoun Circle and a good branch on Ilya Abu Madhi St in Shmeisani (Map p85).

Midrange

Abdoun Circle and Shmeisani offer the densest concentration of restaurants in Amman. Abdoun Circle (Map p68) is particularly good if you can't make up your mind; just pick between the dozen or so restaurants and cafés lining the roundabout.

Fakhr el-Din (Map p68; ☎ 4652399; www.fakhreldin.com; 40 Taha Hussein St, Jebel Amman; mezze JD1-2, main meals JD4-5.500; ⏰ 12.30-3.30pm & 7.30-11.30pm) The highly recommended Lebanese food and elegant, classy setting in a 1950s villa make this a great place for a minisplurge. In addition to the extensive à la carte selections of hot and cold mezze and meaty mains, there's also a good set menu for JD10 (minimum four people), which is good value. Alcohol is served. It's about two blocks behind the Iraqi Embassy in Jebel Amman.

Abu Ahmad Orient Restaurant (Map p68; ☎ 464 1879; www.abuahmedorient.com; 3rd Circle, Jebel Amman; mezze JD0.600-1.500, mains JD2-4.500; ⏰ noon-midnight) Another excellent midrange Lebanese place, with a particularly nice outdoor terrace in summer. The standard grilled meats are all present here but the real highlights are the hot and cold mezze. Try a *buraik* (meat or cheese pie; JD1) or *yalenjeh* (stuffed vine leaves; JD1.250). Lunch specials are a steal at JD4 and the set menu for three costs JD7 to JD8 per person.

Books@café (Map p82; ☎ 4650457; Omar bin al-Khattab, downtown; mains from JD2.500; ⏰ 10am-midnight) For a slice of coffeehouse chic and good Western food this mellow restaurant, bar and café is hard to beat. Genuine Italian pizzas (JD3.500 to JD5) and pasta (from JD2.500) are joined by good salads (JD3). The food is excellent, the service discreet and the atmosphere supercool with plenty of hip young Jordanians lounging on sofas in cosy corners. Hot drinks are a steep JD2, although the 'hot strawberry' may just be worth it. The bar area has a decent selection of wines (JD4 a glass) and beers (JD2 to JD4.500). The special Friday brunch (9am to 1pm; JD5), with French toast and pancakes, is great value.

Wild Jordan Café (Map p82; ☎ 4633542; Othman Bin Affan St, downtown; ⏰ 11am-midnight; mains JD4.500-7.500; ☒ ▣) After checking out the Wild Nature shop, grab a bite at this stylish and modern café. The emphasis is on light and healthy, with smoothies, wraps and organic salads, plus strong veggie options like the spinach and mushroom salad. The glass walls and open-air terrace offer terrific views over Amman, particularly at night. On Fridays and Saturdays there's a great breakfast (JD5) with apple muesli, pancakes and smoked salmon with cottage cheese. Many dishes incorporate fresh organic herbs brought in from the RSCN's nature reserve projects.

Noodasia (Map p68; ☎ 5936999; Abdoun Circle; mains JD4-5) The shiny chrome and dark woods of this stylish pan-Asian diner feel like they have been lifted straight from the cooler quarters of Shanghai. The menu stretches to Chinese, Thai and Japanese snacks and main dishes. The green curries, Thai beef salad and sushi combos are all good and the service is excellent.

Ristorante Casereccio (Map p68; ☎ 5934722; Abdoun Circle; pizzas JD2-4, pastas JD4, mains JD5-6; ⏰ 1-4pm & 7pm-midnight) An unpretentious and casual pizza and pasta place just off the trendy Abdoun Circle. Save space for the Nutella-stuffed pizza with strawberries.

Vinaigrette (Map p85; ☎ 5695481; Howard Johnson Alqasr Plaza Hotel, 3 Arroub St, Shmeisani; mains JD6-12) Salad and sushi rule at this unique and stylish restaurant on the top floor of the Howard Johnson Hotel. Build your own salads (from JD1.950) or try a sushi combo (JD7 to JD18). The daily specials are also worth a look. Mellow jazz complements the superb views over the city, making it a great place for a light dinner before hitting the dance floor downstairs at Nai (p97). The food is brought to you by the same people who run Fakhr el-Din and Wild Jordan Café.

Whispers (Map p65; ☎ 5921850; Abdul Rahman Alawi St, Umm Utheina; sandwiches JD3-4, mains JD6-9) A short walk from the Sheraton, Whispers is a good choice for quality Western food. The contemporary décor is fun (baby sharks circle the huge fish tanks eyeing up all the customers' steaks), it has a good bar and there's one of the best salad bars in town (JD6). Vegetarians will like the tofu scramble.

There are several decent Chinese restaurants in town including the good-value **Shanghai Restaurant** (Map p68; ☎ 4619945; Abbas Mahmoud al-Aqad St, Jebel Amman; dishes JD1.500-2) and the authentic **Taiwan Tourismo** (Map p65; ☎ 5924670; Abdul Rahman Alawi St, Umm Utheina; dishes from JD2; ⏰ noon-3.30pm & 6.30-11.30pm). The latter has great General Tso's chicken and toffee bananas.

Top End

Amman's most classy and expensive places are in Shmeisani or Western Amman, so unless you're staying there, factor in taxi fares to the total bill for the evening. Remember

AMMAN

that most top-end places add a whopping 26% tax to the quoted prices. The places listed below are those we consider to be worth the splurge. All the places listed below are air-conditioned.

Bonita Inn (Map p68; ☎ 4615061; off Al-Kulliyah al-Islamiyah St, Jebel Amman; tapas JD1.500-5.500, mains JD7-8; ☽ noon-midnight) A very good choice with European (primarily Spanish) cuisine and tapas is this inn with a romantic, rustic farmhouse feel. The steaks have a citywide reputation, while the paella Valenciana (JD15 for two; 30 minutes required) and gazpacho soup are as good as you'll get in Amman. Other highlights include the extensive tapas menu, with plenty of calamari, octopus and salads, and wide-ranging wine list. Grab a pre-dinner drink in the pub next door as your paella simmers to perfection. It's near 3rd Circle.

La Terrasse (Map p85; ☎ 5662831; 11 August St, Shmeisani; mezze JD1.250, mains JD5-9, bottle of wine JD20-25; ☽ 1pm-1am) Does decent European cuisine, strong on steaks, in a pleasant and low-key setting. The wine list is extensive, with labels representing Jordan and much of the Mediterranean rim (JD20 to JD25 a bottle). Most nights after 10pm the tiny stage is given over to live Arab singers and musicians, making it a popular venue for well-to-do local families.

Houston's (Map p85; ☎ 5620610; off Abdul Hameed Shoman St, Shmeisani; starters JD2.900-4.500, mains JD5-9; ☽ noon-midnight) A popular American-style family restaurant that gets good reviews from homesick expats. It specialises in Mexican dishes and margaritas (JD4.500), but it also does steaks, burgers and a good salad bar (JD5.500; open noon to 5pm Sunday to Thursday) – you know the deal.

Tannoureen Restaurant (Map p65; ☎ 5515987; Shatt al-Arab St, Umm Utheina; starters JD1-3, mains JD4-9; ☽ 12.30-4.30pm & 7.30-11.30pm) Worth the trek for good Lebanese food, especially mezzes (try the spinach and pine-nut pie) and salads, but it also does a wide selection of Western dishes, grills and fish (around JD8). Reserve a table in the bright and airy conservatory. The restaurant is easily missed – look for the green wall.

Diwan al-Sultan Ibrahim Restaurant (Map p65; ☎ 5517383; Ocean Hotel, Shatt al-Arab St, Umm Utheina; starters JD1-2, mains JD3.750-8; ☽ noon-midnight) The Diwan comes highly recommended by wealthy locals and expats for its quality Arab food. Among the entrées are frogs legs with garlic and coriander (JD5.500) and deep-fried brains (JD2.250), the latter an acquired taste. The fresh fish selection is good, the *batrkh* (roe) is popular, and there are good salads and some Western dishes.

Romero Restaurant (Map p68; ☎ 4644227; www .romero-jordan.com; Mohammed Hussein Haikal St, Jebel Amman; mains JD6-10) Without doubt the best Italian restaurant in town: upmarket, formal and a stone's throw from the InterContinental Hotel. The salads are imaginative (chicken with rocca, mushroom, orange, pine nuts in a honey balsamic dressing), as are the steaks, seafood (red snapper and mussels) and a wide range of pasta and risotto. Desserts are predictably wonderful – crêpes with crème de banana, Grand Marnier and Cointreau, or homemade hazelnut and vanilla ice cream. Reservations are recommended. It's part of the Romero chain with branches in Aqaba, Pella, Umm Qais and Madaba.

Reem al-Bawadi (Map p65; ☎ 5515419; Tlaa al-Ali, Jubilee Gardens; starters JD1, mains JD3-6) and **Tawaheen al-Hawa** (Map p65; ☎ 5349986; Wasfi al-Tal Rd, Jubilee Gardens; mains JD3-6) are two huge restaurant complexes popular with tour groups and Jordanian families. They're a bit far from the centre but are a good option if you want to try some upper-end Jordanian and Lebanese food. Both menus include a wide range of mezze and grills, giving you a chance to explore beyond the normal felafel and hummus dishes. You can eat on brass tables in the cavernous main halls or in Bedouin tents, either way the live music gets things going between 10pm and midnight. The Reem has a traditional bread oven and is perhaps better for couples. If you're headed to Tawaheen al-Hawa, look for the windmill symbol on the wall as there's no English sign.

The top-end hotels all have good restaurants. The Grand Hyatt (p91) has a weekly seafood buffet (JD19; currently Wednesday) and a Friday brunch (JD12.500) in its Grand Café, with Belgian waffles and a kids' clown. The Four Seasons (p91) serves afternoon tea (JD12) from 4pm to 7pm in its classy foyer and terrace. Local expats flock to the wi-fi Internet, deli sandwiches (JD4) and wide selection of wines at the Deli Café in the Jordan InterContinental Hotel (p91).

Patisseries & Ice-Cream Parlours

Sweet tooths can find a spiritual home just about anywhere in Amman. **Habibah** (Map p82; Al-Malek al-Hussein St, downtown) is probably the best bet for Middle Eastern sweets and pastries, though the other long-time stalwarts Jerusalem Restaurant (p92) and Jabri Restaurant (p92) next door are also great. Habibah has a phenomenally busy takeaway branch a couple of minutes southeast in an alley off Al-Malek Faisal St.

Ata Ali (Map p85; ☎ 5812310; Abdul Hameed Sharaf St, Shmeisani; ☷ 7.30am-midnight) Does excellent sweets and ice creams.

Gérard's (Map p68; Abdoun Circle; desserts JD1-3) As soon as you get a whiff of this sweet, hot and sticky place you'll be hooked. It's all about hot waffles, ice cream, shakes, crêpes, frozen yoghurt and iced coffees. Think Brad Pitt in *Thelma and Louise* – all bad but, oh, sooo good.

Caffe Mokka (Map p68; ☎ 5926285; Al-Qahira St, Abdoun; ☷ 7.30am-11pm) A good place to start; serves pastries (from 500 fils) and delicious cakes (from JD1.200), as well as sandwiches and great coffee (JD1.500). There's a breakfast buffet on Fridays (8.30am to noon; JD7).

Self-Catering

Although there are small grocery stores throughout the capital, the larger supermarkets are located in the more affluent and remote suburbs.

There is an outlet of **Safeway** (Map p85; ☎ 5685311; Nasser bin Jameel St, Shmeisani; ☷ 24hr) around 500m southwest of the Sports City junction, and another **Safeway** (Map p65; ☎ 5815558; Sweifieh) just southwest of 7th Circle.

C-Town Shopping Centre (Map p65; ☎ 5815558; Zahran St, Sweifieh; ☷ 7am-midnight) also has a branch close to 7th Circle, as well as in Shmeisani (Map p85; Abdul Hameed Sharaf St; ☷ 7am-midnight).

More central is **Haboob Grand Stores** (Map p68; ☎ 4622221; Al-Kulliyah al-Islamiyah St, Jebel Amman; ☷ 7am-midnight), between 1st and 2nd circles; it sometimes closes on Fridays.

DRINKING

There is plenty of nightlife in Amman, although little that's salubrious in the downtown area. The areas of Shmeisani, Abdoun and, to a lesser extent, Jebel Amman have numerous trendy cafés, bars and a few nightclubs that stay open late, some of which have live music.

Bars

Several bars in downtown, patronised almost exclusively by men, are tucked away in the alleys near the Cliff Hotel. If you're willing to move beyond downtown, there are a range of enjoyable options where women will feel much more comfortable.

MOSTLY MEN

Orient Bar & Restaurant (Map p82; ☎ 4636069; off Al-Amir Mohammed St, downtown; beer from JD1.750; ☷ 11am-late) Also known as 'Al-Sharq', this is a spit-and-sawdust bar that serves a range of beers, spirits and the local arak (if you dare) for JD4. Cheap meals are also available with the slowest service in central Amman thrown in at no extra cost. If you've had a bit to drink, mind your head on the stairs on the way down.

Salamon Bar (Map p82; ☎ 079 5902940; off Al-Amir Mohammed St, downtown; ☷ noon-midnight) Next to the entrance to the Venecia Hotel; this is more modern than the others mentioned here and has beer on tap, but it's tiny and full of smoke.

Other local dives include the **Auberge Café** (Map p82; Al-Amir Mohammed St, downtown; ☷ 10am-midnight) and **Jordan Bar** (Map p82; ☎ 079 5796352; off Al-Amir Mohammed St; ☷ 10am-midnight), a cosy place with an earthy charm that hasn't changed in years. A large Amstel here costs JD1.750.

WOMEN WELCOME

Among the midrange hotels, Hisham Hotel (p90) has a cosy 'English pub' where a pint of draught lager costs about JD2.500.

Rovers Return (Map p65; ☎ 5814844; Ali Nasouh al-Taher St, Sweifieh; beer JD2.750-4.300; ☷ 1pm-late) A godsend for homesick *Coronation St* junkies, this is a popular and cosy English pub with wood panelling and a lively atmosphere, though the drinks aren't cheap at JD4.300 (over US$6) for a pint of Kilkenny. The comfort food (mains JD4.500 to JD5.500) includes authentic fish and chips and roast beef with gravy. The entrance is round the back of the building and can be hard to find; look for the red 'Comfort Suites' sign.

Big Fellow Irish Pub (Map p68; ☎ 5934766; Abdoun Circle; pint of Guinness/Kilkenny JD4.600; ☷ noon-2am) It looks like an Irish pub, it even smells like an Irish pub, but with Arabic music sliding out of the stereo, it doesn't really sound like an Irish pub. If in doubt, tucking into a Guinness pie (JD5.500) and a bread and butter pudding (JD2.500) should put you in the right frame of mind. There are live screenings of international sports events. As it's run by the Sheraton, prices for food and drinks are higher than elsewhere, with 26% tax.

Grappa (Map p68; ☎ 4651458; Abdul Qader Koshak St, Jebel Amman; beer JD2.500-4, mains JD2.500-7.500; ☗ 6pm-1.30am) Stylish wooden benches and B&W photos on the wall give this rustic bar a hip feel but it's the views, huge windows and summer terrace seating that really draw the crowds. There are decent pizzas, salads and *manaqeesh* (Arabic bread with herbs) but the drinking takes priority.

Champions (Map p85; ☎ 5607607; Amman Marriott, Isam al-Ajlouni St, Shmeisani; ☗ 6pm-midnight) An upmarket but popular American-style sports bar at the Amman Marriott.

Living Room (Map p68; ☎ 4655988; Mohammed Hussein Haikal St; ☗ 1pm-1am) Part lounge, part sushi bar and part study (think high-backed chairs, a fireplace and today's newspaper), the Living Room is so understated that it's easily missed. There's a full bar and quality bar meals, from North American steaks to salmon with cream cheese. The fine music seals it as a great place to hang out over a delicious iced tea with lemon grass and mint.

Blue Fig Café (p92) is a great place to spend an afternoon or evening, with a chic crowd, pleasant atmosphere, live music on most Wednesday and Saturday nights and occasional exhibitions. A glass of wine costs JD1.700 to JD3.

Cafés & Juice Bars

Some of the cafés in downtown are great places to watch the world go by, write letters, smoke a scented nargileh, meet locals and play cards or backgammon. The first group of cafés listed below are generally men only with scarcely a local woman to be seen, although foreign women with some gumption and very modest attire, especially if accompanied by a male, will be welcome.

MOSTLY MEN

Arab League Café (Map p82; Al-Malek Faisal St, downtown; ☗ 10am-midnight) This is a popular male domain, full of retirees playing cards.

Auberge Café (Map p82; Al-Amir Mohammed St, downtown; ☗ 10am-midnight) One floor below the Cliff Hotel and very popular with local men. You'll have to make your way through the tobacco haze to reach the balcony which overlooks the main street and is a good place to smoke a nargileh (JD1). There are no pretensions to luxury but it wears a certain downmarket authenticity as a result.

Peace Café (Map p82; ☎ 079 5297912; Al-Amir Mohammed St, downtown; ☗ 9am-midnight) This place is reached via a filthy staircase and is fairly basic, but if you can get one of the two balcony tables overlooking the street, you'll have one of the prime vantage points in downtown.

WOMEN WELCOME

Around Hashemite Sq and along Hashemi St, the dozen or more cafés are decent places for people-watching, especially in summer.

The place in Amman to be seen at night is anywhere around Abdoun Circle and there are plenty of very cool cafés. You could probably take your pick – fashions change frequently in this part of Amman.

Al-Rashid Court Café (Map p82; ☎ 4652994; Al-Malek Faisal St, downtown; tea or coffee 400 fils; ☗ 10am-midnight Sat-Thu, 1-11pm Fri) Also known as the Eco-Tourism Café, the 1st-floor balcony here is the place to pass an afternoon and survey the chaos of the downtown area below. Competition for seats is fierce! It's also one of the best places for the uninitiated to try a nargileh (JD1.250). Although you won't see any local women here, they're well accustomed to foreign tourists. To find it look for the flags of the world on the main façade; the entrance is down the side alley.

Al-Sendabad Coffee Shop (Map p82; downtown; ☎ 4632035; ☗ 10am-midnight) About 150m west of the Roman Theatre, this place has great views over the city (though not the theatre) and is kept clean by the friendly staff. It's a great place to smoke the nargileh (JD1), especially on the roof in summer.

Shaher's Penthouse Cafeteria (Map p82; Sahat al-Malek Faysal al-Awal St, downtown; coffee 500 fils; ☗ 9.30am-11pm) Has a traditionally decorated indoor dining area and a better outdoor terrace overlooking the street far below. Hussein, the resident musician, will happily play the oud or violin to provide a cultured counterpoint to the street noise below.

Darat al-Funun (Map p82; Nimer bin Adwan St, downtown; drinks 300 fils) Definitely the most peaceful place to escape from downtown, surrounded by the ruins of a Byzantine church and the ghosts of TE Lawrence. Drinks are cheap, with coffee at JD1 and tea for 300 fils.

El Farouki (Map p85; ☎ 5678580; 11 August St, Shmeisani; coffee JD1.500) Not hip but a solid old-fashioned coffee shop if you need a quiet break, with good coffee, crêpes and cakes. The coffee comes with a biscuit, a chocolate and 26% tax.

Tche Tche Café (Map p68; ☎ 5932020; Abdoun Circle; ☽ 10am-11pm) You'll have to arrive early to get a seat in this bright and buzzy café. Far from a traditional teahouse it's full of Jordanian women smoking the nargileh, sipping on fruit smoothies and nodding their heads to Arabic pop. The ice cream and pecan waffles are great.

Palestine Juice (Map p82; Al-Malek Faisal St; ☽ 7am-11pm) An overflowingly fertile juice stand that serves refreshing carrot or orange juice, or banana with milk for 500 fils (small glass) or JD1 (large).

ENTERTAINMENT
Cinemas
There are several modern cinema complexes that offer recent releases. Tickets cost JD4 before 6pm and JD5 after 6pm but the quality of sound, vision and chairs is high. Programmes for cinemas are advertised in the English-language newspapers (see p67).

Century Cinemas (Map p68; ☎ 4613200; www .century-cinemas.com; 3rd Circle, Jebel Amman) In the Zara Centre behind the Grand Hyatt, with several fast-food outlets.

Cine Le Royal (Map p68; ☎ 4603022; 3rd Circle)

Galleria (Map p68; ☎ 5934793; Abdoun Circle)

Grand Theaters (Map p65 ☎ 5518411; Mecca Mall) Far from the centre unless you are shopping.

A few other cinemas show kung fu flicks and other B-grade movies but these are often dubbed into Arabic and, apart from the violence, are heavily censored. In downtown, the better ones are **Al-Hussein Cinema** (Map p82; Cinema al-Hussein St) and the **Raghadan** (Map p82; Basman St).

Also in downtown, Books@café (p93) has film nights on Mondays (JD2). The various cultural centres (p66) also show foreign films regularly.

Exhibitions & Music
The various foreign cultural centres regularly organise lectures, exhibitions and also musical recitals. The large, modern **Royal Cultural Centre** (Map p85; ☎ 5661026; Al-Malekah Alia St, Shmeisani) occasionally hosts concerts and plays, usually in Arabic, as does the **King Hussein Cultural Centre** (Map p68; ☎ 4739953; Omar Matar St, Al-Muhajareen). Events are sometimes advertised in the local English-language newspapers.

Darat al-Funun (p83) often features recitals of classical and traditional music; check with the gallery for a schedule of upcoming events. The Jordan National Gallery of Fine Arts (p84) sometimes has visiting exhibitions of contemporary art.

Nightclubs
JJ's (Map p68; Grand Hyatt Amman, Al-Hussein bin Ali St, Jebel Amman; admission Thu JD5; ☽ 8.30pm-late Mon-Sat) The Grand Hyatt's disco is particularly popular on Thursday night when you'll pay for the privilege of rubbing shoulders with Amman's beautiful people.

Harir Lounge (Map p68; ☎ 5925205; Abdoun Circle; ☽ 1pm-1am, until 3am Sat & Sun) Less style and more glamour at this ostentatious upper-floor lounge and restaurant. DJs or a live band (Monday and Thursday) provide the bass and there are sometimes international DJs on the weekends.

Nai (Map p85; ☎ 5689671; Howard Johnson Alqasr Plaza Hotel, 3 Arroub St, Shmeisani; ☽ 6pm-2am) A Howard Johnson hotel is not the first place you'd look for a superhip Ottoman-style lounge/club/mezze bar but Nai is definitely one of the hottest places in town. Mondays and Thursdays get people off the sofas with international DJs and a cover charge (JD10; bookings advised) and there's an Arabic band the first Thursday of the month. The daily specials (6pm to 9pm) are a nice touch, from Saturday and Tuesdays all-you-can-eat sushi (JD15) to Wednesday's all-you-can-drink cocktails (JD10).

Kanabayé (Map p68; ☎ 4642830; 3rd Circle, Jebel Amman) A quieter cool place for a drink, the low orange couches (*kanabayé* in Arabic) and dark seductive browns lend this lounge bar a sexy feel and there's a summer terrace during the day. Thursday is clubbing night, Friday and Saturdays have DJs, Wednesday is Ladies' Night and Tuesday is Latin salsa night.

AMMAN

Sport

Football (soccer) is followed religiously by most locals. The capital's two main teams are Wahadat (generally supported by Palestinians) and Faisaly (supported by other Jordanians). The games are mostly played on Friday at the Amman International Stadium, located near Sports City in Shmeisani (around JD2).

SHOPPING

Amman is the best place in Jordan to shop for souvenirs. There are several high-quality handicraft boutiques, concentrated on Rainbow St and near the InterContinental Hotel, which are run to benefit women, threatened communities and the environment. The main hotels also have branches of the top-end Souq Zara boutiques.

For the latest in Saddam Hussein memorabilia (bank notes, photos etc), check out the stalls en route to the Roman Theatre in downtown.

Mall mania is sweeping through areas of Amman. The biggest monster is **Mecca Mall** (Map p65; ☎ 5527945; Makkah al-Mukarramah Rd) in the northwestern suburbs, with a cinema, bowling alley, video arcade and dozens of restaurants. **Abdoun Mall** (Map p65; ☎ 5920246; Al Umawiyeen St) is a smaller version of the same thing. More are bound to follow.

Amman has a **duty-free shop** (Map p85; ☎ 5678147; Tunis St, Shmeisani; ☒ 8am-10pm Sat-Thu, 2-10pm Fri) Tourists can buy duty-free products here, including 1L of booze and 200 cigarettes, during the first 14 days of their visit. Bring your passport.

Photography & Film

There are plenty of places around town that sell film, although the better places for developing tend to be in Shmeisani or Abdoun. You can get passport photos taken on the spot in downtown at places on Al-Malek al-Hussein, Hashemi, Al-Malek Talal and Quraysh Sts.

Salam Centre (Map p68; ☎ 5922744; Abdoun Circle; ☒ 9am-9pm) One good place, among many, offering memory cards, battery chargers and video cassettes.

Souvenirs

Al-Alaydi Jordan Craft Centre (Map p68; ☎ /fax 4644555; off Al-Kulliyah al-Islamiyah St, Jebel Amman; ☒ 9am-6pm Sat-Thu) It's difficult to leave here

without spending money, with an overwhelming selection spread over several floors. Items include jewellery, Hebron glassware, Palestinian embroidery, kilims and wood carvings, with old kitchen implements and Bedouin tent accessories on the top floor. Prices are marked in both dinars and US dollars.

Al-Burgan (Map p68; ☎ 4652585; www.alburgan .com; 12 Tala't Harb St; ☒ 9.30am-6.30pm Sat-Thu) Has a smaller selection of items but the staff are knowledgeable and prices are reasonable. It's behind Jordan InterContinental Hotel.

Artisana (Map p68; ☎ /fax 4647858; Mansour Kraishan St, Jebel Amman; ☒ 9.30am-6pm Sat-Thu) In the same area, this is another excellent smaller showroom with a wide range that includes scarves, bottles of holy water from the Jordan River and repros of the famous 6000-year-old statues from Ain Ghazal.

Bawabet al-Sharq (Map p82; ☎ 4637424; Abu Bakr as-Siddiq St; ☒ 9am-7pm) The 'Gate of the Orient' has locally made (some on site) home décor items tending towards the kitsch. Sales benefit several Jordanian women's groups.

Beit al-Bawadi (Map p65; ☎ 5930070; Fawzi al-Qawoaji St; ☒ 9am-6pm Sat-Thu) The place for quality ceramics, created to support local artisans, who you can see working in the basement. Designs are both traditional and modern (lampshades and dinner sets), some decorated with Arabic calligraphy, and pieces cost around JD30 to JD60. The top floor has the discounted items. Credit cards are accepted.

Jordan River Foundation (Map p82; ☎ 4613081; Bani Hamida House, Fawzi al-Malouf St, downtown; ☒ 8.30am-7pm Sat-Thu, 10am-6pm Fri) There's an emphasis on home design here, with cushions, camel bags, candles, embroidery, baskets (from Wadi Rayan in the Jordan Valley) and Dead Sea products, all at high prices to match the high quality. Also here is the showroom of Bani Hamada (see p163), which has excellent community-made weavings (a 1.8m by 1.27m weaving costs JD297).

Oriental Souvenirs Store (Map p68; ☎ 4642820; 3rd Circle, Jebel Amman; ☒ 8am-7pm Sat-Thu) More rustic than the others listed here but it's something of an Aladdin's Cave. It's friendly and family run.

Silsal Ceramics (Map p65; ☎ 5931128; Innabeh St, North Abdoun; ☒ 9am-6pm Sat-Thu) Has a small showroom of superb modern pottery with price tags that are surprisingly reasonable. If you're coming along Zahran St from 5th Circle, it's the third small street on the right.

Wild Jordan (Map p82; ☎ 4633587; Othman bin Affan St, downtown; ⏰ 9am-7pm) The nature store at the Wild Jordan Centre sells ecotourism products made in Jordan's nature reserves, including silver, organic herbs and jams from Dana, painted ostrich eggs from Shaumari, and candles made by Bedouin women as part of an income-generation project in Feinan, all decorated with unique nature-inspired designs. All profits go back to the craftspeople and the nature reserve projects.

GETTING THERE & AWAY

For information about international services to/from Amman, see p254.

Air

Amman is the main arrival and departure point for international flights, although some touch down in Aqaba as well.

Royal Jordanian Airlines head office (Map p85; ☎ 5607300; www.rja.com.jo; Al-Malekah Noor St) is inconveniently located in the Housing Bank Centre (9th floor) in Shmeisani. There are more convenient offices in the **Jordan InterContinental** (Map p68; ☎ 4644267; fax 4642152) and along **Al-Malek al-Hussein St** (Map p68; ☎ /fax 5663525), up from the Abdali bus station.

The Royal Jordanian subsidiary, **Royal Wings** (☎ 4875201; fax 4875656), has an office at Marka Airport, but it's easier to book and confirm tickets at any Royal Jordanian office in town.

See p254 for a list and contact details of airlines offices that fly to Amman.

Bus

Tickets for private buses should be booked at least one day in advance.

BUS, MINIBUS & SERVICE TAXIS

At the time of research, the three main bus stations in Amman were Abdali bus station for transport to the north and west, Wahadat bus station for the south, and Raghadan bus station for Amman and nearby towns.

However, the Abdali bus station has been slated for closure for some years now, with services due to move to a new station on the northern outskirts in Tabarbor, or possibly to the newly rebuilt Raghadan bus station in downtown. Ask your hotel or the Ministry of Tourism office for more information.

Service taxis are generally faster and take less time to fill, but they're also more expensive. They depart from the same stations as the minibuses and departures are more frequent in the morning.

Abdali Station

Abdali bus station (Map p68; Al-Malek al-Hussein St) is a 20-minute walk (2km uphill) from downtown; service taxi 6 or 7 from Cinema al-Hussein St goes right by. Regular service taxis depart Abdali for Wahadat bus station (150 fils) throughout the day.

Minibuses take up the top end of the station, then (going downhill) there are the service taxis, private bus company offices, service taxis for Irbid, King Hussein Bridge and Damascus and then buses for Madaba and Mafraq.

From Abdali, minibuses leave for the following destinations (when full):

Destination	Cost (fils)	Duration (hr)
Ajlun	500	2
Deir Alla (for Pella)	500	1
Fuheis	150	¾
Irbid	600	2
Jerash	400	1¼
Madaba	270	¾
Ramtha	500	2
Salt	200	¾
Zarqa	200	½

From Abdali station, there are also service taxis to Irbid (JD1), Ramtha (JD1), Salt (450 fils, 45 minutes) and the King Hussein Bridge (JD2, 45 minutes), as well as international destinations (see p257).

It's worth bearing in mind that there are far fewer departures on Friday, when the lower half of the bus station is transformed into a giant flea market.

Raghadan Station

The newly renovated Raghadan station (Map p82) in downtown Amman is a few minutes' walk east of the Roman Theatre. It had not reopened at time of research but expect it to operate service taxis (for surrounding suburbs), local city buses and, most probably, minibuses to Madaba (270 fils, 45 minutes), Salt (200 fils, 45 minutes), Wadi as-Seer (200 fils, 30 minutes) and Zarqa (200 fils, 30 minutes).

AMMAN

Wahadat Station

Almost all buses and service taxis headed south leave from Wahadat station (Map p65), way out in the southern suburbs by Middle East Circle (Duwaar Sharq al-Awsat). To reach the station, take a service taxi or bus 23 from Abdali station, or service taxi 27 from Italian St (Map p82). A private taxi will cost around JD1 from downtown.

For Petra (actually Wadi Musa) minibuses and service taxis (JD3) depart when full from the far corner of the lot between around 7am and 4pm. The local fare is JD1.800 but minibus drivers almost always charge foreigners JD3. If you have a dispute over fares go to the nearby blue huts of the tourist police. A chartered service taxi should cost JD15 to Petra.

Buses to Aqaba (JD3.500, five hours) leave every hour or so until midnight. There are regular buses to Karak (800 fils, two hours), Shobak (JD1.500, 2½ hours) and Ma'an (JD1.100, three hours). Most services dry up around 4pm.

For Dana there is one bus a day at around 11am for Qadsiyya (JD1.500, three hours); otherwise take a bus to Tafila (JD1.100, 2½ hours) and change.

Buses and minibuses also leave regularly for Madaba (350 fils, 1 hour) but it's more convenient to catch one from Abdali or Raghadan station.

There are semiregular service taxis to Karak (JD1.400, two hours), Ma'an (JD1.200, three hours) and also infrequently to Aqaba (JD5, four hours).

Muhajireen Bus Station

If you want to go to the Dead Sea, minibuses leave from the small minibus station opposite the Muhajireen Police Station (the corner of Al-Ameerah Basma bin Talal Rd and Ali bin Abi Taleb Rd; see Map p68). You may find a local bus direct to Suweimah (600 fils) or even Amman Beach; if not you'll have to go to Shuneh al-Janubiyyeh (South Shuna; 500 fils, 45 minutes) and change for Suweimah, from where you'll have to hitch.

Minibuses leave frequently from the same station for Wadi as-Seer (130 fils, 30 minutes).

PRIVATE COACHES

The domestic **JETT office** (Map p85; ☎ 5664146; Al-Malek al-Hussein St, Shmeisani) is about 500m north-west of the Abdali bus station. Services to Petra and Hammat Ma'in have been cut in recent years but it might be worth asking if they've been reinstated. There are currently five buses daily to Aqaba (JD4.300, four hours) between 7am and 5pm and one bus to King Hussein Bridge (JD6.500, one hour, 6.30am), for crossings into Israel & the Palestinian Territories.

Trust International Transport (Map p65; ☎ 581 3427) has seven daily buses to Aqaba (JD5, four hours) between 7.30am and 7pm. All buses leave from the office inconveniently located at 7th Circle, near the Safeway shopping centre – it's best to charter a taxi to/from downtown. Trust also has a **booking office** (Map p68; ☎ 4644627) at the Abdali bus station.

Afana (Map p85; ☎ 4614611) is a slightly less reliable private company with five departures a day to Aqaba (JD3.500) between 7am and 7pm from its office next to the JETT International office.

Hijazi (Map p68; ☎ 4638110) has regular buses to Irbid (870 fils, 1½ hours) from Abdali station.

Car

Listed are some of the more reliable car-rental agencies. Most take major credit cards and offer cars no more than three years old. Read p265 before hiring a car. Most companies have an office at Abdullah Gardens (Map p85), where there is a collection of around 50 car-rental companies, allowing you to shop around and compare prices. Charges, conditions and insurance costs (and waiver fees in case of accident) can vary considerably; most don't include 16% tax. The smaller companies offer compact cars for as low as JD15 per day but aren't as reliable as the bigger players listed here:

Avis (Map p85; ☎ 5699420, 24hr 777-397405; www .avis.com.jo; King Abdullah Gardens) Branches at the airport, Hotel Le Royal and Hotel InterContinental. Daily rate from JD30. Free drop off at King Hussein Bridge or the airport; elsewhere JD25.

Budget (Map p85; ☎ 5698131; budget@go.com.jo; 125 Abdul Hameed Sharaf St) Charges from JD25 per day including unlimited kilometres and theft insurance.

Eagle Rent-a-Car (Map p85; ☎ 5693399, 24hr ☎ 079 5546021; eaglerentacar@wanadoo.jo; Abdul Hameed Sharaf St) Rates start from JD25 per day with unlimited kilometres, plus JD7 Collision Damage Waiver (CDW) per day.

Europcar (Map p85; ☎ 5655581; Isam Al-Ajlouni St; www.europcar.jo) Branches at Radisson SAS and Abdullah

Gardens. Weekly hire JD140, CDW JD10 per day, free drop in Aqaba. Contact Jeff Abdel Massih.

Firas Car Rental (Map p68; ☎ 4612927, 079 5846454; alamo@nets.com.jo; 1st Circle) Rates are JD25 to JD28 per day with unlimited kilometres. CDW is JD7 per day. Firas is the agent for Alamo Car Rental.

Hertz (Map p85; ☎ 5624191, 24hr line at airport ☎ 4711771; www.hertz.com; King Abdullah Gardens). Offices at the airport, Grand Hyatt & Sheraton. Daily/weekly rates JD35/210. CDW costs JD10 per day with no deductible, or JD7 with a deductible of JD100. Drop off at offices in Aqaba, Petra or Mövenpick Dead Sea Resort cost JD20.

National Car Rental (Map p85; ☎ /fax 5601350, 24hr line ☎ 079 5591731; www.1stjordan.net/national) Offices in Amman Marriott, Le Meridien & Shepherd Hotels. Charges are from JD25 per day (including CDW); daily/weekly rates around JD30/200.

Reliable Rent-a-Car (Map p65; ☎ 5929676, 079 5521358; www.reliable.com.jo; 19 Fawzi al-Qawoaji St, Abdoun) Cars JD20 to JD25, CDW JD5 extra. Offers free drop off and pick up in Madaba and the airport, will deliver the car to you anywhere in Amman and even drive you to the edge of town if you are nervous about Amman traffic. Baby seats are available. You can reserve online; contact Mohammed Hallak.

GETTING AROUND
To/From the Airports

Queen Alia International Airport is 35km south of the city. The **Airport Express bus** (Map p68; ☎ 0880 022006; 4451531) runs between the airport and the upper end of Abdali station, passing through the 4th, 5th, 6th and 7th Circles en route. Buses (JD1.500, 45 minutes) run every half-hour or so between 7am and midnight. From the airport, buses depart from outside the arrivals hall of Terminal 2. Buy your ticket from the booth at the door. The last buses to the airport leave at 10pm and midnight; the first bus leaves at 6am.

With the impending scaling down of the Abdali bus station, the service could shift to either the new station at Tabarbor or the Raghadan bus station.

Anyone travelling on Royal Jordanian can check in their bags, pay the departure tax (JD5) and catch a shuttle bus (JD2, half-hourly between 8am and 9pm) to Queen Alia International Airport from the **Royal Jordanian city terminal** (Map p65; ☎ 5856855; fax 5857224), but it's inconveniently located on 7th Circle. Make sure to check in at least three hours before departure.

There are branches of **Avis** (☎ 4459040) and **Hertz** (☎ 4711771) at the airport and most other car-rental companies will meet you at the airport or otherwise let you pick up the car there.

The other option is a private taxi (JD12 to JD15). With the convenience of the Airport Express, it's difficult to see why you'd need to take a taxi, unless you have a very early flight.

To get to Marka Airport, take a service taxi from Raghadan station (150 fils).

Public Transport
BUS

The local bus system is confusing, with nothing labelled in English. Buses 26, 27, 28, 41 and 43 can be useful for getting to downtown. If bus travel is your thing, ask around the bus section of Raghadan station to see what's headed your way, but you'll need patience and decent Arabic. Tickets cost around 50 fils.

For 7th circle, take bus 41 or anything headed to Wadi as-Seer.

TAXI
Private Taxi

Most drivers of private taxis use the meter as a matter of course, but gently remind

---

AMMAN'S TAXIS

On any given day, Jordan's capital is home to an estimated 16,000 yellow taxis and counting. One will never be far away and they often find you before you find them – hopeful honking at tourists in case they missed the obvious is a favourite pastime. Although Amman inducted its first female taxi driver in 1997, all the others are male. Most drivers are fast and friendly, often more interested in finding out where you're from than keeping an eye on the road.

Making the effort to talk with them is illuminating, shedding light on the latest citywide gossip or scandal, to their take on the problems of the Middle East (many are Palestinians with stories to tell). Most work very hard for their money. A good day can yield JD35 (before overheads) in winter, and double that in summer. A bad day will bring as little as JD15 – not much for up to 15 hours' work.

SERVICE TAXI ROUTES

All departure points are listed on the Map p82.

Service taxi 1 From Basman St for 4th Circle.

Service taxi 2 From Basman St for 1st and 2nd Circles.

Service taxi 3 From Basman St for 3rd and 4th Circles.

Service taxi 4 From the side street near the central post office for Jebel Weibdeh.

Service taxi 6 From Cinema al-Hussein St for the Ministry of the Interior Circle, past Abdali station and JETT international and domestic offices.

Service taxi 7 From Cinema al-Hussein St, up Al-Malek al-Hussein St, past Abdali station and King Abdullah Mosque, and along Suleiman al-Nabulsi St for Shmeisani.

Service taxis 25 & 26 From Italian St, downtown, to the top of Jebel al-Ashrafiyeh' and near Abu Darwish Mosque.

Service taxi 27 From Italian St to Middle East Circle for Wahadat station.

Service taxi 35 From opposite the Amman Palace Hotel, passing close to the Muhajireen Police Station.

Service taxi 38 From downtown to Makkah al-Mukarramah Rd.

---

them when they don't. You need to be especially careful when you're laden with bags and searching for your hotel or heading out in the evening to an expensive restaurant.

The flagfall is 150 fils and fares are cheap; from downtown to Abdali costs around 600 fils while to Shmeisani shouldn't cost much more than JD1.

Service Taxi

Most fares cost about 130 fils per seat and you usually pay the full amount regardless of where you get off. After 8pm, the price for all service taxis goes up by 25%.

There can be long queues at rush hour (8am to 9am, and 5pm to 6pm). The cars queue up and usually start at the bottom of a hill – you get into the last car and the whole line rolls back a car space and so on. Always double check that your taxi is going to your destination before climbing in.

Car & Motorcycle

If you must drive in downtown Amman and are fortunate enough to find a parking spot, remember that parking machines operate along many main streets. It costs 150/250 fils for 30 minutes/one hour.

AROUND AMMAN

There are a number of worthwhile sights within easy reach of Amman, including Salt – an attractive town with good remnants of Ottoman architecture – and Wadi as-Seer, just outside the bustling capital, which combines evocative ruins with beautiful landscapes.

Also within striking distance of Amman is the Dead Sea (p143), Madaba (p150), Jerash (p108) and Bethany-Beyond-the-Jordan (p141), which are high on the list of must-sees for most visitors to Jordan. The desert castles (p133) are another popular day trip from the capital.

KAN ZEMAN   كان زمان

The historic 19th-century inn of **Kan Zeman** (☎ 4128391; fax 4128395; lunch/dinner buffet JD8/12; ⏰ noon-4pm & 7pm-midnight) is one of Amman's longest standing top-end restaurants. Expats in Amman give the food mixed reviews and it's definitely aimed at tour groups but the vaulted ceilings lend it a unique ambience and there's live music after 7pm. If you don't want the full buffet, snack on a *manaqeesh* (baked thyme pastry), washed down with a glass of *sefeeha* (a lemon and mint drink) or the local Kan Zeman red wine (JD2.500). The restaurant is part of a tourist complex with a few **handicraft stores** (most open after 6pm).

Kan Zeman is a bit of a hike from Amman, around 15km south of 8th Circle in the village of Al-Yadoudeh, 3km east of the Desert Highway, so you'll have to factor in a significant taxi fare (at least JD4 one way). If driving, take the signed turn off to Al-Yadoudeh village and follow the signs for 3km to the hilltop site. It's sometimes known as the Sahtain Restaurant.

WADI AS-SEER & IRAQ AL-AMIR
عراق الأمير وادي السير

The narrow, fertile valley of Wadi as-Seer, to the west of Amman, is quite a contrast to the bare treeless plateau around Amman to the east. Spring (particularly April and May) is the best time to visit, when black iris (the Jordanian national flower) and other colourful flowers are plentiful.

Wadi as-Seer is a largely Circassian village, and now virtually part of sprawling western Amman. About 10km down the lovely valley is the village of Iraq al-Amir with its castle and caves. Along the way (about 4km past Wadi as-Seer), and next to the sleepy Al-Yanabeea Restaurant, is part of an ancient **Roman aqueduct** on the right. Shortly after, look up to the hillside on the left to a façade cut into the rock, known as **Ad-Deir** (monastery), although it was probably a medieval dovecote (a place to house pigeons). The actual façade is fenced off.

The **Iraq al-Amir** (Caves of the Prince) are on the right of the road about 6km past Al-Yanabeea Restaurant if you're coming from Amman. The caves are arranged in two tiers – the upper one forms a long gallery (partially damaged during a mild earthquake in 1999) along the cliff face. The 11 caves were apparently used as cavalry stables and locals have used them to house their goats

and store chaff. Steps lead up to the caves from the paved road; opposite is the village of Iraq al-Amir and the **Iraq al-Amir Handicraft Village** (☒ closed Fri), which has a small weaving centre supporting 61 women who produce pottery, fabrics, foodstuffs, carpets and paper products.

About 700m further down the road, just visible from the caves, is the small but impressive **Qasr Iraq al-Amir** (admission free; ☒ daylight hr), also known as the Qasr al-Abad (Palace of the Slave). Mystery surrounds its construction, and even its precise age, but most scholars believe that Hyrcanus, of the powerful Jewish Tobiad family, built it between 187 and 175 BC as a villa or fortified palace. It's one of the very few examples of pre-Roman construction in Jordan. Although never completed, much of the palace has been reconstructed.

The place is unique because it was built from some of the biggest blocks of any ancient structure in the Middle East – the largest is 7m by 3m. The blocks, however, only 20cm or so thick, making the whole edifice quite flimsy and susceptible

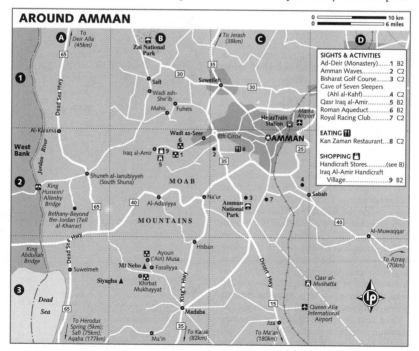

AROUND AMMAN

0 ——— 10 km
0 ——— 6 miles

to the earthquake which flattened it in AD 362. Today, the setting and the animal carvings on the exterior walls are the highlights. Look for the carved panther fountain on the ground floor, the eroded eagles on the corners and the lioness with cubs on the upper storey of the back side.

The gatekeeper will open the interior, as well as a small museum (which includes drawings of what the complex once looked like) for a tip of JD1. If he's not around, ask for the *miftah* (key) at the small shop near the gate.

Getting There & Away

Minibuses leave regularly from the station on Al-Ameerah Basma bin Talal St (Map p68) in Amman for Wadi as-Seer village (130 fils, 30 minutes); and less frequently from the Raghadan station in downtown. From Wadi as-Seer, take another minibus (100 fils) – or walk about 10km, mostly downhill – to the caves; look for the signpost to the Iraq al-Amir Handicraft Village, which is virtually opposite the stairs to the caves. Alternatively take bus 26 from Shabsough St in downtown to its terminus and then change to a bus for Wadi as-Seer or take a taxi. From the caves, it's an easy stroll down to the *qasr* (but a little steep back up).

If you're driving, head west from 8th Circle and follow the main road which twists through Wadi as-Seer village.

CAVE OF SEVEN SLEEPERS (AHL AL-KAHF) أهل الكهف

The legend of the 'seven sleepers' has several parallels throughout literature. It involves seven Christian boys who were persecuted by the Roman Emperor Trajan, then escaped to a cave and slept there for 309 years. This is one of several locations (the most famous being Ephesus in Turkey) that claim to be that cave. Inside the **main cave** (admission free; 8am-6pm) – also known as Ahl al-Kahf (Cave of the People) – are eight smaller tombs which are sealed, though one has a hole in it through which you can see a creepy collection of human bones. Above and below the cave are the remains of two mosques. About 500m west of the cave is a large **Byzantine cemetery**, whose tombs are sadly full of rubbish.

The cave is to the right of a large new mosque complex in the village of Rajib, off the road from Amman to Sabah. Buses from Amman to Sabah pass 500m from the mosque; catch them at Wahadat station (couple of 100 fils, 15 minutes). Alternatively, take a minibus from Quraysh St in downtown, ask for 'al-Kahf' and the driver will show you where to get off to change for a Sabah bus. The easiest way there is by chartered taxi (JD3 one way).

SALT السلط
05 / pop 66,000

The friendly town of Salt is about 30km northwest of downtown Amman and set in a steep-sided narrow valley. It was the region's administrative centre under Ottoman rule, but was passed over as the new capital of Trans-Jordan in favour of Amman. Con-

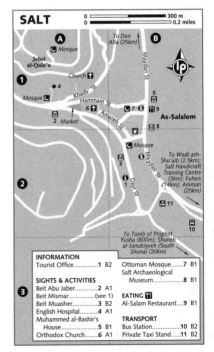

SALT
0   300 m
0   0.2 miles

INFORMATION
Tourist Office............1 B2

SIGHTS & ACTIVITIES
Beit Abu Jaber............2 A1
Beit Mismar..............(see 1)
Beit Muasher.............3 B2
English Hospital.........4 A1
Muhammad al-Bashir's
House...................5 B1
Orthodox Church.......6 A1

Ottoman Mosque......7 B1
Salt Archaeological
Museum...............8 B1

EATING
Al-Salam Restaurant...9 B1

TRANSPORT
Bus Station.............10 B2
Private Taxi Stand.....11 B2

sequently, Salt, which has a large Christian population, has retained much of its charm. Salt was apparently named from the Greek word *saltus* meaning 'forests' (although these are long gone); or from *sultana* for the grapes that were once abundant in the region.

Salt is pleasant and easy to walk around but isn't one of Jordan's highlights, so you could miss it if you don't have much time. The friendly **tourist office** (☎ 3555652; Dayr St; ☯ 8am-3pm Sun-Thu) is upstairs in the impressive old residence of Beit Mismar, but is of minimal use.

Sights & Activities

There are some fine examples of **Ottoman architecture** (see right) in town dating from the late 19th- and early 20th-century. Few of these gracious limestone buildings are open to the public, but some of the façades are quite elegant. The town has recently renovated several façades and rebuilt a series of stairways leading up to fabulous views from atop Jebel al-Qala'a.

Salt Archaeological Museum (☎ 3555651; admission free; ☯ 8am-7pm, to 4pm winter Nov-Apr) is well laid out in a nice Ottoman-era building. Downstairs focuses on glass and pottery (some dating back 5000 years), spanning the Roman, Byzantine and Islamic eras, mostly from around Salt but also from Deir Alla and Tell Nimrin (from where Joshua is thought to have led the Israelites across the River Jordan into the Promised Land). Upstairs are some examples of local traditional dress, displays on traditional farming activities and mosaics fragments from churches around Salt. Fifteen minutes should do it.

Visitors can watch weaving, pottery, mosaics and other handicrafts being made at the **Salt Handicraft Training Centre** (☎ 3550279; Nageb al-Daboor district; ☯ 8am-3pm Sun-Thu), 3km out of town. The centre specialises in both training and production and has a showroom for the finished products. A taxi here costs JD1 to JD2 from the centre; ask for the Balkhar Islamic School (*Bejanib Maddaris al-Balkhar al-Islamiy*). The turn-off is at a set of traffic lights by a bridge, 2km from Salt along the road to Amman.

If you have a car it's worth exploring **Wadi ash-Shu'aib**, a refreshing valley named after the prophet Jethro (Shu'aib in Arabic), which offers some hiking opportunities and interesting caves.

The tomb of Prophet Yusha (Joshua) is a 10-minute walk south of town but is of little specific interest.

Walking Tour of Salt

The following route takes you on a circular tour of Salt's backstreets, taking in its bazaars and old Ottoman architecture. Budget around an hour, including a short visit to the museum.

From Salt bus station walk up Dayr St, past the impressive doorway of **Beit Mismar** and the lovely balcony columns of **Beit Muasher**, both grand old Ottoman residences. Continue along Dayr St as it passes the curved walls of Salt's Orthodox church to the recently restored **Beit Abu Jaber**, which is due to reopen in 2006 as a local museum. Head across the plaza and take the stairs up to the right of the mosque, curving round to the entry of the former **English Hospital** (look for the letters 'E.H.' on the green gate). From here you could wind your way uphill for fine views over the town.

Alternatively, return to the plaza and head down **Hammam St**, Salt's most atmospheric backstreet, past the ornate **Ottoman mosque** to the junction with Maydan St. Across the street is the colonnaded entry of **Muhammed al-Bashir's House** (built 1890–1910), now a traditional coffeehouse (with a tree in front). Next door is Beit al-Sulibi (1920–30).

Break for lunch at the **Al-Salam Restaurant** (below) and then visit the **archaeological museum** (left) before heading back to the bus station or taking a taxi to the **Salt Handicraft Training Centre** (left).

Sleeping & Eating

There is nowhere to stay in Salt.

The northern end of Maydan St is lined with traditional cafés, full of men drinking tea and smoking nargilehs. Basic restaurants along the same street and by the bus station serve kebabs.

Al-Salam Restaurant (☎ 3552115; Maydan St; meals JD1.500; ☯ 7am-10.30pm Sat-Thu) One of the best places in town for cheap Arab food, including chicken and shish kebabs. It's opposite the Arab Bank.

Getting There & Away

The bus station is on the main road south of the town centre. There are minibuses to Salt (200 fils, 45 minutes) from Amman's Abdali and Raghadan stations, via Amman University, and occasional service taxis (450 fils) from Abdali. From Salt, minibuses head down the Jordan Valley to Shuneh al-Janubiyyeh (South Shuna; 250 fils, 45 minutes), and to Wadi as-Seer (200 fils, 30 minutes) and Fuheis (200 fils, 30 minutes), with which Salt can be combined as a day trip from Amman. Taxis (JD5) can be chartered to Amman.

FUHEIS فحيص
☎ 06

This pleasant village, located at a cool 1050m above sea level (15km northwest of Amman), is famous in Jordan for producing fruit and cement, but is of more interest to visitors for its fine places to eat. First built in about 2000 BC, Fuheis is now an overwhelmingly Christian village, with several Orthodox and Catholic **churches**, three of which are just down from the minibus stop.

Fuheis used to have several galleries and workshops producing ceramics, mosaics, paintings and embroidery but at the time of research only one was operating, in the Zuwwadeh Restaurant.

Eating
Fuheis has two excellent restaurants, both easy to spot from the final minibus stop in the Al-Rawaq neighbourhood. The food is excellent, the atmosphere is charming and alcohol is served.

Zuwwadeh Restaurant (☎ 4721528; starters JD1-2, mains JD2-6; ☽ 10am-midnight) The food here is fabulous, especially the *fatteh* (fried bread) with hummus, meat or chicken and pine nuts (JD3.500/5.500/7.500 for a small/medium/ huge), which is almost worth the trip from Amman on its own. The 'wedding *fatteh*' adds tomato and cardamom. Choose between shady outdoor tables or a pleasant indoor dining area. Most nights there are also live oud performances upstairs (after 7pm). Bookings are a good idea at weekends.

Hakoura Restaurant (☎ 4729152; starters 800 fils, mains JD2.500-5; ☽ 10am-midnight) Similarly good and a little cheaper (a small *fatteh* costs JD2.500), Hakoura is an artistic place with a commitment to traditional hospitality, soulful music and modern art, with some excellent food thrown in. There's live music on Thursday evenings.

Getting There & Away
Fuheis is easy to reach by minibus from Abdali bus station in Amman (200 fils, 45 minutes). The town is also connected to Wadi as-Seer and Salt (each 200 fils, 30 minutes), so you could visit all three places in a day. If you're eating at one of the restaurants until late, you may need to prearrange a chartered taxi back to Amman (before/after 6pm JD3/5).

The minibus stop in the older Al-Rawaq neighbourhood (also known as il-balad) is at a roundabout, close to the two restaurants and marked by a statue of St George (known locally as Giorgis) slaying a dragon.

Jerash & the North
جرش & الشمال

The area to the north of Amman is the most densely populated in Jordan, with the major centres of Irbid and Jerash, as well as dozens of small towns dotted in among the rugged and relatively fertile hills.

These are the biblical Hills of Gilead, peppered with olive groves and pine forests that lend a distinctly Mediterranean feel to the region. This is also the heart of Jordan's increasingly important olive oil industry. The well-watered plateau is drained by the Yarmouk and Zerqa (the ancient Jabbok) Rivers, the two biggest tributaries of the Jordan River, the latter marking the ancient border between Ammon and Gilead.

In this area lie the ruins of the ancient Roman Decapolis cities of Jerash (Gerasa) and Umm Qais (Gadara), both of which are well worth a visit. The impressive Islamic castle at Ajlun is also nearby and can be combined with pleasant walking trails at nearby Ajlun Nature Reserve.

Northeast of Irbid, the country flattens out to plains that stretch away into Syria. To the west lies the steamy Jordan Valley, one of the most fertile patches of land in the Middle East and pockmarked by ancient tells and archaeological remains.

In general northern Jordan is a good place to have a car, especially around Ajlun, which combines lovely scenery with light traffic, but it is still possible to see most things with public transport.

HIGHLIGHTS

- Wander the ruins and watch chariot racing at the wonderfully preserved Roman provincial city of **Jerash** (p108) with its superb Oval Plaza, theatres and temples
- Combine some pleasant hiking in the cool, shady **Ajlun Nature Reserve** (p116) with a visit to the fairy-tale Islamic fort of nearby **Qala'at ar-Rabad** (p114)
- Wander the excellent **Museum of Archaeology & Anthropology** (p117) at the vibrant Yarmouk University in Irbid, a great place to meet Jordanian students
- Take in awesome views over the Sea of Galilee from the off-beat Roman and Byzantine ruins of **Umm Qais** (p120)
- Dig through layers of time at tranquil **Pella** (p124), an ancient site which contains traces of all eras of Jordanian history

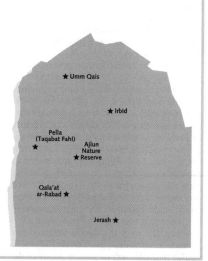

★ Umm Qais

★ Irbid

Pella
(Taqabat Fahl)
★

Ajlun
Nature
★ Reserve

Qala'at
ar-Rabad ★

Jerash ★

JERASH جرش

☎ 02

The ruins at **Jerash** (☎ 6351272; adult/student & child under 15 JD5/2.500; ⏰ 8am-4pm Oct-Apr, to 7pm May-Sep) are one of Jordan's major attractions and still have the power to evoke the ghosts of Rome. It's one of the best examples in the Middle East of a Roman provincial city, and is remarkably well preserved.

In its heyday, Jerash (known in Roman times as Gerasa) had a population of 15,000 to 20,000 inhabitants and, although it wasn't on any major trade route, its citizens prospered from the good agricultural land that surrounded it. The ancient walled city that survives today was the administrative, commercial, civic and religious centre of Jerash. The bulk of the inhabitants lived on the eastern side of Wadi Jerash (now the modern town of Jerash) and the two centres were linked by causeways and processional paths.

As you wander Jerash try to imagine life 2000 years ago: the centre bustling with shops and merchants, lined with cooling water fountains and dramatic painted façades. Picture today's empty niches filled with painted statues; buildings still clad in marble façades and decorated with carved peacocks and shell motifs; and churches topped with Tuscan-style terracotta tiled roofs. For a visual reconstruction of Jerash's finest buildings, check out the drawings at the visitor centre.

History

Although there have been finds to indicate that the site was inhabited in Neolithic times, Jerash rose to prominence from the time of Alexander the Great (333 BC).

In the wake of the Roman general Pompey's conquest of the region in 64 BC, Gerasa became part of the Roman province of Syria and then a city of the Decapolis (see opposite). Over the next two centuries, trade with the Nabataeans (the creators of Petra) flourished and the city grew extremely wealthy. Local agriculture and iron-ore mining in the Ajlun area contributed to the city's wellbeing. A completely new city plan was drawn up in the 1st century AD, centred on the classical features of a colonnaded main north–south street intersected by two side streets running east–west.

When the emperor Trajan annexed the Nabataean kingdom (around AD 106) more wealth found its way to Gerasa. Many of the old buildings were torn down to be replaced by more imposing structures. Construction again flourished when Emperor Hadrian visited in AD 129. To mark a visit of such importance, the Triumphal Arch (now known as Hadrian's Arch) at the southern end of the city was constructed.

Gerasa reached its peak at the beginning of the 3rd century, when it was bestowed with the rank of Colony. Its ascendancy was, however, short lived – disturbances such as the destruction of Palmyra (Syria) in 273, the demise of the overland caravans and the development of sea trade pushed the city into a slow decline. The only respite came during the reign of Diocletian (around 300), which saw a minor building boom.

From the middle of the 5th century, Christianity was the major religion and the construction of churches proceeded apace. Under the Byzantine emperor Justinian (527–65) seven churches were built, mostly out of stones pillaged from the earlier Roman temples and shrines.

With the invasion of the Sassanians from Persia (now Iran) in 614, the Muslim con-

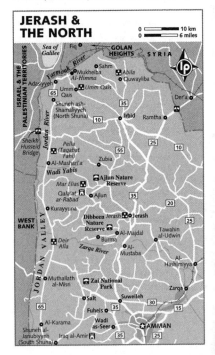

THE DECAPOLIS

The Roman commercial cities of what is now Jordan, Syria, Israel & the Palestinian Territories first became known collectively as the Decapolis in the 1st century AD. Despite the etymology of the word, it seems that the Decapolis consisted of more than 10 cities, and possibly as many as 18. No one knows for certain the reason behind such a grouping. In all likelihood the league of cities served a double function: to unite the Roman possessions and to enhance commerce. In Jordan, the main Decapolis cities were Philadelphia (Amman), Gadara (Umm Qais), Gerasa (Jerash), Pella (Taqabat Fil), and possibly Abila (Qweilbeh) and Capitolias (Beit Ras, near Irbid).

The cities were linked by paved roads that allowed wagons and chariots to circulate rapidly; at Umm Qais and Jerash, the ruts carved by these wagons can still be seen in the stones of the city streets. The cities flourished during the period of Roman dominance in the east, but fell into decline with the dawn of the Umayyad dynasty, which was based in Damascus. Afterwards, the shift to Baghdad as the centre of the Muslim world dealt the Decapolis a final blow.

---

quest in 636 and the devastating earthquake in 747, Gerasa's glory days passed into shadow and its population shrank to about one-quarter of its former size.

Apart from a brief occupation by a Crusader garrison in the 12th century, the city was completely deserted until the arrival of the Circassians from Russia in 1878, after which the site's archaeological importance was realized and excavations began.

Information
BOOKS & MAPS

The free *Jerash* brochure published by the Jordan Tourism Board includes a map, some photos and a recommended walking route. It can be found at the visitor centre in Jerash or the Jordan Tourism Board in Amman.

Anyone with a particular interest in the history of Jerash should pick up one of the three decent pocket-sized guides: *Jerash: The Roman City*; *Jerash: A Unique Example of a Roman City*; or the most comprehensive and readable *Jerash*. All three are available at bookshops in Amman (around JD3 to JD5 each). *Jerash* by Iain Browning is a more detailed and expensive historical book.

ENTRANCE

The entrance to the site is south of the ancient city, close to Hadrian's Arch. The **ticket office** is in the complex of souvenir shops, along with a post office and café. Tickets are checked later at the South Gate.

Next to the South Gate is the **visitor centre**, which has informative descriptions and reconstructions of many buildings in Jerash as well as a good relief map of the ancient city. There are toilets at the Jerash Rest House (p114), visitor centre and the souvenir shops area at the site entrance.

Allow at least three hours to see everything in Jerash and make sure you take plenty of water, especially in summer. It's best to visit Jerash before 10am or after 4pm because it's cooler, there will be less glare in your photos and also far fewer people at the site. Most of the buildings are at their best close to sunset. Remember, however, that public transport to Amman is limited after 5pm. It's possible to leave luggage at the Jerash Rest House while you visit the site, for no charge.

GUIDES

Anyone with a special interest in the history of Jerash may wish to hire a guide (JD5). Guides are available at the ticket checkpoint in front of the South Gate.

Sights
THE RUINS

At the entrance to the site is the striking **Hadrian's Arch**, also known as the **Triumphal Arch**. It's still an imposing structure, but it was originally twice as high when first built in AD 129 to honour the visiting Emperor Hadrian. The central arch is the highest at 13m and all three supported wooden doors. An unusual feature of the construction is the wreath of carved acanthus leaves above the base of each pillar. The arch was originally erected as a new southern entrance to the city, but the area between the arch and the South Gate was never completed.

Behind the arch is the partially restored **hippodrome**, built sometime between the

JERASH & THE NORTH

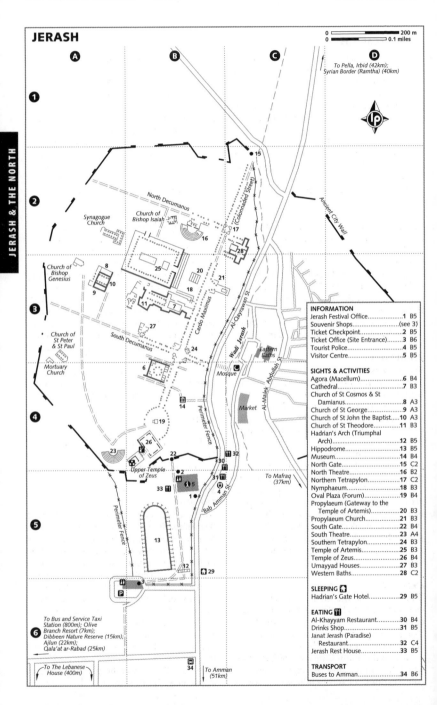

JERASH

0 — 200 m
0 — 0.1 miles

To Pella, Irbid (42km);
Syrian Border (Ramtha) (40km)

INFORMATION
Jerash Festival Office...............1 B5
Souvenir Shops...................(see 3)
Ticket Checkpoint..................2 B5
Ticket Office (Site Entrance)....3 B6
Tourist Police......................4 B5
Visitor Centre.....................5 B5

SIGHTS & ACTIVITIES
Agora (Macellum)..................6 B4
Cathedral............................7 B3
Church of St Cosmos & St
  Damianus.........................8 A3
Church of St George...............9 A3
Church of St John the Baptist...10 A3
Church of St Theodore...........11 B3
Hadrian's Arch (Triumphal
  Arch)..............................12 B5
Hippodrome.......................13 B5
Museum.............................14 B4
North Gate..........................15 C2
North Theatre.....................16 B2
Northern Tetrapylon..............17 C2
Nymphaeum........................18 B3
Oval Plaza (Forum)...............19 B4
Propylaeum (Gateway to the
  Temple of Artemis)...........20 B3
Propylaeum Church...............21 B3
South Gate.........................22 B4
South Theatre.....................23 A4
Southern Tetrapylon..............24 B3
Temple of Artemis................25 B3
Temple of Zeus....................26 B4
Umayyad Houses...................27 B3
Western Baths.....................28 C2

SLEEPING
Hadrian's Gate Hotel.............29 B5

EATING
Al-Khayyam Restaurant..........30 B4
Drinks Shop........................31 B5
Janat Jerash (Paradise)
  Restaurant.......................32 C4
Jerash Rest House................33 B5

TRANSPORT
Buses to Amman...................34 B6

THE RETURN OF BEN HUR

In summer 2005 chariot races returned to Jerash for the first time in around 1500 years, thanks to the vision of **Jerash Chariots** (☎ 6342471; www.jerashchariots.com; ☻ 11am-3pm, 2pm winter, except Fri), a joint Swedish-Jordanian venture. The group plans to run chariot races daily, recreated as authentically as possible, down to the use of Latin commands.

The show starts off with the entrance of around 40 Roman legionnaries (actually Jordanian special forces) who parade around the hippodrome, train for war and complete a range of military drills from the tortoise manoeuvre to the use of a catapult, followed by four pairs of gladiators fighting it out with tridents, nets and *gladius* (sword). This is all a warm up for the main event: four chariots duking it out over seven laps around the hippodrome's central wooden *spina*.

There's currently space for about 500 spectators in the hippodrome, just 3% of the original capacity. You'll have to imagine the original crowd of 15,000 who packed in here; and while you're at it, just picture the spectacle of the Circus Maximus in Rome, which once roared with 157,000 spectators.

Performances are scheduled to take place in the hippodrome daily around noon. They last about an hour and cost JD20 per person. Check the website for more details.

1st and 3rd centuries AD. This old sports field (244m by 50m) was once surrounded by seating for up to 15,000 spectators and hosted mainly athletics competitions and chariot races. Recent excavations have unearthed remains of stables, pottery workshops and indications that it was also used for polo by invading Sassanians from Persia during the early 7th century.

About 250m beyond Hadrian's Arch is the **South Gate** (AD 130), originally one of four along the city wall. It also bears acanthus leaf decoration atop the pillar bases.

The **Oval Plaza** or **Forum** is one of the icons of Jerash. It's unusual because of its oval shape and huge size (90m long and 80m at its widest point). Some historians attribute this to the desire to gracefully link the main north–south axis (cardo maximus) with the Temple of Zeus. The Forum was typically a market and a meeting place. The site may also have been a place of sacrifice linked to the temple. The 56 reconstructed Ionic columns surrounding the plaza are very impressive, and the centre is paved with limestone. The central fountain was added in the 7th century.

On the south side of the Forum is the **Temple of Zeus**. It was built in about AD 162 over the remains of an earlier Roman temple. A Byzantine church was later built on the site. The temple once had a magnificent monumental stairway leading up to it from a lower sacred enclosure, itself supported by a vaulted corridor built to compensate for the unhelpful local topography. The lower level

temenos (sacred courtyard) had an altar and served as a holy place of sacrifice. A French team is reconstructing the dramatic upper temple. To get here walk up the former monumental staircase, past dozens of gigantic fallen pillars.

The **south theatre**, behind the Temple of Zeus, was built between AD 81 and 96 but wasn't opened until the second century AD. It could seat 5000 spectators and can still hold 3000 in its 32 rows. The back of the stage was originally two-storeys high, and has now been rebuilt to the first level. From the top of the theatre there are superb views of ancient and modern Jerash, particularly the Oval Plaza; just prior to sunset is the best time. The theatre is a testament to the wisdom of the ancients, boasting excellent acoustics as quickly becomes clear to anyone attending performances here during the Jerash Festival (see p113). If you are lucky you'll get to see the crazy Jordanian Scottish pipe band that sporadically belts out military tunes on their bagpipes to illustrate the excellent acoustics.

Heading northeast from the Forum, the **cardo maximus** (the city's main thoroughfare, also known as the **colonnaded street**) is another highlight. Stretching for 800m from the Forum to the North Gate, it was originally built in the 1st century AD, and rebuilt and redesigned several times since. It is still paved with the original flagstones, and the ruts worn by thousands of chariots are still clear, as are the manholes for the drains below. Some of the 500 columns that once lined the street were deliberately built at an uneven height to complement the façades of the buildings that once stood behind them. Most of the columns you see today were reassembled in the 1960s.

Just prior to the intersection with the **south decumanus** (main street, running from east to west), and where the columns are taller, is the entrance to the **agora** (sometimes referred to as the **macellum**), where the main market was held and people gathered for public meetings around the central fountain.

Where the cardo maximus joins the south decumanus and north decumanus, ornamental tetrapylons were built. The **southern tetrapylon** consisted of four bases, each supporting four pillars topped by a platform and a statue. They are in varying stages of reconstruction; the southeastern one is the most complete. This intersection was made into a circular plaza in the 3rd century.

To the east of the intersection of the cardo maximus and south decumanus lay the former residential areas of Jerash, now buried beneath the modern town. To the west of the intersection are the ruins of some **Umayyad houses** dating from the 7th and 8th centuries.

About 100m north of the intersection are steps belonging to the 4th-century **cathedral** (probably little more than a modest Byzantine church despite the name). The gate and steps actually cover the remains of an earlier temple to the Nabataean god Dushara, and later rededicated to Dionysus.

Next along the main street is the elegant **nymphaeum**, the main ornamental fountain of the city, dedicated to the water nymphs. Built in about AD 191, the two-storey construction was elaborately decorated, faced with marble slabs on the lower level, plastered on the upper level and topped with a half dome. Water would cascade over the façade into a large pool at the front, with the overflow pouring out through seven carved lions' heads into drains in the street below.

Further along to the west (left) is the **propylaeum** (AD 150), the gateway to the Temple of Artemis. The gateway's portico lies in pieces in the street opposite the gateway. A stairway, flanked by shops, originally ran from here to the eastern residential area. The **propylaeum church** was later built over part of the stairway. From here you can still see the remains of a bathhouse in the modern town below.

Behind the propylaeum, and on top of a small hill, is the well-preserved **Temple of Artemis**, dedicated to Artemis, the goddess of hunting and fertility (and daughter of Zeus). The temple was built between AD 150 and 170, and had 12 columns (11 are still standing), but the marble floors and statues have disappeared. Large vaults had to be built to the north and south of the temple to make the courtyard level; the vaults were used to store the temple treasures. After the edict of Theodorius in AD 386 permitting the dismantling of pagan temples, many of the materials were taken away for construction elsewhere. The temple was fortified by the Arabs in the 12th century, but was later substantially destroyed by the Crusaders.

At the intersection of the cardo maximus and the north decumanus is the more intact **northern tetrapylon**, dedicated to the Syrian wife of the emperor Septimus Severus. It was probably built as a gateway to the north theatre. This tetrapylon differs in style from the southern one. If its condition looks too good to be true that's because it is – it was rebuilt in 2000.

Just downhill (to the southeast) is the rubble of the huge **western baths**, measuring about 70m by 50m. Dating from the 2nd century AD, they represent one of the earliest examples of a dome atop a square room. Once an impressive complex of hot-, warm- and cold-water baths, they were partially destroyed by various earthquakes.

The **north theatre** is smaller than the south theatre and differs considerably in shape and design. It was built in about AD 165 for government meetings rather than artistic performances, and in 235 it was doubled in size. It has been magnificently restored and still holds about 2000 people. Look for the exuberant carvings of musicians and dancers at the base of the stairs.

The cardo maximus ends at the comparatively unimpressive **North Gate**. Built in about AD 115, it has not been restored as well as its southern counterpart and is probably not worth the detour. It linked the cardo maximus with the ancient road to Pella.

On the way back, check out the ruins of several **churches** that lie south and west of the Temple of Artemis. In all, 15 churches have been uncovered in Jerash and more are likely to be found. Behind (west of) the cathedral, above a fountain courtyard, the

Church of St Theodore, built in AD 496, has some limited mosaics. The **Church of St Cosmos and St Damianus** was dedicated to twin brothers, both doctors. It once had marvellous mosaic tiles, but most are now in the Museum of Popular Tradition in Amman. The **Church of St John the Baptist** was built in about AD 531, but is badly damaged. The **Church of St George**, built in about AD 530, is also destroyed.

Surrounding the ancient city for about 4.5km are remnants of the **city walls**, which were between 2.5m and 3.5m thick when built in the 4th century AD, although most of what remains dates from the Byzantine era. There were also originally 24 towers along the walls.

MUSEUM

Before you finish exploring the ancient city, try to visit the small **museum** (☎ 6312267; admission free; ⏰ 8.30am-6pm Oct-Apr, to 5pm May-Sep) just to the east of (and uphill from) the Oval Plaza. It houses a small but good selection of artefacts from the site, such as mosaics, glass and gold jewellery, as well as coins found in a tomb near Hadrian's Arch. All items on display are well labelled in English. No photographs are allowed.

Just as interesting as the exhibits are the inscriptions, tombs and pillars lying higgledy-piggledy in the gardens outside the museum.

SOUND-AND-LIGHT SHOW

With the recent downturn in tourism the summer **sound-and-light show** (☎ 6351053; admission free) has been cancelled, though it may start up again. Check with the visitor centre.

Sleeping & Eating

Surprisingly, there's still no hotel in Jerash. We spotted Hadrian's Gate Hotel by Hadrian's Gate but it was closed every time we visited. If it opens while this book is being printed it will be a useful addition. There are a couple of decent places to stay in Ajlun (see p115). With an early start, you could cover Jerash and Ajlun in a day trip from Amman.

Olive Branch Resort (☎ 6340555; www.olivebranch .com.jo; s/d JD15/25, breakfast JD2.750; P ☒) Around 7km from Jerash, off the road to Ajlun, this secluded and well-run place has great Tuscan-like views, with modern, comfortable rooms and good clean bathrooms. Some rooms come with a balcony. You can also camp in your/their tent for JD4/5 and use the nearby barbecue grills, hot showers and swimming pool (April–November). There's also a games room with billiards and foosball table and a good restaurant (mains JD3 to JD5). A taxi from Jerash costs JD2 one way; to Amman costs JD10 to JD12. Drive 5km from Jerash towards Ajlun, turn right for 1km and then right again for another 2km.

JERASH FESTIVAL

Since 1981 the ancient city of Jerash has hosted the annual Jerash Festival, under the sponsorship of Queen Noor. Events are held in the South Theatre, North Theatre and Oval Plaza in Jerash, as well as the Royal Cultural Centre in Amman, and other places like Umm Qais and Mt Nebo. Special programmes for children are also held at the Haya Cultural Centre in Amman.

The festival is held over 17 days from mid-July to mid-August. It features an eclectic array of performances including plays, poetry readings, opera and musical concerts from around the world, plus craft displays. More information is available from the **organisers in Amman** (☎ 06 5675199; www.jerashfestival.com.jo). Events are listed in English in the official souvenir news sheet, the *Jerash Daily*, printed in English every day of the festival, and the English-language newspapers published in Amman.

Tickets cost at least JD5 for events in Jerash, and about JD20 for more formal events in Amman and elsewhere. They are available from the Royal and Haya Cultural Centres, and (sometimes) the domestic JETT bus office in Abdali in Amman (see p100). JETT also offers one-way and return transport to Jerash during the festival (especially useful when public transport finishes at night). There is also a Jerash Festival office, next to the visitor centre near the South Gate, for information and buying tickets but it's not open at other times of the year and you'd be well advised to buy your tickets well in advance of arriving in Jerash.

Lebanese House (☎ 6351301; starters JD0.700-1, mains JD2.500-5; ✆ noon-11pm) A five- to 10-minute walk from Jerash's centre, this is a local favourite, with outdoor seating and a kids' play area. The Lebanese-style mezze range from frog's legs to *shinklish* (tangy white cheese). Culinary daredevils can try a pair of hot testicles (JD1.750), washed down by a glass of local Machereus white wine. Maybe just stick to the starters…

Jerash Rest House (☎ 6351437; starters JD1-2, mains JD3-7; ✆ noon-5pm) This tour group restaurant by the main gates has decent à la carte meals but most people opt for the lunch buffet (JD5, plus 26% tax).

You'll find cheaper meals opposite the visitor centre, including at the **Al-Khayyam Restaurant** (barbecued meats JD2.500) or the **Janat Jerash (Paradise) Restaurant** (Al-Qayrawan St; mains JD2.500), both with nice terraces.

Getting There & Away

Jerash is 51km north of Amman, and the roads are well signed from the capital, especially from 8th Circle.

From Abdali bus station in Amman, public buses and minibuses (400 fils, 1¼ hours) leave regularly for Jerash, though they can take up to an hour just to fill up.

Jerash's new bus and service taxi station is a 15-minute walk west of the site, at the second set of traffic lights, behind the big white building. You can pick up a minibus to the station from outside the visitor centre (100 fils). Plenty of minibuses travel regularly to Irbid (300 fils, 45 minutes) and Ajlun (300 fils, 30 minutes) until around 4pm. If you don't want to head to the bus station you can normally flag down the bus to Amman from the main junction in front of the site.

If you're still in Jerash after 5pm, be prepared to hitch back to the capital. Service taxis sometimes leave as late as 8pm (usually later during Jerash Festival) but expect a wait. The tourist police are usually happy to cajole a passing motorist into offering a free ride back to Amman. A private taxi one-way costs around JD10; you may be able to bargain down to JD7. To Irbid costs JD8.

AJLUN عجلون
☎ 02

Ajlun (or Ajloun) is another popular and easy day trip from Amman, and can be combined with a trip to Jerash if you set off early. In Ajlun town the mosque, just southwest of the main roundabout, has a minaret dating back some 600 years.

The highlight of the trip, however, is unquestionably the towering **Qala'at ar-Rabad**, 3km west of town. The countryside of pine forest and olive groves is good for hiking and is popular with picnicking locals in summer, when the surrounding hills are a few degrees cooler than the rest of Jordan. If possible, visit on a clear day – the views are superb.

Information

Housing Bank is located just south of the main roundabout in Ajlun, which changes money and has an ATM.

Tourist office (☎ /fax 6420115; ✆ 7am-1pm Sun-Thu) In the restaurant complex at the foot of the castle.

Sights

Qala'at ar-Rabad (Ar-Rabad Castle; admission JD1; ✆ 8am-4pm Oct-Apr, to 7pm May-Sep), built atop Mt 'Auf (about 1250m), is a fine example of Islamic military architecture. The castle was built by one of Saladin's generals (and also nephew), 'Izz ad-Din Usama bin Munqidh, in AD 1184–88, and was enlarged in 1214 with the addition of a new gate in the southeastern corner. It once boasted seven towers, and was surrounded by a dry moat over 15m deep.

The castle commands views of the Jordan Valley and three wadis leading into it – the Kufranjah, Rajeb and Al-Yabes – making it an important strategic link in the defensive chain against the Crusaders, and a counterpoint to the Crusader Belvoir Fort on the Sea of Galilee (Lake Tiberias) in present-day Israel & the Palestinian Territories. With its hilltop position, Qala'at ar-Rabad was one in a chain of beacons and pigeon posts that enabled messages to be transmitted from Damascus to Cairo in a single day.

After the Crusader threat subsided, the castle was largely destroyed by Mongol invaders in 1260, only to be almost immediately rebuilt by the Mamluks. In the 17th century an Ottoman garrison was stationed here, after which it was used by local villagers. The castle was 'rediscovered' by the well-travelled JL Burckhardt, who also stumbled across Petra (see p177). Earthquakes in 1837 and 1927 damaged the castle badly, but its restoration is continuing.

There is a useful explanation in English just inside the main gate, although nothing else is signposted. It's fun to explore and the views are superb.

The castle is a tough uphill walk (3km) from the town centre, but minibuses very occasionally go to the top (about 100 fils). Alternatively, take a taxi from Ajlun (JD1 one way) or hitch a ride. A return trip by taxi from Ajlun (JD3), with about 30 minutes to look around, is money well spent.

Sleeping & Eating

There are two hotels on the road up to the castle; good options if you want to enjoy the sunset. Prices are negotiable at both.

Qalet al-Jabal Hotel (☎ 6420202; s/d/tr JD24/32/45 plus 10% tax) About 1km before the castle, this is probably the pick of the two, though it's a bit overpriced. The comfortable but slightly old-fashioned rooms come with a balcony, but the highlight is the fantastic outdoor terrace garden where meals can be served in summer (it's worth coming here for a drink if you have your own car). The family triples have their own private terrace with castle views. The hotel is 1.3km from Ajlun, by the turn-off to Mar Elias.

Ajlun Hotel (☎ 6420524; fax 6421580; s/d with tax & breakfast Oct-Apr JD13/20, May-Sep 18/30JD) The cheaper option is 500m down the road from the castle. Although it has smaller rooms, it isn't bad. Sadly only the top floors take advantage of the fine views. Hot water can be unpredictable.

Abu-Alezz Restaurant (meals 1.500) by the main roundabout in Ajlun town, does the usual dish of chicken, hummus, salad and bread for around JD1.500. There are also shwarma stalls, such as the good **Al-Raseed** (meals 1.500), on the main roundabout. An alternative is to come prepared to join the locals for a picnic in the surrounding hills.

There are drink stands next to the castle ticket office and a new restaurant is planned next to the tourist office at the foot of the castle hill.

Getting There & Away

Ajlun is 73km northwest of Amman, and 22km northwest of Jerash. The castle can be clearly seen from most places in the area. If you're driving or walking, take the signposted road (Al-Qala'a St) heading west at the main roundabout in the centre of Ajlun.

From the centre of Ajlun, minibuses travel regularly to Jerash (300 fils, 30 minutes along

a scenic road) and Irbid (320 fils, 45 minutes). From Amman (500 fils, two hours), minibuses leave a few times a day from the Abdali bus station; an early start will let you see Ajlun and Jerash in one day, returning to the capital late in the afternoon.

AROUND AJLUN

The sights of Ajlun, Mar Elias and Ajlun Nature Reserve combine to make a fine day trip from Jerash, with the option of staying the night in Ajlun town or in the funky tree houses of the Ajlun Nature Reserve.

Mar Elias   مار الياس

The little-visited archaeological site of **Mar Elias** (admission free; ⊙ 8am-7pm Apr-Oct, to 4pm Nov-Mar) gives you just the excuse you need to explore the countryside around Ajlun. It's not a spectacular site but can be part of an enjoyable day out by rented car.

The prophet Elias is mentioned in both the Quran and the Old Testament and is thought to have been born around 910 BC in the village of Lesteb, next to Mar Elias. The prophet died not far away in Wadi al-Kharrar (see p142), before ascending to heaven on a flaming chariot. During Byzantine times a pilgrimage site grew up around the place under the guidance of the nearby Bishopric of Pella. In 1999 excavations unearthed a church complex dating back to the early 7th century.

From the car park, stairs lead up above the ruins of the earliest church, the apse of which has a tree growing directly above it. The foundations of the main cross-shaped church are easy to make out and are decorated with wonderfully fresh floor mosaics partially covered by plastic. You can make out a lovely tree motif and an interesting swastika motif. Look for tomb chambers to the back right of the church and an earlier chapel with plain white tiles to the south. Water cisterns and bits of masonry dot the rest of the site.

GETTING THERE & AWAY

There's no public transport to the site and it's only really worth a visit if you have a car and can combine a trip to Qala'at ar-Rabad and the nearby nature reserve. From Ajlun take a right by the Qalet al-Jabal Hotel, climb the hill for 1km and take a left at the junction, heading downhill after this for 2.7km. At the junction/army post take a right for another 1.8km until you see a signpost pointing left (the right branch leads to Ishfateena and the Ajlun Nature Reserve). After 1km take the left track for 400m up to the site (a total of 8.3km from Ajlun).

If you're headed on to Ajlun Nature Reserve take a left when you get back to the junction, 1.4km from the site, and head towards Ishfateena. After 1.6km you hit the main road; take a right here and after 5km you'll see the reserve signposted to the left, 300m before the main Irbid–Ajlun highway.

Ajlun Nature Reserve

محمية عجلون الطبيعية

Lost among the forests surrounding Ajlun is this small 13-sq-km **nature reserve** (☎ 02 6475672, ☎ /fax 6475673; adult JD3; 🕙 15 Mar-31 Oct), established by the Royal Society for the Conservation of Nature (RSCN) in 1988 to protect oak, pistachio and strawberry forest, and to reintroduce the native but locally extinct roe deer (of which there are at least 13 in a captive breeding programme). Other local residents include wild boar, stone martens, polecats, jackals and even hyena and grey wolves.

The scenery is lovely (though not spectacular) and makes for a quiet break from Amman. Book accommodation and meals in advance with the RSCN through their Wild Jordan Centre in Amman (see p70). You should be able to catch sight of a roe deer in the large enclosure by the visitor centre.

There are two **hiking trails**. The 2km Roe Deer Trail (can be self-guided) takes about an hour and starts from the accommodation area, looping over a nearby hill, past a 1600-year-old stone wine press and lots of spring wildflowers (April), and returning via the roe deer enclosure. The Rockrose Trail is a longer trail of around 8km (four hours) that involves some scrambling and requires a guide (JD15 per group).

The reserve operates 10 **tented bungalows** (s/d/t/r/q per person incl entry fee JD20/17/16/15), which are comfortable and fun, on a tree-house-style wooden platform. A toilet and solar-heated shower block is a short walk away. Bring mosquito repellent between June and October.

Meals are available in the tented rooftop-restaurant given some notice (breakfast JD3.500, lunch or dinner JD7) or you can cook for yourself on the public barbecue grills. From the rooftop there are great views of snowcapped Jebel ash-Sheikh (Mt Hermon; 2814m) on the Syria-Lebanon border.

Getting here is a bit of an adventure in itself; no public transport goes anywhere close. A one-way taxi from Ajlun (9km) costs around JD2.500; ask the reserve visitor centre to book one for your departure. If you're driving, take the road from Ajlun towards Irbid and take a left turn by a gas station 4.8km from Ajlun towards the village of Ishfateena. About 300m from the junction take a right and follow the signs a further 3.8km to the reserve, next to the village of Umm al-Yanabi.

DIBBEEN NATURE RESERVE

متنزة دبين الوطني

☎ 02

This small area of Aleppo pine and oak forest is Jordan's most recent RSCN-managed nature reserve, established in 2004. Facilities are currently very limited and not yet on par with other RSCN reserves. Check with the RSCN before heading out here as new regulations or facilities might be in place.

There are some short, marked (but unmapped) **hiking** trails through the park. In March and April carpets of red crown anemones fill the meadows beneath the pine-forested and sometimes snowcapped hills. Most trails are either small vehicle tracks or stony paths, some of which continue beyond the park's boundaries. The area is very popular for local picnickers on Fridays and litter can be a problem.

In the middle of the park is **Dibbeen Rest House** (☎ 6339710; d/tr JD25/32), a tourist complex with a children's playground, restaurant and rest house. The comfortable 'chalets' (which sleep three) have a basic kitchen, large bathroom with hot water, TV and fan; it's worth negotiating. Visitors can pitch their own tent in the grounds for JD3 per person, and have access to toilets and hot showers.

Public transport here is very limited. From Jerash, the minibuses heading to the villages of Burma or Al-Majdal goes through the park and can drop you off within 1km of the tourist complex entrance – a detour to the complex can be arranged with the driver for an inducement of about JD1. Chartering a taxi from Jerash is the best idea, and will cost about JD4 one way. If you're driving from Jerash, Ajlun or Amman, follow the initial signs close to Jerash and then ask directions to the Rest House; there are few signs.

IRBID   إربد

☎ 02 / pop 500,000

Irbid is a university town and, perhaps as a consequence, is one of the more lively and progressive of Jordan's large towns. In the area around Yarmouk University, south of the city centre, the streets are lined with outdoor restaurants, Internet cafés and pedestrians out strolling, particularly in the late afternoon. The university also hosts arguably Jordan's finest museum, the Museum of Archaeology & Anthropology.

The area around Irbid has yielded artefacts and graves suggesting that the area has been inhabited since the Bronze Age, although there is little evidence in the town of such antiquity. Jordan's second-largest city is nonetheless a good base from which to explore Umm Qais, Al-Himma and even Jerash, Ajlun and Pella.

Information

Irbid has plenty of banks for changing money and most have ATMs. The police station is above the market area, and offers great views of the city.

There are literally dozens of Internet cafés along the southern end of University St (Shafeeq Rshaidat St) near Yarmouk University; most are open around 10am to 3am (some 24 hours) and charge 500 fils per hour.

Global Internet (500 fils per hour) The nearest Internet café to downtown; it's on the 2nd floor, in a plaza off King Hussein St.

Malkawi Express (☎ 7277876; King Hussein St) A professional photo lab where you can buy and develop print film (750 fils plus 100 fils for each print) and print digital pictures (150 fils per print). King Hussein St is also known locally as Baghdad St.

Post office (King Hussein St; ☼ 7.30am-5pm Sat-Thu, to 1.30pm Fri)

Royal Jordanian Airlines (☎ 7243202; cnr King Hussein & Al-Jaish Sts)

Sights

There are two museums in the grounds of the vast **Yarmouk University** (www.yu.edu.jo), which opened in 1977 and now boasts over 22,000 students from across the region. Foreigners are welcome to wander around the university and it's a good place to meet young Jordanians.

The **Museum of Archaeology & Anthropology** (☎ 7271100, ext 4260; admission free; ☼ 10am-1.45pm & 3-4.30pm Sun-Thu) is highly recommended and features exhibits from all eras of Jordanian history, including a great reconstruction of a traditional Arab pharmacy. The labels are in English. Out back is a Numismatic Hall with some surprisingly interesting displays on the history of money over the last 2600 years.

Jordan Natural History Museum (☎ 7271100; admission free; ☼ 8am-5pm Sun-Thu) contains a range of stuffed animals, birds and insects, as well as rocks from the region, but very little is explained in English. It's good for birders, with some beautiful bee-eaters and rollers on display. The museum is in the huge green hangar No 23.

Beit Arar (off Al-Hashemi St; admission free; ☼ 9am-5pm Sun-Thu) was set up to host cultural events and is located in a superb old Damascene-style house. The rooms are set around a courtyard paved with volcanic black stones and there are manuscripts and photo displays of Arar, one of Jordan's finest poets.

Sleeping

The cheapest hotels are in the city centre in the blocks immediately north of King Hussein (Baghdad) St.

Al-Ameen al-Kabeer Hotel (☎ 7242384; al_ameen _hotel@hotmail.com; Al-Jaish St; dm/s/d JD2/5/8) This is by far the best of the cheapies with friendly management, simple but well-tended rooms and clean shared bathrooms with a hot shower. The rooms overlooking the street can be noisy before 9pm but they are still the better option, though bear in mind that few of the windows lock. The three-bed dorms are men only.

Abu Baker Hotel (☎ 7242695; Wasfi al-Tal St; dm JD2) This is on the 2nd floor of the Bank of Jordan building and has a mostly local (male) clientele. The views over Irbid from the upper floor rooms are superb. There's no lift and only squat toilets. There's hot water in the shared bathroom, but only when you don't really need it (11am–8pm).

Omayed Hotel (☎ /fax 7245955; King Hussein St; s/d with private bathroom & satellite TV JD15/20) This is a cut above the cheapies in both price and quality, and, though it's a bit frumpy, the rooms are spacious, clean and most have nice views. Rooms at the back are quieter.

JERASH & THE NORTH

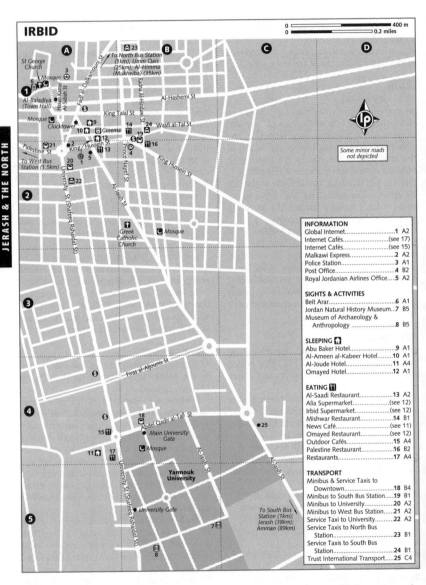

IRBID

The staff are friendly and it's a good place for women travellers.

Al-Joude Hotel (☎ 7275515; joude@go.com.jo; off University St; s/d/tr incl buffet breakfast JD25/35/45, ste JD60) This is Irbid's finest, located near the university, offering friendly staff, a classy ambience and attractive rooms which include private bathroom, satellite TV and a fridge. An extra 35 rooms were added in 2005, pushing the hotel up to four stars. The restaurant here is decent, as is the downstairs News Café (see opposite).

Eating

There are dozens of restaurants to suit most budgets along the southern end of University

St. It's a great place in the evening when the street is crowded with young students. When we asked local university students which was their favourite place, most said 'it will change tomorrow' so, rather than recommend particular places, we suggest that you do what the locals do and stroll along the street until you find one that appeals; most have menus with prices posted outside. There are great cafés on the main roundabout northwest of the university that stay open late.

Al-Saadi Restaurant (☎ 7242454; King Hussein St; starters JD0.500-1.500, mains from JD2.500; ⏱ 8.30am-9.30pm) This is one of the better places in the centre, with a pleasant dining area and decent service; they also have a breakfast menu, with cheese, omelette, fuul and mosabaha (hummus with whole chickpeas).

Omayed Restaurant (☎ 7240106; King Hussein St; starters from JD0.500, mains JD2-4; ⏱ 8am-9.30pm) Another good choice, with reasonable food and nice décor. The window seats have great views over the city. Take the lift to the 3rd floor.

News Café (off University St; pizza JD2.500) Downstairs from the Al-Joude Hotel, this is a great place for Irbid's cool set to hang out. It's warm and inviting, offering coffee, milk shakes, pizza and other snacks, along with plenty of scented nargileh (water pipe).

Mishwar Restaurant (Wasfi al-Tal St) One of several choices in the centre of town for budget-priced felafel, shwarma and juices.

Palestine Restaurant (King Hussein St) Another decent cheapie but not much English spoken here.

Alia Supermarket (☎ 7245987; King Hussein St) A good option for self-caterers and picnickers, as is the next-door Irbid Supermarket. They're by the Omayed Hotel.

Getting There & Away

See p260 for details of service taxis from Irbid to Syria and p259 for buses from Irbid to Israel & the Palestinian Territories. For the latter, the office of **Trust International Transport** (☎ 7251878; Al-Jaish St) is near Al-Hasan Sports City. Trust also has three direct services a day to Aqaba (JD8, five hours).

Irbid is 85km north of Amman and easy to reach from just about anywhere in Jordan. There are three main minibus/taxi stations in town, a long way apart from each other.

From the North bus station, there are minibuses to Umm Qais (250 fils, 45 minutes), Mukheiba (for Al-Himma; 350 fils, one hour) and Quwayliba (for the ruins of Abila; 170 fils, 25 minutes).

From the large South bus station (New Amman bus station), air-conditioned Hijazi buses (900 fils, 90 minutes) leave regularly for Amman's Abdali bus station until about 7pm. To Amman (Abdali) there are also less comfortable buses and minibuses (600 fils, about two hours) and plenty of service taxis (900 fils). Minibuses also leave the South station for Ajlun (320 fils, 45 minutes) and Jerash (500 fils, 45 minutes). Buses go from here to Ramtha (250 fils), for the Syrian border.

From the West bus station (*Mujamma al-Gharb al-Jadid*), about 1.5km west of the centre, minibuses go to Al-Mashari'a (400 fils, 45 mins) for the ruins at Pella; Sheikh Hussein Bridge (for Israel & the Palestinian Territories; 750 fils, 45 minutes) and other places in the Jordan Valley, such as Shuneh ash-Shamaliyyeh (North Shuna; 270 fils, one hour).

Getting Around

Getting between Irbid's various bus stations is easy, with service taxis (120 fils) and minibuses (100 fils) shuttling between them and the centre. Service taxis and minibuses to the South bus station can be picked up on Radna al-Hindawi St, while for the North station head to Prince Nayef St. For the West station take a bus from Palestine St, just west of the roundabout.

The standard taxi fare from the centre (*al-Bilad*) to the university (*al-Jammiya*) is 500 fils; few taxis use meters in Irbid. A minibus from University St to the university gate costs 110 fils. Otherwise it's a 25-minute walk.

If you have a car be aware that the one-way roads and lack of parking can make driving a stressful experience.

ABILA (QUWAYLIBA)   أبيلا (قويليبا)

Possibly one of the Decapolis cities (see p109), the ancient city of **Abila** (admission free; ⏱ daylight hr) was built in the Early Bronze Age (about 3000 BC) between two small hills, Tell Abila and Tell Umm-al-Amad.

There is, however, little to see because what was left after the earthquake in AD 747 remains largely unexcavated, so this is probably a site for the committed fan of remote ruins. Nothing is labelled or set up for visitors and it can be hard to see what you're looking for without a guide, but there are enough **tombs** and eerie **caves** dotted around the fields to interest archaeology buffs. The **theatre** is fairly obviously carved out of the hill, and there are also some **columns** from the markets, temples and baths lying around the site.

The Abila site is close to the village of Quwayliba, about 15km north of Irbid. Buses leave from the North bus station in Irbid (170 fils, 25 minutes) for Quwayliba; ask the driver to drop you off at the ruins.

UMM QAIS (GADARA)　　أم قيس
☎ 02

> And when he came to the other side, to the country of the Gadarenes, two demon-possessed met him, coming out of the tombs, so fierce that no one could pass that way. And behold, they cried out, "What have you to do with us, O Son of God? Have you come here to torment us before the time?" Now a herd of many swine was feeding at some distance from them. And the demons begged him, "If you cast us out, send us away into the herd of swine". And he said to them, "Go." So they came out and went into the swine; and behold, the whole herd rushed down the steep bank into the sea, and perished in the waters.
>
> *Matthew 8:28-32*

In the northwest corner of Jordan are the ruins of another ancient town, Gadara (now called Umm Qais). The ruins are less visually impressive than at Jerash but in recompense you'll probably have the luxury of having the site to yourself. The ruins are interesting because of the juxtaposition of the ruined Roman city and a relatively intact Ottoman-era village. The site also offers awesome views over the Golan Heights *(Murtafa-at al-Jawlan)* in Syria and the Sea of Galilee (Lake Tiberias) in Israel & the Palestinian Territories to the north, and the Jordan Valley to the south.

According to the Bible, it was at Gadara that Jesus cast demons out of two men into a herd of pigs, and the site was an early Christian place of pilgrimage, although an alternative Israeli site on the eastern shore of Lake Galilee also claims this miracle.

History
The ancient town of Gadara was captured from the Ptolemies by the Seleucids in 198 BC, and then the Jews under Hyrcanus captured it from them in 100 BC. Under the Romans, the fortunes of Gadara, taken from the Jews in 63 BC, increased rapidly and building was undertaken on a typically grand scale.

Herod the Great was given Gadara following a naval victory and he ruled over it until his death in 4 BC – much to the disgruntlement of locals who had tried everything to put him out of favour with Rome. On his death, the city reverted to semi-autonomy as part of the Roman province of Syria.

With the downfall of the Nabataean kingdom in AD 106, Gadara continued to flourish, and was the seat of a bishopric until the 7th century. By the time of the Muslim conquest, however, it was little more than a small village. Throughout the Ottoman period the village was substantially rebuilt.

In 1806 Gadara was 'discovered' by Western explorers and the local inhabitants claim to have formed the first government in Jordan, as well as signing the first agreement with the British in 1920. Excavations did not commence until 1982, when locals were finally repatriated to modern Umm Qais village. The site has recently been restored with German funding.

Information
The easiest way to enter ancient **Gadara** (admission JD1; ☑ 8am-5pm) is from the western end of the car park. The site is open 24 hours and there are no ticket checks.

There are a few signs in English. The brochure about Umm Qais published by the Jordan Tourism Board is useful; ask at the museum. *Umm Qais: Gadara of the Decapolis*, published by Al-Kutba (JD3), is ideal for anyone who wants further information. Guides (JD5 per 10 people) are also available at the ticket office in the car park.

There are toilets in the Umm Qais Resthouse. The tourist police are along the laneway from the museum to the resthouse.

The souvenir shop just east of the parking area is run by the former site curator, who is a great source of informal information on the area's archaeology.

Sights

The first thing you come to from the south is the well-restored and brooding **west theatre**, which once seated about 3000 people. Like the north theatre, it was made from black basalt.

Just to the north is the **basilica terrace** complex, about 95m by 35m, with a **colonnaded courtyard** of lovely limestone, marble and basalt colours. The western section housed a row of **shops** (the shells of which remain), but the most interesting remains are of the 6th-century **church**, with an unusual octagonal interior sanctum, marked today by the remaining basalt columns. The church was destroyed by earthquakes in the 8th century.

You'll soon hit the **decumanus maximus**, the main road that once linked Gadara with other nearby ancient cities such as Abila and Pella, and eventually reached the Mediterranean coast.

West along the decumanus maximus are the overgrown **baths**. Built in the 4th century, this was an impressive complex of fountains, statues and baths, but little remains after the various earthquakes. Almost opposite is the decrepit **nymphaeum** (the eastern of the two nymphaeums).

The decumanus maximus continues west for another 1km or so, leading to some ruins of limited interest, including **baths**, **mausoleums** and **gates**. Japanese and Iraqi archaeologists are currently excavating here. Most interesting is the basilica built above a **Roman mausoleum**. You can peer down into the subterranean tomb through a hole in the basilica floor. The sarcophagus of Helladis that once lay here can be seen in the Museum of Anthropology & Archaeology in Irbid.

When you find yourself flagging, head back and grab a reviving drink at the Umm Qais Resthouse (p122), with its stunning views over Gallilee, the Golan and the snowcapped peaks of Lebanon beyond. You can see the minarets of al-Himmah below and the lakeshore city of Tiberias in the distance.

From the resthouse continue on to Beit Russan, a former residence of an Ottoman governor, and now a **museum** (☎ 7500072; admission free; ☽ 8am-5pm Oct-Apr, to 6pm May-Sep). It is set around an elegant and tranquil

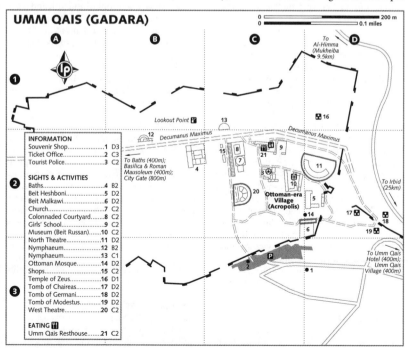

UMM QAIS (GADARA)

To Al-Himma (Mukheiba 9.5km)

Lookout Point

Decumanus Maximus

Decumanus Maximus

To Baths (400m); Basilica & Roman Mausoleum (400m); City Gate (800m)

Ottoman-era Village (Acropolis)

To Irbid (25km)

To Umm Qais Hotel (400m); Umm Qais Village (400m)

courtyard. The main mosaic on display (dating from the 4th century and found in one of the tombs) contains the names of early Christian notables and is a highlight, as is the headless, white marble statue of the Hellenic goddess Tyche, which was found sitting in the front row of the west theatre. Look out also for the wonderful carved basalt door. Exhibits are labelled in English and Arabic.

Surrounding the museum are the ruins of the **Ottoman-era village** dating from the 18th and 19th centuries and also known as the acropolis. If you have time and interest you can check out two intact houses, **Beit Malkawi** (now used as an office for archaeological groups) and the nearby **Beit Heshboni**. In the southeast corner is the **Ottoman mosque**, and in the far north are the remains of the **girls' school**.

Northeast of the museum is the **north theatre**, now overgrown and without its original black basalt rocks, which were cannibalised by villagers in other constructions.

Finally, around the eastern entrance from the main road are several tombs, including the **Tomb of Germani** and the **Tomb of Modestus**. About 50m further west, the **Tomb of Chaireas** dates from AD 154.

Sleeping & Eating

Umm Qais Hotel (☎ 7500080; s/d with shared bathroom JD6/12, with private bathroom 8/16) Few people spend the night in Umm Qais but this is a comfortable place on the main street of the modern village, about 400m west of the ruins. The simple rooms are clean, quiet and sunny, with 24-hour hot water, and the management is friendly. Guests can use the small kitchen or there's a small ground-floor restaurant and a rooftop café in summer.

Umm Qais Resthouse (☎ 7500555; www.romero-jordan.com; starters JD0.600-0.850, mains JD3-4.500, plus 26% tax; ☒ 10am-7pm, to 10pm Jun-Sep) Inside the ruins, this is a pleasant place to grab a glass of wine, kick back and savour the spectacular views. The restaurant is part of the Romero group and so both food and service are good. There's also a small crafts shop here.

A few basic eateries are scattered around the modern village; otherwise come prepared for a picnic in the ruins.

Getting There & Away

Umm Qais village, and the ruins a few hundred metres to the west, are about 25km

northwest of Irbid, and about 110km north of Amman. Minibuses leave Irbid's North bus station (250 fils, 45 minutes) on a regular basis. There's no direct transport from Amman.

With a car you can drive direct from Umm Qais to Pella along the Jordan Valley road, via the village of Adasiyyeh. The turn-off to the left is halfway to Al-Himma (below). The occasional minibus runs down this road to Shuneh ash-Shamaliyyeh but if you are relying on public transport to get to Pella you'll most likely have to backtrack to Irbid and take another minibus from there.

AL-HIMMA (MUKHEIBA)

الحمى (مخيبا)

☎ 02

The Al-Himma hot springs in the pleasant village of Mukheiba are worth a quick side trip from Umm Qais, especially in winter. Borderholics will get a buzz simply from being a stone's throw from the Golan Heights, currently occupied by Israel & the Palestinian Territories. In contrast to the bare, steeply rising plateau of the Golan to the north, the area is muggy, subtropical and lush and it can get very hot in summer. The springs, which reach about 33°C, were famous in Roman times for their health-giving properties and are still popular today.

The place is overrun with local tourists (mostly young men) on Friday and you may find accommodation full on Thursday and Friday nights.

Activities

The village's public **baths** (☎ 7500505; admission JD1; ☒ 8am-8pm) consist of three pleasant indoor hot pools and a dirtier and less popular outdoor pool. There are separate bathing times for men and women, which alternate every two hours. At the time of research men ruled the roost from 10am to noon, 2pm to 4pm and 6pm to 8pm, with women welcome at other times. The baths are on the right as you enter the village. There are rumours that a foreign company may upgrade the facilities, which will inevitably bring much higher fees.

Sleeping & Eating

Chalets (☎ 7500505; d/tr JD8/10, family apt JD25-35; ☒) The basic chalets overlooking the public baths are rundown and not much fun, although the big balconies are a plus. The family-style apartments are more comfortable and come with a hot-water bathroom and air-conditioning.

Sah al-Noum Hotel (☎ 7500510; tr with private bathroom JD6) Has simple and bright triple rooms with a fan, squat toilet and shower, although some are cleaner than others. There's a large, shady restaurant and pleasant private bathing area out the back which is nice but not exactly the place to share a hot tub with that special someone. The hotel is signposted at the fork in the road near the public baths.

Al-Hameh Restaurant (☎ 7500512; starters from 400 fils, mains JD1.250-2.500, large beer JD1.750; ☺ 9am-8pm) The nice terrace overlooking the baths is a good place to grab some lunch, though there is not much going on here during weekdays.

Getting There & Away

Mukheiba is 10km north of Umm Qais, down the hill towards the Golan via a very scenic road. There are reasonably regular minibuses (100 fils, 15 minutes) between Mukheiba and Umm Qais on most days, with plenty on Friday. Direct minibuses from Irbid's North station (350 fils, one hour) also pass along the main street of Umm Qais.

Make sure you bring your passport as there's a military checkpoint just past the turn-off to the Umm Qais ruins. This is also a good place to hitch a ride.

SHUNEH ASH-SHAMALIYYEH (NORTH SHUNA)   الشونة الشمالية
☎ 02

This junction town also has a **hot springs complex** (admission JD1; ☺ 8am-9pm). Irbid locals say the springs are cleaner than those at

---

THE JORDAN VALLEY

Forming a part of the Great Rift Valley of Africa, the fertile valley of the Jordan River was of considerable significance in biblical times and is now the food bowl of Jordan.

The hot dry summers and short mild winters make for ideal growing conditions, and (subject to water restrictions) two or three crops are grown every year. Thousands of tonnes of fruit and vegetables are produced annually, with the main crops being tomatoes, cucumbers, melons and citrus fruits. You'll see dozens of greenhouses and nurseries as you travel through the valley.

The Jordan River rises from several sources, mainly the Anti-Lebanon Range in Syria, and flows down into the Sea of Galilee (Lake Tiberias), 212m below sea level, before draining into the Dead Sea. The actual length of the river is 360km, but as the crow flies the distance between its source and the Dead Sea is only 200km.

It was in the Jordan Valley, some 10,000 years ago, that people first started to plant crops and abandon their nomadic lifestyle for permanent settlements. Villages were built, primitive irrigation schemes were undertaken and by 3000 BC produce from the valley was being exported to neighbouring regions, much as it is today.

The Jordan River is highly revered by Christians because Jesus was baptised in its waters by John the Baptist at the site of Bethany-Beyond-the-Jordan (see p141). Centuries earlier, Joshua led the Israelite armies across the Jordan near Tell Nimrin (Beth Nimrah in the Bible) after the death of Moses, marking the symbolic transition from the wilderness to the land of milk and honey.

And while all Israel were passing over on dry ground, the priests who bore the ark of the covenant of the Lord stood on dry ground in the midst of the Jordan, until all the nation finished passing over the Jordan.

Joshua 3: 17

Since 1948 the Jordan River has marked the boundary between Jordan and Israel & the Palestinian Territories, from the Sea of Galilee to the Yarbis River. From there to the Dead Sea marked the 1967 cease-fire line between the two countries; it now marks the continuation of the official frontier with the Palestinian Territories.

During the 1967 War with Israel, Jordan lost the West Bank and the population on the Jordanian east bank of the valley dwindled from 60,000 before the war to 5000 by 1971. During the 1970s, new roads and fully serviced villages were built and the population has now soared to over 100,000.

Al-Himma and they're cheaper, but they're not as well set up.

There are simple **chalets** (☎ 6587189; chalet for 4 persons JD30) in the complex, as well as a shady restaurant, although the sulphur smell can be a little overpowering.

Shuneh ash-Shamaliyyeh is accessible by minibus from Irbid (West bus station; 270 fils; 45 minutes) and has connections to anywhere along the Jordan Valley road (Hwy 65), including to Al-Mashari'a (for Pella) and Deir Alla.

PELLA (TAQABAT FAHL)　　　بيلا
☎ 02

In the midst of the Jordan Valley are the ruins of the ancient city of Pella (Taqabat Fahl), one of the 10 cities of the Decapolis (see p109). Although not as spectacular as Jerash, Pella is far more important to archaeologists because it has revealed evidence of 6000 years of settlement, from the Stone Age through to medieval Islamic ruins.

Many of the ruins are spread out and in need of excavation, so some walking and imagination are required to get the most

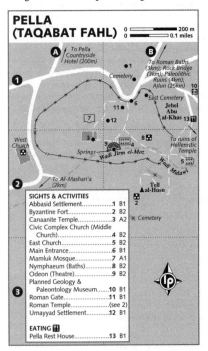

PELLA (TAQABAT FAHL)

SIGHTS & ACTIVITIES	
Abbasid Settlement	1 B1
Byzantine Fort	2 B2
Canaanite Temple	3 A2
Civic Complex Church (Middle Church)	4 B2
East Church	5 B2
Main Entrance	6 B2
Mamluk Mosque	7 A1
Nymphaeum (Baths)	8 B2
Odeon (Theatre)	9 B2
Planned Geology & Paleontology Museum	10 B1
Roman Gate	11 B1
Roman Temple	(see 2)
Umayyad Settlement	12 B1

EATING 🍴	
Pella Rest House	13 B1

from the site. That said, the setting is superb and there are some fine views over the Jordan Valley.

History
Pella was inhabited as early as 5000 BC, and Egyptian texts make reference to it in the 2nd millennium BC.

Pella really only flourished during the Greek and Roman periods. The Jews largely destroyed Pella in 83 BC because the inhabitants were not inclined to adopt the customs of their conquerors. It was to Pella that Christians fled persecution from the Roman army in Jerusalem in the 2nd century AD.

The city reached its peak during the Byzantine era, and by AD 451 Pella had its own bishop. The population at this time may have been as high as 25,000. The defeat of the Byzantines by the invading Islamic armies near Pella in 635 was quickly followed by the knockout blow at the Battle of Yarmouk (near modern Mukheiba) the next year.

Until the massive earthquake that shook the whole region in 747, Pella continued to prosper under the Umayyads. Archaeological finds show that even after the earthquake the city remained inhabited on a modest scale. The Mamluks occupied it in the 13th and 14th centuries, but afterwards Pella was virtually abandoned.

Information
The **site** (admission free) is officially open 8am to 6pm, but if the main entrance is closed, you can enter via the Pella Rest House on the hill.

Anyone with a specific interest should buy *Pella*, published by Al-Kutba (JD3) and available in major bookshops around Jordan.

Sights
THE RUINS
At the base of the main mound (on your right as you enter through the main entrance) are the limited remains of a **Roman gate** to the city. Atop the hill are the ruins of an **Umayyad settlement**, which consisted of shops, residences and storehouses. The small, square **Mamluk mosque** to the west dates from the 14th century. Carved into the south side of the hill is the recently excavated **Canaanite temple**, which was constructed in around 1270 BC and dedicated to the Canaanite god Baal.

The main structure, and indeed one of the better preserved of the ruins at Pella, is the Byzantine **civic complex church** (or **middle church**), which was built atop an earlier Roman civic complex in the 5th century AD and modified several times in the subsequent two centuries. Adjacent is the **odeon** (a small theatre used for musical performances). It once held 400 spectators, but you will need considerable imagination to picture this now. East of the civic complex church are the low-lying remains of a Roman **nymphaeum**.

Up the hill to the southeast is the 5th-century **east church**, which is in a lovely setting. From there a trail leads down into Wadi Malawi and then climbs **Tell al-Husn** (note the remains of tombs cut into the hillside), atop which are the stones of a **Byzantine fort** and **Roman temple**. There are good views of the Jordan Valley from here.

Outside the main site, there are the ruins of a small **Abbasid settlement** about 200m north of the main entrance. There are also a few limited **Palaeolithic ruins** (4km), **Roman baths** and a **rock bridge** (3km) reached via the road past the turn-off to the Pella Rest House.

Also, ask at the rest house how to get to the rubble of a **Hellenistic temple** high on Jebel Sartaba to the southeast; from there, Jerusalem is visible on a clear day. Figure on a couple of hours for the return hike.

A **Geology & Palaeontology Museum** (www.pella museum.org) has been planned for a while now on a site behind the rest house. The museum is the brainchild of famous Jordanian architect Ammar Khammash, but construction had been put on hold during our latest visit.

Sleeping & Eating

Pella Countryside Hotel (☎ 079 5574145; fax 6560899; s/d half board JD20/25) The manager of the Pella Rest House runs this B&B from the back of his house. It has a lovely family feel and a nice outlook towards the ruins. From February to May, black irises, the national flower of Jordan, bloom in the owner's garden. The seven rooms are well kept, with private bathroom and hot shower. Tea and coffee

are complementary and it's well signposted on the road to the site. It's a good place to kick back for a few days and the family can arrange picnics in the surrounding hills.

Pella Rest House (☎ 079 55574145; meals JD6, beer JD2.500; ✆ noon-7pm) Commands exceptional views over Pella and the Jordan Valley; Israel & the Palestinian Territories is visible to the right of the communications towers, the West Bank is to the left, and the Jenin Heights and Nablus are in the middle. Chicken and fresh St Peter's fish (from the Jordan River) are the order of the day and the food is good.

Getting There & Away

From Irbid's West bus station, minibuses go to Al-Mashari'a (400 fils, 45 minutes); get off before Al-Mashari'a at the junction. Pella is a steep 2km walk up from the signposted turn-off but you should be able to find a seat in a minibus up to town (100 fils) or the rest house (250 fils). Check the price first as many of these unlicensed drivers are sharks. There is no direct transport from Amman.

With your own car you can take the newly built back roads to Ajlun (25km), but is best to get good directions from the rest house before setting off.

DEIR ALLA   دير علا

The conical mound of Deir Alla, 35km north of Shuneh al-Janubiyyeh (South Shuna), is one of those places that's more interesting to read about than actually visit. It was first settled around 1500 BC as an early temple, market and cult centre, and is thought to have been the biblical town of Succoth, before it was destroyed in 1200 BC. Various finds from the site are on display in the museum at Salt.

A notice board at the base of the ruins has some limited explanations, or you could ask at the Antiquities Office across the road. The site can be combined with Pella in a day trip from Irbid or Ajlun. Minibuses run along the Jordan Valley road and pass right by the ruins.

The Eastern Desert
شرقي الأردن

The deeper you go into the desert, the closer you come to God.

Arab proverb

To the east of Amman the suburbs gradually peter out, replaced by the *badia*, a stony black basalt desert that stretches to Iraq and Saudi Arabia. The desolate region has long been cut by pilgrimage and trade routes to Mecca and Baghdad; today it's the Trans-Arabia Pipeline and the increasingly strategic Hwy 10 to Iraq. If it wasn't for these, eastern Jordan would probably be left to the Bedouin and their goats. Out in the east you are quickly reminded that Jordan's lonely deserts make up 80% of the country's land, yet support only 5% of its population.

The main attractions for visitors are the hunting lodges, bathhouses, forts and pleasure palaces, collectively known as the 'desert castles', which dot the inhospitable landscape. Azraq holds the region's only real accommodation and is also the site of its greatest environmental disaster, which has seen the region's greatest oasis destroyed in the space of a generation. On a brighter note, the nearby Azraq and Shaumari wildlife reserves offer a rare chance to spot some impressive desert wildlife, including the oryx and wild ass, both reintroduced from the brink of extinction.

Public transport is limited in eastern Jordan, so travelling around in a chartered taxi, organised tour or rented car is a popular and often necessary alternative. Beyond the main highways you'll need a 4WD and preparation for a desert adventure.

THE EASTERN DESERT

HIGHLIGHTS

- Clamber through the brooding basalt ruins of **Umm al-Jimal** (p128), worth exploring for their remote setting
- Explore the desert headquarters of the enigmatic TE Lawrence at **Qasr al-Azraq** (p134), the most accessible – and one of the more interesting – of Jordan's desert castles
- Drink in the details of the wonderful and risqué frescoes of **Qusayr Amra** (p135), a Unesco World Heritage site
- Wander the maze-like corridors of the mighty caravanserai-style **Qasr Kharana** (p136), seemingly lost in the middle of the desert

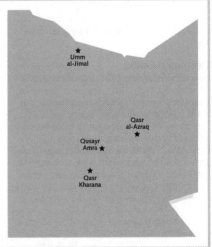

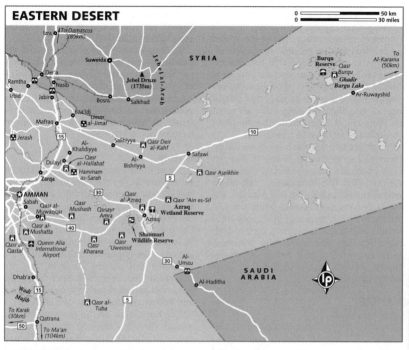

Getting Around

The four desert castles that most visitors see are Qasr al-Hallabat (with nearby Hammam as-Sarah), Qasr al-Azraq, Qusayr Amra and Qasr Kharana, in this order (ie clockwise from Amman) but they can, of course, be visited in the reverse order.

With hired transport you need a full day to visit all four, with lunch in Azraq and a possible visit to Azraq Wetland and/or Shaumari Wildlife reserves. If you start really early (and pay more), it's possible to fit in Umm al-Jimal. Qasr al-Mushatta is probably best visited from the airport or from the Desert Highway.

It is feasible to visit the four main castles in a single day using a combination of minibuses and hitching, though only the castles at Hallabat and Azraq are directly accessible by public transport. You could also base yourself in Azraq town, and use public transport, hitch or charter a vehicle from there.

If you have rented a car for a few days to tour around Jordan, consider renting it for an extra day for a jaunt around the castles and reserves. If driving from Amman, head east of Raghadan bus station towards Zarqa, and follow the signs to Azraq or the individual castles.

TOURS

Jumping on an organised tour of the desert castles from Amman makes a lot of sense, and is one of the few times when an independent traveller on a tight budget will find it worthwhile to bite the bullet and pay for a tour.

Tours can be arranged at the Cliff, Farah and Palace Hotels in Amman (see p87), which charge about JD10 per person for a full-day trip. You're unlikely to get a better deal by negotiating directly with the driver of a service taxi or private taxi in Amman, and regular taxi drivers may not speak English or know the way.

ZARQA   الزرقاء

☎ 09 / pop 700,000

The third largest city in Jordan (after Amman and Irbid), Zarqa is now virtually part of the continuous urban sprawl of northern

Amman. There's not much to this gritty working-class city except a string of truck stops and refugee camps, but you may end up in Zarqa waiting for onward transport.

Zarqa is currently most (in)famous for being the home town of Jordanian terrorist Abu Musab al-Zarqawi, thought to be behind many of the kidnappings and bombings in neighbouring Iraq. Zarqawi spent six years in jail in Jordan during the 1990s before being released in an amnesty.

There are two terminals for buses, minibuses and service taxis. Transport to/from both Raghadan and Abdali bus stations in Amman (200 fils, 30 minutes), and places near Amman such as Salt and Madaba, use the New (Amman) station. From the Old station in Zarqa, there is public transport to smaller villages in the region, such as Hallabat (for Qasr al-Hallabat and Hammam as-Sarah), Mafraq and Azraq. Minibuses shuttle between the two terminals in Zarqa every few minutes.

MAFRAQ   المفرق
☎ 04 / pop 32,000

Despite its appearance on some maps, Mafraq is much smaller than Zarqa. There is nothing to see and nowhere to stay, but travellers heading to eastern Jordan may need to go there for onward transport.

Like Zarqa, Mafraq has two terminals for buses, minibuses and service taxis. The larger Bedouin station has minibuses and service taxis to most places, including Abdali and Raghadan bus stations in Amman (250 fils, one hour), Salt, Zarqa, Madaba, Umm al-Jimal (200 fils, 30 minutes), Deir al-Kahf (for Qasr Deir al-Kahf) and Ar-Ruwayshid (for Qasr Burqu). From the Fellahin station, buses, minibuses and service taxis go to places in northern Jordan, such as Jerash and Irbid, and Ramtha and Jabir on the border with Syria.

UMM AL-JIMAL   أم الجمال

Comparatively little is known about the strange, black city of **Umm al-Jimal** (Mother of Camels; admission free; ☉ daylight hr). There are no grand temples or theatres like those in Jerash. Much of what remains at this large site (800m by 500m) is unpretentious urban architecture; over 150 simple buildings, including 128 houses and 15 churches, which provide a fascinating insight into rural life

during the Roman, Byzantine and early Islamic periods. It's great fun scrambling around the ruins.

Although mostly in ruins, many of the buildings are still discernible because, compared to others, the city was rarely looted or vandalised, and superior materials were used in its construction: Umm al-Jimal is notable for the 'corbelling' method of constructing inverted V-shaped roofs from large bricks of black basalt.

History

Umm al-Jimal was probably founded in the 1st century BC by the Nabataeans, but was quickly taken over by the Romans, who used it as part of their defensive cordon against the desert tribes. Roads led north to Bosra (in present-day Syria) and southwest to Philadelphia (modern Amman). Because it served as an important trading station for Bedouins and passing caravans, the city prospered. The city grew further during the Byzantine period; churches were constructed and Roman buildings were demilitarised.

The boom time was in the early Islamic period when this thriving agricultural city boasted about 3000 inhabitants. The key to the city's prosperity lay in its sophisticated method of storing water (you can still see many of the town's reservoirs).

However, Umm al-Jimal declined soon after the invasion by the Sassanians from Persia in the early 7th century AD; the city's death knell was sounded by an earthquake in 747. The ruins were occupied by Druze refugees fleeing persecution in Syria early in the 20th century, and used as an outpost by French soldiers during WWI.

Information

It's a good idea to allow several hours to explore the ruins. Visit early in the morning, or late in the afternoon, when the light shines dramatically on the black basalt and it's not too hot (there is little shade).

For more details about the site, look for the hard-to-find booklet *Umm el-Jimal* (JD3), published by Al-Kutba and available sporadically at bookshops in Amman.

Sights

The large structure just past the southern entrance is the **barracks**, built by the Romans. The towers were added later and,

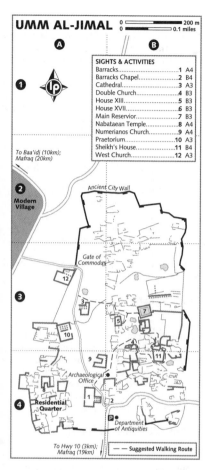

UMM AL-JIMAL

0   200 m
0   0.1 miles

SIGHTS & ACTIVITIES
Barracks...........................1 A4
Barracks Chapel..............2 B4
Cathedral........................3 A3
Double Church.................4 B3
House XIII........................5 B3
House XVII.......................6 B3
Main Reservior.................7 B3
Nabataean Temple...........8 A4
Numerianos Church..........9 A4
Praetorium....................10 A3
Sheikh's House...............11 B4
West Church..................12 A3

To Baa'idj (10km);
Mafraq (20km)

Modern Village

Ancient City Wall

Gate of Commodus

Archaeological Office

Residential Quarter

Department of Antiquities

To Hwy 10 (3km);
Mafraq (19km)

- - - Suggested Walking Route

fine corbelled ceilings, decorated doorways and carved pillars point to the fact that it was built by a wealthy family. A few metres to the south is the **sheikh's house**, which is notable for its expansive courtyard, stables and stairways. Look for the gravity-defying stairs to the north and the precarious corner tower. You can just make out a double stairway to the east of the courtyard. After exiting the building you get a good view of the lovely arched window and vaulted semicircular basement in the exterior eastern wall.

About 150m north of the double church, steps lead down to the **main reservoir**, one of several around the city. Less than 100m to the left (southwest) is **house XIII**, originally a stable for domestic goats and sheep, and later renovated and used as a residence by Druze settlers.

To the west (about 100m) is the **cathedral**, built in about AD 556, but now mostly in ruins. The **praetorium** (military headquarters) is less than 100m to the southwest. Built in the late 2nd century AD by the Romans, it was extended by the Byzantines, and features a triple doorway.

About 200m to the north, through one of the old city gates, is the **west church**, easily identifiable with its four arches and ornate Byzantine crosses.

Getting There & Away

Umm al-Jimal is only 10km from the Syrian border, and about 20km east of Mafraq. With an early start, it is possible to day trip from Amman by public transport. From the Abdali or Raghadan bus stations in Amman, catch a bus or minibus to Bedouin station in Mafraq (possibly with a connection in Zarqa), and from Mafraq catch another minibus to Umm al-Jimal (200 fils, 30 minutes).

If you're driving, head east of Mafraq along Hwy 10 for 16km towards Safawi, then take the signed turn-off north for 3km to Umm al-Jimal. If you have chartered a taxi from Amman for a day trip around the desert castles, it is possible to include Umm al-Jimal on the itinerary for a little extra (maybe JD5) – but start early to fit it all in.

AZRAQ   الأزرق

☎ 05 / pop 6000

The oasis town of Azraq ('blue' in Arabic) lies 103km east of Amman. Once an important meeting of trade routes from Baghdad to

like the castle at Azraq, it has a swinging basalt door that still functions. The **barracks chapel** was added to the east of the barracks during the Byzantine period (around the 5th century). About 150m to the left (west) of the barracks is what some archaeologists believe is a **Nabataean temple**, because of the altar in the middle.

About 100m north of the barracks is the **Numerianos church**, one of several ruined Byzantine churches. Another 100m to the northeast is the **double church**, recognisable by its two semicircular naves, a wonderful structure that was renovated and extended several times over the centuries. About 80m to the right (east) is **house XVII**, whose double-door entryway, interior courtyard,

THE EASTERN DESERT

Jerusalem, and strategic stop on the pilgrim route to Mecca, it performs a similar function today, although the belching camels have been replaced by belching trucks. It forms a junction of roads heading northeast to Safawi and Iraq (230km away), and southeast to Saudi Arabia. The town itself is fairly unattractive and the roads are dominated by truck transport and diesel fumes.

Azraq was once one of the very few sources of water in the region (see opposite). It is also home to Qasr al-Azraq (p134).

Orientation

Azraq is divided in two settlements located north and south of the T-junction of Hwy 5 from Safawi and Hwy 30 from Amman.

Azraq al-Janubi (South Azraq) was founded early last century by Chechens fleeing Russian persecution and stretches for about 1km south of the junction, while Azraq ash-Shomali (North Azraq), where the castle is located, starts about 5km to the north and is home to a minority of Druze, who fled French Syria in the 1920s.

Information

South Azraq is basically a truck stop, with a strip of restaurants, cafés and mechanics. Although it is far less appealing than North Azraq, the southern end has the only budget hotel, cheap restaurants, moneychangers and private telephone agencies. The post office is located in North Azraq.

Sleeping

Zoubi Hotel (☎ 3835012; r with bathroom JD10) Apart from several insalubrious truck stops, this is the only budget accommodation in town. The rooms are comfortable, with clean bathrooms and charming old-fashioned furniture. It is located behind the Refa'i Restaurant in South Azraq, about 800m south of the T-junction.

Al-Azraq Hotel & Resthouse (☎ 3834006; fax 3835215; s/d/tr with bathroom & breakfast JD25/32/45) This semiluxurious resort is surprisingly good value, and includes both comfortable and spacious rooms, satellite TV and a pleasant swimming pool area. The turn-off is located about 2km north of the T-junction, from where it is a further 1.5km to the resthouse.

Azraq Lodge (☎ 3835017) The former British military hospital in south Azraq has recently been renovated by the Royal Society for the Conservation of Nature (RSCN) as a base from which to explore the eastern desert. It's a friendly place with a nostalgic 1950s colonial feel.

Eating

A bunch of small kebab restaurants lines the 1km stretch of road south of the T-junction, rich with the aroma of grilled mutton and diesel. The best are arguably Turkey Restaurant, Cave Restaurant and Refa'i Restaurant, although you could pretty much take your pick from whatever appeals.

Azraq Palace Restaurant (☎ 079 5030356; buffet JD6; ☽ noon-4pm & 6-11pm) This is probably the best place to eat in town and is where most groups stop for lunch. For something lighter try the salad-only buffet for JD4. Evenings are à la carte. The restaurant serves alcohol, which attracts Saudis from across the border.

Getting There & Around

Minibuses (650 fils, 1½ hours) travel between the post office (north of the castle in North Azraq) and the Old Station in Zarqa, which is well connected to Amman and Irbid. Minibuses run up and down the road along northern and southern Azraq in search of passengers before hitting the highway to Zarqa. Use this minibus to travel between the two parts of Azraq.

AZRAQ WETLAND RESERVE

محمية واحة الأزرق

The Qa'al Azraq (Azraq Basin) comprises a huge area of mudflats, pools and marshlands. Before some of this was declared an 'internationally important wetland' in 1977, the wetlands suffered appalling ecological damage (see opposite).

The RSCN has now taken control of the wetlands and established a small (12 sq km) reserve (☎ 3835017; admission JD2, combination ticket with Shaumari Wildlife Reserve JD3; ☽ 9am-sunset). Until more water is pumped into the wetlands to attract the birds, there's not that much to see, but it is easy to reach, just 500m east of town, and can be combined with a trip to the desert castles and Shaumari Wildlife Reserve.

Information

A new **visitor centre** (☎ 3835017), run by the RSCN, marks the entrance to the reserve.

WHAT HAPPENED TO THE WETLANDS?

The Azraq Basin originally fanned out over 12,710 sq km (an area larger than Lebanon). Excavations clearly indicate that it was home to early communities thousands of years ago and once supported roaming herds of animals, including elephants, cheetahs, lions and hippos.

But the wetlands have become an ecological disaster. Extraction of the water from the wetlands to the developing cities of Amman and Irbid started in the late 1960s. Some of the water was 'fossil water' – around 10,000 years old – and was being replaced less than half as quickly as it was being pumped out. Experts believe that 3000 cu metres of water filled the wetlands every year about 40 years ago. The figure plummeted to a catastrophic 10 cu metres per year in 1980, and by 1991 the wetlands had dried up completely. A generation ago there was surface water, but in the 1990s the water level dropped to over 10m below the ground. At this time, salt water seeped into the wetlands, making the water unpalatable for wildlife, and hopeless for drinking and irrigation.

The effect on wildlife has been devastating. The oasis was once a staging post for migratory birds en route from Europe to sub-Saharan Africa, but a simple statistic tells the tale: on 2 February 1967 there were 347,000 birds present in the wetlands; on 2 February 2000, there were just 1200 birds. The wetlands were also home to a species of killifish (Aphanius sirhani), a small fish of only 4cm to 5cm in length and found nowhere in the world outside Azraq. Believed extinct in the late 1990s, a few somehow survived and the RSCN is trying to ensure the killifish population is again able to grow.

Despite efforts in the 1960s to declare the Azraq wetlands a protected national reserve, it was not until 1977 that the RSCN finally established the Azraq Wetland Reserve.

Since 1994, serious funding and commitment from the UN Development Program (UNDP), Jordanian government and RSCN has successfully halted the pumping of water from the wetlands to urban centres. Around 1.5 million cu metres of fresh water is now being pumped back into the wetlands every year by the Jordanian Ministry of Water, an ongoing process which, it is hoped, will enable 10% of the wetlands to be restored, thereby decreasing salinity and attracting wildlife again to the region. It is estimated, however, that more than 500 illegal wells still exist in the area.

THE EASTERN DESERT

It contains an informative interpretation room, an education room (to raise awareness of the wetlands plight and for the training of guides) and an RSCN Nature Shop.

Products from the nature shop are made in the **handicrafts centre** (9am-4pm Sun-Thu), 800m from the visitors centre, where you can see the painting of ostrich eggs, silk screening and embroidery.

Wildlife

The RSCN estimates that about 300 species of resident and migratory birds still use the wetlands during their winter migration from Europe to Africa. They include raptor, several species of lark, desert wheatear, trumpeter finch, eagle, plover and duck. A few buffaloes wallow in the marshy environs, and there are jackals and jerbils at night. The best time to see birdlife is winter (December to February) and early spring (March and April), although the raptors arrive in May. How many birds you actually get to see depends largely on water levels in the reserve.

A 1.5km pathway through the reserve known as the **Marsh Trail** takes 30 minutes to walk, and is ideal for **bird-watching**, although serious birding enthusiasts could take much longer, stopping at the bird hide en route. A viewing platform overlooks the Shishan springs, which once watered the entire marshlands. The path then continues along an ancient Roman or Umayyad water control wall.

SHAUMARI WILDLIFE RESERVE

محمية الشومري

The **Shaumari Wildlife Reserve** (Mahmiyyat ash-Shaumari; www.rscn.org.jo; admission JD2, combination ticket with Azraq Wetland Reserve JD3; 8am-4pm) was established in 1975 and was the first of its kind in Jordan. Its aim was to reintroduce wildlife that had disappeared from the region, most notably the Arabian oryx (see p132) but also Persian onagers (wild

SAVING THE ARABIAN ORYX

The last time the Arabian oryx was seen in Jordan was in 1920 when hunting drove the animal to local extinction. In 1972 the last wild Arabian oryx was killed by hunters in Oman and the oryx was declared extinct in the wild. The nine lonely oryxes left in captivity were pooled and taken to the Arizona Zoo for a breeding programme. They became known as the 'World Oryx Herd'.

In 1978 four male and four female oryxes were transported to Jordan and three more were sent from Qatar the following year. In 1979 the first calf, Dusha, was born and Jordan's oryx began the precarious road to recovery. By 1983 there were 31 oryxes in Shaumari and they were released into the large enclosures. Since that time, they have been treated as wild animals to facilitate their eventual release into the wild.

The Arabian oryx is a herbivore, and, although its white coat had traditionally offered camouflage in the searing heat of the desert, it was also highly prized by hunters, as were its long curved horns, thereby precipitating its near extinction. Oryxes live in herds – even in the enclosures of Shaumari the animals have divided into two or three small herds. Every two to three years, younger males challenge the leader of the herd for dominance, locking horns in a battle in which the loser often dies.

Well adapted to their desert environment, oryxes once had an uncanny ability to sense rain on the wind. One herd is recorded as having travelled up to 155km, led by a dominant female, to rain. In times of drought, oryxes have been known to survive 22 months without water, obtaining moisture from plants and leaves. In Shaumari, according to the RSCN, a whole year's rainfall is only just enough to get your feet wet so the oryxes here are provided with water.

Most oryx calves are born in winter with an 8½-month gestation period. Mothers leave the herd just prior to birth to make a small nest, returning to the herd two or three months after the birth of the calf (which can be up to 5kg in weight). Oryxes have a life span of about 20 years.

In a significant landmark for environmentalists the world over, a small group of oryxes was reintroduced into the wild in the Wadi Rum Protected Area in 2002 – a small, tentative step in what is hoped will be the recovery of the wild oryx in Jordan. The next step is to introduce oryx to the Burqu area in the far northeast.

ass), goitered gazelle and ostrich. Despite poaching and natural predators, four species of wildlife have flourished, a testament to RSCN efforts.

The small (22 sq km) Shaumari Wildlife Reserve is not the place to go to see wildlife roaming the plains unhindered – the animals you'll see are kept in large enclosures – but it is worth a quick visit to see some of the region's most endangered wildlife and the environmentally significant work being done by the RSCN, and it's generally a hit with children.

Orientation & Information

At the entrance to the reserve is a shop selling RSCN products. To the right as you pass through the gate is the nature centre, detailing the fight to save the oryx. Further in is a small picnic area and children's playground, which leads to the **observation tower** and telescope, from where most of the animal species can be seen, including the ornery ostriches.

If you want to get closer, take the **Oryx Safari** (JD10 for up to 10 people, one hour) that drives through the desert to spot oryx. Night safaris are also possible.

Wildlife

Shaumari is home to four main types of wildlife: the Arabian oryx (87 now in the reserve); the blue-necked and red-necked ostrich (40), which was long ago hunted to extinction in the wild in Jordan; the Sabgutu Rosa and Dorcas gazelles (six); and the Persian onager or wild ass (eight).

Nearly 250 species of bird have been identified, including raptor, golden eagle and Egyptian vulture. The best time of year to see birds and wildlife is spring (March to May) and early winter (December).

Sleeping & Eating

You can sleep in the 11 tents of the reserve **campground** (s/d/tr/q per person incl admission fee JD13/11/10/9). With permission from RSCN staff, you can also pitch your tent and use the toilets and cold showers for free. You'd need to be self-sufficient with food, though you can use the kitchen.

Getting There & Away

Shaumari is well signposted on the road from Azraq south to the Saudi border. From the T-junction in Azraq, the turn-off is 7km to the south, while the small road to the reserve runs for a further 6km. The last kilometre is gravel. It is relatively easy to charter a minivan to the reserve from Azraq (JD5), but make sure you arrange for the driver to wait, unless you want to hike 5km back to the main road.

DESERT CASTLES

A string of buildings (pavilions, caravanserais, hunting lodges, forts) and ruins – known collectively (if a little erroneously) as the desert castles – pepper the deserts of eastern Jordan. Most were built, or taken over and adapted, by the Damascus-based Umayyads (AD 661–750) in the earliest years of Islam, though the foundations of two castles, Al-Azraq and Al-Hallabat, date from Roman times. The interiors were richly decorated with mosaics, frescoes, marble, plaster and painted stucco, providing oases of pleasure in the harsh desert.

There are various theories about their use. The early Arab rulers were still Bedouin at heart and their love of the desert probably led them to build (or remodel) these pleasure palaces, which once teemed with orchards and wild game. They pursued their pastimes of hawking, hunting and horse-racing for a few weeks each year. The evenings were apparently spent in wild festivities with plenty of wine, women, poetry and song. They also served as popular staging posts for pilgrims travelling to Mecca and along trade routes to Syria, Arabia and Iraq (never underestimate the luxury of a hot bath in the desert!).

Some historians say that only here did the caliphs (Islamic rulers) feel comfortable about flouting Islam's edicts against the representation of living beings and the drinking of wine. Others have suggested that they came to avoid epidemics in the

big cities or even to maintain links with, and power over, the Bedouin, the bedrock of their support in the conquered lands.

Information

Some of the more remote castles are locked, so you may have to find the caretaker. If he opens any door especially for you (or provides a commentary), a tip (about 500 fils) is obligatory. The five main castles listed following (except Qasr al-Mushatta) have useful explanations inside their entrances. All are building visitor centres and an entry fee of around JD2 may soon follow.

Before setting off, make sure you pick up a free copy of the excellent *Desert Castles* brochure, published by the Jordan Tourism Board (JTB) and available at the JTB office in Amman (see p70). If you want more information about the castles, pick up the small *The Desert Castles,* published by Al-Kutba (JD3) and available from the larger bookshops around Jordan.

See p127 for information on tours and transport to the castles.

QASR AL-HALLABAT قصر الحلابات

This first stop for many visitors on a day trip from Amman is not necessarily the most interesting, so this could be missed if you're pushed for time.

A new visitor centre has been built at the entrance to the site and an entry fee may soon follow. Restoration is continuing under Spanish direction.

Hallabat is a good place to watch the sunset, so if you have your own transport, and don't mind driving back to Amman in the dark, try to finish at Qasr al-Hallabat late in the afternoon.

History

The *qasr* was originally a Roman fort during the reign of Caracalla (AD 198–217), a defence against raiding desert tribes, although there's evidence that Trajan before him established a post on the site of a Nabataean emplacement. In the 6th century, it was renovated and became a Byzantine monastery, but was abandoned during the Sassanian invasion from Persia in the early 7th century. About 100 years later, the Umayyads strengthened the fort, and the hedonistic caliph Walid II converted it into a pleasure palace. In its heyday it

THE EASTERN DESERT

boasted baths, with frescoes and mosaics, a mosque, several reservoirs and an entire farming community.

Sights

Today, the ruins are a jumble of crumbling walls and fallen stones, with only two buildings of much interest.

The white limestone of the square **Umayyad fort** was built on top of the existing black basalt of the earlier Byzantine palace. The fort once contained four large towers, and was three-storeys high. Look for the mosaics above the large central cistern. In the northwest corner are ruins of the smaller original **Roman fort**.

Just east of the fort is the rectangular **mosque**, built in the 8th century. Three walls are still standing, with a lovely cusped arch on the west wall, and the foundations of the original mihrab to the south.

Scattered around the fort you can spot the remains of several cisterns, a huge reservoir and a village that was home to an entire community of palace servants.

Getting There & Away

Qasr al-Hallabat is in the village of Hallabat, and is one of the few castles that can be visited by public transport. Hallabat has a few basic shops selling food and cold drinks, but has no restaurants or places to stay.

From Amman (either Abdali or Raghadan bus station), take a minibus to the New (Amman) station in Zarqa, another minibus to the Old station in Zarqa, and another to Hallabat village (250 fils, 45 minutes).

HAMMAM AS-SARAH   حمام الصرح

Hammam as-Sarah (☼ daylight hr) is a hammam (bathhouse) and hunting lodge built by the Umayyads and linked to the complex at Qasr al-Hallabat. Built from limestone, the building has been well restored and you can still see the underfloor heating system and steam pipes that were used to heat the hot, cold and tepid bathing rooms. Outside the main building is a **well**, nearly 20m deep, an elevated tank and the remains of a nearby **mosque**.

The building is along the main road to Hallabat village, about 3km east of Qasr al-Hallabat and 5km from the main road. The minibus to Hallabat village drives past Hammam as-Sarah, and can drop you off (ask the driver) at the turn-off.

QASR AL-AZRAQ   قصر الأزرق

Azraq fort (admission free; ☼ daylight hr) is the most accessible desert castle, and one of the more interesting. Comparatively little is known about its history and there's been relatively little excavation and renovation. For most visitors, the most compelling attraction is the historical link to TE Lawrence.

> It was to be Ali's first view of Azrak, and we hurried up the stony ridge in high excitement, talking of the wars and songs and passions of the early shepherd kings, with names like music, who had loved this place; and of the Roman legionaries who languished here as garrison in yet earlier times.
>
> *TE Lawrence,*
> Seven Pillars of Wisdom

History

Greek and Latin inscriptions date earlier constructions on the site to around AD 300 – the reign of the Romans. The building was renovated in the Byzantine period, and the Umayyad caliph Walid II used it for hunting and as a military base. It was substantially rebuilt in 1237 by the Damascus-based Ayyubids. It was then occupied by the Ottoman Turks, who stationed a garrison here in the 16th century.

It is most famous because TE Lawrence and Sharif Hussein bin Ali based themselves here in the winter of 1917–18 during the Arab Revolt against the Turks. Lawrence set up his quarters in the room above the southern entrance, while his men used other areas of the fort and covered the gaping holes in the roof with palm branches and clay. They were holed up here for months in crowded conditions with little shelter from the intense cold. Much of the building collapsed in an earthquake in 1927.

Sights

This large building was constructed out of black basalt stone, and was originally three storeys high. Some **paving stones** in the main entrance have small indentations, carved by former gatekeepers who played an old board game using pebbles to pass the time. By the courtyard entrance look for the carvings of animals and various inscriptions.

Above the entrance is **Lawrence's Room**, strategically overlooking the entry and offset with arrow slits for defence. Opposite the entrance, and just to the left, are the remains of a small **altar**, built in the 3rd century AD by the Romans. In the middle of the expansive **courtyard** is a small **mosque**, angled to face Mecca. It dates to the Ayyubid period (early 13th century), but was built on the ruins of a Byzantine church. In the northeast corner of the courtyard, a hole with stairs leads down to a **well**, full of water until about 20 years ago. In the northwest corner are the ruins of the **prison**.

The northern sections are residential areas with barely discernible ruins of a **kitchen** and **dining room**, and nearby **storerooms** and **stables**. The **tower** in the western wall is the most spectacular, and features a huge **door** made of a single massive slab of basalt. Lawrence describes in his book *Seven Pillars of Wisdom* how it 'went shut with a clang and crash that made tremble the west wall of the castle'.

Getting There & Away

Qasr al-Azraq is easy to reach from Amman by public transport. The castle is situated in Azraq ash-Shomali (North Azraq), about 5km north of the T-junction at the end of the highway from Amman. See p130 for details about travelling to and around Azraq, and p130 for information about places to stay and eat.

QUSAYR AMRA   قصر عمرا

Heading back towards Amman along Hwy 30, a turn-off south leads to Hwy 40 and **Qusayr Amra** (admission free; 8am-6pm May-Sep, 8am-4pm Oct-Apr). It's one of the best preserved desert buildings of the Umayyads, and the fascinating and still vibrant 8th-century frescoes are the highlight of a trip out to the eastern desert.

The building was part of a greater complex that served as a caravanserai, baths and hunting lodge, possibly in existence before the arrival of the Umayyads. The word *qusayr* means 'little castle'.

History

Although historians are undecided, the general consensus is that the building was constructed around AD 711 during the reign of Umayyad caliph Walid I (AD 705–15), who also built the Umayyad Mosque in Damascus. A Spanish team of archaeologists began excavations in the mid-1970s; the frescoes have been restored with the assistance of governments and private institutions from Austria, France and Spain. The building is a Unesco World Heritage site.

Information

Entrance to the complex is through the excellent **visitor centre**, which has a relief map of the site, and some detailed descriptions of the site's history and the frescoes, plus some public toilets.

Photography of the interior doesn't seem to be regulated but bear in mind that flash photography will harm the frescoes.

Sights

The entrance of the main building opens immediately to the frescoed **audience hall**, where meetings, parties, exhibitions and meals were held.

As your eyes grow accustomed to the light you are greeted by two topless women that are painted on the arches, holding bowls of food (or money) against a blue background; look for the rich details in the cloth.

On the right side of the right wall is a scene of wrestlers warming up. To the left is the image of a woman who is bathing in what looks like an 8th-century thong. To the left of this painting are the defaced images of the Umayyad caliph surrounded by **six great rulers**, four of whom have been identified – Caesar, a Byzantine emperor; the Visigoth king, Roderick; the Persian emperor, Chosroes; and the Negus of Abyssinia. The fresco either implies that the Umayyad ruler was their equal or better, or it is simply a pictorial list of Islam's enemies. Above is a hunting scene. The left corner depicts a reclining woman with two attendants holding fans. Above her are twin peacocks and the Greek word for victory.

The main chamber alcove here features women's faces on a barrel vault topped off by a king seated on a throne surrounded by floral motifs.

The entire left wall is a huge hunting scene with dogs driving wild onagers into a trap of nets. The ceiling has a clear depiction of the construction of the baths, from the quarrying, moving the stones by camel, to carpentry and plastering of the walls.

A small doorway leads to the left through the three small rooms that made up the

---

THE FRESCOES OF QUSAYR AMRA

The information boards in the visitor centre at Qusayr Amra assure the visitor that: 'None of the paintings of Qusayr Amra portray scenes of unbridled loose-living or carryings-on'. Given the context of early Islam's prohibition of any illustrations of living beings, it's difficult to agree.

Just how far these boundaries were pushed is evident on the western wall of the audience hall, where there is a depiction of a nude woman bathing. Some historians speculate that she may have been modelled on the favourite concubine of the ruler of Amra. The more your eyes roam the walls, past images of musicians, naked dancers, hunters, cherubs, baskets of fruit (and even a bear playing a banjo!) the more the heresy of the frescoes becomes apparent.

And the purpose of all these paintings? Some Islamic scholars blame the Ghassanids, a pagan Arab tribe that ruled the region at the time of Rome, others mumble about rogue rulers who were not true to Islam. But most admit privately that it seems as though the rulers were simply enjoying themselves on a boys' night out, away from the confines of the court.

---

baths. The **apodyterium**, or changing room, has three blackened faces on the ceiling, said to depict the three stages of man's life. Local Christians believe the central figure to be a depiction of Christ. The left wall has a crazy hallucinogenic painting of an exuberant bear playing the banjo, egged on by an applauding monkey. The right wall depicts a musician and female dancer.

The **tepidarium** (where warm water was offered and warm air circulated beneath the floor) has scenes of naked women bathing a child.

The final room is the hot water **calidarium**, which is closest to the furnace outside. The highlight here is the Dome of Heaven, upon which is depicted a map of the northern hemisphere sky accompanied by the signs of the zodiac – one of the earliest known attempts to represent the universe on anything other than a flat surface. You can make out the centaur-like Sagittarius, the Great Bear and several other zodiac signs (see the map in the visitor centre for details).

Outside, a few metres north of the main building, is a partially restored 36m-deep stone **well** and a restored *saqiyah* – a pump turned by a donkey that raised the water to a cistern that supplied water for the baths and for passing caravans.

Getting There & Away

Qusayr Amra is right on the main road and hard to miss, but there are no buses so you'll have to hitch along Hwy 40. It's on the north side of the road, 26km from Azraq, south-west of the junctions of Hwys 30 and 40. From Azraq, take a minibus towards Zarqa as far as the junction, then hitch. You could charter a taxi from Azraq and combine it with a visit to Qasr Kharana.

QASR KHARANA   قصر خرانه

Located in the middle of a treeless plain, this mighty two-storey **building** (admission free; ☉ daylight hr) clearly looks like a fortress, but historians are divided; the narrow windows were probably for air and light rather than for shooting arrows, and though it looks like a *khan* (caravanserai), it wasn't located on any major trade route. The most recent supposition is that it was a meeting room for Umayyad rulers and local Bedouin.

Although small (35 sq metre), the castle has been nicely restored and is worth visiting.

History

A painted inscription above one of the doors on the upper floor mentions the date AD 710, making it one of the earliest forts of the Islamic era. The presence of stones with Greek inscriptions in the main entrance suggests it was built on the site of a Roman or Byzantine building, possibly as a private residence.

Information

A new **visitor centre** has been built at the site, with some displays on local history.

Sights

About 60 rooms (known as *beit*) surround the **courtyard** inside the castle. The long rooms either side of the arched **entrance** were used as **stables**, and in the centre of the courtyard was a **basin** for collecting rainwater.

Make sure you climb to the top levels along one of the elegant **stairways**, passing en route some rooms with vaulted ceilings. Most of the rooms in the upper levels are decorated with well-restored **carved plaster medallions**, set around the top of the walls, which are said to indicate Mesopotamian influence. Stairs in the southeast and southwest corners lead to the 2nd floor and the roof, from which there are great **views** of the surrounding *badia* – although the nearby highway and power station spoil the ambience somewhat.

Getting There & Away

This castle is 16km further west along Hwy 40 from Qusayr Amra. Like Qusayr Amra, it can't be missed from the highway, but there's no public transport along the highway. Either hitch from Azraq or Amman, or charter a vehicle from Azraq and combine it with a visit to Qusayr Amra.

QASR AL-MUSHATTA   قصر المشتى

Of the five major desert castles, the 'winter palace' of the **Qasr al-Mushatta** (admission free; ☽ daylight hr) is the most difficult and time consuming to reach. For this reason it's not included on most tours.

However, the ruins are fairly extensive and fun to wander around. Many pieces have disappeared over the years, ending up in museums around the world; the elaborate carving on the façade was shipped off to Berlin (it's now in the Pergamon Museum) after the palace was 'given' to Kaiser Wilhelm in 1903 by Sultan Abd al-Hamid of Turkey.

Because the castle is located near sensitive areas – primarily the airport – make sure you have your passport ready to show the guards along the way.

History

Qasr al-Mushatta was planned as the biggest and most lavish of all the Umayyad castles, but it was never finished. It was probably started in about AD 743, under caliph Walid II (who intended to establish a city in the area). He was later assassinated by angry labourers, many of whose colleagues had died during construction due to a lack of water in the area, so building was never completed.

Sights

There isn't much to see because the castle was looted, and partially destroyed by earthquakes – with most columns and watchtowers having collapsed. However, the huge exterior wall and carved façades still hint at the original grandeur and beauty of the site.

Right of the entrance are the ruins of a **mosque**, with its obviously rebuilt mihrab. The northern sections have the remains of a vault **audience hall** and **residences**. Segmented pillars lie scattered around like broken vertebrae. One unusual feature of the site is that the vaults were made from burnt bricks (an uncommon material in buildings of this style) rather than black basalt.

Getting There & Away

Qasr al-Mushatta is impossible to reach by public transport or hitching. Furthermore it's badly signposted, and involves going through at least two military checkpoints. If you're driving from Amman, head towards the Queen Alia International Airport, turn left off the Desert Highway to the airport, then turn right at the roundabout just past the Alia Hotel. Leave your passport at the first security check and then follow the road for 12km around the perimeter of the airport, turning right by the second and third checkpoints.

One alternative is to charter a taxi from the airport – a great idea if you have a long wait for a flight – or combine a taxi to the airport with a visit to the ruins. A visit can be made from the airport in an hour.

OTHER CASTLES

There are numerous other castles in eastern Jordan but they are mostly in ruins and of interest only to archaeologists; they're often impossible to reach by public transport and sometimes only accessible by pricey 4WD.

Qasr 'Ain es-Sil   قصر عين السيل

This is not really a castle or palace but a farmhouse built by the Umayyads, possibly over the fortifications of a Roman building. It is small (17 sq metres), and was built from basalt brick. There are some ruins of a **courtyard** (flanked by seven houses), equipment for making bread and olive oil, and some **baths**.

It is located just off the main road through Azraq ash-Shomali (North Azraq), and only about 2km from Qasr al-Azraq.

Qasr Aseikhin   قصر الشيخين

This small Roman fort, built from basalt in the 3rd century over the ruins of a 1st-century Nabataean building, has great views from the hilltop, but nothing else to justify a detour. It's about 22km northeast of North Azraq, and only accessible by 4WD. Go along the road north of Qasr al-Azraq for about 15km, and follow the signs to the fort.

Qasr Deir al-Kahf   قصر دير الكهف

Deir al-Kahf (Monastery of Caves) is another Roman fort, built in the 4th century, also from black basalt. The ruins are more extensive than some others but it is still very difficult to reach. There is an access road north of Hwy 10, or look for the signs along the back roads east of Umm al-Jimal.

Qasr Mushash   قصر موشاش

This large (2 sq km) Umayyad settlement is mostly in ruins. The highlights are the remains of the **palace**, a large **courtyard** surrounded by a dozen rooms, the **baths** and **cisterns**, and **walls** built to protect against possible flooding. It's only accessible by 4WD. Look for the sign along Hwy 40.

Qasr al-Muwaqqar   قصر الموقر

This former caravanserai was built in the Umayyad period, but the ruins are so decrepit that it's not worth bothering to find. There are some remains of **reservoirs**, **Kufic inscriptions** and **columns**, but little else to see; the most interesting item, a 10m stone tower with Kufic inscriptions, is now in the National Archaeological Museum in Amman. The views are wonderful, however.

The ruins are located about 2km north of Hwy 40.

Qasr al-Qastal   قصر القسطل

This ruined Umayyad settlement was ornately renovated by the Mamluks in the 13th century AD, but very little remains. The main building still standing is the 68-sq-metre **palace**, but there are ruins of an **Islamic cemetery** and **baths** nearby. It is located just to the west of the Desert Highway, before the turn-off to the airport, but is poorly signposted.

Qasr al-Tuba   قصر التوبة

This is one of the most impressive of the lesser-known castles, but is also the most difficult to reach. It was erected by the Umayyad caliph Walid II in about AD 743, but (like Qasr al-Mushatta) it was never finished after he was assassinated. The castle was probably going to be a caravanserai, and is unusual because it's made out of bricks. You can see an impressive doorway from the site at Amman's National Archaeological Museum.

The castle is only accessible by 4WD along a poorly signed dirt track (35km) west of the Desert Highway, or an unsigned dirt track south (50km) of Hwy 40. Because the roads are so difficult to find and follow, a knowledgeable guide is recommended.

Qasr 'Uweinid   قصر عويند

This Roman military fort was built in the 3rd century AD to protect the source of Wadi as-Sirhan (now in Saudi Arabia), but was abandoned less than 100 years later. It is only accessible by 4WD, and is about 15km southwest of Azraq al-Janubi (South Azraq); look for the turn-off along the road towards Shaumari Wildlife Reserve.

Qasr Burqu   قصر بورقو

You'd have to be pretty dedicated to visit this brooding black basalt fort and it's certainly too difficult to reach to be a part of a day trip around the desert castles. The fort was originally built in the 3rd century AD by the Romans, became a monastery during the Byzantine period and was restored by the Umayyads in about AD 700.

It's the remote location of the castle on the edge of the **Ghadir Burqu** lake, and the apparent incongruity of the lake in the harsh desert, which makes this place so special. With a tent and a 4WD you could have an adventurous desert trip out here.

The lake is home to a number of bird species (such as finch, stork and pelican) that come to roost because the water level rarely changes, even in summer. The lake also hosts wildflowers and animals such as gazelles, foxes and hyenas.

The RSCN hopes to establish Burqu as a protected reserve and organise trips there from its base in Azraq, though this will take a few years. Contact the RSCN in Amman (see p70) before heading out here.

The good news for the flora and fauna, and the bad news for visitors, is that Burqu is only accessible by 4WD – and with a guide. The lake and castle are about 25km northwest of Ar-Ruwayshid, which is on the road from Mafraq to the Iraqi border. Although public transport is available between Mafraq and Ar-Ruwayshid, there is no chance of even hitching north of the highway to Burqu, and the access road to Burqu is very rough.

Dead Sea Highway

The Dead Sea – known locally as Al-Bahr al-Mayit or Bahr Lut (Sea of Lot) – is one of the world's most extreme locations. About 65km long, with waters six times saltier than the ocean, the depression lies sweltering and sticky at the lowest point on earth. As you descend from the central Jordanian plateau into the Rift Valley the air gets warmer, thicker and muggier. The scenery turns barren brown and a spectacular blue lake opens up before your eyes.

Most people come to the Dead Sea to float in the weirdly buoyant waters or to pamper themselves in a seashore spa, but a trip here doesn't necessarily have to end with a been-there-done-that dip in the salty sea. The wonderful Wadi Mujib Nature Reserve in particular offers great scope for some wet and wild adventure, from hiking and ibex-spotting to swimming and waterfall rappelling.

There's also plenty of archaeological interest. The site of Bethany-Beyond-the-Jordan, where Jesus was baptised by John, is one of the most remarkable historical discoveries of recent years. Further south, Lot's Cave points the way to the intriguing possible locations of those quintessential biblical bad boys, Sodom and Gomorrah.

The Dead Sea Highway is best explored with a car. Public transport is very limited and you'll appreciate having the freedom to stop where you wish. The lowest spot on earth is oppressively hot and muggy in summer, and is best visited in winter or the shoulder months of April or October.

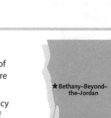

HIGHLIGHTS

- Visit **Bethany-Beyond-the-Jordan** (p141), one of the most important biblical sites in Jordan, where Jesus is believed to have been baptised

- Pack a newspaper and enjoy the bizarre buoyancy of floating in the **Dead Sea** (p143) and finish off with a mudpack to polish the pores

- Splash, swim, float and hike your way through the canyons and pools of the **Wadi Mujib Nature Reserve** (p146)

- Splurge on a day pass to the pools and/or spas of the **Dead Sea Resorts** (p145), followed by a fine meal or a sunset cocktail overlooking the Dead Sea

★ Bethany–Beyond–
the–Jordan

★ Dead Sea
Resorts

*Dead
Sea*   Wadi Mujib
★   Nature Reserve

DEAD SEA HIGHWAY

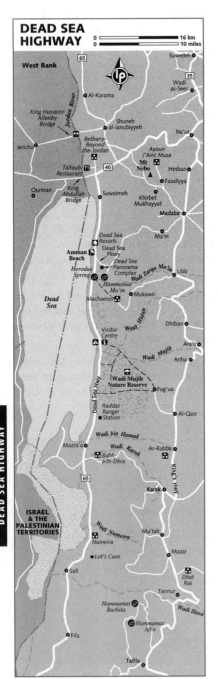

History

Throughout its history, the Dead Sea has changed names as often as it has shifted shorelines. The prehistoric lake, known as Lake Shagour or Lisan Lake, filled the entire Jordan Valley up to the Sea of Galilee until it split in two some 15,000 years ago. The sea was known in biblical times variously as the Salt Sea, the Sea of the Arabah or the Sea of the Plain. Local Arabic names translate as the Sea of Zo'ar, the Stinking Sea and the current name, the Sea of Lot.

The southeast corner of the sea is thought to be the location of Sodom and Gomorrah (see p147). Furthermore, archaeologists now believe that the other 'Five Cities of the Plain' (group of early city states on the Dead Sea plain, referenced in ancient texts and the Bible and sought for years by archaeologists) – Bela/Zoar (modern Safi), Admah (Fifa) and Zeboiim (Khanazir) – can be linked to the nearby towns and wadis of Safi, Fifa and Khanazir respectively, all supplied by fresh water wadis and located next to bitumen processing centres.

The Greeks and Romans named the lake the 'Pitch Sea' after the bitumen traded by the Nabataeans to the Egyptians (who used it for waterproofing and mummification). Ships laden with bitumen regularly crossed the sea in ancient times, as illustrated in a section of the 6th-century Madaba mosaic map (see p152). Trade in indigo, sulphur and sugar was also important historically, as was copper; the world's earliest copper mines are by the shores of the Dead Sea.

Hot springs pepper the sea's shores and have been popular since Roman times. Herod himself sailed across the sea to the spa at Callirhöe near Herodus Spring to get treatment for a skin complaint. Byzantine Christians also regularly travelled to the area, following pilgrim roads to Bethany, Mt Nebo and Lot's Cave.

The northern half of the sea's western shore belonged to Jordan when the famous Dead Sea scrolls were discovered by a Bedouin shepherd at Qumran in 1947. Israel took control of the entire western shore in 1967 after the Six Day War.

Getting There & Away

The Dead Sea Highway (Hwy 65) is the least used of the three main highways crossing Jordan from north to south, but

---

FAST FACTS

- The Dead Sea is the lowest spot on earth at 408m below sea level
- The Dead Sea has shrunk by 30% in recent years
- Jordanians call the Dead Sea depression 'al-Ghor', or the Sunken Land

---

it's a quicker and more interesting alternative to the Desert Highway if you're driving between Amman and Aqaba. Some scenery along the Dead Sea shoreline is superb, especially at the southern end. Around Safi, however, there are numerous trucks from the nearby potash factory and the southern stretches of the highway south of the Dead Sea are barren and desolate.

If you're driving, be aware that there are few petrol stations and places to eat, and there is no access to Petra from the highway, although there is a road to Karak. Much of the highway runs along the border of Israel & the Palestinian Territories, so keep your documents handy, including passport, driver's licence, rental contract and *ruksa* (registration card) for the car.

Getting Around

There is a lack of public transport south of Suweimah so you'll probably have to hitch between Suweimah and Safi. This is a good place to have a car and you can combine a visit to the Dead Sea with the Dead Sea Panorama and Madaba.

BETHANY-BEYOND-THE-JORDAN (AL-MAGHTAS)   المغطس

> Then Jesus came from the Galilee to the Jordan to be baptised by John.
> *(Matthew 3:13)*

> This took place in Bethany beyond the Jordan, where John was baptizing.
> *(John 1:28)*

Known in Arabic as Al-Maghtas, the 'Baptism Site' has been identified by archaeologists as the place where John the Baptist preached, where Jesus was baptised by John, where the first five apostles met and thus where the foundations of the early

Christian faith were laid. Jesus is said to have come here to meet en route from Galilee and Umm Qais and is believed to have spent three days here before heading off to spend 40 days in the nearby wilderness. John was later arrested and beheaded by Herod at Machaerus, also in Jordan (see p162).

The site was known to the Greeks as Sapsafas and to the Bible as Bethany, from the Aramaic Beit Anniya ('House of the Crossing'). Pilgrim churches, guesthouses and a 6th-century pilgrim road grew up around the site, which was visited, as it is today, en route from Jerusalem to Mt Nebo.

As early as 1899, works along the east bank of the Jordan River revealed ancient remains. It wasn't until works were carried out by archaeologists and activists clearing landmines (following the 1994 peace treaty with Israel & the Palestinian Territories) that the remains of churches, caves, extensive wells and water channels, as well as several baptism pools, were found. After much debate, scholars declared the area as the site of John the Baptist's mission and Jesus' baptism, locating it from descriptions in the Bible and from 3rd- to 10th-century pilgrim accounts. Events culminated with Pope John Paul II conducting a massive open-air mass at the site in the spring of 2000.

In addition to the celebrated baptism, Bethany-Beyond-the-Jordan is where Jesus 'went back across the Jordan to the place where John had been baptising to escape persecution from Jerusalem' (John 10:40). Many also believe that it was from here that the prophet Elijah (who was born in Mar Elias in north Jordan) ascended to heaven in a whirlwind:

> And as they still went on and talked, behold, a chariot of fire and horses of fire separated the two of them. And Eli'jah went up by a whirlwind into heaven.
> *2 Kings 2:11*

Beyond its religious significance the site has a fine location, with views of the Dead Sea, Mt Nebo, Jericho (12km away), Jerusalem (27km away) and the Jordan River. The Royal Society for the Conservation of Nature (RSCN) wants to protect the

DEAD SEA HIGHWAY

surrounding marsh and reed lands, and the birds and insects that rely on it.

Information

All vehicles must park at the entrance to the **site** (adult/Jordanian/under 12 JD5/1/free; ☺ 8am-3pm winter Nov-Mar & Ramadan, 8am-5pm summer Apr-Oct). Pick up a brochure and map at the main gate, where there are toilets, souvenir shops and a restaurant. Even the flies here are of biblical plague proportions. The entry fee includes a guided tour, and a free shuttle bus takes you down to the main site close to the sensitive border with Israel & the Palestinian Territories. Most tours last one hour but you can request a longer tour for no extra charge.

The Site

The shuttle bus makes a brief stop at Tell Elias (see right), where the prophet Elias is said to have ascended to heaven after his death, and then normally continues to the last parking lot, where there is a modern pool for baptisms in filtered water from the Jordan River (the river itself is deeply polluted). The tour visits the **Spring of John the Baptist**, one of several places where John is believed to have been baptised. Most baptisms were actually carried out in the spring-fed waters of the Wadi al-Kharrar, rather than in the Jordan River. The path leads through thickets of tamarisk and *argul* (wild cherry) and the yellow rose of Jericho in spring.

The main archaeological site is the remains of three churches, one on top of the other. Steps lead down to what was once the water level and a small building nearby marks the likely **site of Jesus' baptism**. Byzantine churches grew up to mark the site during the 5th and 6th centuries, rebuilt on the same site twice after they were destroyed by flooding. You can see traces of original mosaics.

The trail passes a new golden-roofed Greek Orthodox church, then past border guards to the **Jordan River**, in reality a brown sludgy mess. You can be baptised in the Jordan – if you had the foresight to bring your own priest. Facing off across the river (and the border) is a rival Israeli baptism complex. This is the only place where civilians can currently touch the Jordan River as the remainder lies in a militarised no-man's-land.

Tours often return via the **House of Mary the Egyptian**, a reformed sinner who lived and died in the two-room house in the 4th century. The trail continues left, then on up some wooden stairs (originally a rope) to a two-room **hermit cave** burrowed into the soft rock.

On the way back you can ask to be dropped at **Tell Elias** (Elijah's Hill). The fixing of Tell Elias was important in locating the baptism site as there are strong theological links between Elijah and John the Baptist. The rebuilt arch marks the 5th- to 6th-century pilgrim chapel, where the late Pope John Paul II authenticated the site in March 2000. The nearby rectangular prayer hall is the earliest structure at the site and one of the earliest Christian places of worship ever discovered, dating from the 3rd century when the young religion was still illegal.

The hill behind holds the presumed cave of John the Baptist, a 5th-century monastery which was built around the site and the **Rhotorios Monastery**, which has a mosaic floor with Greek inscriptions. You can see the 3rd- to 4th-century baptism pools and water cisterns used by early pilgrims who would descend steps into the plaster-lined pools. In the early years of Christianity, John was a more celebrated figure than Jesus and this was the more important of the two pilgrimage sites. Muslims venerate John as the prophet Jahia bin Zakharia (there is no baptism in Islam).

Other sites such as the faint remains of a pilgrim resthouse and more pools can be visited during the longer tour.

Eating

Talloubi Restaurant (☎ 079 5574020; fish JD3.850; ☺ lunch & dinner) A better bet than John's Retreat if you have a car, this great fish restaurant is run by Jordan Fisheries, which specialises in excellent tilapia (*talloubi* in Arabic). It's popular at weekends, particularly at dusk, as the sun sets over distant Jerusalem. It's a 2km detour off the road halfway between the baptism site and the main Amman–Dead Sea road.

John's Retreat (mains JD3-5) This normally deserted place at the visitors centre has cold beer (JD2.750) if you need a break.

Getting There & Away

There are signs to the 'Baptism Site' along the road from Amman to the Dead Sea.

Take any minibus to Suweimah. About 5km before the town, the road makes a 90-degree turn; the Dead Sea is to the left, the baptism site to the right. There is no public transport for the 5km to the visitor centre so you'll have to hitch, charter a taxi or walk (take plenty of water).

A taxi from Madaba to the site, taking in the Dead Sea and Mt Nebo en route costs around JD20.

SHUNEH AL-JANUBIYYEH (SOUTH SHUNA)   الشونة الجنوبية
☎ 05

This nondescript town is simply a junction for public transport to the Dead Sea and north through the Jordan Valley. The town is well connected by minibus with Amman's Dead Sea bus station (500 fils, 45 minutes), as well as with Madaba (350 fils, 45 minutes) and Salt (250 fils, 45 minutes).

There are a few cheap restaurants in town, as well as places to buy food for a picnic. Because of the limited public transport to places like Bethany-Beyond-the-Jordan, chartering a taxi from Shuneh al-Janubiyyeh to visit several sites in a few hours is a good idea (JD5 to JD10), and cheaper than chartering in Amman.

DEAD SEA RESORTS   منتجعات البحر الميت
☎ 05

Part of the border between Jordan and Israel & the Palestinian Territories goes through the Dead Sea, a lake with such high salinity that your body floats – suicidal travellers should note that drowning would be quite a feat here. The main centre of tourism on the Jordanian side of the sea is a collection of plush resorts and a nearby public beach, about 5km south of Suweimah, and this is where most visitors will get their first salty taste of the sea.

The Dead Sea is about 65km long and from 6km to 18km wide. Its main source is the Jordan River, but it has no outlet. It's an intense blue lake enclosed by red and browns of the surrounding desert hills.

The name is apt because the incredibly high salt content (30%) is over six times greater than the ocean, so plant and animal life is impossible. The only thing swimming in the Dead Sea are a few tourists.

THE DEAD SEA IS DYING

Every year record books have to be rewritten, as the world's lowest spot gets a little lower. Water levels have fallen from 392m to 408m below sea level (some experts put the water level at closer to 420m), and about 30% (approximately 350 sq km) of the original area has vanished. The level of the Dead Sea has been falling by about 500cm every year for the past 20 years or more, mainly because there is no longer any regular inflow from the near-stagnant Jordan River, water is diverted from the sea for irrigation (only 10% of the natural inflow now reaches the sea), and because evaporation is so high. Additionally more than one million tonnes of water are pumped daily into vast evaporation ponds in the south, covering some 10,000 hectares, in the manufacture of about four million tonnes of potash annually. This southern basin hasn't been connected to the main sea since the 1980s. At this rate some experts even believe the lake may dry up completely in 50 years.

In a bid to reverse the trend, a 180km canal from the Red Sea down to the Dead Sea (known as the Two Seas or Red to Dead canal project) is planned. The aim is to reverse the drop and then restore to historical levels and create enough hydroelectricity along the way to power desalination plants in Jordan and Israel & the Palestinian Territories. Around 45% of the water transferred would be transformed into fresh water.

The biggest hurdle is not the US$4 to US$6 billion required to fund the project but the fact that it requires cooperation between Israel, the Palestinian Territories and Jordan, and thus a resolution of the peace process itself. And that may take some time. Still, agreement was reached on a US$20 million feasibility study in May 2005.

Environmental organisations want the sea to be recognised as a World Heritage site, which would offer it some protections.

For more information on the dangers to the Dead Sea, contact the **Friends of the Earth – Middle East** (www.foeme.org; info@foeme.org).

Swimming here is also difficult because you're too high in the water to stroke properly, but of course you can always float on your back while reading the newspaper and have your picture taken. The buoyancy you'll experience is the sort of thing that you can only understand once you've been and you will invariably hear squeals of surprise from people visiting here for the first time. While paddling about you will probably discover cuts you never knew you had (don't shave before visiting), and if any water gets in your eyes, be prepared for a few minutes of agony.

The concentration of salt has nothing to do with the Dead Sea being below sea level; rather it comes about because of the high evaporation rate which has, over the years, led to a build-up of salts.

At the southern end of the lake, Jordanians are exploiting the high potash content of the mineral-rich water, making Jordan one of the world's largest producers. The Dead Sea also contains various other minerals, many of which are apparently excellent for one's health and skin. Most souvenir shops in Jordan stock various 'Dead Sea' creams, lotions, gels and soaps, all of which contain extractions from the lake, thereby exacerbating the environmental damage.

Most budget travellers choose to take a day trip from either Amman or, increasingly, Madaba. The main reason to stay is to enjoy the spectacular sunset.

Information

Try to avoid Fridays and public holidays when the hotels and public areas are in chaos and public transport is crowded; on any other day there will be few other people around. Always take lots of water as the humidity and heat (over 40°C in summer) can be dehydrating and there's little shade.

Swimming

After a dip in the Dead Sea, you'll find yourself coated in uncomfortable encrustations of salt that are best washed off as soon as you can. A shower (and shampoo and soap) afterwards is vital. If showers are not available, some readers have recommended bringing a few bottles of water for an abridged version of the same thing.

The most expensive way to swim in the Dead Sea is at one of the upmarket hotels

---

THE DEAD SEA ULTRA MARATHON

For most visitors, the Dead Sea is a place to relax and enjoy the novelty of floating at the world's lowest point or being pampered at an upmarket spa complex. And then for others, there's the Dead Sea Ultra Marathon. Starting at Safeway on 7th Circle in Amman, it involves a 50km run (individually or in a relay) down to the Dead Sea at Amman Beach, as well as a half-marathon, a 10km fun run and a kid's run of 4km (none of us here could even manage that). In case you think that this is the preserve of a few mad locals, bear in mind that around 1000 runners take part every year. The race generally takes place on the second Friday in April so if you're keen for a bit of extreme sport, contact the **Amman Rd Runners group** (☎ 06 5677660; www.deadseamarathon.com) or any tourist office for details.

(see opposite), about 5km south of Suweimah, where you pay at least JD10, and probably more, for access to their beaches and other facilities, including shower and swimming pool. The Mövenpick charges JD20 for access to its pools and beach, or JD27 for its spa, pools and beach. The Marriott charges JD15. The Dead Sea Spa Hotel charges JD10 (JD5 for kids), which entitles you to a discounted rate for their buffet (JD8). An all-body Dead Sea 'mud pack' is reported to do wonders for your skin.

AMMAN BEACH   شاطئ عمان
This public **beach** (☎ 3560800; adult/child/Jordanian JD4/2/1; ⏰ 24hr), 2km south of the main hotel strip, is run by Amman municipality as an affordable option for both locals and travellers, and so it is the most popular place for budget travellers to enjoy a dip in the sea. The beach is clean, with sun umbrellas, fresh-water showers and a vibrant local scene that is missing from the sanitised five-star resorts.

It can get very busy at weekends (Thursday night and Fridays), when locals bring their own food and fuel for the public barbecue grills, rent a lounge bed (JD1) and party overnight. There is a restaurant (JD7 buffet), some drinks stalls, basketball courts and an amusement park next door. Swimming pools are also planned.

Locals will generally swim fully clothed, though foreigners shouldn't feel uncomfortable in modest swimming costumes.

HERODUS (ZARA) SPRING   نبع هيرودس

All along the eastern shore of the Dead Sea are areas where you are free to float, although you'll have no showers and you'll probably have to hitch a ride from near Suweimah unless you have your own transport. One free place to swim is at the popular Herodus Spring, 10km south of the main hotel strip, though the place can be jammed at weekends. It's marked by a bridge and large military base, and there's fresh (but undrinkable) water in the nearby Wadi Zarqa Ma'in – ideal for washing afterwards. The water's edge is a short walk down the hill, under the bridge. There's little privacy here and it's not a great place for unaccompanied women.

Nearby is the site of ancient **Callirhöe**, a favourite of Herod who came here in 4 BC to get treatment for a skin condition. There's a small archaeological site (discovered in 1807) to the south of the wadi and there are some remains of the ancient harbour (Herod travelled here by boat). The site is marked on the Madaba mosaic map.

Sleeping & Eating

About 5km south of Suweimah along the Dead Sea Highway are a number of upmarket pleasure palaces so opulent that they issue their own hotel maps to help guests find their way to their rooms. The pools and lush grounds are particularly wonderful on balmy spring and autumn nights. You'll need a booking for the weekend (Thursday night, Friday and Saturday).

Crowne Plaza (☎ 3560110; 🐾) On the northeastern shore of the lake, in Suweimah, the former government rest house is currently being redeveloped by Holiday Inn into a luxury resort.

Dead Sea Marriott (☎ 3560360; www.mariotthotels .com/qmdjv; r from JD93, plus JD10/20 for pool view/poolside r, plus JD10 for weekend stay; ✗ 🐾 🛎) Lovely and stylish but more ostentatious then the Mövenpick. Dining options include the Mosaico buffet (JD20; Monday night is seafood), Jo's Brasserie (good for steaks), the very pleasant Acacia Bar, a poolside bar and Champions sports bar. Good kids' facilities include a jungle playground, a mini waterfall, movies and a family pool.

Mövenpick Resort & Spa (☎ 3561111; www.mo evenpick-deadsea.com; r standard/superior/deluxe JD120/

SPLASH OUT!

Herod the Great and Cleopatra were among the many firm believers in the curative powers of a Dead Sea spa. The low levels of UV rays and high oxygen levels are good for your health and the Dead Sea mud contains calcium and magnesium, good for allergies and bronchial infections; pungent bromine to help with relaxation; iodine to alleviate certain glandular ailments; and bitumen to improve the skin. If you feel like a little pampering, book one of these spas in advance.

Zara Spa (☎ 3561110; www.zaraspa.com; 🕗 8.30am-8.30pm) at the Mövenpick is touted as the best in the Middle East. Entry costs JD27 for nonguests (and even costs JD17 for guests!) and includes access to a gym, private beach, pool, sauna, steam room, foot massage pool, infinity pool, aquapressure pool and Dead Sea saltwater pool (27% salt). Extra services include a mud wrap (one hour JD39), dry flotation, hot stone therapy, shiatsu and other massages (from JD23 for 25 minutes) and facials. A day package costs JD100 to JD136 for 2½ hours of treatments, or blow out with the three-day package for JD255.

Spa (🕗 8am-10pm, treatments 9am-8.30pm) at the Dead Sea Marriott is free for guests or JD15 for nonguests (JD25 with the beach, pools and gym), and includes a heated pool, Dead Sea saltwater pool, Jacuzzi, steam room, sauna and 24-hour gym. Treatments are run by the Sanctuary of London and include massage (JD57 per hour), body wraps, salt scrubs, phytomer facials, mud facials, dry flotation and hydro baths. Weekday packages (Sunday to Wednesday) range from JD45 to JD109.

Dead Sea Spa (🕗 5601554; 🕗 9am-6pm), at the Dead Sea Spa Hotel, has more of a focus on medical treatments, with an in-house dermatologist and physiotherapist. Entry to the beach, pools and spa costs JD12 and includes a fitness room, solarium and Dead Sea saltwater pool. A full-body Swedish massage or mud application costs JD22. A JD50 day's package includes a Swedish massage, mud pack and the use of the pool and gym.

140/160; ☒ ☒ ☒) The resort to beat, with a kasbah-style village concealing luxury accommodation, tennis courts, swimming pools (including an 'infinity pool'), Zara Spa (p145) and a private beach. There are nine bars and restaurants, including Asian and Italian restaurants, a poolside bar, Al-Saraya buffet (JD15), Thursday night barbecues (JD18) and Friday brunch (JD18). All rooms come with a balcony. Poor staff let the facilities down at times.

Dead Sea Spa Hotel (☎ 3561000; www.jordandead sea.com; s/d JD71/85, ste from JD156; ☒ ☒) About 200m south of the Mövenpick, this complex is a definite notch down in luxury but is still nice if you haven't seen the luxury neighbours. There's a medical/dermatological spa (see the boxed text, p145), a decent beach, a big pool and separate kids' pool with slides. Choose from rooms in the main block or bungalows. There's a Lebanese restaurant or hit the buffet (JD13).

The **Kempinski Hotel Ishtar** (www.kempinski.com) is currently being built in the location between the Mövenpick and the Dead Sea Spa Hotel, and should open in 2006.

Getting There & Away
HITCHING
Hitching back to Amman from Amman Beach is relatively easy; Friday and Sunday are the best days.

MINIBUS
Public transport only runs as far as Suweimah. Some budget hotels in Amman organise day trips to the Dead Sea so ask around. For details of getting to/from the Dead Sea from the capital, see p100. See p158 for details of reaching the Dead Sea from Madaba.

TAXI
A return taxi costs about JD30 for the day or JD15 for a one-way drop from Amman, and far less from Shuneh al-Janubiyyeh. It's a bit pointless if you're only interested in a long and leisurely bathe, but it does allow you to seek out better (and free) bathing spots along the shore.

DEAD SEA PANORAMA
بانوراما البحر الميت

This **lookout**, **museum** and **restaurant** complex, opened in 2005 high above the Dead Sea, offers some breathtaking views. As part of the

project, the Dead Sea Parkway winds down from the Madaba–Hammamat Ma'in road to the Dead Sea Highway, offering a great new route between the Dead Sea resorts and Madaba. See p162 for details.

WADI MUJIB NATURE RESERVE
محمية الموجب

The lower Wadi Mujib gorge is now part of the vast Wadi Mujib Nature Reserve (*Mahmiyyat al-Mujib*; 215 sq km), which ranges from an altitude of 900m above sea level to 400m below. It was established by the RSCN for the captive breeding of the Nubian ibex but it also forms the heart of an exciting ecotourism project.

The reserve supports a surprising variety of over 400 species of plants (including rare orchids), 186 species of birds and 250 animal species. The wildlife includes the Nubian ibex, Syrian wolf, striped hyena, caracal and Blandford's fox. It is also an important staging post for migratory birds travelling between Africa and Europe.

Challenges to the reserves ecosystems include illegal hunting by local Bedouin tribes, overgrazing by goats and the demands of mining companies for licenses to start mineral extraction.

Information
First stop is the **visitor centre** (☎ 03 2313059; admission JD1), right by the Dead Sea Highway, about 20km south of the Dead Sea resorts, where you'll pay entry fees and pick up a guide if required. Guides are compulsory for the trails and should be booked in advance through the RSCN in Amman (see p70). Only 25 people per day are allowed on each trail and there's a minimum group size of five. Apart from the Ibex Trail, children are not allowed on the trails. Life jackets are provided.

The Malaqi, Mujib Canyon and Siq trails are only open between 1 April and 31 October, due to the risk of flash floods, but the actual opening dates depend on local water levels and the state of the trails, so ring in advance. Other trails are accessible year-round. The region is extremely hot and dry in summer, so get going early in the morning and take sunscreen and lots of drinking water. For the water trails, bring a swimming costume, towel, some shoes that can get wet, and a waterproof bag for your valuables and camera.

The campground has a solar-powered boat which visitors can rent for JD30 per half-hour.

Hiking

The RSCN allows hiking along half a dozen trails in the reserve, all of which require a RSCN guide.

The easiest activity on offer is the **Siq Trail** (JD8 per person), a lovely 2km splash up into the gorge, ending at a dramatic waterfall. Imagine hiking up Petra's Siq, with a river running through it. The weir at the entrance to the gorge diverts fresh water from the wadi for human use.

The **Malaqi Trail** (JD40 per person) is a guided half-day trip that involves a hot and sweaty hike up into the wadi, a visit to the lovely swimming pools of Wadi Hidan and then a descent (often swimming) through the siq, finally rappelling down the 18m waterfall (not appropriate for nonswimmers or those with a fear of heights). It's not cheap but it's definitely one of the most exciting things you can do in a day in Jordan. If you have limited time you can do a shorter version of the trail, the **Mujib Canyon Trail**, for JD30. The trail starts 3km south of the visitor centre.

Other options include the year-round **Ibex Trail** (JD8 per person), a half-day guided hike that leads up to a Nubian ibex enclosure at the Raddas ranger station, along a ridge that offers views of the Dead Sea, with an optional excursion to the ruined Qasr Riyash.

The **Mujib Trail** (JD25 per person) starts from the ranger station at Fag'ua near the King's Highway and descends down wadis to the Raddas ranger station or Wadi Mujib gorge (JD40 per person).

The **Mukawir-Zara Trail** (JD20 per person) is on the northern boundaries of the park and descends 700m in 6km to the Herodus (Zara) Hot Springs on the Dead Sea Highway (see p145).

Sleeping

The reserve operates a windy 15-tent **campground** (s/d/tr per person JD20/17/16; ☺ 1 April-15 Oct) on the shores of the Dead Sea but you must use the tents provided. Day use of the camp costs JD5. The small gravel beach and fresh-water showers allow you to swim in the sea, or just enjoy the views of the sea from your tent. Food is available if booked in advance (through the campground itself

---

IN SEARCH OF SODOM

Most archaeologists agree that the world's wickedest town lay somewhere around the southern end of the Dead Sea, but that's where the agreement ends. Some scientists believe that the site has been underwater off the east bank of the Dead Sea since biblical times.

Most archaeologists now believe that the Bronze Age site of Babh adh-Dhra (the Gate of the Arm), an archaeological site on the edge of Wadi Karak that was destroyed and abandoned in 2300 BC, is the actual site of Sodom. Intriguingly, the former town of 1000 holds the remains of 20,000 tombs, holding an estimated half a million bodies. Both Babh adh-Dhra and the nearby site of Numeirah, believed to be Gomorrah, are covered in a foot-deep layer of ash, suggesting the cities ended in a great blaze.

The Book of Genesis (Gen 19:24–25) outlines God's displeasure at the locals' behaviour. The last straw came when local Sodomites demanded to have sex with the angels who had been sent by God to visit Lot. In response 'the Lord rained upon Sodom and upon Gomorrah brimstone and fire…and he overthrew those cities, and all the plain, and all the inhabitants of the cities, and that which grew upon the ground…'

Fanciful legends of a fevered biblical imagination? Not necessarily. The whole area is located on a major fault line, and it would not have been the first time that such a zone has been simply swallowed up when the ground collapsed in a cataclysmic slip or a kind of massive implosion, known as 'liquefaction', or collapse of the soil. Another possibility is that an earthquake released large amounts of underground flammable gas and bitumen for which the region was famous (the 'slime pits' referred to in the Old Testament). These substances could have been ignited by fire or a lightening strike.

The observer reporting for the Book of Genesis may well have been describing a terrible natural disaster. Whether or not it was caused by the wrath of God remains a question of faith.

or RSCN/Wild Jordan when booking your accommodation).

Getting There & Away

There's no public transport to the reserve so you need to rent a car or take a taxi from Amman (125km), Madaba or Karak.

LOT'S CAVE   كهف لوط

> Now Lot went up out of Zo'ar, and dwelt in the hills with his two daughters, for he was afraid to dwell in Zo'ar; so he dwelt in a cave with his two daughters.
>
> *(Genesis 19:30)*

One of the few sights along the southwestern side of Jordan is **Lot's Cave** (admission free; ⏱ daylight hr), where Abraham's nephew Lot and his daughters lived for years after fleeing the destruction of Sodom and Gomorrah (see the boxed text, p147). Lot's wife famously turned into a pillar of salt after looking back at the smouldering city.

In an eyebrow-raising incident of incest that's remarkable even for the Bible, Lot's two daughters then spiked their father's drink, had sex with him and then nine months later gave birth to his grandsons/ sons Moab and Ben-Ammi, the forefathers of the Moabite and Ammonite peoples.

The actual cave is on the side of the hill and surrounding it are the ruins of a small Byzantine church (5th to 8th centuries), reservoir and some mosaics, which were excavated by the British Museum. Remains from the cave date to the early Bronze Age (3300–2000 BC) and an inscription in the cave mentions Lot by name. The views west are of the evaporating pools of the local potash industry.

At the base of the hill is the brand new **Lowest Point on Earth Museum**, which has displays on the archaeology of the general region, a café and a couple of hotel rooms.

The archaeological site is 2km north of the phosphate-mining town of Safi (Ghor as-Safi), itself believed to be the historical site of Zo'ar. The cave is known locally as Deir 'Ain Abata, after a local spring, or Kahf Lut, after the Islamic name for the prophet Lot.

The site is signposted from the Dead Sea Highway, and private or chartered vehicles can drive almost to the cave. Regular minibuses run between Karak and Safi (550 fils, one hour). If you're relying on public transport or hitching, be prepared for a 2km walk from the highway, though some minibuses pass the museum en route to Safi.

King's Highway
الطريق الملوكي

The King's Highway – known in Arabic as At-Tariq as-Sultani (Rd of the Sultan) – is of great historical and religious significance. Over the last 3000 years it has been traversed by the Israelites en route to the Promised Land, Nabataeans to and from Petra, Christian pilgrims to Moses' memorial at Mt Nebo, Crusaders to their castle fortifications and Muslim pilgrims heading to and from Mecca.

These are the ancient lands of Moab and Edom, squeezed between the desert and the Rift Valley and cut by numerous deep and hidden wadis. These hidden valleys, from Wadi Mujib to Wadi Dana, hide some of Jordan's most unexpected scenery and greatest adventures.

Of Jordan's three highways running from north to south, the King's Highway is by far the most interesting and picturesque, with a host of attractions. The highway connects the lovely mosaic town of Madaba to wondrous Petra via the Crusader castles, Roman forts, biblical sites and a windswept Nabataean temple.

The road also traverses some epic landscapes, including the lovely Dana Nature Reserve and the majestic Wadi Mujib valley. Dana in particular is fast becoming a must-stop sight and offers one of the best opportunities to just hang out and do some hiking.

Unfortunately, Wadi Mujib is the reason why public transport along this road can be difficult. If you only hire a car or taxi in one part of Jordan, do it here. A drive along the King's Highway is a veritable ride through the centuries, along the spine of history.

HIGHLIGHTS

- Consider making the historic small town of **Madaba** (p150) an alternative base to Amman, as you explore its vibrant Byzantine mosaics and nearby sights

- Visit Herod's castle at **Mukawir** (p162), the site where Salome danced and John the Baptist was beheaded

- Explore **Karak** (p165), Jordan's most impressive storybook Crusader castle, complete with moat, dungeons and a keep

- Take a day off and hike, relax and read at **Dana Nature Reserve** (p171), where 21st-century ecotourism meets a 15th-century Ottoman village

- Feel the hair raise on the back of your neck as you descend the pitch-black secret tunnels of the **Shobak** (p173) Crusader fortress

- Enjoy the views of the Promised Land from **Mt Nebo** (p158) – if they were good enough for Moses, then they are good enough for us

Mt Nebo
★ Madaba

★ Mukawir

Dead Sea

★ Karak

★ Dana Nature Reserve

Shobak
★

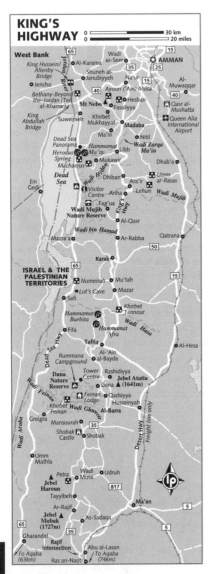

FAST FACTS

- The website **Ancient Routes** (www
  .ancientroute.com) offers a historical
  route description of the King's Highway

- The King's Highway runs for 297km
  between Madaba and Petra

chapter by such methods, you would need
up to a week.

One option to consider is the transport
(minimum three passengers) organised by
the Mariam Hotel in Madaba (see p158) or
the Palace Hotel and other budget places in
Amman (see p87) which runs to Petra in a
day, with stops in Wadi Mujib, Karak and,
sometimes, Dana and Shobak. Chartering a
taxi is also possible for the same journey.

The only alternative is to take a regular
minibus from Madaba to Dhiban, charter a taxi to Ariha, then take a minibus to
Karak. From Karak minibuses run to Tafila,
where you can take another to Qadsiyya
(for Dana). Public transport south of Qadsiyya (near Dana) is infrequent, so you may
need to take a minibus to Ma'an and then
another to Wadi Musa (Petra).

MADABA مادبا
☎ 05 / Pop 50,000

This easy-going town is best known for its
superb and historically significant Byzantine-
era mosaics. The town has a strong sense of
its unique history, making it a major stop
on the tourist trail. Madaba is the most important Christian centre in Jordan, and has
long been an example of religious tolerance,
a place where the Friday call to prayer from
the mosque coexists with Sunday church
bells; Muslims make up two-thirds of the
population, and Christians one-third.

Madaba is compact and easily explored
on foot, with some excellent hotels and
restaurants, and is less than an hour by
regular public transport from Amman, so
it's worth considering as an alternative to
Amman as a place to stay. It's even possible
to come straight by taxi from Queen Alia
International Airport, bypassing Amman
altogether.

Madaba is also a good base for exploring the Dead Sea, Bethany-Beyond-the-
Jordan (Jesus' baptism site; see p141) and

Getting Around

Public transport along the King's Highway
is neither frequent nor complete, with the
stretch between Dhiban and Ariha devoid
of any regular public transport. Hitching
can be a good way to get around, but be prepared for long waits on deserted stretches.
To explore all of the sites covered in this

other local sites such as Mt Nebo, Mukawir (Machaerus) and Umm ar-Rasas.

History
The region around Madaba has been inhabited for around 4500 years. The biblical Moabite town of Medeba was one of the towns divided among the 12 tribes of Israel at the time of the Exodus. It's also mentioned on the famous Meshe Stele, raised in about 850 BC by the Moabite king Mesha (see the boxed text, p165) to commemorate his victory over the Israelites.

By 165 BC the Ammonites were in control of Madaba; about 45 years later it was taken by Hyrcanus I of Israel, and then promised to the Nabataeans by Hyrcanus II in return for helping him recover Jerusalem. Under the Romans from AD 106, Madaba became a prosperous provincial town with the usual colonnaded streets and impressive public buildings. The prosperity continued during the Christian Byzantine period, when there was a large drive towards church construction; most of the mosaics in Madaba date from this period.

The town was eventually abandoned for about 1100 years after a devastating earthquake in AD 747. In the late 19th century, 2000 Christians from Karak migrated to Madaba after a bloody dispute with Karak's Muslims and within their community. They found the mosaics when they started digging foundations for houses. News that a mosaic map of the Holy Land had been found in St George's Church in Madaba reached Europe in 1897, leading to a flurry of exploratory activity that continues to this day.

The well-governed town has plans for a restoration project in the town's souq, which might be worth keeping an eye on over the next few years.

Orientation
MAPS
The brochure *Madaba and Mount Nebo*, published by the Jordan Tourism Board (JTB), provides a brief but satisfactory explanation of the attractions in Madaba. It's available at tourist offices and, usually, the visitor centre. The JTB also publishes several smaller brochures: *Madaba Mosaic Map*, which has slightly more detailed information about the mosaics in St George's Church; and the excellent *Mount Nebo* (see p159).

Information
BOOKSHOPS
If you need more information about the mosaics and other historical buildings in Madaba, pick up the definitive but weighty *Madaba: Cultural Heritage* (around JD22), which is published by the American Center of Oriental Research. Much cheaper (JD8) and more portable is the *Mosaic Map of Madaba* by Herbert Donner, with a foldout picture of the map and detailed text. The best one is the pocket-sized and affordable *Madaba, Mt Nebo* published by Al-Kutba (JD3).

The **bookshop** across from the Burnt Palace sells a good range of current international newspapers.

EMERGENCY
Tourist Police Office (☎ 191; Talal St; ☽ 24hr) Just north of St George's Church.

INTERNET ACCESS
Waves Internet (Talal St; per hr JD1; ☽ 24hr)

MONEY
Arab Bank (Palestine St) Visa and MasterCard. Has an ATM.
Bank of Jordan (cnr Palestine & King Abdullah Sts) Changes cash and travellers cheques.
Housing Bank (Palestine St) Visa; has an ATM.
Jordan National Bank (cnr King Abdullah & Talal Sts) Changes cash and travellers cheques.

POST
Post office (Palestine St; ☽ 8am-5pm) Long-distance telephone calls can be made from inside.

TOURIST INFORMATION
Ministry of Tourism & Antiquities (☎ /fax 3245527; tourism@mota.gov.jo) Has an office above the Burnt Palace for specialised information about Madaba's preservation efforts.
National Society for the Preservation of Madaba and its Suburbs (☎ 3244679; Hussein bin Ali St) Located in front of the Burnt Palace. Possibly worth visiting if you have an interest in what's being done to preserve Madaba's architectural and cultural heritage.
Visitor Centre (☎ 3253536; Abu Bakr as-Seddiq St; ☽ 8am-5pm Oct-Apr, to 7pm May-Sep) Adjacent to the Madaba Mosaic School. There is a helpful information office with a few brochures, toilets and a handy car park. Check out the side room of old photos of Madaba, with a map of all the old buildings; look especially for the 1924 photo of a much smaller Madaba.

Sights

A combined ticket to the Archaeological Park, Madaba Museum and Church of the Apostles costs JD2. Children under 12 are free. There's no student price. It's not possible to purchase cheaper tickets for the individual sites if you only want to visit one.

ST GEORGE'S CHURCH & MOSAIC MAP

This 19th-century **Greek Orthodox church** (Talal St; admission JD1; ☺ 8am-6pm Sat & Mon-Thu, 10.30am-6pm Fri & Sun) was built over a Byzantine church.

Unearthed in 1884, the mosaic on the church floor was a clear map with 157 captions (in Greek) depicting all the major biblical sites of the Middle East (see opposite). The mosaic was constructed in AD 560, and was originally around 25m long (some experts claim 15m is more accurate) and 6m wide. It once contained more than two million pieces but only one-third of the original mosaic has survived.

The map itself, while of enormous historical significance, can be difficult to take in with all its fragments. It's definitely worth seeing, but you need to take your time to get the map's bearing. A room across from the church displays a full size copy of the map for easier viewing.

Don't forget to check out the rest of the church, including some lovely icons with silver halos, an image of St George (St Giorgis) slaying the dragon, and an embroidered depiction of Jesus' death in the

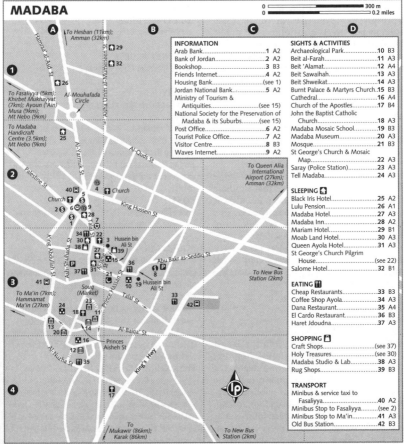

MADABA

0 ——— 300 m
0 ——— 0.2 miles

INFORMATION
Arab Bank	1 A2
Bank of Jordan	2 A2
Bookshop	3 B3
Friends Internet	4 A2
Housing Bank	(see 1)
Jordan National Bank	5 A2
Ministry of Tourism & Antiquities	(see 15)
National Society for the Preservation of Madaba & its Suburbs	(see 15)
Post Office	6 A2
Tourist Police Office	7 A2
Visitor Centre	8 B3
Waves Internet	9 A3

SIGHTS & ACTIVITIES
Archaeological Park	10 B3
Beit al-Farah	11 A3
Beit 'Alamat	12 A4
Beit Sawaihah	13 A3
Beit Shweikat	14 A3
Burnt Palace & Martyrs Church	15 B3
Cathedral	16 A3
Church of the Apostles	17 B4
John the Baptist Catholic Church	18 A3
Madaba Mosaic School	19 A3
Madaba Museum	20 A3
Mosque	21 B3
St George's Church & Mosaic Map	22 A3
Saray (Police Station)	23 A3
Tell Madaba	24 A3

SLEEPING 🏠
Black Iris Hotel	25 A2
Lulu Pension	26 A1
Madaba Hotel	27 A3
Madaba Inn	28 A2
Mariam Hotel	29 B1
Moab Land Hotel	30 A3
Queen Ayola Hotel	31 A3
St George's Church Pilgrim House	(see 22)
Salome Hotel	32 B1

EATING 🍴
Cheap Restaurants	33 B3
Coffee Shop Ayola	34 A3
Dana Restaurant	35 A4
El Cardo Restaurant	36 A3
Haret Jdoudna	37 A3

SHOPPING 🛍
Craft Shops	(see 37)
Holy Treasures	(see 30)
Madaba Studio & Lab	38 A3
Rug Shops	39 B3

TRANSPORT
Minibus & service taxi to Fasaliyya	40 A2
Minibus Stop to Fasaliyya	(see 2)
Minibus Stop to Ma'in	41 A3
Old Bus Station	42 B3

To Hesban (11km); Amman (32km)
To Fasaliyya (5km); Khirbet Mukhayyat (7km); Ayoun ('Ain) Musa (9km); Mt Nebo (9km)
To Madaba Handicraft Centre (3.5km); Mt Nebo (9km)
To Queen Alia International Airport (27km); Amman (32km)
To Ma'in (7km); Hammamat Ma'in (27km)
To New Bus Station (2km)
To New Bus Station (2km)
To Mukawir (86km); Karak (86km)

Hammar al-Asd St
Abha Dinin al-Muheeret St
Al-Mouhafada Circle
Al-Quds St
Palestine St
King Hussein St
Al-Yarmouk St
King Abdullah St
St Saint Paul St
Ash-Shuhada St
Hussein bin Ali St
Abu Bakr as-Seddiq St
Prince Hassan St
Hussein bin Ali St
Talal St
Al-Baiqa' St
Princes Aisheh St
Al-Nuzha St
King's Hwy
Souq (Market)

NAVIGATING THE MADABA MAP

The first thing to do as you take in the Madaba map is to get orientated. As you look at the map, the map's north is to the left. Thus the Mediterranean is at the far west of the map.

Pride of place is the detailed mini map of Jerusalem, depicting city walls, gates, the central road (cardo) and the Church of the Holy Sepulchre in the northeast of the city. South of Jerusalem is Bethlehem (marked in red letters) and Judah. Above Jerusalem are Nablus (Neapolis – the capital of Samaria), Hebron and the oasis of Jericho, surrounded by palm trees.

The central Dead Sea has boats crossing it. The Jordan River is to the side, crossed by cable-drawn ferries and with fish desperately swimming away from the salty water! The site marked as 'Sapsafas' is Bethany-Beyond-the-Jordan, positioned just under a gazelle fleeing a defaced lion. Northeast of the Dead Sea is Herod's spa at Callirhöe (Zara), marked by three springs and two palm trees. Southeast of the sea is Lot's Cave, just above the settlement of Safi (Balak or Zoara), one of the 'Five Cities of the Plain' and marked by more palm trees. The dark line above is Wadi Zered, now known as Wadi Hasa.

The walled city of Karak is at the far eastern edge of the map (ie the top). To the far right, Mt Sinai is recognisable by its coloured mountains; nearby in the far south is the multichannelled Nile Delta. On a mosaic fragment in the far east are the Palestinian and Israeli towns of Gaza and Akkra, finishing off the tour of the Holy Land.

---

southwest corner. A small shop by the exit sells copies of the map and reproduction Orthodox icons.

On Friday and Sunday morning, the church opens at 7am for mass at which visitors are welcome, but viewing the map at these times is not permitted.

ARCHAEOLOGICAL PARK

Some careful restoration and excavation in the early 1990s led to the creation of the **Archaeological Park** (☎ 3246681; Hussein bin Ali St; admission combined ticket JD2; ✹ 8am-5pm Oct-Apr, to 7pm May-Sep), a collection of ruins as well as mosaics from the Madaba area.

As you enter, you'll see a 1st-century BC mosaic from Machaerus, which is said to be the oldest mosaic found in Jordan. Follow the walkway to the right, past mosaics from Massuh (10km north of Madaba), then above the Roman street, which ran east to west between the Roman city gates and was lined with columns, to the faded but fine mosaics of the **Church of the Prophet Elias** (built AD 607). Look for the details (such as the fine green bird) and then descend to the earlier crypt (AD 595).

The large roofed central structure in front of you contains the most impressive mosaics on the site. On the north side of the area under the roof is **Hippolytus Hall**, an early-6th-century Byzantine villa. The main border has decorations depicting the four seasons in the four corners, and the lower

section has pictures of flowers and birds. The middle section (divided by the base of a wall) depicts characters from the classic Greek oedipal tragedy of Phaedra and Hippolytus. The upper image shows a topless Aphrodite positioned next to Adonis and spanking a naughty winged Eros. Also here are the Three Graces (three daughters of Zeus, representing joy, charm and beauty) and, in the top left corner, personifications of the towns of Madaba, Rome and Gregoria, beside a couple of sea monsters.

The **Church of the Virgin Mary** was built in the 6th century above the villa and was unearthed under the floor of someone's house in 1887. The central mosaic, thought to date from AD 767, is a masterpiece of geometric design.

Finally, before leaving, there are more mosaics from Madaba and Ma'in, dating from AD 720.

CHURCH OF THE APOSTLES

This **church** (Al-Nuzha St; admission combined ticket JD2; ✹ 9am-5pm Oct-Apr, 8am-7pm May-Sep) contains a remarkable mosaic dedicated to the 12 apostles, although it can be difficult to see clearly. The embroidery-like mosaic was created in AD 568 and is one of the few instances where the mosaicist (Salomios) put his name to his work. The central portion shows Thalassa, a woman who represents the sea, surrounded by fish and some slippery marine creatures (check out the

KING'S HIGHWAY

comical little octopus). In the same mosaic are representations of less threatening native animals, birds, flowers and fruits, and cherubic faces in the corners.

MADABA MUSEUM

The **Madaba Museum** (☎ 3244056; Al-Baiqa' St; admission combined ticket JD2; ☒ 8am-4pm Oct-Apr, to 7pm May-Sep) is housed in several old Madaba residences.

The first room to the left has a 6th-century mosaic depicting a naked satyr, which some sources say is Bacchus, the god of wine. The rather naughty image of Ariadne, dancing with cymbals on her hands and feet, has been partially destroyed.

Also here is the **Folklore Museum**, featuring jewellery, traditional costumes and a copy of the Mesha Stele (see p165). Other mosaics in the courtyard depict two rams tied to a tree, a popular image that recalls the biblical tale of Abraham prepared to slaughter his son Isaac.

The last hall features artefacts from Hesban, Umm ar-Rasas and Machaerus castle near Mukawir (see p162).

There have long been plans to move the museum to the Saray (see opposite) but nothing has come of this yet.

BURNT PALACE & MARTYRS CHURCH

The **Burnt Palace** (Hussein bin Ali St; admission free; ☒ 8am-5pm Sun-Thu Oct-Apr, to 7pm May-Sep) was a late-6th-century luxury private mansion destroyed by fire and earthquake around AD 749. It contains more mosaics and there are walkways throughout for viewing the site. The **east wing** (down the steps to the left as you enter) contains some good hunting mosaics, while the **west wing's** highlight is the image of a lion attacking a bull. A fragment of a four seasons mosaic is all that remains of the **north wing**. On the site is the continuation of the ancient **Roman road**, which once connected with the road in the Archaeological Park, as well as the 6th-century **Martyrs Church**, which was destroyed in the 8th century. The site requires more imagination than the other sites around town; five minutes should do it.

MADABA MOSAIC SCHOOL

The **Madaba Mosaic School** (☎ 3240723, Hussein bin Ali St; admission free; ☒ 8am-3pm Sun-Thu) was set up in 1992 by the Jordanian Government and is the only school of its kind in the Middle East. Its primary aims are to train Jordanian artists in the production and restoration of mosaics, spread awareness of mosaics in Jordan and to actively preserve mosaics throughout the country. Its restoration work is evident in the Archaeological Park, the Church of the Apostles and at Khirbet Mukhayyat.

The mosaic school consists of a workshop, which includes a partial reproduction of the mosaic map in St George's Church; it

---

MAKING MOSAICS

Mosaics are traditionally made from tiny squares called tesserae, chipped from larger rocks. The tesserae are naturally coloured, and carefully laid on a thick coating of wet lime and ash. Unlike mosaics found in other countries (eg Italy), mosaics found in and around Madaba were made for the floor, and were hardy enough to withstand anything – except massive earthquakes.

The larger mosaics found in and around Madaba required painstaking effort and great skill, taking months or years to complete. As a result, they were only commissioned by wealthier citizens and for important buildings (particularly churches). For some reason, very few of the artists signed their names on the mosaics, possibly because so many people were involved over many years, although other names are often listed, such as the donors and church clergy.

Designs were fairly standard, copied from pattern books, and featured scenes from everyday life, such as animals, fish, plants and people; activities such as hunting and viniculture; personification of the seasons; and various religious events or mythological Greek and Roman gods and goddesses. It's details that are so captivating – the bell on a gazelle's neck, the palm trees at an oasis on the Madaba map, or the expression on a person's face. Most were topped off with intricate braided borders and dazzling geometric designs.

Mosaic making continued for the first century of the Muslim Umayyad dynasty but following the Caliph Yazid II's edict against the representation of living beings, many of the mosaics depicting people were sadly destroyed or replaced with white mosaics.

is displayed on the wall, making it easier to photograph. This is an active school so all visitors should first visit the administration office staff who are usually happy to show visitors around, although the classrooms are understandably off limits.

TELL MADABA

This important archaeological site in the heart of Madaba is still under excavation and there's not much to see. Like many sites around Madaba, it was discovered by accident by a local when he started digging the foundations for his house. It contains remains of a **Byzantine villa** and parts of an **Iron Age wall** or fortification, the largest of its kind in Jordan and visible from above the arch on the top level.

To get the most from this site you'll need a trained eye. For more on the excavations see www.utoronto.ca/tmap. Tread carefully as much remains to be excavated.

Walking Tour

Madaba is compact so all the main attractions can be easily visited on foot. Allow two to three hours for the walk, longer if you want to spend more time admiring the mosaics.

The obvious place to start is **St George's Church** (1; p152), with its mosaic map. From there, head south along Talal St and visit the complex of restaurants and craft shops in **Haret Jdoudna** (2; p157), a wonderfully restored example of traditional Madaba architecture built in 1905. Return north along Talal St, and then turn right (southeast) along Hussein bin Ali St. This takes you to the **Burnt Palace & Martyrs Church** (3; opposite). Further down the hill, at the end of Hussein bin Ali St, turn right (southwest) into Prince Hassan St, then immediately left to reach the **Archaeological Park** (4; p153). Next door is the **Madaba Mosaic School** (5; opposite) and then the **Madaba Visitor Centre** (6; p151). Return to Prince Hassan St and head up the hill, past the new mosque, to the decaying but elegant 1898–1904 **Beit al-Farah** (7) at the corner to the right (west).

For a detour, backtrack up the hill to the solid **Saray** (8; built in 1896 and now the police station) and curve round the building, taking a left, past the **John the Baptist Catholic Church** (9), with its Roman column fragments built into the walls. Turn left onto Princess Aisheh St and Al-Baiqa' St,

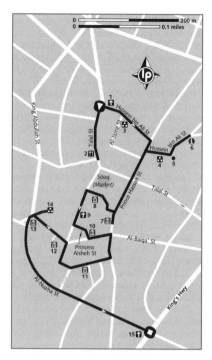

with the 1916–20 **Beit Shweikat** (10) on the corner. Take a right back onto Prince Hassan St and then another right, passing the 1913–22 **Beit Alamat** (11) to the left (south) and the lonely ruins known as the 'cathedral' on the right. The road curves round to rejoin Al-Baiqa' St.

Down an alley running left (south) off Al-Baiqa' St is the entrance to the **Madaba Museum** (12; opposite). Continue further west along Al-Baiqa' St to the junction with An-Nuzha St where there are some more old houses, including **Beit Sawaihah (13)**. Around 50m northeast of the junction, above an open patch of ground, are the ruins of **Tell Madaba** (14; left). Al-Nuzha St then leads south and then southwest, taking you to the junction of the King's Highway, where the **Church of the Apostles** (15; p153) stands.

Sleeping

Madaba has an excellent range of hotels, almost all run by Arab Christians, and all within easy walking distance of Madaba's main sights. Prices include breakfast and private bathroom unless otherwise noted

Mariam Hotel (☎ 3251529; www.mariamhotel
.com; Aisha Umm al-Mumeneen St; s/d/tr JD18/22/26;
❲P❳ ❲✗❳ ❲▯❳ ❲▯❳) The Mariam is doubtless the
best place to stay in town, with spotless
rooms and bathrooms, good breakfasts,
some of the most comfortable beds in Jordan and, best of all, Charl, the superfriendly
owner. A swimming pool, bar and poolside restaurant were added in 2005, which
makes the place great midrange value. Reservations are recommended. The hotel is
located in a quiet residential district, two
blocks northeast of the Al-Mouhafada Circle, an easy 10-minute walk from the town
centre. Charl can organise a taxi to/from
the airport (around JD10) and transport
south along the King's Highway to Petra
(see p158 or to the Dead Sea (see p158).

Salome Hotel (☎ 3248606; salomeh@wanadoo.jo;
Aisha Umm al-Mumeneen St; s/d/tr Sep to mid-Nov & Mar-May
JD15/20/25, rest of year JD13/18/22; ❲P❳ ❲✗❳ ❲▯❳) Connected to the Mariam next door (it's sometimes used an overspill) this new 17-room
hotel is another very comfortable choice.

Black Iris Hotel (☎ 3250171; www.blackirishotel
.com; Al-Mouhafada Circle; s/d/tr/q JD15/20/27/32) Another friendly family-run place with very
reasonable prices, it also comes warmly recommended by readers. The stylish rooms,
some overlooking a pleasant garden, have
spotless bathrooms and there's also a nice
café/reading area. The top-floor quad has
its own private roof terrace, which is great
in the summer. The hotel is easy to spot
from Al-Mouhafada Circle.

Lulu Pension (☎ 3243678; fax 3247617; Hamraa' al-
Asd St; s/d/tr with shared bathroom JD10/20/30, s/d/t with private bathroom & balcony JD15/25/35) Has a family feel
to it, and the rooms are very comfortable and
the welcome is warm. The cheaper rooms are
in the basement. Guests have access to the
satellite TV room and a self-service kitchen
that's great for making cups of tea.

Madaba Hotel (☎ /fax 3240643; Al-Jame St; s/d with
shared bathroom from JD7/12, s/d with private bathroom
JD8/15) This is the best budget option, with
clean, simple rooms and a friendly family feel. The shared bathrooms are spotless, with hot water in the morning and
evening, and there's a ground floor lounge
and kitchen that guests can use. In summer you can probably sleep in the rooftop
Bedouin tent (JD3). Breakfast costs JD1.

Moab Land Hotel (☎ /fax 3251318; moablandhotel@
wanadoo.jo; Talal St; s/d JD15/20 high season Sep-Nov,

Mar-Apr JD20/25, suite JD30) Directly opposite St
George's Church, this place is run by a
Greek Orthodox family. It's an attractive,
clean and airy place, staff are friendly and
the location is excellent. Rooms are warm
and cosy. In summer savour a slow breakfast on the great rooftop terrace. The reception is on the upper floor.

Queen Ayola Hotel (☎ /fax 3244087; Talal St; s/d
with shared bathroom JD10/17, with private bathroom
JD12/20) Rooms here vary and the price does
not always match the quality, so try to have
a look at several rooms. It lacks the family-run charm of Madaba's other hotels; if you
can afford a few dinars more, there's better
elsewhere.

Madaba Inn (☎ 3259003; www.madabainn.com; Talal
St) This brand-new 33-room hotel had not
yet opened at the time of research but should
provide a central midrange option, said to be
managed by Grand Palace Amman.

St George's Church Pilgrim House (☎ 3244984;
Talal St; per person JD7) Christian pilgrims are
the core clientele in this hostel but staff
are generally happy to take in stray tourists. Rooms are simple but very clean, with
fresh sheets and a towel, and you get a small
but clean private bathroom with hot water.
Some rooms have a church view.

Eating & Drinking

Most of Madaba's restaurants serve alcohol
and there are liquor stores dotted around
the town.

Coffee Shop Ayola (☎ 3251843; Talal St; snacks
around JD1; ◷ 8am-11pm) Almost opposite St
George's Church, this is a charming, relaxed place that caters to both tourists and
locals. It serves delicious toasted sandwiches (JD1), all types of coffee (500 fils
to JD1), tea (500 fils) and cans of cold beer
(JD1.500). It's also a good place to spend
time with a nargileh (water pipe).

Dana Restaurant (☎ 3245749; Al-Nuzha St; starters 500-750 fils, mains JD3-4; ◷ 9am-11pm) Not far
from the Church of the Apostles, the atmosphere here is pleasant, though can be
deathly quiet in the evenings. When there's
a group around they serve lunch (sometimes dinner) buffets (JD4); at other times
the owners recommend the sajieh, a baked
dish of chicken, onion and bread (JD4).

El Cardo Restaurant (☎ 3251006; Hussein bin Ali
St; starters JD1-2, mains JD5, buffet JD5; ◷ 8am-midnight)
Opposite the Archaeological Park, the food

here is determined by the presence, or lack of, a tour group; ie either a lunchtime buffet or slim pickings (grilled). A large bottle of Amstel costs JD3. The décor is attractive and the service good.

Haret Jdoudna (☎ 3248650; Talal St; starters from 800 fils, mains JD4-7, pizzas JD2-4, plus 26% tax; ☯ 9am-midnight) A classy complex of craft shops (below), cafés, bars, pizzerias and restaurants, all set in one of Madaba's restored old houses. The food is a notch above the standard, with interesting mezze such as *mutaffi bethanjan* (fried eggplant with sesame), good *fatteh* (fried bread with garlicky yoghurt and hummus, sometimes with chicken) and *sawani* (meat or vegetables cooked on trays in a wood-burning oven), and dessert specials like the pastry flakes and walnuts served with pistachio ice cream (JD2). You can sit either indoors or in the pleasant courtyard, though either way the service borders on the indifferent. There is a small bar (wine JD2.500 a glass) and live music from 9pm.

For cheap felafel, shwarma and chicken places try the King's Highway opposite the former bus station.

There's little going on in Madaba after dark, except drinks in the bar at Haret Jdoudna or poolside at the Mariam Hotel.

Shopping

Madaba is famous for its colourful rugs, which can be bought around town (especially between the entrance to the Burnt Palace and St George's Church) although much of what's on offer comes from elsewhere. There are plenty of souvenir shops in the area.

Next to the entrance to the Burnt Palace, the National Society for the Preservation of Madaba and its Suburbs (p151) has a necessarily long sign and friendly staff. The organisation aims to preserve Madaba's heritage, with a particular focus on protecting the architectural and historical integrity of the old houses around town. It's partly funded by the sale of maps, books and souvenirs from its shop. Opening hours are erratic.

Craft shops (☎ /fax 3248650; Haret Jdoudna complex, Talal St; ☯ 9am-9pm) Have a classy and extensive range of items on offer, including jewellery, books, clothing, mosaics, furniture, textiles and ceramics. Most items come from local nonprofit organisations such as the Noor Al-Hussein Foundation (see p248).

Embroidered items come from the Arab Cultural Society, which supports Jordanian war widows. There's a small silversmiths on site.

Holy Treasures (☎ 3248481; Talal St) Opposite St George Church, this showroom has an expensive but extensive range of good quality Dead Sea products.

Madaba Studio & Lab (☎ 3245932; Talal St; ☯ 8am-9.30pm) One of the better places for developing film. It charges JD5 to develop 36 prints, and sells print film (from JD2.500 for 36 shots), slide film (JD7), memory cards and video cartridges (from JD5). It's near the Moab Land Hotel.

The Madaba Handicraft Centre is a tour group stop 3.5km outside Madaba, on the road to Mt Nebo. It's worth a stop if you have a car and are interested in some shopping.

Getting There & Away

The new bus station, 2km east of the King's Highway, opened in 2005. A taxi to the station costs around JD1 and minibuses and/or service taxis run there from the King's Highway.

There are several attractions that are located around Madaba, but most (with the exception of Mt Nebo and Mukawir) are time-consuming to reach by public transport. If you don't have time to wait around for infrequent minibuses, charter a taxi in Madaba. A half-day trip (JD20 to JD25) could take in Mt Nebo, Khirbet Mukhayyat, Ayoun Musa and Hammamat Ma'in. A full day (around JD35) could also take in Mukawir, Umm ar-Rasas and Wadi Mujib.

TO/FROM THE AIRPORT

If you want to bypass the bustle of Amman, it's possible to reach Madaba from Queen Alia International Airport, although there is no public transport. Private taxis cost around JD12, but most hotels in Madaba can arrange a taxi from the airport for JD10 if you notify them in advance.

TO/FROM AMMAN

From Raghadan, Wahadat and, less often, Abdali bus stations in Amman, there are regular buses and minibuses (350 fils, one hour) throughout the day for Madaba. Minibuses return to Amman until around 9pm (earlier on Fridays), though check which bus station in Amman they are headed to.

TO/FROM THE DEAD SEA

Minibuses also leave from the Madaba bus/ minibus station to Shuneh al-Janubiyyeh (South Shuna; 350 fils, 45 minutes), from where you can catch another minibus to Suweimah (250 fils, 30 minutes). Returning to Madaba, you'll need to take a minibus (before 5pm) for Amman and ask the driver to let you out just before Na'ur, from where a minibus will take you to Madaba (total of JD1.250, 1½ hours).

Charl of Mariam Hotel can often organise a taxi tour to Bethany-Beyond-the-Jordan, Amman Beach on the Dead Sea and the Dead Sea Panorama complex for around JD20 (JD18 without Bethany), with an hour stop at each sight. Ask at the hotel if there are enough passengers to warrant a trip.

With the completion of a new road connecting Mt Nebo with the Dead Sea, it is possible to visit Mt Nebo, the Dead Sea and Bethany-Beyond-the-Jordan in a long day, returning to Madaba in the evening, although you'd have to hitch sections (including the 6km to/from Bethany and from Suweimah to Amman Beach).

For those with their own transport, the new (2005) Dead Sea Parkway road offers a useful and scenically dramatic new route to the Dead Sea from Madaba, linking the Dead Sea resorts and Hammamat Ma'in spa to the King's Highway.

SOUTH ALONG THE KING'S HIGHWAY

Public transport along the King's Highway is patchy and, across Wadi Mujib between Dhiban and Ariha, nonexistent. One worthwhile option is to take the service organised by the Mariam Hotel (you don't have to be staying there). Leaving at 10am, it goes to Petra (arriving around 6pm), with stops at Wadi Mujib for photos, and an hour in Karak. You can get off at Dana, but you'll have to pay the full fare. The service requires a minimum of three people (the hotels ring around Madaba to find other passengers) and costs JD13 per person.

The only alternative is to take a minibus to Dhiban (250 fils, 45 minutes) and then charter a taxi across to Ariha.

TO/FROM ELSEWHERE

It is possible to travel to Karak on a daily minibus (JD1.500, two hours) from the main bus station, although it travels via the less interesting Desert Highway. The bus, which usually leaves sometime after 6am, is the university bus for Mu'tah, but it stops at (or close to) the minibus station in Karak. Be aware, however, that although this minibus claims to run daily, it often doesn't operate when the university is on holidays so check the day before you want to travel.

From the bus station in Madaba, minibuses go to Mukawir (for Machaerus castle; 350 fils, one hour) several times throughout the day, the last at around 5pm.

See p160 for details of getting to and from Mt Nebo.

Getting Around

If you're laden with bags, private taxis are plentiful; from the new bus station to the centre of town costs JD1.

If you are driving, avoid the central area with its fiendish one-way system. Parking is available at the visitor centre.

MT NEBO   جبل نيبو

> Go up unto…Mount Nebo in Moab, across from Jericho, and view Canaan, the land I am giving the Israelites as their own possession. There on the mountain that you have climbed you will die.
>
> *(Deuteronomy 32:49-50).*

Mt Nebo (admission JD1; ⏱ 7am-5pm Oct-Apr, to 7pm May-Sep) is where Moses is said to have seen the Promised Land, a land he was himself forbidden to enter. He died (aged 120) and was later buried in the area, although the exact location of the burial site is the subject of conjecture. The site flickered briefly into the international spotlight with the visit of Pope John Paul II in 2000.

The Mt Nebo region features several peaks, including Siyagha ('monastery' in Aramaic and the modern Arabic name for the site) – known to the Greeks as Mt Pisgah – on which the Moses Memorial Church was built. It's a pleasant side trip from Madaba, just 9km away, and some readers rate the mosaics here as better than those at Madaba. Aside from its religious significance, Mt Nebo commands sweeping views of the ancient lands of Gilead, Judah, Jericho and the Negev – the Promised Land.

History

The existence of the church was first reported by a Roman nun, Etheria, who made a pilgrimage to the site in AD 393. This original three-apsed church was quite modest and only a fraction of the size of what you see today. A nave was added in the 5th century, the first baptistry chapel (with the mosaic) was added in AD 530 and the main basilica was completed in AD 597. It was during this time that a large Byzantine monastery was built surrounding the church.

By this time Nebo had grown into an important pilgrimage site and a turn-off to the site was marked on the main Roman road through the region (a Roman mile marker lays in the church courtyard). Byzantine pilgrims would travel to Jerusalem, Jericho, Bethany, Ayoun Musa and Mt Nebo, before descending to Hammamat Ma'in for some serious post-pilgrimage soaking.

The church was abandoned by the 16th century and the modern site was relocated using 4th- and 5th-century pilgrim travelogues. The Franciscans bought the site in 1932 and have excavated most of the ruins of the church and the monastery, as well as reconstructing much of the basilica.

Information

The entrance to the complex is clearly visible on the Madaba to Dead Sea road, next to a huge new shopping and parking complex. Next to the entrance are some toilets and there's a permanent tourist police presence. Smoking and mobile phones are not allowed in the complex.

The hefty *Town of Nebo* by Fr Sylvestre J Salter and Fr Bellarmiro Bagatti also details other Christian sites in Jordan and is a good reference. More portable and affordable (JD4) is *Mount Nebo* by Michelle Piccirillo. Both are usually available inside the church. The two brochures published by the Jordan Tourism Board – *Madaba and Mt Nebo* and especially *Mount Nebo* – are very informative and available at the tourist office in Madaba. The encyclopaedic *Mosaics of Madaba* is on display inside the church.

Sights

Before you get to the **Moses Memorial Church** pop into the **museum**, which has a good collection of mosaics from around Nebo and a 3-D map of the area. From here, walk round to the back of the church.

As you enter the **basilica**, the nave and specifically the presbytery straight ahead mark the oldest section of the church, which was built around 4th-century foundations in AD 597. Pilgrims light candles near the altar as they have done on and off now for some 1500 years. Next to the altar is the lovely mosaic of a braided cross.

To the left is the Diaconicon/baptistry and the exceptionally well preserved main **mosaic** (AD 530), measuring about 9m by 3m. This mosaic is yet another quite remarkable work of patient artistry, depicting hunting and herding scenes interspersed

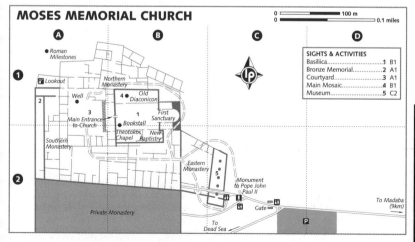

MOSES MEMORIAL CHURCH

0 ——— 100 m
0 ——— 0.1 miles

SIGHTS & ACTIVITIES
Basilica	1 B1
Bronze Memorial	2 A1
Courtyard	3 A1
Main Mosaic	4 B1
Museum	5 C2

Roman Milestones

Lookout

Northern Monastery

Well

Old Diaconicon

Main Entrance to Church

First Sanctuary

Bookstall

Theotokos Chapel

New Baptistry

Southern Monastery

Eastern Monastery

Monument to Pope John Paul II

Private Monastery

Gate

To Madaba (9km)

P

To Dead Sea

with an assortment of African fauna, including a zebu (humped ox), lions, tigers, bears, boars, zebras, an ostrich on a leash and a camel-shaped giraffe. The inscription below names the artist.

The newer **baptistry** to the southeast has smaller mosaics, with a fine image of a gazelle and some pomegranate trees.

From the **lookout** at the back (west) of the **courtyard**, the views across the valleys to the Dead Sea, Jericho, the Jordan River and Jerusalem (just 46km away), are superb, but they're often concealed by the haze and pollution. A direction finder points you in the right direction.

Nearby, a huge Italian-designed **bronze memorial** symbolises the suffering and death of Jesus on the cross and the serpent that 'Moses lifted up' in the desert.

There is little else to see around the complex except the ruins of part of the original monastery. Some of the complex is part of a functioning monastery and is, therefore, off limits to visitors.

To enjoy the views away from the crowds, pack a picnic and hike along the road downhill from the site for 100m and take the track to the left to the nearby hilltop.

Eating

For food, head about 1km back along the road towards Madaba where there are a few restaurants including the recommended **Siyagha Restaurant** (☎ 3250226; mains JD2-5).

Getting There & Away

From Madaba shared taxis run to the mosque at Fasaliyya, for 150 fils a seat. For an extra JD1 or so the service will drop you at Mt Nebo, 3km further.

A return trip in a private taxi from Madaba, with about 30 minutes to look around, shouldn't cost more than JD4 per vehicle.

From Mt Nebo the road continues down for 17km into the Jordan Valley to meet the main Amman–Dead Sea highway, offering excellent views over the valley. There's not much public transport but is a good short cut if you have a car.

AROUND MT NEBO
Khirbet Mukhayyat   خربة مخيط

The village of Khirbet Mukhayyat marks the original site of ancient Nebo village, as mentioned on the 9th-century-BC Mesha

Stele (see p165) and in the Bible. Also here is the **Church of SS Lot and Procopius**, which was originally built in AD 557. Inside this unremarkable building is a remarkable **mosaic**, with scenes of daily life, such as agriculture, fishing and wine-making (the cutting and carrying of grapes). If the church is closed look for the gatekeeper, who lives only a few hundred metres away – a 500 fils tip is appreciated.

On top of a nearby hill lie the obvious ruins of the earlier **Church of St George**. Built in AD 536, very little of the church remains and it's officially off limits to tourists.

The turn-off to Khirbet Mukhayyat is well signposted ('Al-Makhyt') to the south, about 6km from Madaba and about 3km before reaching the church complex at Mt Nebo. A good road leads 2.5km into the village, but the final 100m to the Church of SS Lot and Procopius is steep. There is no regular public transport to the village or the churches and hitching requires patience, though it's not a bad walk. If you have chartered a taxi to Mt Nebo, pay a little more (around JD2 extra) for a side trip to Khirbet Mukhayyat.

Ayoun ('Ain) Musa   عين موسى

Ayoun Musa ('Spring of Moses') is one of two places where the great man is believed to have obtained water by striking a rock (see also p196). The scrappy site is disfigured by a ruined water plant building and there's little to see except the low-lying **ruins** of a couple of churches nearby.

The obvious turn-off to the right (north) is about 1km before the church at Mt Nebo and opposite the Siagha Restaurant. There is no public transport to the site, and hitching is almost impossible. A trip can be combined with a visit to Mt Nebo by chartered taxi, although the switch-backing 2.4km road down to Ayoun Musa is steep and potholed and taxi drivers are reluctant to go along this road unless given substantial financial incentive. Walking down from the main road is easy; coming back is a killer.

HESBAN   حسبان

Amateur archaeologists will like **Tell Hesban** (admission free; ☉ daylight hr), 11km north of Madaba. Over the last few thousand years this strategic hill has been a Bronze Age settlement, an Amorite capital (900–500 BC), a Hellenistic fortress (198–63 BC), a Roman settlement called Esbus (63 BC–AD 350), a Byzantine ecclesiastical centre (AD 350–650), an Umayyad market town (650–750), a regional capital of the Abbasids (750–1260) and Mamluks (1260-1500) and, finally, an Ottoman village. All these layers of history are on view, albeit faintly.

The site is well signed, and you can make out multiple layers of history, including a Byzantine church (the mosaics are displayed in Madaba), a Roman temple and the remains of Hellenistic fort. There are lots of caves and cisterns both here and in neighbouring Wadi Majar. The largest Bronze Age cave can be explored with a torch (flashlight).

Travellers recommend the local caretaker, Abo Nour, who is very knowledgeable about the site. You can locate him in the graffiti-covered house next to the site. Read up on the site beforehand at www.hesban.org.

Minibuses run frequently from Madaba (100 fils, 20 minutes) to Hesban or otherwise take a taxi for JD2.500. The tell is right by the road; at the central junction head up the hill, taking an early right and then swinging around the back of the hill. Any minibuses headed north can take you to Amman.

HAMMAMAT MA'IN
حمامات ماعين (زرقاء ماعين)

☎ 05

About 60 thermal springs have been discovered in the area south and west of Madaba, of which the most famous is **Hammamat Ma'in** (admission per person JD5, per vehicle JD5; ☼ 6am-midnight), which has been developed into a hot-springs resort. The water is hot (at least 45°C), and contains potassium, magnesium and calcium, among other minerals.

Information

The complex at Hammamat Ma'in was run for a time by the French Mercure group but has been taken over by a Saudi company, so facilities and prices were in flux at the time of research.

Day-trippers are welcome to use (free of charge after paying the entrance fee) the Roman baths, the family pool at the base of the waterfall closest to the entrance, and the swimming pool. Visitors are in theory not allowed to bring food and drink into the complex.

Sights & Activities

There are two main baths open to the public. The **Roman baths** have clean indoor hot baths (separate for men and women). There is also a small **family pool** beneath a waterfall, which is one of the first signs to the right as you come down the hill from the gate. In general this pool is restricted to women, families or couples, although this is often not enforced. The water is over 60°C when it leaves its underground spring, but is closer to 50°C by the time it tumbles down the rock. There is a small cave behind the cascading water.

There is also a large, clean cold-water **swimming pool** (☼ closed Oct-Apr) that often closes around 4pm. There is a larger and very picturesque hot–water waterfall immediately to the right (north) of the hotel, but visitors are discouraged from climbing up to it.

The **spa** is part of the resort, and you can expect a range of treatments including mud-wrapping, jet showers, hydrotherapy treatment, massages, hydrojet beds and beauty treatments.

It should be possible to **hike** from the springs down the steep Wadi Zarqa Ma'in to the Herodus Spring on the Dead Sea Highway. Trails are in theory controlled by the Mercure resort, which charges for a guide and provisions.

Sleeping & Eating

There are two sleeping options inside the complex, both of which are administered by the resort. The choice is between the main **Ma'in Spa Hotel** (☎ /fax 3245500) and a cheaper group of attached chalets.

For meals, your only option is the resort restaurant, which looks out onto the main waterfall. There are (sometimes) snacks and soft drinks available next to the Roman baths.

Getting There & Away

Although just 4km from the Dead Sea Highway, the main access road is from Madaba, 27km to the northeast. If you're driving, the last 4km descent into Hammamat Ma'in is scenic but very steep, so use a low gear.

From Madaba, minibuses regularly go to Ma'in village (200 fils, 15 minutes), from where you'll have to hitch the remaining 22km (traffic is light except on Fridays). Alternatively take a taxi from Madaba (JD6

KING'S HIGHWAY

one way, or JD12 to JD15 for a return journey, including around an hour's waiting time). Remember that if your taxi enters the gate (from where it's a 300m walk down the hill to the start of the complex), you'll have to fork out JD5 for the car to enter.

DEAD SEA PANORAMA

This lovely new complex has absorbing views over the Dead Sea and offers a great new route to the sea from the King's Highway. Sunset is a particularly good time to visit. At any time you'll need your own transport.

The **Dead Sea Museum** (☯ 7.30am-4.30pm) is an excellent introduction to the geology, history and environment of the Dead Sea. A **restaurant** is due to open here in early 2006. The complex is just about at sea level.

The complex is 2km west of the turn-off down to Hammamat Ma'in, along a new road opened in 2005 to connect the Desert Highway with the Dead Sea. No public transport runs along the road. The new road makes it possible to make a day trip loop from Madaba, via Hammamat Ma'in, the Panorama Complex, the Dead Sea, Bethany and Mt Nebo, either by hired car or taxi (JD 20 through Charl at the Mariam Hotel – see p158).

MUKAWIR (MACHAERUS)
مكاور (مكاريوس)

☎ 05

Just beyond the village of Mukawir (pronounced Mu-*kar*-wir) is the spectacular 700m-high hilltop perch of Machaerus, the castle of Herod the Great. The hill was first fortified in about 100 BC, and expanded by Herod the Great in 30 BC. The ruins themselves are of minor interest, but the setting is breathtaking and commands great views out over the impossibly steep surrounding hills and the Dead Sea. Most days you'll even have the place to yourself. Machaerus is known locally as Qala'at al-Meshneq (Castle of the Gallows).

Machaerus is renowned as the place where John the Baptist was beheaded by Herod Antipas, the successor to Herod the Great. John the Baptist had denounced Herod Antipas' marriage to his brother's wife, Herodias, as Jewish law forbade a man marrying his brother's wife while he lived. Bewitched by his stepdaughter Salome's skill as a dancer, the king promised to grant her anything she wished. To take revenge on the Baptist, Herodias told her daughter to ask for his head on a platter:

> And she went out, and said to her mother, "What shall I ask?" And she said, "The head of John the Baptiser."
> (Mark 6:24)

So, at the request of Salome, John was killed at Herod's castle, Machaerus. Provocative Salome has inspired painters and writers alike over the centuries.

There is nowhere to stay in Mukawir and only a few basic grocery stores, so bring your own provisions.

Sights

From the car park, a stone staircase leads down to the main path along the path of an old viaduct. Shortly after the path starts to climb, a small path leads around the main hill to the right. It leads past a number of **caves**, one of which legend says is where the gruesome execution took place, although it's not labelled. You take this path at your peril as it's uneven, often covered with loose stones and narrow.

The main landscaped path is much safer and winds all the way up to the **castle**. At the top, the modest ruins are unlabelled. The reconstructed columns southwest of the deep cistern mark the site of Herod Antipas' **palace triclinium**; this is the site where Salome danced. You should also be able to make out the low-lying remains of the eastern **baths** and defensive **walls**.

The Romans built a **siege ramp** on the western side of the hill when taking the fort from Jewish rebels in AD 72 and the remains are still visible.

The castle is about 2km past Mukawir village and easy to spot.

Activities

This is a great area for **hiking**, with plenty of shepherds' trails snaking along the valley walls. One particularly worthwhile track leads steeply down the west side of the castle hill from the top and along a ridge line towards the Dead Sea. The views are magnificent, particularly at sunset.

It's also possible to follow the shepherds' trails (or the 4WD road) down to the hot springs at Hammamat Ma'in. You must exercise extreme caution if taking any of these trails as the terrain falls steeply away and many paths are only for the sure-footed. Women in particular should never hike alone.

You can arrange with the Royal Society for the Conservation of Nature (RSCN) to hike from Mukawir through the Wadi Mujib Nature Reserve to Zara/Herodus Hot Springs; see p147.

Shopping

At the end of the village, and the start of the road to the castle, is a weaving centre and gallery, a women's cooperative run by the Bani Hamida Centre (see the boxed text below). Visitors are always welcome to look around the small **showroom** (☽ 8am-3pm Sun-Thu) where some of the fine woven products are on sale. The women who run it speak little English, but are keen to help and show how the weaving is done. They also have a display video that shows many of the skills used by the women who work as part of the cooperative.

Getting There & Away

From outside the bus/minibus station in Madaba, minibuses (350 fils, one hour) go frequently to the village of Mukawir, via Libb (the last around 5pm).

Unless you've chartered a taxi from Madaba, you'll probably need to walk the remaining 2km (a pleasant downhill stroll most of the way) to the castle. Otherwise, your minibus driver may, if you ask nicely (and sweeten the request with a tip), take you the extra distance. Return traffic between the castle car park and the village borders on the nonexistent. The best way

to visit is in your own car, allowing you to take as long as you want to explore the surrounding hills and even pause for a picnic.

UMM AR-RASAS   أم الرصاص

Umm ar-Rasas, 32km from Madaba, is thought to be the village of Kastron Mefaa, mentioned in the Bible as the Roman military outpost of Mephaath. It was designated as a Unesco World Heritage site in 2004.

A shed hangs over the main ruins of the **Church of St Stephen** (admission free; ☽ 8am-5pm), one of four churches in the original village. Inside the shed are some marvellous **mosaics** dating back to about AD 785. The main mosaic clearly depicts hunting, fishing and agriculture, scenes of daily life (such as boys enjoying a boat ride), and the names of those who helped pay for the mosaic. A panel consisting of 10 cities in the region includes Umm ar-Rasas, Philadelphia (Amman), Madaba, Esbounta (Hesban), Belemounta (Ma'in), Areopolis (Ar-Rabba) and Charac Moaba (Karak). A northern panel depicts Jerusalem, Nablus, Casearea, Gaza and others. The edges of the mosaic are particularly decorative.

By the end of 2006 a new visitor centre and shelter over the church should be in place, most likely along with an entry fee.

Beyond are the expansive ruins of **Kastron Mefaa** village, with another four churches and impressive city walls. Arches rise up randomly from the rubble like sea monsters and you can spot cisterns and door lintels everywhere, but a lack of signposts makes it hard to grasp the structure of the town.

About 1.5km north of the ruins is an enigmatic 15m-tall **stone tower**, the purpose of

---

THE BANI HAMIDA STORY

One of the several organisations in Jordan that sell handicrafts to fund local community development projects (see p248) is Bani Hamida, named after a group of people who settled in the remote village of Mukawir.

Created under the auspices of the Save the Children Fund, with the continuing assistance of the Canadian and US governments and now administered by the Jordan River Valley Foundation, the Weaving Project Center & Gallery was established in Mukawir. Its aims included reviving traditional weaving practices, raising money for the development of villages in the area and improving the independence of local women. The project now employs over 1400 women who work in the gallery at Mukawir, or at home in one of the 12 nearby villages.

Some of the items available for sale both here and at the Jordan River Foundation shop in Amman (see p98) include pottery, baskets, jewellery, rugs, cushions and bags. Most of the items are created using traditional looms and are coloured with natural dyes.

which baffles archaeologists because there are no stairs inside but several windows at the top. It was most likely a retreat for a stylite, a group of Christian hermits, popular at the time, who lived in seclusion on the top of pillars. Crosses decorate the side of the tower and several ruined monastery buildings lie nearby.

As part of the development of facilities at Umm ar-Rasas, a new museum is to be built at the archaeological site of **Lehun** (or Lejjun), a garrison town built a few kilometres away in AD 300 to house the 4th Roman Legion, and part of a line of Roman forts called the Limes Arabicus which defended the remotest borders of Rome. The site is 7km east of Dhiban and might be worth checking out once the complex is finished in 2006. See the website www.lehun -excavations.be for details.

Getting There & Away
A few minibuses go directly to Umm ar-Rasas, via Nitil, from the bus/minibus station in Madaba. Alternatively, catch anything going to Dhiban, and hitch a ride from there. Another option is to charter a private taxi from the obvious turn-off at the roundabout in the middle of Dhiban, but taxi drivers can demand as much as JD5/7 one way/return, including waiting time. Umm ar-Rasas is also accessible from the Desert Highway by private or chartered vehicle.

The Church of St Stephen isn't signposted from the village. Take the dirt track beside the post office for 500m to the site. The post office is 500m north of the T-junction of the road between the King's and Desert Highways and the signposted road leading north to Nitil.

WADI MUJIB GORGE   وادي الموجيب
Stretching across Jordan from the Desert Highway to the Dead Sea (covering a distance of over 70km) is the vast and beautiful Wadi Mujib gorge, rather optimistically known as the 'Grand Canyon of Jordan'. Aside from being spectacular, it is also significant as the historic boundary between the ancient Amorites (to the north) and the Moabites (to the south). Moses is also believed to have walked through Wadi Mujib, when it was known as the Arnon Valley.

Don't confuse the Wadi Mujib gorge here with the Wadi Mujib Nature Reserve (see p146), which lies further downstream and is normally accessed from the Dead Sea Highway.

The canyon, which is 1km deep and 4km from one edge to the other, is definitely worth seeing even if you don't intend going further south to Karak along the King's Highway. Although the canyon is only 4km wide, the road takes 18km to cross the gorge.

Dhiban is the last town you'll pass through (if coming from the north) before you begin the descent down into Wadi Mujib. Once the powerful town of Dibon, the capital of an empire carved out by King Mesha in the 9th century BC, Dhiban is where the Mesha Stele was discovered (see opposite). There is nothing left of the ancient city.

About 3km down (south) from Dhiban is an awesome **lookout** over Wadi Mujib. To admire the views without crossing the valley, walk (or charter a taxi) to the lookout from Dhiban. At the bottom of the valley the main road crosses the large Mujib dam before winding up the far side in a series of switchbacks.

At the point where you will start to again breathe easy after negotiating the perilous climb, you will see the strategically placed **Trajan Rest House** (☎ 079 5903302; bed in shared room JD3, with breakfast & dinner JD10), which is also signed as 'Trajan Restaurant'. The restaurant only serves open buffets for tour groups but you can get hot and cold drinks and breakfast (dinner can be arranged if you are staying overnight) here. The accommodation here is basic, with curtains for doors. It is a good place to hitch a ride down into the valley.

Ariha is the first village you'll reach as you climb up the southern wall of Wadi Mujib, although the village is about 2.5km off the main King's Highway.

Getting There & Away
Dhiban is where almost all transport south of Madaba stops. At the moment, the only way to cross the mighty Wadi Mujib from Dhiban to Ariha (about 30km) is to charter a taxi for JD4 each way. Finding a taxi in Ariha is a lot harder. Bargain hard. Hitching is possible, but you can expect a long wait.

A STELE AT TWICE THE PRICE

The original Mesha Stele was found by a missionary at Dhiban in 1868. It was a major discovery because it not only provided historical detail of the battles between the Moabites and the kings of Israel, but was also the earliest example of Hebrew script to be unearthed. After surviving intact from about 850 BC (when it was raised by King Mesha of Moab to let everyone know of his successes against Israel) to AD 1868, it quickly came to a rather unfortunate end.

After finding the stele, the missionary reported it to Charles Clermont-Ganneau at the French consulate in Jerusalem who then made a mould of it and went back to Jerusalem to raise the money which he had offered the locals for it. While he was away, the local families argued over who was going to get the money and some of the discontented lit a fire under the stone and then poured water over it, causing it to shatter. Although most pieces were recovered, inevitably some were lost. The remnants were gathered together and shipped off to France, and the reconstructed stone is now on display in the Louvre in Paris. Copies can be seen in the museums at Amman, Madaba and Karak.

KARAK   الكرك

☎ 03 / Pop 20,000

The ancient Crusader stronghold of Karak (or Kerak) lies within the walls of the old city and is one of the highlights of Jordan. The fortified castle that dominates the town was a place of legend in the battles between the Crusaders or Franks and the Islamic armies of Saladin (Salah ad-Din). Now among the most famous, the castle at Karak was just one in a long line built by the Crusaders stretching from Aqaba in the south to Turkey in the north.

Often ignored by travellers speeding south towards Petra, Karak is worth the effort to get here.

History

Karak lies on the route that ancient caravans travelled from Egypt to Syria in the time of the biblical kings, and was also used by the Greeks and Romans. The city is mentioned several times in the Bible as Kir, Kir Moab and Kir Heres, capital of the Moabites, and later emerges as a Roman provincial town, Charac Moaba. The city also features on the famous mosaic in St George's Church in Madaba.

The arrival of the Crusaders launched the city back into prominence and the Crusader king Baldwin I of Jerusalem had the castle built in AD 1142. Even today, its commanding position and strategic value are obvious, and stands midway between Shobak and Jerusalem. It became the capital of the Crusader district of Oultrejourdain and, with the taxes levied on passing caravans and food grown in the district, helped Jerusalem prosper.

The castle was passed on to the de Milly family and through marriage fell into the sadistic hands of Renauld de Chatillon who delighted in torturing prisoners and throwing them off the walls into the valley 450m below; he even went to the trouble of having a wooden box fastened over their heads so they wouldn't lose consciousness before hitting the ground. Hated by Saladin for his treachery, de Chatillon had arrived from France in 1148 to take part in the Crusades and from Karak he was able to control the trade routes to Egypt and Mecca, thereby severely disrupting the supply lines of the Islamic armies.

De Chatillon was later executed at the hands of Saladin (the only Crusader leader to suffer such a fate), whose Muslim armies took the castle in 1183 after an epic siege. The Mamluk sultan Beybars took the fort in 1263 and strengthened the fortress, deepening the moat and adding the lower courtyard, but three towers collapsed in an earthquake in AD 1293.

Little more is known of the castle until Jean Louis Burckhardt (the Swiss explorer who rediscovered Petra) passed through Karak in 1812, describing the castle as 'shattered but imposing'.

In the 1880s, religious fighting compelled the Christians of Karak to flee north to resettle Madaba and Ma'in; peace was only restored after thousands of Turkish troops were stationed in the town.

Orientation

The old city of Karak is easy to get around on foot, although beware the madden-

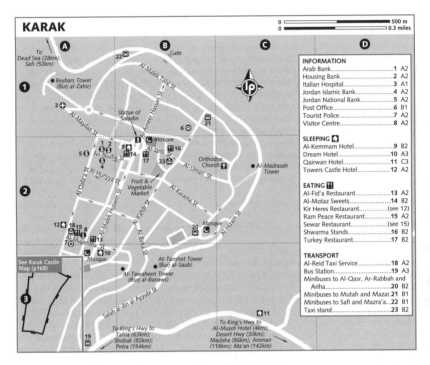

KARAK

INFORMATION	
Arab Bank.....................1	A2
Housing Bank..................2	A2
Italian Hospital................3	A1
Jordan Islamic Bank...........4	A2
Jordan National Bank..........5	A2
Post Office.....................6	B1
Tourist Police..................7	A2
Visitor Centre.................8	A2

SLEEPING	
Al-Kemmam Hotel.............9	B2
Dream Hotel..................10	A3
Qairwan Hotel................11	C3
Towers Castle Hotel..........12	A2

EATING	
Al-Fid'a Restaurant...........13	A2
Al-Motaz Sweets.............14	B2
Kir Heres Restaurant......(see 12)	
Ram Peace Restaurant........15	A2
Sewar Restaurant.........(see 15)	
Shwarma Stands..............16	B2
Turkey Restaurant............17	B2

TRANSPORT	
Al-Reid Taxi Service..........18	A2
Bus Station...................19	A3
Minibuses to Al-Qasr, Ar-Rabbah and	
Ariha.......................20	B2
Minibuses to Mutah and Mazar..21	B1
Minibuses to Safi and Mazra'a..22	B1
Taxi stand....................23	B2

ing one-way system if you are driving. The modern town centre radiates around the statue of Saladin. The plaza near the entrance to the castle has been recently redeveloped and it's in the surrounding streets that you'll find most of the tourist hotels and restaurants.

Tourist authorities have recently built two panorama points a couple of kilometres southeast and northwest of the castle, which provide useful stopping points if you are driving.

Information

If you need to change money here, look no further than An-Nuzha St, a small block located south of the Saladin roundabout. There are at least four banks that change money, and most have an ATM for Visa and MasterCard.

Italian Hospital (Al-Maydan St)

Post office (Al-Khadr St) In the lower (northern) part of town.

Tourist police (☎ 191; Al Qala'a St)

Visitor centre (☎ 2351150; Al-Mujamma St; ☒ 8am-3.30pm Sat-Thu)

Karak Castle

The gate to Karak Castle (admission JD1; ☒ 8am-6pm, to 4pm winter) is reached from the southern end of Al Qala'a St.

Throughout the castle are informative display boards with detailed descriptions of the history and function of each structure. It's worth bringing a torch (flashlight) to explore the darker regions, and some doorways are quite low so watch your head. Reconstruction and excavation work within the castle is ongoing.

The main entrance, known as **Ottoman's Gate**, is at the end of a short bridge over the dry moat. The old entrance or **Crusader's Gate** was once reached via a wooden bridge, 50m to the east, but has not yet been opened to the public.

From Ottoman's Gate, head past the ticket office and take the path leading up to the left. Resist the temptation to head into the vaulted corridor straight ahead and instead follow the path that leads hard left (north). The long chamber you enter to the right is known as the **Crusader Gallery** or stables.

Near the far end of the gallery, steps lead down to the Crusader's Gate. Those entering the castle did so via a narrow winding passage (separated from the Crusader Gallery by a wall). This is typical of Crusader castles, ensuring the entrance could be easily defended as it was not possible to enter the castle in large numbers. On the north wall is a (now headless) **carved figure** which local legend claims to be Saladin, but which actually dates from the 2nd century AD and is believed by scholars to be a Nabataean funerary carving. A small staircase leads up to the site of the ruined **northeast tower**; watch your step.

From the carving, a long passageway leads southwest. Along the left side were the **soldiers' barracks** with small holes for light, walls of limestone and straw and a few Byzantine **rock inscriptions** on the walls. Across the corridor is the **kitchen**, which contains large round stones used for grinding olives and huge storage areas for oil and wheat. In a dark tunnel (only visible with a torch) are some **Greek inscriptions** of unknown meaning. A door from the kitchen leads to the right (west) to the huge **oven**.

Continuing southwest along the main passage, you leave the cool, covered area and emerge into the light. Down to the left is the plunging **glacis**, the dizzyingly steep rocky slope that prevented invaders from climbing up to the castle and prisoners from climbing down. This is where Renauld de Chatillon delighted in expelling undesirables.

If you turn hard right (west, then northwest), you'll enter the overgrown **upper court**, which has a large **cistern** and the largely unexcavated remains of what are believed to have been the domestic **residences** of the castle. At the northern end of the castle is the **terrace**, directly above the Crusader Gallery, which affords fine views over the castle and down to the moat. Above the far (southern) end of the castle rises **Umm al-Thallaja** (Mother of Snows), the hill which posed the greatest threat to the castle's defences during times of siege. To the west is the village of **Al-Shabiya**, which was once called Al-Ifranj because many Crusaders (Franks) settled here after the fall of the castle.

Returning to where you emerged from the long corridor, head southwest. On the left is a **tower** and what is believed to have been a **Mamluk mosque**. On the right is the castle's main **Crusader church** with a **sacristy** down the stairs to the right (north). Note how in this lowered room there are arrow slits in the walls suggesting that this originally formed part of the castle's outer wall.

If you continue to the southern end of the castle, you'll find yourself in front of the impressive, reconstructed **Mamluk keep**. Because it faces Umm al-Thallaja, it was here that the defences were strongest, with 6.5m-thick walls, arrow slits on all four levels and a crenellated section at the top. The keep was built from 1260 by the Mamluk sultan Beybars. It's possible to climb upstairs, past a series of blind niches, to a hidden set of stairs leading up to the upper level.

From the keep, walk northwest, around to the stairs which lead down to the **Mamluk palace**, which was built for Sultan al-Nasir Muhammad in 1311 using earlier Crusader materials. The open-air **reception hall** is a variation of the classic Islamic design of four *iwans* or chambers off the main hall; on two sides are barrel-vaulted rooms. On the one side was the **mosque**, which was probably reserved for palace notables, with the clearly visible mihrab facing Mecca.

A CHIVALROUS SIEGE

In the winter of AD 1183, a gathering of all the important Frankish (Crusader) nobles took place in Karak. They came to celebrate a carefully choreographed wedding, organised as a means of reconciling quarrelling Frankish factions. Saladin, the leader of the Islamic armies, seized on the opportunity and captured the town but met stiffer resistance at the castle. With the catapult assault under way, legend has it that the wedding celebrations within continued unabated. Lady Stephanie, the heiress of Karak, sent out some of the wedding dishes for Saladin. Saladin in turn asked in which section of the castle the young couple were celebrating their wedding night and ordered that this part of the castle was not to be bombarded – a symbol of the chivalry that characterised many of the battles at the time. Saladin's armies withdrew when Frankish reinforcements were sent from across the hills from Jerusalem.

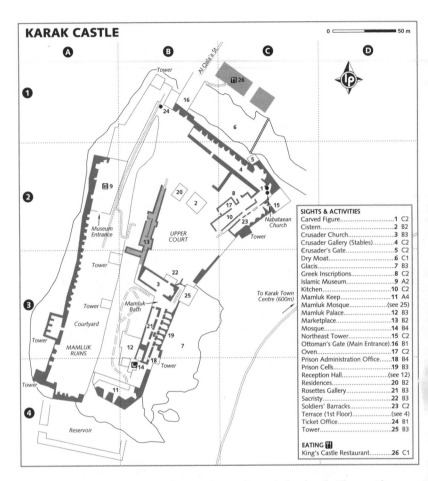

KARAK CASTLE

0   50 m

Before continuing, pause near the top of the stairs for some good **views** down Wadi Karak, towards what is believed to be the site of the condemned cities of Sodom and Gomorrah (see p147). Return to the main Crusader church; immediately south some stairs lead down. Two corridors run off to the southwest. The left (east) corridor leads past seven **prison cells** and at the southern end was the **prison administration office**. The right (west) passage leads from the foot of the stairs through the **Rosettes Gallery**, named after the carved rosette at the foot of the stairs.

If you're game, take the third passage to the left of the steps, which leads northwest through the bowels of the castle, roughly

underneath the church. The corridor turns right (north) and you emerge into the better-lit areas of the delightful underground **marketplace** with various **shops** and **cellars** feeding off it.

At the northern end of the market, the path leads back to the entrance (also the exit) or you can detour to the southwest down the hill to the **Mamluk ruins** and the excellent **Islamic Museum** (8am-around 3pm). If you're lucky you may be able to persuade the curator to open up the nearby underground tunnel for you to explore.

Sleeping

Towers Castle Hotel (2352489; fax 2354293; Al-Qala'a St; dm/s/d JD3/8/12, s/d with private bathroom from JD9/16, new s/d JD12/18) This is the obvious choice, with a good location, a good variety of rooms and friendly Egyptian management. The rooms, many with great views, are large, bright and clean. Prices include breakfast.

Dream Hotel (☎ 077 745762; karak_dream_hotel@ yahoo.com; Al-Mujamma St; s/d with private bathroom JD12/16) The friendly touch of the Towers Castle is lacking here (even though the owners are the same) but it's not bad value, with reasonable rooms. Breakfast costs an extra JD2.500 per person.

Al-Kemmam Hotel (☎ 079 5632365; Al-Maydan St; bed in shared r JD3; s/d JD5/6) A local men-only dosshouse and the only one in the modern town centre. It's not much fun but guests can use the kitchen and there's hot water in the shared bathrooms. There are only four rooms.

Qairwan Hotel (☎ 2396022; fax 2396122; King's Highway; s/d standard JD15/20, deluxe JD20/25; ⚒) This comfortable converted home has a relaxed B&B feel. The nine rooms are all unique and colourful with some nice attempts at decoration and all come with satellite TV and fridge. The upper floor is probably quieter. The hotel is 500m from the bus station, outside the main town of Karak.

Al-Mujeb Hotel (☎ 2386090, fax 2386091; King's Highway; s/d/tr with private bathroom, tax & breakfast JD22/ 30/45) Budget tour groups like this place for the best rooms in Karak (with satellite TV, towels and a fridge) and the attentive staff. It is around 5km from Karak, by the junction on the road to Ar-Rabba, and therefore inconvenient without your own vehicle (a taxi costs around JD2.500 one way).

Eating

Most restaurants are near the castle on Al-Mujamma St or near the statue of Saladin in the modern town. There are some cheap shwarma stands in the streets around the statue of Saladin, particularly east along Al-Jami St.

Ram Peace Restaurant (☎ 353789; Al-Mujamma St; mezze JD1, mains JD3; ⏲ 8am-10pm), next to Al-Reid Taxi Service office, is friendly but the local food is better than the Western variations. The next-door **Sewar Restaurant** (Al-Mujamma St; mezze JD1, mains JD3) is similar.

Al-Fid'a Restaurant (☎ 079 5037622; Al-Mujamma St; mains JD2.500-3.500; ⏲ 8am-10pm) Another popular place with excellent value with main courses,

dips and salads for decent prices. The service is good and the atmosphere cosy.

Kir Heres Restaurant (☎ 2355595; Al-Qala'a St; starters JD1-2.500, mains JD5-7; ⏲ 9am-10pm) In the same building as the Towers Castle Hotel, this is a notch up in quality and a welcome addition to the Karak culinary scene. Though relatively expensive, it has good food and service, and a pleasant ambience. The mezze are best, including good fattoosh, eggplant salad and *matafayah* (eggplant dip). Ask about the ostrich steak.

Turkey Restaurant (☎ 079 5730431; Al-Jami St; mains JD1.500; ⏲ 7am-9.30pm) One of several local restaurants offering roast chicken, hummus and other standard local fare.

Al-Motaz Sweets (☎ 2353388; An-Nuzha St; ⏲ 8am-10pm) One of the better places in town for those with a sweet tooth, serving a range of pastries and sweets.

King's Castle Restaurant (☎ 2396070; lunch buffet JD6; ⏲ noon-4pm) The daily buffet here is popular with day-tripping tour groups and it's a pretty good deal, with pleasant outdoor seating and over 20 salads to choose from. The eastern building is worth a visit for its impressive relief display of the castle as it stood in its original form.

Getting There & Away

As with anywhere along the King's Highway, Karak can be difficult but not impossible to reach by public transport. The main bus station is outside the town, at the bottom of the hill, by the junction of the King's Highway.

MINIBUS

From the main bus station, minibuses go to Amman's Wahadat station (around 800 fils, two hours) via the Desert Highway on a semiregular basis. Minibuses also run every hour or so along the King's Highway from Karak to Tafila (700 fils, around 1 hour), the best place for connections to Qadsiyya (for Dana Nature Reserve) and Shobak. To Wadi Musa (for Petra), take a minibus to Ma'an (JD1.500, two hours) and change there. Alternatively, leapfrog on minibuses to Tafila, Shobak and then Wadi Musa.

Buses to Aqaba (JD2, three hours) travel in the mornings via the Dead Sea Highway about four times a day. In the afternoon you're better off taking the Amman bus to Qatrana on the Desert Highway and changing for a bus headed south to Aqaba.

There are smaller minibus stands around town (indicated on map) for services to Safi (550 fils) and Mazra'a (350 fils) on the Dead Sea Highway, south along the King's Highway to Mu'tah (150 fils) and Mazar (150 fils), and north to Al-Qasr, Ar-Rabba and Ariha.

TAXI

From Amman it's possible (with considerable bargaining) to charter a taxi to Karak via the Desert Highway for about JD18 one way. From Amman via the King's Highway, with a few stops in Wadi Mujib and Madaba, expect to pay at least JD22.

From Karak, taxi fares cost around JD30 to Amman, JD35 to Petra and JD20 to Madaba. Try **Al-Reid Taxi Service** (☎ 2352297; Al-Mujamma St) or just head down to the taxi stand on Umari St.

Getting Around

The old city of Karak has a tricky system of narrow one-way streets. If you're driving, study the map carefully to avoid some serious frustration.

AR-RABBA   عرابه

The holy and historical city of Ar-Rabba came under the rule of King Mesha (9th century BC), then Alexander the Great (mid-4th century BC) and later the Nabataeans (from the 2nd century BC to the 2nd century AD). The Greeks named it Areopolis after Ares, the god of war, and the Romans based their Arabian governor here. It was known locally as Rabbath Moba.

At the northern end of the small town are the small **ruins** of a Roman temple from the end of the 3rd century AD, with two niches that contained statues of the Roman emperors Diocletian and Maximian, and other Roman and Byzantine buildings. None of the ruins are signposted.

The ruins are permanently open, free to enter and located to the east of the main road. Ar-Rabba is easily accessible by minibus from Karak, 16km to the south, but is best visited on a 15-minute stop en route between Madaba and Karak.

MU'TAH   مؤته

☎ 03

Mu'tah is a nondescript town that boasts one of the best **universities** (www.mutah.edu.jo) in Jordan, home to 12,000 students. Mu'tah

is also famous as the location of a battle in AD 632 (some historians say 629), when Christianity first clashed with the armies of Islam (the Byzantine forces defeated the Arab Muslims but they turned the tables four years later). At the main junction in the south of Mu'tah, you'll find a **monument** that commemorates the battle and its *shaheed* (martyrs).

At Mazar (meaning 'tomb'), 3km south of Mu'tah, there is also an impressive **mosque** complex containing the **tombs** of some of the Prophet Mohammed's companions killed in battle.

Minibuses regularly run between Karak and Mu'tah. From Madaba, try the daily university minibus (JD1.500, two hours) from the main bus station, which travels via the Desert Highway. Be aware, however, that it often doesn't operate during the university holidays so check the day before you want to travel.

KHIRBET TANNOUR   خربة التنور

As the King's Highway climbs out of the impressive Wadi Hasa valley (the biblical Zered Valley), at a turn in the road, a dirt track leads off 1.5km to the west to a small hill. A steep 15-minute hike to the top of the hill reveals the ruined 2000-year-old Nabataean temple of **Khirbet Tannour** (admission free; ☉ daylight hr), in an epic location across from a brooding piece of black volcanic hillside.

In all truth there's not much left here to see except for some column bases and the outlines of a temple courtyard and three side rooms (possibly banqueting halls set around a central pool), but most people find the wild location worth a visit for the hike and setting alone.

Copies of the site's famous statue of Nike reside in Amman's National Archaeological Museum and the University of Jordan's Museum of Archaeology; the original is in Cincinnati. A statue of the goddess Atargatis unearthed here is currently in Amman's National Archaeological Museum.

There's no public transport here so you'll have to have a car or hitch. The turn-off is 36km south of Karak town, at the crest of the hill; the 1.5km access road is OK for cars. Park by the communication tower and watch out for the local herders' dogs.

The turnoff signpost is marked as 'AT TA NOURAN I QUI ES SI', which isn't a Latin inscription, but a weather-beaten version of 'At-Tannour Antiquities Site'!

HAMMAMAT BURBITA & HAMMAMAT AFRA

حمامات بربيتا & حمامات عفرا

Hammamat Burbita (or Burbayta) and Hammamat Afra are two thermal hot springs near Wadi Hasa, but the springs and baths at Hammamat Ma'in, near Madaba, are better (although they're more expensive). Women are likely to feel uncomfortable at these two hot springs if local men are around in any numbers. Wadi Afra is currently being upgraded so expect facilities to improve and prices to rise.

The two springs are signposted about 23km north of Tafila; from the turn-off it's about 13km to Burbita, a green patch at the base of a wadi with a small uninviting rock pool and makeshift galvanised iron roof. Another 6km further on, the road ends at the nicer Hammamat Afra. Both spots are popular on Fridays.

There is no public transport to either spot. If you're driving, signposting is confusing and you'll need to ask directions along the way. A chartered taxi from Tafila to Afra costs around JD12 return, including waiting time.

TAFILA

الطفيله

☎ 03

Tafila (also spelled Tafileh) is a busy market centre and transport junction. There is nothing to see, except the very decrepit exterior ruins of a **Crusader castle** (the interior is closed to visitors). It was in Tafila that one of the Prophet Mohammed's emissaries was beheaded, leading to the military conquest by the Islamic armies from AD 632.

Afra Hotel (s/d with shared bath JD5/7) is the only place to stay and is very drab.

Plenty of cheap places sell felafel and shwarma around town. **Adom Rest House** (meals JD4), at the southern end of Tafila on the highway to Dana, is about the best place to eat.

Minibuses from Karak (700 fils, one hour) to Tafila cross the superb scenery of Wadi Hasa. There are also direct minibuses to/from Wahadat station in Amman (JD1, 2½ hours) via the Desert Highway; Aqaba (JD1.200, 2½ hours) via the Dead Sea Highway; Ma'an (JD1, one hour) via the Desert Highway; and just down the King's

Highway to Shobak (800 fils, one hour) and Qadsiyya (for Dana Nature Reserve; 350 fils, 30 minutes).

DANA NATURE RESERVE

محمية دانا الطبيعية

☎ 03

The **Dana Nature Reserve** (adult/student JD6/3) is one of Jordan's hidden gems, as well as its most impressive ecotourism project. Down off the King's Highway, and the main gateway to the reserve, is the charming 15th-century stone village of **Dana**, which clings to a precipice overlooking the valley and commands exceptional views. It's a great place to chill out and spend a few days hiking, reading and relaxing. Most of the reserve is only accessible on foot.

The reserve is the largest in Jordan and includes a variety of terrain, from sandstone cliffs and peaks over 1500m high to a low point of 50m below sea level in the Rift Valley of Wadi Araba, about 14km to the west. The red rock escarpments and valley protect a surprisingly diverse ecosystem, including about 600 species of plants (from citrus trees and desert shrubs to tropical acacias), about 180 species of birds, and over 45 species of mammals (of which 25 are endangered), including ibex, mountain gazelle, sand cat, red fox and wolf. The lower western areas of the reserve can be very hot in July.

There are almost 100 archaeological sites in the reserve, most still being excavated by British teams. Of most interest are the ruins of **Khirbet Feinan**, at the mouth of Wadi Feinan and Wadi Ghuweir. The copper mines here date back 6000 years, when they were the largest metal smelting operations in the Near East (they are mentioned in the Bible). The Romans later worked the mines using Christian slaves. You can explore the ruins of three churches, a Roman tower and the remains of slag heaps where the copper was mined. The main mines of Umm al-Amad are a 13km return hike up in the surrounding hills and you'll need a guide from Feinan Lodge (p173) to reach them. The hills still contain copper, but despite intense lobbying from mining companies, the Jordanian government has agreed not to allow mining in the reserve.

Dana village itself dates from the Ottoman period but was largely abandoned less than a generation ago as locals moved to nearby Qadsiyya in search of jobs. About 50 Bedouin families live inside the reserve.

The reserve was taken over by the RSCN in 1993 and was the first of its kind in Jordan – an attempt to promote ecotourism, protect wildlife and improve the lives of local villagers in an integrated project. The reserve directly or indirectly employs over 40 locals, and income from tourism has helped to rebuild Dana village and provide environmental education in local schools. Villagers also make excellent local crafts (organic herbs, fruit rolls, jams, olive-oil soaps, candles and silver jewellery) that are sold by the RSCN throughout Jordan. The leather goods and candles produced by local Bedouin women at Feinan Lodge, in particular, give local women economic power and an incentive to move away from environmentally damaging goat herding.

Information

The **Visitor centre** (☎ 2270497; dhana@rscn.org.jo; ☽ 8am-8pm) in the guesthouse complex in Dana village includes an RSCN shop, nature exhibits, craft workshops (closed by 3.30pm) and a food-drying centre for making organic food. This is also the place to obtain further information about the reserve and its hiking trails, and arrange a guide. The staff at the centre are knowledgeable, enthusiastic and friendly, and you sense a genuine commitment to the cause. The views from the balcony are stupendous.

Activities

To get the most out of the park you need to explore on foot. The visitor centre can give information on the following **hikes**. Most require a guide, which costs from JD15 for up to two hours to JD32 for a full day, per group. The trails from Al-Barra require a short drive to get to the trailhead (RSCN charges JD6 for a shuttle). The major trails include the following (those marked with an asterisk are only available 1 Mar–31 Oct):

Cave Trail (1km, one hour, can be self-guided) From Rummana Campground to nearby caves and Byzantine ruins.

Nabataean Tomb Tour (2.5km, two hours, guides required, JD10) From Al-Barra to Shaq al-Reesh; short but strenuous.

Palm Trees Wadi Tour (16km, six to eight hours, guides required, JD30 per group) From Al-Barra down through the oases, palm groves and pools of Wadi Ghuweir to Feinan Lodge. A spectacular but difficult hike.

Rummana Campground Trail (one or two hours, can be self-guided) A circular route around the campground, good for bird-watchers (there's a bird hide) and for spotting griffon vultures.

Rummana Mountain Trail (one to two hours, can be self-guided) From Rummana Campground to the nearby Rummana (Pomegranate) Peak, for great views over Wadi Araba.

Steppe Trail (8km, three hours, guides required, JD10 per group) From Dana village to Rummana Campground. Takes you past dramatic wadi escarpments and through terraced gardens.

Wadi Dana to Feinan (14km, four to five hours, can be self-guided) The most popular trail, it takes you down through the quietly impressive scenery of Wadi Dana. The trail is easy to follow. The downside is that it's a killer uphill hike on the way back. After an hour you get to a dry waterfall from where you can explore a mini-*siq* (gorge or canyon); an hour later the trail crosses the wadi floor and this is a good place to turn back. The last third takes you through litter-filled Bedouin camps. It would be a very long day to hike to Feinan Lodge and back. Either stay the night or arrange with the RSCN office for a car to take you back to Dana via Greigra and the Dead Sea Highway (JD36).

Waterfalls Area (2.5km, 2½ hours, guides required, JD10 per group) From Al-Barra to the springs and ruins of Nawatef and back. A great short walk.

It's also possible to do an ambitious two-day trip to Feinan Lodge, hiking in via Wadi Ghuweir, overnighting at the lodge and returning via Wadi Dana. Hotels in Dana can help organise longer treks to Shobak (two days) via Wadi Feinan, Wadi Ghuweir and the village of Mansourah, and on to Petra (four days).

Mountain-bike trails are planned for around Feinan Lodge.

Sleeping & Eating

The RSCN operates three excellent places to stay, for which bookings should be made in advance through the Wild Jordan centre in Amman (see p70). Camping in the reserve is not allowed.

Dana Hotel (Sons of Dana Cooperative; ☎ 2270537; sdqe@nets.com.jo; s/d JD5/10, with private bathroom JD8/12) This ethically run place is the best budget option in town, with simple but stylish rooms and helpful management. The hotel is part of a village cooperative that provides medical and social programs to around 150 local residents. Meals cost JD4 per person and are served in the rooftop Bedouin tent. Room prices include breakfast.

Dana Tower Hotel (☎ 2270226, 079 5688853; dana_tower2@hotmail.com; dm/s/d JD1.500/3/6, s/d with private bathroom JD4/8, full board per person JD8) This rather unsightly privately owned place occupies a prime location overlooking the gorge, but sadly hasn't made any use of the splendid views. That said, it's a welcoming place and a funky, grungy option that's popular with younger backpackers. There's free tea, a washing machine, shared hot showers, rooftop seating and friendly management. It's just downhill from the Dana Hotel.

Dana Guest House (☎ 2270497; dhana@rscn.org.jo; s JD34, d/tr with balcony JD43/53, q with bunk beds JD57, s/d with bathroom JD53/57) The RSCN runs this sleek and highly recommended lodge. The nine rooms are comfortable and stylish, decorated with traditional kilims and ibex-motif bedspreads, and those with a balcony have breathtaking views. Only one room has a private bathroom, but the shared facilities have 24-hour hot water. It's a great place for a splurge. Room prices include breakfast. Other meals (JD7) are available but book them in advance.

Rummana Campground (s/d/tr tent incl breakfast & park entry fee JD18/33/49; ⏲ 1 Mar-31 Oct) This lovely RSCN campsite is a bit pricey but located in a superbly peaceful spot, surrounded by several fine hiking trails. Tents come with mattresses and kerosene lamps and there's a cold-water shower block. You can drive here (see right) or hike in three hours from Dana village (opposite). As with all nature reserves, book through RSCN/Wild Jordan in Amman, though it's also possible to book through the visitor centre. Book meals in advance (JD3 to JD8) or use the barbecue grills (bring your own food and fuel). There is a 20% discount for students.

Feinan Lodge (s/d/tr/q incl breakfast JD35/44/54/60; Wadi Feinan; ⏲ 1 Sep-30 Jun) This remarkable one-of-a-kind ecolodge opened in late 2005 and is only accessible on foot from Dana or by 4WD from the Dead Sea Highway via the Bedouin village of Greigra. The 26 lovely rooms are all unique and most have a balcony. At night the lodge is lit solely by locally made candles (they get through more than 4000 a month!), adding to a unique atmosphere that sits somewhere between medieval monastery and desert fortress (think *Name of the Rose* meets Moroccan kasbah!). It gets very hot here in summer (there is air-conditioning) and you should

bring a torch and mosquito repellent. The hot water is solar-heated so is a bit unreliable. Book through the RSCN.

Getting There & Away

The easiest way to get to Dana by public transport is from Tafila. Minibuses run every hour or so between Tafila and Qadsiyya (350 fils, 30 minutes). The turn-off to Dana village (the faded sign simply says 'Dana Hotel') is 1km north of Qadsiyya; from here it's a 2.8km (steep downhill) walk to Dana village. Headed out of Dana ask around the hotels for a ride as you don't want to walk back up that hill, believe me… A daily bus to Amman (JD1.500, three hours) leaves Qadsiyya at 6.30am.

If you're chartering a taxi in Karak, expect to pay around JD15 one way. From Ma'an to the south, an irregular minibus (750 fils, 1½ hours) should go to Qadsiyya en route to Tafila, but check before boarding.

The Dana Tower Hotel claims that it will pick up travellers for free from Qadsiyya or even Petra if you ring in advance and stay at their hotel. They can arrange a taxi to Petra for between JD10 and JD15.

If you're driving from Tafila or Karak, the first signpost you'll see off to the right (west) only goes to the Rummana Campground; it's better to continue on to the turn-off just before Qadsiyya.

To get to Rummana Campground from Dana village, head 4.5km north of Qadsiyya along the King's Highway and take the signposted left turn for 6km. RSCN can arrange transport from Dana village for around JD6. You must park your vehicle at the Tower entrance and take a free shuttle or walk 2km downhill.

SHOBAK CASTLE   شوبك
☎ 03

Shobak, formerly called Mons Realis (Mont Real, or Montreal – the Royal Mountain), was built by the Crusader king Baldwin I in AD 1115. It withstood numerous attacks from the armies of Saladin before succumbing in 1189, a year after Karak, after an 18-month siege. It was later occupied in the 14th century by the Mamluks, who built over many of the Crusader buildings.

Shobak Castle (admission free; ⏲ daylight hr) has a wild, remote feel to it and perhaps for this reason some readers prefer it to the more touristed (but more impressive) Karak Castle. It's worth a visit despite tricky transport.

Built on a small knoll right at the edge of a plateau, the castle is especially imposing when seen from a distance. Restoration work is ongoing and hopefully this will include some signs explaining the castle's various elements. In the meantime, the caretaker shows visitors around for about JD5. It's a good idea to bring a torch (flashlight) for exploring the castle's many dark corners.

As you climb up from the entrance, there are some **wells** on the left. Soon after passing these, you'll see the reconstructed **church**, one of two in the castle, down to the left. It has an elegant apse supported by two smaller alcoves. The room leading off to the west was the **baptistry**; on the north wall there are traces of water channels leading from above.

Returning back to the main path, turn left (west). After you pass under the arches, a door leads you right (north) into the extensive **market**. If you take the path to the left of the door, some 375 steps lead down into an amazing **secret passageway** that bores into the black bowels of the castle to a subterranean spring, finally surfacing via a ladder outside the castle, beside the road to Shobak town. Tread carefully, use a torch and don't even think about coming down here if you are claustrophobic. If instead you continue past the tunnel, heading west, after about 50m you pass a large two-storey building with archways, built by the Crusaders but adapted by the Mamluks as a **school**.

At the northern end of the castle is the semicircular **keep** with four arrow slits for defending the castle. Outside and to the east, dark steps lead down to the **prison**. If heading to the northeast corner of the castle, you can see **Quranic inscriptions**, possibly dating from the time of Saladin, carved in Kufic script around the outside of the keep. Heading south along the eastern perimeter, you'll soon pass the entrance to the **court of Baldwin I**, which has been partly recon-

structed; see if you can tell which of the stones are originals. The court was later used as a **Mamluk school**.

Continuing south, you'll pass some **baths** on the right (west). Off to the left (east) is a reconstructed **Mamluk watchtower**. Just past the tower is the second **church**. On a room to the left (north) as you enter, you can see above a door in the east wall a weathered carving of a **Crusader cross**. In the church proper, the arches have been reconstructed and from here you can see more **Kufic inscriptions** on the wall of the watchtower.

Beneath the church are the **catacombs**, which contain some Islamic tablets, some Christian carvings, large spherical rocks used in catapults and what is said to be Saladin's very simple throne. From the catacombs, the path leads back down to the gate.

Sleeping & Eating

There is nowhere to stay in Shobak (properly known as Musallath) village but the **Shobak Castle Campground** (☎ 2164265; per person JD5) is sign-posted both from the village and the castle (2.5km). It's set in a tranquil spot with nice views, although it can get cold at night.

There are a few grocery stores and cheap restaurants in Shobak village.

Getting There & Away

Occasional minibuses link Shobak village with Amman's Wahadat station (JD1.500, 2½ hours), Aqaba and Karak. Also some minibuses travelling between Wadi Musa and Ma'an pass through Shobak. There are less reliable minibuses between Shobak and Tafila (800 fils, one hour).

If driving, there are two well-signposted roads from the King's Highway to the castle and there are signs from Shobak village. Otherwise, from Shobak village to the castle, you'll have to charter a taxi (up to JD3 to JD4 return including waiting time; around 3km each way).

Petra
بترا

If you only go to one place in Jordan, make it Petra. Hewn from towering rock walls of multi-coloured sandstone, the imposing façades of its great temples and tombs are an enduring testament to the vision of the desert tribes who sculpted them. The Nabataeans – Arabs who dominated the region in pre-Roman times – chose as their capital a place concealed from the outside world and fashioned it into one of the Middle East's most remarkable cities.

Almost as spectacular as the monuments themselves are the countless shades and Nea-politan swirls formed in the rock. Petra is often called the 'Rose-red City' but even this hardly does justice to the extraordinary range of colours that blend as the sun makes its daily passage over the site.

Few buildings in Petra are freestanding; the bulk were chiselled and bored out of the rock face. Until the mid-1980s, many of these caves were home to the local Bedouin and a handful of families still pitch their black goat-hair tents inside Petra, or even live in the caves.

The site itself is huge and you need a couple of days to get to grips with the place. Budget an extra day here – you'll thank yourself for it later. There are tombs and carvings in every nook and cranny, which makes the place perfect for some off-the-beaten-track exploration.

HIGHLIGHTS

- Feel the excitement build as you walk the **Siq** (p181), the long, dramatic chasm that links the ancient city with the outside world
- Stare in awe at the **Treasury** (p182) – Al-Khazneh, as it's locally known – arguably Petra's most spectacular and most photographed sight
- Explore the towering **Royal Tombs** (p184), offering great views of the old city centre
- Hike steps up to the **Monastery** (p188), perched surreally on a mountain top, and just as impressive as the Treasury
- Get your lungs moving on the great hike to the **High Place of Sacrifice** (p184), along a Nabataean processional way, with superb views and hidden tombs on the way down
- Exploring the Siq and the Treasury in silence and by candlelight during **Petra by Night** (p192) is an unforgettable experience and one that evokes the lost atmosphere of past Petra

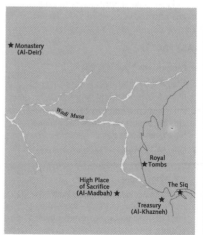

★ Monastery (Al-Deir)

Wadi Musa

Royal ★ Tombs

High Place of Sacrifice (Al-Madbah) ★

The Siq ★

Treasury (Al-Khazneh)

PETRA

History

Excavations in the 1950s unearthed a Neolithic village at Al-Beidha, just to the north of Petra, which dates from about 7000 BC (see p201). This puts it in the same league as Jericho on the West Bank as one of the earliest known farming communities in the Middle East.

Between that period and the Iron Age (from 1200 BC), when the area was the home of the Edomites, little is known. The Edomite capital Sela (mentioned in the Bible) was thought to have been on top of Umm al-Biyara (p190), although the actual site of Sela may lie to the north, about 10km south of Tafila.

The real stars of Petra were the Nabataeans, a nomadic tribe from western Arabia who settled in the area around the 6th century BC, pushing the Edomites west into Judea (where they became known as the Idumaeans). The Nabataeans soon became rich, first by plundering and then by levying tolls on the trade caravans that traversed the area under their control. The most lucrative of these trades was the frankincense, myrrh and spices that were transported by camel caravan to Petra along the Incense Route from southern Arabia. The Nabataeans enjoyed trade agreements with the Minaeans and the Sabaeans of southern Arabia that made them sole handlers not only of the region's famous frankincense but also the spices that had been shipped to Arabia by boat from traders in Somalia, Ethiopia and India.

Suburbs at the four corners of Petra received the caravans and handled the logistics, processing products and offering banking services and fresh animals before moving the goods west across the Sinai to the ports of Gaza and Alexandria, to be shipped to Greece and Rome.

The Nabataeans never really possessed an 'empire' in the common military and administrative sense of the word; instead, from about 200 BC, they established a 'zone of influence' that stretched to Syria and Rome. As the Nabataean territory expanded under King Aretas III (84–62 BC), more caravan routes came under their control and their wealth increased accordingly. At their peak they controlled and taxed trade throughout the Hejaz (northern Arabia), the Negev, the Sinai, and the Hauran of southern Syria. Nabataean communities were influential as far away as Rome and Nabataean tombs still stand at the impressive site of Madain Saleh in Saudi Arabia.

Petra's glory days came under King Aretas IV (8 BC–AD 40), when the city was home to around 30,000 people. Expert hydraulic engineers, the Nabataeans built dams, cisterns and water channels to protect the site and grand buildings were raised in a blend of Greek, Roman and local styles. They also created their own cursive script; the forerunner of Arabic.

The Roman general Pompey, having conquered Syria and Palestine in 63 BC, tried to exert control over Nabataean territory, but the Nabataean king, Aretas III, was able to buy off the Roman forces and retain his independence. Nonetheless, Rome exerted a deep cultural influence and the buildings and coinage of the period reflect the Graeco-Roman style.

The Nabataeans weren't so lucky when they chose to side with the Parthians in the latter's war with the Romans, finding themselves obliged to pay Rome heavy tribute after the defeat of the Parthians. When the Nabataeans fell behind in paying the tribute, they were invaded twice by Herod the Great. The second attack, in 31 BC, saw him gain control of a large slice of territory.

By the time of the Nabataean King Rabbel II, the Nabataeans had lost much of their commercial power – with Palmyra having taken much of the Silk Rd trade from Asia and a knowledge of the monsoon winds had

---

FAST FACTS

- Petra means 'rock' in Greek

- The local Nabataean (ie Aramaic) name of the city was Rakeem or Rekem

- Petra was once home to 20,000 inhabitants but almost no residential buildings have been discovered

- Only 5% of Petra has been excavated

- Petra's al-Siq was created by tectonics not water erosion

- The Cave Bar in Wadi Musa is built inside a Nabataean tomb – surely the most unusual place you've ever downed a pint!

'IBRAHIM' BURCKHARDT

Johann Ludwig (also known as Jean Louis) Burckhardt was born in Switzerland in 1784. As preparation for a long-planned expedition to the source of the Niger River in West Africa, he moved to Aleppo (Syria) for two years, where he learned to dress, eat, sleep and speak Arabic like a Bedouin. He converted to Islam and took the alias of Sheikh Ibrahim bin Abdullah, travelling around Syria to hone his disguise.

In 1812, while en route from Damascus to Cairo, he visited Jerash, Salt, Amman, Shobak and Karak, where he was detained for 20 days as a 'prisoner' of the local sheikh, forced to sleep in a different house each night to appease the locals' numerous offers of hospitality.

On the way south, he heard locals tell of some fantastic ruins hidden in the mountains of Wadi Musa valley, but the people of the region were suspicious of outsiders. To make the detour, he had to think of a ploy so that suspicions were not raised by his guide and porters, as he explained in his posthumously published journal, *Travels in Syria and the Holy Land:*

> I, therefore, pretended to have made a vow to have slaughtered a goat in honour of Haroun (Aaron), whose tomb I knew was situated at the extremity of the valley, and by this stratagem I thought that I should have the means of seeing the valley on the way to the tomb.

He was able to examine, albeit very briefly, a couple of sites including the Treasury (Al-Khazneh) and the Urn Tomb, and reported that 'it seems very probable that the ruins at Wadi Musa are those of ancient Petra', concluding that:

> the situation and beauty of which are calculated to make an extraordinary impression upon the traveller, after having transversed...such a gloomy and almost subterranean passage (the Siq)...it is one of the most elegant remains of antiquity existing.

Burckhardt later discovered Abu Simbel in Egypt and explored the holy city of Mecca, still in disguise, but contracted fatal dysentery in 1817. He died at only 33 years old, and is buried in the Islamic Cemetery in Cairo.

boosted sea trade routes up the Red Sea to Rome, bypassing Petra. Finally in AD 106 the Romans took Petra, creating the province of Arabia Petraea, with a capital at Bosra (Syria), and set about imposing the usual plan: a colonnaded street, baths, and so on. The Emperor Hadrian visited the city in AD 131. Later in the 3rd century the region was reorganised into the province of Palaestrina Tertia, with Petra as the capital.

During the Byzantine period, a bishopric was created in Petra and some Nabataean buildings were turned into churches. Earthquakes in 363 and 551 ruined much of the city and, by the time of the Muslim invasion in the 7th century, Petra was fast passing into obscurity. The only activity in the next 500 years was in the 12th century when the Crusaders moved in briefly and built two forts.

From 1189 (when Saladin conquered the Crusader castles) until the early 19th century, Petra was a forgotten outpost, a 'lost city' known only to local Bedouin. These descendants of the Nabataeans were reluctant to reveal its existence because they feared (perhaps not without reason) that the influx of foreigners might interfere with their livelihood. Finally, in 1812, a young Swiss explorer, JL Burckhardt, ended Petra's blissful isolation, riding into the city disguised as a Muslim holy man.

Petra soon became caught up with the Victorian-era's romantic obsession with the Orient. The site was visited by a slew of amateur archaeologists, travellers, poets and artists (including the famed painter David Roberts in 1839) and a powerful myth grew up around the 'Rose-red City'. The first English archaeological team arrived in 1929 and excavations continue to pull up major finds. In 1992 the mosaics of the Petra Church were unveiled and in 2003 a tomb complex was found underneath the Treasury. After 150 years of attention, Petra still has many secrets left to reveal.

Orientation

Petra is only a three hours' drive from Amman, two hours from Aqaba and 1½ hours from Wadi Rum.

The village of Wadi Musa is the transport and accommodation hub for Petra, as well as other attractions in the vicinity that are well worth seeing if you have more time (and energy).

In the 1980s many of the B'doul Bedouin who had lived in Petra for generations were resettled to hastily built breeze-block villages, such as neighbouring Umm Sayhoun, an arrangement many are less than happy with.

Dangers & Annoyances

Many find the constant hard sell and frequent overcharging in both Petra and Wadi Musa a little wearying; remember that most traders are just trying to scratch out a living in what is a very competitive market. Once you break down the barrier with a smile, you'll find almost all will reciprocate in kind.

Some locals have a mischievous sense of humour, with camels being offered as 'air-conditioned taxis' and at least one inventive young woman offering handicrafts with the words 'Look for free and buy for money or look for money and buy for free'.

If you are hiking through the wadis, especially from November to March and in September and October, pay careful attention to the weather, as these narrow canyons are susceptible to flash flooding.

Getting There & Away

Petra is just three hours' drive from Amman and two hours' drive from Aqaba. See p199 for details on transport options.

Getting Around

Horses with guides can be rented for JD7 for the 800m stretch between the main entrance and the start of the Siq. The price can be negotiated down to as little as JD2 going back up to the entrance. It costs around JD20 for a two-hour horse ride around the surrounding hills.

Horses and carriages with guides are only allowed between the main entrance and the Treasury (2km). These are officially for the disabled and elderly, but are often rented by tired hikers. They officially cost JD20 for a two-person carriage; JD40 to the museum.

Donkeys accompanied with guides are available all around Petra for negotiable prices. They can go almost to the top of the Monastery (about JD3 one way), and all the way to the High Place of Sacrifice (about JD5 one way), and can be rented for trips as far as the Snake Monument and to Jebel Haroun. Leading donkeys is a genuine occupation for local Bedouin, but animal lovers may think twice about hiring one to climb the incredibly steep and narrow paths.

Camel rides are more for the novelty value, and are available for short rides and photographs near the Theatre and Qasr al-Bint. A trip between Qasr al-Bint and the Treasury, for example, costs about JD7.

If you happen to see any animal being cruelly treated, please report it to the Brooke Hospital for Animals (see below).

THE ANCIENT CITY
Orientation

If you are coming down the hill from Wadi Musa, head for the Petra visitor centre plaza across from the Mövenpick Hotel.

BROOKE HOSPITAL FOR ANIMALS

Just to the left of the main entrance to Petra is a large expanse of ground dotted with horses. At the back is the **Princess Alia Horse Clinic** (☎ 2156379; fax 2156437), affiliated with the London-based **Brooke Hospital for Animals** (Map p194; www.brooke-hospital.org.uk), which has a number of animal hospitals in Egypt, Pakistan and India.

Founded in 1988 at the request of Princess Alia, the clinic in Petra aims 'to improve the condition and wellbeing of working equine animals'. It cares for abused horses, educates locals and children in the area about the treatment of animals, provides free preventive measures against disease and operates mobile clinics to remote regions. It also provides sun shelters and water troughs for horses, and gives (second-hand) saddles and other equipment to owners of working animals. Over 20,000 horses, and 250 other animals, were treated by staff in 1997.

If you see a genuine case of any animal being badly treated (rather than being worked hard) please contact the clinic.

MAPS

Very little in Petra is signposted or captioned so a map and guidebook are essential. For most visitors planning to see the major sights over one or two days, this book will be more than sufficient.

If you plan to hike long distances in Petra without a guide, the best map is the Royal Jordanian Geographic Centre's contoured 1:5000 *Map of Petra* (2005). It's usually available at bookshops in Wadi Musa and at the small stand next to the Nabataean Museum for JD3.

The *Petra: The Rose-Red City* brochure, published by the Jordan Tourism Board, has an easy-to-read map, a few explanations and useful photos that help identify certain places. Try to get one before coming to Petra as the visitor centre often runs out.

Information

The **ticket office** (Map p194; ☎ /fax 2156020; ⏱ 6.30am-5pm Oct-Apr, 6am-5.30pm May-Sep) is located in the visitor centre. Although tickets are not sold after the times specified above, you can remain in Petra after this time, usually until sunset.

Entry fees are currently JD21/26/31 for one-/two-/three-day passes. If you bring an international student card you can get a 50% discount. A three-day pass is valid for longer than three days but you'll need to get the extra dates written on the back of the ticket and stamped. Multiday tickets are nontransferable and signatures are checked. Children under 15 get in for half price.

If you're contemplating trying to enter Petra without paying, don't. Apart from the fact that tickets are checked, it's worth remembering that the ongoing preservation of Petra depends on the income from tourists. It may be a lot of money, but it's worth it.

Don't underestimate the size of Petra and the heat in summer. Always take a good hat, sturdy footwear, sunscreen, plenty of rolls of film or a large memory card, snacks and/or a packed lunch and, especially in summer, lots of water.

In general the best time to visit Petra is from mid-October to the end of November, and late January to the end of May. This avoids the coldest, wettest (when floods are possible) and hottest times of the year.

PETRA ON THE WEB

- For background and general travel info on Petra visit **Go 2 Petra** (www.go2petra.com)

- 'Everything you wanted to know about the Nabataean Empire' can be found at **Nabataea Net** (http://nabataea.net)

- See the online Petra exhibition at the **American Museum of Natural History** (www.amnh.org/exhibitions/petra)

- Take an online tour of the excavations of the Great Temple at **Brown University** (www.brown.edu/Departments/Anthropology/Petra)

- A great collection of current and archived links on Petra can be found at the **Complete Petra** (www.isidore-of-seville.com/petra)

BOOKS

There are plenty of souvenir and coffee-table books about Petra. One of the best guidebooks, *Petra: A Traveller's Guide* by Rosalyn Maqsood, includes lots of history and culture, and describes several hikes. The pocket-sized *Petra: The Rose-Red City*, by Christian Auge and Jean-Marie Dentzer, is lightweight and excellent, especially on Petra's historical context. Jane Taylor's *Petra* (JD10) is another good paperback introduction to the site. Taylor also writes the excellent but heftier *Petra & the Lost Kingdoms of the Nabataens,* now available in paperback.

There's a chapter on hiking in Petra in Tony Howard and Di Taylor's *Jordan – Walks, Treks, Climbs & Canyons.* For reconstructions of how Petra's monuments once appeared, *Jordan, Past & Present – Petra, Jerash, Amman* isn't bad.

These books are generally available at shops and stalls around Wadi Musa and Petra but will probably be cheaper to buy at home.

TOILETS

There are toilets at the visitor centre, opposite the Theatre (set in a gorgeous rock-hewn cave and worth a visit in itself!), at the back of Qasr al-Bint and at the two nearby restaurants. If at all possible, avoid going

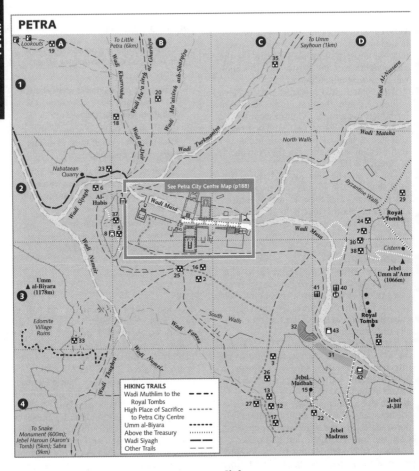

PETRA

HIKING TRAILS
Wadi Muthlim to the Royal Tombs
High Place of Sacrifice to Petra City Centre
Umm al-Biyara
Above the Treasury
Wadi Siyagh
Other Trails

to the toilet elsewhere as it spoils it for the people coming after you.

TOURIST INFORMATION

The first stop for all visitors should be at the **Petra visitor centre** (Map p194; ☎/fax 2156020; 🕑 6am-9pm), just before the entrance. It houses a helpful information counter, a couple of shops and toilets. There are plans to rebuild the visitor centre as part of a much larger complex with an auditorium and shops.

The information counter is also the place to arrange a **guide** (2½hr tour JD15, full-day incl Monastery or High Place of Sacrifice JD35). Tours are available in English, French, Spanish and Arabic.

Sights

There are over 800 registered sites in Petra, including some 500 tombs, but the best things to see are easy to reach. From the gate, an 800m path heads downhill through an area called **Bab as-Siq** (Gateway to the Siq).

DJINN BLOCKS

Five minutes' walk past the entrance are three enormous monuments, known as the Djinn (Spirit) Blocks (map pp180–1, built by the Nabataeans in the 1st century AD. (The Arabic word *djinn* is the source of the English word 'genie'). Their exact functions remain a mystery, but they could have been tombs, or built as dedications to the Nabataean god, Dushara. The largest block has

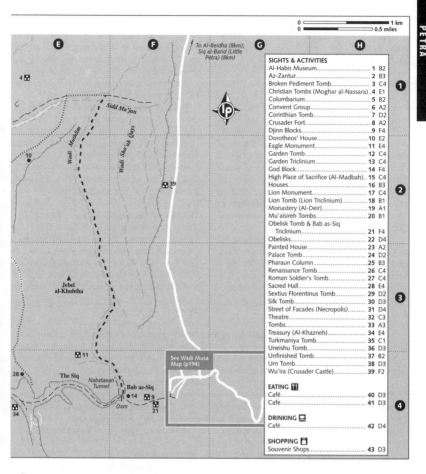

a depression on top, thought to have been used during funeral rites.

OBELISK TOMB & BAB AS-SIQ TRICLINIUM
Further along the path to the left is a tomb (map pp180–1) with four pyramidal obelisks, built as funerary symbols by the Nabataeans in the 1st century BC. The eroded human figure in the centre, along with the four obelisks, is believed to represent the five people buried in the tomb. The combination of Greek, Egyptian and local styles is intriguing.

Underneath is a Nabataean triclinium (three-banked dining room; map pp180–1), with its three small chambers, where annual feasts were held to commemorate the dead. The carved columns flanking the entrance

give a sense of the original façade, while the Doric frieze above the door is also worth a look. Inside, the U-shaped bench is all that remains.

Further down the track, a detour up a signed track to the right leads to several tomb chambers and stepped tombs carved into the top of some domed hills. It's a secret little place, missed by almost everyone in their rush to get to the Siq.

THE SIQ   Map pp180–1
The 1.2km *siq* starts at an obvious bridge, which is, in fact, part of a new dam. The dam was built in 1963, on top of one built by the Nabataeans in about AD 50, to stop water from Wadi Musa river flowing

through the Siq. To the right (north), Wadi Muthlim heads invitingly through a Nabataean tunnel – the start (or finish) of a great hike (see p189).

The entrance to the Siq was once topped by a Nabataean monumental arch. It survived until the end of the 19th century, and some remains can be seen at twin niches on either side of the entrance to the Siq.

The Siq often narrows to about 5m (at some points to just 2m) wide, and the walls tower up to 200m overhead. The original channels cut into the walls to bring water into Petra are visible, and in some places the 2000-year-old terracotta pipes are still in place. One section of the Roman paving was revealed after excavations in 1997 removed 2m of floor accumulation.

The Siq is not a canyon (a gorge carved out by water), but is actually a single block that has been rent apart by tectonic forces; at various points you can see where the grain of the rock on one side matches the other.

At one point the Siq opens up to reveal a lovely square tomb next to a fig tree. A couple of hundred metres further, and a bend in the canyon, look for a weathered but wonderfully evocative carving of a camel and caravan man on the left wall. The water channel passes behind the carving.

Further along, the walls close in still further, and at times almost meet overhead, shutting out the light and seemingly the sound as well. The Siq can seem to continue forever, and the sense of anticipation builds as you look around each corner for your first glimpse of the Treasury. It's a magical introduction to the ancient city.

TREASURY (AL-KHAZNEH)   Map pp180–1

Tucked away in such a confined space, the Treasury (known locally as Al-Khazneh) is protected from the ravages of the elements, and it is here that most visitors fall in love with Petra. The Hellenistic façade is an astonishing piece of craftsmanship, with the

---

SUGGESTED ITINERARIES

Almost everything in Petra is a highlight in itself, and the combined effect of the ancient city is truly astonishing. There are, however, some specific sites that should not be missed. These include the Treasury, High Place of Sacrifice, the Street of Façades, the Theatre, Royal Tombs and the Monastery. Don't restrict yourself to these, but on no account miss them.

It's vital to plan your trip around Petra to make efficient use of your time. Start your exploration early. The tour buses start arriving before 9am and the enchanting *siq* (gorge) is best experienced in quietness and away from large crowds. If you want to see the Treasury bathed in sunlight, you can enter Petra early, visit a few other sites such as the High Place of Sacrifice and the Theatre, and then return at around 9am. The Monastery and Royal Tombs are at their best in the late-afternoon light.

If your time is limited, you may wish to follow these suggestions:

Half-day (about five hours) You will have little time to explore much, so concentrate on the Siq, the Treasury (Al-Khazneh), the Theatre, the Royal Tombs; everything along the Colonnaded Street, Petra Church and the Nabataean Museum.

One Day (about eight hours) One day is really the minimum time needed to do Petra any justice. Try not to rush around in one day if you have time to visit for two: pay the extra for a two-day ticket and explore the site more slowly and thoroughly. In one day, explore the places mentioned above, and allow time for a walk up to the Monastery or the High Place of Sacrifice, or even above the Treasury on Jebel al-Khubtha, if you have any remaining time and energy.

Two Days This is an ideal amount of time, and allows leisurely exploration, hikes to more remote areas, and a long lunch on one or both days. On the first day, allow time to visit the places mentioned under 'Half-day', and climb to the Monastery. On the second day, enter Petra along the stunning Wadi Muthlim; climb to the High Place of Sacrifice from the Theatre and continue along the back of the mountain to the city centre (or vice versa); and hike above the Treasury on Jebel al-Khubtha (best in the morning).

Three Days A three-day ticket allows plenty of time to explore the sites and hike off the beaten track. For the first two days, follow the itinerary listed earlier. On the third and/or fourth days, climb up Umm al-Biyara; explore one of the more remote corners of the site (see p189) and allow some time to explore Siq al-Barid (Little Petra) and the ruins of Al-Beidha village.

NABATAEAN RELIGIOUS PROCESSIONS

Some historians speculate that the primary function of the Siq was akin to the ancient Graeco-Roman Sacred Way. Some of the most important rituals of Petra's spiritual life began as a procession through the narrow canyon, while it also represented the endpoint of the pilgrimage by Nabataean pilgrims. Many of the wall niches that are still visible today along the Siq's walls were designed to hold figures or representations (called *baetyls*) of the main Nabataean god, Dushara. These small sacred sites served as touchstones of the sacred for pilgrims and priests, offering them a link to the more ornate temples, tombs and sanctuaries in the city's heart, reminding them that they were leaving the outside world, and on the threshold of what was for many a holy city.

---

sophistication, symmetry, scale and grandeur of the carving enough to take away the breath of first-time visitors.

As you pause to take in the view, the individual details become more apparent. Atop the six columns at ground level are floral capitals, while the triangular pediment depicts a gorgon's head emerging from the surrounding flora. The carved figures alongside horses on the ground level are thought to be the sons of Zeus. On the top level, in the sunken niches, are two winged Victories, with four more figures of unknown origin alongside. The central figure above the entrance pediment is the source of much speculation; most scholars believe it to be an assimilation of the Egyptian goddess Isis and the Nabataean goddess Al-'Uzza, while others suggest Tyche, the Roman goddess of fortune. Two eroded eagles stand sentry at the very top. Regularly spaced niches on either side of the façade suggest the builders' secret weapon – scaffolding.

Although carved out of the solid iron-laden sandstone to serve as a tomb for the Nabataean king Aretas III, the Treasury gets its name from the story that the Egyptian Pharaoh hid his treasure here (in the urn in the middle of the second level) while pursuing the Israelites. Some locals clearly believed the tale because the 3.5m-high urn is pockmarked by rifle shots, the results of vain attempts to break open the solid-rock urn.

The date of the Treasury's construction has also been a subject of debate, and estimates range from 100 BC to AD 200.

As with all the rock-hewn monuments in Petra, it's the façade that captivates; the interior is just an unadorned square hall with a smaller room at the back. The Treasury, which is 43m high and about 30m wide, is at its most photogenic in full sunlight between about 9am and 11am.

From the Treasury, the Siq turns off to the right (northwest), and diagonally opposite is a **Sacred Hall**, which may have had ritual connections with the Treasury.

STREET OF FAÇADES   **Map pp180–1**

Heading towards the centre of the city, and just before the Theatre, are over 40 tombs and houses built by the Nabataeans in a 'crow step' style reminiscent of the Assyrians. Colloquially known as the Street of Façades, the tombs here are similar to the hundred or more all around Petra, but are certainly the most accessible. It's easy to forget about these when the majestic Theatre comes into view, but the tombs are worth exploring.

The first tomb (number 67) is unusual in that it has a funeral chamber in the upper story. The low entryway highlights how the valley floor has risen over the centuries thanks to the debris washed down during flash floods. Nearby, tomb 70 is unusual in that it is freestanding, with a ziggurat-style top that makes it look like a miniature fort.

THEATRE   **Map pp180–1**

Originally built by the Nabataeans (not the Romans) over 2000 years ago, the captivatingly weathered Theatre was cut out of rock, slicing through many caves and tombs in the process. The seating area *(cavea)* had an original capacity of about 3000 in 45 rows of seats, with three horizontal sections separated by two corridors. The orchestra section was carved from the rock, but the backdrop to the stage or *frons scaenae* (which is no longer intact) was constructed (as opposed to carved) in three storeys with frescoed niches and columns overlaid by marble. The performers entered through one of three entrances, the outlines of which are still partially visible.

NABATAEAN RELIGION

Surprisingly little is known about Nabataean religion considering that the Nabataeans' pre-occupation with death clearly dominates most of the major structures of Petra.

As the cosmopolitan Nabataeans came into contact with surrounding cultures, the early desert polytheistic religion of the original Arabian tribes absorbed Roman, Greek, Egyptian and even Edomite and Assyrian beliefs, to create a unique faith.

The main Nabataean god was Dushara, the mountain god, who governed the natural world. Over the years he came to be associated with the Greek god Dionysus, the Roman Zeus and the Egyptian god Osiris.

For fertility, the Nabataeans prayed to the goddess Al-'Uzza (the Very Strong), who became associated with Aphrodite and Isis. Al-Kutba was the god of divination and writing, linked to Hermes and Mercury. Allat (literally 'Goddess') was associated with Athene.

Early representations of the Nabataean gods were non-figurative. Divine stones known as *baetyls* marked important wadis, junctions, canyons and mountain tops, representing the presence of the divine, much as the Kaaba stone at Mecca still does for Muslims. Religious processions to Petra's spiritual 'High Places' were an important part of the community's religious life, culminating in a sacrifice (some say human) and ritual purification. You can still see these altars and basins atop the High Place of Sacrifice.

The Theatre was renovated and enlarged (to hold about 8500, or around 30% of the population of Petra) by the Romans soon after they arrived in AD 106. To make room for the upper seating tiers, they sliced through more tombs. Under the stage floor were storerooms and a slot through which a curtain could be lowered at the start of a performance. From near the slot, an almost-complete statue of Hercules was recovered.

The Theatre was badly damaged by an earthquake in AD 363, and parts of it were then removed to help build other structures in Petra.

HIGH PLACE OF SACRIFICE (AL-MADBAH)
Map pp180–1

The most accessible of the many sacrificial places high in the mountains is the High Place of Sacrifice, referred to locally as Al-Madbah (the Altar). Located on top of Jebel Madbah, the altars are fairly unimpressive, but the views of the city to the northwest, Wadi Musa village to the east and the shrine on top of Jebel Haroun to the far southwest are superb. About 50m down (north) over the rocks from the High Place are more staggering views, this time of the Royal Tombs.

The steps to the High Place of Sacrifice, which start about 200m before (to the southeast of) the Theatre just past a couple of souvenir stands, are fairly obvious, but not signposted. The climb up takes about 45 minutes, and is better done in the early

morning when the sun is behind you. It's marginally easier than the hike up to the Monastery, but it's still steep and taxing at times. Donkey owners will implore you to ride one of their poor animals for a negotiable JD5/7 (one way/return).

As you near the summit, the trail leads straight ahead into the flatter valley of Jebel Madrass. While you may wish to explore this area, the High Place is to the right (take the right fork at the rubble of a stone building). At the top, near a small café, pass the two **obelisks** dedicated to the Nabataean gods, Dushara and Al-'Uzza; the altars are further along to the north and at the highest point in the immediate area. The top of the ridge was levelled to make a platform, and large depressions with drains were dug to channel the blood of sacrificial animals. It's not clear whether the site was used to conduct ceremonies honouring the gods or to perform funeral rites, or both.

You can return the same way (ie back along the steps and finishing near the Theatre), but if you have the energy it's better to continue on to the city centre via a group of interesting tombs on the west side of the mountain. See p190 for details of this hike.

ROYAL TOMBS
Map pp180–1

The Wadi Musa river bed widens out after the Theatre. To the right (or north), carved into the cliff face, are the impressive burial places known collectively as the 'Royal Tombs'.

The first (and most southern) is **Uneishu Tomb**, dedicated to a minister of Nabataean Queen Shafialt II (the wife of Aretas IV). It's virtually opposite the Theatre, and easy to miss.

The **Urn Tomb**, recognisable by the enormous urn on top of the pediment, is accessible from a stairway next to the café. It has an open terrace over a double layer of vaults, probably built in about AD 70 for King Malichos II (AD 40–70), or Aretas IV (8 BC–AD 40). Of the three tombs carved between the pillars, the central one still has its closing stone, carved with a bust of the king. Above the four half-columns was an architrave (a decorative space between the columns and pediment) decorated with four figures representing deities. The room inside is enormous, measuring 18m by 20m, and the patterns in the rock are striking. It's difficult to imagine how the smooth walls, sharp corners and three small chambers at the top were carved out with such precision. A Greek inscription on the back wall details how the building was used as a Byzantine church in the mid-5th century.

Further up (north) is the **Silk Tomb** which is the most unimpressive of the group in terms of the surviving state of its carvings, due in large part to earthquake damage. It is, however, noteworthy for its stunning swirls of pink, white and yellow veined rock.

The **Corinthian Tomb** is something of a hybrid, with elements of both Hellenistic and Nabataean influences. The portico on the lower level of the tomb is distinctively local in origin, while the upper decorative features are more Hellenistic in style. The top level is reminiscent of the Treasury. The tomb gets its name from the Corinthian capitals adorned with floral motifs. By no means the most ornate of the Royal Tombs – it has suffered centuries of exposure to the elements – it's nonetheless worthy of a visit.

The **Palace Tomb** is a delightful three-storey imitation of a Roman or Hellenistic palace, and is one of the largest and most recent monuments in Petra. Its rock-hewn façade, the largest in Petra, is thought to owe more to ornamental exuberance rather than to any religious significance. The two central doorways are topped by triangular pediments, while the two on either side have

---

THE TOMBS OF PETRA

There are more tombs dotted around Petra than any other type of structure and for years visitors assumed that the city was just one vast necropolis. The simple reason why so few dwellings have been discovered is that the Nabataeans lived in tents, much like some Bedouin do today.

Petra's earliest rock tombs date from the 3rd century BC. The size and design of the tombs depended in large part on the social status and financial resources of the deceased, ranging from simple cave-like tombs to the ornate façades of the Royal Tombs, the high point of Nabataean funerary architecture.

Better sculptors than architects, the Nabataeans quickly realised that it was easier to carve tombs out of the soft sandstone rock than to build free-standing buildings that were vulnerable to earthquakes. The larger tombs were carved out of the rock from the top down, using scaffolding support, and the façades were then plastered and painted (almost none of this decoration remains).

The dead were buried in graves *(loculi)* carved from the plain walls inside the tomb, while the exterior decoration was made to represent the soul (and sometimes likeness) of the deceased. All but the most simple contained banqueting halls where funerals and annual commemorative feasts were held. Some rooms were frescoed and you can still see traces of coloured decoration in Wadi Siyagh's Painted House (see p191) and in the Siq el-Barid in Little Petra (p200).

The Nabataeans were a nomadic desert people without an architectural heritage of their own but as traders they were a cosmopolitan people who readily borrowed elements of art and architecture from neighbours. Thus you'll see Egyptian, Assyrian, Mesopotamian, Hellenistic and Roman styles throughout Petra, as well as unique local architectural inventions such as the Nabataean horned column. If you combine this eclecticism with the organic nature of Petra's cave-like tombs, the stunning natural colour of the rock and natural grandeur of the landscape and it's easy to see how Petra has captured the imagination of generations of travellers.

arched pediments. The doors lead into typically simple funerary chambers. The 18 columns on the upper level are the most distinctive and visually arresting elements of the tomb. The top left corner is built – rather than cut out – of stone because the rock face didn't extend far enough to complete the façade.

A few hundred metres further around (northeast) is the **Sextius Florentinus Tomb**, built from AD 126 to AD 130 for a Roman governor of Arabia, whose exploits are glorified in an inscription above the entrance. This tomb is largely neglected, but is worth the short walk. Narrower than the tombs to the southwest, it has some dazzling rock colourings. The gorgon's head in the centre of the façade above the columns is eroded, but it is still possible to distinguish the vine tendrils emanating from the head. The horned capitals are a uniquely Nabataean creation. Unlike many of the other tombs, the interior is worth a look for the clearly discernible *loculi* (graves), with five carved from the back wall and three on the right as you enter.

There is plenty of room here for wider exploration of more photogenic tombs, and other temples and religious sites in the area. If you have the time and energy, the steps between the Palace and Sextius Florentinus tombs lead to a wonderful position above the Treasury – see p191.

COLONNADED STREET   Map p188

Further west along Wadi Musa are the re-erected columns of the Colonnaded Street that form Petra city centre. Built in about AD 106 (around the same time as that of the similar street in Jerash), over an existing Nabataean thoroughfare, the Colonnaded Street follows the standard Roman pattern of an east-west decumanus, but without the normal cardo maximus (north-south axis). Columns of marble-clad sandstone originally lined the 6m-wide carriageway, while the shops that lined either side were entered through covered porticoes.

At the start of the Colonnaded Street is the **Nymphaeum**, a public fountain dedicated to the nymphs probably built in the 2nd century AD. It was probably here that the waters from the Siq were channelled. Typical of its kind, it had a large semicircular niche decorated with statues and fountains. Little can be

seen today; it's really only recognisable by the huge 450-year-old pistachio tree, a welcome respite from the endless sun in summer.

On the left (south) of the colonnaded street are the limited remains of the market area, archaeologically divided into a **Lower Market** (also known as the Upper Terrace), **Middle Market** and **Upper Market**. Further up on the right (north) are the unrecognisable ruins of the **Royal Palace**.

The street finishes at the **Temenos Gateway**, built in the 2nd century AD with three arches, huge wooden doors and side towers. It marked the entrance to the temenos (sacred courtyard) of the Qasr al-Bint, marking the movement from the commercial area of the city to the sacred area of the temple. Its design is reminiscent of a Roman triumphal arch but with Nabataean touches, such as the floral capital atop at least one column. Look closely for the few remaining floral friezes and a figure with an arrow, which suggest that this was once a very grand structure. Opposite (south) are the decrepit ruins of the **Nabataean baths**.

GREAT TEMPLE   Map p188

Excavations of the Great Temple have been under way since 1993 and have yielded impressive results. It was built as a major Nabataean temple in the 1st century BC and, despite being badly damaged by an earthquake not long after, was in use (albeit in a different form) until the late Byzantine period. The first set of stairs was fronted by a monumental propylaeum (gateway) while the courtyard at the top of the first stairs marked the lower temenos (sacred courtyard), flanked on the east and west sides by a triple colonnade. The upper level housed the temple's sacred enclosure, with four huge columns (made from stone discs and clad in marble) at the entrance. A *theatron* (miniature theatre) stands in the centre. The temple was once 18m high, and the enclosure was 40m by 28m. The interior was originally covered with striking red and white stucco work.

QASR AL-BINT   Map p188

One of the few free-standing structures in Petra, this temple was built in around 30 BC by the Nabataeans, adapted to the cult of Roman emperors and destroyed in about the 3rd century AD. Despite the name given

SAVING PETRA FROM ITSELF

Petra is in danger of being loved to death. At its peak in the late 1990s the site was visited by more than 400,000 people a year. The combination of thousands of footprints a day, increased humidity levels from the breath of thousands of tourists in the most popular tombs and the effects of adventurous travellers clambering over the crumbling tombs and steep hillsides is accelerating severe erosion at the site.

Moreover, the Nabataeans built sophisticated hydraulic systems to divert flood waters from along the Siq to other wadis, and for irrigation and storage. After centuries of neglect, erosion and earthquakes, these are ironically causing serious damage to the Siq and various monuments because their bases are now often in underground water, loaded with salt that works its way up the walls and destroys the sandstone. The damage to the Treasury is the most worrying.

Various foreign governments and Non-governmental Organisations have undertaken surveys, including a team of advisors from the US National Parks Service, and some urgently needed restoration of the Nabataean hydraulic system has taken place, notably along the Siq. Germany has been instrumental in cleaning and stabilising some of the tomb faces, though the main benefactor is the Swiss government, which feels some kindred spirit with Petra because the 'discoverer' of Petra, Burckhardt (see p177), was born in Switzerland.

Part of the problem is the lack of a clear structure in the preservation process. About 25% of Petra's ticket revenue filters back to the **Petra Regional Authority**, which is responsible for developing tourism in an area of some 853 sq km, of which 264 sq km have been designated as an 'Archaeological Park'. Add to this the private **Petra National Trust**, which is involved in training guides, studying the impact on Petra from tourism, managing the number of souvenir stalls and creating dedicated walking trails. Then there is the specialist German-Jordanian **Conservation and Restoration Centre in Petra (CARCIP)**, which offers specialist advice on technical reconstruction.

to it by the local Bedouin – Qasr al-Bint al-Pharaun (Castle of the Pharaoh's Daughter) – it was almost certainly built as a dedication to the Nabataean god, Dushara (and possibly the fertility goddess Al-'Uzza), and was one of the most important temples in the ancient city. In its original form, it stood 23m high and had marble staircases, imposing columns topped with floral capitals, a raised platform for worship, and ornate plaster and stone reliefs and friezes – small traces of which are still evident. The central 'holy of holies', known as an *adyton*, would have housed an image of the deities. The sacrificial altar in front, once overlaid with marble, indicates that it was probably the main place of worship in the Nabataean city and its location at street level suggests that the whole precinct (and not just the temple interior) was considered sacred.

TEMPLE OF THE WINGED LIONS   Map p188
The recently excavated Temple of the Winged Lions is named after the carved lions that once topped the capitals of each of the columns. The temple was built in about AD 27 and dedicated to the fertility goddess, Atargatis, who was the partner of the main male god, Dushara, although some scholars speculate that the goddess Al-'Uzza may also have been worshipped here.

This was a very important temple, centred around a raised altar, and with a colonnaded entry of arches and porticoes that extended down to and across the wadi at the bottom. Fragments of decorative stone and painted plaster found on the site, and now on display in the Nabataean Museum, suggest that both the temple and entry were handsomely decorated. Although there's not much to see, the views are good.

PETRA CHURCH   Map p188
An unmistakable awning covers the remains of the Petra Church (also known as the Byzantine Church). The structure was originally built by the Nabataeans, and then redesigned and expanded by the Byzantines around AD 530. It eventually burned down, and was then destroyed by repeated earthquakes, before being lovingly restored by the American Center of Oriental Research in Amman.

PETRA

Inside the church are some exquisite By-zantine floor **mosaics**, some of the best in the region. The mosaics originally continued up the walls. A helpful map and explanations in English are located inside the church.

AL-HABIS   Map pp180–1
Beyond the Qasr al-Bint is the small hill of Al-Habis (the Prison). From the Nabataean Tent Restaurant steps lead up the face of Al-Habis to the small **Al-Habis Museum** (🕙 8am-4pm). The classical statues, tiny figurines and painted stuccowork on display lend a human dimension to the huge scale of the site, though the Nabataean Museum (oppos-ite) is more impressive.

A lovely trail leads from the museum around the hill for 100m or so to the junc-tion of Wadi Siyagh and Wadi Numeir, continuing around the back of Al-Habis, past the **Convent Group** of tombs, eventually arriving at a series of steps at the southern end of the hill.

At the top of the steps, on top of Al-Habis, are the limited ruins of a small **Crusader fort**, built in AD 1116 by Baldwin I. The ruins

are not impressive, but the **views** of the city centre certainly are. If you poke around the northeastern corner you'll discover cham-bers, sacrificial altars and ruined Nabataean steps that lead down precariously to the west side of the hill.

At the eastern base of Al-Habis are two interesting remains that can be seen as you descend the hill behind Qasr al-Bint. The **Unfinished Tomb** is unique in Petra and offers a rare glimpse at the way the Nabataeans constructed their rock tombs, starting at the top on a platform of scaffolding and working their way down. Nearby is the enigmatic **Columbarium**, whose multiple niches remain a mystery; some suppose they housed votive images or urns, others say this was a dovecote for pigeons.

MONASTERY (AL-DEIR)   Map pp180–1
Similar in design to the Treasury, the spec-tacular Monastery (known locally as Al-Deir) is far bigger (50m wide and 45m high) and just as impressive. Built in the 3rd century BC as a Nabataean tomb, perhaps to King Obodas I (ruled 96–86 BC), the Monastery

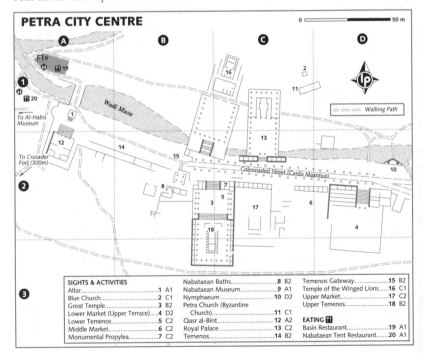

PETRA CITY CENTRE

0 ———— 50 m

Wadi Musa

To Al-Habis Museum

To Crusader Fort (300m)

Colonnaded Street (Cardo Maximus)

Walking Path

gets its name from the crosses carved on its inside walls, suggesting that the building was used as a church in Byzantine times. The building has towering columns and a large urn flanked by two half-pediments. The three-dimensional aspect of the upper level beautifully complements the lower façade, an element thought to be derived from Hellenistic influences. The courtyard in front of the Monastery was once surrounded by columns and was probably used for sacred ceremonies.

It was once possible to climb up a steep trail to a point above the Monastery, but this is currently not allowed for the sake of preserving the Monastery and its tourists – with one visitor falling to her death a few years ago.

Opposite the Monastery there's a strategically placed drinks stall in a cave with a row of seats outside where you can sit and contemplate the majestic sight.

Beyond the drinks stand a trail leads up to two lookouts, with stunning views west over Wadi Araba into Israel & the Palestinian Territories and south to the peak of Jebel Haroun, topped by a small white shrine. A couple of hundred metres behind the drinks stand, tomb 468 is worth exploring for its fine façade, some defaced carvings and excellent views.

The climb to the Monastery takes about 40 minutes, and is best started in mid-afternoon when there is welcome shade along the way and the Monastery is at its most photogenic. The spectacular ancient rock-cut path of more than 800 steps follows the old processional route and is easy to follow (though uphill all the way). It's a spectacle of weird and wonderfully tortured stone and there are several side paths to explore if you have the time. If you really don't want to walk, donkeys (with a guide) can be hired for about JD3/5 one way/return.

The start of the trail to the Monastery starts from behind (to the northwest of) the Basin Restaurant and Nabataean Museum. If in doubt look for weary hikers coming down.

The path to the Monastery passes the **Lion Tomb** (Lion Triclinium), set in a small gully. The two lions that lent the tomb its name are weather-beaten, but can still be made out, facing each other at the base of the monument.

OFF THE BEATEN TRACK

Explore the following hidden corners of Petra and you'll probably have them all to yourself (for locations see Map pp180–1):

- Tombs above Wadi Mu'asireh
- The Christian Tombs of Moghar al-Nassara
- The southern end of the Royal Tombs
- Hillside tombs north of the Theatre
- Tombs at the base of Umm al-Biyara
- Upper Wadi Farasa, north of the Garden Triclinium
- Turkimaniya Tomb, with the longest Nabataean inscription in Petra

---

NABATAEAN MUSEUM   Map p188

In the same building as the Basin Restaurant, this **museum** (9am-5pm, to 4pm Oct-Mar) has an interesting display of artefacts from the region, including mosaics unearthed in Wadi Musa. The historical explanations in English are comprehensive, and will help most visitors better understand the history of Petra. A shop inside the main building sells detailed maps of the area.

Hiking

Anyone with enough energy, time and enthusiasm, who wants to get away from the crowds, see some stunning landscapes, explore unexcavated tombs and temples and, perhaps, meet some Bedouin villagers, should pack an extra bottle of water and go hiking.

None of the following hikes are all that strenuous and none involve camping overnight (which is not allowed). Only the hike to Sabra really needs a guide. Hikers should pick up the contoured *Map of Petra* mentioned on p179. Please note that the approximate hiking times are just that, and do not include the time needed to explore the site and/or linger to admire the views.

Guides can be hired from Petra visitor centre and travel agencies (pricey at JD25 to JD55 per day) or you can find a cheaper Bedouin guide inside Petra.

WADI MUTHLIM TO THE ROYAL TOMBS
Map pp180–1

This adventurous canyon hike (1½ hours) is an exciting alternative route into Petra if you've already taken the main *siq* path. It's not difficult or strenuous but there are places where you'll need to lower yourself down some boulders. Bring sandals in case you need to wade through small water pools.

The trail starts just before the entrance to the Siq, where a trail drops down to the right into an incredible 88m-long **Nabataean tunnel** (there's light at the end of the tunnel). At the far end you'll find yourself in narrow Wadi Muthlim.

Before the tunnel it's possible to make a short side-trip to the **Eagle Monument**, a faint carving of an eagle just northwest of the tunnel. Take the trail to the right of the tunnel, past a god block and over the top of the tunnel, diagonally across to the side valley.

Back on the hike, Wadi Muthlim gradually narrows into a metre-wide *siq* and at a couple of places you'll have to lower yourself down a couple of 2m-high boulder blockages. After 25 minutes look for the remains of a Nabataean dam above you. Thirty minutes from the start of the hike you'll meet a T-junction where the trail hits Wadi Mataha. A painted arrow points to the left; follow this. The sinuous *siq* winds through some residual water pools (you may get your feet wet here) and passes some Nabataean niches before spitting you out blinking into the sunlight 10 minutes later.

(If doing this hike in the opposite direction you can find the entry to the Siq by following the curved man-made wall around to the right – more niches mark the entry to the Siq).

From here it's easiest to just follow the cliff face to the left, past a series of little-visited tombs, including **Dorotheos' House** and the **Tomb of Sextius Florentinus**, until you reach the Royal Tombs. Alternatively, you can explore the interesting so-called 'Christian Tombs' of Moghar al-Nassara.

Note that some parts of the Siq may be impassable if it's been raining. There is a genuine possibility of flash floods along Wadi Muthlim, because the dam at the start of the Siq diverts water down this wadi. It's important that you don't start this trek if it's raining, or is likely to.

HIGH PLACE OF SACRIFICE TO PETRA CITY CENTRE   Map pp180–1
This one-hour hike starts from the High Place of Sacrifice. Refer to p184 for infor-

mation about getting to the High Place up the steps from near the Theatre. It's possible to do this hike in reverse, which makes for a good afternoon exit from the site.

As you face the drinks stand from the top of the path, near the Place of Sacrifice, a trail heads down towards Wadi Farasa (Butterfly Valley). The start of the trail is not immediately obvious, so look for the helpful piles of stones indicating the trail, or ask for directions at the drinks stand.

On the way down is the **Lion Monument**, where water was channelled to pour out of the lion's mouth from the rock face above – an example of Nabataean engineering at its cleverest. The lion is about 5m long and 2.5m high. A stone **altar** diagonally opposite suggests the fountain had some religious function. The steps wind further down the side of the cliff to the **Garden Tomb**, which archaeologists believe was probably a temple. To the right (east) are the remains of a wall, part of the huge water cistern above.

A little further down, on the left (west), is the elegant **Roman Soldier's Tomb**, named for the statue over the door. Almost opposite (east) is the **Garden Triclinium**, a hall used for annual feasts to honour the dead placed in the Soldier's Tomb. The hall is unique in Petra because it has carved decoration on the interior walls. The tomb and triclinium were once linked by a colonnaded courtyard.

A few minutes further down, the trail then branches to the right, above the dry valley. At the ridge ahead take a left (the right branch takes you to the Royal Tombs) and walk past **Az-Zantur**, a 1st-century AD palace that's still under excavation. Nearby is a collection of ruined Nabataean and Roman houses, one of the few traces of habitations so far discovered in Petra. The trail continues west along the ridge to the **Pharaun Column**, the only surviving column of another Nabataean temple. If you're disoriented, the pale-green roof over the Petra Church, north of the Colonnaded Street, is a good landmark for the direction you need to head.

UMM AL-BIYARA   Map pp180–1
He the Judaean king, Amaziah was the one who defeated ten thousand Edomites in the Valley of the Salt and captured Sela in battle...

(2 Kings 14:7)

The return trip from Qasr al-Bint to Umm al-Biyara (the Mother of Cisterns) takes about three hours and offers some of the best views over Petra. It's a fairly strenuous hike up hundreds of steps but the trail is easy to follow. Start the hike in the mid-afternoon when most of the path is in shade but don't leave it too late as you don't want to come down these steps in poor light.

Umm al-Biyara is the flat-topped mountain (1178m) to the southwest of the city centre. On top may have been the Edomite capital of Sela, from where the Judaean king Amaziah (who ruled from 796 to 781 BC) threw 10,000 prisoners to their deaths over the precipice.

From behind Qasr al-Bint, head up to the Pharaun Column and descend to the road that leads along Wadi Thughra to the Snake Monument. The path up the rock face starts from just to the left of the largest of the rock-cut tombs on the southeast face of the mountain – a jeep track leads up to the start of the steps. After a couple of minutes' climbing you'll pass an impressive ceremonial ramp.

On top of the mountain are the ruins of a 7th-century BC **Edomite village**, as well as several cisterns. There are also many unexcavated **tombs** along the base of the eastern cliffs. Take a picnic and savour the views (look for the Monastery to the north).

ABOVE THE TREASURY   Map pp180–1
For dramatic and unusual views of the Treasury, far from the madding crowds, make this 1½-hour return hike from the Palace Tomb, with the option of returning via the Urn Tomb. Start this hike in the early morning to get the Treasury in good light, or in mid-afternoon when some parts are in the shade.

An obvious set of steep processional steps leads up the valley from about 150m northeast of the Palace Tomb. The stiff climb takes about 20 minutes and flats out at a hilltop Nabataean **cistern**. Along the way there are wonderful views of the Roman Theatre.

Continue south from the cistern along a less obvious dirt path, down the dry wadi for another 15 minutes, and then down a small ravine, until you come to a dramatic position about 200m above the Treasury, with fantastic views of the mighty edifice; watch your step. You may have the place to yourself (there's not a drink stand in sight), and the only noise you can hear is

the echo of the tour groups marvelling at the Treasury below. It is easy to get disoriented while finding the path back to the top of the steps, so look out for landmarks on the way down.

Just before you get back to the cistern a tiny cleft in the rock to the left reveals worn steps (take care with your footing) that lead down a gully to a point next to the **Urn Tomb**. The trail isn't all that clear but is doable with some care. If you are not sure about it then take the main path back down the way you came up.

WADI SIYAGH   Map pp180–1
For a leg-stretcher that doesn't require walking straight up the side of a hill, try the trail which follows the dry riverbed to the northwest of Al-Habis hill (it's most easily accessed from in front of the Basin Restaurant) and follows Wadi Siyagh. Once a residential suburb of Petra, the wadi and the nearby slopes have unexcavated tombs and residences to explore and offer some nice picnic spots away from the crowds and the noisy restaurant generator.

As you walk down the wadi from the Basin Restaurant you'll soon see steps leading up on the right side to the **Painted House**, one of the very few tombs in Petra that still has traces of Nabataean frescoes. Further down, at a bend in the valley, is a **Nabataean quarry**.

The main attraction further down the valley is the dense ribbon of green bushes, water pools and even waterfalls (in winter) that lines the wadi. In spring, the flowers are beautiful.

The trail along Wadi Siyagh is easy to follow, but becomes a bit rough in parts as it ascends the wadi walls. Just go as far as you want, but remember that you must come back the same way. Don't walk along the wadi if rain is imminent because flash floods are a real possibility.

JEBEL HAROUN
Aaron will be gathered to his people: he will die there. Moses did as the Lord commanded: they went up to Mount Hor in the sight of the whole community.

(Numbers 20:26-27)

This trip from Qasr al-Bint to Jebel Haroun via the Snake Monument takes around six hours return. Some people hire a donkey (JD20, with a guide) or even a camel for the trip, though this isn't strictly necessary.

Jebel Haroun (1350m) is thought to be biblical Mt Hor, where Moses' brother Aaron (Haroun to Muslims) is believed to be buried. The small white **shrine** on top of Jebel Haroun was built in the 14th century, apparently over Aaron's tomb. There are some excavations of a religious complex under way nearby. The views towards the Monastery and the Dead Sea are worth the effort of getting here, as one reader discovered:

> The path passes Bedu settlements and from the top of the mountain the 360° views to Petra's Deir and the Dead Sea rift are stunning…the walk from/to the entrance of Petra is about three hours each way…a total of about 18km return. The track is easy to find even without a guide. My kids found four different species of lizards at the top, including some big ones.
>
> *Jeroen Peters*

The trail to Jebel Haroun starts at the Pharaun Column, and follows the dirt road past Bedouin settlements to the **Snake Monument**, a curled stone on a rock pedestal that faintly resembles a snake. Just continue to the southwest towards the obvious white shrine (which can look deceptively close); the trail is not steep until the last bit. At the bottom of the mountain, find the caretaker if you want to see inside the shrine. A guide is recommended but not obligatory.

SABRA

The trip from Qasr al-Bint to the suburban Nabataean remains of Sabra takes a minimum of five hours return and takes you to a remote corner of Petra, where trade caravans once unloaded their precious cargoes at the fringes of the main city. The remains at Sabra include some ruined walls, temples, bridges and a small Roman theatre. A guide is needed to even find the trail from Snake Monument. A return trip on donkey costs around JD30.

An exciting option offered by some travel agencies is the adventurous two-day hike from Tayyibeh, through the *siq*-like Wadi Tibn, to Sabra, camping overnight and continuing on to Petra the next day.

Tours

Petra by Night (adult/child under 12 JD12/free) is a magical way to see the old city and can be one of the highlights of a trip to Petra. The walk starts from the Petra visitor centre at 8.30pm on Monday and Thursday nights (it doesn't run when it's raining), and lasts two hours, taking you along the Siq (lined with hundreds of candles) in silence as far as the Treasury, where traditional Bedouin music is played and mint tea is served. There are often performances of Bedouin storytelling.

Tickets are available from a few travel agencies in town or from the Petra visitor centre.

Eating

At the western end of the Colonnaded Street, near Qasr al-Bint, two restaurants offer similar all-you-can-eat buffets.

The upmarket **Basin Restaurant** (lunch buffet JD8.500, beer JD3; 11.30am-4pm) is run by the Crown Plaza Resort. It's expensive but the food is good and includes a barbecue. Alternatively, pay JD5 for salad and mezze only.

Nabataean Tent Restaurant (lunch buffet JD7, drinks JD1; 11.30am-4.30pm) is similar and has nice tables on the grass.

Throughout the site, including at the High Place of Sacrifice and the Monastery, stalls sell cold drinks, bottled water and some basic foodstuffs as well as souvenirs. Prices are high, with bottled water around JD1.500.

WADI MUSA   وادي موسى
☎ 03

The village that has sprung up around Petra is Wadi Musa (Valley of Moses), formerly known as Elji but now named after the valley it follows. It's a patchy mass of hotels, restaurants and shops stretching about 5km down from 'Ain Musa to the main entrance of Petra.

After the signing of Jordan's peace agreement with Israel & the Palestinian Territories in 1994, Wadi Musa became a boom tourist town, transformed almost overnight from a small town with few visitors and a traditional Bedouin society to a sprawling competitive place overrun by visitors laden with cash. Large numbers of Israelis began to visit, along with other tourists, encouraged by moves towards peace in the region. Some locals have coped with these changes better than others – see the boxed text, p212.

Many locals are aware of tourists flocking to Petra with big wallets and little time and this is one of the few places in Jordan where you'll get consistently overcharged.

Orientation

'Wadi Musa' refers to everywhere between 'Ain Musa and the entrance to Petra. The obvious village centre is around the Shaheed roundabout, about 3km from the Petra gates, which is where you'll find most tourist facilities. There is a second collection of mid- and top-end hotels, restaurants and souvenir shops a couple of kilometres downhill close to the Petra entrance.

Information
BOOKSHOPS

Inside Petra, behind the visitor centre and along the main road through Wadi Musa, souvenir stands sell books about Petra, but everything is more expensive than in Amman. See above for information about books and maps.

EMERGENCY

Police station (☎ 2156551, 191) In Wadi Musa, adjacent to the Police roundabout.
Tourist police station (☎ 2156441, 196; ⏰ 8am-midnight) Opposite the Petra visitor centre. A few tourist police can be found lounging around in the shade inside Petra.

INTERNET ACCESS

Petra Internet Café (☎ 2157264; alpetra@hotmail .com; per hr JD3; ⏰ 9am-midnight) Fast ADSL connections, with 50% discount for guests of most of the local hotels. Located up the hill from the Shaheed roundabout.
Rum Internet (☎ 2157906; per hr JD1; ⏰ 10am-midnight) Located down the hill from the Shaheed roundabout.

LAUNDRY

Most hotels will do laundry for around JD1 per piece, though most of it gets sent to the dry cleaners at the Amra Palace Hotel. The Valentine Hotel washes 1kg of laundry for JD2.500 (JD3 for nonguests).

MEDICAL FACILITIES

Queen Rania Hospital Is of a high standard and open for emergencies without referral. Located 5km from the Police roundabout on the road to Tayyibeh.
Wadi Musa Pharmacy Has a decent selection of toiletries. Located near the Shaheed roundabout.

MONEY

There are surprisingly few moneychangers in Wadi Musa, although many hotels will change money, albeit at a poor rate. It's generally better to change travellers cheques before you come to Petra.

The Housing Bank and Jordan Islamic Bank up from the Shaheed roundabout are good for money-changing; both have ATMs. The Arab Bank is down from the roundabout. Closer to the gate into Petra, the Arab Jordan Investment Bank, and the Cairo-Amman Bank in the Mövenpick Hotel, change cash and (usually) travellers cheques with a minimum of fuss. The banks are open from about 8am to 2pm, Sunday to Thursday and (sometimes) 9am to 11am on Friday. A couple of moneychangers near the Silk Rd Hotel keep longer hours.

POST

Main post office (⏰ 8am-5pm Sat-Thu) Located inside a mini-plaza on the Shaheed roundabout.
Post office (⏰ 8am-5pm Sat-Thu) Small office by the Mussa Spring Hotel in 'Ain Musa.
Visitor centre post office (⏰ 7.30am-5pm) The attraction of using the small post office behind the Petra visitor centre is that mail is postmarked 'Petra Touristic Post Office', rather than Wadi Musa.

TELEPHONE

International telephone calls can be made from private agencies along the main streets of Wadi Musa village for around 800 fils per minute. A domestic call costs 150 fils.

TOURIST INFORMATION

The best source of information is the Petra visitor centre near the entrance to Petra (p180). For information about minibuses and other transport, you're better off asking at your hotel or one of the restaurants around the Shaheed roundabout.

Activities
HAMMAMS

A 'Turkish bath' is perfect to ease any aching muscles after walking the trails of Petra. The two places in town generally only have male masseurs. The service includes a steam bath, massage, scrub and 'body conditioning' for a standard JD15. It's a good idea to book in advance.

In the passage under the Silk Rd Hotel (enter from the main road), **Petra Turkish Bath**

WADI MUSA

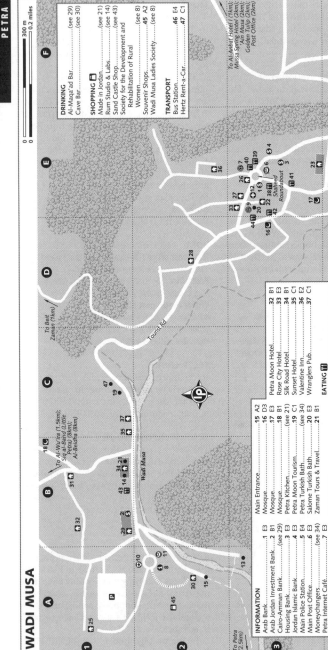

INFORMATION
Arab Bank....................................1 E3
Arab Jordan Investment Bank.......2 B1
Cairo-Amman Bank..............(see 29)
Housing Bank.............................3 E3
Jordan Islamic Bank....................4 E3
Main Police Station....................5 E4
Main Post Office........................6 E3
Moneychangers.....................(see 34)
Petra Internet Café.....................7 E3
Petra Visitors Centre (Ticket Office)..............................8 A2
Rum Internet..............................9 E3
Tourist Police Station................10 A2
Visitor Centre Post Office..........11 A2
Wadi Musa Pharmacy...............12 E3

SIGHTS & ACTIVITIES
Brooke Hospital for Animals......13 A3
Jordan Experience.....................14 B1
La Beduina.............................(see 43)

Main Entrance...........................15 A2
Mosque....................................16 D3
Mosque....................................17 E3
Mosque....................................18 B1
Petra Kitchen........................(see 21)
Petra Moon Tourism.................19 C1
Petra Turkish Bath....................20 E3
Salome Turkish Bath.................21 B1
Zaman Tours & Travel...........(see 34)

SLEEPING
Al-Anbat Hotel II......................22 E3
Amra Palace Hotel.....................23 E3
Cleopetra Hotel.........................24 E4
Crown Plaza Resort Hotel..........25 A1
El-Rashid Hotel.........................26 E3
Elgee Hotel...............................27 E3
Moon Valley Hotel....................28 D2
Mövenpick Hotel......................29 B1
Petra Guest House.....................30 A2
Petra Inn..................................31 B1

Petra Moon Hotel......................32 B1
Rose City Hotel.........................33 E3
Silk Road Hotel........................34 B1
Sunset Hotel.............................35 C1
Valentine Inn............................36 E2
Wranglers Pub..........................37 C1

EATING
Al-Afandi Quick Restaurant.......38 E3
Al-Arabi Restaurant...................39 E3
Al-Saraya Restaurant.............(see 29)
Al-Wadi Restaurant...................40 E3
Cleopetra Restaurant & Coffee Shop.....................................41 E3
Oriental Restaurant...............(see 43)
Petra Nights Restaurant.............42 E3
Red Cave Restaurant.................43 B1
Sanabel Bakery.........................44 D3
Sandstone Restaurant............(see 43)

DRINKING
Al-Maqa'ad Bar.....................(see 29)
Cave Bar................................(see 30)

SHOPPING
Made in Jordan......................(see 21)
Rum Studio & Labs................(see 14)
Sand Castle Shop...................(see 43)
Society for the Development and Rehabilitation of Rural Women.................................(see 8)
Souvenir Shops.........................45 A2
Wadi Musa Ladies Society.......(see 8)

TRANSPORT
Bus Station...............................46 E4
Hertz Rent-a-Car......................47 C1

To Al-Wu'ira (1.5km); Siq al-Barid (Little Petra; 8km); Al-Beidha (8km)

To Bet Zaman (1km)

Tourist Rd

Wadi Musa

To Petra (2.5km)

Shaheed Roundabout

Police Roundabout

To Al-Anbat Hotel (1km); Mussa Spring Hotel (2km); Al Anbat Hotel (2km); Golden Tulip (2km); Post Office (2km)

To Petra Marriot (4km); Petra Panorama Hotel (5km); Nabatean Castle Hotel (5km); Queen Rania Hospital (5km); Tayyibeh (10km); Sofitel Taybet Zaman (10km)

300 m
0.2 miles

(☎ 2157085; ☽ 10am-11pm) is closest to the entrance of Petra, although it's not the cleanest place. It's in the process of building a separate women's baths.

Locals prefer **Salome Turkish Bath** (☎ 2157342; ☽ 4pm-10pm), though it's sometimes booked out by tour groups. Located near Al-Anbat Hotel II.

The Amra Palace Hotel (☎ 2157070; www .amrapalace.com), see p196, also has an excellent hammam, with separate sections for men and women.

Tours

The most professional agency in Wadi Musa for arranging trips inside Petra and around Jordan (including Wadi Rum and Aqaba) is **Petra Moon Tourism** (☎ 2156665; www.petramoon .com), which has an office on the road to Petra. They can arrange horses to Jebel Haroun, expensive fully supported treks to Dana (four to five days), hikes from Tayyibeh to Petra, and camel treks to Wadi Rum. Hiking guides cost around JD55 per day, horses JD20 to JD35 per day.

Other reliable agencies include:
Jordan Experience (☎ 2155005; www.jordan experience.com.jo)
La Beduina (☎ 2157099; www.labeduinatours.com)
Zaman Tours & Travel (☎ 2157723; www.zaman tours.com) In the same building as the Silk Rd Hotel.

A couple of the budget (and a few midrange and top-end) hotels can also arrange simple day trips around Petra and further afield.

Courses

If you've always wanted to know how to whip up wonderful hummus or bake the perfect baklava, **Petra Kitchen** (☎ /fax 2155900; www.petra kitchen.com, petrakitchen@petramoon.com; cookery course per person JD30) is for you. It offers a nightly cookery course where tourists can learn from local women how to cook Jordanian mezze, soup and main course in a relaxed family-style atmosphere. Dishes change daily and the evening starts at 6.30pm (7.30pm in summer), or you can arrange to go early to shop for ingredients. The price isn't cheap but includes food and soft drinks. Reservations are recommended.

Sleeping

Things have changed just a little over the years in Petra. Back in 1908, Macmillan's guide to *Palestine and Syria* had the following advice:

> At Petra, there is no sleeping accommodation to be found, and travellers therefore have to bring with them camp equipment, unless they prefer to put up with the inconvenience of sleeping in the Bedwin huts at Elji, half an hour distant from Petra, or spend the night in some of the numerous temples. Such a course cannot be recommended to European travellers, especially if ladies are in the party.

Even as recently as 1991, there were only four official hotels in Petra. Visitors now have a choice of over 70 hotels and camping is no longer permitted inside Petra.

Prices fluctuate wildly in Petra, depending on the season and amount of business. The high season is generally from April to mid-May and in October. Outside these times, prices drop quickly from the official rates, especially if you're staying more than a couple of nights. The biggest discounts are in late May to September.

Most hotels have a variety of rooms in a variety of sizes; some with balcony, others with a bigger bathroom but no natural light. It's often more important which rooms are available than which is the best hotel.

In winter (November to March), make sure there is heating and that it works. Surprisingly few places have fans, and only the more expensive hotels have air-conditioning. The views advertised by some hotels are actually of Wadi Musa valley, not of Petra itself.

Places that are some distance from the entrance to Petra will offer free transport to and from the gate (usually once a day in either direction). Although many hotels offer 'half board' (which includes breakfast and dinner) at a higher rate, you can always obtain a room-only rate if you wish to eat elsewhere.

One last word: have a good idea of where you want to stay before arriving in town. If you get off the minibus at the Shaheed roundabout in Wadi Musa with a backpack, you'll likely be besieged by persuasive touts, so stick to your guns.

BUDGET

There is a sameness to the many budget places. Most will attempt to entice you with

PETRA

offers of watching the *Indiana Jones and the Last Crusade* video and free shuttles to/from Petra. The choice for women is more difficult than elsewhere in Jordan.

Al-Anbat Hotel II (☎ 2157200; alanbath@joinit.com.jo; s/d JD12/14) The cheaper of the two Anbats, the rooms here are quiet and well-furnished, with clean but small private bathrooms, making it especially good value in the heart of Wadi Musa. It's not perfect; the staff are a bit lackadaisical (but friendly) and the satellite TV keeps packing up halfway during a movie. The double rooms at the front are the best choice. Discounts of 30% are possible, especially outside high season. It may well be renovated soon, with a new restaurant planned for next door.

Valentine Inn (☎ 2156423; valentineinn@hotmail.com; dm JD2-3, s/d with shared bathroom JD6/8, s/d with private bathroom JD8/10; 🖳) The good news here is that for men this is the biggest backpacker hangout in town, well attuned to a range of budget travel needs from travel information to laundry, a great veggie dinner buffet (JD3), Internet access, transport to Amman along the King's Highway and more. The rooms are decent but nothing special and the dorms are very cramped. Both male and female travellers have complained of pushy, rude staff and a 'bad vibe'.

Cleopetra Hotel (☎ /fax 2157090; cleopetrahotel@hotmail.com; s/d JD10/14) The rooms here, all with private bathroom and breakfast, are reasonable but smallish but it's a friendly place to hang out, with BBC World and an extensive range of movies playing in the lobby. Discounts of up to 50% are common.

Mussa Spring Hotel (☎ 2156310; musaspring_hotel@yahoo.co.uk; rooftop bed JD2, dm JD3-4, s/d with shared bathroom JD7.500/11, with private bathroom JD8.500/15) In the village of 'Ain Musa, this is as far from the clamour of Petra as you can get and one of the first places you reach en route from Amman or Ma'an. It offers daily free shuttles to/from the gate at Petra, 5km away. The rooms are small and some are windowless, but it's a friendly place with a terrace and decent restaurant (dinner JD3). The rooms at the front with windows and small balconies are the best. Rates drop by 30% when things are quiet.

Moon Valley Hotel (☎ 2157131; moon-valley-hotel@yahoo.com; rooftop bed JD2, smaller s JD7, larger s/d JD10/15) Down the hill on the road to Petra, this is a friendly place and one where the

---

> **MOSES' SPRING**
>
> Then Moses raised his arm and struck the rock twice with his staff. Water gushed out, and the community and their livestock drank.
>
> *(Numbers 20:11)*
>
> 'Ain Musa (Moses' Spring) is one of two possible locations in Jordan for the site where Moses supposedly struck the rock with his staff and water gushed forth to the thirsty Israelites. The simple site is marked by a modern three-domed building occasionally visited by local pilgrims but there's not a great deal to actually see.

---

hard sell is refreshingly absent. It's clean and well-looked after, with a nice lobby sitting area and roof-top café, and gets good reports from travellers. The more expensive rooms are particularly good value.

Elgee Hotel (☎ 2156701; fax 2157002; s/d JD10/15) Across the road from the Rose City Hotel, this is also a passable option, with all rooms having private bathrooms, though the lobby bar and top-floor disco are a bit seedy.

Rose City Hotel (☎ 2156440; fax 2014132; s/d JD7/13) Quieter than most, this is one of the better-value places in the village centre, with friendly staff. Rooms vary a lot, but all have private bathroom and breakfast.

MIDRANGE
All the room rates in this section include breakfast.

Amra Palace Hotel (☎ 2157070; www.amrapalace.com; s/d JD23/35, half board JD25/40; 🏊) The very comfortable rooms, satellite TV, heated outdoor pool, Jacuzzi, summer terrace and excellent Turkish bath (JD15 per person) push this a notch above anything else in Wadi Musa. Rooms at the front have the better views. Visa cards are accepted.

El-Rashid Hotel (☎ 2156800; Shaheed roundabout; s/d from JD10/15) Popular with groups of French tourists, this place is uninspiring but spacious (particularly the new rooms), and has comfortable rooms right in the centre of town. During quiet periods the friendly management is happy to negotiate, which will probably make it good value and accessible to budget travellers. There is satellite TV and a grand lobby.

PETRA

Sunset Hotel (☎ 2156579; fax 2156950; s/d JD15/20) Handy for the entrance to Petra, with a nice breakfast terrace, but you'll pay for the convenience with average, somewhat gloomy rooms.

Al-Anbat Hotel I (☎ 2156265; www.alanbat.com; s/d JD13/16; P 🖵 🖳) Both a good-value and very well-run three-star resort, located on the road between 'Ain Musa and Wadi Musa. The spacious rooms come with satellite TV, and most have a balcony with views over the wadi. Facilities include a Turkish bath (JD12 for guests) and a small pool (in summer). Breakfast costs JD2 and the good dinner buffets are JD5. Free transport to/from Petra is available. Campers (JD3 per person) can use a designated area, with showers and a kitchen, and you can park a camper van. Al-Anbat is the Arabic name for the Nabataeans.

Petra Moon Hotel (☎ /fax 2156220; petramoon hotel@yahoo.com; s/d JD15/20) Up behind the Mövenpick Hotel, this is convenient for the entrance to Petra. The rooms are simple but clean, with decent bathrooms, and the staff are helpful. If you are planning to spend more than two nights, the price per night drops dramatically.

Silk Road Hotel (☎ 2157222; www.petrasilkroad .com; s/d JD25/35) Another decent, if dull, midrange hotel close to Petra, with spacious rooms. The huge restaurant does a buffet dinner for JD6 and is popular with tour groups.

Petra Inn (☎ 2156403; nabatee@go.com.jo; s/d/tr JD25/35/40, low season JD20/25/30) Similarly good value with comfortable rooms and a convenient location not far from the Petra gate. The rooms can be a bit dark with the notable exception of the fabulous end rooms which offer 120° window views. The excellent roof terrace is a great place to catch the sunset in summer.

Petra Palace Hotel (☎ 2156723; www.petrapalace .com.jo; s/d/tr JD31/46/60; 🖵 🖳) This is a much better-run place, offering superb value and nice details like in-room hair dryers and a washing line. Some of the luxury rooms open out onto a terrace with a swimming pool and there's a good restaurant and bar. Renovations planned for 2006 will bring new rooms and another pool, as well as possible noise and disruption. Credit cards are accepted. Located 500m from the Petra entrance.

Golden Tulip (☎ 2156799; resrv@kingsway-petra .com; s/d JD70/85, discounted to JD30/40; 🖳) Sterile but comforting tour group option from the reliable Dutch chain. It's a bit far from the action, out in 'Ain Musa, and there's no shuttle bus so you'll have to shell out for a taxi (JD1.500) to Petra. It has a pool, a terrace and a decent bar.

TOP END
At all of the places listed here, there are some surprising bargains to be found when business is quiet.

Crowne Plaza Resort Hotel (☎ 2156266; www .crowneplaza.com, cprpetra@nets.jo; s/d JD100/110, discounted to JD80/90 plus taxes; 🖳) A great location (close to the Petra gate and overlooking sandstone bluffs) and good discounted online rates make this a good option. The heated swimming pool is useful outside of high summer and a lovely terrace has summer barbecues. The hotel also has a Jacuzzi, sauna, tennis courts, coffee makers in rooms and self-service laundry facilities. The bar and restaurants are good but the pricey (JD6) breakfast isn't included in the room rate.

Petra Guest House (☎ 2156266; ppwnwm@go.com .jo; s/d JD50/60, discounted to JD40/50) You can't get closer to the entrance to Petra without sleeping in a cave. It's a step down in quality from its sister, the Crown Plaza, but you can use the facilities (pool etc) of that hotel so it's good value. The chalets are more charming than the main building, which is due for renovation, pushing it up to four stars. Rooms are a bit motel-like but comfortable.

Mövenpick Hotel (☎ 2157111; www.moevenpick -petra.com; s/d JD92/112; 🖳) One hundred metres from the gate to Petra, this is the most luxurious place in town, and as stylish as you'd expect. There are Mediterranean and buffet restaurants, a good bar, a swimming pool, roof garden, the peaceful Burckhardt Library, a children's playground and upmarket gift shops. Even the hotel brochure describes the hotel as 'posh'.

Beit Zaman The Sofitel chain is due to reopen this wonderful village-style hotel, which was built several years ago along the lines of the similar Taybat Zaman in Tayyibeh. The hotel has languished during the recent tourism downturn so hopefully the facilities have been kept up.

The following four luxury hotels are on the scenic road between Tayyibeh and Wadi

Musa. They offer fine views (the terraces are fantastic places for a sunset drink) but transport can be inconvenient if you don't have your own car. Some close outside of high season.

Nabataean Castle Hotel (☎ 2157201; resort.nabat aean@moevenpick.com; s/d with half board JD110/120, rm discounted to JD77; ☒) Mövenpick run this luxury place (with the region's only heated indoor pool) and runs a daily shuttle bus to and from Petra. It's located 5km south of the Police roundabout.

Petra Panorama Hotel (☎ 2157390; www.petra panorama.com; s/d JD100/115, discounted to JD42/56 full board; ☒) Like most of the hotels along this road, it offers wonderful sunset views and luxurious rooms. Discounts make this four-star place great value. It is likewise located 5km south of the Police roundabout.

Petra Marriott (☎ 2156408; petramrt@go.com.jo; s/d low season with half board JD45/50, high season JD70/75; ☒) Superb luxury, around 4km from the Police roundabout, on the road to Tayyibeh. It has an outdoor pool, several restaurants, a Turkish bath and even a cinema for free use by guests.

Sofitel Taybet Zaman (☎ 2150111, fax 2150101; s/d JD102/129, discounted to JD74) One of the most unique hotels in Jordan, the Taybet Zaman is a stylish and evocative reconstruction of a traditional Ottoman stone village, with luxurious and spacious rooms, a terrace restaurant (set meal per person JD11) with superb views (although the food gets mixed reviews), handicraft shops, swimming pool and Turkish bath (JD12 per person). If we had the money this is where we'd retire to! Located in Tayyibeh village, a taxi here from Petra will cost about JD10 one way.

Eating

The main road through Wadi Musa is dotted with grocery stores where you can stock up on food, munchies and drinks for Petra, although the selection is fairly uninspiring unless you are a big fan of processed cheese. Some hotels can arrange picnic boxes but they are rarely up to much. A felafel sandwich travels well and makes a great picnic lunch.

Sanabel Bakery (☎ 2157925; ☯ 5am-midnight), lo cated around the corner from Rum Inter-net, does a delicious range of Arab sweets and fresh bread that can be handy for a picnic, but check for overcharging.

After a long, dehydrating day hiking in Petra, most find it hard to resist a Swiss ice cream from the window outside the **Möven-pick Hotel** (JD1.300).

BUDGET

Most of the cheapest places to eat are in Wadi Musa village. There are a few places offering felafel and shwarma, especially around the Shaheed roundabout and just up from Sanabel bakery.

Al-Afandi Quick Restaurant (meals from JD1) A simple and friendly place located off the Shaheed roundabout, offering hummus, felafel and shwarma and one of the very few places in town that doesn't habitually overcharge foreigners.

Al-Wadi Restaurant (☎ 2157151; salads 750 fils, mains JD3-4; ☯ 7am-late) One of two good places right on Shaheed roundabout. There's pasta and pizza, as well as a range of vegetarian dishes and local Bedouin specialties such as *gallayah* and *mensaf*, most of which come with salad and rice. It also does breakfast (around JD1.500).

Al-Arabi Restaurant (☎ 2157661; mains from JD1; ☯ 6am-midnight) Almost next door to Al-Wadi is this pleasant place with helpful staff and good meals. A large chicken shwarma with salad and hummus costs JD2.500. Repeat customers get a discount.

Cleopetra Restaurant & Coffee Shop (☎ 079 531 8775; buffet JD3; ☯ 6am-11pm) Just south of the Shaheed roundabout, this canteen does a few à la carte dishes but most people opt for the decent value but average-tasting open buffet, offering a range of Bedouin special-ties. You can also get breakfast (600 fils to JD1.500).

MIDRANGE

All of the places listed here are down the hill from Wadi Musa village and near the entrance to Petra. They're all close together and similar in menu and price.

Oriental Restaurant (☎ 2157087; mains JD4-5, pizzas from JD2.500; ☯ 11am-9.30pm) A popular place with a slightly schizophrenic menu that churns out both Lebanese main courses and Western-style pasta and pizza.

Red Cave Restaurant (☎ 2157799; starters JD1, mains JD4-5; ☯ 9am-10pm) Cavernous, cool and friendly and the menu has a good selection. The Bedouin *gallayah* comes with lamb or chicken as well as rice, onions and a spicy tomato sauce. Bedouin specialties include *mensaf* and *maqlubbeh* (sometimes called 'upside down'). Located a couple of hundred metres east of the main entrance.

TOP END

Sandstone Restaurant (☎ 2157701; starters JD1, mains JD6; ☯ 8.30am-9pm) Next door to the Oriental Restaurant, this is a friendly place with expensive but decent meals. They sometimes do buffets (JD6). The nice outdoor seating is a good place for a beer.

Al-Saraya Restaurant (☎ 2157111; Mövenpick Hotel; ☯ lunch & dinner) If you need a splurge, look no further than the blow-out buffet (lunch JD12.500, dinner JD16.250), or you can just choose the salad, soup and bread for JD6.

Drinking

There's not a lot to do in the evening, other than recover from aching muscles and plan your next day in Petra. Some hotels organise videos or other entertainment, but only when there are enough takers.

Cave Bar (☎ 2156266; ☯ 8am-midnight; small beer from JD2.500, cocktail JD4, plus 26% tax & service) If you've never been to a bar in a 2000-year-old Nabataean rock tomb (and we're guessing you haven't!) then a drink here is a must. The seats are actually in the side tombs; if that's a bit creepy for you, there's also pleasant seating outside. The ambience is classy and there's live Bedouin music from 9pm (except Saturday). When things get busy it has been known to stay open until 4am. They also serve food, including a special menu of 'Nabataean food' served in clay bowls – reserve this a half-day in advance. It's next to the entrance to the Petra Guest House, behind the visitor centre.

Wranglers Pub (☎ 2156723; ☯ 2pm-midnight; beer JD3-5) The Petra Palace Hotel offers this trendy place although it's a bit soulless when things are quiet. Prices are similar to those at the Cave Bar.

Al-Maqa'ad Bar (☎ 2157111; beer from JD2.500, plus 26% tax & service) The Mövenpick hotel bar has a lovely Moroccan-style interior with carved wooden grills and a central chandelier that has to be seen to be believed. The ice-cream specials are fantastic.

Shopping

There are plenty of souvenir shops lining the road down to the entry gate into Petra,

and plenty of blankets piled with jewellery, carvings, coins and pretty rocks, set up by local Bedouins around Petra itself. Throughout Wadi Musa you'll see craftsmen patiently pouring coloured sand into glass bottles; you can even get them to write your name if you give them time. The top-end hotels also have gift shops selling pricey but good-quality handicrafts.

Made in Jordan (☎ 2155700; www.madeinjordan .com, gallery@petramoon.com) The best quality crafts and gifts in Jordan come from various Non-govermental Organisation (NGO) projects, most of which are represented in this excellent shop. Products include olive oil, soap, paper, ceramics, table runners, nature products from Wild Jordan (p70), jewellery from Wadi Musa, baby blankets and embroidery from Safi, camel hair shawls, bags from Aqaba, plus individual pieces from Jordanian women artists and even a Jordanian Monopoly set. The fixed prices are high, as is the quality; credit cards are accepted.

The **Wadi Musa Ladies Society** (☯ 6am-9pm) and the **Society for the Development and Rehabilitation of Rural Women** (☯ 6am-9pm) both have shops at the visitor centre that are worth a visit for a good range of souvenirs, books and crafts.

Sand Castle Shop (☎ 2157326; ☯ until 8pm) You will have to wade past the furry toy camels and Petra baseball caps to get to the kilims and other good stuff out back.

Rum Studio and Labs (☎ 2157467; ☯ 8.30am-10pm) This is the best place for film in Wadi Musa, in front of the Silk Rd Hotel on the main road. A roll of 36 100ASA Kodak film costs JD3; slides cost JD7. To develop and print 36 shots costs from JD4.360 to JD6, depending on the size.

Getting There & Away

Public transport to and from Wadi Musa is less frequent than you'd expect, given that it's a large village and the number-one tourist attraction in Jordan.

CAR

Hertz Rent-a-Car (☎ 2156981) hire cars cost from JD30 per day. A 4WD Pajero costs around JD65 per day.

Petra and Wadi Musa are well signposted all along the King's and Desert highways. The road from Petra to Little Petra has now been extended to rejoin the Wadi Musa to

PETRA

Shobak road and is one of the more scenic alternatives for heading this way. A new road winds down into Wadi Araba for direct access to the Dead Sea Highway. The road to Tayyibeh is also particularly scenic.

MINIBUS

Minibuses generally leave from the bus station in central Wadi Musa. Most minibuses won't leave unless they're at least half full, so be prepared for a wait. There are far fewer services on Fridays.

At least three minibuses travel every day between Amman (Wahadat station) and Wadi Musa (JD3, three hours) along the Desert Highway. These buses leave Amman and Wadi Musa when full every hour or two between 6am and noon.

Minibuses leave Wadi Musa for Ma'an (JD1, 45 minutes) fairly frequently throughout the day (more often in the morning), stopping briefly at the university, about 10km from Ma'an. From Ma'an there are connections to Amman, Aqaba and (indirectly) Wadi Rum. Minibuses also leave Wadi Musa for Aqaba (JD3, two hours), via Tayyibeh, at about 6.30am, 8am and 4pm – ask around the day before to confirm.

For Wadi Rum (JD3, 1½ hours), there is a daily minibus sometime after 6am. It's a good idea to reserve a seat the day before – your hotel should be able to ring the driver. Be wary of anyone who tries to charge you JD1 for 'luggage', offer to buy you overpriced water and hook you onto a substandard tour. Alternatively take the minibus to Aqaba, get off at the Ar-Rashidiyyah junction and catch another minibus or hitch to Rum.

To Karak, a minibus sometimes leaves at around 8am, but demand is low so it doesn't leave every day. Alternatively, travel via Ma'an.

TAXI

Private (yellow) taxis will travel anywhere around Wadi Musa for a price, but negotiation can be an unrewarding process. A few Pajero 4WD taxis are available for much the same cost. One-way trips cost JD30 to Wadi Rum (one hour) or Aqaba (1½ hour); or JD40 to Karak (1½ hours). If you want to travel to Madaba or Amman via the King's Highway, with stops at Karak and possibly Dana or the Dead Sea, expect to be asked for JD80, though JD60 is more reasonable.

Getting Around

The standard, non-negotiable fare anywhere around the central Wadi Musa area is JD1; a little more if you go as far as 'Ain Musa. There are usually plenty of private (yellow) unmetered taxis travelling up and down the main road, especially in the late afternoon, looking for weary travellers.

AL-WU'IRA (CRUSADER CASTLE) وعره

Built by the Crusaders in AD 1116, **Al-Wu'ira** (admission free; ☾ daylight hr) was overrun by Muslim forces only 73 years later. A fantastic bridge (previously a drawbridge) leads over the gorge to a gatehouse and the limited ruins.

Look for the unsigned turn-off, about 1.5km north of the Mövenpick Hotel, and on the left (west) side of the road leading to Siq al-Barid (Little Petra).

SIQ AL-BARID (LITTLE PETRA)
سيق البيضاء (البتراء الصغيرة)

Siq al-Barid (Cold Canyon) is colloquially known as **Little Petra** (admission free; ☾ daylight hr) and, although nowhere near as dramatic or extensive, it's worth a visit. It was thought to have served as an agricultural centre, trading suburb and resupply post for camel caravans visiting Petra. The surrounding area is picturesque and fun to explore.

From the car park, an obvious path leads to the 400m-long **siq**, which opens out into larger areas. The first open area has a **temple**, which archaeologists know little about. Four **triclinia** – one on the left and three on the right – are in the second open area, and were probably once used as dining rooms to feed hungry merchants and travellers. About 50m further along the *siq* is the **Painted House**, another small dining room, which is reached by some exterior steps. The faded, but still vivid, frescoes of vines, flowers and birds on the underside of the interior arch are a rare example of Nabataean painting, though the walls have been badly blackened by Bedouin camp fires. Cut into the rock opposite the room is a large **cistern**; there are also worn water channels cut into the rock at various points along the *siq*.

At the end of Siq al-Barid are some steps. If you climb to the top, there are some great views and plenty of picnicking opportunities. If you have extra time and interest you could explore the Nabataean quarries and cisterns of Umm Qusa, located just before the entrance to Siq al-Barid.

If you come prepared, it's possible to **hike** from Siq al-Barid to the Monastery (Al-Deir) inside Petra itself, or to Petra centre via Wadi Mu'aisireh al-Gharbiya. You'll need a guide for this (ask at the car park by the entry to Siq al-Barid) as route-finding is tricky. You must also have a valid ticket to Petra (you can't get one at Siq al-Barid).

A 10-minute walk from Little Petra is the **Ammarin Camp** (☎ 079 5667771, 2131229; www .bedouincamp.net; per person in tent JD8) in the next-door Siq al-Amti. Accommodation is just a mattress in a Bedouin tent but there is a shower and toilet block. Breakfast is included in the price but dinner is rather expensive. A small ethnographic museum on site spotlights the local Bedouin tribe, the Ammarin. The camp offers guided hikes in the surrounding hills.

Getting There & Away

You may find a tour to Little Petra organised by one of the hotels in Wadi Musa. If not, a private taxi should cost about JD8 one way or JD15 return, including an hour's waiting time.

If you're driving, take the road north of the Mövenpick Hotel and follow the signs to 'Beda' or 'Al-Beidha'. From the fork, take the left road from where it's just under a further 1km to the car park.

It's a fairly pleasant 8km walk following the road. The route passes the village of Umm Sayhoun, the 'Elephant Rock' formation and then 'Ain Dibdibah, which once supplied Petra with much of its water. You can make a short cut across fields to the left about 1km before the junction to Al-Beidha.

Hitching is possible, especially on Friday when local families head out in droves for a picnic.

AL-BEIDHA   البيدا

The Neolithic ruins of **Al-Beidha** (admission free; ☾ daylight hr) date back some 9000 years and, along with Jericho, constitutes one of the oldest archaeological sites in the Middle East. The remains of around 65 round (and later rectangular) structures are especially significant because they pinpoint the physical transition from hunter-gatherer to settled herder-agriculturalist. The settlement was abandoned around 6000 BC, which is why it is still intact (latter civilisations never built upon it), and so the ruins therefore require some imagination. Please follow the marked trails as the site is fragile.

To get there, follow the trail starting to the left (south) of the entrance to Little Petra for about 15 minutes.

Southern Desert & Aqaba
الصحراء الجنوبية
& العقبة

No man can live this life and emerge unchanged. He will carry, however faint, the imprint of the desert, the bind which marks the nomad; and he will have within him the yearning to return, weak or insistent according to his nature. For this cruel land can cast a spell which no temperate clime can match.

TE Lawrence, Seven Pillars of Wisdom

Jordan's far south belongs to the desert and the Bedouin. At the meeting point of the Rift Valley, the Negev Desert, the Sinai peninsula and the Hejaz region of Arabia, it has been criss-crossed for centuries by trade and pilgrimage routes.

Wadi Rum is where the desert sparkles, opening up an enchanting landscape of red sands and towering sandstone peaks. Lawrence of Arabia fell in love with the place, describing its scenery as 'vast, echoing and God-like'. Today this giant sandpit is an adventure-sports playground, offering excellent hiking, camel riding and rock climbing.

This is the best place to get to know the Bedouin; either chatting over a desert campfire, scrambling up to sandstone bluffs with a Bedouin guide or stopping at a goat-hair tent with your driver for a cup of sweet tea.

Aqaba is the other main stop for visitors, primarily for its excellent diving and snorkelling, though it's gaining ground quickly as a regional winter resort. Aqaba is the gateway to Egypt, via ferry across the Gulf of Aqaba. Israel & the Palestinian Territories is a 10-minute drive away.

HIGHLIGHTS

- Hike, scramble and climb all day in the spectacular desert area of **Wadi Rum** (opposite), then camp out under a stunning blanket of stars

- Make the three-day **Camel Trek** (p210) from Wadi Rum to Aqaba, or save your inner thighs and limit it to a half-day excursion around Rum

- Take a break and enjoy the balmy winter climate, great seafood and idyllic setting of **Aqaba** (p216), Jordan's one and only 'resort'

- It's not the Red Sea but it's damn close, so do some **Diving & Snorkelling** (p227) around the remarkable marine life and coral of the Gulf of Aqaba

- Take a break from your holiday on the private **beaches** (p220) of the Royal Jordan Diving Club or Barracuda Beach

★ Aqaba

★ Wadi Rum Protected Area

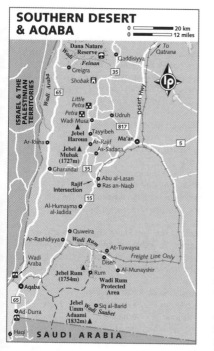

SOUTHERN DESERT & AQABA

WADI RUM

وادي رم

☎ 03

Offering some of the most extraordinary desert scenery you'll ever see, **Wadi Rum** (admission per person JD2, children under 12 free, per vehicle JD5) is a definite highlight of any visit to Jordan. This area, made famous abroad by the exploits of TE Lawrence ('Lawrence of Arabia') in the early 20th century, has lost none of its allure and forbidding majesty. Its myriad moods and dramatic colours, dictated by the changing angle of the sun, best reward an overnight trip so, unless you're really pushed for time, linger here for a day or two, slowing down to the timeless rhythm of desert life, enjoying the galaxy of stars overhead at night and the spectacular sunrises and sunsets. Like most deserts, Wadi Rum is as much to be experienced as it is to be seen.

The jebels of Wadi Rum completely dominate the small village of Rum, which has a few concrete houses, a school, some shops and the 'Beau Geste'-style fort, headquarters of the much-photographed Desert Patrol Corps.

The region known as Wadi Rum is actually a series of valleys about 2km wide stretching north to south for about 130km. Among the valleys is a desert landscape of sand and rocks, punctuated by towering jebels that have eroded into a soft sandstone over a period of up to 50 million years. The valley floors are about 900m above sea level. The epic Jebel Rum (1754m) dominates the central valley and for a long time was considered the highest peak in Jordan; that accolade now goes to Jebel Umm Adaami (1832m), to the south on the Saudi border.

Although conveniently and collectively known as 'Bedouin', the major tribe of Wadi Rum is the Huweitat, who claim to be descendants of the Prophet Mohammed. Villagers and nomads throughout the Wadi Rum area number about 5000. The local Bedouin are proud but very hospitable, particularly once you get out into the desert, away from the competitive environment of the visitor centre and Rum village.

The best months to visit are early spring (March and April) and late autumn (October to November). In winter (December to February) it can rain, and snow on the mountains is not uncommon. In the hot season (May to September) daytime temperatures often soar past 40°C. Throughout the year (including summer), however, night-time temperatures can fall to 0°C, so come prepared if you're camping or watching the sunset.

Wadi Rum was for a while under the management of the Royal Society for the Conservation of Nature (RSCN), who established the Wadi Rum Protected Area in 1988. The area is now controlled by Aqaba Special Economic Zone Authority (ASEZA) but the idea is the same – to promote tourism in balance with the imperative to protect fragile ecosystems. As a result, admission to Wadi Rum is strictly controlled and all vehicles, camels and guides within Wadi Rum must be arranged either through, or with the approval of, the visitor centre.

There is talk of significantly raising the admission fee to around JD7 or JD8 in the future, though no decisions had been made on this at the time of going to print.

History

Wadi Rum was first possibly mentioned in Ptolemy's *Geography* as 'Aramaua', and,

LAWRENCE OF ARABIA

Born in 1888 into a wealthy English family, Thomas Edward Lawrence ('TE' to his friends) studied archaeology, which led him to explore several Crusader castles in Syria, Lebanon and Jordan in 1909 for his thesis. He returned to the Syrian-Turkish border for excavations between 1910 and 1914. With the outbreak of WWI, Lawrence became an intelligence agent in Cairo. Supporting the cause of the Arab Revolt and manifesting his own deep hostility towards French politics in Syria, Colonel Lawrence favoured the creation of a Sunni and Arab state.

But it was the desert revolt of 1917 that stirred the Western imagination and etched his name into legend. At the side of Emir Faisal and with the support of General Allenby, Lawrence and the Arab warriors conquered Aqaba. He entered Damascus in triumph, marking the final defeat of the Ottoman Turks. Syria then became a joint Arab-French state, although not the independent one many Arabs had fought for (and been promised).

He has been widely credited in the West as the reason for this important victory over the Turks, often to the chagrin of Arabs, whose soldiers numbered around 100,000, of whom 10,000 were killed. By all accounts Lawrence, never the most humble of men, did little to alter the perception that he was the figure most responsible for victory. In Lawrence's own words; 'On the whole I prefer lies to truth, particularly when they concern me'.

Returning to England, Lawrence defended his ideas at the Paris Peace Conference and served as the special interpreter of the Hashemites. It was at this time that he started his principal work, *Seven Pillars of Wisdom,* which recounts his adventures. He apparently wrote it twice, because he left the first manuscript in a train station in London! *Seven Pillars of Wisdom* is still suggested reading for British military personnel serving in Iraq.

In 1921, Lawrence was sent to Trans-Jordan to help Emir Abdullah formulate the foundations of the new state. He later left this position and enrolled in 1922 with the Royal Air Force (RAF), under an assumed name, first as a pilot, and then as a simple mechanic.

In 1927 he left on a mission to India but returned home because of rumours that he had encouraged an uprising of Afghan tribes. He left the RAF in February 1935 and died three months later after a motorcycle accident.

For online information on Lawrence check out www.lawrenceofarabia.com, www.telsociety .org and www.telstudies.org.

according to some Islamic scholars, is mentioned in the Quran as 'Ad'. Excavations have confirmed that the area was inhabited between 800 and 600 BC, when it was known as Iram, and was popular with travellers because of the abundance of springs and wild game. By about the 4th century BC Wadi Rum was settled by the Nabataeans, who built temples and left behind inscriptions on the rocks – many of which can still be seen.

The region is probably more famous because the indefatigable TE Lawrence (see above) stayed here in 1917. The serendipitous discovery of a Nabataean temple (behind the Rest House) in 1933 returned the spotlight to the desert but the temple was not completely excavated until 1997, by a team of French archaeologists.

Wildlife

Despite its barren appearance, Wadi Rum is home to a complex ecological system.

Dotted among the desert are small plants that are used by the Bedouin for medicinal purposes, and during the infrequent rains parts of the desert can turn into a colourful sea of purple and blue flowers.

With the extreme heat and lack of water, not many species of animal exist, and sensibly most only venture out at night. If you're really lucky, you may see jackals, wolves, wild goats, the strictly nocturnal Arabian sand cats, and the highly endangered Arabian oryx, a small group of which were released into Wadi Rum in 2002 (see p132). A few birds of prey, such as vultures and eagles, can also be found. And watch out for scorpions, snakes and the scary (but largely harmless) camel spiders.

Orientation

Whether you come by minibus or taxi you'll first arrive at the Wadi Rum visitor centre (around 7km before Rum village), where you'll pay the reserve entry fee. Most people then arrange a 4WD trip at the visitor centre and there are normally dozens of 4WDs waiting for customers. If you want to do your own hiking/climbing etc it is possible to continue to Rum village by jumping quickly back on the bus or hitching the remaining 7km to the village.

BOOKS & MAPS

If you plan to do any short hikes and scrambles, bring a detailed guidebook and map; if you intend to do some serious hiking and rock climbing, it's vital to organise a guide in advance.

The British climber Tony Howard has spent a lot of time exploring Wadi Rum, and has co-written (with Di Taylor) the excellent and detailed *Treks & Climbs in Wadi Rum.* The condensed, pocket-sized and more affordable (JD3 to JD5) version of this is called *Walks & Scrambles in Rum.* Treks and climbs around Wadi Rum are also mentioned in Howard and Taylor's *Walking in Jordan.* Get these books before arriving in Wadi Rum, though if you are lucky you might find something at the Peace Bazar Bookshop a couple of hundred metres south of the Rest House in Rum village.

The colourful Wadi Rum brochure has a map showing the major sites – get one free at the visitor centre. The 1997 *Map of Rum* is contoured and detailed for a small section of northern Wadi Rum (ie around Rum village). The most detailed and informative map is *Wadi Rum Tourist Plan,* published by International Traditional Services Corp, but it's not widely available in Jordan.

Information

Essential items to bring along include a hat (or Bedouin headgear), sunscreen, sturdy footwear and plenty of water. If you're camping anywhere, including the Rest House, bring a torch (flashlight), a book to read and a padlock (many tents are lockable).

The Bedouin are a conservative people, so please dress appropriately. Loose shorts and tops for men and women are OK around the Rest House, but baggy trousers/skirts and modest shirts/blouses will, besides preventing serious sunburn, earn you more respect from the Bedouin, especially out in the desert.

EMERGENCY

Police station (☎ 2017050) Located in the old police fort 400m south of the Rest House. Will not receive complaints (go to the tourist police), but they will come looking for you if you get lost.

Tourist police (☎ 2018215) At the visitor centre.

TOURIST INFORMATION

Visitor Centre (☎ /fax 2090600; rum@nets.com.jo) Inconveniently situated at the entry to the protected area, about 7km north of Rum village.

WADI RUM PROTECTED AREA

In keeping with their efforts to preserve the fragile local environment, the authorities require those making excursions into Wadi Rum to follow a few simple rules, regardless of whether you're in a 4WD, astride a camel or hiking.

- Hunting is prohibited, as is the collection of any animals, flowers, herbs, rocks, fossils or archaeological artefacts
- No camping or climbing is allowed except in official sites set up for this purpose
- Do not damage any trees or graffiti any rocks
- Do not collect firewood or make fires; apart from damaging trees and shrubs, it may also damage the habitat for local animals
- No littering
- Respect the customs and lifestyle of local people and always ask before you take photos

While many of these rules may seem obvious, the scourge of graffiti and cigarette butts (especially at the sunset sites), as well as damage to rock art and safety bolts left on the jebels by climbers, remain as testament to the short-sightedness of some tourists. As the RSCN motto says: 'Leave nothing but footprints, take nothing but memories'.

SOUTHERN DESERT & AQABA

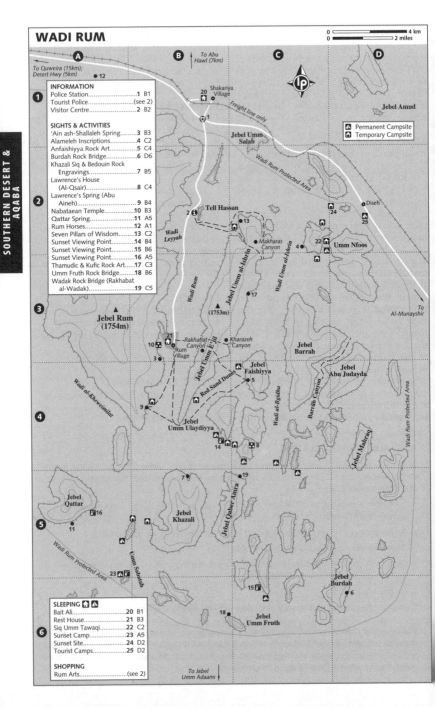

WADI RUM

0 ____ 4 km
0 ____ 2 miles

To Abu Hawl (7km)

To Quweira (15km); Desert Hwy (5km)

INFORMATION
Police Station.........................1 B1
Tourist Police.....................(see 2)
Visitor Centre......................2 B2

SIGHTS & ACTIVITIES
'Ain ash-Shallaleh Spring......3 B3
Alameleh Inscriptions..............4 C2
Anfaishiyya Rock Art..............5 C4
Burdah Rock Bridge................6 D6
Khazali Siq & Bedouin Rock
  Engravings.........................7 B5
Lawrence's House
  (Al-Qsair)...........................8 C4
Lawrence's Spring (Abu
  Aineh)...............................9 B4
Nabataean Temple................10 B3
Qattar Spring......................11 A5
Rum Horses.........................12 A1
Seven Pillars of Wisdom.......13 C2
Sunset Viewing Point...........14 B4
Sunset Viewing Point...........15 B6
Sunset Viewing Point...........16 A5
Thamudic & Kufic Rock Art...17 C3
Umm Fruth Rock Bridge.......18 B6
Wadak Rock Bridge (Rakhabat
  al-Wadak)........................19 C5

SLEEPING
Bait Ali.............................20 B1
Rest House........................21 B3
Siq Umm Tawaqi.................22 C2
Sunset Camp......................23 A5
Sunset Site.......................24 D2
Tourist Camps....................25 D2

SHOPPING
Rum Arts.........................(see 2)

Permanent Campsite
Temporary Campsite

Shakariya Village

Jebel Amud

Jebel Umm Salab

Wadi Rum Protected Area

Diseh

Tell Hassan

Makharas Canyon

Umm Nfoos

Wadi Leyyah

Wadi Rum

Jebel Umm al-Ishrin

Wadi Umm al-Ishrin

To Al-Munayshir

Jebel Rum (1754m)

(1753m)

Rakhabat Canyon

Kharazeh Canyon

Rum Village

Jebel Umm Ejil

Jebel Barrah

Jebel Abu Judayda

Wadi al-Khweimilat

Jebel Faishiyya

Red Sand Dune

Wadi al-Bgaiha

Barrah Canyon

Wadi Rum Protected Area

Jebel Umm Ulaydiyya

Jebel Mahraq

Jebel Qattar

Jebel Qaber Amra

Jebel Khazali

Wadi Rum Protected Area

Umm Sahanah

Jebel Burdah

Jebel Umm Fruth

To Jebel Umm Adaami

TRAVEL AGENCIES & GUIDES

If you arrive in Wadi Rum as an independent traveller without having pre-arranged a guide, the taxi rank principle applies – you take the next guide/driver on the roster. Most of the drivers do a good job but they are primarily drivers not guides and they often don't speak much English or offer any information or guiding during the trip.

If you want a specific guide, contact the guide at least 48 hours in advance and carry a copy of your email correspondence in case the visitor centre asks for it. For longer excursions some planning is required on the part of the guide (eg buying provisions, arranging camels). April, September and October are the busiest seasons for guides.

Guides who have been recommended by readers:

Al-Hillawi Desert Services (☎ /fax 2018867, 079 5940117) Agency with several desert camps, run by the management of the Rest House.

Aouda Abdillah (☎ 2017559; www.aodeh.de/index .htm)

Attallah Sweilhin (☎ 2033508, 079 5802108; attallah_hr@hotmail.com) Also arranges horse trekking with Rum Horses.

Attayak Ali (☎ /fax 2032651, 079 5689373) One of the best climbing and adventure guides. Together with Attayak Aouda, he runs Wadi Rum Mountain Guides (www .bedouinroads.com), a top-notch adventure travel agency.

Attayak Aouda (☎ /fax 2035844, 079 5834736) Recommended as one of the best, if not the best, climbing guide in Rum.

Difallah Ateeg Zelabyeh (☎ /fax 2019135, 077 7309239; difallahz@yahoo.com) Runs a good desert camp.

Hussein Suleiman (☎ /fax 2019645, 079 5583763)

Mohammed Sabah Al-Zalabeh (☎ /fax 2032961, 077 7314688; www.mohammedwadirum.8m.com) Runs the recommended Sunset Camp (see p213).

M'Salim Sabbagh (☎ 079 5660362; moslam_rum@ yahoo.com)

Mzied Atieg (☎ 077 7304501; mzied_co@yahoo.com) Runs a good camp near the Anfaishiyya inscriptions.

Sabagh Eid (☎ /fax 2016238) Official climbing guide.

Salem and Selim Lafi (☎ 079 5127148, 079 5298046; www.rumtrekking.com)

Zedane Al-Zalabieh (☎ /fax 2032607, 079 5506417; zedn_a@yahoo.com)

Some travellers visit Wadi Rum as part of an organised excursion from Aqaba or Petra (generally from JD45 per person for transport, guide and food, although the per person rate drops significantly for more than two

---

DESERT PATROL

The camel-mounted Desert Patrol was set up to keep dissident tribes in order and to patrol the border. Today they've exchanged their camels for blue armoured patrol vehicles and concentrate on smugglers along the Saudi border, though they occasionally rescue a lost tourist.

The men of the Desert Patrol can be quite a sight in their traditional full-length khaki robes, dagger at the waist, pistol and rifle slung over the shoulder – but mostly they now wear just ordinary khaki uniforms. They still revel in their photogenic nature and are happy to pose for those who sit with them and pass the time with a tea.

---

people) but beware, these trips are often a disappointment. Most of the cheaper tours overnight at Diseh instead of Wadi Rum and some never even enter the main protected area. Some agencies have been known to take short cuts on food so you should be clear on exactly what you are getting before handing over your cash. In general it's best to organise something directly and in advance with the Bedouin operators at Wadi Rum.

Activities
EXCURSIONS

For details on reaching many of the sites described here, see the boxed texts on 4WDs (p209) and camel trips (p210). Note that the regulated prices relate only to transportation, and do not include food, tents and blankets. These are a matter for negotiation with your guide but are generally around JD25 per person per day in a fixed camp, with meals; for a mobile camp you'll need to pay more for an extra vehicle to transport items to your camp site each day. If you have your own sleeping bag and tent, and have arranged your own provisions in advance, all you should have to pay is the cost of your four-wheeled or four-legged vehicle.

Short Excursions

Most of the attractions around Wadi Rum can be reached in a 4WD vehicle, on a camel or by hiking. Anyone with less money, time and energy can see a few minor sights on foot in the vicinity of the Government Rest House.

On a small hill located about 400m behind (southwest of) the Rest House (follow the telephone poles) are the limited ruins of a 2000-year old **Nabataean temple**, dedicated to the deity Allat. An interesting explanation (in English and French) of the temple and its excavation is on a wall inside the Rest House. Near the temple are some **inscriptions** by hunters and nomads dating back to the 2nd century BC.

Back in Rum village a new complex near the police station is rumoured to be a new museum of some kind.

About 3km south of the Rest House is **Lawrence's Spring** (Abu Aineh), named after TE Lawrence, who wrote about it in *Seven Pillars of Wisdom*. It's fairly unimpressive compared to the other sights of Wadi Rum. Head south from the Rest House and follow the eastern side of Jebel Rum for 3km. From the obvious water tank at ground level, a 20-minute scramble up some rocks (follow the line of green shrubs) brings you to a small pleasant pool with fine **views** to Jebel Khazali and beyond.

Long Excursions

Most of the major attractions, most dramatic landscapes and better rock formations are further away from Rum village.

The following major sites are the ones featured in the jeep itineraries offered at the visitor centre. The walking, driving or riding distance from the Rest House in Rum village is included in brackets.

Barrah Canyon (14km) This 5km-long valley is worth exploring on foot or on camel.

Burdah Rock Bridge (19km) This is a narrow piece of rock precariously perched about 80m above surrounding rock. It can be reached (up the western side) without gear by anyone in decent shape. See Scrambling p211.

Jebel Faishiyya/Anfaishiyya Rock Art (10km) Some of the best Nabataean and Thamudic inscriptions in Wadi Rum.

Jebel Khazali (7km) The narrow *siq* and rock inscriptions here can be explored on foot for about 150m; beyond this you need ropes and a guide.

Lawrence's House (Al-Qsair) (9km) This is little more than a heap of bricks, apparently once part of a house occupied by Lawrence, and built on the foundations of a Nabataean temple. The remote location and supreme views of the red sands are the main attraction.

Red Sand Dunes (6km) While there are sand dunes in several places around Wadi Rum, this section to which most groups are taken has a small section of beautiful red sand up the slope of Jebel Umm Ulaydiyya.

Seven Pillars of Wisdom (8km) Named after Lawrence's book, this large rock formation is easy to see from the visitor centre.

Sunset & Sunrise (11km) Dusk and dawn are the magical (and cooler) times to be in the desert. The best vantage points differ according to the time of year; the most common is Umm Sabatah. Jeep drivers can take you there and either wait or pick you up later (they are reliable about such things); or arrange a sunset tour which includes a traditional Bedouin dinner for a negotiable price.

Umm Fruth Rock Bridge (13km) This is another small and remote rock bridge that can easily be climbed without gear or a guide. It can be a busy spot at lunchtime.

Wadak Rock Bridge (Rakahbt al-Wadak) (9km) This rock formation, the 'Little Rock Bridge', is easier to climb and more accessible than Burdah Rock Bridge, but is not as impressive. The views across the valley are superb.

Beyond Wadi Rum

Rum's fantastic scenery continues well beyond the confines of the protected area. Wadi Rum Mountain Guides in particular offers trips to beautiful areas in the south of Rum, including Jebel Khasch, Wadi Noghra, Wadi Saabet and 'No-Man's Land', near the Saudi border. This area is best suited to a multi-day camping trip. See their website www.bedouinroads.com for trip ideas.

One great 4WD/hiking combo is to hike up **Jebel Umm Adaami** (1832m), Jordan's highest peak, on the rarely visited southern border with Saudi Arabia. The hour-long uphill hike is marked by cairns and offers fabulous views of Wadi Rum to the north and Saudi Arabia to the south. Find a driver who knows the 45-minute jeep route south to Wadi Saabet, where the hike starts. On the way back stop off at the rock carvings of nearby Siq al-Barid, a lovely spot for a picnic.

Trips out to the remote south are understandably more expensive than to central Wadi Rum.

4WD TRIPS

Rates for 4WD excursions are fixed and listed in the boxed text (opposite). Arranging a trip at the visitor centre is generally hassle free. The tricky thing is finding other travellers who want to do the same trip in order to share costs. The easiest thing is to put together a group in Wadi Musa before taking the bus together to Wadi Rum.

You can opt to visit any combination of sights, especially if you pay for the vehicle for the day. Make sure you discuss your

4WD EXCURSIONS IN WADI RUM

The following prices are per jeep, not per person.

Wadi Rum operators

sites	km	time (hr)	price (JD) per vehicle
Lawrence's Spring	14	1	15
Jebel Khazali (via Lawrence's Spring)	20	2	20
Sunset sites (via Lawrence's Spring & Jebel Khazali)	35	2½	35
Sand dunes (via Lawrence's Spring & Jebel Khazali)	40	3	40
Umm Fruth Rock Bridge (via Lawrence's Spring & Jebel Khazali, Lawrence's House, Anfaishiyya inscriptions and sand dunes)	50	4	40
Burdah Rock Bridge (via Lawrence's Spring, Jebel Khazali, Umm Fruth Rock Bridge, Lawrence's House, Anfaishiyya inscriptions, sand dunes and sunset spot)	60	5	45
Barrah Siq (via Lawrence's Spring, Jebel Khazali, Umm Fruth Rock Bridge and sunset spot)	65	8	50
Day hire	-	8	50
Day vehicle for luggage	-	-	35

Diseh operators

sites	km	time (hr)	price (JD) per vehicle
Alameleh inscriptions	15	1	15
Siq Umm Tawaqi (via al-Hsani Sand dune, Alameleh inscriptions, Lawrence Carving)	18	2	20
Sunset sites (via al-Hsani sand dune, Alameleh inscriptions, Siq Umm Tawaqi)	20	2½	25
Burrah Canyon (Alameleh inscriptions, Umm Ishrin, Lawrence's House, Siq Umm Tawaqi)	40	3	30
Burdah Rock Bridge (via al-Hsani sand dune, Alameleh inscriptions, Umm al-Ishrin, Lawrence's House, Umm Fruth Bridge, Siq Umm Tawaqi)	60	8	50
Day hire	-	8	50

itinerary with the driver and at the visitor centre before you set out, and if you have any complaints of this kind, make sure you report them to the visitor centre when you return to Rum. Most jeeps seat six people and some of the older ones are pick-ups with bench seats in the back (these actually offer better views than the closed-in cabs).

You may be approached by the odd freelance guide in Rum village. Prices may be cheaper (and very negotiable) but there are fewer guarantees to the quality of the trip.

It's important to realise that the maximum times listed are exaggerated and your journey time may be significantly less. On the negative side of things, refunds for excursions shorter than you expected are not possible. On the positive side, Wadi Rum is best enjoyed if you slow down to the pace of the desert and don't race around in a mad rush. Take your time at each site as you'll still have time to complete the itinerary if you linger for a while to admire the view and soak up the silence.

You can easily add on an overnight stay at a Bedouin camp. Your driver will simply drop you off in the afternoon and pick you up the next morning.

CAMELS

If you have the time, travelling around Wadi Rum by camel is highly recommended. Apart from being ecologically sound, it will enable you to experience Wadi Rum as the Bedouin have for centuries and to really appreciate the silent gravitas of the desert. That said, a ride of more than about four hours will leave you sore in places you never even knew existed.

The official rates per person per camel are listed in the boxed text (below). Note that if you take a camel overnight, you will need to negotiate an additional price for food, tents and so on (see p207). You'll enjoy your ride much more if you ride yourself rather than being led. This will cost a bit more as you need to pay for your guide's camel but it's well worth the extra cost.

It is also possible to arrange longer camel excursions from Wadi Rum to Aqaba (three to six nights depending on the route) via the misnamed Lawrence's Rd (he actually took a different route via Wadi Itm); or to near Wadi Musa (for Petra; about five nights). In addition to the usual JD20 per camel per day rate, you'll need to factor in the necessary provisions, tents (if required) and returning the camels back to Rum.

Sunset Camp (p213) offers a two-day trip to Aqaba for around JD75 per person. The last part of the trip to Aqaba is generally done by taxi.

If you ask around you might be able to attend one of the camel races held weekly in winter, generally on a Friday.

HORSE TREKKING

An alternative and memorable mode of four-legged transport through Wadi Rum and surrounding areas is by horse. Expect to pay around JD50 per day. These trips are really for people who have some experience of riding. Among the agencies or guides who can organise such an expedition is **Rum Horses** (☎ 2033508, 077 7471960; www.desertguides.com), a professional French-run trekking, camel and horse trekking agency located on the south side of the road 6km before the turn to Wadi Rum.

HIKING

There are several great hiking routes in Rum, but avoid the extreme heat of summer (May to September). Remember that it's very easy to get disoriented amid the dozens of craggy peaks; temperatures can be extreme; natural water supplies are not common and sometimes undrinkable; passing traffic is rare; and maps are often inaccurate. Walking in sand is particularly exhausting.

The books by Tony Howard and Di Taylor (p205) list a number of hikes in the region.

CAMEL TREKS IN WADI RUM

sites	km	time (hr)	maximum price (JD)
Nabataean Temple	1	½	2
Alameleh Inscriptions	6	2	7
Lawrence's Spring	6	2	7
Sunset Sites (via Alameleh Inscriptions, Siq Umm Tawaqi)	8	1½	10
Jebel Khazali (via Lawrence's Spring)	14	4	16
Sunset sites (via Lawrence's Spring & Jebel Khazali)	22	overnight	40
Sand dunes (via Lawrence's Spring, Jebel Khazali & Lawrence's House)	25	5	20
Burdah Rock Bridge (via Lawrence's Spring, Jebel Khazali & Umm Fruth Rock Bridge)	40	overnight	40
Day Hire	unlimited	8	20
Day Camel for luggage	unlimited	8	20

One excellent do-it-yourself option is to hike southeast across the plain from the visitor centre towards the Seven Pillars of Wisdom and then head up **Makharas Canyon** (take the left-hand wadi when it branches). The wadi narrows after about an hour from the visitor centre and then pops out onto a patch of gorgeous red sand with fabulous views of Jebel Barrah and Umm Nfoos to the east. From here cut north over the sand dunes and plod your way around the northern tip of Jebel Umm Ishrin until you get back to the Seven Pillars of Wisdom. This hike takes about 2½ hours.

You could extend this hike by continuing across the valley on foot or camel to the Alameleh inscriptions, or head even further via the Siq Umm Tawaqi valley (and the carving of Lawrence's head) all the way to Diseh. You'd need a tent, food, plenty of water and a guide for this adventurous overnight option.

Another possible DIY hike is the circumambulation of the southern half of **Jebel Rum** via Wadi Leyyah (eight hours). One great 4WD/hiking combo is to hike up **Jebel Umm Adaami** (see p208).

SCRAMBLING

Scrambling lies somewhere between hiking and climbing. No technical skills are required but you may have to pull yourself up short rock faces at places on the following trips.

If you take a 4WD excursion to **Burdah Rock Bridge**, it's well worth making the hour-long scramble up to the bridge itself. There's nothing technical here but you'll need a guide to find the route up and will need a head for heights on one spot just before the bridge. There are fabulous views from the route up and from the top of the bridge. To continue beyond the bridge you'll need ropes and some climbing skills (one climber fell to his death here in 1999).

With a local guide or a copy of Tony Howard's *Walking in Jordan* you can navigate the labyrinthine *siqs* of **Rakhabat Canyon** for an exciting half-day trip through the heart of Jebel Umm al-Ishrin. The western mouth of the canyon is just by Rum village, but don't confuse it with the more obvious Makhman Canyon to the north. At the far (eastern) end of the canyon you can hike across the valley to the Anfaishiyya inscriptions, 600m south of the Bedouin camp, and then return on foot to Rum via the southern point of Jebel Umm al-Ishrin, with a possible detour to Lawrence's Spring en route. Alternatively, with a guide and some experience of abseiling you can head back west through the mountain ridge along the Kharazeh Canyon for a great loop route.

Another place that offers great scrambling is Jebel Khazali.

ROCK CLIMBING

Wadi Rum offers some challenging rock climbing, equal to if not better than anything in Europe. There's a vast array of climbs right up to French 8 grade.

While rock climbing is still a nascent industry in Wadi Rum and you'll need to bring your own gear, the situation has improved in recent years. There are at least six accredited climbing guides (contactable through the visitor centre), most of whom have been trained in the UK. When arranging a climbing trip, contact a guide at least a few days in advance so that camp equipment and transport can also be organised and prices negotiated. Expect to pay a minimum of JD110 for one to two days' climbing – it may sound expensive but it's not when compared to Europe, and few climbers leave disappointed.

One of the more popular climbs for amateur climbers is up Jebel Rum, because minimal gear is needed and it's close to the Rest House, although a guide is still required to find the best route and to help with the climb. Another popular climbing location is Jebel Barrah.

For information on routes see Tony Howard and Di Taylor's books (p205) and check out the website www.wadirum.net.

OTHER ACTIVITIES

The **Royal Aero Sports Club of Jordan** (Aqaba ☎ 03 2033763, Amman ☎ 06 4873261; www.fly.to/rpacj) offers hot air ballooning over Wadi Rum for around JD135 per person (minimum four people), as well as microlighting (JD90 per hour) and even sky diving (JD145). Contact **Bait Ali** (☎ 2022626, 079 5548133; www.desertexplorer .net) for details of this and other activities such as sand yachting. Bait Ali also rents out mountain bikes, along with maps of possible routes in the dry mud flats north of the camp.

SOUTHERN DESERT & AQABA

The annual **Jebel Ishrin Marathon** (www.whmf .org in German) takes place each September.

Sleeping

Thankfully there is still no hotel anywhere in Wadi Rum, and most of those who stay overnight understandably prefer to sleep out in the desert. Most visitors come as day trippers, so finding a place to enjoy the solitude is easier than it seems.

RUM VILLAGE

The frayed tents out the back of the **Rest House** (☎ 2018867; mattress in two-person tent per person JD3) are pretty much the only option in Rum, but they're only recommended if you arrive in Wadi Rum too late to head into the desert. Some of the mattresses are very thin. You can also pitch you own tent out the back (JD1). You do get access to the toilets and shower block. The site has little security so keep your valuables with you.

It may be possible to find a bed with a family in Rum village. The owner of the Sunset Camp plans to open a **guest house** (half board per person JD10) in Rum village behind his shop and near the telecom tower (500m south of the medical centre).

IN THE DESERT

Experiencing the legendary hospitality of the Bedouins and sleeping out under the stars are among the primary reasons for heading out into the desert. Camping is

---

THE BEDOUIN

All over the east and south of the country, you'll see the black goat-hair tents (*beit ash-sha'ar* – literally 'house of hair') of the Bedouin. The *bedu* (the name means 'nomadic') number several hundred thousand, but few can still be regarded as truly nomadic these days. Most have been crowded out from traditional lands by ever-expanding populations and ill-conceived government resettlement programs. Some have opted for city life, but most have, voluntarily or otherwise, settled down to cultivate crops.

A few retain the old ways – it is estimated that around 40 families still live a nomadic or semi- nomadic existence in the Wadi Rum area. They camp for a few months at a time in one spot and graze their herds of goats, sheep or camels. When the sparse fodder runs out, it's time to move on again, which also allows the land to regenerate.

The Bedouin family is a close-knit unit. The women do most of the domestic work, including fetching water, baking bread and weaving clothes. The men are traditionally providers and warriors, though the intertribal raids that for centuries were the staple of everyday Bedouin life are now reserved for the tales of valour told around the campfire at night.

Tents and houses are generally divided into a women's (haram – forbidden area, from where we get the word 'harem') and men's *(raba'a* or *el shigg)* section, which is where guests are treated to tea and discuss the day's events. Most of the family's belongings and stores are kept in the haram (strangers are not permitted inside).

Most of the Bedouin still living in the desert continue to wear the traditional Bedouin robe known as a *thop,* as well as a dagger – symbol of a man's dignity. The women tend to dress in more colourful garb and rarely veil their tattooed faces (the tattoos take the shape of simple auspicious symbols used to guard against the evil eye).

Although camels, once the Bedouin's best friend, are still in evidence, they are now often replaced by the Landrover or Toyota pick-up – Wilfred Thesiger would definitely not approve! Other concessions to modernity are radios (sometimes even TVs), plastic water containers and, occasionally, kerosene stoves.

The Bedouin are renowned for their hospitality and it is part of their creed that no traveller is turned away. This is part of a desert code of survival. Once taken in, a guest will be offered the best of the available food and plenty of tea and coffee. The thinking is simple: today you are passing through and they have something to offer; tomorrow they may be passing your camp and you may have food and drink – which you would offer them before having any yourself. Such a code of conduct made it possible for travellers to cross the desert with some chance of survival in such a hostile environment. How long this code can survive in an era of mass tourism remains one of the Bedouin's greatest challenges.

permitted only in certain designated areas (these are marked on the Wadi Rum map). If you want to sleep out in the open air, remember that it can get very cold at night. The permanent camp sites marked on the map are run by Bedouin companies and are set up year round; the temporary camp sites are only used occasionally, either by Bedouin groups or tourists.

Sunset Camp (☎ /fax 2032961, 077 7314688; www .mohammedwadirum.8m.com) is out in the desert near Umm Sabatah and has been recommended. A half-/full-day jeep excursion, accommodation and food at the camp and a lift back to Rum village the next morning costs from around JD20 to JD27 per person, dependent on the size of the group. The owner also runs various 4WD and camel treks. It's best to contact the camp in advance.

Most of the operators run their own camps scattered around the desert – see p207.

AROUND WADI RUM

Bait Ali (☎ 2022626, 079 5548133; www.desertexplorer .net; tent/chalet JD12/15) Located 15km from Rum, near Shakariya village, this well-run camp is situated north of the railway line, just west of the turn-off south to Rum village. Rates include breakfast; add JD7.500 for half board. The accommodation is basic but clean – what you are really paying for is the atmosphere and facilities, including an excellent restaurant (nightly barbecues), a bar and comfortable, cushion-filled Bedouin tents that add an exotic Arabian Nights feel. A new splash pool is planned. It's a good base for mountain biking (JD5 per hour, with free route map) and other desert adventures. The camp is 15km from the Desert Highway junction, 9km from the Wadi Rum visitor centre. You can pitch your own tent (JD3) or park a camper van (JD6) and use the clean shower block. Contact Susie.

Eating

Rest House (☎ /fax 2018867; mains JD3.600, breakfast JD3, dinner buffet JD6; ☯ 7am-9pm) A filling meal of kebabs or *shish tawooq*, French fries, and salads and dips is a good deal here, or there are sometimes buffets. Sipping a large Amstel beer (JD2.500) here while watching the sun's rays light up Jebel Umm al-Ishrin is the perfect way to finish off a tough day.

Restaurant Wadi Petra (breakfast JD1.500, dinner or lunch JD3; ☯ 6.30am-11pm) This is a similar choice, outside and visible from the Rest House.

Redwan Paradise (☯ 6am-1am) Along the main road of Rum Village, this cheap and local place serves tea, hummus and felafel for around JD1 and is a favourite place for the younger Bedouin guides to unwind.

Rum Gate Restaurant (☎ 2015995; Wadi Rum Visitor Centre; buffet JD7, sandwich JD3.500) Inconveniently situated in the visitor centre but a decent choice for groups or those with their own transport.

The small grocery stores along the main road through Rum village have mineral water and good supplies, though you'll have greater variety of imported goods if you stock up elsewhere en route to Wadi Rum. The area around Diseh has some of the cleanest aquifer water in Jordan so it's generally not a problem drinking spring water in Wadi Rum.

While out in the desert you may be lucky enough to try a Bedouin barbecue, cooked in an oven buried in the sand known as a *zerb* (see p56).

Shopping

Rum Arts (☎ 2032918; ☯ 8am-5pm) at the visitor centre is worth a look for silver items, embroidered bags and glass designs. Most items are made by local women to whom most of the profits are returned. It's possible to visit the workshop in Rum village if you are interested (closed Friday and Saturday) – ask for directions here or at the Rest House.

Getting There & Away

Public transport is limited because Rum village has a small population and many visitors come on tours organised by agencies or hotels from Wadi Musa or Aqaba. Public transport stops briefly at the visitor centre before continuing to Rum village.

There is talk of starting up a passenger train between Rum and Aqaba along the existing goods line, but don't hold your breath on this one.

HITCHING

Because of the limited public transport to and from Rum village, many travellers (including locals) are forced to hitch – a normal form of transport in this part of Jordan.

The well-signposted turn-off to Wadi Rum is along the Desert Highway at Ar-Rashidiyya, 5km south of Quweira. From Aqaba, take any minibus heading along the highway (but not a JETT bus which won't stop here) and get out at the turn-off (600 fils); from Wadi Musa or other towns to the north, anything headed towards Aqaba will pass the Rum turn-off. From the crossroads you should be able to find a minibus headed your way for JD1 per person; otherwise hitch and negotiate a fare for the 30km ride.

Alternatively, if you have prearranged your excursion through Wadi Rum with a guide, he may come out to pick you up.

You can normally hitch a lift in a pick-up between Rum village and the visitor centre for around JD1.

MINIBUS

At time of research, there was at least one minibus a day to Aqaba (JD1.500, one hour); 7am is the most reliable departure time and there may be a second departure at 8am. From Sunday to Thursday, you should also find one leaving around 12.30pm and possibly again at 3pm, ferrying teachers from the school back to Aqaba. To Wadi Musa (JD3, 1½ hours) there is a daily minibus at 8.30am. It's a good idea to check at the visitor centre or Rest House when you arrive in Wadi Rum to check current departure times.

If you want to head to Ma'an, Karak or Amman, the minibuses to either Aqaba or Wadi Musa can drop you off at the Ar-Rashidiyya crossroads with the Desert Highway (JD1, 20 minutes), where it is easy enough to hail onward transport.

TAXI

Occasionally taxis hang around the visitor centre (and very occasionally the Rest House) waiting for a fare back to wherever they came from – normally Aqaba, Wadi Musa or Ma'an. Count on about JD15 to Aqaba, and JD20 to Wadi Musa (Petra). A taxi from Rum village to the Ar-Rashidiyya crossroads with the Desert Highway costs around JD4.

QATRANA   القطرانه
☎ 03

One of the few towns along the Desert Highway is Qatrana, a couple of kilometres north of the turn-off to Karak, and a former stop on the pilgrim road between Damascus and Mecca. The only reason to stop here (if you have your own transport) is to have a quick look at **Qatrana castle** (admission free), built in 1531 by the Ottomans. It has been nicely restored, but nothing is explained.

The **Ba'albaki Tourist Complex** (d with private bathroom JD32), about 8km north of Qatrana on the highway has souvenir shops and a restaurant (buffets JD5). Breakfast is included in room rates.

MA'AN   معان
☎ 03

Ma'an has been a transport junction and trading centre for many centuries and is now one of the larger towns and administrative centres in southern Jordan. There's little of specific interest here, but the centre of town is pleasant enough and some travellers may have to stay overnight while waiting for transport to Wadi Rum, Wadi Musa (for Petra) and Aqaba.

Ma'an has a reputation of being a religiously conservative town and there has been rioting here in recent years (most recently in 2002), largely against price hikes and the US invasion of Iraq, but we found the mood and people in Ma'an nothing but welcoming and friendly. The town is particularly busy during the haj as it lies on the main pilgrimage route from both Jordan and Syria to Mecca in Saudi Arabia.

Orientation & Information

The main north-south thoroughfare is King Hussein St, centred somewhere around the mosque and the communication tower. Here you'll find restaurants and several banks with ATMs. To get here from the bus station head two blocks west then one block north (a five-minute walk) to the southern end of King Hussein St, where it meets Palestine St. The Kreashan Hotel is a further five minutes' walk north of here.

Horizon Internet Centre (☎ 2131700; King Hussein St; per hr JD1; ⏰ 9am-10pm), opposite the Housing Bank, has fast connections.

Sleeping & Eating

Kreashan Hotel (Krishan Hotel; ☎ 2132043; Al-Bayyarah St; dm JD2, r JD6, 4-/5-bed r JD10/12,) There's really no need to look further than this good central choice, with clean, simple and sunny rooms and clean shared bathrooms. The more expensive rooms are much better value than the faded rooms and dorms of the old wing. It's a small block east of the mosque off the northern end of King Hussein St.

Out on the western edge of town, north of the big roundabout, are two basic truck-stop hotels, the **Hotel Tabok** (☎ 2132452; r JD4) and slightly better **Shweikh Hotel** (☎ 2132427; r JD5), a little further north. Both are noisy and hot.

There is a number of excellent grill and chicken restaurants along King Hussein St, including the **Alroz-Al Bokhary** (King Hussein St; mains JD1-2). There's a tempting sweets shop diagonally across from the corner of King Hussein and Palestine Sts. There are good fruit shops nearby on Palestine St.

Getting There & Away
If you can't get a direct bus to where you want to go in Jordan, chances are that you can find a connection in Ma'an.

The station for buses, minibuses and service taxis is a five-minute walk southeast of the centre. Departures from Ma'an start to peter out around 2pm and stop completely around 5pm.

There are regular minibuses (JD1.150, three hours) and less frequent service taxis (JD3, three hours) to/from Amman's Wahadat bus station. To Aqaba, minibuses (JD1, 80 minutes) and service taxis (JD1.400) are also frequent. For Wadi Rum, take an Aqaba-bound minibus to the junction at Ar-Rashidiyya (500 fils) then take a minibus or hitch from here. For Petra, minibuses to Wadi Musa (500 fils, 45 minutes) leave fairly frequently when full and stop briefly at the university en route. You could also try a service taxi (JD1). To Karak, there are occasional service taxis (JD1.750, two hours) and three minibuses (JD1.500) a day, via Tafila (JD1).

A chartered taxi to Petra/Wadi Musa costs around JD5; to Karak or Aqaba, expect to pay JD15.

DISEH   الديسي
Diseh (or Disi) is northwest of Rum village, about 12km as the vulture flies but 22km by road. Inhabitants and devotees of Wadi Rum insist that Diseh is a very poor cousin. You cannot officially enter the Wadi Rum Protected Area direct from Diseh, but you could easily arrange your transport and guide in Diseh and then enter with them through the main Rum visitors centre. While the scenery is not as spectacular as it is at Wadi Rum, there are some basic camps in Diseh that have been given the thumbs up from budget travellers and you'll still find yourself sleeping in the silence of what is still a beautiful desert. This can be nice, provided you don't mind being in a camp of other tourists and don't need too many luxuries.

Sights
The paved road to Diseh from the turn-off to Rum offers a few accessible jebels and landscapes, which are easy to explore. Locals will happily (and for a price) drive you out into the desert area north of the railway line, which is dotted with Nabataean and Roman dams, artificial rock bridges, rock carvings and inscriptions. The landscape around **Jebel Amud** is the most interesting. A longer trip could take in the 2m-high rock carvings at **Abu Hawl** (Father of Terror), 7km north of the Bait Ali camp, and on to a rock bridge at Jebel Kharazeh. Count on around JD30 for a three-hour trip in a 4WD.

Sleeping & Eating
A number of camps outside Diseh have been recommended by readers. All the following offer beds in cramped individual tents or larger communal Bedouin tents. The first three are next to each other a couple of kilometres southeast of Diseh village.

Zawaideh Desert Camp (☎ 2034525, 079 5840664; zawaideh_camp@yahoo.com; half board per person JD14) Simple but atmospheric, and with hot showers it is decent value.

Captain's Camp (☎ 2016905, 079 5510432; captains@ jo.com.jo; half board per person JD25) A well-run mid-range camp with hot showers, a clean bathroom block and good buffets, but it can be swamped by large tour groups. Contact Rafique Suleiman.

Palm Camp (☎ 2033508, 079 5663410; half board per person JD15) A sociable place with a central campfire and lounging area, but the cramped accommodation makes it a step down from the other two camps.

Getting There & Away
You're unlikely to find a minibus or service taxi headed all the way to Diseh, so follow the instructions for getting to Wadi Rum and get out at the turn-off to Diseh (the police checkpoint 16km after leaving the Desert Highway). From there you'll have to

hitch 8km (be prepared for quite a wait), or the police might, if you ask nicely, ring ahead to one of the camps where someone is usually happy to come out and pick you up.

Minibuses often run from Diseh to the Desert Highway for JD1 per person. A single bus runs to Aqaba daily at 7.30am.

AQABA   العقبة

☎ 03

The balmy winter climate and idyllic setting on the Gulf of Aqaba, ringed by high desert mountains, make this Jordan's aquatic playground. While Amman shivers in winter with temperatures around 5°C and the occasional snowfall, the daytime mercury in Aqaba rarely goes below 20°C and is often

quite a few degrees warmer. In summer, however, the weather is uncomfortably hot, with daytime temperatures over 35°C, but it's often made bearable by the sea breezes. For this reason Aqaba works on siesta time; everything shuts down around 3pm (or earlier) and reopens later in the evening, from around 6pm.

Aqaba is popular with Jordanians from the north (forget trying to get a room during holidays such as Eid al-Adha – see p243), with Saudis from across the border and, somewhat bizarrely, with Hungarian tour groups. It's also an obvious place to break a journey to/from Israel & the Palestinian Territories or Egypt. Diving and snorkelling are Aqaba's main attractions and, while

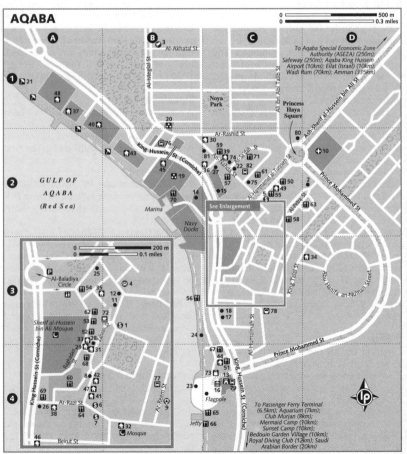

not as extensive as Egypt, it's still a great place to spend a couple of days exploring the underwater brilliance of the coral-rich gulf. The port does mar the view a little and the beaches close to town are fairly unappealing, but there's a laid-back vibe and it's still a good place to kick back and relax from the rigours of life on the road.

Aqaba has big plans for the future. Several new five-star hotels are planned for the southern coast, including the huge Tala Bay resort and condo project. The Ayla Oasis project to the northwest of town involves the creation of lagoons (adding 19km to Aqaba's coastline), a marina, hotels and a golf course, and there's a new shopping and restaurant complex called Ayla Park, which

should materialise soon. Expect Aqaba to change rapidly in the next few years as Jordan gears it up to be the 'new Eilat'.

History

> And king Solomon made a navy of ships in Ezion-Geber, which is beside Eloth (Eilat), on the shore of the Red Sea, in the land of Edom
>
> *1 Kings 9:26*

Excavations at Tell al-Khalifa, 4km west of central Aqaba and right on the border of Jordan and Israel & the Palestinian Territories, have revealed the ancient world's largest copper smelters, thought to be the biblical site of Ezion Geber. Smelting was carried out here from the 10th to 5th centuries BC, with ore coming from mines in Wadi Araba. Ezion Geber was also the ancient port from which King Solomon's fleet departed for the gold mines of Ophir (an unidentified location, possibly Sudan, Ethiopia, Eritrea or Yemen).

As trade with southern Arabia and Sheba (present-day Yemen) developed, the area around Aqaba thrived thanks to its position on one of the Middle East's major trade routes, with routes leading north to Petra, Damascus and Bosra; west to Egypt and Palestine; and south to Arabia. The recent discovery in Aqaba of ceramics from China and Aksumite coins from Ethiopia highlight the cosmopolitan nature of the town.

The town was occupied by the Ptolemies from Egypt during the 2nd and 3rd centuries BC, and then the Nabataeans from about the 3rd to 1st centuries BC. During Roman times the town was renamed Aqabat Ayla (Pass of Alia) and it housed a garrison of legionaries.

Intriguingly, archaeologists working at Ayla recently unearthed a late 3rd-century church, thought to be the world's oldest purpose-built church (earlier churches have been found but these were built for other purposes and later converted). The sanctuary was used for less than a century before it was destroyed by an earthquake.

In the 10th century, a Muslim traveller described Aqaba as 'a great city' and a meeting place of pilgrims en route to and from Mecca. In AD 1024 the town was sacked by local tribes and in 1068 a huge earthquake split the old city of Ayla in two, consigning the town to a minor historical role.

The Crusaders occupied the town in 1116 and fortified a small island nearby – then called Ile de Graye, but now known as Pharaoh's Island (p231). By 1170 both the port and island were in the hands of the Ayyubids, under Saladin (Salah ad-Din). In 1250 the Mamluks took over. By the beginning of the 16th century the town had been swallowed up by the Ottoman Empire, and lost much of its significance when the main trading area of the region was moved to Baghdad in the middle of the 16th century.

For about 500 years, until the Arab Revolt during WWI, Aqaba remained an insignificant fishing village. Ottoman forces occupying the town were forced to retreat after a raid

by the Arabs and TE Lawrence in 1917. From then on, the British used Aqaba as a supply centre from Egypt for the push up through the Trans-Jordan and Palestine regions.

After WWI, the border between Trans-Jordan and Saudi Arabia had still not been defined, so Britain arbitrarily drew a line a few kilometres south of Aqaba. The Saudis disputed the claim but took no action. As the port of Aqaba grew, the limited coastline proved insufficient, so in 1965 King Hussein traded 6000 sq km of Jordanian desert for another 12km of coastline with Saudi Arabia.

Orientation

King Hussein St (also known as the Corniche) is the main axis of Aqaba. It runs more or less north–south along the coast through the centre of town, and follows the Gulf of Aqaba around to the west as far as Israel & the Palestinian Territories, and to the south as far as Saudi Arabia. In the city, a walking path parallels King Hussein St, but it only hugs the coast in small sections because of the private beaches owned by the upmarket hotels, as well as the marina and navy docks. The massive port facilities start a few kilometres south of the centre.

A huge Jordanian flag marks the southern end of the beach, where you'll find a pleasant plaza and the tourist office. It's a pleasant stroll along the beach to get here.

If you stroll too far north of Barracuda Beach you'll probably be sent back by the police, as King Abdullah owns a residence nearby.

Information
BOOKSHOPS

Aqaba has two excellent bookshops that sell a range of international newspapers as well as books about Jordan and the region.

Redwan Bookshop (☎ 2013704; redwanbook@hotmail.com; Zahran St; ⊗ 7.30am-12.30pm & 4-9pm) One of the best in Jordan with an extensive selection of newspapers, hard-to-find Jordanian titles, Lonely Planet guidebooks, and German and French novels.

Yamani Library (☎ /fax 2012221; Zahran St; ⊗ 9am-2.30pm & 6-10pm) A few doors to the north; has a better range of English novels.

EMERGENCY

Police station (☎ 2012411, 191; Ar-Reem St) Opposite the bus station.

Princess Haya Hospital (☎ 2014111) Well equipped and offers decompression chambers (see p228).

INTERNET ACCESS

Aqaba has a good sprinkling of Internet cafés, most of which charge around JD1.

Gate Net (☎ 2017677; Aqaba Gateway; per hr 750 fils, after midnight 500 fils; ☿ 24hr) Has soft drinks for 250 fils.

LAUNDRY

Most visitors stay long enough in Aqaba to get some laundry done – especially useful if you've gathered layers of dust and sand from Wadi Rum.

Frindes Laundry (☎ 2015051; Al-Petra St; ☿ 8am-1pm & 4pm-10pm Sat-Thu) Among the better places, which charges 250/500 fils for t-shirts/shirt or trousers.

Rana Dry Clean (☎ 2013668; An-Nahda St; ☿ 9am-11pm Sat-Thu) Charges are similar.

MONEY

There are dozens of banks and ATMs around the city – see the Aqaba map for locations. Many are located along the southern side of Al-Hammamat al-Tunisieh St.

Numerous moneychangers are congregated around the corner of Zahran and Ar-Razi Sts. They're open longer than the banks, and most change travellers cheques without commission, though check the rate first.

POST

DHL (☎ 2012039, 2011385; Al-Petra St)

General post office (☿ 7.30am-7pm Sat-Thu, 7.30am-1.30pm Fri)

TELEPHONE

Outside the post office is a gaggle of telephone booths, and several stalls nearby sell telephone cards. Other private telephone agencies are located on the main streets, and some moneychangers also offer telephone services. Note that international calls from Aqaba are up to five times cheaper than in Wadi Rum.

TOURIST INFORMATION

Tourist office (☎ /fax 2013363; ☿ 8am-2.30pm Sun-Thu) Next to the Aqaba Museum (head for the huge Jordanian flag) at the western end of Prince Mohammed St. Staff are friendly enough but offer little more than a limited range of brochures. A new visitor centre is planned for central Aqaba.

VISA EXTENSIONS

Aqaba Special Economic Zone Authority (ASEZA; ☎ 2091000, 2091031; www.aqabazone.com, info@aseza .jo) Behind Safeway, by the Central Bank of Jordan. You need to register here if you got a free visa on arrival in Aqaba and will stay in Jordan for more than 14 days (see p250). The website has some useful information about Aqaba.

Police station (☎ 2012411; ☿ 7am-9pm Sat-Thu) Opposite the bus station. An extension for a stay of up to three months is usually available on the spot and is free. It's best to go earlier in the day (8am to 3pm). Aqaba is the only reliable place to get your visa extended outside Amman.

Dangers & Annoyances

Women travellers have reported varying degrees of harassment from local lads on the public beaches. This may even happen on the private beaches belonging to the upmarket hotels, to which you should report anything immediately. On the public beaches, foreign women will feel far more relaxed (but not necessarily more comfortable) wearing loose shirts and baggy shorts. See p220 for more details.

Sights

AYLA (OLD AQABA)

Located along the Corniche, and incongruously squeezed between the marina and the Mövenpick Resort, is the site of **Ayla** (admission free; ☿ 24hr), the early medieval port of Aqaba. The ruins are limited, but worth a quick look if you're in the area. Helpful noticeboards in English clearly pinpoint items of interest and put the place in some perspective.

At the back of the parking space behind the JETT bus office is another small section of the old city, including the city wall and the ancient church.

AQABA CASTLE (MAMLUK FORT)

Aqaba castle (admission JD1, includes the Aqaba Museum; ☿ 8am-4pm Sat-Thu, 10am-3pm Fri Oct-Apr, 8am-7pm May-Sep), measures around 50m by 50m although it is unusual in having sides of slightly uneven length. It is worth looking around as it has been partially reconstructed and gives some sense of its original form.

The first castle may have been built by the Crusaders in the 13th century, but most scholars attribute its construction to the Mamluks during the reign of the sultan Qansur al-Ghuri (1510–17), as attested by the attractive inscriptions in Arabic inside the entrance gate. In one of the eastern rooms off the main courtyard are further inscriptions suggesting that the castle was renovated and enlarged by the Ottomans in both 1587 and 1628. In subsequent centuries the castle was used as a khan (caravanserai) for travelling pilgrims, especially Egyptians, on their way between their homeland and Mecca. The Ottomans occupied the castle until WWI when, in 1917, the fortress was substantially destroyed by shelling from the British Royal Navy. The Hashemite coat of arms above the main entrance was raised soon afterwards as the Arab Revolt swept through Aqaba.

A helpful explanation in English is on a noticeboard at the entrance. You can see stables in the far left corner. The former castle mosque has been turned into offices. Tickets must be purchased at the museum in the visitor centre and entitle you to enter both museum and castle on the same ticket.

AQABA MUSEUM (MUSEUM OF AQABA ANTIQUITIES)

This small **museum** (admission JD1, student 150 fils; 8am-4pm Sat-Thu, 10am-3pm Fri Oct-Apr, 8am-7pm May-Sep) is located inside the visitor centre. Both the centre and museum were previously the home of Sherif Hussein bin Ali – the great-great-grandfather of the present king, Abdullah II – who lived here for a period of time after WWI.

The collection of artefacts includes coins from Iraq and Egypt, ceramics from the excavations of Ayla (Old Aqaba), 8th-century Islamic stone tablets and some late Byzantine reliefs. All captions are in English and there are some informative descriptions of the items and the archaeological history of the area. The ticket also entitles you to enter the castle.

BEACHES

Aqaba promotes itself as a resort (most pictures feature people happily water-skiing and lazing on the beach), but the town itself is not nearly as developed for such activities as it pretends to be. For most of the water sports action and the better beaches, you'll need to head south of town (see p227). Even here there is often little shade and public transport is limited.

Now that the top-end resorts have gobbled up most of the public beaches north of the centre, the main free **public beach** is the stretch of sand lined with cafés between the navy docks and Aqaba castle. This isn't really the place for swimming but offers nice sunset strolls and great people watching.

If you wanted to bare some skin you are better off at a private beach. Of the hotel beaches, the Aquamarina Beach Hotel is the cheapest at JD2.500 but the tiny beach really isn't up to much. The Radisson SAS charges JD10 for its small beach. The Mövenpick Resort is the priciest but best at JD16/19 for weekday/weekend use of its beach, three pools, health club and sauna and includes JD5-worth of drink vouchers.

Barracuda Beach (☎ 2109891; fax 2019892; admission JD5, towel hire JD1; 9am-7pm) offers a good balance between cost and comfort. This new private 100m stretch of clean sandy beach is equipped with hammocks, a cushioned lounge area, a bar, restaurant, pool and lots of water sports. The fun and games include beach buggies, volleyball, Jet Skis, a banana boat, water skiing and weekend beach parties. A dive centre is planned.

Better sandy options further south include the Club Murjan resort, the Royal Diving Centre or the public beaches around the Aqaba Marine Park Visitors Centre (see p227).

Activities
WATER SPORTS

Club Murjan, the Aquamarina Beach Hotel and Barracuda Beach are well set up for various water sports. Nothing is cheap of course: water-skiing and jet-skiing cost around JD1 per minute. Windsurfing (JD5 per hour) and kayaking (JD3 per hour) are cheaper options.

Sindbad (☎ 079 5556076; booth in Aqaba Gateway) operates sunset boat cruises on Thursday and Friday afternoons (JD10 per person) and also a snorkelling boat trip (JD20 per person with lunch). Most hotels can book you on these trips.

GLASS-BOTTOM BOATS

If you can't go diving or snorkelling, the next best thing is a glass-bottom boat. The ride is fun, but the amount of fish and coral is usually disappointing unless you get away from central Aqaba (where much of the coral has died) and hire the boat for two to three hours. The posted rate for a boat (holding about 10 people) is JD15 per hour but, with patience, you may be able to negotiate the price down to half this. Boats congregate along the central public beach or at a jetty in front of Aqaba castle.

The glass-bottom boats can also be hired for longer trips if you want to go swimming, snorkelling or fishing (bring or hire your own equipment); this is a great day out if you can get a group together. Count on about JD35 per day for a boat holding six people. The budget hotels sometimes organise trips for JD10 per person. Mornings bring the calmer weather.

DIVING & SNORKELLING
For details of the diving sites and snorkelling along the coast south of town, see p227.

Several places in town hire out snorkelling equipment for around JD5, including the dive centres and Barracuda Beach.

HAMMAMS
Aqaba Turkish Baths (☎ 2031605; King Hussein St; ☽ 9am-9pm) offers the full works – massage, steam bath and scrubbing – for JD8. Readers have highly recommended this place. Women are welcome to attend, but need to make a reservation in advance and are charged more as 'special arrangements' are made (you'll get the place to yourself). They try to find female attendants in this case, though this isn't guaranteed.

Tours
If you are thinking on taking a tour to Wadi Rum see p207. These are some of the more experienced agencies offering tours to Wadi Rum:

International Traders (☎ 2013757; aqaba. office@traders.com.jo; Al-Hammamat al-Tunisieh St) Expensive but reliable.

Nyazi Tours (☎ 2022801; www.nyazi.com.jo; King Hussein St) Recommended adventure tour company run by Nyazi Shaba'an, former Director of Antiquities & Tourism in Petra. Camping, hiking, jeep tours and camel trips.

Peace Way Tours (☎ 2022665; www.jordantrips.com; King Hussein St) This agency gets mixed reviews from readers (although it seems to depend on the guide).

Red Sea Tours (Zahran St) A budget agency in the Jordan Flower Hotel.

Wadi Rum Desert Services (☎ 2013882; http:// wadirumdesertservice.tripod.com) Near Al-Shami Restaurant, off Zahran St. Another long-standing agency, although with both positive and negative reports from travellers. Also know as Qutaish & Sons, it operates as a branch of Firas Car Rental.

Trips to Wadi Rum start from JD45 per person per day (including transport, food and an overnight stay in the desert). Make sure you find out exactly what you're getting for your money, including how many meals are covered by the price. See p207 for more on this.

Some agencies also organise day trips to Petra (JD40), but this is poor value as your time in Petra will be very limited and the price doesn't include entrance fees – it's better to budget a couple of days and go under your own steam.

Sleeping
Aqaba is a popular place for Jordanian and Saudi tourists in winter (October to March), with the season (and hotel rates) peaking in April, May, October and November. People also flock to Aqaba from northern Jordan during long weekends and public holidays, especially around Eid al-Adha (immediately after the haj), for which you'd need to book weeks in advance. At these times, prices may increase by as much as 30%.

Just about all hotels, including the budget places listed here, have air-conditioning. In the summer air-conditioning is more a necessity than a luxury, and always make sure it's working before forking out any money. In summer, budget travellers may find it cooler to sleep on the roof of their hotel.

Campers, overlanders, beach bums and dive junkies should consider staying at one of the camps along the beach south of Aqaba (see p231).

BUDGET
Unless it is stated otherwise, most places listed here offer (non-satellite) TV, air-conditioning and a private bathroom with hot water (not always reliable). Most places don't include breakfast but can usually rustle up something unsatisfying for around JD1.500. Tariffs in most budget places are negotiable by JD1 to JD3 per person, especially in quieter times.

Al-Amer Hotel (☎ /fax 2014821; Raghadan St; s/d JD12/14) Good upper-budget value here, with sunny, clean rooms. Ask for a room at the front where the views are great.

Al-Naher al-Khaled Hotel (☎ 2012456; zv51@ hotmail.com; Ar-Razi St; s/d JD14/18) Rates here can be negotiated down to JD8/10 in off-season, which is good value. The full rates are much poorer value. Rooms are pleasant, bright and clean. Rooms at the front are noisy because the glass doesn't quite fit properly and those at the back have French windows which don't lock (though you'd be very unlucky to have anything stolen).

Al-Kholil Hotel (☎ /fax 2030152; Zahran St; s/d JD10/12, with balcony JD12/14) One of the better places in the area, though the low ceilings seem to have been designed by hobbits. It's really worth paying extra for a balcony as these make the rooms.

Jordan Flower Hotel (☎ 2014378; s/d with shared bathroom JD7/8, with private bathroom JD10/11) A simple place but probably the best of three cheapies next to each other on Zahran St. The rooms are a bit grubby and vary so look at a few. The pricier rooms come with a balcony.

Petra Hotel (☎ 2013746; s/d without bathroom JD5/7, with private cold-water bathroom JD6/8, with private hot-water bathroom JD8/10) The cheapest options are pretty bleak and most rooms don't have windows but there's a lot of variety so look around. The three rooms with balconies have terrific views. Lone women travellers should probably stay elsewhere.

Jerusalem Hotel (☎ 2014815; s/d JD5/8) Probably the most run-down and least welcoming of the three cheap places located in Zahran.

Three slightly more expensive places are next door to each other at the northern end of Zahran St. They are located in a quiet off-street courtyard with an open-air café out the front and some rooms have balconies. All are friendly places.

Amira Hotel (☎ /fax 2018840; s/d JD12/18) Best of this bunch and one of several other budget hotels that bizarrely have exactly the same furniture. Aim for a clean bathroom, a small balcony and a quiet room away from the street. Prices include breakfast.

Belal Hotel (☎ 2019284, fax 2019285; s/d JD12/18) The Belal is slightly better than the Dweikh if you can score one of the 'non-fragrant' rooms. Satellite TV and a decent bathroom are a bonus. The hotel was formerly known as Nairoukh I.

Dweikh Hotel I (☎ 2012984; fax 2012985; s/d JD10/15) From the puke-green corridors to the poky bathrooms, the rooms at the Dweikh are a bit knackered.

MIDRANGE
Every place listed here has a fridge, air-conditioning, TV (usually satellite), tele-

phone and private hot water bathroom. If you can negotiate a discounted price, these places are great value. Prices include breakfast unless otherwise stated.

Al-Zatari Hotel (☎ 2022970; fax 2022974; King Talal St; side rooms s/d/tr JD18/28/35, front-view rooms JD20/32/39, plus tax; P) Well-run and highly recommended, with well-appointed rooms, a balcony and a nice coffee shop/restaurant. The staff are also friendly. It's just a short walk downhill to the town centre. Front-facing rooms are worth the extra money as they are bigger and have better views.

Nairoukh II Hotel (☎ 2012980; nairoukh2hot@hot mail.com; King Hussein St; s/d JD 15/22) Despite the mind-bending carpet, this is good value: close to the centre; modern rooms; helpful staff; and great views over the gulf. Single rooms are smaller and don't have the views. Single/double room rates rise to JD19/27.500 in April, May, October and November.

Moon Beach Hotel (☎ /fax 2013316; King Hussein St; s without sea view JD12, s/d with sea view JD17/30) A stone's throw from the castle and hence removed from (but easy walking distance to) the bustle of central Aqaba. The rooms are clean and pleasant and most have great views. Five new rooms come with beach views. Credit cards are accepted. A good family option.

Crystal Hotel (☎ 2022001; fax 2022006; Ar-Razi St; s/d JD20/30) Walk into the plush marble lobby and you'll feel like you're in an upmarket hotel. The rooms are very comfortable and spacious, if a little sterile; the large corner rooms are by far the best. Add JD3 per person for breakfast. The official rates of JD40/55 rarely apply.

Al-Shula Hotel (☎ 2015153; alshula@wanadoo.jo; Raghadan St; s/d JD15/20) Right in the heart of the action, the rooms here are smaller than some other hotels, but it's quiet and well run and rooms on the west side have excellent views of Eilat in Israel & the Palestinian Territories. Add JD5 in high season. Don't get too excited when you arrive; the lobby is grander than the rooms.

Shweiki Hotel (☎ 2022657; fax 2022659; Hammamat St; s/d/tr JD16/24/28) Another good-value central option. Rooms are spacious with good bathrooms and some come with nice coastal views. Rooms without balcony are a little cheaper; all rates are open to discussion.

Al-Cazar Hotel (☎ 2014131; alcsea@alcazar.com.jo; An-Nahda St; s/d JD25/35; 🏊) This is a big tour-group hotel, with pleasant spacious rooms with balcony, a swimming pool, pub, and on-demand DVD cinema, though it's getting a bit faded these days and can be gloomy during low season. One big plus is that guests get free access to Club Murjan, a water sports centre (p231) to which the hotel runs transport twice a day.

Aquamarina Beach Hotel (☎ 2016250; www.aquamarina-group.com, aquama@go.com.jo; s/d JD25/30, sea view JD30/40; 🏊) This substandard Euro-resort, popular with Hungarian groups, is the faded, ugly sister squeezed in between glamorous siblings the Radisson and InterContinental. Facilities include a swimming pool, a grim video arcade, a bar and a water sports and dive centre (p229). Sea-view rooms are worth the extra money. There's an Arab Bank ATM (for Visa) at the gate. It's a cheap option if you don't mind the old-fashioned interiors.

Golden Tulip (☎ 2031901; www.goldentulip.com, goldtulip@go.com.jo; s/d JD50/60, discounted to JD30/40; 🚫 🏊) A modern and fresh four-star choice, with an interior atrium, decent bar, rooftop plunge pool and good location with lots of restaurants nearby. The 110 rooms are nicely decorated, with cool tiled floors and a balcony.

Aqaba Gulf Hotel (☎ 2016636; www.aqabagulf.com; King Hussein St; JD45/55; 🚫 🏊) Excellent if you can get the discount rates routinely offered when things are quiet. The luxurious rooms, swimming pool, tennis courts, bar, restaurants and service are what you'd expect from a four-star place.

TOP END

Radisson SAS Hotel (☎ 2012426; aqaba@radisson.com.jo; King Hussein St; s/d with city view JD60/65, sea view JD70/75; 🚫 🏊) A comfortable rather than opulent four-star option, with a small beach (flanked by ugly walls), kid's entertainment centre and a beach bar/grill (mains JD5-7).

Mövenpick Resort Hotel (☎ /fax 2034020; www.movenpick-aqaba.com; King Hussein St; standard/seaview/superior d JD78/85/96; 🚫 🏊) Aqaba's finest and most stylish digs, deserving its five stars, with lovely interiors decorated with mosaics and Moroccan lamps. The huge pool and beach complex across the road has three pools, a gym (open 6am–10pm), lovely gardens and the Red Sea Grill. Other restaurants include the Palm Court buffet (JD15), and Italian and Lebanese restaurants, both with a lovely outdoor terrace.

This is the place to spoil yourself with Swiss ice-cream specials, buffet blowouts and a fine health club. Disabled-accessible rooms are available.

The InterContinental and Kempinski are two five-star options under construction at the time of research. The InterContinental is due to have 255 rooms, wi-fi Internet, a 200m beach, the largest pool in Aqaba, six restaurants and its own marina.

Eating

Aqaba has a large range of places to eat to suit almost all budgets, and many travellers will relish the plentiful seafood, although it can be expensive – for the lobster (summer only) expect to pay JD35. Aqaba's signature dish is its *sayadieh* – fish on a bed of rice with a tomato, onion and pepper sauce.

BUDGET

Al-Mohandes Cafeteria (Al-Hammamat al-Tunisieh St; 🕒 7.30am-midnight) Very popular with locals for cheap and tasty shwarma and felafel in a clean and lively setting.

Pearls Fast Food (☎ 2015057; Ar-Razi St; snacks from 500 fils, mains JD2.500-3.500; 🕒 24hr) Ideal if you crave a burger with chips at 3am, and it also does a range of main dishes and breakfast.

Syrian Palace Restaurant (☎ /fax 2014788; Raghadan St; starters under JD1, mains JD2-6; 🕒 10am-midnight) A good option for Syrian and Jordanian food, including fish, at moderate prices. The tables situated by the window are the best and the service is good if a little slow. It's next to the Al-Amer Hotel.

Al-Tarboosh Restaurant (☎ 2018518; Raghadan St; pastries around 200 fils; 🕒 7.30am-midnight) One of two pastry shops that offer a great range of meat, cheese and veggie pastries that they'll heat up for you in their huge oven.

Al-Shami Restaurant (☎ 2016107; Raghadan St; starters under JD1, mains JD2-6; 🕒 10am-1am) In a lane between Raghadan and Zahran Sts, the Shami is another cheap place recommended by readers. The menu (printed in English outside) is extensive and the air-conditioned dining area upstairs has good views.

National Restaurant (☎ 2012207; Zahran St; mains from JD2.500; 🕒 7.30am-midnight) Under Al-Kholi Hotel, this is a busy place and deservedly so. The meat and chicken dishes come with salads and hummus and are a great deal.

Al-Safara'ah Restaurant (King Hussein St; meals from JD1; 🕒 lunch & dinner) One of two good open-air

SOUTHERN DESERT & AQABA

restaurants located next to each other by the entry access to the southern end of the public beach. Good-value shwarma meals and grilled chicken dishes make this the best value place in town.

Ös Urfa Restaurant (☎ 6146020; King Hussein St) A Turkish restaurant nearby that's fast getting a good reputation for its tasty eggplant and meat dishes, a range of Turkish mezze and good grills.

Karmel Restaurant (Raghadan St; ⏲ 7am-1am) Not much more than a collection of open-air tables here next to the Al-Amer Hotel, serving nothing but tea, excellent hummus, fuul and felafel, but it's packed every night.

MIDRANGE & TOP END

Ali Baba Restaurant (☎ 2013901; Raghadan St; starters under JD1, mains JD3-7; ⏲ 8am-midnight) This old-timer draws the crowds for its pleasant outdoor seating and central location but it's trading on its past reputation according to many readers. There's plenty of mezze, grilled meats and fish, including *sayadieh* (JD7), plus breakfast food and good cakes.

China Restaurant (☎ 2014415; Al-Petra St; dishes JD2.500-3, large beer JD1.800; ⏲ 11.30am-3pm & 6.30-11pm) The cook at this good place is Chinese and his restaurant has long maintained a high standard, getting numerous repeat visitors. Prices are reasonable.

Captain's Restaurant (☎ 2016905; An-Nahda St; starters 600 fils-JD6, mains JD3-6; ⏲ 8am-midnight) Near the Chilli House; has a pleasant dining area around the side. Seafood starts from JD5.500, including *sayadieh*, which isn't bad, or try a seafood salad (JD3.500). Breakfast is also served (600 fils to JD1.600).

Mina House Floating Restaurant (☎ 2012699; starters from 650 fils, mains from JD3.500; ⏲ noon-midnight) This is an old favourite but recent travellers' reports suggest that it's now become more of a local male hang-out, so lone women might want to get a second opinion before heading out here. The restaurant is on a boat moored (or rather cemented) to the shore south of Aqaba castle. Fish starts at JD7 per 500g, which is good considering it is always freshly caught, and not frozen as in some other Aqaba restaurants. The setting is very pleasant, with good views over the gulf to Eilat and Taba.

La Dorada Restaurant (☎ 2033137; mezze JD1-2, mains JD3.500, fish JD6; ⏲ lunch & dinner) There's a relaxed Mediterranean fishing port vibe here, serving up *sayadieh,* paella, shrimp, Lebanese mezze and a good selection of wines.

Royal Yacht Club Restaurant (☎ 2022404; www .romero-jordan.com; Royal Yacht Club; starters JD1-2, antipasto JD3-6, mains JD6-12; ⏲ noon-11.30pm) With views of the marina, this is an upscale and elegant place to savour a romantic sunset and mingle with Aqaba's nouveau riche. The Italian menu includes some interesting items like a crab, avocado, shrimp and artichoke salad, and mussels Provençale, before ending abruptly and rather sadly with a 'cheeseburger'. Arrive early and grab a drink at the pleasant bar.

Floka Restaurant (☎ 2030860; An-Nahda St; starters JD4.500-6, mains JD5.500-11; ⏲ 12.30-11.30pm) Many readers have recommend this seafood restaurant and it's a good choice for an upmarket dinner. The catch of the day normally includes sea bream, silver snapper, grouper and goatfish, and there's a good fish stew (JD5.500). Choose between indoor or outdoor seating. Credit cards are accepted.

Silk Road Restaurant (☎ 2033556; As-Sa'dah St; mezze JD1-3, fish dishes JD6-7, seafood JD6-10; ⏲ noon-midnight) One of Aqaba's finest restaurants, this is a great place to blow the budget or celebrate a special occasion. It would be a false economy not to try the delicious seafood salads, chowders or main courses. There are three attractive dining areas, with traditional low seating, and nightly (Russian!) belly-dancers in summer which you can easily enjoy or escape. There's also an extensive, reasonably priced wine and alcohol list (a draught Amstel costs JD2).

SELF-CATERING

The best supermarket is **Humam Supermarket** (☎ 2015721; Al-Petra St; ⏲ 8.30am-2.30pm & 4-11pm). **Safeway** (⏲ 8am-midnight) is quite a hike away, 750m north of Princess Haya Hospital.

The **Fruit and Vegetable souq** hidden at the southern end of Raghadan St is the best place for fruit and vegetables.

The best **bakery** (Al-Hammamat al-Tunisieh St; ⏲ 6am-11pm) is unsigned in English.

CAFÉS & ICE-CREAM PARLOURS

There are popular **beachfront cafés** along north of the Aqaba castle (where the front row seats of the cafés are so close to the water that you can wet your toes while you whet your whistle). No alcohol is served at these public places.

The **juice stands** (750 fils-JD1.500) on Ar-Razi St are popular places for travellers to hang out at and meet others.

Al-Fardos Coffee Shop (coffee 500 fils), just off Zahran St, is a traditional coffeehouse where local men sip coffee, play backgammon and stare open-mouthed at Arabic music videos. It has a pleasant outdoor setting and foreign women are welcome.

To help alleviate heatstroke in summer, head for anywhere that sells ice cream, such as **Hani Ali** (Raghadan St), a sugar-addict's paradise of traditional sweets and delicious ice cream; or **Gelato Uno** (off An-Nahda St) behind the Hertz car rental office.

Drinking

All the top-end hotels have bars, and most offer some kind of happy hour from 6pm to 7.30pm. For traditional Arabic dancing, and somewhat dubious cabaret acts, head to the nightclub in the **Aquamarina Beach Hotel** (☎ 2016250; www.aquamarina-group.com).

Baranda Lounge (☎ 077 7232444; upper story, Aqaba Gateway; beer JD2-3.500) Yes, this is a 'bar and a lounge' and the coolest one in town at that. It's a relaxed and friendly place with sensible prices, a lovely terrace and a patio out back that captures the sea breezes at night. Good food is served until midnight (steaks are JD6.500) and bar snacks until 3am.

Rovers Return (☎ 2032030; Aqaba Gateway; pint of Amstel/Guinness JD2.740/4.300) A branch of the Amman expat favourite but with cheaper drink prices thanks to the lower taxes.

Royal Yacht Club (☎ 2022404; beer JD2.500-3.500) Above the Romero Restaurant in the marina, this is the pick of the upmarket crowd. It's a sophisticated place to enjoy the sunset and catch some late afternoon sea breezes.

Fun Pub (☎ 2034020; Mövenpick Hotel; ⏱ 8pm-2am) The best of the hotel bars, with a happy hour from 8pm to 9pm.

Entertainment

Aqaba Gateway (☎ 2012200; Al-Baladiah Circle) has the best collection of restaurants, fast food, shops, bars and a cinema.

Jordan Experience (☎ 2022200; Aqaba Gateway; jex@aqabagaateway.com; admission JD6) Families will like this multimedia experience that starts off through a Disney-style *siq* and ends with a 40-minute film that simulates a flying-carpet tour of Jordan, complete with moveable seats. There are three shows a day.

Barracuda Beach (p220) has Friday-night beach parties in summer, with a cover charge of around JD10.

Shopping

There are plenty of shops around the centre of Aqaba selling the usual range of tourist souvenirs, including the ever-popular (but rather crap) bottles of coloured sand. You'll have to pick through the tack to find what you're looking for.

One shop which stands out for its quality is the **Noor Al-Hussein Foundation shop** (☎ 2012601; ⏱ 8am-6pm, until 7pm May-Sep), located opposite the museum. Profits from the sale of its high-standard products go to help supporting marginalised communities throughout Jordan. Items include silver jewellery from Wadi Musa, petroglyph designs from Wadi Rum, kilims, clothes, embroidery, basketwear and ceramics. Credit cards are accepted.

Photo Hagop (☎ 2012025; Zahran St; ⏱ 8.30am-11pm) has several branches around town and offers developing (JD4.500 for 36 prints), print and slide film, digital accessories and video cartridges (from JD3.500).

Getting There & Away

AIR

Aqaba has Jordan's only commercial **airport** (☎ 2012111) outside Amman, although it only awakes from its slumber when a flight is about to leave or arrive. There are weekly international flights to Paris and Sharm El-Sheikh in Egypt. Located 10km north of town.

Royal Jordanian (☎ 2014477; www.rja.com.jo; Ash-Sherif al-Hussein bin Ali St; ⏱ 9am-5pm Sun-Thu) Operates flights to Amman's Queen Alia International Airport on Friday and Saturday. This is the place to buy, confirm or change Royal Jordanian or Royal Wings air tickets. Tickets to Amman cost JD39 one way.

Royal Wings (www.royalwings.com.jo) A subsidiary of Royal Jordanian, flies between Aqaba and Amman's Marka airport twice daily.

BOAT

There are two daily boat services to Nuweiba in Egypt. For information about these services see p261.

There is no real need to buy your ticket in advance as they never sell out (except perhaps during the haj – see p243); just purchase the ticket at the ferry terminal when departing.

BUS

From Aqaba to Amman it's worth paying for the comfort, speed and air-conditioning of a JETT or Trust private bus. Try to book tickets for these at least a day in advance. Buses for both companies leave from outside their respective offices.

From the **JETT bus office** (☎ 2015223; King Hussein St), next to the Mövenpick Hotel, buses run five times daily to Amman (JD4.300, four hours), between 7am and 5pm. The office is a 10-minute walk from the centre.

Trust International Transport (☎ 2039480; Just off An-Nahda St) has six daily buses to Amman (JD5, four hours), the first at 7.30am and the last at 6pm. There are also buses to Irbid (JD8, 5½ hours) at 8.30am, 10.30am and 3.30pm.

Ordinary public buses travel between the main bus/minibus station in Aqaba and Amman's Wahadat station (JD3.500, five hours) about every hour between 7am and 3pm, sometimes later. **Afana** has services about every hour between 7am and 10pm from Aqaba bus station to Abdali station in Amman.

There is talk of moving the bus station to the northern outskirts of Aqaba.

CAR

Aqaba has branches of all the major car-hire agencies. Most charge a 'drop fee' (JD25) if you wish to leave the car in Amman or at Queen Alia International Airport. Hiring in Aqaba makes some sense as public transport in the south of the country is less frequent and requires more connections than in the north. Aqaba is also far easier to drive around than Amman.

See p264 for tips on hiring and driving a car in Jordan. If you are a nervous driver it's worth paying the 'collision damage waiver' (CDW) where available, which means you pay nothing additional in the case of an accident.

Al-Cazar Car Rental (☎ 2014131; alcsea@alcazar.com.jo; An-Nahda St) Reliable agency that charges from JD35 per day with unlimited kilometres, plus JD5 for CDW.

Avis (☎ 2022883; avis@go.com.jo; King Hussein St) Charges from JD30 per day for a couple of days' hire, with unlimited kilometres; 4WDs cost JD90. CDW costs JD7 per day. Located inside the Housing Bank Centre.

Europcar (☎ 2019988; An-Nahda St) From JD25 to JD30 per day, plus JD7 for CDW.

Hertz (☎ 2016206; hertz@go.com.jo; An-Nahda St) From JD35 per day with unlimited kilometres. Strangely,

paying the JD10 per day CDW still leaves you with US$100 to pay in the event of an accident.

Thrifty (☎ 2030313; An-Nahda St) Opposite the Al-Cazar Hotel.

You may be faced with a brief customs check as you enter the Aqaba Special Economic Zone by road from the north.

MINIBUS

To Wadi Musa (for Petra), minibuses (JD3, two hours) leave when full between 7am and 2pm; the exact departure times depend on the number of passengers and you may have to wait an hour or two (which is often longer than the actual travel time…). Otherwise, get a connection in Ma'an (JD1.500, 80 minutes) for which there are hourly departures throughout the day.

A couple of minibuses go to Wadi Rum (JD1, one hour), at around 6.30am and, more reliably, 11am. You may find afternoon buses at 1pm and 3pm. On Friday there is usually only one minibus a day. At other times, catch a minibus towards Ma'an, disembark at the turn-off to Wadi Rum at Ar-Rashidiyya and then hitch a ride to Rum village (30km) from there.

Minibuses to Amman (JD4, five hours) leave hourly throughout the day.

All of the above minibuses leave from the main bus/minibus station on Ar-Reem St. Minibuses to Karak (JD2, three hours), via Safi and the Dead Sea Highway, are the exception, leaving from the small station next to the mosque on Al-Humaimah St.

TAXI & SERVICE TAXI

From the main bus/minibus station, service taxis head to Amman (JD5, five hours), but far less regularly than buses and minibuses. To Karak (JD3.250, three hours) they leave from the small station on Al-Humaimah St. Service taxis start lining up at either station at 6am and many have left by 8am so get an early start. Chartering a taxi costs around JD25 one way to Petra and to Wadi Rum return.

Chartering a taxi between Aqaba and the Israel & the Palestinian Territories border costs around JD5. For details on crossing the southern border to/from Israel & the Palestinian Territories, see p257. A few hardy-looking 4WD service taxis go to destinations in Saudi Arabia.

Getting Around

TO/FROM THE AIRPORT

Aqaba's **King Hussein Airport** (☎ 2012111) is located 10km north of town, close to the border with Israel & the Palestinian Territories. There's no bus to the airport, so take service taxi 8 (15 minutes, around JD1) from the main bus station, or take a taxi for around JD5. Be wary of unscrupulous taxi drivers trying to fleece unsuspecting tourists who have just arrived in Aqaba.

TO/FROM THE FERRY TERMINAL & SOUTHERN COAST

Minibuses (250 fils) leave from near the entrance to Aqaba castle on King Hussein St for the Saudi border via the southern beaches, camps, dive sites and Royal Diving Centre, passing en route the ferry terminal for boats to Egypt. Minibuses returning to Aqaba can be full of construction workers heading off shift from 2pm to 3pm. A private taxi from central Aqaba to the ferry terminal shouldn't cost more than JD2, though some try for JD4. A seat in a shared taxi costs JD1.

TAXI

Hundreds of private (yellow) taxis cruise the streets beeping at any tourist (Jordanian or foreign) silly enough to walk around in the heat rather than take an air-conditioned taxi. Taxis are unmetered so prices are entirely negotiable, and the drivers in Aqaba enjoy the sport. Most rides cost between 500 fils and JD1.

SOUTH OF AQABA

The road south of Aqaba stretches about 18km to the Saudi Arabian border at Ad-Durra. Much of the coastline is taken up by the massive port facilities, but there are a few beaches, as well as some excellent diving and snorkelling spots. Minibuses run down the road from near Aqaba castle on King Hussein St to the Saudi border.

Diving & Snorkelling

The northern end of the Gulf of Aqaba enjoys high salinity, and the winds from the north and minimal tides mean the water stays clear. The temperature of the water is warm (an average 22.5°C in winter and 26°C in summer), attracting a vast array of fish, and helping to preserve the coral.

The **Jordan Royal Ecological Society** (☎ 06 5679142; www.jreds.org) says the gulf has over 110 species of hard coral, 120 species of soft coral and about 1000 species of fish. These include colourful goatfish, leopard flounder, clown fish, trigger fish; various species of butterfly fish, parrot fish, angel fish; and the less endearing spiky sea urchin, poisonous stonefish, scorpion fish, sea snakes, jellyfish and moray eels. Green turtles and hermit crabs can also be found

---

RED SEA AQABA MARINE PARK

Jordan's only stretch of coastline is the northern part of the Gulf of Aqaba, and it's home to over 300 types of coral and numerous species of fish and marine life. Jordan's only port (and the region's major shipping lane) and resort cause real problems for the fragile marine environment.

In an attempt to halt the damage, the **Aqaba Marine Park** (☎ 2019405; fax 2014206) was established in 1997. The park stretches for about 8.5km, from the Marine Science Station to the Royal Diving Club, and extends about 350m offshore and 50m inland. The park contains about 80% of Jordan's public beaches and most of the decent diving and snorkelling spots, so the park managers are trying to find the right balance between promoting tourism and preserving the marine environment.

Local and foreign environmentalists have managed to ban fishing and limit boating in the park, and have established jetties into the sea so that divers and snorkellers can jump into the water rather than wade out over coral from the beach. Park rangers ensure that visitors and locals obey the strict environmental protection laws.

The park managers also hope to conduct a public awareness campaign for locals (particularly children) and all divers and snorkellers, lobby the government to enforce local environmental laws, and conduct further research into the damage caused by tourism and pollution. The Marine Science Station, south of Aqaba, is also deeply involved in the preservation of the marine environment.

and even (harmless) whale sharks pay a visit in summer.

One unwelcome natural visitor in the area is the Crown of Thorns Starfish (known as COTS), which feeds on and kills local coral. Divers are requested to notify their dive master if they spot these starfish.

BOOKS

Lonely Planet's *Diving and Snorkeling Guide to The Red Sea* concentrates on sites along the Egyptian coast, but has a detailed section about diving around the Gulf of Aqaba. The major bookshops in Aqaba (see p218) have a good range of books about diving, such as the *Introduction to the Marine Life of Aqaba*. The Redwan Bookshop sells the plastic *Red Sea Fishwatchers Field Guide,* which can be taken underwater to identify species of fish and coral.

HEALTH

If you're cut by coral, or stung by a stonefish, see above for advice and remedies. The **Princess Haya Hospital** (☎ 2014111) in Aqaba is well equipped for diving mishaps, and even has a

decompression chamber (☎ 2014117), where staff are trained to deal with diving accidents. **Dr Jamil Refari** (☎ 077 7411345, 02 2015021) is one doctor who has been recommended. The reputable dive centres are equipped with emergency oxygen tanks, a first-aid kit and a mobile phone.

It's important to remember that, if you dive to any depth, it is dangerous to gain altitude until at least 12 hours after your dive. This applies to the roads to Petra and Amman, as well as flights. Deeper dives require an even longer time period.

DIVING & SNORKELLING SITES

The coast between Aqaba and the Saudi Arabian border boasts about 30 diving and snorkelling sites. Of these, about 25 can be enjoyed by snorkellers and all but one is accessible from a jetty or beach.

Sites are not signposted, nor are they remotely obvious from the road; if you want to dive or snorkel independently you'll have to ask for directions, or take pot luck. Snorkellers will find it far better to pay the extra money and use the private beaches run by the Royal Diving Club or Club Murjan.

The following are the more popular sites (listed in order from Aqaba). You can also snorkel at Pharaoh's Island, which is in Egyptian waters; see p231.

First Bay Offshore from the Marine Science Station, it has good coral gardens for divers at a depth of 8m to 15m.

*King Abdullah Reef Named after the king (an avid diver) and offshore just north of the Mermaid Camp, it has good visibility and decent but unspectacular coral. It's easily accessible from the beach, and the coral starts about 20m offshore.

*Black Rock Offshore from Mermaid Camp, this site boasts diverse species of soft coral, with occasional visits by turtles, and is good for snorkellers.

Cedar Pride This Lebanese freighter was deliberately sunk to create a diving site in 1985. It's only 200m offshore, and in water about 20m deep. The wreck is covered with bright, soft coral and is home to schools of colourful fish. The waves can be a bit harrowing at times, however, and the sea urchins can be a pain. Sadly, this is also the site with the most litter.

*Japanese Garden Located just south of the Cedar Pride, this site is ideal for snorkellers and has a stunning array of coral.

*Gorgonian I This reef is probably the best place for snorkelling, although the waves can be difficult. The coral is superb, and there's plenty of marine life and the chance to see sea turtles.

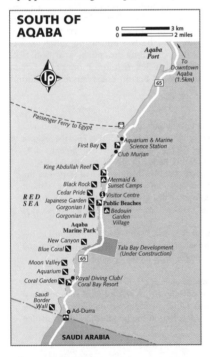

SOUTH OF AQABA

0 —————— 3 km
0 —————— 2 miles

Aqaba Port

To Downtown Aqaba (1.5km)

65

Passenger Ferry to Egypt

First Bay

Aquarium & Marine Science Station
Club Murjan

King Abdullah Reef

Black Rock
Cedar Pride
Japanese Garden
Gorgonian I
Gorgonian II

R E D
S E A

Mermaid & Sunset Camps
Visitor Centre
Public Beaches
Bedouin Garden Village

Aqaba Marine Park

New Canyon
Blue Coral

Moon Valley
Aquarium
Coral Garden

65

Tala Bay Development (Under Construction)

Royal Diving Club/ Coral Bay Resort

Saudi Border Wall

Ad-Durra

SAUDI ARABIA

RESPONSIBLE DIVING & SNORKELLING

To help preserve the ecology and beauty of the reefs, please consider the following tips when diving or snorkelling:

- Do not touch or feed fish, and minimise your disturbance of marine animals. In particular, do not ride on the backs of turtles as this causes them great anxiety. Feeding fish may disturb their normal eating habits, encourage aggressive behaviour or be detrimental to their health.

- Do not touch or remove any marine life or coral, dead or alive, from the sea or beach. Dragging equipment across the reef can also do serious damage. Polyps can be damaged by even the gentlest of contact. Never stand on coral – instead use a jetty (or boat) to reach the water, even if the coral looks solid and robust.

- Be conscious of your fins. Even without contact, the surge from heavy fin strokes near the reef can damage delicate organisms. When treading water in shallow reef areas, take care not to kick up clouds of sand. Settling sand can easily smother the delicate organisms of the reef.

- Do not throw any rubbish into the sea or leave it on the beach. Plastics in particular are a serious threat to marine life. Turtles can mistake plastic for jellyfish and eat it.

- Ensure that boat anchors are on buoys, and not attached to precious coral, and take care not to ground boats on coral

- Practice and maintain proper buoyancy control. Major damage can be done by divers descending too fast and colliding with the reef.

- Resist the temptation to buy coral or shells. Aside from the ecological damage, taking marine souvenirs depletes the beauty of a site and spoils the enjoyment of others – and is illegal in Jordan.

---

*Gorgonian II This is similar in size, accessibility and standard to Gorgonian I, but the coral is not as good; there are numerous moray eels.

*New Canyon A sunken WWII Russian tank lies 30m offshore and at a depth of just 5m. Further into the sandy canyon, the walls are lined with coral.

Blue Coral This is another sloping reef, with hard and soft coral at shallow depths.

Moon Valley Accessible from the beach, about 800m north of, and run by, the Royal Diving Club, this sandy area has a sloping reef and a varied, but unremarkable, array of fish and coral. Napoleon fish are often found at greater depths.

Aquarium Not to be confused with the aquarium at the Marine Science Station, this is the name given to the reef accessible from the jetty at the Royal Diving Club. There are enough colourful fish, and soft and hard coral, to impress all divers and snorkellers. The southern area offers the best opportunity for underwater photography.

Saudi Border Wall The coral is perfectly preserved but, because it's only about 300m north of the Jordan/Saudi border, divers should take great care – the best sections are not accessible by snorkellers.

* best snorkelling sites

DIVING CENTRES

Most of the dive agencies have offices in Aqaba where you can arrange your equip-ment and destination. The price per dive invariably decreases the more you do. The most professional agencies include:

Aqaba Adventure Divers (☎ 079 5843724; www .aqaba-adventure-divers.com) Runs a dive shop in downtown Aqaba, and operates dives in conjunction with Bedouin Garden Village Camp. A single dive with equipment costs JD24, open water course JD240, advanced JD180. Snorkelling gear is JD5. Contact Talal Abumahfooz.

Aqaba International Dive Centre (☎ /fax 2031213; diveaqaba@yahoo.com) Off King Hussein St. This popular, friendly and well-equipped centre charges JD17 per dive including transport and all equipment (JD15 if you do two dives on the same day). An open-water Professional Association of Diving Instructors (PADI) course costs JD200.

Arab Divers (☎ 2031808; arabdivers@hotmail.com; King Hussein St) On the 2nd floor, next to Nairoukh II Hotel. This friendly dive company has been highly recommended by a number of readers; it charges JD16 for the first dive with full equipment, JD30 for a introductory dive, JD25 per person per night dive (minimum of two people) and JD210 for the open-water PADI course. The company also runs other courses and the instructors speak English, German, French and Japanese. All dives are beach dives.

Dive Aqaba (☎ 2034849; www.diveaqaba.com) A dive with all equipment costs JD25; day trip with two dives, drinks and lunch JD55; day trip snorkelling JD20; discover diving for novices with two dives JD70; open water course

SOUTHERN DESERT & AQABA

SAFETY GUIDELINES FOR DIVING & SNORKELLING

Before embarking on a diving or snorkelling trip, careful consideration should be given to making it a safe as well as enjoyable experience. You should:

- Possess a current diving certification card from a recognised scuba diving instructional agency
- Obtain reliable information about physical and environmental conditions at the dive site (eg from a reputable local dive centre)
- Be aware of marine park regulations and etiquette about marine life and the environment; see p229
- Dive only at sites within your realm of experience; if you can, engage the services of a competent, professionally trained dive instructor or dive master
- Be aware that underwater conditions vary significantly from one region, or even site, to another: seasonal changes can significantly alter any site and dive conditions, which influences the way divers dress for a dive and what diving techniques they use
- Ask about the environmental characteristics that can affect your diving and how local trained divers deal with these considerations

---

JD235; advanced open water JD185. Also offers boat dives and internships. Located opposite Golden Tulip. Contact Rod Abbotson.

Red Sea Diving Centre (☎ 2022323, 2018969; www .redseadivecentre.com) One of the more long-standing dive centres in Aqaba, it charges about JD25/42 for two dives without/with equipment hire, or JD25 for a single dive with equipment hire. Off King Hussein St.

Royal Diving Club (☎ 2017035; www.rdc.jo) Around 12km south of the city centre. In operation since 1986, this experienced company is very professionally run. Charges start at JD26 for the first dive with equipment (JD40 for two in the same day). A refreshment dive (if you haven't been diving for a year) costs JD37 with equipment, as does a night dive (minimum three people). It's JD255 for the open-water PADI course. All dives are shore dives. Ask about dive programmes for children and people with a disability.

Sea Star (☎ 2014131; Al-Cazar Hotel; www.seastar -watersports.com) Each dive with full equipment and dive master accompaniment costs JD30, while rates decrease the more dives you do. Night dives (extra JD10) are also available with prior notice.

All of the above diving centres can also organise night dives. Underwater camera hire costs around JD10. Other costs include: an underwater torch (flashlight), about JD5 per trip; wetsuits, about JD3.300/6.600 for a short/long one; and fins, about JD1.500.

Most of the diving centres run PADI courses, most commonly a five-day open-water course (JD200 to JD250) or a three-day advanced open-water course (JD180 to

JD200). If you've never been diving you can try an introductory dive under the supervision of a dive master. Most places offer tuition for children. Courses are often run by Europeans who speak English, French, German and/or Italian.

SNORKELLING

All of the diving centres mentioned earlier hire out flippers, mask and snorkel for around JD5 per day.

If you have your own gear and want to go snorkelling away from the beach, ask the diving agencies about the cost of accompanying a scuba-diving trip. Diving staff are generally happy to point out the best snorkelling spots. The cheapest place to snorkel is Club Murjan (JD4 plus equipment), while the Royal Diving Club charges JD7 (plus JD5 for equipment). Arab Divers will hire you snorkelling equipment and drop you off and pick you up at snorkelling sites for JD8.

Aquarium   الحوض المائي

Part of the Marine Science Station complex, the **aquarium** (☎ 2015145; admission JD2; ☹ 8am-5pm) is quite run down and only worth a visit if you don't get a chance to go diving or snorkelling. The tanks provide a colourful glimpse at coral, moray eels, turtles and stonefish. The aquarium is located about 7.5km south of Aqaba, 500m south of the ferry passenger terminal.

Club Murjan   نادي المرجان

About 1.3km south of the Marine Science Station is **Club Murjan** (☎ 2012794), the beach and diving centre run by Al-Cazar Hotel in Aqaba. Guests of the hotel, and divers using the hotel's diving centre, can enjoy the facilities at Club Murjan for no charge, while the public can use the good beach, swimming pool and showers during the day for JD4, including return transport from Al-Cazar Hotel (departures at 9am and 1.30pm). Hire of snorkelling gear costs JD7 per day. Water-sports gear such as canoes and paragliders are also normally available. There is a bar and restaurant on the site.

Aqaba Marine Park Visitors Centre

متنزه العقبة البحري ومركز الزوار

The headquarters of the **marine park** (☎ 203 5801; mpark@aseza-env.gov.jo), around 12km south of Aqaba, has the largest section of free public beach, with sun shades and a jetty, museum, gift shop and park offices. The Al-Sanbouk Café sits here on a moored boat.

There's another large free public **beach** just to the south, with several cafés. Both beaches are near the Japanese Garden and Gorgonian I dive sites and can be very busy on Fridays.

Beach Camps   مخيمات الشاطىء

Bedouin Garden Village (☎ 079 5602521; bedwin jamal@yahoo.com; per person camping JD2-3, s/d JD15/20, large room JD20/30, meals JD5; 🛠) Beach or dive bums will like this place, located about 10km south of the town centre on the east side of the road. Accommodation is basic, cramped and overpriced, and there is no air-conditioning, but you can camp or park a camper van for cheap. There's a Bedouin tent for hanging out in, a small pool, a dive centre (see p229), restaurant and shared showers for campers and divers. They can arrange Bedouin music performances in the evenings if there are enough people, and hire out snorkelling gear (JD5 per day). A taxi here costs JD2 to JD3.

Other camps, such as the **Mermaid Camp** (☎ 079 5567761) and **Sunset Camp** (☎ 077 7786023; www.sunsetcamp.com; reefdiverjo@yahoo.com) are due to relocate next to the Bedouin Garden Village, to (maybe) create a Dahab-style budget beach community. If that pans out, this will be the place to head for if you are camping, overlanding or just diving on the cheap. The current site of these camps is expected to be developed as a five-star resort.

Tala Bay   تالى باي

Located just north of the Royal Diving Club (and about 11km south of Aqaba), **Tala Bay** (☎ 2017222; www.talabay.jo) is an ambitious development project that should start to open during the life of this book. The first phase is for a marina, golf course, five-star and three-star hotels and a water sports club. More hotels (2500 rooms in total), villas, apartments, shops and restaurants will come in the years ahead. Developers are working closely to ensure that it has minimal impact upon the environmental protections demanded by the Red Sea Aqaba Marine Park.

Royal Diving Club   مركز الغوص الوطني

Located about 12km south of Aqaba, and close to the Saudi border, is the **Royal Diving Club** (☎ 2017035; www.rdc.jo), which is an excellent place for swimming, diving and snorkelling. It has a lovely swimming pool, restaurant and a decent beach, where women are able to feel relaxed.

The entrance fee of JD7/3.5 for adults/children (aged five to 12) allows guests to use the facilities. Snorkelling gear costs an extra JD5 per day. Hotels in Aqaba can often arrange entry for JD5, including transport (but without a towel), which is cheaper than just turning up. Entrance and transport is free for anyone scuba diving with the Royal Diving Club (see p229).

Attached to the dive centre is the new **Coral Bay Resort** (☎ 2017035; s/d JD53/63; 🛠), with comfortable, clean and modern rooms, some with sea views. Only the 2nd-floor rooms have a balcony. Divers should be able to negotiate a discount on the room rate, which includes breakfast. Add JD10 for half board.

The minibus provided by the centre picks up guests from outside most of the hotels in Aqaba at 9am, 10am, 11am and noon, and returns at 12.30pm, 3pm, 4pm and 5pm. Ring the Royal Diving Club the day before to arrange a lift. Alternatively take the public minibus from near the Aqaba castle. A private taxi costs around JD4 one way, but it can be difficult to find one going back to Aqaba.

Pharaoh's Island   جزيرة فرعون

This picturesque island (*Jazirat Fara'un* in Arabic) is 15km south of Aqaba, but only a few hundred metres from Taba, in Egypt. It's actually in Egyptian waters, but travelling to or from Egypt this way is not permitted.

Excavations suggest that the island was inhabited as far back as the Bronze Age. The fantastic Crusader **Salah ad-Din Fort** is fun to explore; and there is really good swimming and snorkelling in the lagoon, and diving further out which is only accessible by boat.

Top-end and good midrange hotels can book day trips to the island for JD24 per person, which includes the entrance fee to the island, Egyptian visa, lunch and transport. Two days' notice is often required to allow time for the visas to be processed.

Directory

CONTENTS

PRACTICALITIES

- **Newspapers & Magazines** English-language papers worth reading are the daily *Jordan Times* (200 fils; www .jordantimes.com) and weekly *Star* (500 fils; www.star.com.jo). *JO* (www.jo.jo) is a cool local magazine published in Amman, but can be hard to find. Imported newspapers include *The Times* (JD3.500), *Guardian Weekly* (JD1.500), *Le Monde* and *Le Figaro* (JD1.500). The *International Herald Tribune* (JD1) has a regional section from Lebanon's *Daily Star*. Magazines include *Time* (JD2.700) and *Newsweek* (JD2.800).

- **Radio** Check out Radio Jordan (96.3 FM in Amman, 98.7 FM in Aqaba) or the BBC World Service (103.1 FM in Amman and 1323AM across the country). Try 99.6 FM for popular hits.

- **Electricity** Jordan's electricity supply is 220V, 50 AC. Sockets are mostly of the European two-pronged variety, although some places use European three-pronged sockets.

- **Weights & Measures** Jordan uses the metric system. See the front of this guidebook for a conversion table.

ACCOMMODATION

Jordan has a good range of accommodation options to suit most budgets, although away from the main tourist centres there's not a great deal of choice. However this is generally not a problem because Jordan is so compact most attractions can be easily visited in day trips from the main centres.

Peak season is considered to be September, October, March, April and part of May and you can expect tourist numbers and hotel prices to be at their highest (or rather discounts at their lowest) during these months. Holiday weekends are also extremely busy at resorts at Aqaba and the Dead Sea. Outside of these months, and if tourism numbers remain low, you can negotiate discounts on most hotels' published rates.

Camping

Bringing a tent just to save money on accommodation doesn't make much sense. There's no camping allowed in Jordan's nature reserves or at Petra, but cheap rooms are plentiful. Finding a secluded place to pitch a tent in a densely populated country like Jordan is far from easy so always check with the local authorities before setting up.

Some places to discreetly pitch a tent are near Umm Qais, and Ajlun castle. The only camp sites where pitching your own tent is allowed are south of Aqaba (tents catch the sea breezes in summer) and Wadi Rum and

DIRECTORY

TOP FIVE PLACES TO STAY

The following five offer unique top-end options and are *so* worth the splurge:

- Feinan Lodge, Dana Nature Reserve (p173) – Arabesque meets medieval monastery in a 21st-century ecolodge
- Mövenpick Aqaba (p223 or Dead Sea p145) – simply luxurious
- Dana Guest House, Dana (p173) – stunning views and sleek style
- Under the stars at a Bedouin camp in Wadi Rum (p212)
- Sofitel Taybet Zaman (p198), near Petra – designery boutique hotel in a restored Ottoman village

---

Shaumari Reserve, although some hotels (eg the Olive Branch Resort near Jerash) allow you to pitch a tent in their grounds.

Pre-set tents are available in Wadi Mujib and Dana nature reserves, though they are surprisingly expensive options. These should be booked in advance through Wild Jordan (p70).

One popular option is to spend the night in a Bedouin camp in the desert at Wadi Rum. Facilities can be basic but it's a great experience – see p212 for more details.

Hotels

A surprising thing about accommodation in Jordan is that some towns have no hotel at all. Other towns, like Ajlun, offer little or nothing at the budget end of the market.

In places with hotel accommodation, prebooking a room is rarely needed and you'll have little trouble finding a hotel in any price range if you just turn up, except in Aqaba at peak times (see p221 for details).

Most budget and some midrange places charge an extra JD1 to JD2 for breakfast, which is invariably little more than bad tea/coffee, bread and jam. It's cheaper to buy this sort of food at a grocery store and make your own breakfast, or you can get a better local breakfast for about the same money at a budget-priced restaurant. Breakfast is generally included in the price at midrange and top-end hotels; the latter generally have generous buffet-style breakfasts.

BUDGET

There are no youth hostels in Jordan. Some places, especially those catering to backpackers, allow guests to sleep on the roof – which, in summer, is a good place to be – for about JD2 per person. Private rooms start at about JD3/6 for singles/doubles, but anything decent will cost about JD6/10. Prices are negotiable, especially when things are quiet.

Most budget places have 'triples' (rooms with three beds), and often rooms with four beds, so sharing a room with friends, or asking to share a room with another guest, is a way of reducing accommodation costs considerably. Some cheaper places have two accommodation choices: basic rooms with a shared bathroom, and nicer, more expensive ones with a private bathroom.

Especially in Amman, cheap places can be incredibly noisy because of the traffic and the hubbub of cafés and shops below. Try to get a room towards the back of the building. Many budget places are located above shops and cafés, which means climbing several flights of stairs to your room.

MIDRANGE

There is a reasonable selection of midrange hotels, with at least one in most towns you're likely to visit, but only in Amman, Wadi Musa (near Petra) and Aqaba will you have much choice. Rooms in midrange hotels usually have colour TV (sometimes featuring satellite stations such as CNN), fridge, heater (essential in winter) as well as telephone. For budget travellers, a quiet, clean room with reliable hot water and a private bathroom in a midrange hotel is sometimes worth a splurge; prices start at about JD15/22 for singles/doubles. Negotiation is always possible, especially if business is quiet or you're staying for several days – so it is sometimes possible to get a nice room in a decent midrange hotel for a budget price.

TOP END

There is no shortage of top-end hotels in Amman, Wadi Musa (near Petra), the Dead Sea and Aqaba. They all feature the sort of luxuries you'd expect for the prices. Most guests at these sorts of places are on organised tours; in quieter times negotiation is possible, and surprising bargains are possible when things are quiet. At other times you'll probably get the best rates from a travel agency instead of just walking in. Major credit cards are accepted in almost all top-end places. All top-end hotels add tax and service charge of 26% (see p246) but this is often included in a discounted rate.

Rental Accommodation

In Amman, the two main English-language papers, and notice boards at the cultural centres (p66), at Books@café (p93) and the University of Jordan Language Center office (p240) are the best places to check for apartments and houses to rent. Alternatively, wander around the nicer areas (just off the road between 1st and 5th circles, or Shmeisani) and look for signs on residences or shop windows advertising places to rent.

You'll pay at least JD200 per month for a furnished apartment in a reasonable area of Amman; a little less if unfurnished. A furnished apartment or small house in a working-class suburb is possible for as little as JD100 per month (usually closer to JD150), but not much in this range is advertised so ask around. For this price, don't expect everything to work.

Short-term rentals are available in Aqaba, where prices for a furnished two-bedroom apartment with a kitchen start at JD10 per night in the low season and JD20 in the high season. Most apartments in Aqaba can only be rented for a minimum of one week, however, and must be prebooked in the peak season.

Resorts

The two main concentrations of resorts are on the Dead Sea (see p143) and Aqaba (p223), where you'll find branches of the luxurious Mövenpick, Kempinski (in Amman – and soon to be in Dead Sea and Aqaba) and Marriott chains, with multiple beaches, pools and everything else you'd expect.

ACTIVITIES

Perhaps surprisingly, Jordan offers some of the best outdoor activities in the Middle East, from hiking and climbing in its stunning deserts and wadis, to scuba diving and snorkelling in the turquoise waters off Aqaba. Don't head home without trying at least a couple of these fantastic adventures.

Aero Sports

The **Royal Aero Sports Club of Jordan** (☎ Amman 06 4873261, Aqaba 03 2033763; www.fly.to/rpacj) offers microlighting (JD50 per hour), skydiving (JD150), gliding, paragliding and even hot air ballooning from Marka Airport in Amman or, by arrangement, over the dramatic scenery of Wadi Rum.

Archaeological Digs

Many ancient sites in Jordan are still being excavated and it's possible to join an archaeological dig; note that such work is usually unpaid and you may even have to pay for the privilege.

Plan well ahead if you're interested in working on archaeological excavations. No dig director will welcome an inquiry two weeks before a season begins. Permits and

---

TOP FIVE ARCHAEOLOGICAL WEBSITES

- American Expedition to Petra (http://petra-archaeology.com)
- Franciscan Cyberspot (http://198.62.71.1/www1/ofm/fai/faimain.html) – super detail on Madaba and Mt Nebo regions, including Madaba map and mosaics of Mt Nebo
- Madaba Plains Project (www.hesban.org) – overview and history of Hesban from Andrews University
- Virtual Karak Resources Project (www.vkrp.org) – good on history and detail on Karak castle
- East of the Jordan (www.asor.org/pubs/new.html) – online text of the book by Burton MacDonald

security forms may have to be completed, so allow up to six months for all possible bureaucratic niceties. Much of the work is also seasonal. Opportunities are nonetheless growing as field project leaders realise the advantages of taking on energetic and motivated amateurs.

When you write to dig directors, tell them what you can do. If you have special skills (like photography or drafting), have travelled in the region or worked on other digs (or similar group projects), let them know. Locals are usually employed to do the basic spade work.

To get an idea of what is going on, and where and when, contact one of the organisations listed below. All are based in Amman (☎ 06).

American Center for Oriental Research (ACOR; ☎ 5346117; www.bu.edu/acor; PO Box 2470, Jebel Amman, Amman 11181) ACOR is part of the Archaeological Institute of America (AIA), and prepares an extensive annual listing of field-work opportunities in the Middle East. Write to: AIA, 135 William St, New York NY 10038.

American Expedition to Petra (http://petra -archaeology.com/index.htm) Operates a six-week dig at Petra's Temple of the Winged Lions in June/July for US$2800. An application pack costs US$25. Contact Dr Philip C Hammond, 15810 Chicory Dr, Fountain Hills, AZ 85268, USA.

American Schools of Oriental Research (www.asor .org) Affiliated to the American Center for Oriental Research (see above).

Biblical Archaeological Society (www.bib-arch.org) Produces the magazine *Biblical Archaeological Review* and runs archaeological tours. The website lists archaeological digs that accept paying volunteers.

Council for British Research in the Levant (☎ 5341317; www.cbrl.org.uk; PO Box 519, Al-Jubeiha, Amman 11941)

Friends of Archaeology (FoA; ☎ /fax 5930682; www .arabia.com/foa, foa@nets.com.jo; PO Box 2440, Amman 11181) Established in 1960, this Jordanian-run, non-profit organisation aims to 'protect and preserve the archaeological sites and cultural heritage of Jordan'. FoA operates educational field trips for members only.

Institut Français d'Archéologie du Proche Orient (☎ 4640515; www.ifporient.org; PO Box 5348, Amman 11181)

University of Jordan: Archaeological Department (Map p65; ☎ 5355000, ext 3739; www.ju.edu.jo)

One particularly active programme is run at picturesque Pella, in northwestern Jordan, by the University of Sydney. For details, contact the volunteer coordinator at **Pella Volunteers** (☎ 02 93514151; http://acl.arts.usyd.edu.au/research/pella /pellavols.html) in Australia. The nine-week programme costs around A$3200.

Other paying digs also include those at **Tell Jalul** (www.andrews.edu/archaeology), 5km east of Madaba; **Khirbet al-Mudyana** (Wilfred Laurier University in Ontario), 48km south of Amman; and **Ya'amun** (www.uark.edu/~jcrose), 19km southeast of Irbid. Prices range from US$1700 to US$3500 for a six-week dig.

Boats & Other Water Sports

In Aqaba, trips on a glass-bottom boat are fun, although the amount of fish and coral that can be seen is sometimes disappointing and you need at least a couple of hours to get to the better areas. The boat trip from Aqaba to Pharaoh's Island is a good day trip that combines history and snorkelling.

A couple of resorts and private beaches in Aqaba offer everything from kayaking and windsurfing to jet-skiing.

Camel Treks

The camel is no longer a common form of transport for Bedouin; most now prefer the ubiquitous pick-up truck – in fact, it's not unusual to see a Bedouin transporting his prized camel in the back of his Toyota! For visitors, however, one truly rewarding experience is a camel trek. Enterprising Bedouin are happy to take visitors on three- to six-night camel treks from Wadi Rum to Aqaba or Petra (see p210), as well as shorter trips.

Diving & Snorkelling

The coastline between Aqaba and the Saudi border is home to some of the world's better diving spots. Although the diving and snorkelling is perhaps not quite as good as Egypt's Red Sea sites, there's plenty of coral and colourful marine life and the crowds are noticeably missing.

The advantages are that all sites are accessible from a major town (Aqaba), easy to reach for snorkellers and accessible from a jetty or the beach, so a boat is not required (which reduces the cost considerably). Also, visibility in the Gulf is usually excellent (as much as 40m, although it's usually closer to 20m), the tides are minimal, the water is shallow and drop-offs are often found less than 50m from shore.

Diving is possible all year. The best time is early February to early June for water and outside temperatures, visibility and marine life, although March and April are not good because of algae bloom.

For specific information about diving and snorkelling activities around Aqaba, see p227.

Hiking

Hiking is an increasingly popular pastime in Jordan, with the Dana Nature Reserve, Mukawir, Petra, Wadi Mujib and Wadi Rum among the most rewarding options.

Any hike will take longer, and take more out of you, than you think – walking in sand is not easy, nor is going uphill in the hot sun. Allow yourself plenty of time, and also give yourself time to linger and enjoy the view, chat with passers-by or simply sit in the shade during the heat of the day.

Getting reliable maps is a problem, partly because they don't always exist and because they can be hard to read because of confusing topography. Try to get maps abroad as there are very few available in Jordan.

Most wadis are unsafe during winter (November to March) due to the danger of flash floods. Paths are often washed away every spring and so routes change every year according to conditions. Bear in mind that Global Positioning System (GPS) units and mobile phones are unreliable in the steep canyon walls of many wadis.

WADI WALKING

Jordan's most exciting hikes are through the surprisingly lush gorges, waterfalls, pools and palm trees of its dramatic wadis (seasonally dry river beds). You'll need some help arranging a hike here, largely because you need transport to drop you off at the beginning and pick you up at the end of your hike (generally a different location and accessed from different roads). Moreover, route-finding is difficult (there are no defined trails) and trails change year to year due to seasonal flooding. Hikes are only safe from late March/early April to early October and you should always check the weather forecast for rain and get local advice before heading off on a hike.

The following are Jordan's best wadi options:

- **Wadi Hasa** – A moderate two-day, 24km trek, all downhill, often in water, through a water playground of pools and waterfalls (including a hot waterfall) and changing scenery. One of the most beautiful wadis in Jordan. There is currently a police check along the road to the start of the trail. The full trek ends near Safi.

- **Wadi Yabis** – Day hike (12km, six to seven hours), accessed from Hallaweh village, 15km from Ishfateena, north of Ajlun. The trail descends 700m past a spring and 2000-year-old olive trees, down a canyon to a 50m waterfall and on to Wadi Rayyan dam. Spring brings wonderful wildflowers and is the best time to visit.

- **Wadi bin Hammad** – A 10km day-hike from the start of the trail at a set of hot springs to the Dead Sea Highway, 6km north of Mazra'a. The hot springs and upper (eastern) stretches are popular with day trippers, especially on Fridays. The full hike ends at the Dead Sea, or alternatively you can just do the first 90 minutes through the dramatic narrow gorge. It's a one-hour drive from the King's Highway tot he start of the trail but it's hard to find without a guide; the turn-off is 11km north of Karak.

- **Wadi Fifa (Feifa)** – Walk up the wadi as far as you want from the Dead Sea Highway. A 4km hike brings you to a small waterfall and continues past water pools, a *siq* and lots of palm trees. The trail starts at -240m so is hot in summer – bring lots of water.

- **Wadi Ghuweir** – Full day hike (12km, seven hours) from Mansoura (near Shobak) to Wadi Feinan, past dramatic geological formations. The trail is accessed from near Shobak via a steep downhill drive, or you can start from Dana Nature Reserve. See p171.

- **Wadi Zarqa Ma'in** – From the hot spring resort of Hammamat Ma'in to the Dead Sea. Check trail regulations at the Hammamat Ma'in spa.

- **Wadi Numeira** – This wadi starts 10km north of Lot's Cave and quickly leads to a dramatic *siq* with pools and waterfalls. The upper wadi is only accessed via a 1.5m rope ladder.

The best places for some DIY hiking are Petra (p189), Dana Nature Reserve (p172; though most trails here require a guide), Wadi Rum (p210), Ajlun Nature Reserve (p116) and the half-day hike from Al-Beidha (p201) to Petra's Monastery.

Several longer routes are also possible if you have a tent and stove. In particular, Dana to Petra is an excellent four-day trek that takes you through Wadi Feinan, Wadi Ghuweir (see the boxed text, p237) and Little Petra.

BOOKS

British climbers Tony Howard and Di Taylor have spent a lot of time exploring the hiking, trekking and rock-climbing possibilities in Jordan. Their books include the detailed *Treks & Climbs in Wadi Rum,* the condensed, pocket-sized and more affordable *Walks & Scrambles in Rum,* published in Jordan by Al-Kutba; and *Walking in Jordan.* These books are only sporadically available inside Jordan.

Although it can be difficult to find, *Trekking & Canyoning in the Jordanian Dead Sea Rift* by Itai Haviv contains numerous trekking and canyoning routes in the wadis of Central Jordan and is well worth picking up, even though many routes are dated now.

HIKING AGENCIES

Only a tiny fraction of Jordanian travel agencies have experience in organising hiking or trekking expeditions. Those that do are generally very expensive, with an organised overnight trek costing several hundred US dollars. For a list of some agencies see p262.

Yamaan Safady (☎ 077 7222101; www.adventure jordan.com) is one of the best young hiking guides in the country. From March to October he leads weekly hiking trips for expats and locals to wonderful places such as Wadi Yabis, Wadi Hasa and beyond, as part of the Adventure Jordan Hiking Club. To get on his email list, which details upcoming hikes, send an email to yamaan@adventurejordan .com. Costs for day hikes generally start at JD25 per person with transport and guide.

The **Royal Society for the Conservation of Nature** (RSCN; ☎ 06 5350456; www.rscn.org.jo; PO Box 6354, Amman 11183) offers a wide range of guided hikes in Wadi Mujib and Dana nature reserves and can also arrange long-distance treks if given prior notice.

WHAT TO BRING

If you intend to hike while in Jordan, make sure that you come prepared. A lightweight windproof top is recommended, as is a thin fleece jacket for the evening. Lightweight waterproofs can be a good idea in spring. Bring some trainers that can get wet, plus a back up pair of shoes, if you intend to walk any of the wet wadis.

It's not advisable to wear shorts or sleeveless tops – it's inappropriate dress for conservative villages in the countryside, and you'll get burnt to a crisp anyway. Don't forget a hat, sunscreen, medical kit, knife, moleskin (for blisters), a torch (flashlight) and matches. Water purifiers and insect repellent will also be very useful.

If you plan to do a lot of hiking, a backpack hydration system such as those made by Camelbak (www.camelbak.com) can be very useful.

WHEN TO GO

The best time for hiking is undoubtedly the middle of spring (mid-March to late April), when it's not too hot, the rains should have finished, the flowers should be in bloom and the wells and springs should be full. At this time, however, Wadi Mujib and some of the wadis in Petra may still be susceptible to flooding or impassable in places – Wadi Mujib generally opens on 1 April. Always check local conditions before setting out. From late September to mid-October is also good; it's dry but not excessively hot.

Rain and floods can occur throughout the months from November to March. This is not a good time to hike or camp in narrow wadis and ravines because flash floods can sweep unheralded out of the hills.

Horse Riding

It's possible to explore the deserts around Wadi Rum on Arabian stallions, though this is for experienced riders only.

Rum Horses (☎ 2033508, 077 7471960; www.desert guides.com) is a professional French-run trekking, camel and horse trekking agency. It's on the south side of the road 6km before the turn to Wadi Rum.

Hot Springs

Jordan boasts dozens of thermal hot-water springs, where the water is usually about 35°C to 45°C. The water contains potassium, magnesium and calcium, among other minerals – popular for their apparent health benefits. The most famous and popular is Hammamat Ma'in, near Madaba. Other popular spots around Jordan include Hammamat Burbita and Hammamat Afra, west of the King's Highway near Tafila; and Al-Himma springs in Mukheiba village, very close to the northern border with Israel & the Palestinian Territories. All are currently being upgraded.

Women are likely to feel more comfortable at Hammamat Ma'in, which has an area for families and unaccompanied women, and the public baths at Al-Himma – which allocates special times solely for the ladies.

Rock Climbing

Wadi Rum offers some challenging and unique rock climbing, equal to just about anything in Europe. The most accessible and popular climbs are detailed in the excellent books written by Tony Howard and Di Taylor (see opposite). Guides are necessary, and you'll need to bring your own climbing gear. See p211 for more details.

For more information see the websites www.n-o-m-a-d-s.demon.co.uk and www.wadirum.net.

Adventure Peaks (☎ 015 3943 3794; www.adventure peaks.com; Central Buildings, Ableside, Cumbria, LA22 9BS) runs week-long climbing trips to Wadi Rum from the UK.

Running

Long-distance runners may want to combine a trip to Jordan with the annual Dead Sea Marathon (p144) or Jebel Ishrin Marathon (www.whmf.org, in German), the latter in Wadi Rum each October. Half-marathons and shorter runs are also arranged during both events.

The local branch of the Hash House Harriers ('drinkers with a running problem') organise local runs each Monday from Amman – check out www.geocities.com /hashemitehhh.

Swimming

The number of public beaches in Aqaba is slowly diminishing as they are gobbled up by upmarket hotels. The best beaches are now along the coastline south of Aqaba, but most spots have little shade and can be very busy on Fridays. The private beaches

in Aqaba are clean and available to the public for a few dinars.

Most visitors head for a float in the Dead Sea, where swimming is almost impossible because of the incredible buoyancy of the salt water. See p143 for more details.

Turkish Baths

If your muscles ache from traipsing around vast archaeological sites like Petra and Jerash and climbing up and down the jebels (hills) of Amman, consider a hammam (also known as a Turkish bath). The best places are in Wadi Musa and Amman, though there is a public hammam in Aqaba. Prices are around JD8 to JD15. At the better places you'll sweat it out in a dry- or wet-steam bath and then be scrubbed with woollen gloves, soaped with olive-oil soap, massaged and laid to rest on a hot marble platform.

Women are welcome, sometimes at separate times to men, but should make a reservation so that female attendants can be organised.

BUSINESS HOURS

Government departments, including most tourist offices, are open from about 8am to 2pm every day apart from Friday – and sometimes they also close on Saturday. Visitor centres keep longer hours. Banks are normally open from 8.30am to 3pm every day but Friday and Saturday. The opening times for post offices vary from one town to another, but tend to be from about 8am to 6pm every day except Friday, when they close about 2pm. Many sights, government departments and banks close earlier in winter.

Almost all major tourist attractions are open every day, normally during daylight hours.

Smaller shops and businesses are open every day from about 9am to 8pm, but some close for a couple of hours in the middle of the afternoon, and some do not open on Thursday afternoon and Friday. The souqs (markets) and street stalls are open every day and, in fact, Friday is often their busiest day.

CHILDREN

Taking the kids adds another dimension to a trip in Jordan, and of course it's not all fun and games. First, it's a good idea to avoid coming in the summer because the extreme heat could really make your family journey quite unpleasant. Keeping your kids happy, well fed and clean is the main challenge.

The good news is that you'll rarely have to embark on really long journeys in Jordan, and chartering a taxi or renting a car is easy, so this shouldn't pose too great a problem.

Fresh and powdered milk is available; otherwise, stick to bottled mineral water, soft drinks or canned juices, which are plentiful. Kids already eating solids shouldn't have many problems. Cooked meat dishes, the various dips (such as hummus), rice and the occasional more or less Western-style burger or pizza, along with fruit (washed and peeled) should all be OK as a nutritional basis.

With infants, the next problem is cleanliness. It's impractical to carry more than about half a dozen washable nappies with you, but disposable ones are not so easy to come by. As for accommodation, you'll want a private bathroom and hot water.

The good news is that children are as loved in Jordan as anywhere else in the Middle East. Few people bring their young ones to this part of the world, so you'll find that your kids are quite a hit. In that way they can help break the ice and open the doors to contact with local people with whom you might never have exchanged glances.

Some of the more interesting attractions for older kids will be visiting the beaches and snorkelling at Aqaba, exploring castles at Karak, Shobak and Ajlun, riding a camel at Wadi Rum or Petra, checking out the ostriches and oryx at Shaumari Wildlife Reserve, floating in the Dead Sea, beach sports and swimming pools in Aqaba and walking and enjoying picnics in a few of the nature reserves.

For more comprehensive advice about travelling with children, pick up a copy of Lonely Planet's *Travel with Children* by Cathy Lanigan.

CLIMATE CHARTS

Climate in Jordan is conditioned partly by altitude, with the lowest areas such as the Jordan Valley and Gulf of Aqaba suffering from the worst summer heat and humidity. The higher central and northern areas, in

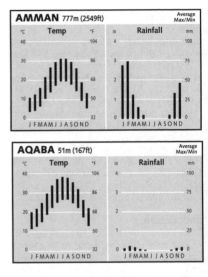

contrast, can be quite cold in winter (November to February).

COURSES
Food

For cooking courses see p60.

Language

For those taken enough by the mystery of the Arab world to want to learn something of the language, there are several possibilities, mostly in Amman (refer to the relevant chapters for full contact details of the universities and cultural centres):

British Council (☎ 06 4636147; www.britishcouncil .org.jo) Can put individuals in touch with a private tutor.
University of Jordan Language Center (☎ 06 535500, ext 3436; www.ju.edu.jo; University of Amman) Offers two-month summer courses (Jul-Aug) in Modern Standard Arabic (MSA) for JD500, as well as four-month spring and autumn semesters for JD750. Tuition is 20 hours a week and there are six levels of proficiency. It's also possible to arrange evening language classes.
Yarmouk University (☎ 02 7271111; www.yu.edu .jo; Irbid) Offers 14-week spring & autumn semesters for JD1050, less for subsequent courses & an intensive 10-week summer course.

CUSTOMS

The usual goods are prohibited, eg drugs and weapons, as are 'immoral films, tapes (cassettes) and magazines' – but customs are not tough on this unless it's pornography.

Duty-free allowances for 'non-residents' (tourists) are: 200 cigarettes or 25 cigars or 200g of tobacco; two bottles of wine or one bottle of spirits; and a 'reasonable amount of perfume for personal use'.

Jordan has no restrictions on the import and export of either Jordanian or foreign currency.

DANGERS & ANNOYANCES

Jordan is very safe to visit and travel around; remarkably so considering the turmoil, restrictions and difficulties in other nearby countries. The best general advice for all travellers is to take care – but not to be paranoid. Women who have travelled through places like Turkey will probably find that Jordan is comparatively relaxed and hassle free, but women who have not visited the region before may be annoyed at the leering and possible harassment from local men.

It is always a good idea to check the prevailing security situation before commencing your journey:

Australian Department of Foreign Affairs and Trade (www.smarttraveller.gov.au)
UK Foreign and Commonwealth Office (www.fco.gov.uk/travel)
US Department of State (http://travel.state.gov)

Minefields

Although the risk to travellers is very small, there are several minefields that were laid along the border with Israel & the Palestinian Territories before and during 1967. These are in the Jordan Valley (near Lake Tiberias); north of Aqaba; and in the southern Jordan Valley near the Dead Sea (they have even been known to float into the Dead Sea during flash floods). The minefields are well off the tourist trails, but if you're in these areas please take heed of warnings not to enter. It's hoped that Jordan will be mine-free by 2009.

Public Disorder

During rare political or economic crises (such as an increase in the price of staple goods or when the US invades a neighbouring country), occasional impromptu protests and acts of civil disobedience can occur. There are also frequent demonstrations in support of the Palestinians. These most often take place in Karak, Tafila and Ma'an, while the university areas of Irbid, Mu'tah and northern Amman are sometimes volatile.

Foreigners are never targeted during these protests, but it is certianly best to avoid becoming involved. The best sources of current information are the English-language newspapers published in Amman or your embassy/consulate in Jordan.

Theft & Crime

Theft is not a real problem in Jordan, especially for people who take reasonable care. Leaving your bag under the watchful eye of a member of staff in the office of a bus station or hotel for a few hours should be no cause for concern. Shared rooms in hotels are also quite OK as a rule, but don't take unnecessary risks, and it can be a good idea to keep your luggage secured with a padlock. Be careful very late at night outside nightclubs in Amman that are patronised by intoxicated, vulnerable and comparatively wealthy foreigners.

The military keep a low profile and you'd be unlikely to experience anything but friendliness, honesty and hospitality from them, as with most Jordanians. It's generally safe to walk around day or night in Amman and other towns, but women should be a little more cautious.

Theft is not a real problem in Jordan but it's always wise to take basic precautions. Always carry your wallet (if you have one) in a front pocket, and don't have too much cash in it. The bulk of your money, travellers cheques and documents are better off in a cotton money belt worn close to the skin. It's also sensible to leave some of your money hidden as a separate stash in your luggage (eg rolled up in a pair of thick socks) in case you find yourself in deep trouble at some point.

DISABLED TRAVELLERS

In late 2000, Jordan celebrated its first ever Olympic gold medal, won by the female athlete Maha Barghouthi in the Sydney Paralympics. Jordanians are very proud of this achievement and it threw the spotlight onto people with disabilities. The benefits of this will take a long time to filter through and for now Jordan is still not a great place for disabled travellers. Although Jordanians are happy to help anyone with a disability, the cities are crowded and the traffic is chaotic, and visiting tourist attractions, such as the

DIRECTORY

vast archaeological sites of Petra and Jerash, involves lots of walking on uneven ground.

The Jordanian government recently legislated that wheelchair access must be added to all new public buildings, but nothing will ever be done to accommodate wheelchairs elsewhere. Horse-drawn carriage can be used as transport for disabled visitors part of the way into Petra. Some travellers with a disability have reported having little difficulty getting around most of Petra on a combination of donkey, horse and carriage.

The Royal Diving Club is a member of the **Access to Marine Conservation for All** (AMCA; www.amca-international.org), an initiative to enable people with disabilities to enjoy scuba diving and snorkelling.

DISCOUNT CARDS

Student discounts of 50% are available at most tourist sites, but the discounts are applied unevenly. Note that the card must be an International Student Identity Card (ISIC) and not just a university ID card.

EMBASSIES & CONSULATES
Jordanian Embassies & Consulates

All of the following are embassies unless otherwise indicated:'

Australia Canberra (☎ 02 6295 9951; www.jordan embassy.org.au; 20 Roebuck St, Red Hill, ACT 2603)

Canada Ottawa (☎ 613 238 8090; 100 Bronson Ave, Suite 701, Ottawa, Ontario ON K1R 6G8)

Egypt Cairo (☎ 02 748 5566; fax 760 1027; 6 Al-Shaheed Basem al-Khatib, Doqqi)

France Paris (☎ 01 46 24 23 78; amb.jor@wanadoo.fr; 80 Blvd Maurice Barres, 92200 Neuilly-Seine)

Germany Berlin (☎ 030 36 99 60 0; www.jordan embassy.de; Heerstrasse 201, 13595)

Israel Tel Aviv (☎ 03 751 7722; fax 751 7712; Rehov Abbe Hillel Silver 14, Ramat Gan suburb)

Lebanon Beirut (☎ 05 922 500; fax 922 502; Rue Elias Helou, Baabda)

Netherlands The Hague (☎ 070 416 7200; www .jordanembassy.nl; Badhuisweg 79, 2587 CD)

Syria Damascus (☎ 11 333 4642; fax 333 6741; Al-Jala'a Ave, Abu Roumana)

Turkey Ankara (☎ 0312 440 2054; fax 440 4327; Mesnevi Ded Korkut Sokak 18, Çankaya); Istanbul (☎ 0212 230 1221, 241 4331; Kalipci, Sokak 119/6, Tesvikiye)

UK London (☎ 020 7937 3685, 0870-005 6952; fax 020 7937 8795; www.jordanembassyuk.org; 6 Upper Phillimore Gardens, W8 7HB)

USA New York (☎ 212 832 0119; 866 Second Ave, 4th fl, NY 10017); Washington (☎ 202 966 2664; www.jordan embassyus.org; 3504 International Drive NW, DC 20008)

Embassies & Consulates in Jordan

The following embassies and consulates are in Amman (☎ 06). Egypt also has a consulate in Aqaba (see p251 for visas to surrounding countries). In general, the offices are open 9am to 11am Sunday to Thursday for visa applications and again 1pm to 3pm for collecting visas. (Note: At the time of writing the Australian, Canadian and UK embassies were closed temporarily due to security threats.)

Australia (Map p65; ☎ 5807000; www.jordan .embassy.gov.au; 3 Youssef Abu Shahhout, Deir Ghbar)

Egypt Embassy (Map p68; ☎ 5605175; fax 5604082; 22 Qortubah St; ⌚ 9am-noon Sun-Thu) Single/multiple entry visa costs JD15/19, bring a photo; pick up your visa around 3pm the same afternoon. Located between 4th and 5th circles. Consulate (Map p216; ☎ 03 2016171; cnr Al-Isteglal & Al-Akhatal Sts, Aqaba; ⌚ 8am-3pm Sun-Thu).

France (Map p68; ☎ 4641273; www.ambafrance-jo .org; Al-Mutanabbi St, Jebel Amman)

Germany (Map p68; ☎ 5930367; fax 5685887; 31 Bin Ghazi St, Jebel Amman) Between 4th and 5th circles.

Iraq (Map p68; ☎ 4623175; fax 4619172; Al-Kulliyah al-Islamiyah St, Jebel Amman) Located near the 1st circle.

Israel Consulate (Map p85; ☎ 5524686; Maysaloon St, Shmeisani)

Lebanon (Map p68; ☎ 5922911; fax 5929113; Al-Neel St, Abdoun) Near the UK embassy.

Netherlands (Map p68; ☎ 5902200; www.nether landsembassy.com.jo; 22 Ibrahim Ayoub St) Located near the 4th circle.

New Zealand Consulate (Map p82; ☎ 4636720; fax 4634349; 99 Al-Malek al-Hussein St, downtown) Located on the 4th floor of the Khalas building.

Saudi Arabia Consulate (Map p68; ☎ 5920154; fax 5921154; 1st Circle, Jebel Amman)

Syria (Map p68; ☎ 5920648, 5920684; Al-Salloum St, Jebel Amman) Located near the 4th circle.

UK (Map p68; ☎ 5909200; www.britain.org.jo; Dimashq St, Wadi Abdoun, Abdoun)

USA (Map p65; ☎ 5920101; http://usembassy-amman .org.jo; 20 Al-Umawiyeen St, Abdoun)

Yemen (Map p68; ☎ 5923771; Al-Ameer Hashem bin al-Hussein St, Abdoun Circle)

FESTIVALS & EVENTS

Jordan's best-known cultural event is the Jerash Festival (p113). In summer, traditional concerts and plays are held at the Odeon and Roman Theatre in Amman, as well as in the towns of Salt and Fuheis.

FOOD

In this guide we generally order restaurants by budget, starting with the cheapest. Expect to pay JD1 to JD3 for a budget meal of roast chicken, around JD3 to JD6 for a main dish in a midrange place and anywhere from JD8 upwards for a meal in a top-end restaurant. See p55.

GAY & LESBIAN TRAVELLERS

There is some confusion over the legal status of homosexuality in Jordan. Most sources state that gay sex is not illegal and that the age of consent for both heterosexuals and homosexuals is 16.

There is a subdued underground gay scene in Amman, so if you're keen to explore it, make very discreet enquiries. Public displays of affection by heterosexuals are frowned upon, and the same rules apply to gays and lesbians, although two men or women holding hands is a normal sign of friendship.

A few places in Amman are gay-friendly, such as the multipurpose Books@café (p93), or Abdoun's trendy cafés, such as the Blue Fig Café (p92 and p96), which pulls in a young, mixed, but discreet gay and straight crowd. Other suggested meeting places are the Roman Theatre/Hashemite Square, the top-end hotel bars in Amman and the Corniche in Aqaba.

Possible further sources of information include www.gaymiddleeast.com and the Gay and Lesbian thread of Lonely Planet's Thorn Tree bulletin board (www.lonelyplanet.com).

HOLIDAYS

As the Islamic Hejira calendar is 11 days shorter than the Gregorian calendar, each year Islamic holidays fall 11 days earlier than the previous year. The precise dates are only fixed a short time beforehand because they depend upon the sighting of the moon.

Public Holidays

During the public holidays listed below, most government offices and banks will close. Most shops, moneychangers and restaurants will remain open, and public transport will still function normally on most public holidays, although most shops will close during Eid al-Fitr and Eid al-Adha.

Try to avoid any archaeological site, nature reserve or park on a public holiday or Friday, as they are often swamped by enormous groups of excitable kids on a school outing.

New Year's Day 1 January
King Abdullah's Birthday 30 January
Arab League Day 22 March
Good Friday March/April
Labour Day 1 May
Independence Day 25 May
Army Day & Anniversary of the Great Arab Revolt 10 June
King Hussein's Birthday 14 November
Christmas Day 25 December

The main Islamic holidays are listed below. See the Table of Islamic Holidays for equivalent dates in the Western calendar:

Islamic New Year First Day of Muharram.
Prophet's Birthday Celebrated on 12 Rabi' al-Awal.
Eid al-Isra Wal Mi'raj Another feast which celebrates the nocturnal visit of the Prophet Mohammed to heaven.
Ramadan Ninth month of the Muslim Calendar, see p244.
Eid al-Fitr Also known as Eid as-Sagheer (small feast), starts at the beginning of Shawwal to mark the end of fasting in the preceding month of Ramadan.
Eid al-Adha This is the commemoration of Allah sparing Ibrahim (Abraham in the Bible) from sacrificing his son, Isaac. It also marks the end of the Haj. Every year about 350,000 sheep are sacrificed throughout the Muslim world at this time.

The 'big feast' of **Eid al-Kabir** is not a holiday but it is when Muslims make the haj (pilgrimage to Mecca). Accommodation in

TABLE OF ISLAMIC HOLIDAYS

Hejira Year	New Year	Prophet's Birthday	Ramadan Begins	Eid al-Fitr	Eid al-Adha
1427	31.01.06	11.04.06	24.09.06	24.10.06	31.12.06
1428	20.01.07	31.03.07	13.09.07	13.10.07	20.12.07
1429	10.01.08	20.03.08	01.09.08	01.10.08	08.12.08
1430	29.12.08	09.03.09	22.08.09	20.09.09	27.11.09
1431	18.12.09	26.02.10	11.08.10	10.09.10	16.11.10

Aqaba can be in short supply and the ferry between Aqaba and Nuweiba is much busier just before and after these dates. This period lasts from 10 to 13 Zuul-Hijja.

Ramadan

Ramadan is the ninth month of the Muslim calendar, when Muslims fast during daylight hours to fulfil the fourth pillar of Islam (see p39). During this month, pious Muslims will not allow anything to pass their lips in daylight hours. One is even supposed to avoid swallowing saliva.

Although many Muslims in Jordan do not follow the injunctions to the letter, most conform to some extent. Foreigners are not expected to follow suit, but it's generally impolite to smoke, drink or eat in public during Ramadan (see p58).

Business hours during Ramadan are more erratic and it can be difficult dealing with anyone during the day who's hungry, thirsty or, worse, craving a cigarette.

Ramadan can be inconvenient at times for visitors, but all tourist attractions remain open and public transport generally functions normally. Hotel restaurants will be open, as will tourist-oriented restaurants.

INSURANCE

A travel insurance policy to cover theft, loss and medical problems is a good idea, but check the small print before you hand over the cash. Check that the policy covers ambulance fees and emergency flights home.

Some policies specifically exclude 'dangerous activities', which can include scuba diving, motorcycling and even trekking. You should have insurance if you plan to dive in Aqaba – decompression chamber treatment can cost JD14,000!

You may prefer a policy that pays doctors or hospitals directly rather than making you pay on the spot and claim later. If you have to claim later make sure you keep all documentation. Some policies ask you to call back (reverse charges) to a centre in your home country where an immediate assessment of your problem is made. See also p271.

INTERNET ACCESS

Jordan is now truly part of the cyber community, and boasts numerous Internet Service Providers (ISPs), including **Cyberia** (www.cyberia.jo).

Almost every town in Jordan has at least one public Internet centre. The most competitive rates, and the highest number of Internet centres, are found outside major universities such as Yarmouk University (Irbid) and the University of Jordan in northern Amman. Costs range from about 750 fils per hour to JD2 per hour. You'll generally pay a minimum of an hour, even if you were actually online for less.

If you have a laptop it's possible to connect to the Internet from top-end and a few midrange hotels that have direct-dial phones. **AOL** (☎ 06 5606241; www.aol.com) offers a local Internet access number as part of its global roaming services.

The easiest way to collect mail through Internet centres is to open a web-based account such as **Hotmail** (www.hotmail.com) or **Yahoo! Mail** (mail.yahoo.com). Most places are also set up for the various online chat services, such as MSN Messenger.

LEGAL MATTERS

The Jordanian legal system is something of a hybrid. Civil and commercial law is governed by a series of courts working with a mixture of inherited British-style common law and the French code. Religious and family matters are generally covered by Islamic Sharia courts, or ecclesiastic equivalents for non-Muslims.

Foreigners would be unlucky to get caught up in the machinations of Jordanian justice. Penalties for drug use of any kind are stiff and apply to foreigners and locals alike. Criticising the king can bring a jail term of up to three years! Traffic police generally treat foreign drivers with a degree of good-natured indulgence, so long as there are no major traffic laws broken. However, excessive speeding, drunk driving and not wearing a seat belt will land you in trouble. If you do get into strife, there is little your embassy can do for you but contact your relatives and recommend local lawyers.

MAPS

For most visitors the maps in this guidebook will be more than sufficient but, if you're doing some hiking or intensive exploration, a detailed map of Jordan is a good idea.

The Jordan Tourism Board's free *Map of Jordan* is worth getting hold of. The Royal

Geographic Centre of Jordan publishes a series of decent maps, including a good hiking map of Petra.

Several detailed maps should be available in your own country: ITMB's good 1:700,000 map of *Jordan* is probably the easiest map to find; Bartholomew's *Israel with Jordan* is OK, but it includes Israel & the Palestinian Territories at the expense of eastern Jordan; *Jordan* by Kümmerly and Frey is good, and probably the best if you're driving around Jordan; and the third edition of GEO Project's *Jordan* (1:730,000) also includes an excellent map of Amman.

MONEY

The currency in Jordan is the dinar (JD) – it's known as the *jay-dee* among hip young locals – which is made up of 1000 fils. You will sometimes hear *piastre* or *qirsh,* which are both 10 fils (10 qirsh equals 100 fils). Often when a price is quoted the unit will be omitted, so if you're told that something is 25, it's a matter of working out whether it's 25 fils, 25 piastre or 25 dinars! Although it sounds confusing, most Jordanians wouldn't dream of ripping off a foreigner.

Coins are 10, 25, 50, 100, 250 and 500 fils, and one dinar. Notes come in denominations of JD1, 5, 10, 20 and 50. Try to change larger notes as often as possible at larger restaurants and when paying your hotel bill.

Changing money is very easy in Jordan, and most major currencies are accepted in cash and travellers cheques. US dollars are the most accepted, followed by UK pounds and euros; you'll get nowhere with Australian or New Zealand dollars.

There are no restrictions on bringing dinars into Jordan. It's possible to change dinars back into some foreign currencies in Jordan, but you'll need to show receipts to prove that you changed your currency into dinars at a bank in Jordan.

Syrian, Lebanese, Egyptian, Israeli and Iraqi currency can all be changed in Amman, usually at reasonable rates, though you may have to shop around. Egyptian and Israeli currency are also easily changed in Aqaba. It's a good idea to talk to travellers arriving from across the border you're about to cross; you can find out the in-country rates, so you know how much to change.

Banks seem to offer slightly better rates than moneychangers for cash, but the difference is not worth worrying about unless you're going to change a huge amount. Most large hotels will change money (sometimes for guests only) but rates are always lower than those offered by the banks and moneychangers. There are small branches of major banks at the borders and at the airports.

Some of the banks are fussy about the older US dollar notes, and possibly may not even accept them.

ATMs

It is possible to survive in Jordan almost entirely on cash advances, and ATMs abound in all but the smaller towns. This is certainly the easiest way to travel if you remember your PIN.

There are no local charges on credit card cash advances but the maximum daily withdrawal amount is around JD500, depending on your particular card. All banks have large signs (in English) outside indicating which credit cards they accept.

Visa is the most widely accepted card for cash advances and using ATMs, followed by MasterCard. Other cards, such as Cirrus and Plus, are also accepted by many ATMs (eg Jordan National Bank and HSBC).

If an ATM swallows your card call ☎ 06 5669123 (Amman). Emergency numbers to contact in Amman if you lose your credit card:

American Express (☎ 06 5607014)
Diners Club (☎ 06 5675850)
MasterCard (☎ 06 4655863).
Visa (☎ 06 5680554)

Credit Cards

Most major credit cards are accepted at top-end hotels and restaurants, travel agencies, larger souvenir shops and bookshops. However, always be sure to ask if any commission is being added on top of your purchase price. This can sometimes be as much as 5%; if so, it may be better to get a cash advance and pay with the paper stuff.

International Transfers

Some major banks (such as the Arab Bank and Jordan National Bank) can arrange the international transfer of money. The Cairo-Amman Bank is part of the international service offered by **Western Union** (www.western union.com). **MoneyGram** (www.moneygram.com) has agreements with several banks. Fees are high with both, so obtaining a cash advance with a credit card might be a better bet.

Moneychangers

Generally, moneychangers offer slightly lower rates than banks for cash. In theory, they do not charge commission on travellers cheques but in practice many do, so shop around. Moneychanger offices are smaller and easier to use than banks, and are generally open daily until around 9pm. Always check the rates at banks or in the English-language newspapers before changing money.

Tax

Jordan has a sales tax of 16% but this is generally only added to midrange and top-end restaurants. Midrange and top-end restaurants and hotels may also add on an additional 10% service charge. The sales tax on hotel rooms has been lowered to 7% in an effort to bolster tourism, but this figure could change at any time. The Aqaba special economic zone has a sales tax of only 5% and many Jordanians head there on shopping sprees to take advantage of the lower consumer prices.

See p248 for information on tax rebates for tourists.

Tipping

Tips of 10% are generally expected in better restaurants. Elsewhere, rounding up the bill to the nearest 250 fils or with loose change is appreciated by underpaid staff, including taxi drivers. Hotels and restaurants in the midrange and, especially, top-end categories generally add on an automatic 10% service charge.

Travellers Cheques

Most flavours of travellers cheques are accepted, with the most recognised being American Express (Amex). Always check the commission before changing.

PHOTOGRAPHY & VIDEO
Airport Security

All airports in Jordan have X-ray machines for checking luggage. Despite assurances that the machines are safe for camera film, it's best to keep your unexposed film in a clear Ziploc bag so it can be easily removed

for hand inspection. Don't ever put film in your check-in luggage.

Film & Equipment

Most Western brands of print film are available throughout Jordan at prices comparable with the West. Prices at tourist sights (especially Petra) are marked-up, as you'd expect. A roll of print film costs around JD3 for 36 shots, plus a similar amount to develop it.

A decent price for 100 ASA Elitechrome (36 shots) is JD5.500, but slide film is getting increasingly hard to find due to the rise of digital formats. There's currently only one place in Jordan that develops slide film and it's expensive, so wait until you get home.

Digital accessories and memory cards are widely available, though they are pricier than abroad (a 256MB memory stick/compact flash costs JD61/40). Many camera shops can burn photos onto a CD and print digital pictures.

Blank video cassettes are available in major towns in Jordan (from JD3.500 up to JD12 for digital).

Photographing People

If you take pictures of anything suggesting any degree of squalor, even the activity of the marketplace, it can offend some people's sense of pride, although hostility is rare.

A zoom lens is great for taking people shots, usually without being noticed. Some Jordanians, women in particular, object to being photographed, so ask first. Persisting in your snapping if unwelcome can lead to ugly scenes, so exercise caution and common sense. Children will generally line up to be photographed.

Restrictions

Photography in military zones such as 'strategic areas' like bridges and public buildings is forbidden. Take particular care out in the Eastern Desert as there are several sensitive military sites not far from the desert castles.

Technical Tips

The single biggest factor to take into account is light. Taking pictures in the middle of the day will almost guarantee a glary, washed-out shot. The strong contrasts of light and shade are particularly hard for your camera to deal with. Where possible, try to exploit the softer light of the early morning and late afternoon, which enhances subtleties in colour and eliminates problems of glare. If you do need to take shots in bright light use a lens filter. As a rule, 100 ASA film is what you'll need most.

If you want your camera to continue working for your next trip make absolutely sure you don't get sand in it. A large Ziploc plastic bag and a lens brush will help keep your camera clean.

POST
Postal Rates
Normal-sized letters and postcards cost 325 fils to the Middle East, 475 fils to the UK and Europe and 625 fils to the USA and Australia.

Parcel post is ridiculously expensive, so Jordan is not the best place from which to send souvenirs home. To send anything by air to Australia, for example, the first 1kg costs JD11.600, and JD6.200 for each subsequent 1kg. To the UK and Europe, the first 1kg is JD12.350 and then JD3.400 per extra 1kg; and to the USA and Canada, it costs JD12.800, then JD7 per extra 1kg.

Amman is the best place to send parcels – see p69 for more information.

Sending Mail
Stamps are available from all post offices, and most souvenir shops where postcards are sold. Postcards and normal-sized letters can be dropped in any of the post boxes around most towns. Letters posted from Jordan take up to two weeks to reach Australia and the USA, but often as little as three or four days to the UK and Europe. Every town has a post office, but you're well advised to send things from major places like Amman, Madaba, Karak, Wadi Musa (near Petra) and Aqaba.

Of the international courier companies, **FedEx** (www.fedex.com.jo) has an office in Amman, and **DHL** (www.dhl.com) has offices in Amman and Aqaba. They are reliable but expensive (half a kilo costs around JD50 to most countries, although the per kilo rate decreases dramatically the more you send). There are also a few home-grown versions.

SHOPPING
Jordan has an interesting selection of crafts and souvenirs, though prices reflect the generally high quality. Amman is the best place to shop for souvenirs, with everything from unimaginable tourist kitsch to superb and high-quality handicraft boutiques on offer.

Bargaining
As in most countries in the region, many prices are negotiable, except public transport, food in grocery shops and restaurants. Bargaining, especially when souvenir hunting, is essential, but shopkeepers are less likely than their Syrian and Egyptian counterparts to shift a long way from their original asking prices.

Carpets, Kilims & Embroidery
While it's still possible to stumble across an aged handmade 'Persian rug' from Iran, chances are it was knocked together in an attic above the shop. This is not to say that the carpets are lousy, but it's worth taking a close look at quality. Inspect both sides of the carpet to see how close and strong the knots or weaving are.

Designs generally tend to consist of geometric patterns, although increasingly the tourist market is being catered to with depictions of monuments, animals and the like. Rugs and tapestries made by Bedouin and Palestinian women are popular, but you need to look carefully to make sure that they are actually handmade. Madaba is famous for its traditional rugs.

Palestinian embroidery is particularly striking, usually employing red thread on a black background.

Copper & Brassware
From Morocco to Baghdad, you'll find much the same sorts of brass and chased copper objects for sale. The good thing about this stuff is that it's fairly hard to cheat on quality, but check for leaks before buying anything you actually wish to use. Popular items include large decorative trays and tabletops, Arabic coffeepots and complete coffee sets with small cups.

Duty Free
There are duty-free shops at Queen Alia International Airport and next to the Century Park Hotel in Amman (p98), plus small ones at the three border crossings with Israel & the Palestinian Territories.

Most upmarket shops offer tax rebates, meaning that if you spend over JD50, keep your receipts, fill out a tax rebate form and leave the country within 90 days, you can get the 16% tax refunded to you at a booth at the airport, just before check-in.

Export Restrictions

Exporting anything more than 100 years old is illegal, so don't buy any souvenir that is deemed by the salesman to be 'antique' – if only because it probably isn't. You may be offered 'ancient' coins around some of the archaeological sites. These may be genuine, but buying them – and taking them home – is highly illegal. If you're unsure about what is an 'antique', contact the **Customs Department** (☎ 06 4623186) in Amman.

Gold, Silver & Jewellery

Gold shops are scattered all over the bigger cities of Jordan, including downtown Amman's glittering gold souq. As a rule, gold is sold by weight, and all pieces should have a hallmark guaranteeing quality. Verifying all this is difficult, however, so the best advice is to buy items you're happy with even if you find out at home that the gold content is not as high as you were told by that nice salesman.

Silver is the most common material used by Bedouin women to make up their striking pieces of jewellery, such as earrings, necklaces and pendants laden with semi-precious stones. Silver is not only used in women's jewellery, but to make carry cases for miniature Qurans and other objects.

Take most of the talk about 'antique jewellery' with a shaker full of salt, and remember customs regulations about antiques (see above).

Handicrafts

Several chains of shops around Jordan sell high-quality handicrafts and souvenirs made by Jordanians, mostly women. Profits from the sale of all items go to local NGOs that aim to develop the status of women, provide income generation for marginalised families, nurture young artists or protect the local environment.

Products from these small-scale initiatives include silver jewellery from Wadi Musa; handmade paper products from Iraq al-Amir, Aqaba and Jerash; ceramics from Salt; painted ostrich eggs from Shaumari; weavings from Iraq al-Amir; and traditional clothing from across Jordan. Most also produce a wide range of stylish home decor items aimed at the foreign market, including cushions, tablecloths and wall hangings.

Bani Hamida Weaving cooperative with a store in Amman. See p163.

Jordan River Foundation (www.jordanriver.jo; p98) Profits go to support the foundation, which aims to preserve traditional communities of the Jordan River Valley and Wadi al-Rayan. The main shop is located in Amman.

Noor Al-Hussein Foundation (www.noor.gov.jo/nhf .htm) This centre helps preserve traditional handicraft skills and supports vulnerable women's communities. Products are sold in shops throughout Jordan, including Aqaba (p225), though direct sales have been scaled back in recent years.

Wild Jordan (p99) Proceeds from the gift shops go to the Royal Society for the Conservation of Nature's environmental programmes and to local communities. RSCN shops can be found in Amman, Azraq, Dana and Wadi Rum.

Other places that have an excellent range of ethically produced handicrafts include **Haret Jdoudna** in Madaba (p157) and **Made in Jordan** in Wadi Musa/Petra (p199).

Other Souvenirs

The ubiquitous nargileh water pipes are about the most vivid reminder possible of a visit to Jordan. Remember to buy a supply of charcoal to get you going if you intend to use the thing when you return home – a couple of spare tubes would not go astray either. This would have to be about the most awkward souvenir to cart around, however, or post home – and the chances of it surviving either way are not good.

Another simple souvenir that is much easier to carry around is the traditional Arab headcloth, or keffiyeh, and *agal* (the black cord used to keep it on your head), so characteristic of the region. The quality of keffiyehs does vary considerably. The elegant flowing ankle-length Bedouin robe known as a *jalabiyya* is available at shops all over Jordan.

A few stalls in downtown Amman sell either ouds (Arabic lutes) or *darbukkas,* the standard Middle Eastern-style drums. The latter can go quite cheaply, and even the ouds are hardly expensive. Such an item's musical value must be considered unlikely to be high – it's the kind of thing you'd buy more to display than to play.

Other souvenirs include bottles of olive oil (the best are produced by Jordan Treasure), miniature reproduction mosaics from Madaba and Hebron-style glassware from the town of Naur (outside Amman). Jordan's shopping capital of kitsch is Wadi Musa, which overflows with t-shirts, Petra reproductions and those ubiquitous bottles of coloured sand, carefully created through tiny funnels in several shops in town.

Woodwork
Also popular with foreigners are woodwork items, ranging from simple jewellery boxes to elaborate chess sets and backgammon boards. Better-quality stuff tends to be made of walnut and inlaid with mother-of-pearl. If the mother-of-pearl gives off a strong rainbow-colour effect, you can be almost sure it's the real McCoy. The actual woodwork on many of these items tends to be a little shoddy, even on better-quality items, so inspect the joints and inlay carefully.

SOLO TRAVELLERS
There's not much of a backpacker scene in Jordan, except in Wadi Musa and, to a small extent, Amman. The tours run by the budget hotels in Amman are one of the best ways to share travel expenses and meet other travellers.

When choosing a room bear in mind that single rooms are generally much smaller than doubles, so always try to negotiate a double room for a single price.

TELEPHONE
The telephone system in Jordan has recently been privatised, and there are no longer any public telephone offices to make calls from, so visitors must either use a private telephone agency, call from a hotel or shop, or buy a telephone card for one of the 1000 or more pay phones throughout Jordan.

The local telephone system is quite reliable. Local calls cost around 100 fils for three minutes and the easiest place to make a call is your hotel, where local calls are often free. Otherwise, most shopkeepers and private telephone agencies will make their telephones available for about 250 fils.

The cost of overseas calls from Jordan varies wildly. The cheapest places are the private telecommunication agencies, where calls are placed through computers or, more likely,

a mobile phone. Rates at these centres are between 150 fils and 500 fils per minute. Always check the rate beforehand.

Overseas calls can be made at any card pay-phone or from hotels but will be substantially more expensive. It's best to call overseas and then get the recipient to ring you back at your hotel. Reverse-charge telephone calls are normally not possible.

Mobile Phones
Mobile phones in Jordan use the GSM system. Mobile telephones can be rented from companies such as **Mobilcom** (☎ 5857777; www .mobile.com.jo; code 077) or **Fastlink** (☎ 06 5823111; www.fastlink.com.jo; code 079), which offer a full range of plans and pre-paid cards. Rates for signing up can start at JD60 including 20 minutes mobile-to-mobile time or 50 minutes mobile-to-land time. If you have your own phone and purchase a local SIM card, expect to pay around JD25 to get started. Both companies offer pay-as-you-go services.

Per minute mobile charges are around JD1.400 for international, 120 fils around the country, or 200 fils to 280 fils to neighbouring countries.

TIME
Jordan is two hours ahead of GMT/UTC in winter and three hours ahead between 1 April and 1 October, when daylight savings time is introduced. Note that Jordan's daylight savings time is slightly out of sync with summer clock changes in Europe. There are no time differences within Jordan.

Jordan is on the same time zone as Israel & the Palestinian Territories, Syria and Egypt: see the World Times zones map on p290.

TOILETS
Most hotels and restaurants, except those in the budget category, now have Western-style toilets. Otherwise, you'll be using the local Arab (squat) variety, which are generally flushed by pouring a jug of water down them.

Toilet paper is rarely offered, except in the midrange and top-end hotels and restaurants, but is widely available in shops throughout Jordan. Always carry an emergency stash with you. Remember that the little basket which is usually provided in the toilet is for toilet paper; use it or the toilet's contents will return to you as an overflow on the floor.

TOURIST INFORMATION
Local Tourist Offices

Jordan has a network of good tourism offices and, increasingly, visitor centres. The main tourist office in Amman is located on the ground floor of the **Ministry of Tourism and Antiquities** (www.tourism.jo) in Jebel Amman (see p70). Tourist visitor centres are located at Madaba, Aqaba, Karak, Jerash, Petra, Qasr Amra and Wadi Rum, with more to come.

The Jordan Tourism Board (JTB) publishes an array of excellent brochures in most languages. Pick one up from a JTB office overseas or from any tourist office in Jordan.

Tourist Offices Abroad

You can get most information from the website of the **Jordan Tourism Board** (www.see-jordan.com). The following offices will send you a package of brochures and maps if you contact them in advance:

France (☎ 01 55 60 94 46; gsv@article.com; 122 rue Paris, 92100 Boulogne-Billancourt, Paris)

Germany (☎ 069 9231 8870; jordan@adam-partner.de; Weser Strasse 4 60329 Frankfurt)

UK (☎ 020 7371 6496, brochure hotline 0870 7706933; info@jordantourismboard.co.uk; 115 Hammersmith Rd, London, W14 0QH)

USA (☎ 1 877 733 5673, 703 2437404; www.seejordan.org; Suite 102, 6867 Elm St, McLean, VA 22101)

VISAS

Visas are required by all foreigners entering Jordan. These are issued with a minimum of fuss at the border or airport on arrival (JD10). Note that visas are not issued at the King Hussein Bridge if you plan to enter from Israel & the Palestinian Territories. At the airport immigration counters, join the normal immigration lines to get your visa. There are moneychangers adjacent to the counters; ATMs are only available after immigration.

Tourist visas are valid for three months (ie you must enter the country within three months of the date of issue) for stays of up to one month from the date of entry, but can be easily extended for stays of up to three months (see p70).

Visas can also be obtained from Jordanian consulates or embassies outside the country.

The cost is usually around JD14/28 for a single/multiple entry visa. They are issued within 24 hours and two photos are required. In the Middle East, visas are available from Jordanian embassies in Turkey, Lebanon, Syria, Israel & the Palestinian Territories (avoid this if you wish to travel elsewhere in the region), Egypt, Iraq, Yemen and the Gulf States. See p242 for the location of other Jordanian diplomatic missions.

The only reason to apply for a visa from a Jordanian consulate or embassy is if you wish to obtain a multiple-entry visa, as these are not issued at the border, or if you plan to arrive via the King Hussein Bridge.

One exception worth knowing about is that if you arrive in Aqaba by sea from Nuweiba in Egypt (and presumably also by land from Eilat) your visa should be free because Aqaba has been designated as the Aqaba Special Economic Zone Area (ASEZA) set up for free trade. If you plan to stay in Jordan for more than two weeks you have to register with the ASEZA office in Aqaba (rather than the police station). It's also theoretically possible to enter through another border crossing and ask for a special 'Aqaba visa'. Your visa should then be free but you must go straight to Aqaba and register with ASEZA within 48 hours of your arrival in Jordan. Failure to do this will incur the JD10 visa fee and a fine of JD1.500 per day.

If you will be in Jordan for less than 24 hours en route to a third country you can request a free-of-charge transit visa. This also exempts you from the JD5 departure tax but you must leave Jordan within 24 hours of arrival.

Visa Extensions

A single-entry visa is valid for one month after arrival in Jordan (it used to be two weeks but this changed in June 2005 – check what is written on your visa), after which time you need to register at a police station in order to get the full three months of your visa. Failure to do so will result in a fine of at least JD1.500 per day for every day you have overstayed.

One visa extension of two or three months is easy to obtain, and often in less than 30 minutes. Extensions are technically possible in major provincial capitals such as Aqaba, Irbid and Karak, but are best done in Amman (see above). An extension costs nothing, and no photos are needed. After a stay of three months you may require an HIV test (JD20), though some travellers report that this is sometimes required after only one month. The maximum stay allowed is six months.

If you want another extension, wish to reside in Jordan, or there is something unusual about your visa (eg a curious number of Israeli stamps), you may be sent to the **Directorate of Residency & Borders** (Map p85 ☎ 5623348; Majed al-Idwans St, Shmeisani, Amman; ◷ 8am-3pm

GETTING OTHER VISAS IN JORDAN

Jordan is generally not a good place to get visas for neighbouring countries other than Egypt. For addresses of embassies and consulates, see p242.

Egypt

Most nationalities are issued a visa on arrival in Egypt, including at Cairo airport and at Nuweiba for those arriving by ferry from Aqaba (the Egyptians demand payment in US dollars); however, it's important to request a visa that is valid for all of Egypt – not just the Sinai peninsula (ie as far as Sharm el-Sheikh).

The easiest place to obtain an Egyptian visa (up to three months duration) is from the consulate in Aqaba, where you'll need one passport photo, one to two hours and JD12/15 for a single-/multiple-entry tourist visa. The relatively chaotic Egyptian embassy in Amman charges a little more and issues visas the same day.

Iraq

Travel to Iraq is not advised at present. Visa applications take two to three weeks to get approval from the Ministry of Interior in Baghdad.

Israel & the Palestinian Territories

Staff at the heavily fortified Israeli embassy actively discourage visa applications as visas are available at most border crossings and many nationalities do not require them. At the King Hussein Bridge three-month Israeli visas are available, while visas of just one month's duration are available at Sheikh Hussein Bridge and the Wadi Araba/Rabin crossing.

Lebanon

Lebanese visas are readily available at Lebanese entry points but not at the Lebanon embassy in Amman. Remember that, if you are travelling to Lebanon via Syria, you will need to obtain your Syrian visa *before* you arrive in Jordan.

Saudi Arabia

The only visas currently issued to tourists seem to be transit visas, which sometimes allow you to travel along the Tapline (Trans-Arabia Pipeline) in three days, but sometimes only let you fly in and out, and spend a day in Riyadh.

Syria

If you intend to travel to Syria, make sure you have a Syrian visa before you arrive in Jordan. Only foreign residents in Jordan (ie expatriate workers and diplomats) and residents of a country without Syrian representation can be issued a Syrian visa at the embassy in Amman. Some readers have received a Syrian visa after obtaining a letter of recommendation (in Arabic) from their embassy in Amman, but this is definitely more the exception than the rule and should not be counted on.

Visas are theoretically available at the Syria/Jordan border if there is no Syrian representation in your country of residence.

You will be refused a Syrian visa, and entry to Syria, if there is any indication in your passport of entry to Israel & the Palestinian Territories.

Sun-Thu, 8am-1pm Sat) for further checking and paperwork. Take service taxi 6 or 7 to Sh-meisani from downtown, from where it's a 15-minute walk. The office is next to the Shmeisani central police station (*markaz mudiret ash-shurta;* مركز مديرية الشرطة).

WOMEN TRAVELLERS

As a woman travelling alone around Jordan for three weeks, I have found the people only helpful, hospitable and friendly.

K Millar, UK

Attitudes Towards Women

Attitudes to foreign women in Jordan can be trying to say the least. The reasons for this are complex and, of course, it would be foolish to lump everyone together into the same category. These largely Muslim socie-ties are, by contemporary Western stand-ards, quite conservative when it comes to sex and women, and most men have little or no contact with either before marriage – you'll soon discover that your marital status (whether you're male or female) is a source of considerable interest to pretty much any-one you meet. 'Are you married?' usually figures among the first five standard ques-tions locals put to foreigners.

Western movies and TV also convince some men in these countries that all foreign women are promiscuous and will jump into bed at the drop of a hat.

Precautions

There will probably be times when you have male company that you could well live with-out. This may go no further than irritating banter or proposals of marriage and declar-ations of undying love. Harassment can also take the form of leering, sometimes being fol-lowed and occasionally being touched up.

You cannot make this problem go away and, where possible, you should try to ig-nore it or you'll end up letting a few sad individuals spoil your whole trip. Plenty of women travel through Jordan, often alone, and never encounter serious problems, so please do not become paranoid.

The first rule of thumb is to respect standard Muslim sensibilities about dress – immodest dress is still the major source of irritation to locals. Aim for knee-length dresses or loose pants and cover the shoul-ders and upper arms. Some women go to the extent of covering their head as well, though this is not really necessary in Jordan. Bear in mind that smaller towns tend to be more conservative than big cities like Amman, and smaller towns are generally more re-laxed than tiny villages in the countryside. In the trendy districts of Amman such as Abdoun and Shmeisani you'll feel comfort-able dressing as you would at home.

Female travellers have reported varying degrees of harassment from local lads on the public beaches in and near Aqaba. Bi-kinis are permitted on the private beaches run by the hotels and diving centres (where harassment is also possible), but elsewhere in Aqaba, and along the Dead Sea (except at the upmarket hotels), dress conservatively – ie baggy shorts and loose tops, even when swimming. Never go topless.

Some women also find it's not worth summoning up the energy to acknowledge, for example, being brushed up against but some behaviour may well warrant a good public scene, emphasising the shame and dishonour involved. You'll be surprised how quickly bystanders will take matters into hand if they feel one of their own has overstepped the mark. If you have to say something to ward off an advance, *imshi* (clear off) should do the trick.

In theory, the chances of getting harassed are greater in budget hotels where there are fewer controls on who comes and goes.

Lastly, some advice for single female travellers from single female readers:

- don't go to any bar unaccompanied
- avoid eye contact with any man you don't know – wearing dark glasses can help
- a wedding ring will add to your respect-ability in Arab eyes, even if you're not mar-ried; a photo of your children/husband (real or fake) will clinch it
- don't sit in the front seat of a chartered private or service taxi
- on public transport do sit next to a woman if possible
- don't go outside with wet hair, as this apparently implies that you've had sex recently!
- don't venture alone to remote regions of large archaeological sites such as Petra – including Siq Al-Barid (Little Petra) – and Jerash

- always check for peep holes in rooms and bathrooms (particularly cigarette holes in curtains)
- always place a chair against your locked hotel room door in case of 'accidental' late-night intrusions
- Be particularly circumspect about declarations of undying love from Jordanian guides, even (and especially) the handsome ones!

If you suffer any harassment go to a police station, or tourist police booth, which can be found at most tourist sights. The tourist police in Jordan take reports seriously. Should the need arise, do not hesitate to call the nationwide **Halla Line/tourism complaints number** (☎ 80022228) especially for tourists, and is staffed by English-speaking police officers.

Most toiletries are easily found in Jordan, though tampons are not always readily available. You should bring your own contraceptives and any special medications.

Restaurants, Bars & Coffeehouses

Some activities, such as sitting in coffeehouses, are usually seen as a male preserve and, although it's quite OK for Western women to enter, in some places the stares may make you feel uncomfortable.

A few restaurants have a 'family section' where local and foreign women, unaccompanied by men, can eat in peace. In some of the local bars and coffeehouses there is only one toilet, so try to avoid using these (same advice goes for male travellers!). Midrange bars and cafés in Amman almost always welcome women – see the Amman chapter, p95.

WORK

Working in Jordan is not really an option for most foreigners passing through, but it is possible for anyone with the right qualifications or interests who has done some planning before leaving home. Your employer in Jordan should be able to deal with the bureaucratic requirements of working permits.

Diving

If you are a qualified diving instructor, you may be able to get some work at one of the diving centres in Aqaba, particularly during the peak season (about September to March). Dive Aqaba takes a limited number of interns. See p229 for contact details.

Language Teaching

Teaching English is the most obvious avenue of work for travellers. One of the top schools in Amman is run by the **British Council** (☎ 06 4636147; www.britishcouncil.org.jo). The minimum requirements for teaching are the RSA Preparatory Certificate (the Diploma is generally preferred) or equivalent and two years' work experience. Most of the recruiting for teaching roles is done from the UK. For details contact their **head office** (☎ 020 7930 8466; www.britishcouncil.org; 10 Spring Gardens, London SW1A 2BN) before coming to Jordan. If you are already in Jordan, casual vacancies occasionally arise so it can be worth dropping off your CV, addressed to the Teaching Centre Manager.

The **American Language Center** (☎ 06 5523901; www.alc.edu.jo) runs the other top language school. Like the British Council, it mainly recruits in its own country.

Volunteer Work

Those hoping to work with Palestinian refugees should contact the public information office of the **UN Relief & Works Agency** (Map p85; UNRWA; ☎ 06 5609100, ext 165; jorpio@unrwa.org; Mustapha bin Abdullah St, Shmeisani, Amman). There is no organised volunteer programme, but if you are in Jordan for a few months (they prefer longer-term commitments, rather than just a few weeks) and have a particular professional skill in education, relief or health, you may be able to arrange something. Contact them at least three months in advance.

For other volunteer opportunities check out www.jordandevnet.org.

Transport

GETTING THERE & AWAY

Most visitors come to Jordan as part of a jaunt around the Middle East. Amman is well connected with most cities in the Middle East and Europe, but no airline has direct flights between Amman and Canada, Australia or New Zealand, and there are very few direct services between Amman and the USA. The overland borders between Jordan and Israel & the Palestinian Territories, and Jordan and Syria are popular and generally trouble-free, though you'll have to consider the implications of a trip to Israel & the Palestinian Territories if headed on to some other states in the Middle East (see p258). The ferry trip to Egypt is another popular option.

ENTERING THE COUNTRY

Entering Jordan is painless, whether by land, air or sea, and visas and money exchange are available at all borders.

Arriving in Amman by air you'll find an airport foreign exchange booth before immigration and two after, with an ATM after immigration. Obtaining a visa on arrival takes less than a minute – queue up in the normal immigration aisle.

Passport

Your passport should be valid for at least six months after you arrive in Jordan. Always carry your passport with you when travelling around sensitive areas such as near the border of Israel & the Palestinian Territories – which means most of the Jordan Valley and anywhere along the Dead Sea Highway. Checkpoints and passport checks are common in these areas.

AIR
Airports & Airlines

The national airline, **Royal Jordanian** (www.rja.com.jo, www.rj.com), is well run and has direct flights to most major cities in Europe and all over the Middle East. **Royal Wings** (www.royalwings.com.jo), a subsidiary of Royal Jordanian, has smaller planes for short flights from Amman to Tel Aviv (daily), Aqaba and Sharm el-Sheikh (four weekly).

The modern **Queen Alia International Airport** (☎ 06 4452000), about 35km south of Amman, is the country's main gateway. There are two terminals, only 100m apart and opposite each other. Terminal 1 is used for most Royal Jordanian flights and Terminal 2 is used by other airlines. Both terminals have ATMs, foreign exchange counters, a post office and a left luggage counter. The departure lounge has a decent café if you need to use up your remaining dinar.

The only airport hotel here is the **Alia Hotel** (☎ 4451000; aliahotel@index.com.jo; s/d JD70/85), a cou-

---

THINGS CHANGE

The information in this chapter is particularly vulnerable to change: prices for international travel are volatile, routes are introduced and cancelled, schedules change, special deals come and go, and rules and visa requirements are amended.

The upshot of this is that you should get opinions, quotes and advice from as many airlines and travel agents as possible before you part with your hard-earned cash. Details given in this chapter should be regarded as pointers and are not a substitute for your own careful, up-to-date research.

ple of kilometres from the airport terminal. You should be put up here if your flight is delayed or has an enforced overnight stopover. Otherwise, you can get a 50% discount on the room rate if you have an international ticket on Royal Jordanian. If you are just transiting Amman for a few hours you can use the pool for JD5.

The former military airfield in Marka, northeast of central Amman, is used by Royal Wings for a few flights to Aqaba and Tel Aviv in Israel & the Palestinian Territories. The only other international (and domestic) airport is at Aqaba, and some international carriers stop in Aqaba en route to Amman. There are occasional charter flights between Europe and Aqaba.

The following airlines fly to Jordan and have offices in Amman (☎ 06):

Air France (Map p85; airline code AF; ☎ 5666055; www.airfrance.com; hub Charles de Gaulle, Paris)

Austrian Airlines (Map p85; airline code OS; ☎ 5694604; www.aua.com; hub Vienna)

British Airways (Map p65; airline code BA; ☎ 5828801; www.ba.com; hub Heathrow, London)

Emirates (Map p68; airline code EK; ☎ 4615222; www.emirates.com; hub Dubai)

Gulf Air (Map p68; airline code GF; ☎ 4653613; www.gulfairco.com; hub Bahrain)

KLM (Map p82; airline code KL; ☎ 4655267; www.klm.com; hub Amsterdam)

Kuwait Airways (Map p85; airline code KU; ☎ 5685246; www.kuwait-airways.com; hub Kuwait City)

Lufthansa Airlines (Map p85; airline code LH; ☎ 5601744; www.lufthansa.com; hub Frankfurt)

Middle East Airlines (Map p82; airline code ME; ☎ 4603500; www.mea.com.lb; hub Beirut)

Qatar Airways (Map p85; airline code QR; ☎ 5656682; www.qatarairways.com; hub Doha)

Turkish Airlines (Map p68; airline code TK; ☎ 4659102; www.turkishairlines.com; hub İstanbul)

Tickets

Cheap tickets to Jordan are rare and you may find cheaper deals to Cairo, İstanbul or Tel Aviv. Foreigners with a Jordanian residence card get cheaper fares inside the country.

Online ticket sales work well if you are doing a simple one-way or return trip on specified dates, but you'll have to invest some time to find the best fares.

Always remember to reconfirm your onward or return flight at least 72 hours before departure on international flights.

> **DEPARTURE TAX**
>
> Jordan's departure tax for foreigners is JD5, whether you are departing by air, land or sea. Middle Eastern citizens go free but Jordanians pay JD25! If you've been in Jordan for less than 72 hours (24 hours if departing by a land border) you should be exempt from the departure tax, but only if you ask.
>
> Air tickets purchased inside Jordan from 2005 onwards should have the departure tax included in the ticket price – check with a travel agent when buying your ticket.

Australia

There are no direct flights between Australia and Jordan and most flights go via Southeast Asian capitals. One of the cheaper routes to Amman from Melbourne or Sydney is with Qantas Airways or Thai Airways International to Bangkok, and on to Amman with Royal Jordanian. Return low/high season fares start at A$1450/1700. Gulf Air and Emirates fly from Sydney and Melbourne to hubs in the Middle East.

Flight Centre (☎ 133 133; www.flightcentre.com.au)

STA Travel (☎ 1300 733 035; www.statravel.com.au)

Trailfinders (☎ 1300 780 212; www.trailfinders.com.au)

Continental Europe

KLM-Royal Dutch Airlines and Lufthansa Airlines offer the most direct flights to Amman, and have excellent connections all around Europe and the UK. Amsterdam and Frankfurt are the two major hubs for discounted air transport in continental Europe.

One cheap airline worth considering is Cyprus Airways, which flies to Amman via Larnaca (Cyprus) from many European capitals. Royal Jordanian has weekly direct flights between Paris and Aqaba.

From Frankfurt, air fares start at €1050 for a return flight. A recommended agency is **STA Travel** (☎ 069 7430 3292; www.statravel.com), which has branches in major cities across Germany and the rest of Europe.

In Italy, recommended travel agents include **CTS Viaggi** (☎ 06 462 0431; www.cts.it), a student and youth specialist with branches in major cities. Expect to pay €660 for a return flight to Amman.

Recommended in Paris is **OTU Voyages** (☎ 0820 817 817; www.otu.fr), which has branches across France. Other recommendations include **Voyageurs du Monde** (☎ 01 42 86 16 00; www .vdm.com) and **Nouvelles Frontières** (☎ 08 25 00 07 47; www.nouvelles-frontieres.fr), with branches across the country. Return fares to Amman start at €1100.

Readers have recommended both www .connections.be and www.taxistop.be for discounted online tickets to Jordan.

Middle East

Jordan is a decent base from which to explore the Middle East, and there are regular flights from Amman all around the region. Flights are not particularly cheap, however, but specials (eg over the Thursday/Friday Islamic 'weekend') are sometimes available.

These are some approximate one-way fares from Amman: Abu Dhabi JD180, Baghdad JD380, Beirut JD100, Cairo JD125–JD135, Damascus JD70, Dubai JD175, İstanbul JD180, Kuwait City JD200, San'a JD220, Tripoli JD250 and Tel Aviv JD80. In Amman, the best places to start looking for air tickets are the agencies along Al-Malek Al-Hussein St, near the flyover.

In Tel Aviv, try the **Israel Student Travel Association** (ISSTA; ☎ 03 524 6322; 128 Ben Yehuda St). There's also a branch in Jerusalem (☎ 02 625 2799; 1 HaNevi'im St).

In İstanbul there are lots of travel agencies on the northern side of Divan Yolu in Sultanahmet, all of them specialising in budget air tickets. **Orion-Tour** (☎ 212 232 6300; www.oriontour.com; Halaskargazi Caddesi 284/3, Marmara Apartimani, Sisli 80220) is recommended.

The area around Midan Tahrir in Cairo is teeming with travel agencies, but don't expect any amazing deals. One of the best agencies in Cairo, though it's way down in Ma'adi, is **Egypt Panorama Tours** (☎ 02 359 0200; www.eptours .com) just outside Al-Ma'adi metro station.

New Zealand

Flights to Jordan from New Zealand generally run via Frankfurt or Bangkok. From New Zealand, you can expect to pay around NZ$1650 for a return flight to Amman in the low season.

Flight Centre (☎ 0800 243 544; www.flightcentre.co.nz)
STA Travel (☎ 0508 782 872; www.statravel.co.nz)

UK

London and other cities in England are well connected with Amman, although some of the cheapest airlines do not fly there directly and require a lengthy (even overnight) stopover. Some of the airlines mentioned below offer 'open jaw' tickets which, for example, allow you to fly into Amman, but out of Beirut (Lebanon) or Damascus (Syria).

Some of the cheapest flights from the UK to Amman are on Lufthansa (via Frankfurt); Olympic Airways (via Athens); Turkish Airlines (via İstanbul); and Tarom (via Bucharest). Low season return fares start from £320.

Royal Jordanian flies direct between London and Amman daily. Expect to pay £420 for a return fare. One way to London in Amman costs JD305. British Mediterranean (part of British Airways) flies daily, mostly direct but once a week via Beirut so check the routing before booking.

The tour company **Voyages Jules Vernes** (☎ 020 7616 1000; www.vjv.co.uk) operates charter flights to Aqaba for its clients and may sell extra seats to the public.

STA Travel (☎ 0870 160 6070; www.statravel.co.uk)
Trailfinders (☎ 020 7938 3366; www.trailfinders.com)

Online travel agencies include www.last minute.com, www.cheaptickets.co.uk and www.expedia.co.uk.

USA & Canada

There's little direct traffic between the USA and Jordan, so most flights change in Europe (London for British Airways, Paris for Delta/Air France or Amsterdam for Northwest/KLM). Alternatively, get a connection in a country near Jordan on a Middle Eastern airline. The cheapest option may be to fly into Tel Aviv and then cross the border into Jordan by bus or service taxi. However, this means that your passport will have those dreaded Israeli entry stamps – see p258.

Royal Jordanian (☎ 1800 223 0470) has direct flights between Amman and New York, Chicago and Detroit, with onward codeshare flights with America West. Flights from New York start around $900, or $1100 from Los Angeles (via Detroit).

Air Canada and Royal Jordanian offer flights, via London or Frankfurt, from Canada to Amman. Canadian discount air tickets are about 10% higher than those sold in the USA.

STA Travel (☎ 800 781 4040; www.statravel.com) Has offices throughout the US.

Travel CUTS (☎ 1866 416 2887; www.travelcuts.com) Canada's national student travel agency has offices in all major cities.

Online booking agencies include:
Cheap Tickets (www.cheaptickets.com)
Expedia (www.expedia.com)
Orbitz (www.orbitz.com)
Travelocity (www.travelocity.com)

LAND

Crossing the border overland into Jordan from Saudi Arabia is nigh on impossible for non-residents and travel to Iraq is curently on hold, so most travellers generally come overland from Syria or Israel & the Palestinian Territories, or by ferry from Egypt. However, there are three important things to note:

- *Any* indication of travel to/from Israel & the Palestinian Territories will mean that you cannot enter Syria, Lebanon and most other Middle Eastern countries, although Jordan is OK. See p258 for details
- All travellers who intend to travel to Syria should ensure they obtain a visa for Syria *before* coming to Jordan – see p251
- Jordanian visas are not available at the Israel/Jordan border at King Hussein Bridge (though they are available at other crossings)

Most travellers arrive in Jordan by bus or service taxi if travelling overland, although it's no problem bringing your own car or motorcycle (see p264).

Iraq

Travel to Iraq is not recommended at the present. Land transport crosses at the al-Karama/Tarbil border post, which is located 330km from Amman. **Jordan Regular Transport** (☎ 4622652) at Abdali bus station in Amman currently operates service taxis and minibuses to Baghdad, mostly for Iraqi citizens and using Iraqi drivers. Services leave Amman at midnight in order to get to the border at dawn. Vehicles then travel in convoys for safety into the notorious 'Sunni triangle', passing Fallujah before *(in sha'Allah)* arriving in Baghdad. A seat in a service taxi costs JD25 and JD15 in a minibus. A private car should cost around JD140.

Israel & the Palestinian Territories

Since the historic peace treaty between Jordan and Israel & the Palestinian Territories was signed in 1994, three border crossings have opened to foreigners – King Hussein Bridge, Sheikh Hussein Bridge and Wadi Araba.

BORDER CROSSINGS

Before crossing into Jordan from Israel & the Palestinian Territories, there are a few things you need to remember:

- Only change as much money as you need because the commission charged by moneychangers is often ridiculously high
- Israeli visas of one month's duration are issued at the Wadi Araba (Rabin) and Sheikh Hussein Bridge crossings, but those issued at the King Hussein Bridge are usually for three months
- Jordanian visas cannot be obtained on arrival at the King Hussein Bridge
- If you want to visit Israel & the Palestinian Territories, use the King Hussein Bridge crossing and then return to Jordan within 14 days (or three months if you extend your visa in Jordan before leaving), you do not need a second or multiple-entry Jordanian visa
- Private vehicles cannot drive across the King Hussein Bridge, but they can be taken across the other borders
- Refer to p258, for information about how to deal with the Israeli passport-stamp issue

On both sides of all three borders there are moneychanging facilities, places to eat and drink, and duty-free shops. On the Jordanian side of all three borders there is a post office and a **tourist information counter** (⏰ 8am-2pm, closed Fri).

You can expect borders to be closed on the Jewish holiday of Yom Kippur and the Islamic holiday of Eid al-Fitr (see p243).

King Hussein (Jisr al-Malek Hussein)/Allenby Bridge

Only 40km from Amman and 30km from Jerusalem, this **border crossing** (⏰ 8am-6pm Sun-Thu, 8am-12pm Fri & Sat) offers travellers the most direct route between the two cities. It is a common way to exit, but not enter, Jordan, because Jordanian visas are not

TRANSPORT

TRANSPORT

ISRAELI BORDER STAMPS

Most countries in the Middle East and North Africa (with the exception of Jordan, Egypt, Turkey, Tunisia and Morocco) will not grant visas, or allow entry, to anyone who has *any* evidence of visiting Israel, or the Palestine Territories (which includes the West Bank). This includes Israeli exit stamps from any of the three borders with Jordan (ie from Eilat, King Hussein Bridge and Sheikh Hussein Bridge); Israeli exit stamps or Egyptian entry stamps at Rafah and Taba, both on the border; and any Jordanian entry stamps at the border of Israel & the Palestinian Territories. Travellers have even been turned away from Syria's border with Jordan for having unexplained periods of time in their passport, such as three weeks in Jordan without any evidence of a Jordanian visa extension.

Even if you do things in a convoluted fashion – eg visit Israel & the Palestinian Territories from Egypt, return to Egypt and go to Jordan on the ferry – you run a good chance of acquiring unwanted evidence in your passport. Even if the Israelis do not stamp you in or out, the Egyptians may well do so (at Rafah at least). And then if you apply for a Syrian visa, or attempt to cross the Jordan/Syria border, without a Jordanian entry stamp you'll probably be denied a visa or entry.

The only foolproof method is to visit the countries that will not accept evidence of a visit to Israel & the Palestinian Territories *before* going there, and then go to countries, such as Egypt and Jordan, that will accept Israeli visas/stamps – and later get a new passport. If you have dual citizenship, try to get two passports, but keep them separate and make sure you get the correct visas and stamps in the right passport.

If none of the above is possible or feasible, cross the border from Jordan to Israel & the Palestinian Territories at the King Hussein Bridge and go back to Jordan the same way. To be sure, leave and re-enter Jordan within the time limit specified on your Jordanian visa (ie within 14 days of your original visa or within the duration of any extension). But make sure you ask for all Jordanian and Israeli stamps to be placed on a separate piece of paper. People who have crossed from Jordan to the West Bank in small groups have asked for stamps on separate pieces of paper, but have still been caught out; for some reason, Israeli immigration officials may not stamp the first two or three passports, but then they'll stamp the next few – so it's best to cross individually or in groups of two.

If you get an Israeli or Jordanian exit or entry stamp in your passport, there's little you can do. If you report that your passport is 'lost' to your embassy in any country in the Middle East, it may be met with extreme cynicism, and even rejection. And some countries may also be highly sceptical, and even refuse you a visa or entry, if you have a brand new, unused passport issued in the Middle East.

issued at this border – so get a Jordanian visa at an embassy/consulate beforehand, or use another border crossing.

Public transport in Israel & the Palestinian Territories doesn't run during the Jewish Shabbat between sunset Friday and sunset Saturday. On Friday and Saturday it's better to arrive before 11am.

Due to the ongoing *intifada* (uprising) in the Palestinian Territories, no Jordanian buses were crossing King Hussein Bridge at the time of research. Instead, service taxis run throughout the day from Amman's Abdali bus station to (but not across) King Hussein Bridge (JD2.500, 45 minutes) or there's a single daily JETT bus (JD6.500) at 6.30am. These services may move to the

Wahadat station in the future, so check with your hotel.

The ride to the Israeli & Palestinian Territories side, although extremely short, can seem to last an eternity with repeated stops for passport and bag checks. At the time of research, it was not possible to walk, hitch or take a private car across. Buses (JD2) shuttle between the two borders. There are money-changing facilities on your way to the exit.

The historic oddity of this crossing has remained enshrined in the fact that, on leaving Jordan, you're not really considered to be leaving Jordan. Prior to 1988, Jordan laid claim to the West Bank as its own territory, and somehow this idea has remained in the approach to visas. If you wish to return to Jordan from the Palestinian Territories on your current Jordanian visa, you need only keep the stamped exit slip and present it on returning by the same crossing (it won't work at the other crossings). You must return within the validity of your Jordanian visa or its extension.

At the Israeli border post, plead with the officials to stamp your Jordanian visa stamp rather than your passport (see opposite).

Travelling into Jordan, the Israeli exit tax is a hefty 127 NIS (around US\$29; compared to around 70 NIS elsewhere), supposedly because you're paying to leave Israel & the Palestinian Territories. Note that, if you intend to return to Israel, you must keep the entrance form given to you by the Jordanians – they may well insist on you prolonging your stay in Jordan if you cannot present it.

To get to Jerusalem from the border, take a *sherut* (Israeli shared taxi; around US\$40 for the car) to Jerusalem's Damascus Gate. Alternatively take a cheaper bus to Jerusalem or, if that's not running, a bus to Jericho and then a *sherut* to Damascus Gate. Much of the public transport in the West Bank was not running when we were there.

In all, crossing the border can take up to three hours, depending on Israeli security measures; avoid 11am to 3pm when delays are more common.

Sheikh Hussein Bridge (Jisr Sheikh Hussein)

The northernmost **crossing** (Jordan Bridge to the Israelis; 🕑 6.30am-10pm Sun-Thu, 8am-8pm Fri & Sat) links northern Jordan with Beit She'an in Galilee (Israel & the Palestinian Territories), 6km away. It's handy if you wish to visit northern Jordan, and it's the closest crossing to Jerusalem and Amman that will issue Jordanian visas on arrival.

From Irbid, regular service taxis leave the West bus station for the border (750 fils, 45 minutes). From the bridge it's a 2km walk (or hitch) to the Israeli side, from where you have to take a taxi to the Beit She'an bus station for onward connections inside Israel & the Palestinian Territories.

If you're coming from Israel & the Palestinian Territories, take a bus to Tiberias, and change at Beit She'an (6km from the border). From there, take another bus to the Israeli border (allow enough time because there is only a handful of buses per day). After passport formalities and paying Israeli exit tax (70 NIS), a compulsory bus takes you to the Jordanian side.

From the Jordanian side, either wait for a minibus or shared taxi to Irbid (from where there are regular connections to Amman), go to Shuneh ash-Shamaliyyeh (North Shuna) by private or service taxi, or walk (3km) to the main road and flag down a minibus or service taxi.

Wadi Araba

This handy **crossing** (formerly Arava, now the Yitzhak Rabin crossing to the Israelis; 🕑 6.30am-10pm Sun-Thu, 8am-8pm Fri & Sat) in the south of the country links Aqaba to Eilat. To get there from Aqaba you'll have to take a taxi (JD5). Once at the border you can just walk across. From the border, buses run to central Eilat, only 2km away. All in, Aqaba to Eilat takes about an hour.

If you're travelling from Jerusalem and you want to skip Eilat, ask the driver to let you out at the turn-off for the border, a short walk away. Israel & the Palestinian Territories exit tax is 68 NIS here. On the Jordanian border take a taxi into Aqaba (JD5, 15 minutes) or you could negotiate a taxi fare direct to Petra (around JD25, two hours) or Wadi Rum.

BUS

Several cities in Jordan are now regularly linked to cities in Israel & the Palestinian Territories. Travelling by bus directly between Amman and Tel Aviv will save you the hassle of getting to/from the borders, but it's more expensive than crossing independently, and you'll have to wait for all passengers to clear customs and immigration.

From Amman, **Trust International Transport** (Map p65; ☎ 06 5813427) has buses from its office at 7th Circle to Tel Aviv (JD21, six hours), Haifa (JD18, seven hours) and Nazareth (JD18, seven hours), departing daily except Saturday at 8.30am. Services cross the border at the Sheikh Hussein Bridge. Buses leave from the Trust office in **Irbid** (☎ 02 7251878) at around 10am. Book tickets the day before.

CAR & MOTORCYCLE

If you're driving from Israel & the Palestinian Territories, use the border crossings at Sheikh Hussein Bridge or Wadi Araba/ Rabin (it is not possible to drive over the King Hussein Bridge).

Saudi Arabia

Getting a visa, even a transit visa, to Saudi Arabia is a very difficult feat – see p251, for details.

The main land route for public transport into Saudi Arabia is at Al-Umari, which is located along the highway south of Azraq. The other two crossing points are Ad-Durra, located south of Aqaba, and further east at Al-Mudawwara. Several companies run services to Jeddah and Riyadh from Amman's Abdali bus station.

Syria

If you want to travel directly between Damascus and Amman, it's worth taking a direct bus or service taxi. Otherwise you may end up spending more time and money once you catch a service taxi to Der'a, organise your own transport across the border, get another lift to Ramtha, perhaps another to Irbid, and then a connection to Amman. The only reason to travel this way is if you want to stop off en route at places such as Ezra'a and Bosra ash-Sham (Syria), or Jerash and Umm Qais.

If you are headed to Syria from Jordan, make sure you get a Syrian visa before arriving in Jordan (see p251), either in your home country or in İstanbul, Ankara or Cairo.

BORDER CROSSINGS

The two border crossings between Syria and Jordan are efficient and relatively painless on both sides. If you intend to drive between Jordan and Syria, the better border to cross is at Der'a/Ramtha.

Der'a/Ramtha and Nasib/Jabir are both open for 24 hours every day. The Jordanian sides both have a post office and **tourist office** (🕗 8am-5pm Sat-Thu, 8am-2pm Fri), moneychangers (open most of the time) where Jordanian dinars and Syrian pounds are changed, and places to eat and drink.

Der'a/Ramtha

Ramtha is the border most commonly used by foreigners who are using nondirect public transport and/or detouring to sights in northern Jordan. You can get direct transport between Damascus and Irbid or Amman, without stopping in Ramtha, though there are also buses to Ramtha from Amman's Abdali station (500 fils, two hours) and Irbid (250 fils). From Ramtha, service taxis and

minibuses run regularly to the border. If hitching, ask the immigration office on the Jordanian side to flag down a vehicle for a lift to the Syrian border.

Nasib/Jabir

Most service taxis between Amman and Damascus now use this crossing. It's also useful if you plan a detour to eastern Jordan (eg Azraq), as the border at Jabir is useful for connections to Zarqa or Mafraq.

BUS

The air-conditioned **Jordan Express Travel & Tourism** (JETT; Map p85; ☎ 5664146; Al-Malek al-Hussein St, Shmeisani) buses travel between Amman and Damascus (JD5, five hours) twice a day, at 7am and 3pm; book a day in advance. JETT also has a daily bus to Aleppo (JD7.500, eight hours) at 2.30pm. JETT's international terminal is just up from the Abdali bus station in Amman. **Afana** (Map p85; ☎ 4614611), next door, also has an evening bus to Damascus (JD5, five hours), leaving at 9pm, but it arrives very early in the morning and services aren't quite as reliable. Buses drop passengers off at the Baramke garage in Damascus.

The Palace Hotel in Amman (p88) has started a useful minibus service which runs between Amman and Damascus, with stops en route at Jerash, Bosra and Shaba (JD25 per person). They require a minimum of four passengers.

SERVICE TAXI

The service taxis to Damascus (three hours) are faster than the buses and run at all hours, although you'll have to wait longer in the evening for one to fill up. Service taxis take less time to cross the border than trains or buses because there are fewer passengers to process, and the drivers are experienced in helping passengers with immigration and customs formalities. These taxis are huge, yellow (or white) and American-made.

From Amman, service taxis for Damascus ('ash-Sham' in Arabic) leave from the eastern or lower end of the Abdali bus station (Map p68); from Damascus, they leave from the Baramke garage. The trip costs JD7 from Amman, and S£500 from Damascus. Service taxis also travel between Damascus and Irbid (South bus station, 2½ hours) in northern Jordan for slightly less.

THE HEJAZ RAILWAY

The Hejaz Railway was built between 1900–1908 to transport pilgrims from Damascus to the holy city of Medina, reducing the two-month journey by camel and on foot to as little as three days. For Jordan, and Amman in particular, this meant an increased boom in trade. The 1462km line was completely funded by donations from Muslims – but functioned for less than 10 years.

The trains and railway line were partially destroyed in the Arab Revolt of 1917 during WWI. The line was rebuilt as far south as Ma'an, but is now only used for cargo. There is occasional talk of introducing a tourist passenger service between Aqaba and Wadi Rum.

TRAIN

Services on the Hejaz Railway between Amman and Damascus leave Amman and Damascus on Monday and Thursday at 8am, but very few travellers take this service because it is so much slower than a service taxi (you have to change trains at the border, so figure on at least nine hours to Damascus). Tickets cost JD3 (half-priced for kids under nine). The charming old station is located on King Abdullah I St, approximately 2.5km east of the Raghadan station in Amman.

The **ticket office** (☎ 06 4895413) is officially only open from 7am on the morning of departure, although you may well find someone around at other times. To get to the station, take a service taxi from Raghadan station, or a private taxi (around 800 fils).

Elsewhere in the Middle East

For other destinations in the Middle East, travellers need time, patience – and most importantly – the necessary visas. These trips are long and hence most people end up flying.

From Abdali bus station, service taxis depart frequently for Beirut (JD20) and less frequently to Kuwait (JD30). Hijazi (see p100) has buses to Dubai (JD45), usually once a week.

JETT has services to the following surrounding cities from its international bus office in Amman:

destination	days	one way	hours
Beirut	Sun & Thu	15JD	6
Cairo	Sun & Tue	US$58	24
Doha	daily	44JD	30
Dubai	daily	52JD	36
Kuwait	Fri	30JD	18
Manama	daily	35JD	24

Note that the fare to Cairo must be paid in US dollars, and includes the Aqaba–Nuweiba ferry ticket.

SEA

There are two boat services to Nuweiba in Egypt which leave from the passenger terminal just south of Aqaba. With both services, departure times can be subject to change so call the **passenger terminal** (☎ 03 2013240; www.abmari time.com.jo/english) before travelling to check the departure time.

The fast boat, which leaves Aqaba daily (except Saturday) at noon (get there by 10.30am), takes about an hour and costs JD26 or US$36; children aged two to 12 pay JD14 or US$20. It's more expensive (US$45) to come the other way due to the difference in government taxes. You need your passport to buy a ticket. The return ferry leaves Nuweiba around 3pm.

There is also a slower ferry service (which doubles as a car ferry) that officially leaves at noon but often doesn't leave until 5pm or later, depending on the number of trucks trying to get on board. When it does leave, it should take three hours but it usually takes longer. There is sometimes talk of another service, at 6pm, but this is only during exceptionally busy times (like the haj). The cost for the slow ferry is US$25. A car in either direction costs an extra US$110.

Tickets for either service can be paid for in Jordanian dinars or US dollars. It's not possible to buy return tickets. Beware of buying ferry tickets in Amman because you may be charged for nonexistent first-class seats – buy the tickets in Aqaba. The worst time for travelling is just after the haj, when Aqaba fills up with *hajis* (pilgrims) returning home from Mecca to Egypt.

Most nationalities can obtain Egyptian tourist visas on arrival at Nuweiba. If you only need a visa valid for the Sinai region you can get this on the boat. If you wish to travel further than Sharm el-Sheikh you need a full visa for Egypt. You can get this at the consulate at Aqaba (see p251) or on arrival at Nuweiba.

Whichever direction you travel in, you will have to hand in your passport to immigration authorities on the boat and pick it up at the immigration offices in Aqaba or Nuweiba.

Travellers from Eastern Europe may want to get their Egyptian visa before boarding the boat as some have been refused entry onto the ferry at Aqaba because they had no Egyptian visa.

There are money exchange facilities at the terminals at Nuweiba and Aqaba. The Jordanian side offers a decent exchange rate (at the time of research JD1 equalled €1.2) but avoid travellers cheques, which attract a huge commission.

There is a sporadic twice-weekly catamaran trip between Aqaba and Sharm el-Sheikh (officially US$45, three hours) but this wasn't operating at the time of research.

If you are travelling from Egypt you will arrive in Aqaba too late for public transport to Petra or Wadi Rum so you'll have to overnight in Aqaba or arrange a taxi.

One thing to consider, if you don't mind an Israeli border stamp (see p258), is that it's quicker and cheaper to travel overland via Israel & the Palestinian Territories. Take a taxi from Taba to the border then another taxi on to the Arava border crossing with Jordan (or go by bus changing at Eilat bus station); the whole thing takes about an hour. Going to Egypt bear in mind that you can't get a full Egyptian visa at the border with Israel & the Palestinian Territories at Taba, only a Sinai peninsula visa, so get one in Aqaba or Amman before you go.

TOURS

Organised tours from abroad are generally divided into cultural/historical tours, overland adventures that combine several Middle Eastern countries, or activity-based holidays that involve some hiking and camel riding. See p269 for details of companies inside Jordan that can organise individual tours and itineraries.

Australia
Adventure World (☎ 02 8913 0755; www.adventure world.com.au)

Peregrine Adventures (☎ 03 9663 8611; www .peregrineadventures.com, www.geckosadventures.com)
Yalla Tours (☎ 1300 362 844, 03 9510 2844; info@yallatours.com.au)

Israel & the Palestinian Territories
Desert Eco Tours (☎ 972 8637 4259; www.deserteco tours.com) Specialises in camel, hiking and 4WD tours; based in Eilat.

UK
Abercrombie and Kent (☎ 0845 070 0610; www .abercrombiekent.co.uk)
Alternative Travel Group (☎ 0186 531 5678; www .atg-oxford.co.uk; 69-71 Banbury Rd, Oxford OX2 6PJ) Activities in Dana, Wadi Rum and Aqaba.
Cox & Kings (☎ 020 7873 5000; www.coxandkings .co.uk)
Dragoman (☎ 0870 4994 4750; www.dragoman.com)
Exodus (☎ 0870 240 5550, 020 8675 5550; www .exodus.co.uk)
Explore (☎ 0870 333 4001; www.explore.co.uk)
High Places (☎ 0114 275 7500; www.highplaces.co.uk) Ten-day hiking and scrambling trip in Wadi Rum, including a Christmas departure.
Idrisi Travel (☎ 31 0492 340632; www.idrisitravel .co.uk; Molenakkers 25, 5761 BS Bakel, Netherlands) Hiking and archaeology. British company based in the Netherlands.
Imaginative Traveller (☎ 0800 316 2717, 020 8742 8612; www.imaginative-traveller.com)
Martin Randall Travel (☎ 020 8742 3355; www .martinrandall.com)
Tribes (☎ 017 2868 5971; www.tribes.co.uk)
Voyages Jules Vernes (☎ 020 7616 1000; www.vjv .co.uk)

USA
Archaeological Tours (☎ 212 9863054; www.archaeo logicaltrs.com; 271 Madison Ave, suite 904, NY, NY 10016) A 14-day historical tour with archaeologists.
Journeys Unlimited (☎ 800 255 8735, 734 665 4407; www.journeys-intl.com)
Ya'lla Tours (☎ 503 977 3758; www.yallatours.com)

GETTING AROUND

Jordan is so small that you can drive from the Syrian border in the north to the Saudi border in the south in just over five hours. There is only one domestic flight (Amman to Aqaba) and no internal public train service, so public transport here comprises of buses/ minibuses, service taxis and private taxis.

Where public transport is limited or non-existent, hitching is a common way of getting around. Hiring a car is a popular, if more expensive, alternative. Chartering a service taxi (white) or private taxi (yellow) is another alternative, and having a driver will take the hassle out of driving, although the cost will vary depending on your bargaining skills.

AIR

Since only 430km separates Ramtha in the north from Aqaba in the south, Jordan has only one internal flight, between Amman and Aqaba (JD39, 40 minutes). See p225 for details.

BICYCLE

Cycling is a popular option, but not necessarily always a fun one. March to May and September to November are the best times to get on your bike.

The disadvantages are: the stifling heat in summer; the few places to stop along the highways; the unpredictable traffic, with drivers not being used to cyclists; the steep streets in some cities, such as Amman and Karak; the paucity of spare parts because so few locals ride bikes; and the tendency of Jordanian children to throw stones at unwary cyclists.

There is no way to cycle along the King's Highway without getting stoned. We read it in your guidebook before leaving, but thought that kids would not stone three male adults with beards and long trousers who are looking angry. We were wrong. And there are not only *some* groups of kids who try to stone you, but basically it's becoming a major hobby for all male children between three and 20... Cycle in the morning when children are at school and plan to spend plenty of time discussing and waiting; you probably won't do more than 40km a day.
Bernhard Gerber, Switzerland

The good news, however, is that the road system is satisfactory, the roads are generally smooth and the main cities and tourist attractions are well signposted in English.

With some preparation, and an occasional lift in a bus, cyclists can have a great time. Most major sights are conveniently placed

less than a day's ride apart, heading south from the Syrian border – ie Irbid-Amman-Madaba-Karak-Dana-Petra-Ma'an-Wadi Rum-Aqaba. All these places have accommodation of some kind and restaurants, so there's no need to carry tents, sleeping bags and cooking equipment. Most other attractions can be easily visited on day trips, by bike or public transport.

The King's Highway is the most scenic route, but also the most physically demanding. The Desert Highway is boring and the traffic is heavy, while the Dead Sea Highway has extremely few stops, and is always hot. Two stretches along the King's Highway where you may want to take public transport are across the extremely wide and steep Wadi Mujib valley between Madaba and Karak, and between the turn-off to Wadi Rum and Aqaba, which is very steep, has appalling traffic and plenty of treacherous turns. The steepest climbs are those from the Jordan Valley up onto the eastern plateau in the north.

Spare parts are not common in Jordan, so carry a spare tyre, extra chain links, spokes, two inner tubes, repair kit and tool kit with spanner set. Also bring a low gear set for the hills and a couple of water containers; confine your panniers to a maximum of 15kg.

BUS

Public minibuses and, to a lesser extent, public buses are the normal form of transport for locals and visitors.

Tickets for public buses and minibuses are normally bought on the bus. For private buses, tickets are usually bought from an office at the departure point. Tickets for private buses should be bought a day in advance; on public buses and minibuses it's every frail old man, woman, and goat for themselves. Bigger private bus companies like **JETT** (Map p85; ☎ 5664146; Al-Malek al-Hussein St, Shmeisani) (Amman to Aqaba), **Trust International Transport** (Map p65; ☎ 06 5813427) (Amman to Aqaba) and **Hijazi** (Map p68; ☎ 4638110) (Amman to Irbid) are generally the most reliable, comfortable and fastest because they generally don't stop en route to pick up passengers.

Unaccompanied men and women can sit next to each other, but some seat-shuffling often takes place to ensure that unaccompanied foreign men or women do not sit next to members of the opposite sex that they do not know. On smaller minibuses locals signify that they want to get off by rapping a coin on a side window.

Public buses and minibuses normally only leave when full, so you can sometimes wait around for an hour or more before you finally depart. Standing is not normally allowed.

There's little overcharging on minibuses, except for services to/from Wadi Musa (for Petra). Sometimes you will have to pay the full fare even if you're not going the full distance.

CAR & MOTORCYCLE
Automobile Associations
The **Royal Automobile Club of Jordan** (☎ 06 5850626, for carnets 4622467; www.racj.com) can arrange a carnet if you are bringing your own car.

Bringing Your Own Vehicle
Drivers of cars and riders of motorbikes will need the vehicle's registration papers and liability insurance. Strictly speaking you don't need an International Driving Permit (IDP) to drive in Jordan (your na-

tional licence is generally sufficient, unless you have your own car and plan on crossing any borders), but bring one with you to avoid any hassles. You also need a *Carnet de passage en douane,* which is effectively a passport for the vehicle and acts as a temporary waiver of import duty. The carnet will also need to specify any expensive spare parts that you're planning to carry with you, such as a gearbox. This is designed to prevent car-import rackets. Contact your local automobile association for details about all documentation.

At the borders to Jordan (and the ferry terminal in Nuweiba, Egypt) you'll be obliged to take out local insurance of JD35 (valid for one month), plus a nominal 'customs fee' of JD5 for 'foreign car registration'.

Finally, bring a good set of spare parts and some mechanical knowledge, as you will not always be able to get the help you may need. This is especially the case for motorcycles: there are only a few motorcycle mechanics in Jordan who are able to deal with anything modern.

ROAD DISTANCES (KM)

	Ajlun	Amman	Aqaba	Azraq	Irbid	Jerash	Karak	King Hussein Bridge	Ma'an	Madaba	Ramtha	Tafila
Amman	73											
Aqaba	396	328										
Azraq	155	103	415									
Irbid	32	89	408	143								
Jerash	22	51	370	132	38							
Karak	182	118	252	205	202	164						
King Hussein Bridge	78	56	367	152	109	89	151					
Ma'an	279	212	116	289	294	255	154	252				
Madaba	95	32	325	119	115	77	86	64	210			
Ramtha	57	94	410	141	28	40	205	130	296	118		
Tafila	242	180	189	266	267	229	63	215	90	151	296	
Wadi Musa (Petra)	297	230	97	317	313	275	142	268	45	228	316	81

Checkpoints

You may pass through checkpoints in Jordan, particularly when driving along the Dead Sea Highway near the sensitive border with Israel & the Palestinian Territories. Always stop at checkpoints. Foreigners are generally waved through without any fuss, though you may have to show your passport.

Fuel & Spare Parts

Benzin 'adi (regular) petrol costs around 370 fils per litre, and the slightly less frequently available *mumtaz, khas* (super) costs 450 fils, and rising. Remember to check with your car-hire company as to which petrol your car requires; most take super. Best of luck if you're looking for unleaded; *khal min ar-rasas* (unleaded petrol) is only reliably available in Amman and even then at only a few stations. Diesel is available at about 150 fils per litre.

Petrol stations are run by the state monopoly Jordan Petroleum Refinery Co. Stations can mostly be found on the outskirts of major towns, and at some junctions, although you may have to try a few if you're looking for super. Along the Desert Highway there are plenty of stations. There are fewer along the King's Highway, and *very* few along the Dead Sea Highway.

Garages with reputable mechanics can be found in the outskirts of most towns. They can handle most repairs, at negotiable prices, but always check with your car-hire company before getting anything done.

4WDs

Four-wheel drives are only necessary if you're going to out-of-the-way places in the deserts, such as Burqu. However, 4WDs should only be hired – and driven – by someone who is experienced; driving in the desert where there are no signs, and getting bogged in sand in 45°C heat, is one of the more dangerous things you can do in Jordan.

Four-wheel drive vehicles can be hired from reputable agencies in Aqaba (p226) and Amman (p100), but are far more expensive than normal sedans: at least JD65 per day. Also, companies only offer 100 to 200 free kilometres; you then pay extra for each kilometre.

To get around Wadi Rum, you'll need to charter a 4WD jeep with a local driver.

JORDAN'S MOST SCENIC DRIVES

- Umm Qais to Al-Himma – views to Galilee
- Mt Nebo to Suweimeh – views over Jericho and the Promised Land
- Deir Alla to Salt – incredibly steep and affords stunning views
- Dead Sea Highway, between Suweimeh and Safi – views of the salt sea
- Qadsiyya to Dana Guest House – winding views down Wadi Dana
- Across Wadi Mujib, the 'Grand Canyon' of Jordan
- Wadi Musa to Tayyibeh, at sunset
- Around Wadi Rum (4WDs only)
- Dead Sea Panorama to the Dead Sea Highway – the best views of the Dead Sea
- Tafila to Fifa – winding desert wadi scenery

Hire

Hiring a car can be expensive, but if you can split the costs, it's a great way of seeing a lot of Jordan quickly and easily.

It makes little sense to hire a car to travel to places like Petra and Jerash, which need a day or more to be explored properly on foot; or to Wadi Rum, where a 4WD as well as a local driver is needed. Chartering a service or private taxi with a driver is potentially better value in these places. See p16 for some possible itineraries. Three days is sometimes the minimum period allowed by car-hire companies.

There are many agencies in Amman, a few in Aqaba and one or two irregularly staffed offices at Queen Alia airport and the King Hussein border with Israel & the Palestinian Territories. Any car-hire agency elsewhere is usually just an office with one guy, one desk, one telephone and one car for hire (usually his!). You'll get the best deal in Amman (see p100), where competition among agencies is fierce.

Avis (www.avis.com.jo) The biggest car-hire company in Jordan. Offices in Amman, Aqaba and King Hussein Bridge. Free drop-off at King Hussein Bridge or the airport; elsewhere JD25.

Budget (budget@go.com.jo)

TRANSPORT

Eagle Rent-a-Car (eaglerentacar@wanadoo.jo)
Europcar (www.europcar.jo) Free drop in Aqaba.
Firas Car Rental (alamo@nets.com.jo) Firas is the agent for Alamo Car Rental.
Hertz (www.hertz.com.jo) Drop-off at offices in Aqaba, Petra or Mövenpick Dead Sea Resort costs JD20.
National Car Rental (www.1stjordan.net/national) Offices in Amman and at Sheikh Hussein Bridge.
Reliable Rent-a-Car (www.reliable.com.jo) Reliable and recommended. You can reserve online; contact Mohammed Hallak. Baby seats are available.

Expect to pay JD25–JD35 per day for the smallest, cheapest sedan. This doesn't include tax or petrol, but usually includes free unlimited kilometres – undoubtedly a better deal than accepting a cheaper set-rate with a charge per kilometre.

For a three-day hire, companies will often waive the tax and include unlimited kilometres if the daily rate doesn't. Discounts of 15% or more are available for weekly hire; anything longer than one week is up for negotiation. A rate of JD20 per day for a reliable car with unlimited kilometres is a good deal.

Cars can be booked, collected and paid for in Amman or Aqaba and dropped off in the other city, but most companies charge from JD20 to JD25 for this service. Companies need a credit card for a deposit, but payment can be also made with cash; most major credit cards are accepted.

To ensure that you don't break down in the middle of nowhere, you should always hire a car less than three years old – most reputable companies won't offer anything else. Most hire cars have air-conditioning, which is a godsend in summer and vital along dusty tracks. Most cars are 'midrange' sedans though you can find cheaper rates if you are happy to squeeze into a tiny Korean hatchback. Cars with automatic transmission are more expensive, but anyone not used to driving on the right-hand side of the road should consider getting an automatic rather than a manual. Always carry a decent road map – these are not provided by car-hire agencies. Child-restraining seats are generally available for an extra fee.

Some agencies are closed on Friday and public holidays. If so, prearrange collection and delivery to avoid longer hire periods. Check the car over with a staff member for bumps, scratches and obvious defects, and check brakes, tyres, etc before driving off.

Finally, it is important to be aware that there are myriad complicated conditions and charges to remember and consider:

- Most agencies only hire to drivers over 21 years old; some stipulate that drivers must be at least 26 years
- Some offer free delivery and collection within the same city, but this is only during working hours
- Hire is often for a minimum of three days, sometimes two and only reluctantly for one day. Very rarely will any agency give a refund if you return the car early.
- Hire cars are not able to be driven outside Jordan

Insurance

Most car-hire rates come with basic insurance which involves a deductible of up to JD300 (ie in case of an accident you pay a maximum of JD300). Most agencies offer additional Collision Damage Waiver (CDW) insurance for an extra JD7 to JD10 per day, which will absolve you of all accident costs (in some cases a maximum of JD100 excess).

Insurance offered by major companies often includes Personal Accident Insurance and Theft Protection, which may be covered by your travel insurance policy from home. Always read the conditions of the contract carefully before signing – an English translation should always be provided.

If you're driving into Jordan in a private vehicle, compulsory third-party insurance must be purchased at the border for about JD35 (valid for one month). You also pay a nominal customs fee of JD5 for 'foreign car registration'.

Road Conditions

Visitors from any country where road rules are actually obeyed may be shocked by the traffic in Jordan, especially in Amman. But anyone who has driven elsewhere in the Middle East may find the traffic comparatively sedate. Indeed, provided that you can keep driving in Amman down to a bare minimum and have an idea in advance how to get to your destination, you're unlikely to encounter too many difficulties if you take reasonable care.

If you're driving around Jordan, read the following carefully:

- Many road signs are in English, but they are sometimes badly transliterated (eg 'Om Qeis' for Umm Qais or, our favourite, 'AT TA NOURAN I QUI ES SI' for the At-Tannour Antiquities Site!). Brown signs denote tourist attractions, blue signs are for road names and green signs are for anything Islamic, such as a mosque.

- Take care when it's raining: water and sand (and sometimes oil) make a lethal combination on the roads
- The Jordanian road system makes more use of U-turns than flyovers
- One-way streets are often not signposted and can be fiendish in Karak and Irbid
- Always watch out for obstacles: pedestrians who walk along the road; cars darting out of side roads; and herds of goats and camels, even on the major highways
- Roundabouts are often large, and all drivers (local and foreign) find them totally confusing
- Petrol stations are not that common, so fill up as often as you can
- Parking in major towns, especially Amman, is a problem, but it's easy to find (and normally free) at major attractions like Jerash, Petra and Madaba
- Most roads (and even the highways) are dangerous at night because white lines are not common, obstacles (eg herds of camels) are still roaming about, and some cars have no headlights or put them permanently on high beam
- Signposting is erratic: generally enough to get you on your way but not enough to get you all the way to the destination
- Jordanians are extremely reluctant to commit to a single lane, so there's a lot of overtaking using the slow lane

Road Hazards

Despite the small population, and relatively good roads, accidents are alarmingly frequent. In 2001, there were 52,000 road accidents in Jordan with 783 fatalities (an average of 16 for every 10,000 vehicles), with a large number of victims being pedestrians and children. In 2004, nine British holidaymakers were killed in road accidents near Tafileh on the way to Petra.

The roads where accidents are more common are those frequented by long-distance trucks, eg the short stretch of Highway 65 (south of Aqaba to the Saudi border) and Highways 10 and 40 east of Amman.

In the case of an accident in a hire car, do not move the vehicle. Get a policeman from the local station to attend the scene immediately, obtain a police report (Arabic is OK) and contact the car-hire company – not obtaining a police report will normally invalidate your insurance. Depending on where you are, most reputable companies will send someone to the scene within hours. If there's any serious injury to you or someone else, also contact your travel insurance company at home as well as your embassy/consulate in Amman.

If your own private car is involved in an accident, your driving licence and passport will be held by the police until the case has been finalised in a local court – which may take weeks.

Drivers are always considered guilty if they hit a pedestrian, regardless of the circumstances.

Telephone numbers for local police stations are mentioned throughout the book, but two emergency numbers (☎ 191 and ☎ 192) are valid for police emergencies anywhere in Jordan, and should be answered by English-speaking staff. In Amman, there are separate numbers for the **Highway Police** (☎ 06 5343402) and **Traffic Police** (☎ 06 4896390 or 190) – the exact difference between the two, however, is unclear.

Road Rules

Vehicles drive on the right-hand side of the road in Jordan, at least in theory. The general speed limit inside built-up areas is 50km/h or 70km/h on multilane highways in Amman, and 90km/h to 110km/h on the highways. Note that indicators are seldom used, rules are occasionally obeyed, the ubiquitous horn is a useful warning signal and pedestrians must take their chances. The condition of the roads varies; unsigned speed humps are common, as are shallow ditches across the road, usually at the entrance to a town.

Wearing a seat belt is now compulsory, though a recent survey suggested that fewer than 30% of Jordanians used them. Traffic police are positioned at intervals along the highways. Police tend to be fairly indulgent towards foreigners, so long as they do nothing serious.

Road checkpoints are mainly for Jordanian drivers of private vehicles, and for trucks. Buses, minibuses, service taxis and private

TRANSPORT

taxis rarely need to stop; if they do, drivers just quickly show their papers to the police. Sometimes police come into a bus (there's rarely room in a minibus) to check the identification papers of passengers (usually young men). Foreigners are rarely bothered, and if you're asked to show your passport (this is more likely to happen anywhere near a border) it's probably more out of curiosity than anything else.

If you have chartered a private taxi, the driver is often waved through the checkpoint when the policeman sees smiling foreigners, obviously out for a day trip. If you're driving a hired or private vehicle, you may be stopped. Again, there's a good chance you'll be waved on unless the policeman is friendly or bored. You are only likely to be asked serious questions if you seem to be going near the border with Iraq.

Nonetheless, always keep your passport, drivers licence, hire agreement and registration papers handy, especially along the Dead Sea Highway. In recent years hire cars have been used by Palestinian militants to cross into Israel & the Palestinian Territories, so police near the border are unusually vigilant.

HITCHING
Getting a Ride

Hitching is never entirely safe in any country in the world. Travellers who choose to hitch should understand that they are taking a small, but potentially serious, risk. People who choose to hitch will be safer if they travel in pairs and let someone know where they are planning to go.

Despite this general advice, hitching is definitely feasible in Jordan. The traffic varies a lot from place to place, but you generally don't have to wait long for a lift on main routes. Hitching is only really worth it to avoid chartering expensive taxis or where public transport is limited or nonexistent, eg parts of the King's Highway and to the desert castles east of Amman.

Always start hitching early, and avoid 1pm to 4pm when it's often too hot and traffic is reduced while many locals enjoy a siesta. Also, don't start hitching after about 4pm unless it's a short trip on a road with frequent traffic, because hitching after dark increases the risk. The best places to look for lifts are junctions, tourist attractions (eg lookouts) or shops where cars often stop. Police stationed at major junctions and checkpoints are often happy to wave down drivers and cajole them into giving you a lift.

To indicate that you're looking for a lift, simply raise your index finger in the direction you're heading. On a large truck, you may be asked for a fare; in a private vehicle, you probably won't need to pay anything. However, to avoid a possibly unpleasant situation, ask beforehand if payment is expected and, if so, how much the driver wants. Otherwise, just offer a small amount when you get out – it will often be refused.

Finally, a few general tips. Don't look too scruffy; don't hitch in groups of more than two; women should be very careful, and look for lifts with families, or in a car with another local or foreign female; trucks on some steep and windy roads (eg between the Wadi Rum turn-off and Aqaba) can be painfully slow; and make sure you carry a hat and lots of water.

Picking up Hitchhikers

If you have chartered a service taxi or private taxi you are under no obligation to pick up any hitchhikers, but if you're driving a private or hired car, the pressure to pick up people along the way can be intense. It's hard not to feel a twinge of guilt as you fly past locals alongside the road waving their arms frantically. On remote stretches where public transport is limited or nonexistent, eg across the Wadi Mujib valley, you should try to pick up a few passengers.

One advantage about picking up a hitchhiker is the chance to meet a local, and readers have often been invited to a home in return for a lift. Although you may be charged, you should never charge a local for a lift. They will assume that any foreign hitchhiker can afford to pay for transport, and that any foreigner driving a private or hired car doesn't need the extra money.

LOCAL TRANSPORT
Bus

The two largest cities, Amman and Irbid, have efficient and cheap public bus networks, but few have destination signs in English (although some have 'English' numbers), there are no schedules or timetables available and local bus stations are often chaotic. Service taxis are much more useful and still cheap.

Taxi

There are two main types of taxis in Jordan. Yellow private taxis work like taxis anywhere. White service (*servees*) taxis run along set routes within many towns, and between most towns, as well as between Jordan and the neighbouring countries of Iraq, Syria and Saudi Arabia (see p257 for more information).

Both service taxis and private taxis can be chartered. Hiring a service taxi for a day is usually cheaper than hiring your own car. To charter a service taxi along a set route (eg Aqaba to Ma'an), find out the standard fare per person and then just pay for all the seats in a car (normally four). A long-distance trip in a private taxi costs more, but drivers are more amenable to stops and side trips.

If the taxi driver doesn't speak English, use the Arabic script in this guidebook or ask a local who does speak English to write down the destination(s) in Arabic.

PRIVATE TAXI

Yellow private taxis are very common in major towns like Amman, Irbid, Jerash, Ma'an, Madaba, Wadi Musa (Petra) and Aqaba, as well as in important transport junctions like Shuneh al-Janubiyyeh (South Shuna) and Tafila. There is no pricing standard among taxis. Taxis in Amman are metered and most drivers will use the meter; in Wadi Musa there is a standard fare of JD1 anywhere in town; elsewhere you'll just have to negotiate a reasonable fare.

Taxis are not expensive in Jordan and, after climbing up and down the jebels (hills) of Amman, or staggering around in the infernal summer heat of Aqaba, you'll be glad to fork out the equivalent of less than US$2 for a comfortable, air-conditioned ride across town.

SERVICE TAXI

Service taxis are usually battered Peugeot 504 or 505 station wagons with seven seats, or battered Mercedes sedans with five seats. They are always white, and usually have writing and numbers (in Arabic) indicating their route.

Because of the limited number of seats, it usually doesn't take long for one to fill up. They cost up to twice as much as a minibus, and about 50% more than a public bus, but are quicker because they stop less often along the way to pick up passengers. However, they're not always that much more comfortable than a bus or minibus, unless you get the prized front seat. To avoid waiting for passengers, or to give yourself extra room, you can always pay for an extra seat.

Lone female travellers should always ask to sit in the front seat if the back is jammed with men, otherwise it's worth paying for an extra seat. If chartering a taxi, single females should always sit in the back.

Major cities, such as Amman and Irbid, are well served by service taxis that run along set routes within each city, and often go to (or past) places of interest to visitors. As with intercity service taxis, the route is listed in Arabic on the driver's door and drivers wait until they are full before departing.

TOURS

An alternative to a pricey group tour organised from abroad is to arrange your own private mini-tour with a Jordanian travel agency. Many of these can arrange hiking or archaeological itineraries and provide a car and driver.

For hiking and activities in Jordan's nature reserves you are best off contacting the tourism department of the **Royal Society for the Conservation of Nature** (RSCN; www.rscn.org.jo/), who can arrange short activity breaks or entire itineraries (see p53). For an extended trip to Wadi Rum it's best to contact a local Bedouin agency such as **Wadi Rum Mountain Guides** (www.bedouinroads.com).

If you're travelling independently, and on a tight budget, jumping on a budget-priced organised tour from Amman to a remote place like the desert castles of eastern Jordan is far easier, and often cheaper, than doing it yourself. See p87.

The following local agencies are reliable:
Alia Tours (☎ 06 5620501; www.aliatours.com.jo) Standard tours.
Archaeological Adventure Travel & Tourism (☎ 03 2157892; fax 2157891; a-a@index.com.jo)
Atlas Travel & Tourist Agency (☎ 06 4624262; fax 4610198; www.atlastours.net) Also offers side trips to Israel & the Palestinian Territories, Syria and Lebanon.

Desert Guides Company (☎ 06 5527230, 079 5532915; www.desertguidescompany.com; PO Box 9177Amman) Trekking, mountain-bike and adventure trips.

Discovery (☎ 06 5697998; www.discovery1.com)

Golden Crown Tours (☎ 06 5511200; www.golden crowntours.com) Offers archaeological, religious and adventure tours.

International Traders (☎ 06 5607014; fax 566 9905; sahar@traders.com.jo) Expensive but reliable, and the representative for American Express travel services; locations in Amman and Aqaba.

Jordan Beauty Tours (☎ 079 5581644, 077 7773978, 077 7282730; www.jordanbeauty.com; Petra)

Jordan Direct (☎ 06 5938238; www.jdtours.com; Boumedien street, Amman) Located in Amin Marie Complex.

Jordan Eco-Tours (☎ 06 5524534; www.jordaneco tours.com)

Jordan Experience (☎ 03 2155005; www.jordan experience.com.jo; Wadi Musa) A Dutch/Jordanian venture; quite expensive.

Jordan Inspiration Tours (☎ 03 2157317, 079 5554677; www.jitours.com; Petra)

La Beduina (☎ 2157099; www.labeduinatours.com)

Petra Moon (☎ 03 2156665; www.petramoon.com; Wadi Musa) A professional agency that also offers an interesting range of treks in remote areas of Petra and Dana.

Royal Tours (☎ 06 5857154; www.royaltours.com .jo) Part of Royal Jordanian, and good for stopover packages.

Zaman Tours & Travel (☎ 03 2157723; www .zamantours.com; Wadi Musa) Adventure tours, camping, camel treks and hiking.

Health

CONTENTS

Prevention is the key to staying healthy while travelling in the Middle East. Infectious diseases can and do occur in Jordan, but these can be avoided with a few precautions. The most common reason for travellers needing medical help is as a result of traffic accidents. Medical facilities in Jordan are generally very good, particularly in Amman.

BEFORE YOU GO

A little planning before departure, particularly for pre-existing illnesses, will save you a lot of trouble later. See your dentist before a long trip; carry a spare pair of contact lenses and glasses (and take your optical prescription with you); and carry a first-aid kit with you.

It's tempting to leave it all to the last minute – don't! Many vaccines don't ensure immunity for two weeks, so visit a doctor four to eight weeks before departure.

Bring medications in their original, clearly labelled, containers. A signed and dated letter from your physician describing your medical conditions and medications, including generic names, is also a good idea. If carrying syringes or needles, be sure to have a physician's letter documenting their medical necessity.

INSURANCE

Find out in advance if your insurance plan will make payments directly to providers or reimburse you later for overseas health expenditures (in many countries doctors expect payment in cash); it's also worth ensuring your travel insurance will cover repatriation home or transport to better medical facilities elsewhere. Your insurance company may be able to locate the nearest source of medical help, or you can ask at your hotel. In case of an emergency, contact your embassy or consulate. Your travel insurance will not usually cover you for anything other than emergency dental treatment. Not all insurance covers emergency aeromedical evacuation home or to a hospital in a major city, which may be the only way to get medical attention for a serious emergency.

See p244 for more on insurance.

RECOMMENDED VACCINATIONS

Plan ahead for getting your vaccinations: some of them require more than one injection, while some vaccinations should not be given together. Note that some vaccinations should not be given during pregnancy or to people with allergies – discuss this with your doctor.

MEDICAL CHECKLIST

Following is a list of other items you should consider packing in your medical kit.

- Antibiotics (if travelling off the beaten track)
- Antidiarrhoeal drugs (eg loperamide)
- Acetaminophen/paracetamol (Tylenol) or aspirin
- Anti-inflammatory drugs (eg ibuprofen)
- Antihistamines (for hay fever and allergic reactions)
- Antibacterial ointment (eg Bactroban) for cuts and abrasions
- Steroid cream or cortisone (allergic rashes)
- Bandages, gauze, gauze rolls
- Adhesive or paper tape

REQUIRED & RECOMMENDED VACCINATIONS

The following vaccinations are recommended for most travellers to Jordan, though you should check with your local health provider:

- diphtheria & tetanus – single booster recommended if you've had none in the previous 10 years
- hepatitis A – a single dose at least two to four weeks before departure gives protection for up to a year; a booster 12 months later gives another 10 years or more of protection
- hepatitis B – now considered routine for most travellers
- measles, mumps & rubella – two doses of MMR recommended unless you have previously had the diseases. Young adults may require a booster.
- polio – generally given in childhood and should be boosted every 10 years
- typhoid – recommended if you're travelling for more than a couple of weeks
- yellow fever – vaccination is required for entry into Jordan for all travellers over one year of age if coming from infected areas such as sub-Saharan Africa, and parts of South America

For more on these diseases and vaccinations see Infectious Diseases, opposite.

- Scissors, safety pins, tweezers
- Thermometer
- Insect repellent that contains DEET, for the body
- Insect spray that contains Permethrin – for clothing, tents and bed nets
- Sun block
- Oral rehydration salts
- Iodine tablets or other water purification tablets
- Syringes and sterile needles (if travelling to remote areas)

INTERNET RESOURCES

There is a wealth of travel health advice on the Internet. For further information, the Lonely Planet website (www.lonelyplanet .com) is a good place to start. The World Health Organization (www.who.int/ith) publishes a superb book, *International Travel and Health,* which is revised annually and is available online at no cost.

Another website of general interest is MD Travel Health (www.mdtravelhealth.com), which provides complete travel health recommendations for every country, updated daily, also at no cost.

The Center for Disease Control (www .cdc.gov/travel/mideast.htm) offers a useful overview of the health issues facing travellers to the Middle East.

The US embassy in Amman has a list of recommended doctors in Jordan at http:// usembassy-amman.org.jo/cons/doctors.doc.

FURTHER READING

Lonely Planet's *Healthy Travel – Asia & India* is packed with useful information including pretrip planning, emergency first aid, immunisation and disease information and what to do if you get sick on the road. Other recommended references include *Traveller's Health* by Dr Richard Dawood, *International Travel Health Guide* by Stuart R Rose, MD and *The Travellers Good Health Guide* by Ted Lankester, an especially useful health guide for volunteers and long-term expatriates working in the Middle East.

IN TRANSIT

DEEP VEIN THROMBOSIS (DVT)

Deep vein thrombosis occurs when blood clots form in the legs during plane flights chiefly because of a prolonged immobility The longer the flight is, the greater the risk Though most clots are reabsorbed unevent fully, some may break off and travel through the blood vessels to the lungs, where they may cause life-threatening complications.

The chief symptom of DVT is swelling or pain of the foot, ankle or calf, usually but not always on just one side. When a blood clot travels to the lungs, it may cause chest pain and difficulty breathing. Travellers with any of these symptoms should immediately seek medical attention.

To prevent the development of DVT on long flights you should walk about the cabin, perform isometric compressions of the leg muscles (ie contract the leg muscles while sitting), drink plenty of fluids, and avoid alcohol and tobacco.

JET LAG & MOTION SICKNESS

Jet lag is common when crossing more than five time zones; it results in insomnia, fatigue, malaise or nausea. To avoid jet lag try drinking plenty of fluids (non-alcoholic) and eating light meals. Upon arrival, seek exposure to natural sunlight and readjust your schedule (for meals, sleep, etc) as soon as possible.

Antihistamines such as dimenhydrinate (Dramamine) and meclizine (Antivert, Bonine) are usually the first choice for treating motion sickness. Their main side-effect is drowsiness. A herbal alternative is ginger, which works like a charm for some people.

IN JORDAN

AVAILABILITY & COST OF HEALTH CARE

There are modern, well-equipped public hospitals in Amman, Irbid, Aqaba and Karak; smaller hospitals in Madaba, Ramtha and Zarqa; and basic health centres in most other towns. Jordan also boasts over 50 private hospitals, which cater primarily to patients from neighbouring countries, particularly the Gulf States, who are attracted by the lower medical costs. Emergency treatment not requiring hospitalisation is free in Jordan.

Most towns have well-stocked pharmacies, but always make sure to check the expiry date of any medicine you buy in Jordan. It is better to bring any unusual or important medical items with you from home,

and always bring a copy of a prescription. The telephone numbers for pharmacies (including those open at night) in Amman and Irbid, and for hospitals in Amman, Zarqa, Irbid and Aqaba, are listed in the two English-language newspapers. All doctors (and most pharmacists) who have studied in Jordan speak English because medicine is taught in English at Jordanian universities, and many have studied abroad. Dental surgeries are also fairly modern and well equipped.

For minor illnesses such as diarrhoea, pharmacists can often provide valuable advice and sell over-the-counter medication.

For an ambulance in Jordan call ☎ 193.

INFECTIOUS DISEASES
Diphtheria & Tetanus

Diphtheria is spread through close respiratory contact. It causes a high temperature and severe sore throat. Sometimes a membrane forms across the throat requiring a tracheostomy to prevent suffocation. Vaccination is recommended for those likely to be in close contact with the local population in infected areas. The vaccine is given as an injection alone, or with tetanus (you may well have had this combined injection as a child), and lasts 10 years.

Hepatitis A

Hepatitis A is spread through contaminated food (particularly shellfish) and water. It causes jaundice and, although it is rarely fatal, can cause prolonged lethargy and delayed recovery. Symptoms include dark urine, a yellow colour to the whites of the eyes, fever and abdominal pain. Hepatitis A vaccine (Avaxim, VAQTA, Havrix) is given as an injection; hepatitis A and typhoid vaccines can also be given as a single-dose vaccine, hepatyrix or viatim.

Hepatitis B

Infected blood, contaminated needles and sexual intercourse can all transmit hepatitis B. It can cause jaundice, and affects the liver, occasionally causing liver failure. All travellers should make this a routine vaccination. (Many countries now give hepatitis B vaccination as part of routine childhood vaccination.) The US Center for Disease Control says the level of hepatitis B is high in Jordan. The vaccine is given singly, or

HEALTH

at the same time as the hepatitis A vaccine (hepatyrix). A course will give protection for at least five years. It can be given over four weeks, or six months.

HIV

This is spread via infected blood and blood products, sexual intercourse with an infected partner and from an infected mother to her newborn child. It can be spread through 'blood to blood' contacts such as contaminated instruments during medical and dental procedures, acupuncture, body-piercing and sharing used intravenous needles.

Reliable figures aren't available about the number of people in Jordan with HIV or AIDS, but given the strict taboos in Jordanian society about drugs, homosexuality and promiscuity, the disease is relatively rare. Contracting HIV through a blood transfusion is about as unlikely as in most Western countries, and anyone needing serious surgery will probably be sent home anyway.

You may need to supply a negative HIV test in order to get a second visa extension for a stay of longer than three months.

Polio

Generally spread through either contaminated food or water, polio is one of the vaccines given in childhood and should be boosted every 10 years, either orally (a drop on the tongue), or as an injection. Polio may be carried asymptomatically, although it can cause a transient fever and, in rare cases, potentially permanent muscle weakness or paralysis. Polio is not currently present in Jordan but is prevalent in neighbouring countries.

Rabies

Spread through bites or licks on broken skin from an infected animal, rabies is fatal. Animal handlers should be vaccinated, as should those travelling to remote areas where a reliable source of post-bite vaccine is not available within 24 hours. Three injections are needed over a month. If you've come in physical contact with an infected animal and haven't been vaccinated you'll need a course of five injections starting within 24 hours or as soon as possible after the injury. Vaccination does not provide you with immunity, it merely buys you more time to seek appropriate medical help.

Tuberculosis

Tuberculosis (TB) is spread through close respiratory contact and occasionally through infected milk or milk products. BCG vaccine is recommended for those likely to be mixing closely with the local population. It is more important for those visiting family or planning on a long stay, and those employed as teachers and health-care workers. TB can be asymptomatic, although symptoms can include cough, weight loss or fever, months or even years after exposure. An X-ray is the best way to confirm if you have TB. BCG gives a moderate degree of protection against TB. It causes a small permanent scar at the site of injection, and is usually only given in specialised chest clinics. As it's a live vaccine it should not be given to pregnant women or immunocompromised individuals. The BCG vaccine is not available in all countries.

Typhoid

This is spread through food or water that has been contaminated by infected human faeces. The first symptom is usually fever or a pink rash on the abdomen. Septicaemia (blood poisoning) may also occur. Typhoid vaccine (typhim Vi, typherix) will give protection for three years. In some countries, the oral vaccine Vivotif is also available.

Yellow Fever

Yellow fever vaccination is not required for Jordan but you *do* need a yellow fever certificate if arriving from an infected area, or if you've been in an infected area in the couple of weeks prior to arrival in Jordan. There is always the possibility that a traveller without an up-to-date certificate will be vaccinated and detained in isolation at the port of arrival for up to 10 days, or even repatriated. The yellow fever vaccination must be given at a designated clinic, and is valid for 10 years. It is a live vaccine and must not be given to immunocompromised or pregnant travellers.

TRAVELLER'S DIARRHOEA

The chances of getting sick from unhygienic food handling and preparation in Jordan are fairly slim. To prevent diarrhoea:

- Avoid tap water unless it has been boiled, filtered or chemically disinfected (iodine tablets)

- Beware of ice cream that is sold in the street or anywhere it might have been melted and refrozen; if there's any doubt (eg a power cut in the last day or two), steer well clear
- Be careful of shellfish such as mussels, oysters and clams, particularly outside of Aqaba, as well as the raw meat dishes that are available in Lebanese restaurants in Jordan.
- Buffet meals are risky, as are empty restaurants; meals freshly cooked in front of you in a busy restaurant packed with locals are much more likely to be safe

If you do develop diarrhoea, be sure to drink plenty of fluids, preferably an oral rehydration solution containing salt and sugar (weak black tea with a little sugar, soda water, or soft drinks allowed to go flat and diluted 50% with clean water are also good). In an emergency you can make up a solution of six teaspoons of sugar and half a teaspoon of salt to a litre of boiled or bottled water.

A few loose stools don't require treatment but, if you start having more than four or five stools a day, you should start taking an antibiotic (usually a quinolone drug) and an antidiarrhoeal agent (such as loperamide). If diarrhoea is bloody, persists for more than 72 hours, is accompanied by fever, shaking chills or severe abdominal pain, you should seek medical attention.

Where this is not possible the recommended drugs for bacterial diarrhoea (the most likely cause of severe diarrhoea in travellers) are norfloxacin 400mg twice daily for three days or ciprofloxacin 500mg twice daily for five days. These drugs are not recommended for children or pregnant women. The drug for children is co-trimoxazole, with dosage dependent on weight. A five-day course is given. Ampicillin or amoxycillin may be given to pregnant women, but medical care is necessary.

ENVIRONMENTAL HAZARDS
Diving, Snorkelling & Swimming
Stonefish have a very nasty habit of lying half-submerged in the sand, so wear something on your feet if you're walking into the sea (as opposed to jumping into the deep water from a jetty or boat). If stung by a stonefish, see a doctor immediately. Other nasty creatures to avoid are lionfish which, like the stonefish, have poisonous spikes, and jellyfish, whose sting can be painful. If stung by a jellyfish, douse the rash in vinegar to deactivate any stingers which have not 'fired'. Calamine lotion, antihistamines and analgesics (and urine) may reduce the reaction and relieve the pain. Coral cuts are notoriously slow to heal and, if they're not adequately cleaned, small pieces of coral can become embedded in the wound.

It is important to remember that, if you dive to any depth, it is dangerous to go to certain altitudes until six hours have elapsed. This includes the road to Petra and most roads out of Aqaba. Deeper dives require an even longer wait.

Aqaba has an excellent hospital where cuts, bites and stings can be treated. Most importantly, it has decompression chambers for the 'bends'.

Heat Illness
Read this section carefully, especially if you are travelling to Jordan between May and September. Despite the warnings, some visitors get themselves into trouble hiking through the desert in the heat of the day, especially around Wadi Rum.

Heat exhaustion occurs following heavy sweating and excessive fluid loss with inadequate replacement of fluids and salt. This is particularly common in hot climates when taking unaccustomed exercise before full acclimatisation. Symptoms include headache, dizziness and tiredness. Dehydration already occurs by the time you feel thirsty – aim to drink sufficient water such that you produce pale, diluted urine. The treatment of heat exhaustion consists of fluid replacement with water or fruit juice or both, and cooling by cold water and fans. The treatment of the salt loss component consists of salty fluids as in soup or broth, and adding a little more table salt to foods than usual.

Heat stroke is much more serious. This occurs when the body's heat-regulating mechanism breaks down. Excessive rise in body temperature leads to sweating ceasing, irrational and hyperactive behaviour and eventually loss of consciousness and death. Rapid cooling by spraying the body with water and fanning is an ideal treatment. Emergency fluid and electrolyte replacement by intravenous drip is usually also required.

HEALTH

Insect Bites & Stings

Mosquitoes may not carry malaria but can cause irritation and infected bites. Using DEET-based insect repellents will prevent bites. Mosquitos also spread dengue fever.

Bees and wasps only cause real problems to those with a severe allergy (anaphylaxis). If you have a severe allergy to bee or wasp stings you should carry an adrenaline injection or similar. For general bug bites, calamine lotion or a sting relief spray will give relief and ice packs will reduce the pain and swelling.

Scorpion stings are notoriously painful and in Jordan can actually be fatal. Scorpions often shelter in shoes or clothing so check your shoes in the morning.

Bed bugs are often found in hostels and cheap hotels. They lead to very itchy lumpy bites. Spraying the mattress with an appropriate insect killer will do a good job of getting rid of them.

Scabies are also frequently found in cheap accommodation. These tiny mites live in the skin, particularly between the fingers. They cause an intensely itchy rash. Scabies is easily treated with lotion available from pharmacies; people who you come into contact with also need treating to avoid spreading scabies between asymptomatic carriers.

Snake Bites

To minimise your chances of being bitten always wear boots, socks and long trousers when walking through undergrowth where snakes may be present. Don't put your hands into holes and crevices, and be careful when collecting firewood.

Half of those bitten by venomous snakes are not actually injected with poison (envenomed). If bitten by a snake, do not panic. Immobilise the bitten limb with a splint (eg a stick) and apply a bandage over the site, with firm pressure, similar to bandaging a sprain. Do not apply a tourniquet, or cut or suck the bite. Get the victim to medical help as soon as possible so that antivenin can be given if necessary.

Water

Tap water in Jordan is generally safe to drink, but for a short trip it's better to stick to bottled water, or boil water for 10 minutes, use water purification tablets or a filter. In the Jordan Valley, amoebic dysentery can be a problem. The tap water in southern Jordan, particularly Wadi Rum, comes from natural springs at Diseh and so is extremely pure.

TRAVELLING WITH CHILDREN

All travellers with children should know how to treat minor ailments and when to seek medical treatment. Make sure the children are up to date with routine vaccinations, and discuss possible travel vaccines well before departure as some vaccines are not suitable for children less than one year old.

In hot, moist climates any wound or break in the skin may lead to infection. The area should be cleaned and then kept dry and clean. Remember to avoid contaminated food and water. If your child is vomiting or experiencing diarrhoea, lost fluid and salts must be replaced. It may be helpful to take rehydration powders for reconstituting with boiled water. Ask your doctor about this.

Children should be encouraged to avoid dogs or other mammals because of the risk of rabies and other diseases. Any bite, scratch or lick from a warm-blooded, furry animal should immediately be thoroughly cleaned. If there is any possibility that the animal is infected with rabies, immediate medical assistance should be sought.

Travel with Children from Lonely Planet includes advice on travel health for younger children.

WOMEN'S HEALTH

Emotional stress, exhaustion and travelling through different time zones can all contribute to an upset in the menstrual pattern. If using oral contraceptives, remember some antibiotics, diarrhoea and vomiting can stop the pill from working and lead to the risk of pregnancy – remember to take condoms with you just in case. Condoms should be kept in a cool dry place or they may crack and perish.

Emergency contraception is most effective if taken within 24 hours after unprotected sex. The International Planned Parent Federation (www.ippf.org) can advise about the availability of contraception in different countries. Tampons and sanitary towels are easily available in Amman but not necessarily in smaller towns.

Travelling during pregnancy is usually possible but there are important things to consider. Have a medical check-up before embarking on your trip. The most risky times for travel are during the first 12 weeks of pregnancy, when miscarriage is most likely, and after 30 weeks, when complications such as high blood pressure and premature delivery can occur. Most airlines will not accept a traveller after 28 to 32 weeks of pregnancy, and long-haul flights in the later stages can be very uncomfortable. Antenatal facilities vary greatly between countries in the Middle East and you should think carefully before travelling to a country with poor medical facilities or where there are major cultural and language differences from home. Taking written records of the pregnancy, including details of your blood group, is likely to be helpful if you need medical attention while away. Ensure your insurance policy covers pregnancy delivery and postnatal care, but remember insurance policies are only as good as the facilities available.

Language

CONTENTS

Arabic is Jordan's official language. English is also widely spoken but any effort to communicate with the locals in their own language will be well rewarded. No matter how far off the mark your pronunciation or grammar might be, you'll often get the response (usually with a big smile): 'Ah, you speak Arabic very well!'.

Learning a few basics for day-to-day travelling doesn't take long at all, but to master the complexities of Arabic would take years of consistent study. The whole issue is complicated by the differences between Classical Arabic (*fus-ha*), its modern descendant MSA (Modern Standard Arabic) and regional dialects. The classical tongue is the language of the Quran and Arabic poetry of centuries past. For long it remained static, but in order to survive it had to adapt to change, and the result is more or less MSA, the common language of the press, radio and educated discourse. It is as close to a *lingua franca* (common language) as the Arab world comes, and is generally understood – if not always well spoken – across the Arab world.

Fortunately, the spoken dialects of Jordan are not too distant from MSA. For outsiders trying to learn Arabic, the most frustrating element nevertheless remains understanding the spoken language. There is virtually no written material to refer to for back-up, and acquisition of MSA in the first place is itself a long-term investment. An esoteric argument flows back and forth about the relative merits of learning MSA first (and so perhaps having to wait some time before being able to communicate adequately with people in the street) or focusing your efforts on a dialect. If all this gives you a headache now, you'll have some idea of why so few non-Arabs, or non-Muslims, embark on a study of the language.

PRONUNCIATION

Pronunciation of Arabic in any of its guises can be tongue-tying for someone unfamiliar with the intonation and combination of sounds. Pronounce the transliterated words slowly and clearly.

This language guide should help, but bear in mind that the myriad rules governing pronunciation and vowel use are too extensive to be covered here.

Vowels

Technically, there are three long and three short vowels in Arabic. The reality is a little different, with local dialect and varying consonant combinations affecting their pronunciation. This is the case throughout the Arabic-speaking world. More like five short and five long vowels can be identified; in this guide we use all but the long 'o' (as in 'or').

a	as in 'had'
aa	as the 'a' in 'father'
e	short, as in 'bet'; long, as in 'there'
i	as in 'hit'
ee	as in 'beer', only softer
o	as in 'hot'
u	as in 'put'
oo	as in 'food'

Consonants

Pronunciation for all Arabic consonants is covered in the alphabet table on p279. Note that when double consonants occur in the

THE STANDARD ARABIC ALPHABET

Final	Medial	Initial	Alone	Transliteration	Pronunciation
ﺎ			ا	**aa**	as in 'father'
ﺐ	ﺒ	ﺑ	ب	**b**	as in 'bet'
ﺖ	ﺘ	ﺗ	ت	**t**	as in 'ten'
ﺚ	ﺜ	ﺛ	ث	**th**	as in 'thin'
ﺞ	ﺠ	ﺟ	ج	**j**	as in 'jet'
ﺢ	ﺤ	ﺣ	ح	**H**	a strongly whispered 'h', like a sigh of relief
ﺦ	ﺨ	ﺧ	خ	**kh**	as the 'ch' in Scottish *loch*
ﺪ			د	**d**	as in 'dim'
ﺬ			ذ	**dh**	as the 'th' in 'this'
ﺮ			ر	**r**	a rolled 'r', as in the Spanish word *caro*
ﺰ			ز	**z**	as in 'zip'
ﺲ	ﺴ	ﺳ	س	**s**	as in 'so', never as in 'wisdom'
ﺶ	ﺸ	ﺷ	ش	**sh**	as in 'ship'
ﺺ	ﺼ	ﺻ	ص	**ş**	emphatic 's'
ﺾ	ﻀ	ﺿ	ض	**ḍ**	emphatic 'd'
ﻂ	ﻄ	ﻃ	ط	**ţ**	emphatic 't'
ﻆ	ﻈ	ﻇ	ظ	**ẓ**	emphatic 'z'
ﻊ	ﻌ	ﻋ	ع	**'**	the Arabic letter *'ayn*; pronounce as a glottal stop – like the closing of the throat before saying 'Oh-oh!' (see Tricky Sounds, p280)
ﻎ	ﻐ	ﻏ	غ	**gh**	a guttural sound like Parisian 'r'
ﻒ	ﻔ	ﻓ	ف	**f**	as in 'far'
ﻖ	ﻘ	ﻗ	ق	**q**	a strongly guttural 'k' sound; also often pronounced as a glottal stop
ﻚ	ﻜ	ﻛ	ك	**k**	as in 'king'
ﻞ	ﻠ	ﻟ	ل	**l**	as in 'lamb'
ﻢ	ﻤ	ﻣ	م	**m**	as in 'me'
ﻦ	ﻨ	ﻧ	ن	**n**	as in 'name'
ﻪ	ﻬ	ﻫ	ه	**h**	as in 'ham'
ﻮ			و	**w**	as in 'wet'
				oo	long, as in 'food'
				ow	as in 'how'
ﻲ	ﻴ	ﻳ	ي	**y**	as in 'yes'
				ee	as in 'beer', only softer
				ai/ay	as in 'aisle'/as the 'ay' in 'day'

Vowels Not all Arabic vowel sounds are represented in the alphabet. For more information on the vowel sounds used in this language guide, see Vowels (p278).

Emphatic Consonants To simplify the transliteration system used in this book, the emphatic consonants have not been included.

LANGUAGE

transliterations, both are pronounced. For example, the word *al-hammam* (toilet), is pronounced 'al-ham-mam'.

TRICKY SOUNDS

Arabic has two sounds that are very tricky for non-Arabs to produce: the 'ayn and the glottal stop. The letter 'ayn represents a sound with no English equivalent that comes even close. It is similar to the glottal stop (which is not actually represented in the alphabet), but the muscles at the back of the throat are gagged more forcefully and air is released – it has been described as the sound of someone being strangled. In many transliteration systems 'ayn is represented by an opening quotation mark, and the glottal stop by a closing quotation mark. To make the transliterations in this language guide (and throughout the rest of the book) easier to use, we have not distinguished between the glottal stop and the 'ayn, using the closing quotation mark to represent both sounds. You should find that Arabic speakers will still understand you.

TRANSLITERATION

It's worth noting here that transliteration from the Arabic script into English – or any other language for that matter – is at best an approximate science.

The presence of sounds unknown in European languages and the fact that the script is 'incomplete' (most vowels are not written) combine to make it nearly impossible to settle on one universally accepted method of transliteration. A wide variety of spellings is therefore possible for words when they appear in Latin script – and that goes for places and people's names as well.

The whole thing is further complicated by the wide variety of dialects and the imaginative ideas Arabs themselves often have on appropriate spelling in, say, English (words spelt one way in Jordan may look very different again in Syria and Lebanon, with strong French influences); not even the most venerable of western Arabists have been able to come up with a satisfactory solution.

While striving to reflect the language as closely as possible and aiming at consistency, this book generally anglicises place, street and hotel names and the like as the

locals have done. Don't be surprised if you come across several versions of the same thing.

ACCOMMODATION

I'd like to book a ...	*biddee ehjuz ...*
Do you have a ...?	*fi ...?*
(cheap) room	*ghurfa (rkheesa)*
single room	*ghurfa mufrada*
double room	*ghurfa bi sareerayn*

for one night	*li layli waHde*
for two nights	*layltayn*
May I see it?	*mumkin shoofa?*
It's very noisy/dirty.	*kteer dajeh/wuskha*
How much is it per person?	*'addaysh li kul waHid?*
How much is it per night?	*'addaysh bel layli?*
Where is the bathroom?	*wayn al-Hammam?*
We're leaving today.	*niHna musafireen al-youm*

address	*al-'anwaan*
air-conditioning	*kondishon/mookayif*
blanket	*al-bataaniyya/al-Hrem*
camp site	*mukhayam*
electricity	*kahraba*
hotel	*funduq/otel*
hot water	*mai saakhina*
key	*al-miftaH*
manager	*al-mudeer*
shower	*doosh*
soap	*saboon*
toilet	*twalet/bet al-mai*

CONVERSATION & ESSENTIALS

Arabs place great importance on civility and it's rare to see any interaction between people that doesn't begin with profuse greetings, enquiries into the other's health and other niceties.

Arabic greetings are more formal than in English and there is a reciprocal response to each. These sometimes vary slightly, depending on whether you're addressing a man or a woman. A simple encounter can become a drawn-out affair, with neither side wanting to be the one to put a halt to the stream of greetings and well-wishing. As an *ajnabi* (foreigner), you're not expected to know all the ins and outs, but if you come up with the right expression at the appropriate moment they'll love it.

The most common greeting is *salaam alaykum* (peace be upon you), to which the correct reply is *wa alaykum as-salaam* (and upon you be peace). If you get invited to a birthday celebration or are around for any of the big holidays, the common greeting is *kul sana wa intum bikher* (I wish you well for the coming year).

After having a bath or shower, you will often hear people say to you *na'iman*, which roughly means 'heavenly' and boils down to an observation along the lines of 'nice and clean now, eh'.

Arrival in one piece is always something to be grateful for. Passengers will often be greeted with *il-Hamdu lillah al as-salaama* – 'thank God for your safe arrival'.

Hi.	*marHaba*
Hi. (response)	*marHabtain*
Hello.	*ahlan wa sahlan* or just *ahlan* (Welcome)
Hello. (response)	*ahlan beek/i* (m/f)

It's an important custom in Jordan to ask after a person's or their family's health when greeting, eg *kayf es-saHa?* (How is your health?), *kayf il'ayli?* (How is the family?). The response is usually *bikher il-Hamdu lillah* (Fine, thank you).

Goodbye.	*ma'a salaama/Allah ma'ak*
Good morning.	*sabaH al-khayr*
Good morning. (response)	*sabaH 'an-noor*
Good evening.	*masa' al-khayr*
Good evening. (response)	*masa 'an-noor*
Good night.	*tisbaH 'ala khayr*
Good night. (response)	*wa inta min ahlu*

Yes.	*aiwa/na'am*
Yeah.	*ay*
No.	*la*
Please. (request)	*min fadlak/fadleek* (m/f)
Please. (polite)	*law samaHt/samaHti* (m/f)
Please. (come in)	*tafaddal/tafaddali* (m/f)/ *tafaddaloo* (pl)
Thank you.	*shukran*
Thank you very much.	*shukran kteer/ shukran jazeelan*
You're welcome.	*'afwan* or *tikram/tikrami* (m/f)
One moment, please.	*lahza min fadlak/i* (m/f)

Pardon/Excuse me.	*'afwan*
Sorry!	*aasif/aasifa!* (m/f)
No problem.	*mafi mushkili/moo mushkila*
Never mind.	*ma'alesh*
Just a moment.	*laHza*
Congratulations!	*mabrouk!*

Questions like 'Is the bus coming?' or 'Will the bank be open later?' generally elicit the response: *in sha' Allah* (God willing), an expression you'll hear over and over again. Another common one is *ma sha' Allah* (God's will be done), sometimes a useful answer to probing questions about why you're not married yet.

How are you?	*kayf Haalak/Haalik?* (m/f)
How're you doing?	*kayfak/kayfik?* (m/f)
Fine thank you.	*bikher il-Hamdu lillah*
What's your name?	*shu-ismak/shu-ismik?* (m/f)
My name is ...	*ismi ...*
Pleased to meet you. (when departing)	*fursa sa'ida*
Nice to meet you. (lit: you honour us)	*tasharrafna*
Where are you from?	*min wayn inta/inti?* (m/f)
I'm from ...	*ana min ...*
Do you like ...?	*inta/inti bitHeb ...?* (m/f)
I like ...	*ana bHeb ...*
I don't like ...	*ana ma bHeb ...*

I	*ana*
you	*inta/inti* (m/f)
he	*huwa*
she	*hiyya*
we	*niHna*
you	*into*
they	*homm*

DIRECTIONS

How do I get to ...?	*keef boosal ala ...?*
Can you show me (on the map)?	*mumkin tfarjeeni ('ala al-khareeta)?*
How many kilometres?	*kam kilometre?*
What street is this?	*shoo Hal shanki had?*
on the left	*'ala yasaar/shimaal*
on the right	*'ala yameen*
opposite	*muqaabil*
straight ahead	*dughri*
at the next corner	*tanee mafraq*
this way	*min hon*
here/there	*hon/honeek*
in front of	*amaam/iddaam*

SIGNS

Entrance	مدخل
Exit	خروج
Open	مفتوح
Closed	مغلق
Prohibited	ممنوع
Information	معلومات
Hospital	مستشفي
Police	شرطة
Men's Toilet	حمام للرجال
Women's Toilet	حمام للنساء

near	qareeb
far	ba'eed
north	shimaal
south	janub
east	sharq
west	gharb

EMERGENCIES

Help me!	saa'idoonee!
I'm sick.	ana mareed/mareeda (m/f)
Call the police!	ittusil bil shurta!
doctor	duktoor/tabeeb
hospital	al-mustash-fa
police	ash-shurta
Go away!	imshee!/rouh min hoon!
Shame (on you)!	aayb!
(said by woman)	

HEALTH

I'm ill.	ana maareed/mareeda (m/f)
My friend is ill.	sadeeqi maareed (m)/
	sadeeqati maareeda (f)
It hurts here.	beeyujani hon

I'm ...	andee ...
asthmatic	azmitrabo
diabetic	sukkari
epileptic	saraa/alsaa'a

I'm allergic ...	andee Hasasiyya ...
to antibiotics	min al-mudad alHayawi
to aspirin	min al-aspireen
to penicillin	min al-binisileen
to bees	min al-naHl
to nuts	min al-mukassarat

antiseptic	mutahhi
aspirin	aspireen/aspro (brand name)
Band-Aids	plaster

chemist/pharmacy	as-sayidiliyya
condoms	kaboot
contraceptive	waseela lee mana' al-Ham
diarrhoea	is-haal
fever	Harara
headache	wajaa-ras
hospital	mustashfa
medicine	dawa
pregnant	Hamel
prescription	wasfa/rashetta
sanitary napkins	fuwat saHiyya
stomachache	wajaa fil battu
sunblock cream	krem waki min ashilt al-shams
tampons	kotex (brand name)

LANGUAGE DIFFICULTIES

Do you speak English?	bitiHki ingleezi?
I understand.	ana afham
I don't understand.	ana ma bifham

I speak ...	ana baHki ...
English	ingleezi
French	faransi
German	almaani

I speak a little Arabic.	ana baHki arabi shway
I don't speak Arabic.	ana ma beHki arabi
I want an interpreter.	biddee mutarjem
Could you write it down, please?	mumkin tiktabhu, min fadlak?
How do you say ... in Arabic?	kayf t'ul ... bil'arabi?

NUMBERS

0	sifr	٠
1	waHid	١
2	itnayn/tintayn	٢
3	talaata	٣
4	arba'a	٤
5	khamsa	٥
6	sitta	٦
7	saba'a	٧
8	tamanya	٨
9	tis'a	٩
10	'ashara	١٠
11	yeedaa'sh	١١
12	yeetnaa'sh	١٢
13	talaatash	١٣
14	arbatash	١٤
15	khamastash	١٥
16	sittash	١٦
17	sabatash	١٧
18	tamantash	١٨
19	tasatash	١٩

20	'ashreen	٢٠
21	wHid wa 'ashreen	٢١
22	itnayn wa 'ashreen	٢٢
30	talaateen	٣٠
40	arba'een	٤٠
50	khamseen	٥٠
60	sitteen	٦٠
70	saba'een	٧٠
80	tamaneen	٨٠
90	tis'een	٩٠
100	miyya (meet before a noun)	١٠٠
200	miyyatayn	٢٠٠
1000	'alf	١٠٠٠
2000	'alfayn	٢٠٠٠
3000	talaat-alaf	٣٠٠٠

PAPERWORK

date of birth	tareekh al-meelad/-wilaada
name	al-ism
nationality	al-jenseeya
passport	jawaz al-safar (or paspor)
permit	tasriH
place of birth	makan al-meelad/-wilaada
visa	visa/ta'shira

SHOPPING & SERVICES

I'm looking for ...	ana abHath ... aa'n
Where is the ...?	wayn/fayn ...?

bank	al-bank
beach	ash-shaati'/al-plaaj/al-baHr
chemist/pharmacy	as-sayidiliyya
city/town	al-medeena
city centre	markaz al-medeena
customs	al-jumruk
entrance	al-dukhool/al-madkhal
exchange office	al-masref/al-saraf
exit	al-khurooj
hotel	al-funduq/al-otel
information desk	isti'laamaat
laundry	al ghaseel
market	al-sooq
mosque	al-jaami'/al-masjid
museum	al-matHaf
newsagents	al-maktaba
old city	al-medeena al-qadeema/ al-medeena l'ateeqa
passport & immigration office	maktab al-jawazaat wa al-hijra
police	ash-shurta
post office	maktab al-bareed
restaurant	al-mata'am
telephone office	maktab at-telefon/ maktab al-haalef

temple	al-ma'abad
tourist office	maktab al-siyaHa

I want to change ...	baddee sarref ...
money	masaari
travellers cheques	sheeket siyaHiyya

What time does it open?	emta byeftaH?
What time does it close?	emta bi sakkir?
I'd like to make a telephone call.	mumkin talfen min fadlak

Where can I buy ...?	wayn/fayn feeni eshtiree ...?
What is this?	shu hada?
How much?	addaysh/bikam?
How many?	kim waHid?
How much is it?	bi addaysh?
That's too expensive.	hada ghalee kheteer
Is there ...?	fee ...?
There isn't (any).	ma fee
May I look at it?	mumkin shoof?

big/bigger	kbeer/akbar
cheap/cheaper	rkhees/arkhas
closed	msakkar
expensive	ghaali
money	al-fuloos/al-masaari
open	maftuH
small/smaller	sagheer/asghar

TIME & DATES

What's the time?	addaysh essa'aa?
When?	emta?
now	halla'
after	b'adayn
on time	al waket
early	bakkeer
late	ma'qar
daily	kil youm
today	al-youm
tomorrow	bukra
day after tomorrow	ba'ad bukra
yesterday	imbaarih
minute	daqeeqa
hour	saa'a
day	youm
week	usboo'
month	shahr
year	sana
morning	soubeH
afternoon	ba'ad deher
evening	massa
night	layl

Monday	al-tenayn
Tuesday	at-talaata
Wednesday	al-arba'a
Thursday	al-khamees
Friday	al-jum'a
Saturday	as-sabt
Sunday	al-aHad

The Western Calendar Months

The Islamic year has 12 lunar months and is 11 days shorter than the Western calendar, so important Muslim dates will occur 11 days earlier each (Western) year.

There are two Western calendars in use in the Arab world. In Egypt and westwards, the months have virtually the same names as in English (January is *yanaayir*, October is *octobir* and so on), but in Lebanon and eastwards, the names are quite different. Talking about, say, June as 'month six' is the easiest solution, but for the sake of completeness, the months from January are:

January	kanoon ath-thani
February	shubaat
March	azaar
April	nisaan
May	ayyaar
June	Huzayraan
July	tammooz
August	'aab
September	aylool
October	tishreen al-awal
November	tishreen ath-thani
December	kaanoon al-awal

The Hejira Calendar Months

1st	MoHarram
2nd	Safar
3rd	Rabi' al-Awal
4th	Rabay ath-Thaani
5th	Jumaada al-Awal
6th	Jumaada al-Akhira
7th	Rajab
8th	Shaban
9th	Ramadan
10th	Shawwal
11th	Zuul-Qeda
12th	Zuul-Hijja

TRANSPORT
Public Transport

Where is the ...?	wayn/fayn ...?
airport	al-mataar

bus station	maHattat al-baas/ maHattat al-karaj
ticket office	maktab at-tazaakar
train station	maHattat al-qitaar

What time does the ... leave/arrive?	ay saa'a biyitla'/biyusal ...?
boat/ferry	al-markib/as-safeena
(small) boat	ash-shakhtura
bus	al-baas
plane	al-teeyara
train	al-qitaar

Which bus goes to ...?	aya baas biyruH 'ala ...?
I want to go to ...	ana badeh ruH ala ...
Does this bus go to ...?	hal-baas biyruH 'ala ...?
How many buses per day go to ...?	kam baas biyruH ben nahar ...?
How long does the trip take?	kam sa'a ar-riHla?
Please tell me when we get to ...	'umal ma'aroof illee lamma noosal la ...
Stop here, please.	wa'if hoon 'umal ma'aroof
Please wait for me.	'umal ma'aroof istanna
May I sit here?	mumkin a'ood hoon?
May we sit here?	mumkin ni'ood hoon?

1st class	daraja oola
2nd class	daraja taaniya
ticket	at-tazaakar
to/from	ila/min

Private Transport

I'd like to hire a ...	biddee esta'jer ...
Where can I hire a ...?	wayn/fayn feeni esta'jer ...?
bicycle	bisklet
camel	jamal
car	sayyaara
donkey	Hmaar
4WD	jeep
horse	Hsaan
motorcycle	motosikl
tour guide	al-dalee as-siyaaHi/ al-murshid as-siyaaHi

Is this the road to ...?
Hal Haza al-tareeq eela ...?
Where's a service station?
wayn/fayn maHaltet al-benzeen?
Please fill it up.
min fadlak (emla/abee) Ha
I'd like (30) litres.
biddee talaateen leeter

diesel	*deezel*
leaded petrol	*benzeen bee rasa*
unleaded petrol	*benzeen beedoon rasas*

(How long) Can I park here?
  (kam sa'a) mumkin aas-f hon?
Where do I pay?
  fayn/wayn mumkin an addf'aa?
I need a mechanic.
  bidee mekaneesyan
The car/motorbike has broken down (at ...).
  al-sayyaara/-mutusikl it'atlit ('an ...)
The car/motorbike won't start.
  al-sayyaara/-mutusikl ma bit door
I have a flat tyre.
  nzel al-doolab
I've run out of petrol.
  mafi benzeen or *al-benzeen khalas*

I've had an accident.
  aamalt hads

TRAVEL WITH CHILDREN

Is there a/an ...?	*fee ...?*
I need a/an ...	*biddee ...*
car baby seat	*kursee sayyaara leel bebe'*
disposable nappies	*pamperz* (brand name)
nappies (diapers)	*Ha fa daat*
formula (baby's milk)	*Haleeb bebe'*
highchair	*kursee atfaal*
potty	*muneeyai*
stroller	*arabeyet atfaal*

Do you mind if I breastfeed here?
  mumkin aradda hon?
Are children allowed?
  Hal yousmah leel atfaal?

Glossary

This glossary is a list of Arabic (A) words commonly used in Jordan, plus some archaeological (arch) terms and abbreviations.

abu (A) – 'father of...'
agal (A) – black headropes used to hold a keffiyeh in place
agora (arch) – open space for commerce and politics
ain (ayoun) (A) – spring or well
amir (A) – see *emir*
arak – alcoholic spirit
Ayyubids – the dynasty founded by Saladin (Salah ad-Din) in Egypt in 1169

bab (abwab) (A) – gate
badia (A) – stony desert
beit (A) – house
beit ash-sha'ar (A) – goat-hair Bedouin tent
benzin 'adi (A) – regular petrol
bin (A) – 'son of...'; also *ibn*
burj (A) – tower

caliph (A) – Islamic ruler
caravanserai – large inn enclosing a courtyard, providing accommodation and a marketplace for caravans
cardo maximus (arch) – Roman main street, from north to south

Decapolis – literally 'ten cities'; this term refers to a number of ancient cities in the Roman Empire, including Amman and Jerash
decumanus (arch) – Roman main street, from east to west
deir (A) – monastery
duwaar (A) – circle

Eid al-Fitr (A) – Festival of Breaking the Fast, celebrated throughout the Islamic world at the end of *Ramadan*
emir (A) – Islamic ruler, leader, military commander or governor; literally 'prince'

haj (A) – the pilgrimage to Mecca
haji (A) – one who has made the haj
hammam(at) (A) – natural hot springs; sometimes refers to a Turkish steam bath, and toilet or shower
haram (A) – forbidden area
hejab (A) – woman's headscarf

IAF – Islamic Action Front, the largest political party in Jordan
ibn (A) – 'son of...'; also *bin*

il-balad (A) – 'downtown', the centre of town
imam (A) – religious leader
intifada – ongoing Palestinian uprising against Israeli authorities in the West Bank, Gaza and East Jerusalem that started in December 1987
iwan (A) – vaulted hall opening into a central court

jalabiyya (A) – man's full-length robe
janub(iyyeh) (A) – south(ern)
jebel (A) – hill or mountain
JETT – Jordan Express Travel & Tourism, the major private bus company in Jordan
jezira (A) – island
jihad (A) – holy war in defence of Islam, also the personal struggle to be a good Muslim
jisr (A) – bridge
JTB – Jordan Tourism Board

keffiyeh (A) – checked scarf worn by Arab men
khal min ar-rasas (A) – unleaded petrol
khirbat (A) – ruins of an ancient village
khutba (A) – Islamic sermon
Kufic (A) – a type of highly stylised old Arabic script

madrassa (A) – theological college that is associated with a mosque; also a school
maidan (A) – town or city square
Majlis al-Umma (A)- Jordan's National Assembly
malek (A) – king
malekah (A) – queen
Mamluks – literally 'slaves'; Muslim dynasty named for a former slave and soldier class
masjid (A) – mosque
medina (A) – old walled centre of any Islamic city
mezze (A) – starters, appetisers
mihrab (A) – niche in the wall of a mosque that indicates the direction of Mecca
minaret (A) – tower on top of a mosque
minbar (A) – pulpit in a mosque
MSA – Modern Standard Arabic
muezzin (A) – mosque official who calls the faithful to prayer, often from the *minaret*
mumtaz (A) – 'super' petrol or '1st class' (especially on trains); literally 'excellent'

nargileh (A) – water pipe used mainly by men to smoke tobacco
necropolis (arch) – cemetery
nymphaeum (arch) – literally 'temple of the Nymphs'; a place with baths, fountains and pools

oud (A) – Arabic lute

PLO – Palestine Liberation Organization
PNC – Palestinian National Council
PNT – Petra National Trust
PRA – Petra Regional Authority
praetorium (arch) – military headquarters
propylaeum (arch) – grand entrance to a temple or palace

qala'at – (A) castle or fort
qasr (A) – castle or palace
qibla (A) – direction of Mecca
Quran (A) – holy book of Islam
qusayr (A) – small castle or palace

rababa (A) – traditional single-string Bedouin instrument
Ramadan (A) – Muslim month of fasting
ras (A) – cape, point or headland
RSCN – Royal Society for the Conservation of Nature

saqiyah – a pump turned by a donkey
servees – service taxi
shaheed – martyrs
shamal(iyyeh) (A) – north(ern)
sharif (A) – descendent of the Prophet Mohammed (through his daughter, Fatima); general title for Islamic ruler

sheikh (A) – officer of the mosque or venerated religious scholar
sidd (A) – dam
siq (A) – gorge or canyon
souq (A) – market
stele (arch) – stone commemorative slab or column decorated with inscriptions or figures

tell (A) – ancient mound created by centuries of urban rebuilding
temenos (arch) – a sacred courtyard or similar enclosure
tetrapylon (arch) – an archway with four entrances
thop – traditional Bedouin robe
Trans-Jordan – Jordan's original name
triclinium (arch) – dining room in Roman times

Umayyads – first great dynasty of Arab Muslim rulers
umm (A) – 'mother of…'
UNRWA – UN Relief & Works Agency

wadi (A) – valley or river bed formed by watercourse, dry except after heavy rainfall (plural: widyan)

zerb – Bedouin oven, which is buried in the sand

Behind the Scenes

THIS BOOK

This 6th edition of *Jordan* was researched and written by Bradley Mayhew. The Health chapter was adapted from material written by Dr Caroline Evans. The 5th edition of Jordan was researched and written by Anthony Ham, and editions before that by Paul Greenway and Damien Simonis.

THANKS from the Author

Firstly, I'd like to offer my thanks to Charl Twal, Sami and Hamid at the Palace Hotel and Mohammed Hallak of Reliable Rent-a-Car, without whom my research would have been so much less fun. Particular thanks to Charl for helping with the Arabic script. Ruth of Jordan Jubilee (www.jordanjubilee .com) was very helpful, as she is to all travellers to Jordan.

Several people helped with tips and pointers, including Majdi Twal, Walid Nassar, Eid Nawafleh at Petra Moon, Lotus Abu Karaki for info on tourism projects and Yamaan Safadi for an overview on trekking options. Thanks to David Symes for help getting things rolling.

Many people at the RSCN were generous with their time and information; particular thanks go to Ghada al-Sous, Abeer Smadi and Chris Johnson at the Wild Jordan office and to the guys at Wadi Mujib and Dana (Bassam Al-Saudi at Rummana and Abel Razzak Khwalabeh at Dana). Salaam to Ahmad Al-Wazani in Irbid.

Finally and most importantly, thanks and love to Kelli, for when the plane home touches down and life begins again.

CREDITS

Commissioning Editors Kerryn Burgess, Lynne Preston, Janet Austin
Coordinating Editor Trent Holden
Coordinating Cartographer Joshua Geoghegan
Coordinating Layout Designer Wibowo Rusli
Managing Cartographer Shahara Ahmed
Assisting Editors Charlotte Orr, Janice Bird
Assisting Cartographer Amanda Sierp
Cover Designer James Hardy
Colour Designer John Shippick
Project Managers Eoin Dunlevy, Chris Love
Language Content Coordinator Quentin Frayne

Thanks to Alan Murphy, Celia Wood, Darren O'Connell, Jane Thompson, Imogen Bannister, Mark Germanchis, Sally Darmody

THANKS from Lonely Planet

Many thanks to the hundreds of travellers who used the last edition and wrote to us with helpful hints, useful advice and interesting anecdotes:

A Atef & Vaelentina Abu, Lisa Ansbro **B** Paddy Baldwin, Gabrielle & Hilbert Belksma-Rutten, Marylin Bernard, Julia Bishop, Cristina Boglia, Cora Bon, Mike Bonthoux, Kim Boreham, Leah Bower, Pascal Brunet, Faruk Budak, Marit Buis, Natalie Bull, Sean Burberry **C** Andrew Campion, Paul G Chamberlain, Yee Cheng, Elizabeth Chipp, Brian Clifton, Perrine Colignon, Cesar Colmenero Santiago, Simon Corder **D** Colyn Davey, Sandra de Jong, Henk & Nicole de Raad, Joanna Dench, Spencer Dillon, Lendvai Domonkos, Belika Douma, Tonia Dunnette **F** Rachel Farrand, K Fellows, Gloria Fernandez, S W Fielding, Debra Foran, Martin Frederiksen

---

THE LONELY PLANET STORY

The story begins with a classic travel adventure: Tony and Maureen Wheeler's 1972 journey across Europe and Asia to Australia. There was no useful information about the overland trail then, so Tony and Maureen published the first Lonely Planet guidebook to meet a growing need.

From a kitchen table, Lonely Planet has grown to become the largest independent travel publisher in the world, with offices in Melbourne (Australia), Oakland (USA) and London (UK). Today Lonely Planet guidebooks cover the globe. There is an ever-growing list of books and information in a variety of media. Some things haven't changed. The main aim is still to make it possible for adventurous travellers to get out there – to explore and better understand the world.

At Lonely Planet we believe travellers can make a positive contribution to the countries they visit – if they respect their host communities and spend their money wisely. Every year 5% of company profit is donated to charities around the world.

G Warda Gamar, Dorothee Gaudin, Ziegler Georg, Paul Gesalman, Sam Gilroy, Dianne Goldsmith, Craig & Johnna Goodmark, Anna-Karin Guindy **H** Meichael Halasa, Marcella Hallemeesch, Julia Hopkins, Martin Hraba **I** Keith Inman, Alene Ivey **J** Florence Jenny, David Jordan **K** Christin Karlsson, David Kong, Nienke Kramer, Tamas Kutassy **L** Nonie Lazenby, Sunny Lee, Christine Liebrecht **M** I MacDonald, Michael Malone, Marion Marquardt, Michael Martin, Andrew McKinlay, Anton Menning, Caryl Mollard, Chris & Sandy Morgan, Stephen Mosel, Marzena Mularska **N** Peter Nieuwpoort, Alex Nikolic **O** Paula O Donovan, Andrew Osmotherley, Paul Owen **P** Marina Papadopoulou, David Patel, Johan Pettersson, Job Piet, Anne Poepjes, Guillermo Pascual Pouteau, Donald Povey, Evelien Pullens **R** Spela Repic, Vanessa Ringer, Skip Roothans, Cindy Rose **S** Phil Salvador, J Samuel, Monica Sapirstein, Lilia Sassen, Odeh Sawalha, Heidi Schmitt, Char Simons, Davor Skeledzija, Emily Smith, Rafi Spero, Edwin Steenvoorden, Andrea Stenzel, Jeff Stewart **T** Christina Themar, Olivia Thrift, Titti Torstensson, Cressida Trew **V** Cornelis van Dieren, Agnes van Veen, Chris Verrill **W** Helen Walls, Joy Wan, Paul Whillis, Jorien Wiersum, Frances Wiig, Martyn Winfield, Manfred Wolfensberger, Daphne Wong **Y** Greg Yanagihara, Keiji Yoshimura, D C Young **Z** Andreas Zahner

ACKNOWLEDGEMENTS

Globe on the back cover © Mountain High Maps 1993 Digital Wisdom, Inc.

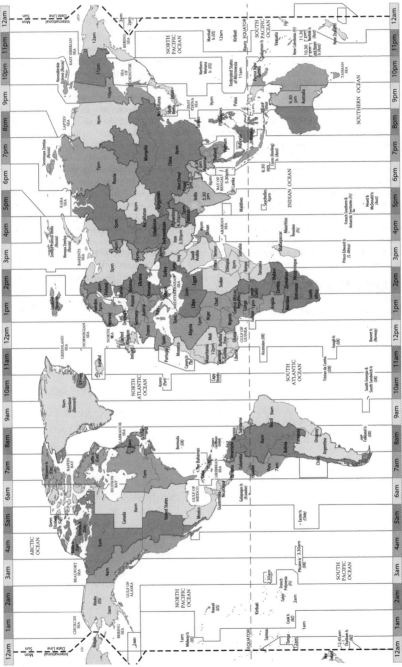

Index

INDEX

304

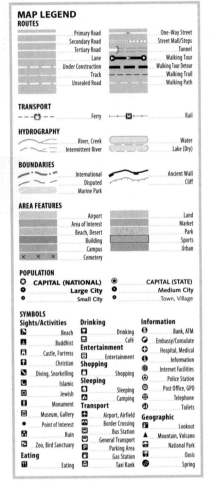

MAP LEGEND

ROUTES

Primary Road	One-Way Street
Secondary Road	Street Mall/Steps
Tertiary Road	Tunnel
Lane	Walking Tour
Under Construction	Walking Tour Detour
Track	Walking Trail
Unsealed Road	Walking Path

TRANSPORT

Ferry	Rail

HYDROGRAPHY

River, Creek	Water
Intermittent River	Lake (Dry)

BOUNDARIES

International	Ancient Wall
Disputed	Cliff
Marine Park	

AREA FEATURES

Airport	Land
Area of Interest	Market
Beach, Desert	Park
Building	Sports
Campus	Urban
Cemetery	

POPULATION

○ CAPITAL (NATIONAL)	● CAPITAL (STATE)
● Large City	○ Medium City
● Small City	○ Town, Village

SYMBOLS

Sights/Activities
- Beach
- Buddhist
- Castle, Fortress
- Christian
- Diving, Snorkelling
- Islamic
- Jewish
- Monument
- Museum, Gallery
- Point of Interest
- Ruin
- Zoo, Bird Sanctuary

Eating
- Eating

Drinking
- Drinking
- Café

Entertainment
- Entertainment

Shopping
- Shopping

Sleeping
- Sleeping
- Camping

Transport
- Airport, Airfield
- Border Crossing
- Bus Station
- General Transport
- Parking Area
- Gas Station
- Taxi Rank

Information
- Bank, ATM
- Embassy/Consulate
- Hospital, Medical
- Information
- Internet Facilities
- Police Station
- Post Office, GPO
- Telephone
- Toilets

Geographic
- Lookout
- Mountain, Volcano
- National Park
- Oasis
- Spring

LONELY PLANET OFFICES

Australia
Head Office
Locked Bag 1, Footscray, Victoria 3011
☎ 03 8379 8000, fax 03 8379 8111
talk2us@lonelyplanet.com.au

USA
150 Linden St, Oakland, CA 94607
☎ 510 893 8555, toll free 800 275 8555
fax 510 893 8572
info@lonelyplanet.com

UK
72–82 Rosebery Ave,
Clerkenwell, London EC1R 4RW
☎ 020 7841 9000, fax 020 7841 9001
go@lonelyplanet.co.uk

Published by Lonely Planet Publications Pty Ltd
ABN 36 005 607 983